CRIMINOLOGY
Perspectives on Crime and Criminality

CRIMINOLOGY
Perspectives on Crime and Criminality

Peter Wickman
State University of New York at Potsdam

Phillip Whitten
General Editor

with the assistance of
Robert Levey

D. C. HEATH AND COMPANY
Lexington, Massachusetts   Toronto

Acknowledgments

Text Credits

Pages 117, 185, data abridged from pp. 80–82 and 87–92 in *Criminology,* 10th ed. by Edwin H. Sutherland and Donald R. Cressey. Copyright © 1978 by J. B. Lippincott Company. Reprinted by permission of Harper & Row, Publishers, Inc.

Picture Credits

Chapter 1   2 © Charles Gatewood; 5 Chicago Tribune-New York News Syndicate, Inc.; 16 Harvard Law School Art Collection; 20 Harvard Law School Art Collection.
Chapter 2   34 Margaret Bourke-White, *Life Magazine,* © Time, Inc.; 37 © 1979 Eric A. Roth/The Picture Cube; 46 © Charles Gatewood; 50 Courtesy of the *Arizona Republic & Gazette,* photo by Lud Keaton.
Chapter 3   60 © Frank Muller/Woodfin Camp & Associates; 68 Courtesy, FBI; 82 © Tim Eagan/Woodfin Camp & Associates; 90 © George W. Gardner.
Chapter 4   94 Charles Gatewood/Stock, Boston; 105 Brent Jones; 108 Frank Siteman/Stock, Boston; 109 Peter Simon/Stock, Boston; 116 Frank Siteman/The Picture Cube; 125 Mary Ellen Mark/Magnum Photos, Inc.
Chapter 5   132 © Charles Gatewood; 136 Jean-Claude Lejeune/Stock, Boston; 141 Eileen Christelow/Jeroboam, Inc.; 154 © Sylvia Johnson/Woodfin Camp & Associates; 157 Susan Meiselas/Magnum Photos, Inc.
Chapter 6   162 Brown Brothers; 164 Radio Times Hulton Picture Library; 173 Copyright © 162 United Artists Corporation. All rights reserved. 180 Emilio Mercado/Jeroboam, Inc.; 183 Lyn Gardiner/Stock, Boston; 186 Wide World Photos, Inc.; 203 Paul Foley.
Chapter 7   212 © 1972 by Paramount Pictures Corporation. All rights reserved. 220 Jonathan L. Barkan/The Picture Cube; 231 United Press International Photo; 239 Brown Brothers; 241 Historical Picture Service, Inc., Chicago; 247 United Press International Photo.
Chapter 8   268 Michael D. Sullivan; 270 Brown Brothers; 272 © Ellen Shub/The Picture Cube; 279 © Janet Fries/Icon; 284 © Charles Gatewood; 293 Ruth Silverman/Stock, Boston.
Chapter 9   306 Robert V. Eckert, Jr./EKM-Nepenthe; 310 © Eric Kroll 1978/Taurus Photos; 318 © Joel Gordon 1979; 324 © George W. Gardner, 1979; 327 © Eric Kroll 1978/Taurus Photos.
Chapter 10   332 © Charles Gatewood/Magnum Photos, Inc.; 337 © Susan Kublin 1979/Photo Researchers, Inc.; 345 © J. P. Laffont/Sygma; 349 United Press International; 354 Peter Menzel/Stock, Boston; 356 Cary Wolinsky/Stock, Boston; 368 Wide World Photos.
Chapter 11   372 © 1978 Jim Anderson/Woodfin Camp & Associates; 376 © Joel Gordon 1979; 392 © B. Klieve/Jeroboam, Inc.
Chapter 12   406 Cary Wolinsky/Stock, Boston; 410 Radio Times Hulton Picture Library; 417 © Charles Gatewood; 418 United Press International Photo; 420 James H. Karales/Magnum Photos, Inc.; 431 John R. Maher/EKM-Nepenthe; 440 © B. Klieve/Jeroboam, Inc.
Chapter 13   452 John Maher/EKM-Nepenthe; 462 Michael D. Sullivan; 488 United Press International Photo.
Chapter 14   492 Lynn Adler/Jeroboam, Inc.; 496 Culver Pictures, Inc.; 500 © Eric Kroll/Taurus Photos; 516 © Shepard Sherbell/Sygma.
Chapter 15   520 Bill Powers/*Corrections Magazine;* 528 Courtesy, Pennsylvania Prison Society; 531 Boston Globe Photo; 548 © 1979 Eric A. Roth; 564 © Eric Kroll/Taurus Photos.
Chapter 16   568 Paul Conklin; 578 © Joel Gordon; 582 Peter Southwick/Stock, Boston; 590 Jeff Albertson/Stock, Boston.

Copyright © 1980 by D. C. Heath and Company.

All rights reserved. No part of this publication may be reproduced or transmitted in any form or by any means, electronic or mechanical, including photocopy, recording, or any information storage or retrieval system, without permission in writing from the publisher.

Published simultaneously in Canada.

Printed in the United States of America.

International Standard Book Number: 0-669-01600-4

Library of Congress Catalog Card Number: 79-89479

PREFACE

Criminology: Perspectives on Crime and Criminality is written for the beginning student in criminology. We have tried to expose the reader to the major perspectives, issues, and diverse concerns and debates that characterize contemporary criminology. We have endeavored to present a balanced "humanistic" view of criminology that is current in content and clearly written so as to stimulate the reader's systematic study of crime, criminality, and criminal behavior. Yet in our effort to maintain a balanced approach to the crime problem, we have not ignored critical or ideological issues and concerns.

The book is organized into four parts. *Part 1* introduces the study of criminology and sets the framework for the book by describing the historical development of major perspectives relevant to the study of crime, criminality, and the criminal law. The major theories are summarized within a historical context, and we present our own viewpoints and ideological commitments relative to the study of the crime problem.

Part 2 describes some of the social correlates of crime and criminality. This section provides an analysis of social factors associated with the phenomenon of crime and its definition. At this juncture we do not link criminal statistics with such factors as age, race, or gender roles in a causal manner. Rather, we describe them as correlates and concomitants of crime and delinquency.

Part 3 focuses on a more comprehensive treatment of theoretical perspectives. Within this framework we set forth a system of typologies for the further descriptive analysis of major crime patterns or systems. These include, among others, comprehensive descriptions of professional, organized, and white-collar crime patterns.

Part 4 presents cogent critiques of the criminal justice system, its history, and the recent development of policies and patterns whereby agents of the state express society's reaction to crime. The emphasis is on the degree of effectiveness and humaneness of efforts to control crime by intervention in the lives of those defined as "criminal." The chapter on corrections and punishment presents cross-national as well as U.S. data. It's based on research by both conventional and critical scholars into the apparent ineffectiveness of programs that seek to control crime or criminals through rehabilitative schemes. Alternative models for the future of corrections are also surveyed. The final chapter on public policy provides a critique of the reluctance of policymakers to link crime policy with social policy and suggests alternative policies that might promote justice. In this instance we leave ourselves open to being labeled "reformists," but if this be the case, it is in a more critical vein than most texts that take the "middle-ground" position. While we avoid utopian solutions throughout the book, still we affirm that social institutions are creations of human effort. As such, they are capable of being redirected by concerted constructive human forces.

The difficult task of preparing a textbook of this scope was made less onerous by the assistance rendered by numerous people. The senior author would particularly like to acknowledge the debt he owes to the work of David Matza. Chapters 4 and 6 reflect a liberal borrowing of his concepts and perspectives. Also, Marshall Clinard and Richard Quinney's typologies have been relied on and adapted in the chapters describing the various crime patterns. Without the cooperation of Dean Richard E. Hutcheson of the State University of New York at Potsdam and the library staff at that college, the writing would have been more difficult. An expression of appreciation is due David Hanson, my colleague and chairman, for his encouragement.

In addition, both the authors want to acknowledge the assistance of those whose time and effort helped to make the book possible. Special thanks go to Phillip Whitten, general editor, who gave unsparingly of his time in editorial work on the manuscript. We are grateful to the reviewers, David Greenberg (New York University), J. Robert Lilly (Northern Kentucky State College), Peter K. Manning (Michigan State University), Clinton Sanders (University of Connecticut), and Lyle W. Shannon (University of Iowa) for their helpful criticisms and suggestions on various parts of the manuscript. The work of Stephen Pfohl (Boston College) in reviewing the book throughout the various stages of its development warrants special notice for the persistent and helpful manner in which he prodded us into more careful presentations of data and clarifications of theoretical perspectives. Adelle Arcus did a particularly fine job in typing the manuscript. Finally, we owe a debt of gratitude to the staff at D. C. Heath and Company.

P. Wickman

CONTENTS

PART ONE
Introduction to the Study of Criminology — 1

1 Criminology: The Study of Crime and Criminality — 3
What Is Crime? — 3
  Images of Crime in American Folklore and History **4**
  Competing Perspectives in the Definition of Crime **6**   What Kind of Behavior Is Crime? **9**   A Legal Definition of Crime and Its Relativity **10**
What Is Criminology? — 12
What Is Criminality? — 13
  Theories of Crime and Criminality **13**   The Classical School **15**   BOX 1. Pioneers in Criminology—Cesare Beccaria (1734–1794) **16**   The Positive School **17**   BOX 2. Pioneers in Criminology—Cesare Lombroso (1835–1919) **20**   The Positive School and Social Reforms **21**
The Development of American Criminology — 22
  Kinds of People Paradigm **23**   Kinds of Environment Paradigm **24**
Changing Paradigms in Contemporary Criminology — 25
Research in Criminology: The Convergence of Theory and Inquiry — 28
Research Methods — 30

2 Criminal Law and the Study of Crime and Criminality — 35
The Nature of the Law — 36
  The Nature of the Law: Natural and Universal or Positive and Rational? **39**   How Social Control Becomes Formal **40**
Social Basis of the Criminal Law: Its Nature, Sources, and Distinctions — 43
  Consensus and Conflict Theories **43**
The Nature of the Criminal Law — 47
  Criminal Law Versus Civil Law **47**   Sources of the Criminal Law **48**   Procedural and Substantive Laws **49**   BOX 1. Miranda Rights **50**
The Social Organization of the Legal System: Problems and Limitations — 52
  Problems in Classification **52**   The Limits of Criminal Responsibility **52**   BOX 2. It's Against the Law . . . **53**   The Overreach of the Law: Crimes Without Victims **56**   Crimes Left Unattended: The Underreach of the Law **56**

PART TWO
Social Correlates of Crime and Criminology — 59

3 Assessing the Magnitude and Cost of Crime — 61
How Much Crime Is There? — 61
  The "Dark Figure" of Crime **62**
The Use and Misuse of Crime Data in Politics and Policy — 63

The Manipulation of Urban Crime Figures **66** Bureaucracy and Crime Statistics **66**

Estimating the Extent of Crime: Official Data — 67
The *Uniform Crime Reports* **67** Variations in Sex, Age, and Race in Arrest Rates **77**

Unofficial Estimates of the Extent of Crime — 82
Victim Surveys — 83
Self-Reports — 85
Estimates of the Cost of Crime — 87

4 Becoming Delinquent: Social Conditions, Group Associations, and the Defining Process — 95

The Study of Delinquency and the Study of Crime — 96
The Concept of Delinquency: Estimates of Officially Defined Juvenile Offenders — 97
Legal Definitions of Delinquency and Status Offenses **97** How Many Are Labeled Delinquent? **100**

Social Correlates of Conforming and Nonconforming Juveniles — 102
Social Institutions as Influences in Social Control **103**

The Position of Youth in Society — 112
Becoming Delinquent: Affinity and Affiliation Perspectives — 113
Personal and Social Predispositions: Affinities **114** Affiliation and Subcultural Theories **116** BOX 1. Youth Gangs: One Member of a Bronx Youth Gang Tells Why It's So Important **118**

Signifying Agents and Organizations: Societal Reaction and Becoming Delinquent — 122
Signifying Agents of Delinquency: The Police **122** The Juvenile Court and the Processing of Delinquents **124** Juvenile Corrections and Noninstitutional Alternatives **127** Suggested Reforms: "Radical Nonintervention" **128**

5 Female Status: Women's Crime and Societal Reaction — 133

Changing Perspectives on Female Crime and Delinquency — 134
Early Explanations of Female Crime **134** Female Criminality: Contemporary Perspectives **135** The Status of Women: Complexities of the Opportunity Perspective **141** BOX 1. Sisters In Crime **142**

Has There Been an Increase in Women's Crime? — 144
The Criminal Justice System and Patterns of Sexism — 153
The Female Offender in Court **154** The Double Standard and Class and Racial Factors **155** Women and the Corrections System: Benign Neglect **158**

PART THREE
Theoretical Perspectives and Crime Patterns as Behavior Systems — 161

6 Theories and Perspectives on Crime and Criminality — 163

The Quest for Answers: Why Do People Break the Law? — 163
The Legacy of Positivism: Emphasis on Explaining Criminal Behavior — 166
Biological and Psychological Affinities **167** BOX 1. The XYY Chromosome Carrier **170** BOX 2. The "Son of Sam": A Study in Contrasts **176** Sociological Affinities **178** Subcultural Affinity **182**

Affiliation Perspectives: Social Process Explanations — 184

BOX 3. Sutherland's Principles of Differential Association **186**

Signification: The Labeling Process — 189
Signification Aspects of the Labeling Perspective **190** Criticisms of Labeling **194**

Conflict Perspectives: Power Relationships and the "Signification" of Criminality — 195
Conflict Perspectives and Critical or Radical Criminology **199** Criticism of the Critical Conflict Perspective **201**

Sociological Theories and the Study of Crime and Criminality: Criminal Behavior Systems — 202
Criminal Behavior or Action Systems: The Typological Approach **204**

7 Professional and Organized Crime Behavior Systems — 213

Professional Crime — 214
History of Professional Crime **214** Professional Burglary: Behavior System **215** Professional Theft: Behavior System **217** BOX 1. The Thief's Work **219** BOX 2. The Ins and Outs of Pickpocketing **221** The Professional Criminal's Self-concept **224** Affiliational Networks: The Support System of Professional Offenders **226** Convergences in Belief and Status Systems **228** Societal Reaction and Social Change **229**

Professional Heavy Crime — 229
BOX 3. Hijacking: A Major American Industry **233**

Organized Crime — 235
History of Organized Crime **241** The Structure and Function of Organized Crime: The "Mafia," Reality or Myth? **243** BOX 4. The Career of Joseph Valachi: A Soldier in Organized Crime **247** Organized Crime Goes "Legit" **254** BOX 5. Takeover of a Garbage Collector Charged to Two Reputed Mafia Men **258** Organized Crime and the Corruption of Criminal Justice **259** BOX 6. Organized Crime and Police Corruption: A Cop Tells Why He Blew the Whistle **260**

8 Patterns of Violent Crime — 269

Focus on Interpersonal Violence — 271
BOX 1. Public Concern over Violent Crime **272**

A Subculture of Violence or a Violent Culture? — 273
Social Economic Status, Race, and Violent Crime **274** Age, Sex, and Violent Crime **275** A Subculture of Violence? **275**

Traditional Patterns of Violent Crime — 278
Types of Homicide **279** The Extent of Homicide **281**

The Victims of Homicide — 282

Patterns of Interpersonal Violence in Family Settings — 286
Is the Family a "Violent Subculture"? **286** BOX 2. The Story of a Battered Wife **288** Child Abuse: Violent Crime or Individual Pathology? **291**

Forcible Rape as a Violent Crime Pattern — 295
The Extent of Rape **295** Patterns of Forcible Rape **296** BOX 3. Rape: Verdict Was Guilty On All Counts **297**

The Identification, Control, and Prediction of Violence — 299

9 Avocational and Commonplace Crime — 307

Avocational Criminal Behavior Systems — 308
Selected Avocational Offense Patterns **308** Criminal Careers and Self-Concept **310** Affiliational Aspects in Avocational Crime Patterns **311** Convergence of Criminal and Conventional Behavior Patterns **313** Societal Reaction to Avocational Crime Patterns **314**

Commonplace or Traditional Criminal Behavior Patterns — 315

Types of Offense Patterns 315   Commonplace Criminal Careers and Self-Concept 316   BOX 1. Tales of a Reformed Car Thief 321   Affiliational Aspects of Commonplace Crime Patterns 323   Convergence of Conventional and Criminal Behavior Patterns 325   Societal Reaction and Definition of Criminality 326   BOX 2. Basketball, Drugs, and the Black Schoolboy 327

10   White-Collar Crime Patterns   333

The Meaning and Scope of White-Collar Crime   334
Types of White-Collar Crime Patterns   336
BOX 1. Arson 337   Occupational White-Collar Crime 339   Corporate White-Collar Crime 340   Official White-Collar Crime 342   Careers and Self-Concepts of White-Collar Criminals 344   BOX 2. Operation CHAOS: The CIA's Special Operations Group 345

White-Collar Crime: Behavior Systems and Affiliation   349
White-Collar Crime: Criminal and Conventional Convergences   352
Occupational White-Collar Crime 353   BOX 3. Rx for Medifraud 354   Corporate White-Collar Crime 357   Multinational Corporations and Convergence of Conventional and Criminal Patterns 358   Advertising and Mass Appeals as Overlap of Conventional and Criminal Patterns 359   BOX 4. The Biggest Bribers 360

Societal Reaction: Deterrence and Social Control of White-Collar Crime   361
Social Control of White-Collar Crime: Regulatory Agencies 362   The Deterrent Effect of Punishment 363   Controlling Occupational White-Collar Crime 364   Controlling Corporate White-Collar Crime 365   Controlling Official White-Collar Crime 367   BOX 5. For Convicted Businessmen, Watergate Is Only a Memory 368

11   Victimless Crimes and Public Order Crime Patterns   373

Are Public Order Crimes Victimless?   374
Selected Patterns of Public Order Crime   375
Sexual Offenses: Prostitution and Homosexual Behavior 376   Drunkenness: Patterns of Blaming the Victim 379

Drug Use and Victimless Crime Patterns   380
Drug Types and Definitions 380   BOX 1. Marijuana Decriminalization, 1980 385

Status Offender Careers: Self-Concept, Group Support, and Convergences   386
Sex Offender Careers 387   Careers of Substance Users 391

Signification: Societal Reaction to Victimless Crimes   395
Signifying Sex Offenders 396   Signifying Substance Use Offenders 398   Problems in Regulating Victimless Crimes 402

PART FOUR
Crime Control and Societal Reaction: Criminal Justice, Intervention, and Prevention   405

12   Law Enforcement: Police, Crime, and the Community   407

The Police: A Visible Symbol   407
Origins of Modern Police: From the "Watch System to Bureaucracy"   409
Early History 409   Federal, State, and Local Police: Fragmentation and Expansion 411

Police Functions in Contemporary Society   414

The Police as Primary Agents of Direct Social Control **416** The Police as Buffers and as a Linkage in the Criminal Justice System **417** BOX 1. Law Enforcement Code of Ethics **418** Comprehensive Service Function of the Police **419** Police as Symbols of Governmental Authority **421** The Occupational Culture and Role Definition of the Police **422**

Police Organization: Management, Operation, and Control — 423
Changing Emphases **425**

Police Work: Patterns and Problems — 428
Patterns of Police Operations **429**

Policing and the Rule of Law — 435
Arrest and Clearance **436** Police Discretionary Power: Use and Misuse **437** BOX 2. The Miranda Warning **440** Police Corruption: "Bad Apples" or Social Patterns? **442**

Politicization of the Police and Other Dilemmas for the Rule of Law — 443
New Technologies: The Police as Technicians **444** Policing and the Community **445** The Ineffectiveness of Present Strategies **446** Improving Police Citizen Cooperation and Minimizing the Fear of Crime **448**

13 The Courts and the Administration of Justice — 453

Processing the Defendant: Applying Criminal Definitions — 454
Stages in Processing: Pretrial and No-Trial **454** Discretionary Aspects of Pretrial and No-trial Processing **457** Negotiated Pleas: Bargain Justice? **459** The Trial Process: Ideal versus Reality **461**

Major Roles in the Court — 465
The Judge **465** The Prosecutor **466** Defense Counsel **467** The Jury **468**

The Structure of the Court System — 470
Federal and State Court Systems: Dual Sovereignty or Fragmentation? **470** Juvenile Courts: "The Worst of Both Worlds"? **472**

Pervasive Problems of the Courts: Limiting Discretion and Capital Punishment — 474
Sentencing Disparities **474** BOX 1. Making Sure Punishment Fits the Crime **476** Indeterminate Sentences and Sentencing Disparity **477** Limiting Discretion: Fixed Sentences or General Principles? **477**

Capital Punishment: Deterrence and Retribution or Irreparable Caprice? — 478
BOX 2. The Case for Capital Punishment **481** BOX 3. The Argument Against Capital Punishment **484** Racial and Social Bias in Capital Punishment **485** Irreversibility **487** Cost-Benefit Analysis **487** BOX 4. The Execution of John A. Spenkelink **489**

14 Jails: Their Function in Detention and Confinement — 493

The Function of Jails in America — 494
A Historical Perspective on Jails **495**

Organization, Administration, and Conditions of Jails Today — 498
Organization and Administration **498** Jail Conditions: Crowding and Neglect **499** Inadequate Physical Facilities **500** Inadequate Staff **501** Administrative Inadequacies **504**

Depopulating the Jail: Alternatives to Pretrial Detention and Diversion — 505
Detention Reform: Citations or Summonses in Lieu of Arrest **506** Depopulating Jails: Bail Reform and Release on Recognizance **507** Speedy Trial Procedures **509** Depopulating the Jails Through Case Screening and Pretrial Diversion **510** Juvenile Diversion in England and the United States **511**

Alternatives for Those Sentenced to Jails — 513

Suspended Sentences **514**   Fines **514**   Probation **514**
Sentence Options Related to the Jail Program **515**
A Changing Role for the Jail — 516
Community Corrections: Fad or Reform? **516**

15 The Dilemma of Corrections: Treatment, Punishment, or Justice? — 521
The Scope of Corrections — 522
The Nature and Extent of Corrections **522**   The Goals of Corrections **525**
The History of the Prison:
Inglorious Reforms and Present Patterns — 527
The Social Structure of the Prison — 532
Formal Organization of Prisons **532**   Organizational Structures **533**   Prison Guards or Correctional Officers? **535**   BOX 1. Jail Guards, Good and Bad **538**
Informal Prison Organization: The Inmate's World — 540
Traditional Views of the Convict World: The Prison Culture **540**   Importation and Interchange Models of Inmate Social Organization **542**   Implications of the "Interchange" Model **544**
The Effects of Correctional Programs: Does Anything Work? — 545
Rehabilitation and Treatment Assumptions **545**   Educational Programs: Academic and Vocational **546**   Individual Therapy (Treatment) **547**   Group Therapy (Treatment) **547**   Behavior Modification: Treatment or Repression? **549**   Work Release **549**   Community-Based Treatment **550**   Probation **550**   Parole **550**   Half-Way Houses **551**   Sentencing and the Effectiveness of Punishment **551**   The Interchangeability of Penal Measures **552**
European Correctional Perspectives — 553
Limiting the Use of Prisons in Northern Europe **553**   BOX 2. No More Prisons? There Are Alternatives **554**   Treatment Ideology: Breakthrough and Reevaluation **555**
The Future of Corrections — 556
BOX 3. Prisons: A Global Problem **557**   The Abolitionists **560**   The "Realists" or Conservative Neoclassicists **561**   The Justice Model **562**

16 Public Policy: Crime and Social Priorities — 569
Perspectives on Crime Control — 569
Crime Policy Reform **572**
Dilemmas of Crime Control Efforts — 573
Justice in the Macro Society — 577
Crime Control Policy for the Future **579**
A Just Criminal Justice System as a Policy to Control Crime — 583
How Might the Criminal Laws Be Made More Just? **583**   What Is the Role of the Police in the Community? To Whom Are They Accountable? **584**   Limiting Judicial Discretion and Promoting Justice as Fairness **584**   Alternatives to Corrections **585**   BOX 1. Criminals: Doing Good Instead of Time **586**   Parole and Reentry: Should Parole Be Abolished? Should Ex-Offenders Receive Amnesty? **589**
By Way of Conclusion — 591

NOTES — 593

INDEX — 625

PART ONE

Introduction to the Study of Criminology

1 Criminology: The Study of Crime and Criminality
2 Criminal Law and the Study of Crime and Criminality

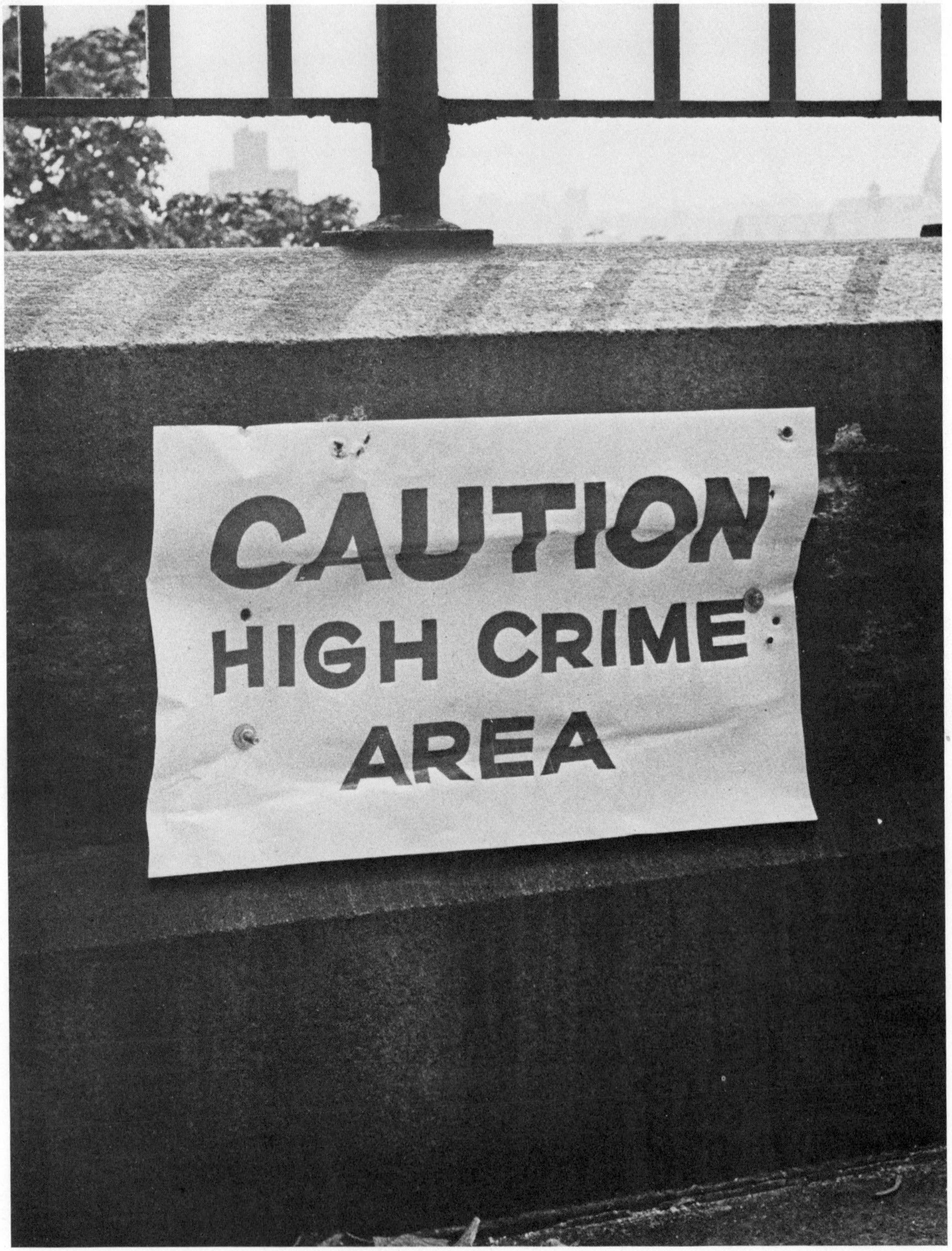
CAUTION
HIGH CRIME
AREA

And such was the state of mind that a few dared to commit the worst crime, many more would have liked to do so, and all acquiesced.
—Tacitus, History I

CRIMINOLOGY: THE STUDY OF CRIME AND CRIMINALITY

In beginning a study of modern criminology—a study that encompasses a variety of competing perspectives—it is essential to pose three basic questions regarding the study of crime and to summarize some of the shared understandings and competing answers.

First, *What is crime?* To what extent are public concerns regarding crime based on fact, and to what extent are they based on misconceptions and myths? What are some of the disagreements regarding the meaning of crime that enliven the field of criminology?

Second, *What is criminology?* What are its major concerns and assumptions? What do criminologists do? Are they concerned mainly with theories and explanations, or with ameliorating and improving both individuals and conditions associated with crime?

Third, *What is criminality?* Who is a criminal? Can the causes of criminal behavior be explained by sociological or psychological theories, or are our only "explanations" the definitions provided by the legal system?

You may already have anticipated some, or even all, of these questions. Indeed, an awareness of the crime problem and a desire to understand it may be one of the reasons you have decided to study criminology. Crime, after all, is an undeniable fact of contemporary society. To the extent that we can think analytically and critically about the crime problem, we should be able to comprehend our modern world more fully.

WHAT IS CRIME?

Most Americans feel they have an idea of what crime is all about. It's no wonder, as we are confronted with a steady diet of fact and fiction, reality and myth, in both the entertainment world and the news media. Since well over one hundred million serious crimes—homicide, aggravated assault, forcible rape, robbery, burglary, larceny, and auto theft—have been reported to the police since 1960, it is likely that each of us has direct knowledge of someone who has been victimized by crime.

Still, for the large majority of Americans, attitudes and definitions of crime are derived largely from vicarious rather than direct personal experience. Thus, when we think about crime, we tend to view it as behavior alien to us or to "normal" society. Our first reaction is to consider "crime in the streets" or "organized crime," for these are the most feared types of crime—the types that receive the most attention in newspapers, television, and popular literature. Yet these crimes make up only a small proportion of the nature and extent of crime in our society.[1]

Given the reliance on the media for much of our information and ideas about such social issues as crime, it is doubtful that many citizens think analytically about the meaning of crime. Even though the crime problem is very much a part of the contemporary scene, the manner in which it is purveyed to us may lead to shared misunderstandings and a limited or distorted perception of its complex nature. The ways in which popular notions of crime influence our perceptions about the extent of crime will be dealt with in Chapter 3. Our inquiry here will focus first on where and how such limited images of crime have been generated in our popular culture and how our folklore influences our perceptions of crime. Then we will survey competing definitions of crime and how certain types of behavior come to be defined as crime. Next we will present a legal definition of crime, and finally, we will discuss the implications of crime.

Images of Crime in American Folklore and History

Many of our misconceptions about crime have come down to us by way of American "popular" culture. The cheap pulp fiction and "dime" novels that were published from the 1880s through the 1940s presented a limited and distorted view of crime in our society.[2] Other popular literary forms, such as the crime comic strip Dick Tracy, which began in 1931, projected a view of crime as the activity of flawed, sinister beings.[3] Motion pictures have presented unreal images of crime and criminals, such as the romanticized heroes in *Bonnie and Clyde*. At the same time, radio and television have reiterated themes quite removed from the reality of crime and the criminal justice system. *Perry Mason*, a series that has endured since 1957, thanks to reruns, depicts a brilliant lawyer who each week not only proves his own client innocent and accused unjustly of a heinous crime, but who also fingers the real criminal, dramatically getting him or her to break down and confess on the witness stand. In so doing, he invariably outwits and humiliates Lt. Tragg, the bumbling police inspector, and the arrogant prosecutor, Berger. More recent television programs have projected similarly unrealistic images of crime and justice in series such as *Baretta, Columbo,* and *Kojak,* although the stars of these programs and

Images of crime in American folklore.

their settings provide characters and urban situations with which we can easily identify.[4]

Popular culture, which occupies much of our society's leisure time, presents a limited, distorted view of crime. While there is considerable shared understanding and agreement among Americans concerning the reality of crime, there is also a folklore and a mythology of crime. The images or stereotypes of crime that do exist—whether from folk traditions, popular literature, films, or other mass media—provide a "reality" of crime that is not based on careful analysis, although often in its own way it is insightful.[5]

As John Conklin has suggested, the "criminal environment" of a society consists of the myths, legends, and images of crime that it holds. These perspectives are influenced by data from a variety of sources. And while the concern with crime that grows from such sources may not necessarily correspond objectively to real dangers that people may confront, conceptions about crime may create the belief that crime is a more serious problem than it used to be.[6] The fear of crime, then, is real, whether or not it is based on accurate data. A public opinion poll conducted for the National Center for State Courts in 1978, for example, indicated that Americans were more worried about street crime than inflation, unemployment, or any other national problem. When asked to note "serious social problems," an overwhelming 88 percent listed "street crimes," 83 percent noted drugs, and inflation and unemployment were third and fourth with 79 and 67 percent, respectively.[7] Perhaps it is this *fear of crime,* rather than any actual increase or decrease in law-violating behavior, that determines whether or not we experience a "crime wave." Indeed, public perception of crime waves appears to be a perennial problem. The Crime Commission noted in one of its task force reports in 1967 that just about every generation since the beginning of our nation has felt threatened by rising crime and violence.[8]

Public perceptions of the crime problem often evoke images of a "criminal element"—outcasts and antisocial aliens in a society that basically is law abiding. But the average citizen is seldom aware of the complexity of crime and its intricate relationship to social structure. As Daniel Bell pointed out more than a quarter century ago, crime can be seen as a distorted mirror that caricatures the morals and customs of society. He was describing organized crime and the manner in which it paralleled the junglelike quality of early American business.[9] Organized criminals, who are relatively invisible, and white-collar criminals, who are the most coddled, are not what the public generally pictures when thinking of criminal types. Obviously, neither organized crimes nor white-collar crimes can be laid at the feet of the "crime-prone," underprivileged classes. But these two types of offenses accounted for about 65 percent of the total estimated cost of crime in 1976—some $125 billion.

Americans do not often think of everyday people as being involved in crime. Even though they might believe that crime is on the increase, they find it difficult to accept the idea that criminal offenses are committed by ordinary people. One reason may stem from public conceptions of crime and criminals that are shaped to some degree by the fictionalized portrayal of stereotypical characters in the movies and on TV. Unfortunately, the characters in *Baretta*, *Kojak*, or *Hawaii Five-O* usually lack the subtlety of real individuals and provide us with very little insight into the crime problem in our society.

Perhaps the best way to deal both with the false conception of crime of the popular media and with public concern over the crime wave is to develop some sense of the problem's complexity. This awareness might temper the assumption that the crime problem can be dealt with in isolation from the conflicts in the social structure of our society.[10] Crime is an ethical, economic, moral, and political issue, as well as an individual or social issue. Unfortunately, it cannot be controlled merely by controlling the offenders.

Competing Perspectives in the Definition of Crime

The general public tends to share a limited and distorted idea about crime. Would specialists from various fields such as criminology, anthropology, law, psychology, sociology, social work, and criminal justice and others concerned with interpreting such behavior provide a more definitive meaning of what crime is? If they were asked, What is crime? would we discover any agreement on the explicit meaning of crime? No. We would not discover much of a consensus not only because of the different perspectives of these specialists but also because crime is not a unitary phenomenon. It covers a wide range of diverse behaviors. There is considerable disagreement, even among criminologists, regarding the exact nature of crime. The positions outlined below highlight these competing views and underscore the complexity of the study of crime.

Natural Law. This position holds that there is a body of universal principles and rules that are basic to the legal and social regulation of human conduct. These rules are assumed to come from a higher source than the enacted (positive) law and are claimed to reflect a natural law. Any violation of this natural law is seen as a crime. The natural law also stands as a set of universal standards against which enacted law can be evaluated.[11] When an enacted law is seen as being out of line with these higher principles, it might be regarded as "unjust." In his "Letter from the Birmingham Jail," Martin Luther King appealed to this higher law when he argued that though we have a responsibility to obey just laws, we also have a moral responsibility to disobey unjust laws.[12]

The idea of natural law can be traced all the way back to the earliest written legal codes, like the Code of Hammurabi (c. 1900 B.C.) and the Ten Commandments of the Judaic–Christian tradition. References to natural law can be found in classical philosophers like Aristotle and Cicero. Cicero, for example, asserted: "There is in fact a true law which in accordance with nature, applies to all."[13] The American Declaration of Independence assumed the "natural right to life, liberty and the pursuit of happiness."

Assuming that natural law is universal, some scholars have sought to identify universal crimes. In the late nineteenth century, the Italian criminologist Raffaele Garofalo, who wrote of the natural or born criminal, attempted to discover whether there were any crimes "which at all times and in all places" would be seen as "punishable acts." He concluded that the idea could not be proved.[14] More recently, criminologist Herman Mannheim noted that the idea of natural law has resulted in varying interpretations. He concluded that the idea comes from a human longing for an absolute measure of "goodness or badness," though no such measure can be found.[15]

Legalistic Determinism. The importance of the criminal law in the definition of crime is stressed in legalistic determinism. Jerome Michael and Mortimer J. Adler, in their cogent critique of criminology, *Crime, Law and Social Science* (1933), argued that since crime is "conduct proscribed by the criminal code it follows that the criminal law is the formal cause of crime." That is, "the criminal law gives behavior its quality of criminality." They concluded that this is the only possible definition of crime.[16]

Legal Realism. This position emphasizes the social and human context of legal definitions of crime, the process by which judges and courts decide whether or not a given behavior is criminal. It recognizes that "judges make law," rather than merely apply it in a neutral manner.[17] The legal realists stress the human aspect of the process and the fact that since law is human it cannot be absolute. Legal precedent and laws are used to support a judge's decision, which is also based on the idea of "justness"—determined in part by his or her personal background. In one of his often quoted essays, Supreme Court Justice Holmes draws on the underlying rationale of the realist position: "A legal duty so called is nothing but a prediction that if a man does or omits certain things he will be made to suffer . . . by judgment of a court."[18]

Lawyer and sociologist Paul Tappan offered an earlier definition of crime in this same vein. He suggested that "only those are criminals who have been adjudicated as such by the courts."[19] He held that the person defined as a criminal has that label imposed on him or her as a result of the social enterprise of whose who are charged by the state with that duty. Tappan in a later work defined crime as "an *intentional* act or omission in *violation* of the criminal law, *committed without defense* of justification, and *sanctioned* by the state as a felony or misdemeanor." [20] The realist position is significant for its emphasis on the manner in which criminal definitions are applied in court proceedings and for the recognition that such labels are bestowed as a result of the law in action, which involves "social action on the part of those who create and enforce the laws as well as the act itself." [21]

Cultural Determinism. Many early sociologists and criminologists tended to seek a broad, "normative" definition of crime rather than rely upon the law, which they viewed as too relative and changeable for systematic analysis. Thus, cultural determinists sought to define crime as behavior that was in violation of the norms of a given society.

Norms are the social rules that constrain our behavior. Following the classification of William Graham Sumner, norms are usually divided into *folkways, mores,* and *laws.* These designations denote the manner in which norms vary in their degree of obligation, specificity, severity of sanction, source of social control, and the agents who enforce them. Thorsten Sellin argued that crime is conduct in violation of "conduct norms," whether or not it involves the violation of a specific criminal law. The search for an objective definition of crime led, in time, to an emphasis on the individual offender and on his or her biological traits, personality, and social factors rather than the act. As a result of this emphasis, the study of law was slighted by early criminologists.[22]

Social Reaction. This perspective sees crime as a result of social interaction—a social enterprise that involves the "rulemakers," "rule enforcers," and "rulebreakers." [23] The focus of this perspective, often referred to as the *labeling perspective,* is not on behavior but on the process of societal reaction by which agents of the state assign the legal status of crime to certain behaviors. The stress is upon explaining why and how the behavior comes to be labeled criminal.[24]

Interest Group Conflict. This perspective also stresses the formation and application of social definitions of crime. But rather than viewing the law (or rules defining crime) as a reflection of a broad normative consensus in society, it perceives law as the result of opposing group interests in a society characterized by social change, conflict, and force.[25] Crime is not necessarily the result of conflict with the collective conscience of society, but rather conflict with those interest groups in society that possess the power to shape public policy through the enactment and enforcement of criminal law. Crime is the expression of such conflict. For instance, the Prohibition laws were the result of a reform movement by rural Protestant interests against urban morality. However, this approach and the interactionist analysis are less applicable—except in rigid ideological versions—to crimes such as murder, rape, and burglary.[26]

New Critical Criminology. Definitions of crime from these perspectives— there are varying emphases, among others, the "natural rights" position and

Marxist positions—move beyond a legalistic conception of crime. The *natural rights* definition of the Schwendingers and others links the definition of crime to definitions of criminal justice. Crime is seen as behavior that denies certain rights to individuals or groups. Thus, the denial of racial or sexual equality becomes the crime of racism or sexism.[27] A more ideological and radical version of critical criminology, such as Richard Quinney's reformulation of the conflict perspective, defines crime in terms of the domination of and accommodation by the working class in the capitalist system. Crime, he argues, is a legal definition assigned by authorized agents of the state to behavior that conflicts with the interests of the ruling class.[28] Some of the implications of these new critical orientations will be discussed more fully below and in Chapter 6.

What Kind of Behavior Is Crime?

Under the law the criminal is a person who has been so defined by the criminal law. Yet, you might ask, "Does such a label apply only to those who have been convicted of a given crime in a court of law? What about those who have, in fact, violated the law but have not yet been found guilty, or those not yet known or arrested?"[29] The problem of the criminal who has not been adjudicated or convicted was a concern of Edwin H. Sutherland. In his study of white-collar crime, Sutherland sought to develop a definition that would include those who had not been sanctioned or sentenced:

> The essential characteristic of crime is that it is behavior which is prohibited by the State and against which the State may react, at least as a last resort, by punishment. The two abstract criteria generally regarded by legal scholars as necessary elements in a definition of crime are legal description of an act as socially harmful and legal provision of a penalty for the act.[30]

In his research on white-collar crime, Sutherland showed that criminal behavior is human behavior, except that when behavior is judged in terms of some standard of conduct, the adjective "criminal" is added. This definition should alert us to the risk of confusing crime as an act with the search for an answer to what causes criminal behavior in the constitutional makeup and environmental forces in the background of the offender. As C. Ray Jeffery has argued, a theory of criminal behavior is *not* a theory of crime, although the explanation of why and how individuals violate the law is a significant focus of criminology.

Jeffery emphasized that "we must ascertain those conditions whereby an act is defined as a crime so as to identify the relationships between legal definitions and other norms, for criminality exists in the social system that controls and regulates behavior, and not in the behavior."[31] (The relationship between the sociology of law and the legal system that defines criminality is discussed at length in Chapter 2.) In other words, if we broaden our definition of crime to include antisocial or undesirable social behavior, we not only neglect the legal status of crime, but rely upon assumed universal social—or, in the case of the radical perspective, political—definitions of right and wrong conduct.

A Legal Definition of Crime and Its Relativity

Behavior is criminal only when it is judged, defined, or labeled by some specific standard of conduct. And it is the criminal law that makes distinctions between criminal and noncriminal action. The question of why and how individuals violate the law is a separate aspect of criminology. What concerns us here is discovering why some acts are seen as criminal and why and how the criminal law is applied to these behaviors.

A legal definition of crime should not ignore the fact that crime is an ethical, moral, political, economic, and social phenomenon. The laws defining crime and the application of the label are influenced by the interplay of all of these forces, both in the present and the past. Our operational definition asserts that *crime is an intentional violation of the law* (commission or omission) *established by the political authority of the state, for which the violator is labeled as criminal and subject to sanctions or punishment by agents of the state.* We concur with that perspective in criminology which holds that crime is a legal status assigned to an act by authorized agents of the state.[32] It is the process and context of societal reaction to the act, as well as the law in action, which set limits to the range of behaviors being defined.

There are at least five interrelated elements that must be present for an act to be defined as a crime.[33]

1. There must be an act of either commission or omission.
2. The act must be in violation of a specific legal code.
3. There must be criminal intent *(mens rea)*.
4. There must be a causal relationship between the act and the harm that it has precipitated.
5. There must be some legally defined sanction or punishment specified for the individual convicted of the act.

These elements may overdraw the formal aspects of the criminal law—or what Sutherland and Cressey have termed its *politicality* (public legal authority), *specificity* (distinctions between criminal and civil law), *uniformity* (assumed evenhanded justice), and *penal sanction* (punitive) aspects—at the risk of glossing over the dynamic, subjective, and relative forces inherent in the application of such definitions.[34] But it should be noted that as a formal means of social control the criminal law represents a balance between social interests. So, when we talk about the *relativity of crime,* we should not just refer to the variations and disparities between jurisdictions. We also need to recognize that definitions of criminality and their development, existence, and application must be examined in a wider social perspective that places such "rules of law" in the context of other unwritten rules by which a society seeks to ensure conformity and to punish nonconformity.

The relativity of crime is evidence of its complexity, for good and bad are not readily defined in the stereotypical manner given us by television's cops-and-robbers morality. Arbitrary definition of crime, as well as deviance or nonconformity, may lead to one form of behavior being prohibited by law, while others, equally or even more injurious, may not be so defined. Nor are all law violators of similar types equally punished or sanctioned. Burglars, for instance, and those convicted of larceny and motor vehicle theft more frequently receive penal sanctions than do white-collar criminals such as those convicted of embezzlement and fraud in the federal courts. And burglars' sentences usually are longer. An understanding of the relativity inherent in the definitions of crime—definitions that sometimes are assumed to be neutral (because they are based on the law)—as well as social injustices (which are linked to the capricious use of discretion in crime control efforts) might be one benefit to be gained from a critical, systematic study of the contradictions inherent in our crime control system.[35]

Legal realism lent credence to the relative nature of the criminal law. As Tappan noted: "In the developed society ... criminal law and its correctional instruments become the ultimate regulators, though their effectiveness, like ... the mores, is circumscribed by public opinion and ... community reaction to constituted authority and those who offend." [36] Over the past several decades, sociologists and criminologists, building upon the ideas of the French sociologist Emile Durkheim (1858–1917), have broadened the relativism of the realists. Durkheim's thesis went beyond the idea of relativism. He argued that crime and deviation are common features of all societies, even one of a "society of saints" composed solely of "exemplary individuals." In such a group, there might well be a heightened sense of morality, and crimes as such might be unknown. But a society of saints might come to define insults and slander as serious offenses against members of the group.[37]

The *social reactionist* or *labeling* perspective takes a more extreme sociological view of crime. Quinney notes that proponents of this view see crime and other forms of deviant behavior as categories created and imposed upon some persons by others.[38] They focus on the process by which members of a society decide what rules to create and apply. The process is seen as inherently political, and thus crime is considered relative rather than absolute.

The related *conflict perspective* has also had a wide influence upon a great many sociologists and criminologists. Studies of reform movements that have influenced public policy, such as child labor laws, juvenile court statutes and Prohibition—have shown that these reforms were not entirely humanitarian, but also served the interests and values esteemed by dominant groups in society. Quinney has commented that "by formulating criminal law (including legislative statutes, administrative rulings, and judicial decisions), some segments of society protect and perpetuate their own interests." Thus, in this view, the criminal law is the result of conflict between groups in society. The law, including criminal definitions, penal sanctions, and policies of crime control and prevention, reflects the interests of those who have power and a stake in regulating those of conflicting interest who have less power.[39] Both the labeling and conflict perspectives focus upon what has become a dominant sociological view of crime and criminality. Crime is seen as the expression of a balance between conflicting social values and pressures; criminality is the consequence of a conflict situation.

This discussion of sociological perspectives has considered an important aspect of criminology: "accounting for the definitions by which specific behavior comes to be considered as crime or noncrime." [40] It has also provided an opportunity to stress a major theme underlying our approach to the problem of crime. Crime is not a unitary phenomenon. There are numerous persistent criminal definitions related to crimes against persons and property, and data concerning the extent of criminal activity are based upon the law. The American criminal justice system and crime control efforts operate within the law. The criminal is the "one who has been defined as such by the criminal law." [41]

WHAT IS CRIMINOLOGY?

The subject matter of criminology embraces ten major concerns. As outlined by Walter Reckless, these include:[42]

1. The compilation of crime data including offenses committed, arrests, and types of violators.
2. A comparative, cross-cultural study of criminal law as related to socio-economic, political systems of societies in transition.
3. Studies of the demographic characteristics of adult and juvenile offenders, with attention to categories at risk and the distribution of offenses and offenders.
4. The formulation and testing of hypotheses that seek to explain patterns of crime and delinquency.
5. The formulation and description of various criminal behavior systems that might be identified within various societies.
6. The study of recidivism, habitual offenders, and those first offenders who relapse or desist.
7. The study of status offenses or victimless crimes as these relate to crimes against public definitions of morality.
8. The systematic study of law enforcement organizations and the effectiveness of law enforcement relative to special offender types.
9. The study of penal measures including the relative effectiveness of treatment in institutions and community-based alternatives.
10. The evaluation of crime and delinquency prevention programs.

The difficulty in developing, or even defining, a unified field of study is evident from the diversity of this list, which includes theoretical, descriptive, and applied topics. In the academic world, theoretical and applied areas usually are separated. The theoretical realm of criminology is broadly defined as the *systematic study of crime and criminals.* In particular it focuses on causes of crime, types of offenders, crime trends and the extent of crime, the process of defining behavior as criminal, and crime control measures, including prevention and correctional efforts. Applied criminology currently is categorized as *criminal justice.* This term refers to the organization and function of those agencies that seek to control or manage crime—the police, courts, and corrections. But the distinction between the two areas is not that simple, for in its study of crime and social reaction to crime, criminologists have studied just about every aspect of the criminal justice process.[43]

There is tension between the theoretical and applied dimensions of criminology, just as there is tension between the different theoretical perspectives. The most persistent area of conflict has been between those criminological perspectives that seek to develop theories of *criminal behavior* as distinct from *noncriminal behavior,* and those perspectives that stress the necessity of explaining why behavior is labeled *criminal* in the first place. This is the problem of explaining *criminality.*[44] Commenting on this conflict some years ago, George B. Vold noted: "There is, therefore, a dual problem of explanation—that of accounting for the behavior as behavior, and equally important, accounting for the definitions by which specific behavior comes to be considered as crime or noncrime."[45]

As we search the history of criminology, this dilemma may become more apparent, both in the theoretical (or scientific), and in the practical dimensions of the multidisciplinary study of crime and criminality.

WHAT IS CRIMINALITY?

Theories of Crime and Criminality

Although many of the substantive concerns that are included in the study of criminology were addressed by classical philosophers, there was no formal study of the causes of crime until the eighteenth century. Before then, crime and criminal behavior were explained by interpretations that rested upon moral or religious beliefs. Crime was defined as sin or immoral behavior. The causes of deviant behavior were thought to be related to one's relationship to the spiritual world. Nonconformers were viewed as sinners or those who chose to be bad. During the reign of Henry VIII in England (1509–1547), much behavior formerly thought of as sin became defined as crime, while behavior previously held to be immoral became illegal. Thus sinners were defined as criminals.

As the state took over efforts to deal with such behavior, a harsh and repressive legal system developed, based on despotism and the arbitrary authority of the king, the church, and the aristocracy. Crimes were ill-defined. On the continent of Europe, police were ruthless and judicial procedures gave the accused little chance of proving their innocence. Punishments were also arbitrary and applied unequally; and the nobility were exempt from the most severe forms. Little progress in criminal legislation, which was based upon principles of intimidation and vengeance, was made during the early Middle Ages.[46]

It was against this backdrop that new views of the individual and society emerged in the intellectual ferment referred to by historians as the "Enlightenment." The *philosophes,* or French social thinkers of the period, appealed to "natural law" and "natural rights," which they interpreted using reason and the new scientific approach. During this time of social upheaval, which even-

When does immoral behavior or sin become crime?

tually led to the French Revolution, attacks upon the *ancien regime* included ideas for reforming the legal system. Thinkers such as Montesquieu and Voltaire condemned the arbitrary powers of the system and demanded that all should be equal before the law. In other parts of Europe similar reforms were being advocated. The scene was set for what has become known as the *classical school* of criminology.[47]

The Classical School

The major contribution of the classical school was not in the development of a theory of crime as such, for the individual was assumed to possess "free will" and the power of choice. Cesare Beccaria, an Italian aristocrat, is usually cited as the founder of this school (see Box 1). His essay, *On Crime and Punishment,* published anonymously in 1764, expressed in cogent and coherent form the new concepts of justice that were emerging from the Enlightenment. Leon Radzinowicz has suggested that the basic ideas of this document comprise what have become the essentials of the "liberal doctrine" of criminal law. In abbreviated form these concluded that:[48]

1. Since criminal law places restrictions on individual freedom, it should be limited.
2. The presumption of innocence should be the guiding principle in the administration of justice.
3. There should be a written code defining in advance both offenses and punishments.
4. Punishment should be retributive—that is, it should allow means whereby the offender might compensate or make redress in a manner that involves his private rights, as his offense has affected others.
5. The severity of punishment should be strictly limited. It should be proportionate to the crime and not go beyond that which is necessary to prevent further offenses or deter others.
6. Punishment should correspond to the nature of the offense. For instance, fines are suitable punishments for simple thefts, corporal punishment is suitable for violent crimes.
7. Punishments should be administered with speed and certainty.
8. The offender should be punished for what he has done and not used for reformatory measures or as an example to society—that is, the right of judges to interpret laws should be narrowly limited and based on the offense committed, rather than vary according to the personality of the offender.
9. The potential offender is seen as an independent, reasoning individual who could consider the consequences of crime. Therefore, all deserve the same punishment for the same offense.
10. It is better to prevent crimes than to punish them. This requires a definite, limited code of laws.

Pioneers in Criminology

BOX 1

Cesare Beccaria (1734–1794)

Cesare Bonesana, Marquis di Beccaria, was born in Milan to aristocratic parents. He graduated from the University of Pavia and subsequently developed an interest in philosophy and literature, especially the writings of the French *philosophes*, Montesquieu, Rousseau, and others.

In 1764 he published anonymously the essay, *Dei delitti et dille pene* (*On Crime and Punishment*), an attack on the arbitrary, abusive, repressive, and barbaric law and criminal justice practices prevalent in eighteenth-century Europe. This little book set forth a new concept of criminal justice based on the concepts of the social contract and natural rights of the Enlightenment.

The essay outlined these basic principles: (1) punishment for crime should be based upon law (the idea of *nullum crimen sine lege*); (2) application of the laws of society should be equal for all, regardless of class; (3) the severity of punishment should be both limited and certain, and it should correspond to the offense; (4) the reasonable basis of punishment is its deterrent effect; and (5) the prevention of crime will come about through the enactment of just laws applied equally to all.

Beccaria's ideas soon became widely accepted, and even the enlightened despots of the eighteenth century adopted some of them, including the abolition of the death penalty in some countries. Some of these principles eventually found their way into our own Declaration of Independence in 1776, the French Revolution's Declaration of the Rights of Man in 1789, and the infamous French Penal Code of 1791, which otherwise, made a mockery of many of the ideals proclaimed by the Revolution.

Source: Abstracted from Elio Monachesi, "Cesare Beccaria," in H. Mannheim *Pioneers in Criminology*. Montclair, N.J.: Patterson Smith, 1972, pp. 36–49.

Beccaria's ideas departed sharply from the harsh, arbitrary nature of the prevailing laws. He even advocated the abolition of the death penalty—even for murder—although this position was inconsistent with the logic of the "liberal creed." Beccaria's ideas were central to what has become known as the *classical school,* and English philosophers and reformers, such as William Blackstone (1723–1780), Jeremy Bentham (1748–1832), and Sir Samuel Romilly (1757–1818), adapted and applied his views to their efforts to reform the English legal system.

Through English law, Beccaria indirectly helped to influence the criminal law in America. Romilly used his arguments to secure reduction in the use of the death penalty. Bentham modified Beccaria's idea of proportionate punishments in the principle of the *felicity calculus:* punishment should be administered in a manner calculated to make the pain of punishment outweigh the pleasure derived from committing the offense, but should not go beyond that required to induce conformity to the law. And Blackstone's *Commentaries on the Laws of England,* which is known to every American legal scholar, was influenced by Beccaria in its discussion of English criminal law, although it was published only a year after Beccaria's essay.[49]

These ideas were altered in the early nineteenth century by neoclassical thinkers who modified the doctrine of free will to take note of mitigating circumstances such as incompetence, insanity, imbecility, or age as they related to responsibility. The M'Naghten case (1843) established the rule in English and American courts for determining the question of sanity or insanity based upon the offender's capability for distinguishing between right and wrong. The M'Naghten rule states that the "insane person" lacks responsibility. Being not guilty by reason of insanity, he is confined in a hospital rather than imprisoned. From their statistical analyses, the neoclassical critics concluded that specific social arrangements were directly related to specific criminal outcomes. The implication was that official crime rates were a regular feature of social activity rather than of individual propensities toward crime.[50]

The basic concepts of the classical school are established in the legal principles of *nullum crimen sine lege* (no crime without law), and *nullen poena sine lege* (no punishment without law)—principles that still dominate our contemporary legal system. The transition from the classical school's emphasis on the free will of the individual actor to the deterministic position was stimulated by the work of a Belgian, Adolphe Quetelet, and a Frenchman, A. M. Guerry. Quetelet and Guerry were the first to apply the scientific method to the study of crime, using crime statistics to explore the relationship between crime and social factors.

The Positive School

The nineteenth century provided us with two contrasting approaches to the study of crime, both essentially deterministic. Each grew out of the scientific developments of that century. The first emphasized crime as the result of social factors, or "kinds of environments." The other viewed crime as the result of the individual's constitution, his or her physical and psychological traits.[51] In twentieth-century criminology these two approaches were to become even more divergent.

The origin of the *positive school*—or, for that matter, the origin of criminology, itself—is often attributed to the theories of Cesare Lombroso (1835–1919). Lombroso influenced two other important Italian social thinkers, Enrico Ferri (1856–1928) and Raffaele Garofalo (1852–1934), and he, in turn, was influenced by them. The positive school is so called because its methods of inquiry were patterned after the objective approach to human behavior set forth by Auguste Comte (1798–1857), the French philosopher. This mode of inquiry sees society as a mechanistic entity governed by laws of cause and effect that, if studied systematically, would enable us to predict and control future events. These positivists sought to apply the natural science model of cause and effect and the scientific method to the study of crime and the criminal. The ideas set forth by Lombroso, expanded and revised in the five editions of his book, *L'uomo deliquente (The Criminal Man)*, between 1876 and 1897, were a synthesis of ideas developed earlier by Darwin, Spencer, Comte, and others.[52]

Although based on natural science, the inspirational "leap of faith" implicit in Lombroso's concept of the "criminal man" is revealed in the following quote from the introduction to a summary of his ideas written for his American followers by his devoted daughter:

> I ... began to study criminals in the Italian prisons, and ... I made the acquaintance of the famous Brigand Vilella. This man possessed ... extraordinary agility.... His cynical effrontery was such that he openly boasted of his crimes. On his death one cold grey November morning, I was deputed to make the postmortem, and on laying open the skull I found on the occipital part, exactly on the spot where a spine is found in the normal skull, a distinct depression which I named the *median occipital fossa*, because of its situation precisely in the middle of the occiput.... This depression, ... was correlated with the hypertrophy of the vermis, known in birds as the middle cerebellum.
>
> This was not merely an idea, but a revelation. At the sight of that skull, I seemed to see all of a sudden, lighted up as a vast plain under a flaming sky, the problem of the nature of the criminal—an atavistic being who reproduces in his person the ferocious instincts of primitive humanity and the inferior animals.[53]

Scholars have long since abandoned the idea of the atavistic, or primitive criminal, but the image of the "depraved being" still surfaces in public perceptions of criminal types.

In his later years, Lombroso modified his ideas to acknowledge the existence of environmental factors. But he still regarded most criminals as defective, degenerate, or inferior in some way. His student, Ferri, was more eclectic in his emphasis on the interrelation of biological and social factors. Ferri attempted both to develop an explanation of the criminal and to advocate means for preventing crime through social and economic reforms. He maintained a continuous attack against the classical (and neoclassical) school's concept of deterrence through punishment. Since he saw criminal behavior as either innate or a result of the social environment, Ferri argued that punishment lacked deterrent value, for it could not change an individual's nature.[54]

Garofalo, the third Italian positivist, also argued against the "penal proportion" ideas of the classical school—that the quantum of punishment should correspond to the quantum of crime. Instead, he advocated that the state intervene to protect the moral order of the community against the behavior of the "natural criminal,"—conduct that offends the basic moral feelings of probity (goodness) and pity (compassion). Garofalo's concept can be seen as a psychological corollary of Lombroso's atavism.[55] He held that an individual's capacity for crime should be weighed against his capacity to adapt or to be made to adapt to society. Both Ferri and Garofalo assented to the Fascist regime of Mussolini, demonstrating an apparent parallel between positivist assumptions about social control of the nonconformer and a totalitarian political system.[56]

Lombroso and his followers focused attention on the individual actor as a criminal type and perpetuated many a myth in the process. Yet, along with the social determinists with whom they engaged in continuing controversy during the latter part of the eighteenth century, they laid the groundwork for modern criminology.

The heritage of positivism retained in twentieth-century America can be summarized in the following trends and emphases in the study of the crime problem:[57]

1. Focus on the individual criminal, rather than the legal act.
2. Emphasis on scientific determinism and rejection of the idea of free will or individual choice.
3. The assumption that the offender is somehow different, "sick," or pathological, and therefore must be treated, corrected, or cured.
4. The rejection of punishment with its assumption of deterrence by correctional treatment based on the therapeutic or medical model, and the institution of penal reforms such as the indeterminate sentence and parole.

The positive school, then, emphasized *bio-psychological determinism*—the idea that crime was the result of constitutional factors, or "kinds-of-people" theories. At the same time, a second school of thought within the emerging field of scientific criminology sought to explain and control human behavior in terms of certain social or environmental theories. These two currents of nineteenth-century thought were equally deterministic. Both supposed that the methods of natural science could be extended to human behavior, and both placed their main emphasis on either "nature" or "nurture."

In the 1830s, Quetelet and Guerry stressed the significance of social factors such as age, sex, education, climate, and race. Their influence can be recognized in the report of the British Royal Commission on Crime in 1863, which concluded that social circumstances, such as the general level of welfare

Pioneers in Criminology

BOX 2

Cesare Lombroso (1835–1919)

Cesare Lombroso, whose dedication to the study of the "criminal man" led both to his being revered and reviled, is often credited with being the "father of modern criminology." Born in Verona, Italy, in 1835, he was an army physician and a professor of medical jurisprudence and psychiatry. The school of thought that he founded has variously been known as the *Italian*, the *anthropological*, the *modern*, and most frequently, the *positive school*.

The distinctive technique of Lombroso's criminal anthropology involved measurements of the cranium and the description of anomalies of the face and body structure. His theory involved three basic ideas. First came the concept of the born criminal. As a result of congenital and pathologic factors, members of this sub-species, *Homo delinquens*, were impelled to a life of crime. Second, this type was atavistic, a "throw-back" or "ghost from the past," similar to children and primitive peoples in their hedonistic, nonintellectual, curious, cruel, and cowardly emotions and behavior. Their behavior, morality, and phenotype was similar to the lunatic, especially the epileptic. Third, Lombroso contended that there is a *criminal type* who can be identified largely on the basis of physical traits and stigmata. Later in his life, Lombroso also described the "criminoloids," men who became criminals because of "vicious training" and "weak natures."

Lombroso noted with pride that his theories had become objects of "almost fanatical adherence," especially in America. He referred to the "brilliant results" obtained by the application of his ideas at the Reformatory at Elmira, New York, and in the development of the parole system and juvenile court.

Lombroso's biological determinism has long been outmoded, but his ideas reemerge every now and then wearing a more modern guise.

Source: Abstracted from Leonard D. Savitz, New Introduction in Gina Lombroso–Ferrero, *Criminal Man* (reprint edition). Montclair, N.J.: Patterson Smith, 1972, pp. vi–xx.

in society and the degree of employment or unemployment, were more influential in affecting the extent of crime than the existing system of punishments.[58]

Social determinism in the writings of Karl Marx, and more particularly in the works of his Dutch disciple, William Bonger, sought to explain crime in terms of the economic structure of society. Marx conceived of the criminal as an individual who is both determined by economic forces and who chooses such forces. He argued that exploitative social arrangements distort our social nature and alienate us. Therefore, criminal classes develop out of the most exploited segments in society—the *Lumpenproletariat*. While Bonger attributed criminal behavior to those individuals "demoralized" by capitalism, he described the criminal as a person in need of social control. Since capitalism produced egoism rather than altruism, he argued, socialism would provide more desirable and effective institutions for social control.[59]

Durkheim's stress on concrete social factors—for instance, changes in population that brought about changes in the normative arrangements leading in turn to *anomie* or deregulation—led him to conclude that without crime there could be no adaptation to change or progress. Thus, crime is a necessary, normal aspect of society. Durkheim also emphasized that crime served to promote the solidarity of the community and functioned to create a boundary-setting effect. In his *The Division of Labor in Society* (1933), he notes that when crime occurs, people react by increasing their social contacts, and attention is given to group solidarity as a result.[60] But this emphasis on complexity is much more subtle than recent interpretations of Durkheim by Robert K. Merton and others might lead us to conclude. His idea that crime was "normal" evoked strong attacks from both the French social theorist, Gabriel Tarde, and Enrico Ferri—two men who had little in common other than their opposition to the idea that crime is an integral aspect of all societies.[61]

The Positive School and Social Reforms

These new criminological theories, stressing bio-psychological and social determinism, did much to weaken the classical assumptions of criminal law. Social reforms in the nineteenth century further eroded these ideas. Reform movements in both America and Great Britain stressed social conditions resulting from industrialization and urbanization and related them to the creation of crime. This emphasis was epitomized in the idea of the "criminal classes" and social evils described in the social novels of Charles Dickens (1812–1870). Later in the century, Charles Booth published *Life and Labors of the People of London*, a multivolume study that also linked harsh social conditions with crime.

Reformers in America sought to reform the jails and almshouses in which criminals, paupers, the insane, and mental defectives were indiscriminately incarcerated. Prison reformers joined with practitioners to found the National Prison Association in 1870. Z. B. Brockway, one of the leaders in this movement, became the warden of the first reformatory for young offenders, which opened in 1876 at Elmira, New York. Here he introduced the *indeterminate sentence* and parole, where the offenders' maximum sentences to prison would depend on their response to imprisonment and where they would be released to serve specified periods of time under the supervision of parole officers.

In 1899, the efforts of reformers resulted in the establishment of the first juvenile court, located in Cook County, Illinois. This reform involved a noncriminal definition of delinquency and the control and prevention of youthful deviance through intervention based on the *parens patriae* powers, the doctrine that permits the state to intervene to protect a child's welfare. In promoting more humane and effective means of social control, the reformers were instrumental in changing the general framework of the criminal justice system. The new social control procedures were grounded in a basic tenet of the positive school—that crime control activities should fit the offender and his or her personality defects.

The ideology of treatment had replaced the idea of proportionate punishment. The convergence of reformist currents with ideas of the positive school has led some to conclude that by focusing exclusively on individuals and ignoring problematic social environments, criminology had an inherent conservative ideological bias. This analysis seems to be fairly accurate when you consider how concerned nineteenth-century criminologists were with the rising incidence of crime and disorder that came with the social changes of the Industrial Revolution. The pragmatic, individualistic, progressive, and reformist emphases of American criminology in the twentieth century have been colored by positivist assumptions regarding the belief in science as a means of describing, predicting, and controlling criminal behavior. Crime has come to be seen as a condition, in the individual or society, that can be corrected or cured. The rise of the therapeutic idea, resting on the *parens patriae* power of the state, came to mean that the criminal law operated for the protection of society and enforcement of social conformity, rather than for the purpose of regarding crime as a political and moral issue within a legal framework that would protect individual rights.[62]

THE DEVELOPMENT OF AMERICAN CRIMINOLOGY

In America, criminology began as a field of study composed of leftovers—bits and pieces of problems adopted from economics, anthropology, sociology, psychology, and from the moral sciences of philosophy and theology. As with sociology, it quickly became an applied, pragmatic, empirical, and individualistically focused discipline. Early criminologists were concerned with amelioration, improvement, and reform. Their emphasis was on how individuals became criminals and how they might be corrected.

Although Radzinowicz suggests that American criminology represented a decisive break with Lombroso's ideas, undertones of a deterministic, positivist bent still remain in current criminology texts. Considerable concern is focused on how individuals become criminals and on how the social conditions that give rise to such "pathological" behavior can be ameliorated. Although early American criminologists were also reformers, C. Wright Mills termed their sociological counterparts "social pathologists," because their emphasis was correctional and tended toward the idea that "bad conditions" caused "bad people."[63] The nature-versus-nurture controversy continued in the constitutional deterministic theories that ranged from claims for inherited criminality and psychoanalytic determinism to a reserved emphasis on social factors.

Criminology has generally been defined in terms of its three major fields of emphasis and their related subdivisions: (1) the explanation of crime and criminal behavior; (2) the study of the development, interpretation, and application of the criminal law; and (3) the administration and operation of the criminal justice system and its three subsystems—law enforcement agencies, the courts, and the correctional system.

Traditionally, both the "kinds-of-people" and "kinds-of-environment" analyses have tended to focus on explanations of criminal behavior and their relationship to strategies for controlling or treating the individual criminal. Until recent years, criminologists have paid less attention to the study of criminal law and the process by which certain acts and actors are declared criminal.

An increased awareness that the crime problem is not sufficiently addressed by the typical approaches was noted by several writers in the 1950s including C. Ray Jeffery, who argued:

> The question "why and how people commit crimes" is an important one; however a theory of behavior is not a theory of crime. Behavior is criminal only when judged by some standard of conduct. The term "crime" refers to the act of judging or labeling the behavior, rather than . . . the behavior itself. Why people behave as they do and why the behavior is regarded as criminal are two separate problems requiring different types of explanation. If we . . . include all antisocial behavior within . . . criminology, we must either state that all deviant behavior is criminal or that criminology is concerned with noncriminal behavior as well as criminal behavior. . . . Only in the criminal law do we find the distinction between criminal and noncriminal behavior.[64]

Kinds-of-People Paradigm

The lingering influence of positivism is evident in the emphasis of early American criminology in the search for the causes of crime within the actor, hence the kinds-of-people paradigm.[65] Even though Charles Goring raised serious questions about the validity of Lombroso's conclusions in *The English Convicts* (1913), numerous attempts have been made to revive the idea that criminals are biologically defective or constitutionally inferior. Johannes Lange's comparative study of identical and fraternal twins in 1930 sought to reassert that criminality is inherited. Earlier studies, such as Richard Dugdale's *The Jukes* (1910) and Harry H. Goddard's *Feeble-Mindedness: Its Causes and Consequences* (1914), related crime and delinquency to low-grade mentality. Neo-Lombrosian ideas which purported to advance the ideas that biological factors such as brain lesions or XYY chromosomal abnormalities are related to crime and violence marked debates regarding biological determinism as recently as the 1970s.

Psychoanalytic theorists, following Freud, substituted for biological factors what David Matza suggests is a form of "overdeterminism," in which the individual behaves as though he or she were captive to repressed conflicts in the unconscious and early childhood traumas.[66] For a number of years the multiple factor approach was dominant in research on crime and delinquency. Eleanor T. and Sheldon Gluecks' work on *Unraveling Delinquency* (1950) included biological, psychological, and social factors in the hope of identifying correlates that would predict delinquency, though their study only identified "delinquency potential." [67]

The kinds-of-people paradigm, with its emphasis on uncovering the basic causes of criminal behavior in the individual, epitomizes what Matza has termed the correctional perspective. This concern with the problem of causation, or etiology, focuses on such root causes in order to remove them, as well as the behavior that results from them.[68] The correctional perspective is also pervasive in the social determinist kinds-of-environments paradigm. Both approaches form the basic assumptions for traditional correctional policies and programs that are based on treating or rehabilitating the individual. This medical model, or treatment ideology, views criminal behavior as a pathology or sickness that must be cured.

Kinds-of-Environment Paradigm

The shift from an emphasis on the individual to that of crime as a product of social conditions represented a form of social determinism. It is evident in kinds-of-environment theories that range from nineteenth- and early twentieth-century Marxist interpretations to social pathology ideas of the early Chicago School and anomie theories stressing poverty, blocked opportunity, and differential association.

The Chicago sociologists revised the earlier forms of European environmental determinism in relating social disorganization to the incidence of high crime and delinquency rates. Their emphasis was on the disorganized patterns of life in the slums and physically deteriorated areas of the city. In his much quoted essay, "Social Structure and Anomie" (1938), Robert K. Merton reformulated Durkheim's concept of *anomie*. He contended that there is a relationship between poverty and pathology in that crime is more prevalent among the lower segment of society due to the dissociation or gap between goals of success defined by society and institutional means for achieving material success. Thus crime and delinquency were seen by Merton as deriving from lower-class individuals who found it necessary to "innovate" illegitimate means to success. This reinterpretation of Durkheim's concept of *anomie* or "normlessness" was later utilized by Richard A. Cloward and Lloyd E. Ohlin in their "opportunity theory," wherein delinquency was viewed as the result of "blocked opportunity" among lower-class youths.

Sociology came to dominate research on crime following Sutherland's formulation of "differential association" in 1939. Sutherland sought a theory to explain why some people became criminal and others did not. He argued that rather than pursuing the evil-causes-evil fallacy, which assumes that "bad conditions" cause people to be bad, we should examine the development of criminal behavior as the normal result of the process of social learning. Borrowing from Gabriel Tarde's imitation theory, Sutherland hypothesized that individuals learn criminal behavior in the same way that they learn law-abiding behavior. Criminality, he argued, is learned because of an excess of definitions (and associations) favorable to law violations over definitions unfavorable to the violation of the law. Differential association, which will be dealt with more fully in chapters 4 and 6, is basic to this learning process since it seeks to explain the circumstances in which the learning takes place.[69] Since Sutherland implied but did not stress human choice in this process, human behavior still seemed determined by social circumstances.

Sutherland did not fully succeed in freeing his theory from the determinism of the positivists. He subsequently turned his attention to the "white-collar" criminal, and in a 1940 article railed against the hypocrisies of those in the higher echelons of the business community. Yet most efforts of American criminology have focused on explanations of personal and social factors that predispose or constrain those in lower-class subcultures to engage in criminal behavior, rather than on the criminality of those in the "respectable" subcultures who are involved in white-collar crime.[70]

These subcultural theories emphasized environmental conditions of offenders, such as their socioeconomic status, educational inadequacies, and their relative lack of opportunity. Those who lived in such conditions were seen as having an affinity for crime. Equality of opportunity was held out as a cure for crime, as in the ill-fated "war on poverty" of the 1960s. Sometimes the effort to provide opportunity yielded evidence that lower-class value systems left people incapable of taking advantage of new conditions. Consequently, kinds-of-environment theories continued to stress the individual, and intervention programs tried to correct the individual or to develop preventive community programs.

While the kinds-of-people and kinds-of-environment paradigms varied in emphasis, they both tended to take for granted the legal definition of crime. Their analyses focused upon the offender, and on his or her characteristics—constitutional or social—within the terms of the legal definitions.

CHANGING PARADIGMS IN CONTEMPORARY CRIMINOLOGY

During the 1960s, the labeling perspective began to consider societal reactions to crime. The proponents of this perspective turned their attention to the legal order and its function in the creation of crime. Howard S. Becker stated that "deviance is not a quality of the act the person commits, but rather a consequence of the application by others of rules and sanctions to an offender." [71] More recently, Richard Quinney has argued that the process of labeling someone a criminal must be understood in terms of the political and economic structure of the larger society. According to Quinney:

> No behavior is criminal until it has been so defined through recognized procedures of the state. In this sense, criminal behavior differs from noncriminal behavior only according to the definition that has been created by others. It is not the quality of the behavior, but the nature of the action taken against the behavior that gives it the character of criminality.[72]

The labeling (or societal reactionist) perspective gained considerable popularity in the study of crime, and by the 1970s it had become conventional wisdom. In their concern with societal reaction to crime and the negative, stigmatizing effect of social control efforts, the labeling theorists challenged commonsense conceptions of criminal behavior as well as the positivistic theories that imputed a propensity for law-violating behavior to lower-class and minority groups. They focused on the micro settings and interactions between social control agents (rule enforcers) within the bureaucratic criminal justice apparatus.[73] In recent years, however, certain conflict theorists have suggested that while the labeling perspective has focused on societal reaction to crime and on those who do the "dirty work" of enforcing the laws, it has not probed deeply into how laws came to be formulated and defined. Nor has it focused sufficiently on crime and criminal law. Extending the insights of the labeling theory, conflict theorists have contended that dominant power groups — the ruling class — use the formulation of laws to control the less powerful segments of society.

Conflict theory assumes a continuing conflict in society over the distribution of power and resources. It seeks an explanation of crime that is political as well as social. Crime is seen as the result of the complex interaction between social institutions and social structures on the one hand, and the consciousness of individuals who live within and respond to such social structures on the other.[74]

Recent conflict theory, as distinct from the earlier version of Vold (1958) — who viewed conflict as contributing to the integration of the social order rather than class conflict — might be seen as following two main currents. The non-Marxist version, epitomized by Austin Turk, has focused upon the criminalization process. Turk has argued that we should study the manner by which legal authorities act as creators, interpreters, and enforcers of rules for individuals in society who are "subjects" of the laws that influence their behavior, but are not the "makers" of the laws. Crime and delinquency result from conflict between those who have not learned the rules and those in power and authority who make them. Consequently, the legal status of criminal is given to such persons by authorized agents empowered by "the state." [75]

The Neo-Marxist orientation of conflict theory, sometimes termed "critical criminology," sees the law, law enforcement agencies, courts, and corrections agencies as the result of basic class divisions in society. The laws and their enforcement are seen as the means through which the powerful impose their standards of conduct on others, protect their material goods and privileges from the have-nots, and define illegal behavior to include actions that might threaten the status quo. Crime may be seen from this perspective as the result of the unequal distribution of wealth and power in a capitalist society.[76]

Both versions of conflict theory have displayed skepticism, not only toward the idea that crime is caused by some pathology on the part of the individual, but also toward the notion that the criminal law represents a set of absolute standards enforced equally against all. Together with advocates of the labeling perspective, they see official crime statistics and the processes involved in social control as part of the crime problem. Conflict theory, in both its versions, has made criminologists more politically aware in their study of crime. Yet as one observer has commented, their achievements have been more rhetorical than empirical. We still lack studies that focus on crimes of the powerful, social control agencies that relate to the wealthy rather than the disreputable, and the corporate rather than the individual law violator.[77]

The contention of "radical," critical criminologists that crime is the product of the economic organization and class oppression of our modern capitalist society seems to contradict the "new neoclassical" criminology of Ernest van den Haag and James Q. Wilson. These men have revised classical theory with a large dose of positivism, to provide a perspective that appeals to law-and-order advocates. However, as Isidore Silver has noted recently, there are some critical, if not ironic, convergences between the two outlooks, for both perspectives are disenchanted with and critical of the liberal democratic state and its crime control system. While both are cynical about the capacity of the modern welfare state to affect the crime problem by instituting programs that will reduce social inequalities, Silver contends that they oversimplify a complex issue. The neoclassicists, in their emphasis on individual responsibility, are not interested in explaining crime but rather in more effective social control. The radicals are not interested in crime but in revolution.[78]

The student of criminology, then, is faced with a number of competing paradigms. There are those that stress kinds of people, kinds of environments, and labeling and power conflicts. And there are those that advocate the elimination of crime by changing the system, either through abolishing capitalism or by making it more efficient, as the "new conservatives" seem to advocate, and perhaps more repressive.

We have only briefly summarized a number of complex perspectives. The major point, however, is that crime is behavior, and like other forms of social behavior it has many dimensions that vary with time, situation, and actors. Consequently, no single, narrow perspective, whether pragmatic, reformistic or ideological, whether physical or environmental, whether deterministic or voluntaristic, is an adequate starting point for the study of crime, for crime is not a unitary phenomenon.

RESEARCH IN CRIMINOLOGY: THE CONVERGENCE OF THEORY AND INQUIRY

If we assume that crime is a socially and legally defined problem, we must inquire into the process by which criminal definitions are formulated. We must understand the process of societal reaction to crime in order to identify the manner in which crime and criminals are defined and processed by the agents of social control. This study involves an analysis of the police, courts, and corrections institutions, as well as criminal behavior.

Criminological research, like all research, relies upon theories. Theories are statements about reality based on assumptions regarding the nature of society, the individual, and the phenomenon under scrutiny.

Criminology is a science to the degree that it seeks to use systematic methods to acquire and organize information about crime. In this process our theoretical commitment or inclination will both inform and influence us. Therefore, before outlining some of the more typical research methods available to the student of criminology, it will be useful to specify some of the areas in which it is assumed that theoretical perspectives converge with applied research methods. Having summarized the strengths and limitations of several competing theories of crime and criminality, we submit that the study of crime and its control should be characterized by the following six requisites and reservations:

1. *Since criminology is voluntaristic, it rejects "hard determinism" and avoids the tendency of positivists and others who seek to emulate the procedures and techniques of the physical sciences in a slavishlike adherence to objectivity that separates the knower from the known.* The idea of causality borrowed from the physical sciences has been used to establish that A causes B, where B is criminal behavior and A represents social factors that are assumed to be pathological, such as poverty. Such an association might be established between variables by using sophisticated statistical techniques, but we still would know nothing about a particular case or individual. Further, we should not assume that crime or criminal behavior can be explained as the result of any single factor or set of factors or circumstances, merely because they are cast as quantifiable variables. To do so is to obscure the variety of ways in which the individual relates to, interacts with, affects, and is affected by his or her social world or total environment.

Criminology, then, is voluntaristic in that we assume that men and women are purposive creatures and innovators of action within the complexities of the social structure; our study of crime and criminality should make a conscious attempt to avoid strict determinism in all its guises. An overly deterministic study would cause us to lose sight of human purpose and instrumentality, as well as the integrity of the individual in the creation of such behavior.[79]

2. *Criminological research should include a high degree of "value-consciousness."* Unlike detective work, criminology involves much more than

"getting the facts." It involves a consciousness of one's own values, those of the public, the persons being studied, and those of policymakers and enforcers. Implicit also is an increased awareness of consequences and alternatives. A consciousness of the role of marijuana laws in the criminalization of thousands of our youths, for instance, should make us aware that it may be easier to develop nonpunitive policies for regulating such activities. An increased *value-consciousness* implies the ability to develop new action alternatives—a difficult task since we are conditioned to thinking in terms of "the causes" of crime. If over the next ten years criminologists study changes in the public's attitudes and values toward laws regulating marijuana use, for example, we might learn a great deal about the function of "values" and their influence on law as a means of crime control. In the process, the awkward phrase "the law may be a cause of crime," might become more meaningful, as we recognize that it may be easier to manipulate the law by changing the lawmakers' and the public's values, at less cost and suffering, than our attempts to change individual status offenders.[80]

3. *Criminological research should recognize the serious problem of validity in both official and unofficial crime data.* We should know the origins of such data, be sensitive to tendencies that might lead to biases or inaccuracies, and cross-check data by using information from multiple sources. Our discussion in Chapter 3 should sensitize us to the need to view all crime statistics, official and unofficial, with considerable skepticism and to recognize that like crime definitions they might tell us as much about the rate-producing behavior of law enforcement bureaucracies and the defining process of control agencies as they do about crime.[81]

4. *Our theories of crime should enable us to make distinctions between characteristics and behavior patterns of the alleged offender prior to efforts to intervene or control (arrest, adjudication, imprisonment) from those attributed to the offender after he or she has become subjected to such control efforts.* Perhaps one of the more serious problems related to the study of crime is the assumption that there is a simplistically clear distinction between criminals or delinquents and noncriminals or nondeliquents. It is too easy to assume that those defined as criminals are a homogeneous group and that noncriminals represent another discrete group. Thus, the identified differences between the groups are related to law-violating or conforming behavior. Yet, as will be noted in Chapter 3, some studies suggest that as much as 90 percent of the population has violated the law. Other studies have indicated that on specific traits, such as intelligence, there may be more similarities than differences between delinquents and nondelinquents. The point is that there are *no* conclusive data that prove that criminals are any more abnormal, maladjusted, or pathological than noncriminals. And unless studies that seek to explain criminal, as distinct from noncriminal, behavior are designed and carried out in a valid manner, we should remain cautious. For example, in a study of prison inmates that identifies the unique characteristics of those incarcerated, how do we distinguish between those traits that may be the result of incarceration and those

presumed to be the cause of criminal behavior? Given existing data, we need to be skeptical about the use of vague concepts based upon specious generalizations.[82] Some law violators suffer from the effects of emotional maladjustments and live in conditions of social disorganization and poverty. But so do many conventional people.

5. *Are our prisons and programs of treatment and rehabilitation in our correctional system as unworkable and counterproductive as recent research seems to infer?* In view of recent research, there seems to be little evidence that corrections has any appreciable influence on reducing recidivism. The recent emphasis on the deterrent effect of severe and certain punishment has been advocated in the absence of concrete evidence on either side of the deterrence debate. Comparative cross-national studies between Scandinavia and the United States suggest an *inverse* relationship between certainty and severity of punishment and deterrence. Yet, with the single exception of South Africa, our society continues to have the longest prison terms among Western nations.[83]

6. *Criminology's study of the agencies of social control, law enforcement, the courts, and corrections should seek to demystify them in order to make them accountable to the various publics (the "consumers") they are intended to serve.* As Marvin E. Wolfgang noted, we need to change our criminological focus, for "we have focused long enough on the offender and his weaknesses. It is time we look to ourselves—to this chaotic, decaying, degrading system and indict it for its failures." [84] The problem becomes one of avoiding an overidentification with the control agents and system without romanticizing the lawbreaker. Research should be focused upon justice in the administration of justice, as well as upon its deterrent effects. A "value-conscious" criminology would recognize that the criminal justice system exercises its power in a more harsh manner, though sometimes benignly, over the least powerful: the poor, the minorities, and the young.

RESEARCH METHODS

Methods of criminological research are numerous, and various combinations of techniques may be used. These methods include (1) statistical analysis of crime trends; (2) statistics on traits and social factors related to criminals; (3) the use of case histories and life studies of individuals; (4) the study of the criminal and/or agents of criminal justice at work, through field observations and ethnographic methods; and (5) carefully designed experimental methods using control groups and "before and after" longitudinal approaches.

The method used will be influenced by the nature of the problem being studied and will be affected by one's theoretical orientation. Since crime represents an incredible range of diverse behaviors, one may want to apply different theories and methods to study different behaviors.[85]

Where the researcher relies on government funding, he or she may tend to orient research to problems defined by the funding agency. Government funding tends to be most plentiful for kinds-of-people and kinds-of-environment studies. This research emphasis is an outgrowth of public and political concern with the rising incidence of crime; the need for cost-benefit analysis due to the rising costs of criminal justice; and the action orientation of many academic criminologists who rely on grants for their research. It is far too easy to become seduced, consciously or unconsciously, into the process of shaping our concepts in such a way that the data will conform to the particular theoretical and/or ideological orientation of the public agency that has funded our research.[86]

Recently, there have been some devastating critiques of the cost-effectiveness of the courts, police, and prisons, suggesting that research of this nature is desired by "conservative" as well as "radical" critics of the system. However, a clash of conflicting perspectives exists within the field of criminology, and those studies that challenge, rather than support the status quo, will more often than not be carried out by independent researchers. As the research seeking to advance these new theories is made available, the new paradigms will undergo critical examination. This is one of the functions of research—to test and prove or disprove theory. Research using the mass of data accumulated from earlier theories about crime and its causes must also be reexamined in the light of new findings and new theories.[87]

The focus of criminology is the study of crime—the social conditions in which crime occurs, the definition of crime, and societal reaction to crime. But the criminologist is not just a technocrat or problem solver. As Nils Christie, the Norwegian criminologist, has suggested, in our concern with rule definition, rule violation, and the application of power against those seen as rulebreakers, we should be problem raisers as well as problem solvers.[88]

SUMMARY

We have noted the public concern and controversies regarding the problem of crime and have concluded that crime represents a vast range of diverse human behaviors and is not in any sense a unitary phenomenon. After summarizing various definitions of crime, we have noted that a basic point of departure is *the criminal law,* which deals with the complexities involved in the distinctions between criminal and noncriminal behavior. The *formulation of criminal definitions* is also an important aspect of study.

The search for explanations of crime and criminal behavior through the ideas of pioneers in criminology was summarized and illustrated in the controversial development of the history of criminology. The ideas of the *classical* and *positive schools* of thought and their influence on modern theory and practice were explored. The continuing influence of the *deterministic focus of the positivists* was described as relying upon either *constitutional determinism*—kinds-of-people—or upon *social determinism*—kinds-of-environments—paradigms. These perspectives were shown to be similar in that both involve simple explanations of a complex subject.

The emerging *labeling* and *conflict perspectives* were presented as challenges to these attempts to explain crime as the simple result of defective heredity, personality maladjustments, or social pathological conditions. These perspectives focused attention on societal reaction efforts and the law and its enforcement as a social control mechanism.

We reviewed a list of requisites for study that recognize the importance of theory in criminological research. The limitations of any single explanation of crime was stressed in order to help us avoid equating the methods of study of a complex social phenomenon with the methods of causation and explanation used in the natural sciences. Humans are much more than reactive beings, and the study of crime involves much more than the technical manipulation of data.

ADDITIONAL READINGS

Becker, Howard S. *Outsiders: Studies in the Sociology of Deviance.* New York: Free Press, 1963.

> A readable, systematic presentation of the "interactionist" or labeling perspective. Becker's seminal work focuses attention on the manner in which social groups create categories of crime and deviance by formulating and applying the rules. The book includes numerous examples based upon historical and observational research.

Christie, Nils, ed. *Scandinavian Studies in Criminology.* Published under the auspices of the Scandinavian Research Council for Criminology. Oslo: Scandinavian University Books, 1965–1974.

> These volumes provide a sampling of the studies and developing theories of Scandinavian scholars. The perspectives vary from reformist to social-radical. Volumes 2–5 are available.

Mannheim, Hermann, ed. *Pioneers in Criminology*, 2nd ed. Montclair, N.J.: Patterson Smith, 1972.

> This expanded edition of an earlier work covers twenty-three pioneers in criminology. These men of ideas are described in terms of the social milieux in which their ideas evolved. The initial chapter by the editor and the final article by C. Ray Jeffery are especially useful in their focus on integrating the contributions of the various theorists to the historical development of criminology.

Matza, David. *Becoming Deviant.* Englewood Cliffs, N.J.: Prentice-Hall, 1969.

> A cogent statement of the interactionist perspective within the framework of earlier and emergent theoretical approaches. The author uses the concept of "naturalism" to emphasize the social process involved in describing crime and deviance as they relate to the signifying reaction of those in authority. In Part II he attempts to synthesize the interrelationship between social factors, associations, and the reaction of legal authorities through the use of the concepts of affinity, affiliation, and signification.

Quinney, Richard. *The Social Reality of Crime.* Boston: Little, Brown & Co., 1970.

> Relying upon the interactionist and conflict viewpoints, the author presents a theoretical perspective that focuses upon explaining how behavior comes to be defined as criminal, the manner in which criminal definitions are applied, and how these relate to criminal behavior patterns and the construction of criminal conceptions.

Vold, George B. *Theoretical Criminology.* New York: Oxford University Press, 1958.

> This book provides a comprehensive review of theoretical orientations in criminology with an emphasis on conflict theory, at the time it was written. The questions raised remain timely, as they probe issues that still face us in the study of criminology.

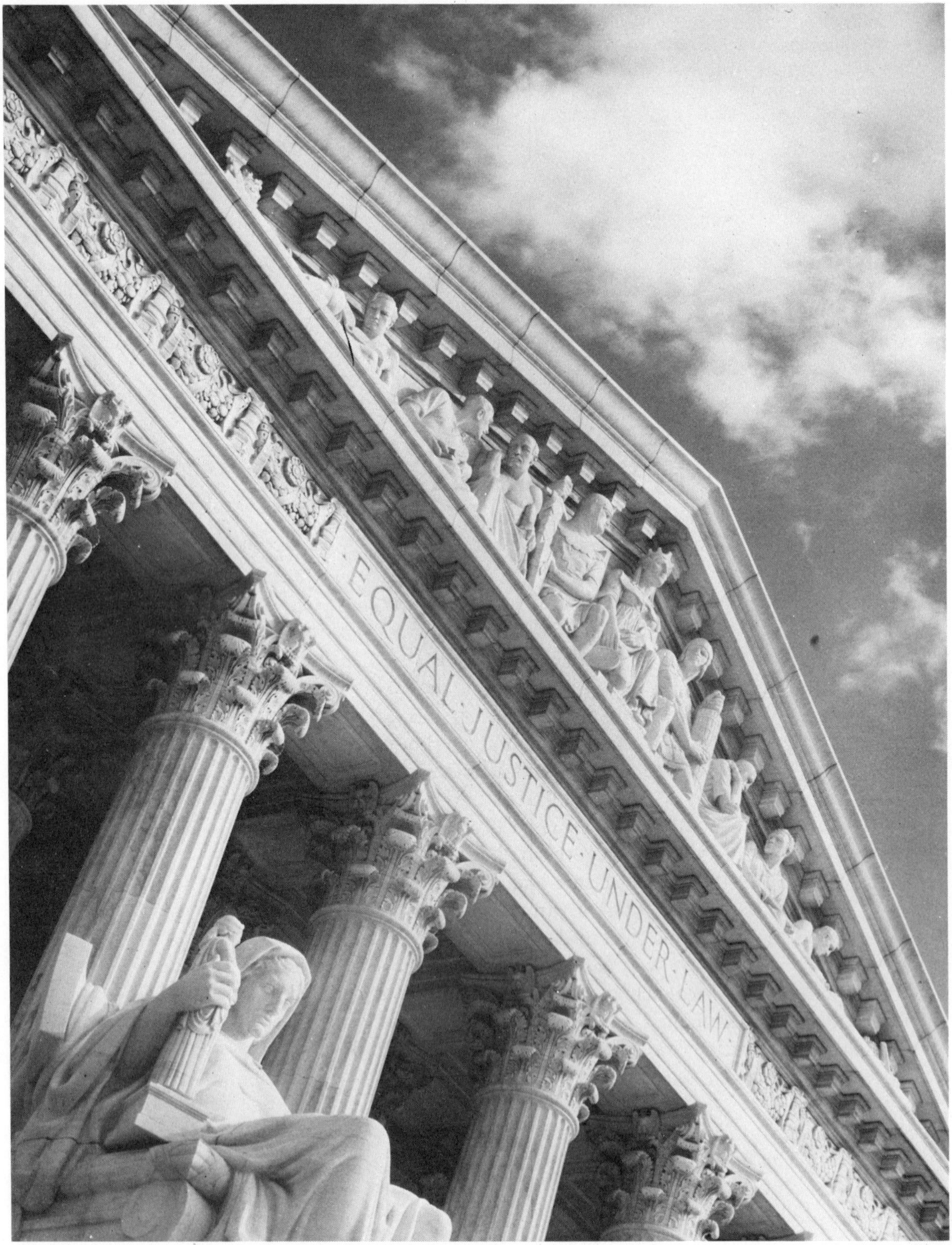
EQUAL·JUSTICE·UNDER·LAW

"If the law supposes that," said Mr. Bumble . . .
"the law is a ass, a idiot."
—Charles Dickens, Oliver Twist

CRIMINAL LAW AND THE STUDY OF CRIME AND CRIMINALITY

You can't break the law unless there is a law to break. Although it seems an obvious point, this notion is central to the study of criminality. Often in history the law has evolved not out of some vision of a better society, but to serve the purposes of powerful interest groups. While some law exists simply to punish behavior that offends prevailing morality, other law exists as a method of social control. The complex streams that join in the development of the law reach back to early religion and ancient governments, and the process continues to be distilled as the "law in action" is played out every day.

In his pioneering text, *Criminology*, published over fifty years ago, E. H. Sutherland noted that "an understanding of the nature of law is necessary in order to understand the nature of crime." [1] Professor Sutherland's work, in attempting to differentiate between "criminal" and "noncriminal" behavior, focused on the political nature of crime and criminality, rather than simply on individual and environmental factors. In recent years the study of criminology has undergone a perceptible shift in this direction, toward a recognition of the study of the sociology of law as a prerequisite for the study of crime.[2]

Although the classical school emphasized the law and its administration and sought to reform them, the influence of the positive school on American criminology has resulted in an inclination to explain criminal behavior without a corresponding stress on the influence of the criminal law.[3] Contemporary criminologists still place considerable stress on description and analysis of the subcultures, behavior systems, and lifestyles of those who are involved in criminal activity. There is, however, a growing realization that it is also necessary to understand how some acts are defined as crimes while others are not and the process by which some individuals are defined as criminal. The most recent edition of Sutherland's text, which has been revised by Donald R. Cressey five times since Professor Sutherland's death in 1950, opens with the observation that "criminology is the body of knowledge which . . . includes within its scope the process of making laws, breaking laws, and of reacting toward the breaking of laws." [4]

When we assert that crime is a complex legal, economic, political, moral, and social issue, we are emphasizing not only the many dimensions of crime; we are also stating that there is a relationship between crime and the law. Conduct that is viewed as "bad," harmful, or immoral, may evoke a negative response. As citizens, we might object to ridicule, or ostracize such conduct. But unless the conduct is defined as illegal, we cannot treat it as a crime. It is the law—specifically, the criminal law—that spells out the conditions under which a given act can be defined as criminal. Although in a formal sense criminal law is the "cause" of crime, as Jerome Michael and Mortimer Adler have argued, the label "criminal" may have as much to do with the characteristics of the person labeled as with his or her behavior. However, the law provides the justification and legitimacy for society's response to behavior defined as illegal.[5]

In the interest of furthering our comprehension of these interrelationships and to provide a more complete understanding of the complexities of crime, we turn now to a survey of the social basis of the law as it relates to crime and criminality. We will focus initially upon the nature of the law as a means of social control and briefly describe its importance in highly developed, industrialized, urbanized societies. We will also discuss the social basis and more recent origins of the criminal law. Finally, we will discuss the social organization of the legal system and relevant problems bearing on administration, classification, legal responsibility, and the overreach of the criminal law.

It should be clear from what has been stated that the study of crime and criminality relies upon some understanding not only of the criminal law, but also of the "law in action" as criminal definitions are applied. Our focus will remain the sociology of law. But this chapter will provide a basis for understanding the nature of criminal laws as they relate to the study of crime and criminality.

THE NATURE OF THE LAW

What is the law? Is it necessary? Both of these are persistent issues in the study of human societies. Lay persons may be inclined to take the answers to both questions for granted, until they find themselves in a situation involving their own interests.

The law obviously means different things to different people. It means one thing to the manager of a television station who must fulfill certain requirements to be licensed. It may mean something quite different to the viewer who is wooed into buying some useless drug being advertised or to the PTA member who lobbies the Federal Trade Commission to prohibit the advertising of

Whom does the law protect?

"junk food" on children's programs. The presence of law is obvious in the numerous taxes we pay on all levels of government, including fees paid for licenses to fish, hunt, own a dog, drive a car, get married, and so on.

These and many other images remind us of the pervasive presence of law in our lives. For example, in one of its many guises the law protects endangered species. In other forms it protects those who pollute the air and water and threaten our social order in various ways. In June 1978, the Supreme

Court upheld the Endangered Species Act of 1973 and ruled that the construction of the Tellico Dam must be halted, since the project threatened a tiny fish known as the snail darter with extinction. At about the same time that the courts were upholding the rights of a group of self-styled Nazis to demonstrate in a suburb of Chicago, demonstrators against nuclear power projects and nuclear weapons were being arrested in various parts of the country.

Evidence of the ubiquitous manner in which the law affects our lives—should you need to be reminded of its presence in our everyday affairs—can readily be noted in the routine activities of the police and courts. For instance, in 1975 the FBI reported over 8 million arrests, 1.9 million for the seven major crimes. If we counted traffic violations and parking tickets, we would include many million more citizens who had direct contact with the law. In the realm of civil law, the impact is further widened by the hundreds of thousands of litigations that are threatened, filed, settled out of court, or go to trial each year. Over a million divorces are processed each year, along with a quarter of a million bankruptcy cases; another million citizens serve on juries. And each year a great proportion of the adult population fills out a tax return for the Internal Revenue Service—a requirement of the law.

The law and the legal system that provides its dynamic aspect represent the most authoritative, formal, and public form of social control in modern society. Social control refers to the means by which a social group promotes conformity to its definitions of proper conduct. Even societies that do not appear to have a system of formal laws have arrangements to promote conformity and to punish those who deviate.[6] As a means of social control, the law is "characterized by (1) explicit rules of conduct, (2) planned use of sanctions to support the rules, and (3) designated officials to interpret and enforce the rules, and often to make them."[7]

Definitions of the law focus upon a society's system of norms or rules, particularly the body of rules that is created, administered, and enforced by the political authority of the state. Max Weber (1864–1920), the German sociologist, defined law as a "legitimized" pattern of rules, based either upon the authority of the state or some other means of external obligation or control. However, Weber made clear distinctions not only between norms such as *custom* and *convention* and laws, but also between the law of the state and that of other organizations. He referred to "extra-state" law, and "state" law, and noted that legal coercion is the monopoly of the state.[8] Weber's perspective can give us insights into the complexities of rules and laws that regulate social relations in industrialized societies such as our own.[9]

Anthropologists have sought to contrast the legal systems of smaller societies with those of more developed societies. Among the earliest of these scholars was Bronislaw Malinowski, who in his classic study of the Trobiand Islands suggested that legal systems are not intentional but rather the end result of "rules . . . sanctioned . . . by a definite social machinery . . . , based upon mutual dependence . . . and reciprocal services."[10] Malinowski's query—Are intentional laws necessary?—has been reflected in questions about the necessity of law raised by social philosophers from Plato to Marx. It is one thing to argue that laws in modern society too often serve the interests of elites and powerful groups and that there should be a basic reordering of our system of justice. It is quite a different matter to argue that in a pluralistic, ethnically heterogeneous society such as the United States, laws are not necessary to promote the social order. Some Marxist theorists argue that once the capitalist social order is gone, the law that serves to protect and strengthen capitalism will no longer be necessary. But in countries that have undergone socialist revolutions, centralized governments are still very much in evidence, and law is buttressed by the coercive power of the state.[11]

The Nature of the Law: Natural and Universal or Positive and Rational?

Throughout Western history, scholars have long been concerned with the nature of law. There has been a continuing argument between "natural" or divine law, and "positive" law based on human rationality. The concept of positive law, which emerged in the nineteenth century along with the growth of science and humanism, is the law of the ruler of the state. It seeks to define in a rational manner relations between the state (the ruler) and the citizen (the ruled).[12]

Early in U.S. history there was a merging of natural and positive law. Colonial law, especially in New England, was based on biblical authority, and morality was enforced through the legal code. When the Constitution was written and it became necessary to append the Bill of Rights in order to secure its ratification, the principles of natural law were enshrined in the first ten amendments. It is assumed that judges, however, interpret the Constitution in terms of its actual content, not in terms of their own ideas of some higher system of law.

Modern law turns the presumption of natural or universal law on its head, for law and the laws are manmade and are constantly changing.[13] For example, in the New England colonies, as noted above, the lawmakers relied on religious ideals as a basis for their criminal law. And until the time of the American Revolution, court records suggest that many were prosecuted for crimes that were also seen as sin, such as adultery or Sabbath violations. By the early nineteenth century, however, the focus of the law shifted from an emphasis on morality to the protection of property.[14] Still, there were some lapses in this general trend. Dramatic attempts to control morality through law lingered into the twentieth century with the enactment of the Eighteenth Amendment (Prohibition) in 1920, the Harrison Act of 1914 (which taxed opiate drugs), and the Marijuana Tax Act of 1937. While the "noble experiment" of Prohibition failed, enforcement of the Harrison Act and passage of the Marijuana Tax Act criminalized both heroin and *cannabis*. The nation's drug problem has been greatly complicated by these punitive measures of the "rulemakers" and "rule enforcers." Drug addicts are stigmatized as "junkies" or "dope fiends," and "pot smokers" are regarded by much of the larger society as self-indulgent and immoral.

Actually, laws such as these might be classified as "natural laws" because of the ideological assumptions that spawned them. A more rational legal approach to laws that seek to control personal morality would be to avoid laws that are based largely upon ideological considerations. But this is easier said than done. Those who strongly advocate a system of positive law have two reasons for attacking the inherent moral quality of statutes that are argued to rest in natural law. First, they claim such laws often are enshrouded in a sanctity to which they are not entitled. Second, the assumption of natural law serves as a barrier to legal reform.[15]

How Social Control Becomes Formal

Social control occurs within all groups, communities, and societies. The mechanisms of social control operate to the extent that an individual may be able to limit the actions of others or have his or her own actions controlled or limited. The means of control are social, because they involve the actions of others. However, over time, individuals often internalize this system of customary and institutional patterns of behavior—a pattern which tends to reflect the morality and values of the groups or society of which they are members.[16]

Even in early, preliterate societies there was a normative order that made it possible for the individual to take part in the group's moral, religious, and conventional relationships. Georg Simmel (1858–1918), the German social thinker, observed that custom operates at a nonspecific normative level, which requires the kind of social units possible in small-scale societies. As a society grows larger, the informal norms of custom become objective and formalized, as in a legal system, while individual morality continues to be governed, at least in part, through the internalization of societal norms.[17]

Simmel contends that the enlargement of a group creates a favorable climate for the translation of less specific norms of custom into more specific forms of rules—in other words, law. He cites as an example the emergence of the county in the New England states for judicial or legal control purposes. However, he notes that the size of the group is related to the development of the system of law only to the extent that its elements form a unity. The scattered ancient Germanic tribes, for instance, were very slow in developing a unified legal system. He concludes that the cohesion of a large group is both the cause and effect of the development of a legal constitution. Simmel's ideas suggest a relationship between informal social change and the emergence of formal legal controls, namely, a system of law.

The United States traces its legal system back to the English common law. As C. Ray Jeffery points out, twelfth-century England under Henry II (1135–1189), the man responsible for the death of Thomas Becket, was going through a period in which the law was consolidated. Henry had quarreled with Becket over the fact that ecclesiastical courts had sole jurisdiction over clergymen accused of crimes. Henry's Constitution of Clarendon formalized the separation of church and state and brought all those charged with crimes into lay courts. This emergence of the king's authority brought state law into existence. Common law became the law of the king and was available to all men.[18]

English Common Law. Jeffery points out that there is no historical foundation for the idea that the common law of England is the same as Anglo-Saxon law. The shift from custom to law occurred, he argues, when a political community not based on kinship or tribe became the basis of social organization. Justice was now the prerogative of the state, which in criminal cases was represented by the prosecutor. Under the law, criminal offenses became offenses against the state. His comparison of tribal and state law shows these major differences:

Tribal Law	State Law
Blood-tie	Territorial tie
Collective responsibility	Individual responsibility
Family as unit of justice	State as unit of justice
Feud or compensation	Punishment

This comparison demonstrates how formal systems of social control developed as societies made the transition from small, compact, informal groups to larger, more complex systems. The study of the sociology of law also provides insights into how the variety of laws came into being and how some of these legal traditions have resulted in abiding contradictions in the criminal justice system. There is growing awareness, even among conventional criminologists, that the law and the agents of the state who carry it out are neither as neutral nor as impartial as one might hope. If the legal system is neutral, it is so only in the sense of it being a rope in a never-ending game of tug-of-war between competing social groups. Behind almost every law is some interest group that was powerful enough to have its interests legitimated.

The Law of Theft. Jerome Hall's study (1952) of theft was an early effort to provide a case study of what happens when social conditions change and the laws of a powerful interest group are no longer protected. Hall traced the origins of modern theft laws to the Carrier Case, which occurred in England in 1473. These are the facts of the case: The defendant was hired to carry certain filled containers, or bales, to Southampton. Instead, he carried them to another place and took the contents. When he was apprehended and charged with a felony, he still had possession of the containers. One judge argued that the defendant had not committed a felony because he had been hired to carry the bales and he still had them in his lawful possession. But a majority of the judges departed from precedent and argued that the case should be decided "according to the law of nature," not by common law. The decision introduced the idea that an individual entrusted with another's property could indeed commit a trespass upon that property. Hall summed it up this way:

> On the one hand, the criminal law at the time is clear. On the other hand, the whole aggregate of political and economic conditions... thrusts itself upon the court. The more powerful forces of the time were interrelated very intimately and at many points; the New Monarchy and the nouveau riche—the mercantile class; the business interests of both and the need for a secure carrying trade.... The great forces of an emerging modern world, represented in the above phenomena, necessitated the elimination of a formula which had outgrown its usefulness. A new set of major institutions required a new rule. The law, ... was brought into a more harmonious relationship with the other institutions by the decision rendered in the Carrier Case.[19]

Vagrancy. William Chambliss has described how another legal concept, the law of vagrancy, evolved out of changing social interests in England. The first such law had been enacted in 1349 to regulate the giving of alms to the able-bodied unemployed. After the plague of the Black Death, there was a shortage of workers, and the law was revised to require those who were available to accept employment at a low wage. The vagrancy laws were revived and strengthened again in the sixteenth century during a period of growing commerce and industry. Chambliss concludes that these laws, like those concerned with theft, were enacted in response to the needs of powerful interest groups in England at the time. In modern times these same laws have come to be used to control people exhibiting "undesirable" behavior. Furthermore, service bureaucracies, such as public welfare agencies, function "to regulate the poor" through the enactment of administrative laws that allow them to process individuals and exercise social control outside of the traditional legal system.[20]

The Legislation of Morality. As our society has become more heterogeneous, secular, and pluralistic in its values and beliefs, interest groups have emerged that seek to promote their own versions of "good" or right conduct. Howard Becker, in his study of the passage of the Marijuana Tax Act of 1937, has suggested that this act was initiated as a consequence of the moral enterprise of the director of the Federal Bureau of Narcotics (FBN). A more recent study by Donald Dickson (1968) has argued that this legislation resulted from efforts by bureaucrats in the FBN to counter the effects of congressional budget cuts and the decline in concern over drug use. As a result of the law, the FBN became more securely entrenched, and the criminal approach that had been used against heroin addicts came to be applied against marijuana users.[21]

According to Joseph Gusfield, the American temperance movement grew out of a conflict between the small-town, rural Protestant middle classes and the urban, Catholic, and Lutheran lower classes who were drinkers. He notes that even when the Prohibition laws were broken, there was no doubt whose laws they were.[22] Stuart Hills has observed that the need for a "symbolic" restatement of the norms in the law increases when the values of the dominant group are under threat—that is, when the criminal law is used to condemn or define private morality as crime (for example, drug use, gambling, public or even private drinking), then the law may not reflect the consensus within the larger community regarding such conduct.

The efforts by particular interest groups to legislate laws for the purpose of regulating private morality become more apparent when there is less agreement regarding moral standards and when dominant societal definitions are under assault.[23] Such laws, according to some authorities, have been recognized for centuries as *mala prohibita,* a term that refers to offenses for which a fine or imprisonment might be levied, although the act in question need not necessarily infer an antisocial state of mind.[24] The phrase has sometimes been used by criminologists and other writers to make a distinction considered meaningful between conduct defined as wrong because it is forbidden *(mala prohibita)* and more conventional crimes termed *mala en se*—wrong in themselves. The infrequency with which such distinctions are made by contemporary criminologists, as well as by those who write in the area of sociology of law, may reflect the credence given to an assumption of the conflict perspective discussed below (that *all* criminal laws are made by those who have the power to translate their interests into public policy).[25] We happen to think that the historical meaning of the term *mala prohibita* merits some recognition. Nevertheless, we will discuss behavior systems related to violation of laws that seek to regulate private morality as "public order" crimes.

Sexual Psychopathy Laws. These laws grew out of the concern beginning in the 1930s that followed widely publicized sex crimes. Influenced by psychiatrists, sexual psychopathy laws specify that those accused of sexual offenses must be diagnosed by psychiatrists. Thus, the myriad sexual psychopathy laws that exist today reflect not only the concerns of an irate public, but the self-interest of psychiatrists as well.[26]

SOCIAL BASIS OF THE CRIMINAL LAW: ITS NATURE, SOURCES, AND DISTINCTIONS

Consensus and Conflict Theories

The law is a formal means of social control. It emerges out of a system of norms as a society becomes more complex. If the law merely encodes a group's mores, it reflects a standard already agreed upon by the society. But if a law does not relate to the common standards of society, or to the definitions of right and wrong of groups within that society, whose interests does it serve? Might such a law lessen the solidarity of the society?

Broadly speaking, these are the two opposing views that have developed regarding the creation and function of law in society. The *consensus* model, or perspective, holds that law exists for the society and is a reflection of group consciousness. The *conflict* perspective holds that law exists to serve the goals and interests of the most powerful members or groups in society who are in positions to influence its enactment and administration.

Contemporary social scientists have been stimulated in their study of both perspectives by the work of legal scholar Roscoe Pound. His point of view has come to epitomize the consensus perspective, although this label was applied after the fact. Pound viewed society as being composed of diverse groups; the law was a means of resolving conflicts as they cropped up among individual, public, and social interests. Since certain interests were quite necessary to the welfare of society, it was important to reconcile conflicts and secure the social order. This could be done through the law. As Pound stated, "the law in an attempt to satisfy . . . , to adjust these . . . conflicting claims and demands . . . so as to give effect to the greatest total of interests or to the interests that weigh most on our civilization, with the least sacrifice to the scheme of interests as a whole." [27] Pound was attracted to the concept of the "law in action," or "the living law," which is not created as a service to special interests but rather as a method of mediating conflicting interests of individuals and groups in society. He saw the living law as the best road toward social harmony.

The opposing conflict perspective is well described in the work of Richard Quinney, who was among several writers who revived an interest in the sociology of criminal law during the 1960s. This perspective calls on ideas developed by a number of social scientists, including Karl Marx and the more recent writings of George Vold, Austin Turk, Howard Becker, William Chambliss, and Robert Seidman.[28] In varying degrees, these writers see society as characterized by change, conflict, coercion (power), and adversity. Building on these views and in distinct contrast with Pound, Quinney argued from the conflict perspective that:

> Though the law may operate to control interests, it is . . . created by interests. . . . Seldom is law the product of the whole society. . . . Law is made by men . . . who have the power to translate their interests into public policy. . . . Law does not represent the compromise of the diverse interests in society, but supports some interests at the expense of others. . . . In the conflict-power model of interest structure . . . politically organized society is held together by conflicting elements and functions according to the coercion of some segments by others. . . . Finally, since law is formulated and administered within the interest structure of . . . society it follows that law changes with modification in that structure.[29]

The consensus perspective is captured by Jerome Hall's argument that the "criminal law represents a sustained effort to preserve important social values from serious harm and do so not arbitrarily but in accordance with rational methods directed towards the discovery of just ends." [30] In other words, consensus assumes shared interests growing out of a consensus of values. This perspective was the conventional posture of criminologists until recent years when the conflict perspective began to gain considerable favor among moderate and "critical" social scientists. These scholars began to reevaluate the assumptions of the "consensus" model in the face of the overuse of the police power of the state in the 1960s in reaction to urban riots and political protests, and in the revelations of the machinations by control agencies, such as the CIA and FBI, that have been exposed in the post-Watergate years.[31]

The conflict perspective offers insight into how certain behaviors come to be defined, proscribed, and penalized by the criminal law. A limited number of empirical studies, some of which we have referred to previously, have shown how the criminal law can be shaped in favor of the interests of powerful groups in society. We need more careful studies of property crimes of the powerful, especially corporate misbehavior or white-collar crime, bribery, and corruption. Criminologists have left analyses of Watergate, for instance, largely to journalists and political commentators. At the same time, we need more information about conventional crimes such as murder, assault, theft, robbery, and rape. Obviously, such conduct is contrary to the definitions of right and wrong held by most groups in society, including those who are relatively powerless. Perhaps conflict theories can do more to explain why some forms of conduct, such as pollution of the environment, false advertising, fraud, and corruption in high places, have only reluctantly been proscribed by law and are so difficult to prosecute.

Both perspectives will endure, since neither totally explains the origin of the criminal law, although each has been critical of its effectiveness. The conflict perspective has challenged the easy assumption that the criminal law defines conduct as criminal to protect the interests of all groups in society. However, the interrelationship of the criminal law with societal mores can also indicate the ineffectiveness of the law. As Sutherland noted some years ago, "when the mores are adequate, laws are unnecessary; when the mores are inadequate, the laws are ineffective." [32]

Sutherland was not necessarily pointing to the specific failure of legal norms, but rather to the limitations of the legal system and means of formal social control when they are unsupported by nonlegal, informal control systems. The ineffectiveness of unsupported law is well illustrated by the general failure of laws that have been passed with the intention of regulating private morality. One result of such attempts has been termed the "patterned evasion" of our laws.[33] For even when certain types of behavior are condemned by the law, there may still be members of society who desire to and do indulge in such forbidden activity. Consensus frequently is insufficient to deter either those who seek such behavior or those who provide them with the desired goods and services.

In his study, *Crimes Without Victims* (1965), Edwin Schur has noted how criminal laws fail to deter and control homosexuality, abortion, and drug addiction. To this list we might add many other forms of sexual deviation, as well as gambling and public intoxication. In addition to illustrating the various limits of legal action—as well as their possible harmful influence—these laws emphasize significant areas in which there are obvious conflicts of interest in society.[34]

Interest groups seek to promote their own versions of morality.

In summary, as Schur has reminded us in another context, laws and legal institutions can, and may, be used to promote the conscious ends of vested interest groups. This does not mean that laws may fail to serve certain normative goals and at times transcend specific political goals. While the legal system may reflect and embody the "wisdom of the ages" contained in the culture of a given society, it is also constantly changing relative to substance and procedure. And laws regulating television advertising, regulation of the pollution emission of automobiles, and so forth, do not wait for the consensus of public opinion. Neither the "order" nor the "conflict" perspective, then, can by itself give us a sufficient understanding of the legal system. For just as society might be seen as a combination of stability and change or consensus and conflict, so might these forces be seen as complementary forces in our legal system.[35]

THE NATURE OF THE CRIMINAL LAW

Just what is the criminal law? Obviously it means different things to different people, and the answer can depend on who is asking the question. Many people think of "the law" in terms of the police or judges who enforce and administer it. Police officers on the beat regard "the law" as the set of rules they are out there to enforce. Judges and lawyers may take a much broader view, extending to the subtle interpretations of existing laws that have occurred over many years. In fact, in the hands of lawyers, "the law" often becomes enmeshed in a network of ideas and terminology that can mystify the lay public —and enhance the prestige of the professional. Criminals have their own perspective toward "the law," centered, quite sensibly, around the prospect for arrest and punishment.

Criminal law has been referred to as the ultimate form of legal control in the state. The political authority of the state assumes the task of redressing wrongs done to its citizens, based upon the idea that the state is harmed when one of its subjects is harmed. In essence, criminal law defines offenses that are seen as contrary to the interests of society, while civil law deals with conduct that is contrary to the individual's interests.[36]

Criminal Law Versus Civil Law

Civil law refers generally to laws regulating relations between individuals and/or groups. These include laws regulating contracts, the family (divorce), property rights, and torts. The general term *torts* refers to actions in which the individual, with the assistance of the state, seeks redress for personal injuries or defamation of character. If a *plaintiff* (an injured party) wins the case, the *defendant* (the offending party) may be ordered by the court to pay the plaintiff an amount of money for harm suffered. The proceedings are considered a private matter between two persons or entities, and the emphasis is on compensation rather than on deterrence or retribution, as in the criminal law.

In criminal violations the state symbolically represents all of society and brings the action against the accused. In a criminal suit, the individual, if convicted, faces some form of punishment. Either a fine, probation, a penal sanction, capital punishment, or some combination of these is "handed down." Since a crime is an action against society, some social purpose is thought to be served by a criminal sanction. Through punishment, the offender must expiate or make amends for the moral wrong he or she has committed against the community. This is related to the matter of retributive justice, which we will deal with in Chapter 14.

But the distinctions between civil and criminal law are not always clearcut. Obviously many civil cases involve harm to some person. In the case of rape, for example, it is possible to bring both criminal and civil actions. If convicted, the offender may be punished under criminal law and at the same time be required to pay compensation to the victim as a result of a tort suit. The technical distinctions are also blurred for other crimes. For instance, white-collar crime can be prosecuted either in a criminal or civil suit. In a case involving the sale of harmful merchandise, for example, the offense may be chargeable under the Pure Food and Drug laws—usually a civil offense—or it may be chargeable as a fraud—a criminal offense—or in a tort suit, where injured parties seek financial redress.

Sources of the Criminal Law

The principle of *stare decisis* evolved around the middle of the thirteenth century. It established the idea that a decision of a higher court becomes a precedent to be followed in future cases of a similar nature. Legislative enactments also began to supplement law created by judicial decision, as political and social changes led to challenges of the English courts.

As these lawmaking bodies and court decisions defined new crimes, legislative bodies enacted legal codes incorporating much of the common law. On the continent of Europe, there has historically been a reliance on written law. These laws have been termed "civil," in contrast with the English common law.

Strictly speaking, law created by legislative enactment is the system of civil law. The criminal law of the United States is an amalgam of the English common law and the continental civil law. The English common law was the law of the original thirteen colonies. Only one state—Louisiana—has a history of civil law.

The criminal code of the United States is drawn from at least four sources that provide a basis for both *substantive laws* (the actual rules governing conduct and sanctions that may be imposed when they are violated) and *procedural laws* (the manner in which the actual laws must be applied). These sources are:

1. *The constitutions of the United States and the fifty states,* which encompass basic principles and guide future legislative actions and court decisions.
2. *Statutory laws enacted by the federal Congress and the fifty state legislatures,* which are compiled as the Criminal Code, the Penal Code, and so on.
3. *Common or case law,* including court decisions which interpret the statutes and the constitutions.
4. *Administrative law,* developed by certain agencies, such as the Federal Trade Commission (FTC), the Federal Communications Commission (FCC), and federal and state prison systems, that Congress and state legislatures empower to make rules and regulations in their areas.

During the twentieth century, there has been an enormous growth in the number of administrative agencies with responsibility for regulating business and commerce and looking after the general welfare of citizens. Their rules and regulations have the weight of law, both in theory and practice, and cases arising under such law may be processed through the state and federal courts. However, many white-collar violations are dealt with through administrative means, and information on decisions in these cases never makes its way into the *Uniform Crime Reports* compiled by the FBI.

Despite a vast proliferation of legal authority, all law in the United States is still limited by and must conform to the federal Constitution, including criminal law defined in the statutes and case law (court decisions), as well as law made by administrative agencies. Individual rights, minority rights, and the rights of suspected or convicted offenders are protected from potential abuse by the Bill of Rights and the Fourteenth Amendment. Since the case of *Marbury* v. *Madison* in 1803, the Supreme Court has exercised the power to interpret the Constitution of the United States.

Procedural and Substantive Laws

Substantive laws have two basic functions: (1) they specify definitions of conduct forbidden in a given jurisdiction and (2) they specify the punishments that may be meted out for each type of offense. In the first instance, distinctions may be made between homicide and involuntary homicide, as in the case of motor vehicle deaths. Such definitions often vary between jurisdictions. In some, a motor vehicle death may even be defined as a misdemeanor if no gross negligence is involved. California, however, amplifies the substantive law. It defines vehicular manslaughter as a felony—a felony being when the action leading to death constitutes a failure to exercise care that would justify a belief that there had been indifference to the property and welfare of others.[37]

Procedural law describes the rules and conditions under which the state may proceed against someone accused of an offense against the substantive law. For instance, the guarantee of trial by jury, the right to cross-examine witnesses, the right to face one's accusers, and the right to appeal are all set forth in the procedural law. If the state violates these rights, it is in violation of "due process," and there are grounds for an appeal that could reverse a conviction. In this sense, procedural law is intended to protect the individual from arbitrary action by the state.

The recent Supreme Court decisions dealing with no-knock laws, wire tapping, and confessions all concern procedural guarantees protected by the Fourth and Fifth Amendments to the Bill of Rights and similar guarantees in state constitutions. For instance, the *Miranda* decision (1966) did not deal with substantive law. Rather it was a reaffirmation of a constitutional procedural guarantee in the Fifth Amendment against the use of undue pressure to obtain a confession. By ordering law enforcement officers explicitly to inform possible suspects in criminal cases of their rights, the Court was using legal procedure as a way to ensure that the law was upheld. What was involved was the Constitution's guarantee that no person can "be compelled in any criminal case to be a witness against himself." (See Box 1.)

Miranda Rights

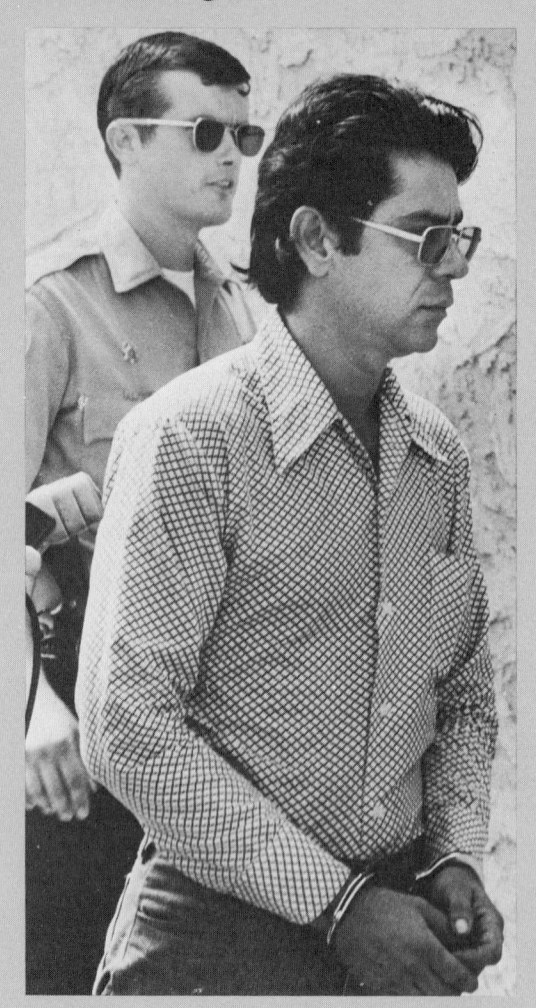

BOX 1

Arrest of Ernesto Miranda

WASHINGTON, Jan. 25 — The Supreme Court ruled today that a suspect who goes to a police station voluntarily and who is not under arrest can be questioned without being given the "Miranda warning" about the right to remain silent and to have a lawyer.

The Court issued the 6-to-3 ruling summarily, without having heard arguments in the case. It represented further restrictions by the present Justices on the landmark Miranda decision by the Warren Court.

Today's decision held that the police may ask a suspect to appear at the station house, tell him that the authorities have evidence incriminating him in a crime and then question him about it behind closed doors without benefit of the Miranda warning.

The Court acted in response to a petition from the State of Oregon asking the Justices to review a decision of the Oregon Supreme Court in a burglary case, in which the Oregon court ruled that Miranda warnings should have been given in such a situation notwithstanding the fact that the defendant was not under arrest.

Recent Trend Continued

The Court's decision, in an unsigned four-page opinion, reverses the Oregon court's ruling. Justices Thurgood Marshall, William J. Brennan, Jr. and John Paul Stevens dissented.

The decision continues the trend of Supreme Court rulings of the last few years taking a restrictive view of the Supreme Court's 1966 Miranda decision, one of the landmarks — and one of the most controversial rulings — of the Court in the Warren era.

It also continues the recent Supreme Court trend of deciding some important issues summarily, without giving them full review — a trend that the Court has been increasingly criticized for, both inside and outside the legal profession.

The executive director of the American Civil Liberties Union, Aryeh Neier, issued a statement today castigating the Court on both points.

Views of the Dissenters

He said that the decision "very substantially negates the Miranda decision." And he said that the way in which the Court issued its ruling was "astounding," adding that, "If they're going to undercut Miranda," such action should be taken only after full review.

Among the dissenters, Justice Marshall said that the ruling was contrary to the "rationale" of the Miranda decision, if not perhaps to the exact Miranda holding. Justice Stevens contended that "the issues presented by this case are too important to be decided summarily." Justice Brennan said that he would have heard argument in the case and that he dissented from the summary ruling.

In the Miranda case, in 1966, the Supreme Court ruled that statements made by a defendant while he was in "custodial interrogation" may not be used against him at trial, unless before making those statements he was given various warnings—that he had the right to remain silent; that if he spoke, what he said could be used against him; that he had the right to a lawyer and that if he could not afford a lawyer one would be provided for him.

The Court defined custodial interrogation as questioning that is initiated by law enforcement officials after a person has been taken into custody "or otherwise deprived of his freedom of action in any significant way."

The Court reasoned that such warnings were necessary to protect the defendant's Fifth Amendment right not to be forced to incriminate himself.

In today's case, the defendant was on parole at the time of the questioning. A state police officer told him he would "like to discuss something" with him and asked him to appear at the state patrol office. The parolee went to the office; once there, the officer said that he was not under arrest but also said there was incriminating evidence against the man. The man then confessed—and was then given his Miranda warnings.

The Oregon court ruled that the man's statements were inadmissible. Under the ruling in the Miranda case, it reasoned that the interrogation had taken place in a "coercive environment," particularly since the defendant was a parolee and the questioning took place in the offices of the state police.

The Supreme Court, in reversing this decision, also relied on the Miranda decision. It stressed, however, that Miranda applied to a custodial situation and that Miranda warnings were required "only when there has been such a restriction on a person's freedom as to render him 'in custody.' "

"Any interview of one suspected of a crime by a police officer will have coercive aspects to it, simply by virtue of the fact that the police officer is part of a law enforcement system which may ultimately cause the suspect to be charged with a crime," the Court said. "But police officers are not required to administer Miranda warnings to everyone whom they question."

Source: *New York Times,* Jan. 25, 1977. © 1977 by The New York Times Company. Reprinted by permission.

Pound's concept of "living law" has most often been manifested in procedural law, which is more open to innovation. Substantive law tends to change more slowly. Even so, the two are often so intermingled that it is not always easy to separate them. But if we assert that there may be no crime without law, it should follow that a "just" substantive criminal law cannot be administered without "just" procedures.

THE SOCIAL ORGANIZATION OF THE LEGAL SYSTEM: PROBLEMS AND LIMITATIONS

Problems in Classification

In the American legal system, crimes are divided into two categories. Relatively minor offenses such as disorderly conduct and petty theft are classified as *misdemeanors*. The more serious offenses such as aggravated assault, rape, robbery, and homicide are called *felonies*.

In the English legal system, the distinction is made between lesser offenses that can be dealt with in a *summary proceeding,* and more serious offense for which a *bill of indictment* is required before prosecution. In American law, criminal cases involving misdemeanors are handled at the local level through municipal courts, and punishments may involve up to one year in jail, a fine, or both. Felony cases are handled in county or superior courts, and punishment can involve sentencing to a state prison, a fine, or both. In the case of a capital offense, the penalty may be life imprisonment or even death.

The distinction between a misdemeanor and felony often can be arbitrary. Local courts have the right to reduce charges, and it is common for individuals charged with felonies to end up convicted of misdemeanors. Similarly, an offense treated as a misdemeanor in one jurisdiction may be considered a felony elsewhere. Thus the same offense can attract a range of punishment, depending on where it is tried.

The Limits of Criminal Responsibility

Although the field of criminology has explored individual behavior as it searches for a unified theory of criminality, it has never fully come to grips with the problem of individual responsibility. But the legal system, as it reacts to criminal behavior, generally has operated on the assumption of free will. Although free will does not exist in the absolute sense, the notion of exacting punishment for criminal violations stems from the presumption that individual choice has been exercised and the offender can be held responsible for his or her acts.

In seeking to understand and predict criminal behavior, positivistic criminology has advanced some scientific explanations that are rooted in economic and social factors, physical or mental abnormalities, or even genetic disabilities—like the recent theories linking aggressive behavior to the XYY chromosome. These various theories are not intended to justify offenders or excuse

It's Against the Law . . .

BOX 2

Sometimes the law just doesn't seem to make sense. In some New England states, for example, "blue laws" remain on the books, and often are enforced. These laws, which date back to Puritan times some three hundred years ago, prohibit commercial activities on Sunday, the "Lord's day."

Despite their apparent violation of the First Amendment, attempts to repeal these laws are defeated annually in state legislatures. Beginning in 1977, however, Massachusetts approved a temporary suspension of the blue laws—but only during the Christmas shopping season.

Massachusetts, though, is not the only state with anachronistic laws on its books. Did you know, for example, that it's against the law in the following states . . .

Alabama: to buy peanuts after sundown?
Arkansas: to blindfold a cow on a public road?
California: to peel an orange in a hotel room?
Colorado: to wear a mask?
Florida: to bathe unless you are fully dressed—even in your own bathtub?
Idaho: to walk around looking peeved or dejected?
Indiana: to take a bath in winter?
Kentucky: for a wife to move furniture around in the house without her husband's permission? Or for a wife to buy a hat without having her husband try it on first?
Maine: to blow your nose in public?
Michigan: to tie a crocodile to a fire hydrant?
Minnesota: to hang male and female underwear on the same clothesline? Or for a man to keep his hat on when meeting a cow?
Mississippi: to give beer to an elephant?
New York: to play cards on a train?
Ohio: to allow your pet out after dark unless it is wearing a taillight? Or for more than one person to drink from the same bottle?
Oregon: to wear roller skates in a public lavatory?
Virginia: to tickle a girl?

their wrongdoing, though at times the matter of guilt or criminal responsibility has been obscured by an emphasis on the offender as a sick person more in need of treatment than punishment. This emphasis on criminal behavior creates a schism between the problem of what to do with the criminal by way of reacting to his or her behavior—that is, treating or correcting it—and the problem that resides in the definition of crime and criminality and its application by agents of the state. You will recall that in Chapter 1 we defined crime as an *intentional violation of the law* (by commission or omission) *established by the state, the definition of which means that the individual who is defined or labeled as a criminal is subject to sanctions or punishment by the state.* The matter before us is, how might we avoid this schism and focus on the legal definitions and their application in defining some acts as criminal and others as noncriminal? The sociology of law studies the limits imposed by the legal code that may help identify when an accused offender may or may not be defined and/or labeled as a criminal.[38]

If we accept a crime as being an intentional act in violation of the criminal law, what limits does the legal code impose on defining the accused as an offender and assigning him the status of criminal? And since crime is forbidden behavior for which punishments are meted out by legal authorities, when should an accused offender *not* be treated as a criminal?

Juvenile Delinquency. In our society, those under a specified age, usually seven, are excluded from criminal responsibility. Between the ages of seven and a specific upper limit, individuals are still legally children and are seen as lacking full capacity for criminal intent. Under the common-law tradition of *parens patriae,* the state may intervene to protect children and treat them as delinquents, not as criminals. This concept is being strained today as younger and younger offenders become involved in the most serious and antisocial kinds of crime and violence and juvenile systems are unable to cope. A more complete discussion of the substantive and procedural dimensions of juvenile law will be presented in chapters 4 and 13. The fact that the juvenile court has mitigated the juvenile's responsibility for his or her conduct and dealt with it as a behavior problem in terms of the medical model (rather than in traditional legal terms) contributes to the difficulty.

Duress. Another example of a criminal act for which one is not held responsible is a deed done under *duress.* If it can be proved that an individual was forced by another to perform a criminal act, he or she will not be held legally responsible for that act.

The Insanity Defense. Although rarely invoked, the insanity defense is a political issue that sparks the public imagination. During the 1960s, for instance, there were only eleven cases in New York State in which the accused was ruled "not guilty by reason of insanity." [39]

In most jurisdictions the M'Naghten test of insanity is one of the standards by which cases are evaluated, although it is the sole test in less than half of the states. M'Naghten was a man who suffered from the delusion that he was pursued by deadly enemies. In attempting to shoot Sir Robert Peel, the prime minister of England, he killed Peel's secretary by mistake. He was found not guilty by reason of insanity.

The court based its decision on testimony that showed that M'Naghten was suffering under the delusion of being persecuted by the prime minister's Tory party and as a result had lost "all power of self-control." His acquittal was based on the state of his mind at the time of the offense, not on his denial of the act with which he was charged. Although his acquittal did not lead to his release, M'Naghten died in a mental hospital twenty-one years later. The verdict was seen as unwarranted leniency. As a result of the public controversy over the verdict, the House of Lords requested the opinion of all fifteen of the common-law judges on the matter, and the M'Naghten rule or legal test for insanity was formulated.[40] This rule required that to be exempt from criminal punishment, the person accused must have been at the time of committing the act "laboring under such a defect of reason, from disease of mind, as not to know the nature and quality of the act he was doing; or if he did know it, that he did not know he was doing what was wrong." [41]

The insanity plea or defense is an exception to the concept of free will and criminal responsibility on which the law is based. In the twentieth century, deterministic, criminological positivism, influenced by new ideas in psychology and sociology, was brought into the courtroom. In an effort to expand the concept, a more comprehensive test of insanity was called for and developed in the Durham rule (1954). This rule originated in the Court of Appeals of the District of Columbia. It states simply that an accused is not criminally responsible of his or her unlawful act if it was the product of mental disease or mental defect. While the Durham rule has since been rejected in the District of Columbia, it has been adopted in Maine and the Virgin Islands, and may be used as a guideline by juries deciding such cases in New Hampshire.[42]

Yet the insanity defense is more than a scholarly struggle: it has taken on political and ideological overtones. Former President Nixon, for instance, concerned that the insanity defense allows dangerous criminals to go free, proposed that it be excluded from the federal courts. To some legal scholars who were critical of the Durham rule, the insanity defense was necessary in that it is the exception to the belief in "freedom of the human will," and "it allows the court to treat every other defendant as someone who chose between *good and evil.*" [43]

The insanity defense represents an insoluble conflict between deterministic theories of causation and the persistent classical free-will theory of moral responsibility, which is related to *mens rea*. The various tests of insanity, including the recent Model Penal Code of the American Law Institute, cannot resolve the issue. As studies of jury deliberations have shown, juries in such cases are more apt to base their conclusions on human feelings. The insanity defense, however, touches on questions of basic social beliefs in its application to specific cases, in that it seeks to make a distinction between those who are morally responsible and those who are not, and between those who should be punished and those who should be treated.[44] It is this aspect of the defense that has resulted in some serious inequities. Although successful insanity pleas may be rare, defendants found not guilty by reason of insanity face mandatory commitment to mental hospitals for indefinite terms.

The controversy over just where mental health ends and crime begins continues. Criminal law prescribes punishment while still recognizing mitigating mental circumstances in some cases. Treating a criminal offense strictly as a health problem may not only jeopardize legal safeguards inherent in the idea that moral responsibility is necessary to determine guilt, but often conceals the fact that crime is a conflict between those who make and enforce laws and those who violate them.

The Overreach of the Law: Crimes Without Victims

It was once assumed that the best way to deal with crime was to pass specific laws against specific behaviors. Today the emphasis has shifted to the enforcement of existing laws. The criminal justice system devotes an enormous amount of energy to dealing with minor offenses. Indeed, over half the more than eight million arrests in 1975 involved lesser crimes. This situation has led many criminologists to the conclusion that the criminal law is overextended and often self-defeating in its attempts to regulate private behavior. The overreach of the criminal law into areas of private activity and private morals not only overloads the system and increases costs, but has the effect of "criminalizing" large segments of the population.

The overreach of the criminal law seems most apparent when it involves offenses generally known as *crimes without victims.* These are the offenses generally defined in *mala prohibita* laws, and usually involve activity that the participants do not bring to the attention of agents of the state. They include crimes like illegal gambling, possession of illicit drugs, proscribed sexual activities between consenting adults, and until the recent Supreme Court decision, abortion. The overreach of the law in prosecuting such activities not only creates great economic costs, but also contributes to a distorted picture of the total crime problem.

Efforts to decriminalize lesser crimes such as public drunkenness are underway in some states. Possession of small amounts of marijuana is now a misdemeanor rather than a felony in at least six states, and a similar redefinition is being considered in others. In such victimless crimes, the relationship between interest groups who maintain the power to assert their particular definition of right conduct and those not in a position to exercise power is most obvious.

Crimes Left Unattended: The Underreach of the Law

Conflict of interests, social status, and power are also relevant to the application of criminal definitions to the more powerful. Those involved in "sharp" business practices, industrial pollution, and government corruption are often afforded differential treatment under the law, although it should be noted that there are laws to prohibit such conduct—laws which in effect are contrary to the interests of the powerful. But as Sutherland pointed out some years ago, unlike conventional criminals, the powerful not only have influence in creating the rules by which they are regulated, but also are frequently able to control access to information about criminal charges and to manipulate societal reaction. In effect, they are in a position to "cover-up" their wrongdoing.[45]

SUMMARY

Since it is in the criminal law that we find distinctions between criminal and noncriminal behavior, and because social definitions of crime lack precision, the starting point for the study of criminology is the *sociology of law*, which provides an understanding of how *legal norms* emerged out of conflict between competing groups.

Historically, societies moved from a reliance on *informal social controls* to a need for *legalized formal social control*. The natural law asserts a rational relationship between *divine law* and/or *natural law* and those laws regulating human conduct. *Positive law* sees laws as man-made, emerging from attempts by the state to regulate public aspects of human behavior.

The major sources from which modern law emerged include *common law, constitutional law, statutes,* and *administrative law*. They provide a basis for *substantive* and *procedural law* as these are variously defined and modified by practice and precedent.

The law distinguishes between serious crimes—*felonies*—and lesser crimes—*misdemeanors*. These definitions can change as social values change. The legal code also specifies *exceptions to criminal responsibility* within the law that may depend on *age, duress, or degree of mental competence*. Distinctions are also made among offenses that are wrong in themselves, those that are wrong because they are prohibited, and those that are offenses against the public interest.

In trying to deal with offenses involving acts that are prohibited, such as illegal drug use or certain sexual activities, there has been an *overreach of the law*. This overreach has extended into the area of public nuisance crimes, like public drunkenness. Efforts continue to decriminalize these kinds of behavior.

These laws provide relevant case studies of the connection between the criminal law and conflict between powerful interest groups that are able to influence criminal definitions. This conflict is also important in the application of criminal definitions. An awareness of the process by which such definitions become a part of the criminal law and the analysis of societal reactions to behavior that comes to be defined or labeled as criminal have been enhanced by recent emphasis on the sociology of law.

ADDITIONAL READINGS

Barkum, Michael, ed. *Law and the Social System.* New York: Lieber-Atherton, 1973.

A collection of five essays that analyze the complex relationship between law and society. The essays focus upon issues related to legal definitions, law and behavior, research into the sociology of law, and legal sanctions, as well as law and the formative process of the social order.

Friedman, Lawrence, M. *Law and Society: An Introduction.* Englewood Cliffs, N.J.: Prentice-Hall, 1977.

A brief historical and comparative introduction to the sociology of law that presents conventional current perspectives on the legal system, primarily focusing on the United States.

Hall, Jerome. *Theft, Law, and Society,* 2nd ed. Indianapolis: Bobbs-Merrill, 1952.

Traces the history of the law of theft and illustrates the relationship between social conditions and emerging social forces in history as these are reflected in the application of the criminal law. This book has become a classic study in the sociology of law.

Quinney, Richard. *Critique of the Legal System.* Boston: Little, Brown & Co., 1974.

A somewhat doctrinaire extension of the conflict perspective. Provides criticisms within the context of a Marxist-oriented indictment of the legal system.

Schur, Edwin, M. *Law and Society: A Sociological View.* New York: Random House, 1968.

Edwin Schur relies upon his background in law and sociology to provide a sociological examination of major areas of law, including the nature and meaning of the law, the law's relationship to social change, and the role of social science evidence in the legal system.

Weber, Max. *On Law in Economy and Society.* Translated by Edward Shils and Max Rheinstein. New York: Simon and Schuster, 1954.

This book contains the basic elements of Weber's most comprehensive statement on the sociology of law. His insights—drawn from primitive and comparative law—attest to the contributions he has made to the modern study of the subject.

PART TWO

Social Correlates of Crime and Criminology

3 Assessing the Magnitude and Cost of Crime
4 Becoming Delinquent: Social Conditions, Group Associations, and the Defining Process
5 Female Status: Women's Crime and Societal Reaction

FINDER
FINGERPRINT READER
Calspan
CONTROL UNIT
CONRAC
PEP-400

3

Any set of crime statistics . . . involves some evaluative, institutional processing of people's reports. Concepts, definitions, quantitative models, and theories must be adjusted to the fact that the data are not some objectively observable universe of "criminal acts," but rather those events defined, captured, and processed as such by some institutional mechanism.
—Albert D. Biderman and Albert J. Reiss, Jr., "On Exploring the 'Dark Figure' of Crime," Annals (November 1967):15.

ASSESSING THE MAGNITUDE AND COST OF CRIME

HOW MUCH CRIME IS THERE?

You are doubtless familiar with the headlines: Rape Up 100%! Crime on the Increase! FBI Figures Show Violent Crime Climbing! In this startling form, most Americans are reminded regularly that they live in a frightening society. When spectacular crimes, particularly senseless murders, span the headlines, it can seem as if all of society is being engulfed by a crime wave: a single man randomly firing his rifle from a tower in Texas; the "Son of Sam" terrorizing the city of New York; the graves of a score of murdered itinerant workers uncovered on some California farmland; the Manson "family." Images of violent crime are etched in the mind. In many large urban areas, the reports of street crimes, such as handbag snatching and housebreaking, leave many citizens with the unsettling sense that they may become part of the crime problem—as victims.

No one will dispute that there is far too much crime in our society. But we have yet to come up with an accurate accounting system for measuring its practical or psychological toll. Even the best of current methods carefully couch all statistics in terms of "estimates." It should not be assumed that current official, or even unofficial, crime statistics can give valid measures of the volume, distribution, variation, or change over time in the crime rate. It is conceivable that if accurate figures could be collected, the totals might reach two to three times the levels reported in official statistics.

The "Dark Figure" of Crime

While the actual extent of crime in our society is unknown, given the nature of criminal behavior, the full extent will probably never be known.[1] The difference between crimes that are known and/or reported to the police and the actual amount of crime that is assumed to take place is often referred to as the "dark figure" of crime. Does the fact that there is much hidden crime necessarily mean that we should zealously seek to control or eliminate it? This question poses both a philosophical and a policy dilemma. There are some obvious hazards in campaigning for law and order when the extent of the problem has not been established. But acknowledging that the actual extent of crime is hidden may have value to the degree that it allows us to put published statistics of crime into a perspective that can help us understand the manner in which certain behaviors are perceived and dealt with in various social contexts.[2]

Crime statistics are significant to the extent that they influence and are influenced by the images of the phenomenon of crime that we hold in our minds. Richard Quinney noted that whether there is more or less "actual criminality" is not the issue. "The crucial question is, why societies and their agencies report, manufacture or produce the volume of crime that they do?"[3] In short, we assume that official crime data are significant since they influence our perceptions of the reality of crime. And these definitions of reality influence the processes by which society deals with nonconforming and unlawful conduct.

When crime data are used as a primary basis for research or are taken to represent the "true" picture of crime in society, they evoke considerable controversy among criminologists.[4] So although most textbooks on criminology characteristically begin with a discussion of crime statistics, their authors invariably qualify their use of such data with warnings and qualifications about their lack of reliability. Then they proceed to use the same data as though we can assume a constant, general ratio between reported crime and hidden crime.[5] Here, for example, are three more or less typical statements drawn from textbooks published in 1930, 1973, and 1978:

> It is not possible to discover or measure with any fair approximation the amount of crime in the United States, or the size of the population as it may be revealed by crime statistics.[6]

> Crime statistics are among the most unreliable and questionable social facts.[7]

> The statistics about crime and delinquency are probably the most unreliable and most difficult of all social statistics.[8]

Heeding these warnings about the limitations, reliability, value, and even validity of official crime statistics, we will begin our analysis of crime data by noting their political nature. We will also explore the origins of the FBI's *Uniform Crime Reports* (UCR) and the extent and variations in crimes reported to the police. In seeking to develop a broader data base over the past decade, the government has developed the National Crime Panel, which has sought to measure the extent of crime through the administration of periodic *victimization surveys* conducted in selected large urban centers across the country. Since these surveys rely upon the responses of victims—whether or not the crimes were reported to the police—they are, in a sense, unofficial data. We will also summarize some of the *self-report studies* in which social scientists have asked a given group about the criminal or delinquent acts they have committed. These have further documented the existence of "hidden criminality." Both victimization surveys and self-report studies have cast doubt on the idea that there is a constant ratio between the "reality of crime" produced by official statistics and the actual amount of crime. However, both of these methods have serious limitations.[9]

THE USE AND MISUSE OF CRIME DATA IN POLITICS AND POLICY

Even though our data are incomplete and unreliable, we probably have compiled more statistics on crime and criminals than on most other types of social behaviors. By 1975, there were nearly 600,000 full-time law enforcement employees, many of whom were involved in some way in recording data about crime. In addition, there were thousands of court and correctional employees gathering information about crimes, offenders, and victims. Still, as Peter Manning points out, "the actual extent of crimes committed in a society is unknown—and in all likelihood unknowable, and therefore crime statistics as well as the crime rate, are simply a construction of police activities."[10]

Those who record and interpret crime statistics are very aware of the "dark figure" of unreported crime, and as their techniques and procedures

"It's finally happened. There are more criminals than victims."

have improved, this pool of "hidden" crime has been reflected in some of the reported increases.[11] For instance, in 1975, the FBI's summary of crime activity, the *Uniform Crime Reports*, "estimated" the number of *index crimes* (the seven most frequent serious offenses listed in Table 3.1) at 11,256,000. This figure represented an increase of about 9 percent over the volume of the previous year, and a 39 percent increase over 1970 (see Table 3.2). Some of this gain, however, reflected more sophisticated methods of reporting. In 1975, for example, the UCR data included 95 percent of the total population compared to 91 in 1970. Statistics were contributed by 13,000 jurisdictions in 1975, compared to 9,200 in 1970. While the 1975 reports tapped 83 percent of the rural population, the 1970 reports covered only 71 percent.[12] So the increase in volume of index crimes between 1970 and 1975 reflects in part the impact of federal money spent to stimulate more efficient reporting of offenses as well as added law enforcement personnel in the rural areas of our society.

Aside from these matters of statistical and reporting bias, there is the problem of the manipulation of crime statistics for political and organizational ends. Public announcements by government bureaucrats that "crime is on the increase" may create the impression that crime is somehow more of a threat than it was in the past.[13] In addition, in their quest for "big news stories," newspapers and other media may become unwitting accomplices in creating a "crime-wave" mentality simply by passing official information along. And the fear of crime may, in turn, set in motion a self-fulfilling prophecy—a circular process that leads to greater efforts at reporting, an ensuing rise in the published crime rate, an escalation of the fear of crime, and public support for more spending for crime control.

It should not surprise us then, that beginning in the mid-1960s, "law and order" emerged as a major domestic concern—and even became a major campaign issue for several presidential candidates who felt it both appropriate and politically valuable to address the public's concern about and fear of crime.[14] Once in office, however, the object is not just to rail against crime, but to prove you have done something about it. Attorney General John Mitchell, chief law enforcement official of the Nixon administration (later to become a white-collar crime statistic himself), faced that dilemma when the FBI was preparing to announce a 13 percent rise in all crime in 1970. Mitchell proceeded to edit the press release to read that the *rate of increase* in violent crimes had slowed by 7 percent to make it appear that the law-and-order policies of the Nixon administration had brought about a decrease in the rate of increase of crime.[15]

On the local level, police chiefs and law enforcement bureaucracies may find themselves pressured by politicians to "do something" about crime. After all, the police have established a claim on the responsibility for crime control. So the police argue for funds for equipment and personnel to carry on their fight against crime. Conversely, law enforcement agencies may manipulate crime data by reporting fewer offenses in order to justify their use of previously allocated funds.[16]

Table 3.1. Estimates of Index Crimes Known to Police, 1975

Area	Population[a]	Total Crime Index	Violent[b] Crime (subtotal)	Property[b] Crime (subtotal)	Murder and non-negligent manslaughter	Forcible rape	Robbery	Aggravated assault	Burglary	Larceny/theft	Motor vehicle theft
Standard metropolitan statistical area	156,133,251										
Area actually reporting[c]	97.3%	9,378,048	897,074	8,480,974	16,257	48,225	440,365	392,227	2,679,939	4,902,559	898,476
Estimated total	100.0%	9,540,537	906,843	8,633,694	16,490	48,894	443,461	397,998	2,729,061	4,989,336	915,297
Rate per 100,000 inhabitants		6,110.5	580.8	5,529.7	10.6	31.3	284.0	254.9	1,747.9	3,195.6	586.2
Other cities	23,680,618										
Area actually reporting	93.0%	979,909	59,116	920,793	1,201	2,984	12,695	42,236	242,985	630,250	47,558
Estimated total	100.0%	1,050,749	63,717	987,032	1,313	3,196	13,685	45,523	261,276	674,718	51,038
Rate per 100,000 inhabitants		4,437.2	269.1	4,168.1	5.5	13.5	57.8	192.2	1,103.3	2,849.2	215.5
Rural	33,310,131										
Area actually reporting	83.3%	579,456	46,850	532,606	2,216	3,395	6,527	34,712	227,235	276,297	29,074
Estimated total	100.0%	665,280	55,724	609,556	2,702	4,003	7,827	41,192	261,792	313,644	34,120
Rate per 100,000 inhabitants		1,997.2	167.3	1,829.9	8.1	12.0	23.5	123.7	785.9	941.6	102.4
United States total	213,124,000	11,256,566	1,026,284	10,230,282	20,505	56,093	464,973	484,713	3,252,129	5,977,698	1,000,455
Rate per 100,000 inhabitants		5,281.7	481.5	4,800.2	9.6	26.3	218.2	227.4	1,525.9	2,804.8	469.4

[a] Population is Bureau of the Census provisional estimate as of July 1, 1975.
[b] Violent crime is offenses of murder, forcible rape, robbery, and aggravated assault. Property crime is offenses of burglary, larceny/theft, and motor vehicle theft.
[c] The percentage representing area actually reporting will not coincide with the ratio between reported and estimated crime totals, since these data represent the sum of the calculations for individual states which have varying populations, portions reporting, and crime rates.

Source: FBI, *Uniform Crime Reports, 1975* (Washington, D.C.: U.S. Government Printing Office, 1975), p. 49.

The Manipulation of Urban Crime Figures

The manner in which crime data may be manipulated by various police agencies was noted by the President's Crime Commission in 1967. The commission went out of its way in its 1967 general report to illustrate how changes in reporting methods between 1959 and 1965 resulted in increases in the various index crimes ranging from 27 to 202 percent. In a comparison of crime reporting on the volume of robberies in the nation's two largest cities, New York and Chicago, the Crime Commission also demonstrated how bureaucratically organized law enforcement agencies may manipulate and manufacture crime statistics to serve their own interests. In the 1930s, Chicago had less than the population of New York, yet it consistently reported eight times as many robberies. The discrepancies in the New York Police Department's crime data were so glaring that the FBI finally decided to exclude New York from the *Uniform Crime Report Summary* in 1949 and for several subsequent years. Meanwhile, after the New York police established a new centralized system in 1950, there was a sudden rise of 400 percent in robberies and 1300 percent in burglaries—surpassing even Chicago's figures. But in 1959, Chicago centralized its data collection, and suddenly its rate of increase in these categories edged past New York's. By 1966, when the Crime Commission was at work, New York once again had the higher rate of increase for robberies. Needless to say, these developments raised some eyebrows on the Crime Commission, now faced with the task of explaining a reported rate in 1966 that was thirteen times greater than the rate in 1940. In the end, the commission strongly questioned the usefulness of considering such inconsistent measurements in trying to ascertain national trends.[17]

Another case of fallible, big-city crime reporting was documented by Daniel Bell in his analysis of the construction of the crime rate by the Philadelphia Police Department. When a new police commissioner was appointed by a reform mayor in 1952, he discovered that estimates of crime had been trimmed by as much as 5,000 complaints in one inner-city precinct. He installed a centralized reporting system, and the 1953 figures showed an increase of 70 percent over 1951.[18]

Bureaucracy and Crime Statistics

Official statistics, then, may be used by police departments to enhance their organizational image of efficiency and to justify their crime control mission. In this regard, Manning notes they are not unlike other bureaucracies in our statistically oriented culture that manipulate data in their claim to be efficient in order to promote the autonomy and survival of the organization.[19]

This strategy involves the use of official statistics such as clearance rates and official FBI data to create the impression of professional efficiency. Those offenses classified as solved become part of the clearance rate, while crimes without victims, where there is no complainant, are not included in the clearance rate. One recent analysis of arrest trends in the United States from 1969 to 1976 illustrates the manner in which such pressure on police to overlook victimless crimes may be reflected in crime statistics. The proportion of arrests for such offenses showed a sharp decrease from 51.5 percent to 35.9 percent during this period. During the same interval, arrests for serious crimes fluctuated around 20 percent, while arrests for nonserious crimes increased from 29.5 to 41.3 percent.[20] This preoccupation by law enforcement bureaucracies with the construction of official statistics is epitomized in the statement, "the more the police enforce the laws, the higher the crime rate."[21]

Certainly it is obvious that crime is a social evil. Yet the social construction and use of crime statistics by police organizations serve to obscure the complexity implicit in Emile Durkheim's statement that crime is a normal condition of society as it serves an integrative social function. We will not be able to understand the complexity of the crime problem until we recognize that the use and misuse of crime data to create a crime wave mentality and to make police bureaucracies appear more efficient is a part of the problem.

ESTIMATING THE EXTENT OF CRIME: OFFICIAL DATA

The Uniform Crime Reports

Whatever the shortcomings of official statistics, criminologists generally still rely on them in their study and analysis of crime. It is obvious that these crime statistics and rates do not measure the total incidence of crime. But they do report those events that are identified, reported to, and recorded by official agencies as violations of the legal definitions of crime.

The earliest crime data collected in America were very sketchy and followed the European model of drawing information from two principal sources: statistics on those prosecuted and convicted in the courts, and statistics on prisons. By 1900, twenty-five states had passed statutory provisions for the collection of judicial statistics, and twenty-three states provided for the compilation of prison statistics. Early critics argued that neither source was as useful or accurate as arrest statistics. Since it was apparent that there were many more crimes committed than there were arrests, offenses known or reported to the police came to be seen as a more complete measure of crime.

In 1927, the International Association of Police Chiefs established a committee to study the matter. Three years later the association proposed a voluntary national program for collecting data on offenses known to the police. The Federal Bureau of Investigation was authorized by Congress to serve as a clearinghouse, and in 1931 it began issuing its reports. Initially the reports were published monthly, then quarterly. In 1958 the present system of major annual reports was adopted. The FBI continues to issue preliminary quarterly reports for cities with populations of over 100,000.

The FBI's *Uniform Crime Reports* (UCR) attempts a nationwide accounting of crime data based on statistics provided by city, county, and state law en-

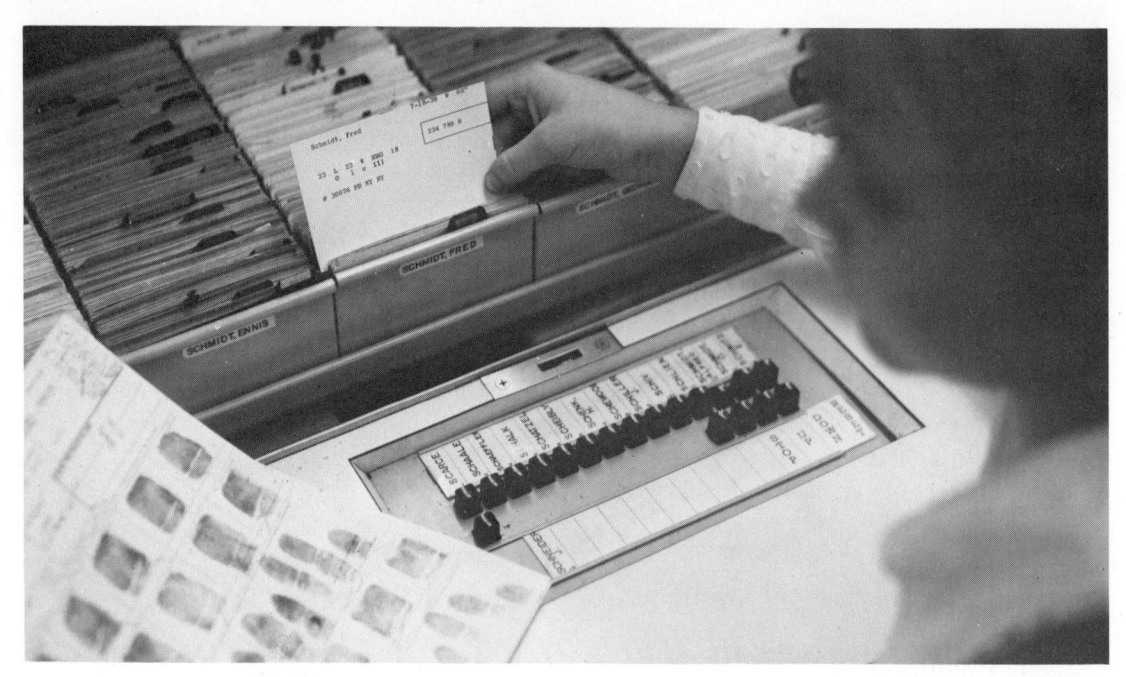

The official construction of the reality of crime.

forcement agencies. It does not include data from federal agencies. Although incomplete and unreliable, the FBI seeks to provide guidance to these agencies responsible for the collecting of data. The UCR organizes the data into two general categories: crimes known to the police and arrests. Included in crimes known to the police are offenses that have been reported to or observed by the police in the categories of crime that are termed "serious" by the FBI. They are called *index crimes.*

In the interest of uniformity, the FBI has adopted standardized definitions in the *Uniform Crime Reports* that try to overcome the variations in the definitions of criminal offenses in the numerous jurisdictions reporting. For instance, the UCR handbook defines larceny as a theft of $50 or more, making it a felony rather than a misdemeanor. Yet, despite these guidelines, some jurisdictions do not report larceny in the felony category unless the theft is $100 or more. With inflation of the dollar, by the way, this $50 larceny definition has made the larceny/felony category more inclusive over the past twenty years.

The FBI has made a determined effort to make the *Uniform Crime Reports* more complete. Only about 400 police departments sent in data when the collecting process started in 1930. This figure increased to 8,000 police departments in 1964 and 9,000 in 1973, covering about 93 percent of the population. The 1975 UCR include data from 13,000 contributors covering 97 percent of those living in standard metropolitan statistical areas (SMSA's), 93 percent of those in other cities, and 83 percent of the rural population—for a combined average of 95 percent of the nation's population. (See Table 3.1.)

Table 3.2. Estimated Extent of Crime, Rate, and Percent Change for 1975 as Compared to 1960, 1970, and 1974

Index Crime Offenses	Estimated Crime 1975 Number	Rate per 100,000 Inhabitants	Percent Changeover 1974 Number	Rate	Percent Changeover 1970 Number	Rate	Percent Changeover 1960 Number	Rate
Murder and nonnegligent manslaughter	20,510	9.6	−1.0	−2.0	+28.2	+21.5	+125.1	+88.2
Forcible rape	56,090	26.3	+1.3	+.4	+47.6	+40.6	+226.3	+174.0
Robbery	464,970	218.2	+5.1	+4.3	+32.9	+26.8	+331.2	+263.1
Aggravated assault	484,710	227.4	+6.2	+5.4	+44.7	+38.0	+214.1	+164.1
Violent (subtotal)	*1,026,280*	*481.5*	+5.3	+4.4	+38.9	+32.5	+255.8	+199.3
Burglary	3,252,100	1,525.9	+7.0	+6.1	+47.5	+40.6	+256.6	+200.0
Larceny/theft	5,977,700	2,804.8	+13.6	+12.7	+41.5	+34.9	+222.2	+171.1
Motor vehicle theft	1,000,500	469.4	+2.4	+1.6	+7.8	+2.8	+204.8	+156.5
Property (subtotal)	*10,230,300*	*4,800.2*	+10.3	+9.4	+39.0	+32.6	+230.5	+178.1
Total	11,256,600	5,281.7	+9.8	+8.9	+39.0	+32.6	+232.6	+179.9

Source: FBI, *Uniform Crime Reports, 1975* (Washington, D.C.: U.S. Government Printing Office, 1975), p. 11.

In terms of pure volume of data, the 1975 UCR may be the most complete set of crime statistics ever assembled in the United States. Yet the data in the UCR can be deceiving. They have been misinterpreted and misused. But despite continuing controversy over their shortcomings, they are a readily available source for research and planning, and critics have yet to come up with an acceptable alternative.

The UCR comes closer to fulfilling the requirements of Thorsten Sellin's principle relative to crime data than the court or prison statistics on which we relied previously. Sellin, who was both a critic and proponent of FBI data gathering, coined the axiom that "the value of criminal statistics as a basis for measurement of criminality in geographic areas decreases as the procedure takes us further away from the offense itself." [22] He emphasized that greater value should be placed upon offenses known to police than upon actual arrests that vary widely, depending on the skills and luck of police professionals. Field surveys of victimization, in which people speak of their own unfortunate encounters with crime — often incidents that are never reported — would be a type of data collection that would adhere even more closely to Sellin's theory.

Types of Crime Data in the Uniform Crime Reports. The twenty-nine offenses itemized in the *Uniform Crime Reports* are divided into two general categories. In *Part I,* the offenses listed include murder, nonnegligent manslaughter, forcible rape, aggravated assault, robbery, burglary, larceny/theft ($50 and over) and motor vehicle theft (see Table 3.1). These seven offenses have been categorized as *index crimes,* both because of their assumed seriousness and the frequency with which they occur. In this sense they are relied upon as indicators, or indices, of crime and crime trends in the United States. The index crimes are subdivided into *violent crimes* (the first four listed) and *property crimes* (the last three). Local police agencies compile their statistics under the seven UCR categories and submit their reports on a monthly basis.

In its arrests reports, the UCR combines these seven index offenses with twenty-two additional categories that are considered "less serious" offenses and which the FBI arbitrarily places under the heading of *Part II* offenses (see Table 3.4). However, only the Part I offenses are referred to as index crimes, and frequently commentators and journalists refer only to the seven index offenses as "serious crimes." Yet some Part II offenses, like fraud and embezzlement, exact a heavier financial and social toll from their victims than several of the index crimes.[23]

An example of UCR data is shown in Table 3.1 and other tables in this chapter. In reading and interpreting data of this nature, there are some particulars of which you must be aware in order to avoid drawing incorrect conclusions. In addition to the seven crime offenses that yield a total for all offenses reported to and recorded by the police in a given year, there are three terms to be kept in mind: (1) *violent crime,* reported in terms of the sum and rate for the four Part I violent offenses (murder and manslaughter, rape, robbery, aggravated assault); (2) *property crime,* reported in terms of the sum and rate for the three Part I property offenses (burglary, larceny/theft, motor vehicle theft); and (3) *crime rate*, the number of offenses reported in a given year per 100,000 population. The crime rate is calculated by:

$$\text{Crime Rate Total Population} = \frac{\text{Total Number Offenses}}{\text{Population}} \times 100,000$$

Estimates of the Extent of Reported Crime. An examination of the data in Tables 3.1 and 3.2 and Figure 3.1 gives us some idea of the extent and rate of crime over the time periods covered — at least in terms of offenses recognized as crime events by local police agencies and reported to the FBI. The changes in reported crime and in the crime rate are plotted in Figure 3.1. We should be cautious in reading the comparative changes in crime rates for violent offenses and property offenses depicted in Figures 3.2 and 3.3. Looking at Table 3.1, for example, we can ascertain that the rate for property crimes is about ten times that of violent crimes (4,800.2 to 481.5). Table 3.2 indicates that the property rate has increased at a slightly higher percentage since 1970. Given the greater volume of these crimes it means that there was a much greater increase in sheer numbers in the three property categories.

In 1975, the volume of larceny/theft alone was nearly six times that of all categories of violent offenses. While the estimated increase in the volume of index crimes over 1974 was nearly 10 percent, the four violent crime categories, which comprise only 9 percent of the total volume, increased at a rate of 5 percent. Among violent crimes, there has been much public concern over the persistent rise in the rate of robbery. Criminologists attribute some of this rise to the nature of the crime itself, maintaining that since robbery is a property crime that involves violence, real or threatened, and the offenders are usually strangers to the victims, the incidents are more likely to be reported to police.

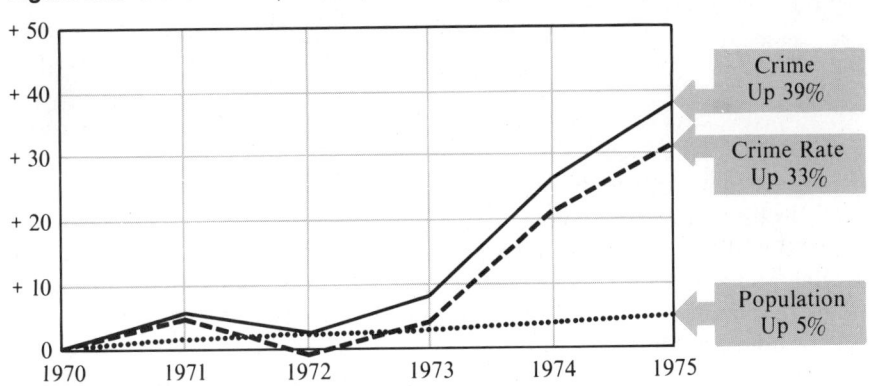

Figure 3.1. Crime and Population, 1970–1975 (percent change over 1970)

Note: Crime = Crime Index Offenses
Crime Rate = Number of Offenses per 100,000 Inhabitants
Source: FBI, *Uniform Crime Reports, 1975* (Washington, D.C.: U.S. Government Printing Office, 1975), p. 12.

Figure 3.2. Crimes of Violence, 1970–1975 (percent change over 1970)

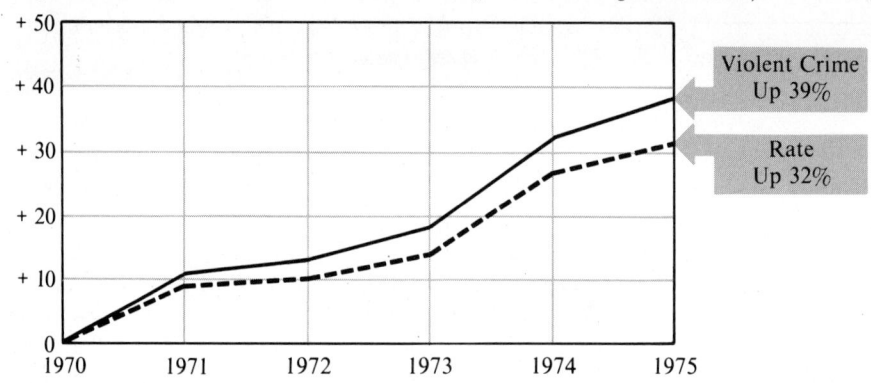

Violent Crime Up 39%
Rate Up 32%

Note: Limited to Murder, Forcible Rape, Robbery and Aggravated Assault
Source: FBI, *Uniform Crime Reports, 1975* (Washington, D.C.: U.S. Government Printing Office, 1975), p. 13.

Figure 3.3. Crime Against Property, 1970-1975 (percent change over 1970)

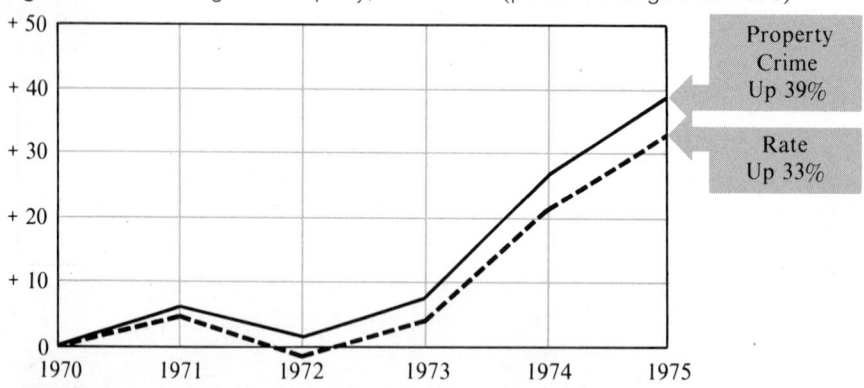

Property Crime Up 39%
Rate Up 33%

Note: Limited to Burglary, Larceny/Theft, and Motor Vehicle Theft
Source: FBI, *Uniform Crime Report, 1975* (Washington, D.C.: U.S. Government Printing Office, 1975), p. 14.

Furthermore, although robbery is included as a type of "violent crime" in the FBI's listing of crimes known to the police, in discussing "crime cleared by arrest" the FBI classifies it with property offenses. Police are more successful in clearing homicides and other violent crimes by arrest than they are in solving the more numerous property offenses (see Figure 3.4), although the clearance rate for homicides has slipped from a level of 86 percent in 1970 to 79 percent in 1975. This is not to dismiss the excessive amount of violent crime in our society and the human suffering it causes. For even though the rate for murder decreased in 1975 for the second time in fifteen years, the homicide rate in the United States, 9.6 per 100,000, is still twice that of Finland—our nearest com-

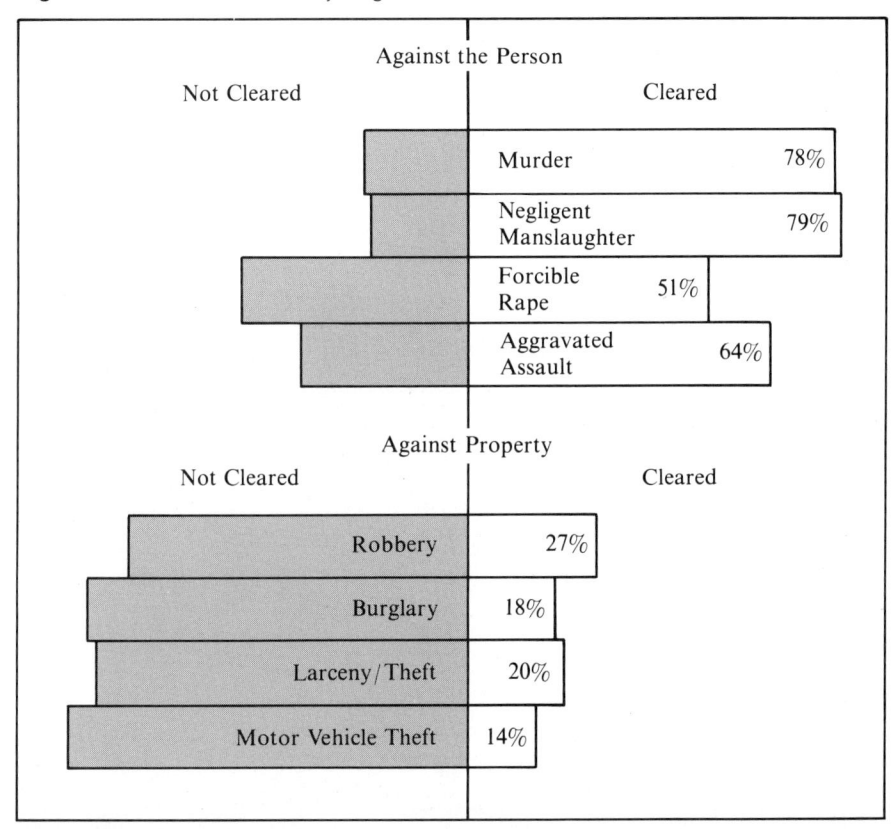

Figure 3.4. Crimes Cleared by August, 1975

Against the Person

	Cleared
Murder	78%
Negligent Manslaughter	79%
Forcible Rape	51%
Aggravated Assault	64%

Against Property

	Cleared
Robbery	27%
Burglary	18%
Larceny/Theft	20%
Motor Vehicle Theft	14%

Source: FBI, *Uniform Crime Reports, 1975* (Washington, D.C.: U.S. Government Printing Office, 1975), p. 40.

petitor among Western developed nations. And although the annual rate of increase for rape is comparatively low, the rate has jumped 174 percent in fifteen years. Some of the increase certainly is due to the fact that women are less reluctant today to report these violent sexual offenses than previously.

Even the FBI cautions that its aggregate figures and methods of reporting should be used carefully. Still, visitors to the new FBI headquarters in Washington, D.C., might miss the cautionary note provided in the UCR when they look up at the "crime clocks" that depict how often various crimes occur (see Figure 3.5). From a superficial glance, you could conclude that the clocks warn of the risk of becoming a victim of a given crime in one's community. Actually, they are based on annual rates that have been tabulated retrospectively, and do not imply any minute-by-minute regularity in the commission of crime. But the compilers of the *Uniform Crime Reports* do maintain that the risk of becoming a victim of crime did increase by about 33 percent between 1970 and 1975.

Figure 3.5. Crime Clocks, 1975

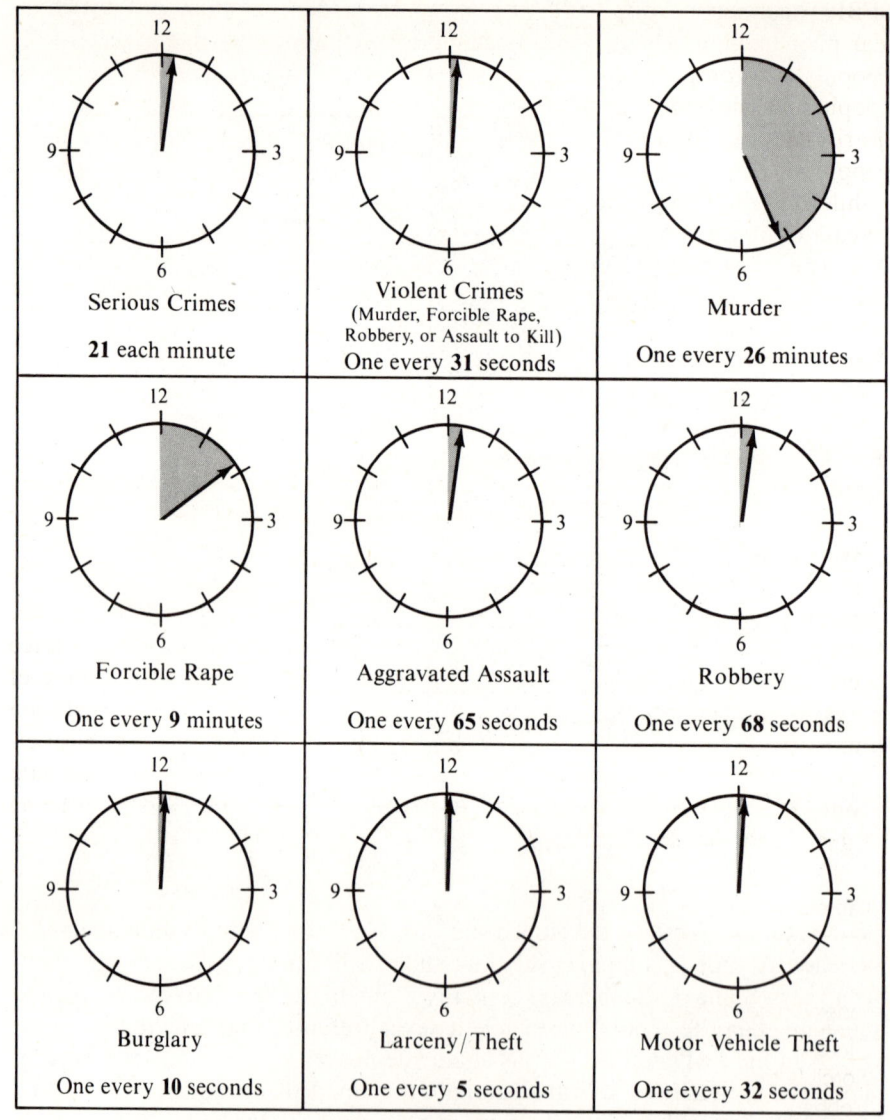

Serious Crimes **21** each minute	Violent Crimes (Murder, Forcible Rape, Robbery, or Assault to Kill) One every **31** seconds	Murder One every **26** minutes
Forcible Rape One every **9** minutes	Aggravated Assault One every **65** seconds	Robbery One every **68** seconds
Burglary One every **10** seconds	Larceny/Theft One every **5** seconds	Motor Vehicle Theft One every **32** seconds

Note: The *Uniform Crime Reports* cautions that these crime clocks should be viewed with care, since they are an aggregate representation of UCR data and are designed to portray the annual reported crime and show the relative frequency of occurrence of the index offenses. This figure does not imply a regularity in the commission of offenses; it represents the annual ratio of crime to fixed time intervals.

Source: FBI, *Uniform Crime Reports, 1975* (Washington, D.C.: U.S. Government Printing Office, 1975), p. 9.

The preface to the 1975 UCR lists thirteen factors claimed to affect the volume and type of crime. They include seven references to the effectiveness of police and criminal justice organizations that seem to reflect the opinion of the FBI. The other six variables acknowledge the reality that crime is not a singular phenomenon. These include, among other things, density and size of the population, composition of the population relative to age, sex, and race, and population movement as related to seasonal variations in the crime rate. These variables are supported by the UCR data. For instance, cities with a population over 250,000 had a 7 percent increase in the crime rate over 1974, while suburban areas still undergoing active population shifts recorded an increase of 10 percent.

The crime rate also varied by region (see Table 3.3). The greatest increase, 12 percent, was reported for the Southern states. Eleven percent was reported for the Northeastern states, 9 percent for the North Central states, and 7 percent for the Western states. Although the overall crime rate is highest in the Western states, murders are highest in the South, where 42 percent of the 20,510 homicides in 1975 were committed.

Climate and seasonal variations in weather conditions have been considered a factor in crime ever since the pioneer work done by the Belgian mathematician, Adolphe Quetelet, in the 1830s. Human associations vary with the seasons, and it is reasonable to relate crimes against persons to those times of the year when people congregate more intensely in group activities. Crimes against persons tend to be high during summer months (see Figure 3.6), but we must not attribute cause to this correlation. The data compiled by Enrico Ferri and other early criminologists indicated a pattern of high volume of crime in the summer, but we would be more critical today of his conclusion that summer crime activity was largely due to the negative psychological effects of hot weather. Until more comparative studies are completed using data from tropical societies, firm conclusions cannot be drawn about weather being a direct causal factor in crime.

Table 3.3. Crime Rate by Region (per 100,000 population)

Index Crime Offenses	Northeastern States	North–Central States	Southern States	Western States
Murder	7.6	8.1	12.7	9.0
Forcible rape	21.0	24.1	25.8	37.6
Robbery	300.4	207.3	168.6	216.5
Aggravated assault	206.4	177.2	253.8	284.0
Violent (subtotal)	*535.4*	*416.8*	*460.8*	*547.1*
Burglary	1,448.0	1,322.2	1,475.1	2,029.4
Larceny/theft	2,295.7	2,911.0	2,582.2	3,708.2
Motor vehicle theft	652.8	431.4	329.8	539.1
Property (subtotal)	*4,396.4*	*4,664.6*	*4,387.0*	*6,276.6*
Total	4,931.9	5,081.3	4,847.8	6,823.7

Source: FBI, *Uniform Crime Reports, 1975* (Washington, D.C.: U.S. Government Printing Office, 1975), p. 11.

Figure 3.6. Crime by the Month

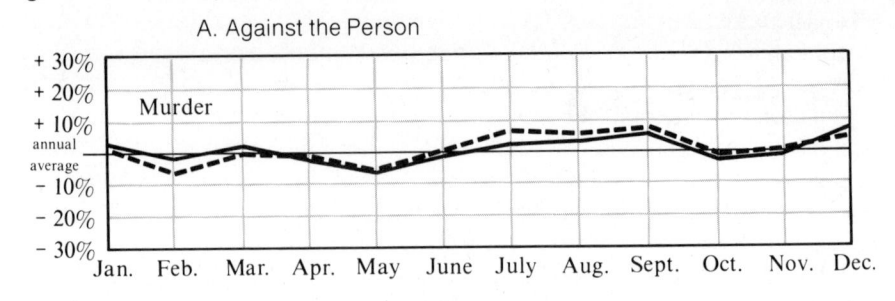

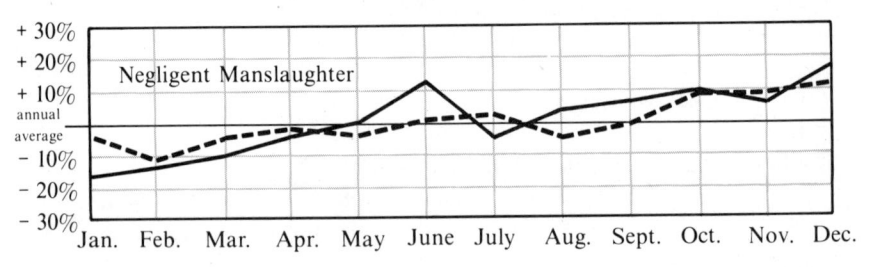

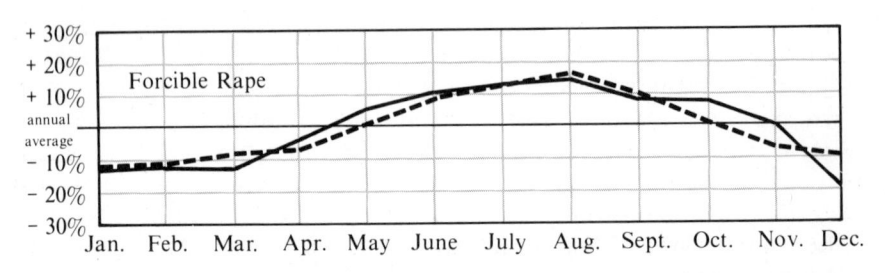

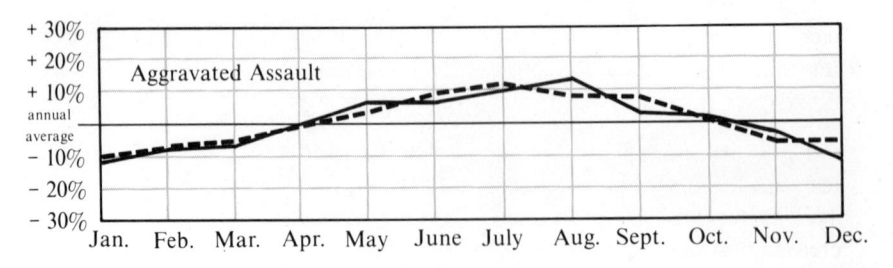

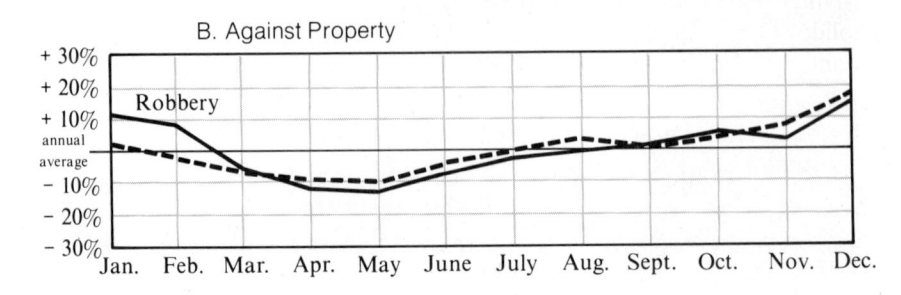

A. Against the Person

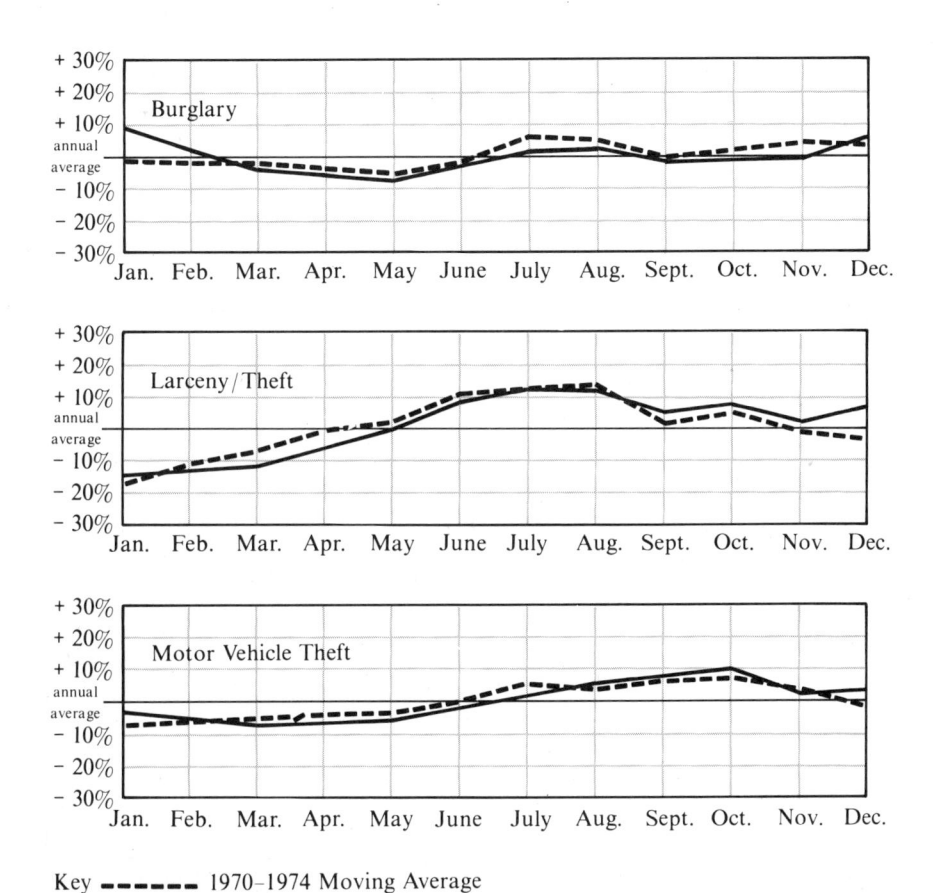

[Charts showing monthly crime rate variations for Burglary, Larceny/Theft, and Motor Vehicle Theft, comparing 1970–1974 Moving Average with Variation from 1975 Annual Average.]

Key ------ 1970–1974 Moving Average
―――― Variation from 1975 Annual Average

Source: FBI, *Uniform Crime Reports, 1975* (Washington, D.C.: U.S. Government Printing Office, 1975), pp. 38–39.

There are monthly variations in crime rates as well. In December, crime rates tend to go up in the categories of murder, negligent manslaughter, robbery, burglary and larceny/theft. This rise may partially be explained by the increased business and social activity during that month and the hazardous driving conditions in some sections of the country. But neither hot weather nor holidays explain why motor vehicle theft tends to reach an annual peak in the months of October and November.

Variations in Sex, Age, and Race in Arrest Rates

The proportion of arrests varies not only according to the specific offense, but also by age, sex, and racial composition of the population. For instance, crime rates have always been much higher for men than for women. But this may be changing. As Rita Simon has stated:

As women become more liberated from hearth and home and become more involved in full-time jobs, they are more likely to engage in the types of crimes for which their occupations provide them with the greatest opportunity. They are also more likely to become partners and entrepreneurs in crime to a greater extent than they have in the past.[24]

Sex. Simon's study challenges the popular impression that women have recently become more involved in crimes of violence than in the past. She suggests that this impression may be due to the fact that women have been more involved in property offenses in recent years. It may also be due to the spectacular and highly publicized exploits of a small number of women—Patty Hearst, "Squeaky" Fromme, Susan Saxe, and Arab and West German terrorists. Simon points out that between 1953 and 1972, the percentage increase for men arrested for violent crimes was nearly four times that of women. For property crimes the situation is almost reversed—the increase in the numbers of women arrested is three times the percentage of increase for males.[25]

The rate of change for women in the arrest statistics is most pronounced in the index crime of larceny/theft and Part II offenses, such as forgery, fraud, and embezzlement. In 1967, the ratio of females to males arrested for larceny was 1 to 3. But by 1975 that ratio had closed to 1 to 2.2 (see Table 3.4). In Part II offenses, the proportion for forgery had decreased from 1 in 4 in 1972, to 1 in 2.5 in 1975. For embezzlement, the proportion of females arrested during the same years dropped from 1 in 3.5 to 1 in 2.2. If these trends continue at the same rate, the arrests of men and women for fraud, embezzlement, and larceny may equalize by 1990.

Table 3.4. Arrest Trends for Major Crimes in the United States by Age and Sex, 1975

Offenses Charged	Total Arrested 1975	Male	Female	Under 25
PART I Index Crimes				
Criminal homicide				
Murder and nonnegligent manslaughter	16,485	84.4	15.6	44.9
Manslaughter by negligence	3,041	88.8	11.2	50.6
Forcible rape	21,963	99.0	1.0	58.0
Robbery	129,788	93.0	7.0	77.0
Aggravated assault	202,217	86.9	13.1	49.6
Violent crime (subtotal)	*370,453*	*89.7*	*10.3*	*59.5*
Burglary, breaking or entering	449,155	94.6	5.4	85.2
Larceny/theft	958,938	68.8	31.2	75.4
Motor vehicle theft	120,224	93.0	7.0	84.6
Property crime (subtotal)	*1,528,317*	*78.3*	*21.7*	*79.0*
Subtotal Part I	*1,901,811*	*80.5*	*19.5*	*75.2*

Table 3.4 (continued)

PART II Offenses				
Other assaults	352,648	86.2	13.8	51.9
Arson	14,589	88.7	11.3	74.7
Forgery and counterfeiting	57,803	71.1	28.9	56.6
Embezzlement	9,302	68.9	31.1	39.6
Fraud	146,253	65.8	34.2	35.8
Stolen property (burglary, receiving, etc.)	100,903	89.3	10.7	71.7
Vandalism	175,865	92.0	8.0	86.0
Weapons, carrying, possession, etc.	130,933	92.0	8.0	51.2
Prostitution, commercialized vice	50,229	25.7	74.3	65.9
Sex offenses, except rape and prostitution	50,837	92.3	7.7	50.8
Narcotic drug laws	508,189	86.2	13.8	77.0
Gambling	49,469	91.2	8.8	18.9
Offenses against family and children	53,332	88.3	11.7	41.9
Driving under the influence	908,680	91.9	8.1	27.1
Liquor laws	267,057	85.7	14.3	80.8
Drunkenness	1,176,121	92.9	7.1	23.9
Disorderly conduct	632,561	82.4	17.6	57.4
Vagrancy	59,277	89.5	10.5	33.2
All other offenses, except traffic	1,037,754	83.9	16.1	60.5
Curfew and loitering violations	112,117	79.7	20.3	100.0
Runaways	188,817	43.1	56.9	100.0
Total arrests for all Part I and Part II offenses	8,013,645	84.3	15.7	56.9

Source: FBI, *Uniform Crime Reports, 1975* (Washington, D.C.: U.S. Government Printing Office, 1975), pp. 190–91.

In the meantime, although the statistical gap between male and female criminality is closing, it varies considerably by the nature of the offense. As social status differences between the sexes diminish, we can expect that there will be a lessening of the statistical difference between the types of crime committed by men and women.

Age. Youth plays a major part in crime statistics. People under the age of twenty-five were involved in 57 percent of the arrests in 1975. Of that total, 42 percent were under age eighteen and 9 percent were under the age of fifteen. This amounted to an increase of 2 percent for those under twenty-five and 3 percent for those under eighteen over the 1974 figures.

Even in the more serious index crimes, a majority of those arrested were under twenty-five (see Table 3.4), and in both the burglary and motor theft categories, five out of six arrests were in this younger age group. Young people also dominate the statistics in arrests for Part II offenses such as vandalism. And, of course, they comprise the entire group arrested as curfew violators and runaways.

Until very recently, the fifteen- through twenty-five-year-old segment of the population was increasing at a rate four times faster than the general population. As the median age of the population starts rising again, it is likely that the crime rate for this group will level off somewhat. Yet it must be considered that young people, particularly minority youth, are grossly overrepresented among the unemployed in the inner cities, and inequality of economic opportunity is a condition that is highly correlated with crime.

Race. "When all offenses are considered together," the President's Crime Commission noted, "the majority of offenders arrested are white, male, and over twenty-four years of age." [26] Even so, race is almost as much a factor as sex in determining the likelihood of arrest in our society. Though blacks comprise only 11 percent of the population, their rate of arrest is disproportionately high for all but two of the offenses shown in Table 3.5. Note that in the categories included in violent crimes, blacks are disproportionately represented, even though the percentage of such offenses for which whites were arrested was slightly larger. In an earlier seventeen-city study of violent crimes, Lynn Curtis reported that in 1967 blacks were offenders and victims in nearly two-thirds of violent crimes, such as homicide, aggravated assault, and forcible rape.[27] He notes in another analysis of these data that racial and economic constraints create social and personal responses (cultural adaptations) that generate aggressiveness toward self and others. This in turn results in suffering

Table 3.5. Arrests for Part I Crimes by Race, 1975

Offenses Charged	Total Arrests				Percent Distribution		
	Total	White	Black	Other[a]	White	Black	Other
PART I Index Crimes							
Criminal homicide							
Murder and nonnegligent manslaughter	15,173	6,581	8,257	335	43.4	54.4	2.2
Manslaughter by negligence	2,971	2,316	558	106	78.0	18.7	3.3
Forcible rape	19,920	10,414	9,050	456	52.3	45.4	2.3
Robbery	110,411	43,598	64,867	1,946	39.5	58.8	2.7
Aggravated assault	180,668	105,226	71,360	4,088	58.2	39.5	2.3
Violent crime[b] (subtotal)	*326,172*	*165,819*	*153,534*	*6,819*	*50.8*	*47.1*	*2.1*
Burglary: breaking or entering	422,032	294,779	119,853	7,400	69.8	28.4	1.7
Larceny/theft	923,127	620,618	282,297	20,212	67.2	30.6	2.1
Motor vehicle theft	110,320	78,029	29,145	3,146	70.7	26.4	2.9
Property crime[c] (subtotal)	*1,445,479*	*993,426*	*431,295*	*30,758*	*68.3*	*29.6*	*2.1*
Subtotal Part I	*1,784,622*	*1,161,561*	*585,384*	*37,677*	*65.1*	*32.8*	*2.1*

Table 3.5. Arrests for Part II Crimes by Race, 1975

Offenses Charged	Total Arrests				Percent Distribution		
	Total	White	Black	Other[a]	White	Black	Other
PART II Offenses							
Other assaults	338,441	217,481	113,608	7,352	64.3	33.6	2.1
Arson	13,667	10,843	2,618	206	79.3	19.2	1.5
Forgery and counterfeiting	53,692	35,615	17,470	607	66.3	32.5	1.2
Fraud	141,866	99,972	40,476	1,418	70.5	28.5	1.0
Embezzlement	8,809	6,030	2,691	88	68.5	30.5	1.0
Stolen property (buying, receiving, possessing)	93,148	60,444	31,462	1,242	64.9	33.8	.3
Vandalism	165,846	138,107	25,149	2,590	83.3	15.2	1.5
Weapons, carrying, possession, etc.	123,114	69,843	51,028	2,243	56.7	41.4	.9
Sex offenses, except rape and prostitution	47,901	47,635	9,259	1,007	78.6	19.3	2.1
Prostitution, commercialized vice	46,727	21,030	25,032	665	45.0	53.6	1.4
Narcotic drug laws	487,287	383,644	96,660	6,978	78.7	19.8	1.5
Gambling	47,798	11,960	34,424	4,001	25.0	72.0	3.0
Offenses against family and children	52,199	36,751	14,616	832	70.4	28.0	1.6
Driving under the influence	893,798	751,024	117,105	25,659	84.0	13.1	2.9
Liquor laws	263,051	233,061	21,337	8,653	88.6	8.1	3.3
Drunkenness	1,161,140	883,383	224,417	53,340	76.1	19.3	4.6
Disorderly conduct	578,630	390,194	174,517	13,919	67.4	30.2	2.4
Vagrancy	58,228	34,010	22,897	1,321	58.4	39.3	2.3
All other offenses, except traffic	986,652	696,160	267,294	23,198	70.6	27.1	2.3
Suspicion	27,133	16,105	10,665	363	59.4	39.3	1.3
Curfew and loitering law violations	111,167	80,517	24,499	2,151	72.4	25.6	2.0
Runaways	186,314	163,515	18,814	3,985	87.8	10.1	2.2
Total arrests for all PART I and PART II Offenses	7,671,230	5,538,890	1,935,422	196,918	72.2	25.2	2.6

[a] Other includes Native Americans, Chinese, etc.
[b] Violent crime includes first four index crimes.
[c] Property crime includes last three index crimes.
Source: FBI, *Crime in the United States, 1975: Uniform Crime Reports* (Washington, D.C.: U.S. Government Printing Office, 1975), p. 192.

inflicted by blacks on themselves as well as on others.[28]

As the President's Commission noted, when comparisons are made of black and white populations living under similar conditions, the differences in arrest rates become insignificant. The inner-city slums, where an inordinate

The black and the poor are disproportionately represented in crime data.

percentage of the nation's black people reside, are extremely high crime areas. And while blacks living in them are involved in a large number of arrests, slum-dwelling blacks are also more apt to become victims of crime.[29]

UNOFFICIAL ESTIMATES OF THE EXTENT OF CRIME

For a century, concern with the difficulty of assessing the extent of crime and the need to develop an effective public policy toward it have sparked development of some alternative techniques for plotting the "dark figure" of hidden crime. Since the crux of the criticisms of official data has always been the problem of validity, unofficial techniques have tried to employ means that were independent of the taint of processing by official law enforcement organizations. Victim surveys and self-reports are the two most frequently used unofficial techniques for measuring crime. Both rely on individual recall of criminal events, but selective recall of past events poses some problems of its own.

In their article, "On Exploring the Dark Figure of Crime," researchers Albert Biderman and Albert Reiss present five generalizations that apply to selective reporting studies: (1) underreporting increases with the length of time between the event and the interview; (2) the degree of social threat or embarrassment is negatively related to the rate of reporting; (3) the greater the involvement in institutional processing, the more likely a crime is to be recalled; (4) respondents report their own experiences better than those of others; and (5) the more events to which one has been subject, the more likely one is to report a known event. "The crucial matter," they write, "is that underreporting is selective among classes of persons and events and by time." [30]

So unofficial as well as official sources of data are faced with the problem of limited validity and lack of reliability. At best, one complements the other. And to this date, there is no source of perfect, or even near perfect, criminal data. No single source represents an objective picture of actual criminal activity, for each source involves the subjective definition and selection of events by those doing the reporting and the processing of such data by some institutional means.

Victim Surveys

The first intensive attempts to use victim surveys to estimate the incidence of crime was initiated by the President's Crime Commission in 1966. The commission reported that "these surveys show that the actual amount of crime in the United States today is several times that reported in the UCR." [31]

The commission's report summarized two surveys to support its generalization. In a National Opinion Research Center (NORC) survey of a sampling of 10,000 households nationwide, respondents were asked whether they or anyone living with them had been victimized by crime during the previous twelve months. The NORC survey reported that the amount of violent crime was nearly twice that reported by the UCR, while the amount of property crime was more than twice the reported UCR figure. The rate for forcible rape was three-and-a-half times higher, and burglaries were three times higher. Only one homicide was reported in the NORC sample, which corresponds roughly to recent national statistics. Only in the category of motor vehicle theft were the figures in the victim survey lower than those in the UCR. The flaws of selective reporting may explain that difference. For example, some cars may have been reported stolen and were recovered later or found to have been misplaced. The respondents, through forgetfulness or embarrassment, may not have mentioned the incidents.[32]

An even greater discrepancy was found between the UCR data and that of a survey of medium and high crime rate precincts in Washington, D.C. Interviews with business and transient victims of crime reflected rates three to ten times as great as those in the official reports.[33]

The Law Enforcement Assistance Administration (LEAA) sponsored several victim surveys during the 1970s. The U.S. Bureau of Census set up a crime panel to conduct two of the surveys. The first of these looked at incidents of crime in the nation's five largest cities in 1972. In each city, interviews were conducted in 10,000 households, representing about 22,000 residents, aged twelve and over. The results showed a crime rate for Philadelphia that was five times the UCR figures. Chicago, Detroit, and Los Angeles had rates nearly three times as great, while New York City had twice the crime rate indicated by the FBI.[34]

Another victim survey was a study of eight American cities conducted during July to November of 1972 and March to May of 1975. The results are compared in Table 3.6 with UCR data for similar offenses in 1975. In the survey period ending in 1975, there was seven times as much rape, nine times as much robbery and burglary, fifteen times the amount of assault, and even five times the auto theft reported in the *Uniform Crime Reports* for 1975.[35]

Exact comparisons are difficult because the categories are not identical, but the vast discrepancies make their point. The victim surveys also cast light on why many crimes go unreported. Those interviewed in the various victimization studies were asked if they had reported the offense to the police and if not, why? The responses to these inquiries for the survey of the five largest cities are summarized in Table 3.7. The results of the surveys are quite similar. Typically, those interviewed were more inclined to report more serious crimes (about 74 percent), while they were less inclined to report Part II offenses

Table 3.6. Comparison of UCR and Eight City Survey Rates, 1971–72, 1974–75 (per 1000 population)

Categories of Crime	Eight City[a] Survey 1971–72	UCR[a]	Ratio	Eight City Survey 1974–75	UCR	Ratio	Percent Change Survey	Percent Change UCR
Rape	2	.2	10:1	2.2	.3	7.3:1	10	50
Robbery[b]	18	1.8	10:1	19.5	2.2	8.9:1	8	22
Assault[b]	30	1.9	15.8:1	35	2.3	15.2:1	17	21
Burglary	138	11.4	12.1:1	14.3	15.3	9.4:1	4	34
Larceny/theft	33.3	20	1.7:1	45.3	28	1.6:1	12	40
Motor vehicle theft	29	4.3	6.7:1	27.2	5	5.9:1	−2	16
Total violent crime[c]	*51*	*4*	*12.8:1*	*58*	*4.8*	*12:1*	*14*	*20*
Total property crime[c]	*125.3*	*35.7*	*3.5:1*	*144.3*	*53.1*	*2.7:1*	*14*	*49*

[a] UCR Reports do not distinguish crimes committed against individuals or households while survey data represent victimization rates for persons over age 12.

[b] Survey data are broken down in terms of subcategories of robbery with injury or without, and aggravated or simple assault.

[c] Detail may not add to totals shown because of rounding.

Source: FBI, *Uniform Crime Reports, 1975* (Washington, D.C.: U.S. Government Printing Office, 1975), p. 49; and U.S. Department of Justice, *Criminal Victimization Surveys in Eight American Cities; A Comparison of 1971/72 and 1974/75 Findings* (Washington, D.C.: U.S. Government Printing Office, 1976), pp. 15–131 *passim*. The eight cities are Atlanta, Baltimore, Cleveland, Dallas, Denver, Newark, Portland and St. Louis.

(about 37 percent). Yet discrepancies were identified in these surveys between offenses that victims claimed to have reported to the police agencies and data on crimes recorded by the police as "known to the police." Apparently this "shrinkage" was due to the police either failing to respond or not regarding an offense as a crime and thus not recording it. It is evident that a change in the inclination of citizens to report crime, or in the processing and recording of such reports by the police, could influence the volume of offenses that constitute official crime data. Although victimization rates are higher than crimes known to the police, the "dark figure" of crime may be due both to the decision of police not to record reported offenses and to the failure of citizens to report crimes.[36]

Table 3.7. Percent Distribution for Not Reporting Victimizations to Police, 1972

Reasons for Not Reporting	Personal Sector	Household Sector	Commercial Sector
Nothing could be done; lack of proof	34	37	33
Not important enough	28	31	34
Police would not want to be bothered	7	8	4
Too inconvenient or time consuming; did not want to become involved	4	3	7
Reported to someone else	9	3	8
Other and not given	12	12	13

Source: National Crime Panel Surveys, *Criminal Victimization Surveys in the Nation's Five Largest Cities* (Washington, D.C.: U.S. Department of Justice, 1975), pp. 63–67, 138.

Self-Reports

Anonymous self-reporting has become an increasingly valuable tool for scholars seeking statistics relating to crime and delinquency that go beyond the data on actual offenses, which focus only on those detected. The pioneering study in this field was A. L. Porterfield's comparison of offenses committed by college students and delinquents in Texas in the 1940s. He found that college students admitted to having been involved in similar acts of delinquent and criminal behavior during their high school years as the juveniles who were officially dealt with by the courts.[37]

The same type of findings turned up in a follow-up study by F. J. Murphy on the Cambridge–Somerville Youth Experiment in 1946. That study identified many boys who admitted involvement in offenses that had gone officially unrecorded.[38] Another survey of upper-income adults in New York in 1947 once again confirmed a pattern of unreported law breaking among "law-abiding" citizens. Over 90 percent of the 1,698 men and women sampled admitted to having committed one or more of the forty-nine offenses on the checklist.[39] In 1957, a similar technique was used to compare the delinquent behavior of high school students with the proven delinquency of a sample of institutionalized juveniles. Although those in the institution reported more serious offenses, there was considerable similarity between the two groups. However, there were differences in terms of frequency and degree of seriousness of delinquency. This supports the findings of other self-report studies of delinquency. It may be "normal" for a juvenile to commit one or two delinquent acts, but it is relatively rare for him to be involved in frequent, consistent delinquent behavior.[40]

Self-report studies indicate the proportion of those studied who admit to having committed certain offenses, and compare those who have been identified as offenders and have been arrested or convicted with those who have not been apprehended. However, they do not provide more than an imprecise estimate of the magnitude of the "dark figure" of crime. Several drawbacks regarding their shortcomings as valid measures have been noted by Roger Hood and Richard Sparks. For example, they note the general absence in such studies of a reliance on representative samples of areas for which there are comparable arrest data, as well as the failure to identify the specific time period in which the violations occurred. Consequently, it is not possible to make reliable comparisons of the number of offenses reported by respondents with the number recorded by the police in the same period; they merely show the proportion of subjects who admit crimes who are also known to the police. It is not possible through such self-report studies to know how many offenses are officially known. Still, it seems that only a small number are apprehended.[41]

M. L. Erickson and L. T. Empey reported in 1963 that none of their matched samples of fifty known and unknown offenders failed to mention their offense in the interviews.[42] In H. L. Voss's research on a sample of 620 seventh-graders, the fifty-two who were known to the police had committed eighty-three offenses, only four of which were not mentioned, inferring a high degree of validity.[43]

In a study of English boys, D. P. Farrington (1973) had similar results. Those officially identified as delinquents confessed that they had committed more offenses (twelve or more) with about three times the frequency that "nondelinquents" reported.[44] Travis Hirschi's study provides a less positive correspondence between self-reports and official records. He found that 15 percent of the white boys in his sample who did not admit to having stolen anything of "medium value" had police records, while 46 percent of those who admitted to having stolen something of "medium value" had police records. Obviously these discrepancies raise some question about the validity of Hirschi's respondents.[45]

The validity of self-report measures was only slightly positive in a study by McCandless et al. They studied black and white boys, fifteen to seventeen years of age. Both groups were from poverty-stricken backgrounds in the South. An index of "committed delinquency" was derived from official data and compared with their responses. The correlation between official and admitted delinquency was very low (.12).[46]

In Kerstin Elmhorn's study of school boys in Stockholm, it was found that although 57 percent admitted to at least one serious offense, 93 percent had not been caught.[47] Another study in Scandinavia found that only about 14 percent of a sample of delinquents in Oslo had any contact with the police or the courts.[48]

Self-report studies of criminal behavior raise additional questions and doubts about the validity and reliability of official police data, and they do not give us a very precise estimate of "hidden" crime. But they do provide a means by which we can find out a little more about the nature and extent of hidden criminality, especially crime involving juveniles. It has been noted that aside from aiding our assessment of those in our society who have committed such offenses, self-report studies serve two important functions. First, they break down the artificial dichotomy between those labeled "delinquents" and nondelinquents. Second, they provide more valid comparisons between the two groups.[49]

Most self-report studies have focused on juveniles, and it should not be assumed that they could be used effectively to correct deficiencies in official crime statistics. But along with the data from victim surveys, they provide needed insights into the "dark figure" of unreported crime.

ESTIMATES OF THE COST OF CRIME

The direct costs of crime, its control, and prevention are massive. When the indirect costs resulting from loss of life, loss of income, and higher costs of goods and services are added, the price tag becomes mind-boggling. Though estimates of the cost of crime must rely on a tenuous base of information, the cost is clearly so enormous and is such a heavy burden on society that in a very real sense every American pays a "crime tax."

Just as it is impossible to come up with accurate statistics on the incidence of crime, so too is there no way to tabulate its exact dollar cost to society. By its very nature, most crime is shrouded in secrecy. Certainly the maneuverings of the barons of organized crime occur out of public view. Balance sheets are not available from which to assess how much money flows into illegal coffers each year. But from time to time, various agencies of government have tried to measure the economic impact of crime. In 1976, the Joint Economic Committee of the United States Congress published an estimate of the cost of crime that exceeded $125 billion per year (see Figure 3.7). Other sources have set the figure at around $50 billion in 1970, to about $100 billion by 1975. In addition, inflation has its effect on everything, even crime.

Although it may serve political or journalistic purposes to come up with "lump sum" estimates, it is more useful to determine the various separate costs of crime and crime control. As the President's Crime Commission wrote in 1967:

Figure 3.7. Estimated Cost of Crime According to Joint Economic Committee Projection for 1976

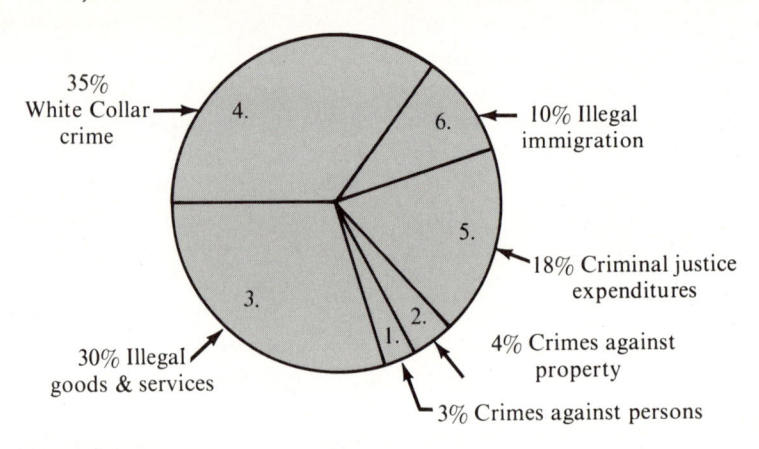

[Pie chart showing:
- 35% White Collar crime (4)
- 10% Illegal immigration (6)
- 18% Criminal justice expenditures (5)
- 4% Crimes against property (2)
- 3% Crimes against persons (1)
- 30% Illegal goods & services (3)]

1. Crimes against persons
   3%, $3.76 billion.

Murder	$3.6	billion
Aggravated assault	$144	million
Forcible rape	$ 18	million

2. Crimes against property
   4%, $5.11 billion

Robbery	$144	million
Burglary (breaking and entering)	$1.226	billion
Theft	$898.9	million
Theft (motor vehicle)	$1.73	billion
Arson	$1.112	billion

3. Illegal goods and services (organized crime)
   30%, $37.68 billion

Narcotics and dangerous drugs	$21.4	billion
Illegal-sale liquor	358	million
Prostitution	10	billion
Illegal gambling	5.918	billion

4. White-collar crime
   35%, $44 billion

   Inter alia, bankruptcy fraud, bribery, payoffs, computer-related crime, consumer fraud, illegal competition, credit card and check forgery, embezzlement and pilferage, insurance fraud, and securities theft and fraud.

5. Total for federal, state and local criminal justice expenditures 18%, $22.7 billion

6. Illegal immigration
   10%, $12 billion

   Total estimated expenditures $125.2 billion

Source: Estimates of Joint Economic Committee, U.S. Congress, dated December 20, 1976. (Received from Senator Humphrey's Office, April 1977.)

> The information available about the economic cost of crime is most usefully presented not as an overall figure, but as a series of private and public costs. Knowing the economic impact of each separate crime aids in identifying important areas for public concern and guides officials in making judgments about priorities for expenditures. Breakdowns of money now being spent in different parts of the criminal justice system, and within each part may afford insights into past errors.[50]

Consistent with this view, the commission developed dollar estimates on the public and private impact of crime in six categories, but did not publicize an aggregate sum. It maintained that it would be a misuse of economic data to add together such unlike factors as loss of earnings due to homicide, unreported commercial theft, abortion fees, costs of police departments, and costs of private crime-fighting apparatus.[51] As Norval Morris and Gordon Hawkins point out, to add the estimated loss due to vandalism to the fees paid to prostitutes makes no economic sense.[52] But as the commission suggests, the picture of crime that emerges from such estimates provides a different view than the data that only portray offenses known to the police. For instance, from an economic point of view, the commission estimated that in 1965, "organized crime," through loansharking, illegal alcohol, gambling, narcotics, prostitution, and other activities, generates about twice as much revenue as the take from all other kinds of crime, including white-collar crime, which in areas like arson, overlaps with organized crime.[53]

In terms of dollars, white-collar crime is among the fastest growing types of criminal activity. Official data now exist to support pioneer criminologist E. H. Sutherland's finding of forty years ago that law violations committed in the course of white-collar business activity cost society more than all the index crimes.[54] In 1977, the Joint Economic Committee report estimated the cost of white-collar crime for 1976 at $44 billion or 3.5 percent of the gross national product; thus it has outstripped the impact of organized crime that was estimated to cost society $37.7 billion annually in 1976.[55]

The growing cost of maintaining a law enforcement establishment to fight crime is also reflected in current figures. The Crime Commission put a price tag of $4.2 billion on law enforcement and criminal justice in 1967. A decade later, the Joint Economic Committee's estimate was up to $22.7 billion, with about 60 percent going to police agencies and the remainder to corrections and the courts.[56]

Police budgets increasingly are weighted in favor of sophisticated hardware like traffic control equipment, riot control weapons, squad cars, and new radio systems. In the corrections field, growing budgets tend to reflect custodial personnel and increased wages rather than new rehabilitative programs. These patterns raise some questions regarding public expenditures for the prevention and control of crime:

> Does the heavy commitment of funds for law enforcement yield appropriate results?

Fear and insecurity add to the price we pay for crime.

Are the costs of incarceration—generally estimated at $11,000 per person, per year—too high?

Are there more humane and less expensive means for controlling offenders, particularly those whose crimes are strictly against property rather than people?

Can better methods be devised for preventing violent crimes?

What can be done to control white-collar crime?

And finally, what does the staggering cost of crime tell us about our professed efforts to build a sane and just society?

The Joint Economic Committee data were used as a primary source for a seven-part television series called, *Cost of Crime and the Crime Tax,* which was aired in the New York area during the fall and winter of 1976–77. Using the $125 billion total as a basis, the final program in the series broke down the per person cost of crime to $584, or $2,336 for a family of four. But the show explained how even crime costs are borne disproportionately by those in lower-income brackets. A family of four with a median income of $10,000 would, by this analysis, be paying 55 percent of its taxes to support the cost of crime to society. At a $25,000 income level, about 24 percent of a family's tax bill would go toward these costs.

Poor citizens in our society not only pay more than an equal share of the cost of crime, they also are more likely to be victims of it and more apt to live in fear of it. "I got bars on every window of my house," one woman said on camera, "and one day washing my dishes I looked out . . . and I thought, what have I done? I have not stopped the robber from getting in. I've imprisoned myself and I don't want to be in prison in this great democracy." It is this kind of fear and insecurity that adds an inestimable premium to the price we all pay for crime.

SUMMARY

While we all agree there is considerable crime in our society, we do not yet have accurate statistics to measure either its extent or costs. The best-known and most complete reporting system is the FBI's annual *Uniform Crime Reports*. Recent increases in crime reported by the UCR are now conceded to have resulted, in part, from more sophisticated methods of data collection and from vigorous efforts on the part of the law enforcement establishment to collect crime data from more jurisdictions. In short, the FBI's *Uniform Crime Reports* give us less an accurate picture of crime than a view of police reactions to crime. The UCR data help us to assess various aspects of American crime as it is seen by the police and other official control agencies. This is the picture purveyed to the public through the media, and it serves to heighten the public's perception of crime.

The limitations of the UCR data and their lack of reliability have led to the development of other means to assess the nature and extent of crime. Over the past decade the federal government has developed *victim surveys* that have provided data on the extent and nature of offenses in our largest cities. Social scientists have also used *self-report studies* to assess the "dark figure" of hidden crime. Neither these methods, based upon unofficial sources, nor the UCR, gives us valid, reliable measures of crime, for the actual amount of crime in society is unknown and unknowable by its very nature. *Victim surveys* and *self-reports* have inherent methodological problems, but they do allow us to assess additional aspects of the crime picture.

The twenty-nine offenses itemized in the UCR are divided into two categories: *Part I and Part II*. Part I offenses include *murder, nonnegligent manslaughter, forcible rape, aggravated assault, robbery, burglary, larceny/theft, and auto theft*. These are known as *index crimes* because of their assumed seriousness and the frequency with which they occur. The index crimes are subdivided into *violent crimes* (murder, manslaughter, rape, and assault) and *property crimes* (robbery, burglary, and theft). Part II offenses cover a wide range of criminal activity including arson, fraud, embezzlement, runaways, and "all other offenses." In spite of their impact, *no Part II offenses are included in the crime index.*

Despite media attention to spectacular crimes of violence, the greatest increase in crime in the past two decades has been in *property-related crime*. In 1975, the four violent crimes comprised only 9 percent of the total volume of reported offenses. Nonetheless, the United States is an unusually violent society. Our murder rate, for instance, is the second highest in the developed world.

Crime rates vary by *region of the country*. Though the overall crime rate is highest in the West, murders are highest in the South. *Season, age, sex, and race* are other variables related to crime. Men commit more crimes than women—though in all but violent crimes women are closing the gap. Young people and black people also commit disproportionate numbers of crimes.

Both the direct and the indirect *costs of crime* are enormous. While exact figures cannot be tabulated, a recent *estimate* placed the annual cost at over $125 billion. Probably the two types of crime with the greatest economic impact are *white-collar crime* and *organized crime*. In addition to dollar costs, crime also exacts a heavy psychological toll. As usual, the poor pay a disproportionate share of both.

In the chapters that follow we will make use of official data as they relate to topics being considered. The reliability of these data should always be open to challenge. Other data will be presented where possible, so that the official data will be less open to misinterpretation and distortion. Nevertheless, the official data are significant in that they provide a necessary perspective regarding the manner in which the criminal justice system deals with crime, processes offenders, and, in effect, produces criminality.

ADDITIONAL READINGS

Bell, Daniel. "The Myth of the Crime Wave." In *The End of Ideology*, edited by Daniel Bell. Glencoe, Ill.: Free Press, 1960, Chap. 8.

    An historical critique that takes issue with data that indicate that crime is more prevalent today than previously. Descriptive and anecdotal.

Biderman, Albert D. and Albert J. Reiss, Jr. "On Explaining the Dark Figure of Crime." *Annals of the American Academy of Political and Social Science* 374 (November 1967):1–15.

    The authors discuss two basic criticisms of official and unofficial crime data and present a history of the development of efforts to illuminate hidden crime. Statistics are seen as a result of processing definitions of crime.

Federal Bureau of Investigation, *Crime in the United States—Uniform Crime Reports*. Washington, D.C.: U.S. Government Printing Office, published annually.

    This is the annual report of crime data collected by the FBI. Each year additional data are included. In 1975 and 1976, it ran to about 300 pages. Published in early fall each year.

Pepinsky, Harold E. "The Growth of Crime in the United States." In *Readings in Criminology*, edited by Peter Wickman and Phillip Whitten. Lexington, Mass.: D. C. Heath, 1978.

> The growth of crime is considered as a problem throughout American history. The assumption that crime is underreported leads to a self-fulfilling prophecy. The author contends that we should report fewer offenses to break the cycle.

President's Commission on Law Enforcement and Administration. *The Challenge of Crime in a Free Society.* Washington, D.C.: U.S. Government Printing Office, 1967.

> A dated but thoughtful report influenced by liberal scholars. Chapter 2, "Crime in America," gives an excellent assessment of crime data in the 1960s.

Simon, Rita. *Women and Crime.* Lexington, Mass.: D. C. Heath, 1975.

> In perhaps the most authoritative book on women and crime, Simon examines in detail the criminal activity of American women. In Chapter 4, male and female arrest statistics over a twenty-year period are compared.

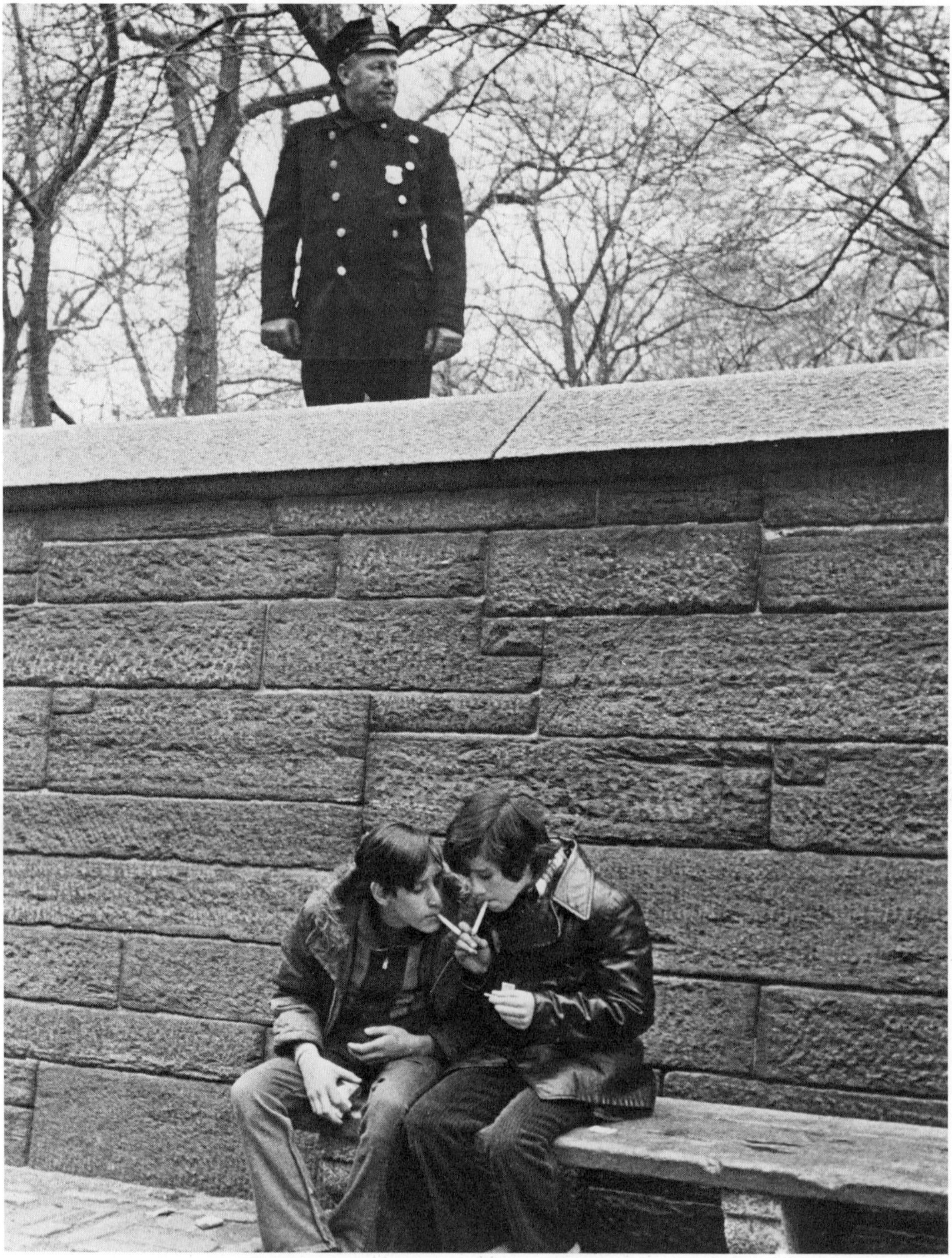

> The chief problem in any community cursed with crime is not the punishment of the criminals, but the preventing of the young from being trained to crime.
> —W.E.B. DuBois, The Souls of Black Folk

4

BECOMING DELINQUENT: SOCIAL CONDITIONS, GROUP ASSOCIATIONS, AND THE DEFINING PROCESS

What young person hasn't had a drink of alcohol or skipped a day of school? How rare is it for an adolescent to engage in any number of activities that are against the law of some state? For the young person, the question of juvenile delinquency is often a matter of whether or not you are caught. The law has created a limbo for the young. In an attempt to accord more enlightened treatment to young offenders, the law, the courts, and the police have elaborated an ambiguous system that on the one hand can divert a youngster away from unlawful behavior and on the other can brand him a juvenile delinquent.

Many different perspectives and theories have been developed to describe and explain delinquency. Until recent years some approaches offered explanations similar to those for adult offenses, emphasizing the individual. Others focused on social factors or "kinds of environments." The past decade has witnessed considerable change in the manner in which scholars have come to view the status of the juvenile offender, but the emphasis of many of the earlier studies still persists. In asking the question, Why do juveniles become involved in delinquent behaviors? the response of social scientists, policymakers, and practitioners has been to focus on factors implicit in the question. Both research and practice have been guided by images of the delinquent and certain assumptions made about him or her that are implied in the question, Why?

These assumptions have been made explicit in approaches that stress the actor's lack of inner control and character defects; social factors such as race, ethnicity, poverty and lack of opportunity; and inadequate family and social institutions related to the socialization of the individual into his or her appropriate social role. In short, the traditional focus has been upon the actor and those social conditions that seem to set the delinquent far apart from conforming youths.[1]

These conceptions of the delinquent have developed within the context of criminology influenced by the positive school. Consequently, relatively little attention has been devoted to how acts and individual actors become collectively and progressively defined as delinquent; likewise, little emphasis has been placed on studying how individuals perceive, respond, and adapt to the labeling process. The traditional object of study has been those who have *already* been apprehended, defined, "tagged," or labeled as *delinquents*.[2] These studies have provided a wealth of valuable insights. But they have given us relatively little information from which we can develop an understanding of how a youngster comes to be defined as delinquent, or gain a feeling for the relationship between the delinquent behavior and the responses of those social agents and organizations involved in the defining process.[3]

It is our assumption that social reaction perspectives can be applied to the study of delinquency more appropriately than to many areas of adult crime. Thus, we will focus upon the manner by which juvenile behavior may come to be seen as delinquent behavior by both formal and informal agents of social control. In analyzing delinquent careers from this perspective, we will summarize some of the more conventional perspectives that have focused on treating the individual and on reforming his or her social environment. We will note convergences between these individualistic explanations and interactional theories that result in a social definition of delinquency.

We will begin by discussing the concept of delinquency, how it is formulated, and the manner in which the application of the legal definition has resulted in organizationally produced statistics. Then we will turn our attention to social correlates, or social structural elements and processes, typically related both to conformity and nonconformity in juveniles. Next, we will turn to the manner in which juveniles are defined and labeled delinquents as they are processed through the juvenile justice system. Finally, we will discuss some emerging alternatives to our present policy toward juvenile delinquency, including "radical nonintervention."

THE STUDY OF DELINQUENCY AND THE STUDY OF CRIME

Even though delinquents generally are assumed to be different from nondelinquents and according to positivistic theories are impelled by personal or social factors to be delinquent, studies underscore the frequency with which delinquents become law-abiding adults. Studies of juvenile delinquency have shown that anywhere from 60 to 85 percent of delinquents do not continue on to become adult violators. This maturational reform apparently occurs whether or not juvenile justice and correctional agencies intervene and whether or not such intervention provides effective, "quality" correctional or rehabilitative services.[4]

More recently, David Greenberg has analyzed the age-specific aspect of most juvenile crimes and has shown that both property and violent offenses decline with age, although violent crime rates decline less rapidly. His argument, supported by crime-specific arrest rates, is that the disproportionate involvement of juveniles in major types of crimes can be understood as a result of the changing position of juveniles in industrialized societies. To the extent that individual and social factors influence such behavior, then, they vary over time and in relationship to the socioeconomic arrangements of a given historical epoch.[5]

Delinquent careers—and doubtless criminal careers as well—need to be perceived within the context of the interrelationships between law-violating and conforming behavior. If we explore the subtle relationships between social factors, intentionality, and human behavior, we may be less inclined to see delinquency as "something special" or depraved or to mystify or romanticize the behavior. As Howard Becker suggests, we might be better able to see crime and delinquency "simply as a kind of behavior some disapprove of and others value, studying the processes by which either or both perspectives are built up and maintained."[6]

THE CONCEPT OF DELINQUENCY: ESTIMATES OF OFFICIALLY DEFINED JUVENILE OFFENDERS

Legal Definitions of Delinquency and Status Offenses

Although there is an apparent consensus among criminologists as well as journalists that delinquency is widespread, the concept of delinquency lacks precision. Legal definitions vary from state to state, and it seems that almost any form of youthful misbehavior or nonconformity can be defined as delinquent.

It becomes clear when we examine past and present legal definitions that the juvenile, as compared with the adult, has been and continues to be evaluated by different standards of conduct. Basic to our criminal law is the idea that a behavior must specifically be proscribed in the law for it to be considered a crime. This is the classical principle of *nullen crimen sine lege*—no crime without a law. Adult codes also provide procedural standards that regulate the power of the state and are designed to safeguard the rights of the accused and even the convicted.

The rationale behind juvenile statutes is entirely different: not only is the juvenile not seen as a hardened criminal, but also as someone in need of protection from society as well as someone from whom society should be protected. Consequently, many acts are considered delinquent only if they are committed by people within a certain age category.

Large numbers of juveniles come to the attention of the police and the courts because they are suspected of violating a law that also applies to adults—assault, burglary, robbery, and larceny are typical examples. A second category included in all statutes, except federal laws, is known as *status offenses*, or acts prohibited to children but not to adults.[7] Under such laws, large numbers of children may be dealt with by the courts for a much broader range of behaviors than would be allowed under adult criminal procedure.

The following list is a compilation of acts or conditions, in addition to the violation of the law, that have been or are still included in juvenile court statutes. They are listed in order of their frequency.[8]

1. Violates any law or ordinance
2. Habitually truant
3. Associates with thieves, vicious or immoral persons
4. Incorrigible
5. Beyond control of parent or guardian
6. Growing up in idleness or crime
7. So deports self as to injure or endanger self or others
8. Absents self from home without consent
9. Immoral or indecent conduct
10. (Habitually) uses vile, obscene, or vulgar language (in public place)
11. (Knowingly) enters, visits policy shop or gaming place
12. Patronizes, visits policy shop or gaming place
13. (Habitually) wanders about railroad yards or tracks
14. Jumps train or enters car or engine without authority
15. Patronizes saloon or dram house where intoxicating liquor is sold
16. Wanders streets at night, not on lawful business
17. Patronizes public poolroom or bucket shop
18. Immoral conduct around school (or in public place)
19. Engages in illegal occupation
20. Smokes cigarettes (or uses tobacco in any form)
21. Frequents place the existence of which is in violation of the law
22. In occupation or situation dangerous or injurious to self or others
23. Is found in place for which adult may be punished
24. Addicted to drugs
25. Disorderly
26. Begging
27. Uses intoxicating liquor
28. Makes indecent proposal
29. Loiters, sleeps in alleys, vagrant
30. Runs away from state or charity institution
31. Found on premises occupied or used for illegal purposes
32. Operates motor vehicle dangerously while under influence of liquor
33. Attempts to marry without consent, in violation of law
34. Given to sexual irregularities

This list makes one wonder if anyone can grow up without qualifying as a delinquent in some jurisdiction, since many of these laws are still on the books. The ambiguous nature of such laws leaves them open to broad interpretation when law enforcement agents, school officials, citizens, and even parents apply them to juveniles.

In its *1967 Task Force Report on Juvenile Delinquency*, the President's Crime Commission summed up the two general categories of delinquency and status offenses as follows:

> Delinquency comprises cases of children alleged to have committed an offense that if committed by an adult would be a crime. It also comprises cases of children alleged to have violated specific ordinances or regulatory laws that apply only to children, such as curfew regulations, school attendance laws, restrictions on use of alcohol and tobacco; and children variously designated as being beyond control, ungovernable, incorrigible, runaway, or in need of supervision . . . according to national juvenile court statistics, the latter two groups account for over 25 percent of the total number of delinquent children appearing before children's courts and between 25 and 30 percent of the population of State institutions for delinquent children.[9]

State legal codes offer a wide variety of definitions of these two aspects of juvenile statutes. These statutes define delinquency and status offenses not only substantively, but also according to age. The range is from sixteen years in five states to twenty-one years in two states. The modal age is eighteen years, though until ERA laws were passed in some states, it was different for females and males. The New York Family Court Law, for instance, formerly read: " 'Persons in need of supervision' means a male less than sixteen years of age and a female less than eighteen years of age . . . ." (section 212b). But this phrase was deleted with the passage of equal rights legislation.

The intent of juvenile delinquency laws, which are based on sociological as well as legal concepts, is to remove a child who violates the law from the regular criminal court and to deal with the offense in its social context, rather than in a criminal context. Specialized juvenile courts are empowered to provide treatment and protection to children who need it. These courts combine the function of diversion of child offenders from the criminal justice system with child welfare protection. But these functions of the court have resulted in a diffuse concept of delinquency, where both law violators and status offenders have been labeled as "delinquents." The idea that children are responsible for their law violations against the social order has been abandoned. In its place we have a system of punishment with treatment. Unfortunately, under the guise of treatment, juveniles have sometimes been denied the legal protection that the criminal law guarantees to adult offenders. For even if there were a uniform legal definition of delinquency—and at present it is what the law specifies in fifty-three different jurisdictions—the problem of applying the definition would still exist. Although in the popular mind the status of the juvenile delinquent may be comparable to that of the adult criminal, the procedural standards for admissible evidence and the court's informal methods for deciding whether or not the juvenile has committed a delinquent act severely limit the civil and legal rights of the juvenile. For instance, it was not until the Supreme Court's decisions in *Kent* (1966), *Gault* (1967), and *Winship* (1970) that a minor's right to due process, counsel, protection against self-incrimination, and rules of evidence were applicable to juvenile court cases. But juvenile courts continue to rely upon data provided by social workers, which may not be related to a specific charge. Thus, a juvenile's general social history often looms more significant than whether or not the child is guilty or innocent.

How Many Are Labeled Delinquent?

Uniform Crime Report Data. In 1975, the FBI reported that 26 percent of all arrests involved juveniles. There were, of course, fewer than the official total of 2,078,459 juveniles apprehended, since some individuals were arrested more than once.[10]

The UCR indicates that a large percentage of those juveniles arrested are "screened out" or "adjusted" (released) in the station house, or are referred to agencies other than the juvenile court. The various alternative dispositions are summarized in Table 4.1. In some studies the rate of police referrals to the court varies from 8.6 to 71.2 percent.

Table 4.1. Disposition of Juveniles Taken into Police Custody, 1975

Disposition	Total	Percentage
Handled within department and released	697,061	41.6
Referred to welfare agency	24,293	1.4
Referred to other police agency	31,663	1.9
Referred to juvenile court jurisdiction	883,736	52.7
Referred to criminal or adult court	38,958	2.3
Total all dispositions	1,675,711[a]	100.0[b]

[a] Includes all offenses except traffic and dependency cases.
[b] Due to rounding, percentages do not add up to total.
Source: FBI, *Uniform Crime Reports, 1975* (Washington, D.C.: U.S. Government Printing Office, 1976), p. 177.

Estimates from Juvenile Court Data. In addition to arrest statistics by age categories published in the *Uniform Crime Reports*, comprehensive data are provided by the Children's Bureau of the Department of Health, Education, and Welfare (HEW). These statistics offer a picture of juveniles who are handled in the courts, both formally and informally, and indicate the extent to which youth are labeled delinquent. It should be noted that other agencies and individuals—school officials, social service or welfare workers, or parents—may refer a juvenile to court. The data reported here, from HEW's Office of Youth Development, reflect both delinquency law violations and status offenses. They include conduct considered as law violating only when committed by children—running away, truancy, and ungovernable behavior—as well as violations of state or local laws, excluding traffic cases.

As Table 4.2 illustrates, based on reports from 1,969 out of 2,973 of the courts serving 75 percent of the population, it is estimated that there were 1,143,700 cases of delinquency processed or adjudicated by juvenile courts in

Table 4.2. Number and Population-Standardized Rate of Delinquency Cases Disposed of by Juvenile Courts, United States, 1957–1973

Year	Child Population 10 through 17 years of age (in thousands)	Delinquency Cases[a]	Percent Boys	Percent Girls	Rate[b]
1957	22,173	440,000	81	19	19.8
1958	23,443	470,000	81	19	20.0
1959	24,607	483,000	81	19	19.6
1960	25,368	510,000	81	19	20.1
1961	26,056	503,000	81	19	19.3
1962	26,989	555,000	81	19	20.6
1963	28,056	601,000	81	19	21.4
1964	29,244	686,000	81	19	23.5
1965	29,536	697,000	80	20	23.6
1966	30,124	745,000	80	20	24.7
1967	20,837	811,000	79	21	26.3
1968	31,566	900,000	79	21	28.5
1969	32,157	988,500	77	23	30.7
1970	32,614	1,052,000	76	24	32.3
1971	32,969	1,125,000	75	25	34.1
1972	33,120	1,112,000	74	26	33.6
1973	33,377	1,143,700	74	26	34.2

[a] Data for 1957–1969 estimated from the national sample of juvenile courts. Data for 1970–1973 estimated from all courts reporting whose jurisdiction included more than three-fourths of the population of the United States.
[b] Based on the number of delinquency cases per 1,000 U.S. child population, ten through seventeen years of age.
Source: U.S. Department of Health, Education, and Welfare, Office of Youth Development, "Juvenile Court Statistics, 1973," 1975, pp. 10–11 (tables 5 & 8).

1973. In other words, about 3 percent of those in the age range of ten through seventeen years were dealt with by the courts. Between 1957 and 1973, the number of cases reported by the courts increased by 160 percent, while the youth population increased by about 51 percent. So the delinquency rate per 1,000 increased by about 73 percent. Most of the increase was reported from suburban courts.

The data in Table 4.2 also indicate that the ratio of male to female delinquency moved from 4 to 1 in the 1960s to about 2.8 to 1 in 1973. This narrowing of the difference in the rate of delinquency has been particularly significant since 1967. Over that six-year interval (1967 to 1973), the rate of delinquency for girls increased by 75 percent, while the rate of increase for boys was less than half—32 percent.

The fact that courts deal with a majority of juvenile cases informally is important in understanding the scope of the court's function. The proportion dealt with informally (compared with those formally processed) increased from 46 to 54 percent between 1957 and 1973. This means that a majority of those youths dealt with by agents connected with the court are now referred to other social service agencies or placed on informal supervision. The fact that a majority of juveniles is diverted from the court through an informal process may very well work to a youth's advantage unless he or she "messes up" at which time the "carrot" may become a "stick" when the youth is returned to the court.

Unofficial Estimates of Delinquency. Some of the numerous attempts to assess the extent of hidden delinquency through self-reports were summarized in the previous chapter. These studies illustrate some of the difficulties involved in estimating the nature as well as the extent of juvenile violations. Although only a few juveniles are arrested in a given year, still fewer end up in court, and a rather insignificant number are committed to institutions. Yet self-report studies have indicated consistently that the percentage of youths who have committed violations of a delinquent nature is about 95 percent.[11]

One of the classic attempts to contrast officially produced statistics with self-report data was the study by James Short and F. Ivan Nye. Among their more controversial findings was the lack of a statistically significant difference in social class when comparing *noninstitutionalized* self-confessed delinquents. Institutionalized youngsters, however, came mainly from the lower socioeconomic status (SES) levels.[12]

SOCIAL CORRELATES OF CONFORMING AND NONCONFORMING JUVENILES

Theories that seek to trace the conditions in which crime and delinquency occur make certain assumptions about the nature of society. Consensus and conflict, the two contrasting models discussed in an earlier chapter, emphasize different aspects of the formal and informal means society uses to control the behavior of juveniles.

In the *consensus model,* a person who violates the law is seen as one who rejects the consensus of society and threatens the stability of the social order. The *conflict model,* on the other hand, stresses the different beliefs and value systems of different groups in society. For instance, the juvenile justice system is run by adults who share a middle-class orientation, while those processed through the juvenile courts are all young and disproportionately lower class.[13] The conflict perspective reminds us of the tremendous variation in beliefs and behavior in our society. The effects of such variation should be kept in mind in the following summary of the various social institutions that provide the structure for socializing individuals into conventional as well as illegal behavior. Social institutions are those social structures—familial, educational, governmental (and legal), religious, and economic—organized by a society to meet the basic needs of its members. They provide the context in which individuals may learn to conform to societal demands, as well as the context in which deviation may occur. The nature of these institutions is not the same in all situations, nor is their influence similarly felt by all.

Social Institutions as Influences in Social Control

Social institutions are the relatively permanent means by which a society meets its basic needs. Once they come into being, institutions and the values that support them are transmitted through the culture of a society. Thus each individual is born into a world of predefined patterns of conduct that initially are imposed upon him or her.

Though social institutions are created by people, they are in a sense external to the individual. Each generation seeks to make the traditional institutions meaningful both to itself and to the succeeding generation. Children are taught proper behavior in terms of traditional values. Yet there is no guarantee that traditional values and patterns of behavior will inexorably become ingrained in the individual in the process of socialization.

Institutions such as the family, education, government (or the law), religion, and in contemporary society, the mass media, all participate in the definition of "right" and "wrong" conduct. Hence, they are related in varying degrees to the control of behavior. To the extent that a society exhibits a high degree of *solidarity,* additional means of social control are less necessary.

Peter Berger and Thomas Luckmann have cogently argued that since social institutions are a human product and are external to the individual, it follows that socialization into the institutional order of society is a social process requiring the establishment of sanctions. In a society with a high degree of solidarity, these sanctions or social controls are largely informal in nature and may be viewed as internal to the individual—an integral part of the person's self-concept. Contemporary industrial urban society does not exhibit such cohesiveness but rather is heterogeneous and pluralistic in its ethnic and ethical composition. Consequently, many of the definitions of right and wrong, of conforming and deviant behavior, are formal ones, since they are external to the individual's initial or primary group. Each person is simultaneously a member of a family—the primary social institution—and numerous other secondary groups that may have different norms, roles, or behavior expectations. In modern society there tends to be a greater reliance on formal social controls, as well as on formally defined rules to control its members.[14]

Socialization: The Development of the "Self." The socialization of the child begins within the family. If the parents belong to a lower socioeconomic stratum of society, the orientation of that social location will be transmitted to the child. Although he or she may share many values with other lower-class children, the individual will also differ from them due to idiosyncratic familial aspects of *primary* socialization. In moving through those less personal associations and institutions that provide secondary socialization, the developing person will come in contact with a variety of beliefs that compete with each other and with any earlier orientation. In neither primary nor secondary socialization is the developing person merely a passive recipient of cultural definitions. But in secondary socialization, the individual may be more aware and conscious of institutional expectations coming from outside the "self."

Both aspects of socialization take place within biological limitations, and both involve the narrowing of acceptable behaviors. In primary socialization, the biological needs of the human animal are adapted to a social framework. For example, children typically learn to eat at regular intervals and to develop socially acceptable sleep patterns. In our society, children learn what is and is not good food and that they are expected to eat three meals a day. Likewise, in most cases they learn appropriate gender roles and controls related to expressing their sexuality. They learn, for example, that a sister or brother is not an appropriate sex object. If primary socialization deals effectively with the frustrations that accompany such learning, the self will develop a set of "inner" controls that will moderate biological demands throughout later life. The individual is involved in a social enterprise in which the limits are set by nature. But the human organism is transformed by human culture, and social institutions which are "humanly produced are continuously interpreted and created." [15]

The idea that the self develops within a social enterprise, or process, which stresses the interaction within the self's social world, represents a radically different perspective from the more traditional social-psychological concept of a dichotomy between self and objective reality. Since the self is always in a process of "becoming," a person's *self-concept* does not represent the stable coherence that is frequently assumed. Moreover, we cannot assume that primary socialization is the only way the individual learns to conform to or deviate from the normative system. Not only must we consider that "significant others" may fail to transmit the norms or rules laid down by dominant groups, but we should also be aware of the roles of other social institutions in influencing behavior. We cannot assume that parents in primary groups, teachers in the schools, ministers, priests, or rabbis in religious institutions, other authority figures such as athletes and actors in the media, and peace officers in law enforcement agencies promote in some simple mechanical manner the norms and role expectations of politically powerful groups in society. Social institutions, however, provide the external, objective structure for the individual's social world within which his or her behavior becomes patterned in interaction with others.

The Family: Focus of Primary Socialization. The family provides the developing individual with her or his initial orientation to the external social world and is expected to inculcate conformity to social conventions. Yet this process is made problematic by the complexity of the external world and by the different subjective understandings of those involved in the process.

Rapid social changes in the twentieth century have modified basic economic, educational, and recreational functions of the family. The family is now more a consumer unit than a production unit. The school, the state, and to a lesser extent, formal religion, loom larger today in preparing the young for adulthood. Changing values and attitudes toward sexuality and courtship have made large families virtually passé. Still, the family is often faulted for the rising rate of delinquency. Family *anomie* (a state of normlessness), lack of control of the young, and the decreasing importance of the nuclear family are seen as related to delinquent behavior. Yet marital conflict, economic insecurity, and lower socioeconomic status due to familial instability are reflections of important social issues in the larger society.

Traditionally there has been wide acceptance of the relationship between broken homes and law-violating behavior—especially delinquency. As early as 1932, Clifford Shaw and Henry McKay challenged this relationship when they concluded that the influence of the family in creating delinquency must be sought in more subtle family relationships than the fact of a broken home.[16] Death of a parent, desertion by the father, divorce, or separation all disrupt family stability and may result in a lowered family economic status. In other words, the relationship between broken homes and delinquency is now believed to be far more complex than formerly thought.

Social control is most effective within a positive family context.

In recent studies, as Karen Wilkenson has noted, the relationship between broken homes and delinquency has been found to be significant only when correlated with other influences, such as poor school achievement or delinquent male friends with poor records of school achievement. Additionally, studies that have examined both the influence of family stability and delinquent male friends have found the broken home to be more important for predicting female delinquency than male delinquency. In studies that sought to control for race, age, and socioeconomic background, it was found that broken homes are more crucial for preadolescents than for adolescents. Such conditions are found to a greater degree among boys and girls charged with incorrigible behavior or running away. These, of course, are "status" offenses and not strictly law violations. It appears that there is no simple relationship between broken homes and delinquency.[17]

More generally, Travis Hirschi has found that the more a child is attached to and identifies with his or her parents, the less likelihood there is of delinquency.[18] Obviously, a strong attachment to or identification with one's parents may be more difficult in a situation of divorce and impossible in the case of death or desertion. But the existence of a broken home may bring other adjustment mechanisms to bear on family relationships. Perhaps the crucial factor is that of *parental control* within the family. Certainly many families with both parents present are disorganized and ineffective in controlling adolescent behavior. One study of juvenile boys on probation suggested that boys from intact homes that evidenced "disorganization" had more emotional problems than those from stable but broken families.[19] Yet to pinpoint the family as the causal factor in delinquent or conforming behavior is too simplistic. The family, like other institutions, is socially created and exists only in relationship to society's other major institutions.

Educational Institutions. Along with the family, schools share a large responsibility for the socialization process. To the extent that schools are formal and impersonal, they are a means for confronting the developing self with some of the external expectations of society. Directly and indirectly, the developing person is reminded by the school of a wider compass of authority than the family.

Over the past century the school has also provided a means for upward mobility—especially for Jewish, Irish, Italian, and other European immigrants. But until recently, schools did not serve these functions for blacks and native Americans. Recent studies have shown that for other poor Americans as well, the schools have functioned to accent and perpetuate class differences, as much as to provide access to upward mobility. The schools present hurdles as well as opportunities through the increased use of personality and "intelligence" tests and curricula that may often be irrelevant to the aspirations and expectations of many children from lower socioeconomic groups.

Writing in the *Task Force Report on Juvenile Delinquency and Youth Crime* for the Crime Commission in 1967, Walter Schafer and Kenneth Polk stated that "delinquency is anchored into social, educational, political, and economic conditions that transcend local communities."[20] They argued that delinquent behavior results in part from linkages between the schools and such behavior. Their inventory of defects in the schools includes:[21]

1. The tensions developed in students due to the conflict between the stress on educational achievement and the imposition of middle-class values on youths who are oriented to lower-class values.
2. The belief in the limited potential of pupils from economic disadvantaged backgrounds.
3. Irrelevant instruction and teaching methods.
4. The reinforcement of failure through testing, ability grouping, and "tracking."
5. A contribution to conditions that lead to a lack of commitment and participation in the educational enterprise and in the community.
6. Responses to misbehavior that degrade, label, and exclude those with deviant tendencies.

Considerable evidence correlates lack of educational skills with both misbehavior in school and delinquency. The fact that a child who cannot read will have difficulty in achieving and maintaining a feeling of self-worth in an English class is related to misbehavior and "acting-out." This seems to be ignored when such problems are treated clinically or when they are referred to juvenile court. Although studies show time and again that low achievement is correlated with delinquency, children often are kept in school without providing them with effective means to improve academic skills. Indeed, in such cases evidence indicates that dropping out of school leads to *diminished* delinquent behavior. As Bernard Rosenberg and Harvey Silverstein have shown, many youths from poverty-level income groups have low aspirations and expectations because of their disadvantaged economic and political position in society. Lower-strata youths are more realistic regarding aspirations and expectations than the middle-class illusion that all share the "American dream" of success might lead us to believe. The Horatio Alger myth is irrelevant to such youths, and keeping them in school may distort their sense of reality with a middle-class illusion.[22]

A study by Martin Gold found that poor school performance is associated with delinquency for boys, but not for girls. Although having friends who are delinquent alters this variable, boys with poor grades averaged twice as many offenses as those with better grades. Those with poor grades and delinquent friends reported four times as many offenses as the other two groups. Gold concludes that delinquency among such youths may be "performance" or "action for approval" of peers. Lacking access to the approval of family and other adults—including teachers—due to poor school achievement, such boys may turn to delinquent friends to gain approval through delinquent activity.[23] Similarly, Hirschi found supporting evidence for the generalization that the better a youth performs in school, the less likely he is to be involved in delinquency.

Positive binds to school decrease the likelihood of becoming delinquent.

Moreover, he found that a favorable attitude toward school tends to insulate a child from delinquency, even in the absence of parents. By virtue of the home situation, an adolescent may have a low stake in conformity. But if the adolescent has a positive attitude toward school, the likelihood of becoming involved in delinquency decreases.[24]

Both the Gold and the Hirschi studies reveal that boys from families of semiskilled and unskilled workers were characteristically found among those who had below average grades or who were school failures. Other studies have shown that "tracking," or separating those with low aptitude and low achievement, is one of the strongest predictors of self-reported delinquency. And so it goes. In the inner-city schools and in schools in small towns, those most in need of the advantages of an adequate education are frequently bypassed. Statistics on the offenders in our nation's prisons and jails indicate that those who are incarcerated fall below the median level of education for the general population.

This is not the place for a polemic against the defects of the educational system. But available evidence might confirm the analysis that Walter Schafer and Kenneth Polk made for the Crime Commission over a decade ago. They suggested that the schools do not need more social workers, counselors, stricter attendance laws, special classes, or programs for troublesome students. Instead, they need to address themselves to basic problems related to delinquency. First, schools must develop programs to maximize each student's chances for educational success. Second, schools must organize their programs and efforts to assist those who fall behind and avoid excluding or "pushing out" those who run afoul of community and school standards of conduct.[25]

Religious Institutions. The relationship between religion, social control, and problematic behaviors such as crime and delinquency is ambiguous. Religion frequently is mentioned as a positive factor that helps deter criminal behavior. It is plain that American society is pluralistic in its religious beliefs and moral values. To assert that religion serves as a social control mechanism in such a society, one must first specify *whose* religion. In our society, we should expect some conflict between norms learned in the primary group and those that reflect the beliefs and interests of the dominant groups in society.

The resurgence of interest in a variety of religious movements among American youth in the 1970s provides contemporary illustrations of the manner in which individual and group religious beliefs and practices can come into conflict with the belief systems of established churches and/or parents. This renewed religious interest has focused largely on groups ranging from

Religion as societal control or youth dissent?

those influenced by Eastern religions to the so-called "Jesus people" and other "charismatic" movements. These religious groups have gained acceptance among five to eight million Americans, mainly in the eighteen to twenty-four age bracket. Many of these movements demand an intensive, personal commitment and full-time participation in group activities. Because of the commitment required and the popular view that new converts have been "duped," parents of youthful adherents have criticized their activities and in some cases taken direct action against them, hiring professional "deprogrammers" to remove their sons and daughters from such groups. Some lower courts in California and several other states have supported such action with decisions in favor of the parents. But by 1977, groups such as the Hare Krishnas and the Unification Church ("Moonies") had taken legal action to protect their members.[26]

Still, some critics of society have associated declining religious interest with the rise in crime and delinquency. But there is ample evidence that the vast majority of children and adults who profess no religious commitment never become identified with criminal or delinquent behavior. Religion may not be a "necessary" means of social control when other belief systems are present.

While there are numerous examples of churches that have moved out of urban slums to avoid problems such as crime when they might have used their influence to promote community development, religious organizations have also been involved in delinquency prevention programs. Joseph Fitzpatrick describes some of these programs in different parts of the country in his article for the Crime Commission's *Task Force Report on Delinquency*.[27]

The Mass Media. Social scientists and other scholars have been engaged in an ongoing conflict regarding the influence of the mass media on human behavior. Some maintain that the media help tie the great variety of groups in our mass population into the major institutions and value systems of our heterogeneous society. Others argue that mass media are alienating influences, depriving individuals of seeking meaningful means for individual growth and enrichment. Both see the media as having powerful influences that may evoke positive or negative behaviors from their millions of consumers.

In recent years considerable discussion of the impact of the media on law-violating and deviant behavior has centered on television. Keep in mind that the effect television has on the viewer is modified by the network of "significant others" and meaningful membership groups in which he or she may be involved. Moreover, the effects of the mass media on the developing "self" have not been established clearly. But the pervasiveness of television is staggering. There is at least one television set in 97 percent of our homes. By the time a youth is eighteen, he or she has been exposed to approximately 22,000 hours of television, twice as much time as that spent in school. Researchers estimate that television depicts five acts of violence per hour. If this estimate is accurate, it means that the typical eighteen-year-old has viewed well over

100,000 violent acts on the tube. Much of this viewing is unsupervised by adults. The addiction to television may have been what the poet Kahlil Gibran had in mind when he wrote about "that stealthy thing that enters the house a guest, and then becomes a host, and then a master." [28]

One early study conducted a content analysis of 100 hours of programs during the so-called "children's hour." It discovered some 124 scenes involving violence, including 12 murders, 16 gunfights, 21 shootings, 21 other gun incidents, and 37 hand-to-hand fights.[29] Ten years later, in 1971, a writer estimated that the number of violent acts per hour presented on a television program had risen to five.[30]

Such studies led the president of the United States to order a study of television violence by the surgeon general in 1969. A number of those appointed to this commission either had served as consultants for the major networks or had been on their payrolls in some executive capacity. The commission released its five-volume report in 1972. Two studies reported in volume 3, *TV and Adolescent Aggressiveness,* are of special interest.

One was the report of a longitudinal study on 900 third-grade children. The data showed that an unpopular child in the third grade tended to watch television with greater frequency over the ten years of the study if he or she remained unpopular. A positive correlation was established between the degree of violent programs preferred and the aggressive behavior of the children. Another study reported on a longitudinal analysis of observations of 2,200 tenth-grade boys throughout the United States between 1966 and 1970. Those boys identified as most aggressive preferred violent fights and television violence more than their less aggressive peers. Both these and other studies show a *correlation* between television and violence. But correlation does not mean *causation,* and studies do not establish whether it was the violence on television that caused violent behavior or simply that those involved in aggressive or violent behavior preferred to watch violent television shows.[31] Some social scientists argue that a steady diet of television viewing influences behavior through the impact of the vicarious experiences which, in turn, may lead to imitation. A vicarious experience may provide an excuse for acting out certain latent impulses in an individual. There have been studies of this "cathartic effect."

The idea that violence in the media may lead to imitation in real life is illustrated, but certainly not documented, by examples from news reports over the past few years. The following are cases in point. A helicopter was used in a prison break from Jackson Prison in Michigan after a similar scene in the movie *Breakout* was aired. A woman in Boston was forced to douse herself with gasoline and was set on fire by a gang of hoodlums two nights after a similar scene in *Fuzz* was shown on TV. The stabbing murder scene in *The Marcus-Nelson Murders* was said to be the reason a woman was stabbed by a seventeen-year-old youth. And a ten-year-old girl was gang-raped with a Coke bottle in San Francisco the day after a television movie shown during the "family hour" depicted a similar crime.

But as Robert Snow argues, children know the difference between imaginary and real situations. We might console ourselves with the fact that most adolescents do not become involved in violent behavior after watching the "tube," although some studies show there are class and race differences correlated with the impact of television on violent behavior.[32]

Blaming television for delinquency is too simplistic an answer to a complex phenomenon such as delinquency. The fact that a developing child might spend 22,000 hours watching television tells us more about the anomie of the family—in which parents neglect to control the television viewing habits of their children—and the gross commercialism of society, than it does about the causes of crime and delinquency. The complexity of the crime problem is not altered by confusing the *correlation* between television watching and a high delinquency rate with *causation*. But there are indications from numerous studies suggesting that violence on television may be an additional factor that can increase the likelihood of violent behaviors in children.

THE POSITION OF YOUTH IN SOCIETY

Although Americans generally think of their society as "child-centered," on closer scrutiny it becomes apparent that the status or social position of the young is a marginal and even ambiguous one. This phase of the individual's life is often referred to by social scientists as a time of stress and turmoil. As child psychologist G. Stanley Hall, who did much to develop the study of adolescence as a special field at the turn of the century, put it, it is a period of *Sturm und Drang*. Because young people in modern society must confront unique problems of adjustment that often lead to emotional problems and deviance, some social scientists have seen them as delinquency prone.

In Western industrial society, youth is a stage in the life cycle characterized by biological maturity and social dependence. Young people are expected to aspire to and prepare for adulthood, but they are constantly reminded by adults who staff the agencies that direct their preparation that they are still children, just "kids." They are not allowed full participation in economic, political, or social matters of concern to them. This subculture of youth does not seem to be integrated in terms of any common core of values or normative system, but rather reflects the pluralism and value conflicts of the adult culture.

David Matza has suggested that in response to this relatively powerless transitional position—where they are neither adults, nor children, yet referred to as possessing the traits of a culture apart and are provided quasi-independence on campuses, playgrounds, and the streets—youth have developed a variety of lifestyles. He characterizes these as ranging from extreme conformity—"scrupulosity"—to rebelliousness. He includes such behavior patterns as bohemianism ("hippie"), radicalism, and delinquency in this latter category. Although the youth subculture reflects the pursuit of fun, thrills, and frivolous leisure, which are subterranean or hidden in our adult, middle-class

Puritan morality, it also exhibits conventional lifestyles of conformity and preparation for adulthood.[33]

There is an ongoing interplay between conventional and deviant behavior in the teenage and youth subcultures. And the experiences indulged in by the participants include many activities that have come to be defined as juvenile *status offenses.* In some respects youth culture may be thought of as a conventional version of what Matza terms "subcultural delinquency."[34]

It is within the context of the social position of youth and their response to their marginal status that we should consider the emergence of the juvenile justice system. Anthony Platt has characterized the reform movement out of which the juvenile court emerged at the turn of the century as the "child-saving" movement. The child savers, however, were more concerned with protecting "respectable citizens" from the children of the poverty-stricken lower classes running loose in the streets than they were with the welfare of the children.[35]

This discussion is relevant to the emergence of the juvenile justice system, for the concept of adolescence had to be created as a social reality—along with the broader social status of youth—before the terms *juvenile* and *juvenile delinquent* could be legally defined.

With the establishment of the first juvenile court in Cook County, Illinois, society asserted its right under *parens patriae*—the state acting in a parental and therapeutic role—to intervene in a juvenile's life.[36] And so the movement to establish juvenile courts assumed vague humanitarian objectives. But it also included a commitment to the positivist emphases on the criminal actor rather than the act. It assumed as well a deterministic model of human behavior and generally focused on abnormal aspects of delinquent behavior.[37] By assuming a parentlike role, the juvenile court sought to correct the behavior or modify those traits that caused it. However, there was considerable disagreement among social scientists, practitioners, and treatment specialists about the causes of the behavior. Various causes were advanced to explain delinquency, including spiritual and character disorders, biological or physical constitution, psychopathogenic factors, and social factors including race, family life, poverty, social class, educational failure, and adolescent turmoil. Intervention policies varied accordingly.[38]

BECOMING DELINQUENT: AFFINITY AND AFFILIATION PERSPECTIVES

Considerable research and theorizing has sought to explain not only the extent of delinquency and its relationship to various aspects of the social structure, but also why some juveniles commit delinquent acts and others don't. More recently, numerous studies have focused on societal reaction to delinquent acts from the interactionist or labeling perspective. In summarizing some explanations that try to answer the question of why juveniles commit delinquent acts, particular attention will be paid to theories stressing social disorganization and subcultural perspectives. We will seek to identify elements within these theories that might later be synthesized with the interactionist perspective. It is our contention that social factors may provide a fuller understanding, not only of the motivational aspects involved in becoming delinquent, but also of the manner in which certain acts come to be defined as delinquent as a result of the process of "tagging" and labeling.

We will organize these studies by using a schema or typology set forth by David Matza. In his provocative work, *Becoming Deviant,* Matza suggests three major concepts around which these three perspectives can be organized. *Affinity* relates crime and delinquency to personal attributes and social disorganization; *affiliation* stresses group associations, especially differential association; and *signification* explores the societal reaction to criminal behavior.[39]

Personal and Social Predispositions: Affinities

Kinds-of-People Affinities. The ideas of Lombroso and the early founders of positive criminology were described earlier. In the 1930s, 40s, and 50s, a number of works sought to explain crime and delinquency in terms of biological or constitutional factors. One of the more influential attempts to prove such a relationship was the work of Sheldon and Eleanor Glueck. They found that institutionalized delinquents were predominantly mesomorphs in body type—athletic and muscular. Unfortunately, such a statistical relationship or association between two variables does not provide insights into the operation of additional factors, like the reaction of social control agents such as judges who may be more inclined to see "husky" juveniles as potentially dangerous and so commit them to juvenile facilities. Other selective social processes might also be operating.[40]

Psychological Affinities. Attempts at explaining delinquency in terms of psychological variables have been widely accepted, perhaps due to the relatively deferential manner in which we regard psychology and psychiatry. Reviews of studies purporting to establish a relationship between personality traits and crime and delinquency were conducted by Karl Schuessler and Donald Cressey (1950) and Gordon Waldo and Siven Dinitz (1967). In all, 207 studies covering several decades were reviewed. The researchers found no solid basis for believing that offenders score differently on personality measures than nonoffenders.[41]

The term *psychopathic personality* has also been used widely to explain delinquent conduct.[42] This term has become a "wastebasket" category, applied to those who do not readily fit into more conventional diagnostic categories but who nevertheless exhibit antisocial behavior. More recently, the term *sociopath* has substituted for *psychopath* in describing the unsocialized delinquent. But both terms involve a form of circular reasoning, and neither is of much explanatory value. Still, such constitutional explanations persist, perhaps as Edwin Schur suggests, because we prefer to see delinquency as a "sickness," rather than evidence of the diverse behavior patterns of youth.[43]

Sociological Affinities. Matza has suggested that the affinity most favored by modern sociologists is the relationship between circumstances of poverty and delinquency and crime. Such an affinity has a long history. Studies documenting the disproportionate existence of delinquents and criminals in deteriorated urban neighborhoods were carried out in England in the nineteenth century.[44] Sociologists of the Chicago school accepted the relation between poverty, social disorganization, and social pathology. Beginning in 1929, Shaw and McKay published a series of studies providing ecological and ethnological analyses of delinquents (*Delinquency Areas,* 1929; *Jack Roller,* 1930; *The Natural History of a Delinquent Career,* 1931). These studies related differential rates of delinquency to social characteristics of communities and to the community disorganization that resulted in reduced control of children and patterns of juvenile delinquency.[45] Matza notes that even though their data verified their thesis, they were based on official statistics or estimates of the extent of delinquency. More significantly, they failed to explain the social processes by which some became committed to delinquency while most remained committed to conventional behavior.[46]

Robert Merton's reformulation of Emile Durkheim's concept of *anomie* has provided an influential framework for later theories of delinquency. In his essay, "Social Structure and Anomie," Merton argues that the cultural values of a society define its goals and the institutionalized means for achieving them. His hypothesis was that deviant behavior may be seen as a symptom of disassociation or disjuncture between culturally defined aspirations and the prescribed means for achieving them. As people learn and strive for socially valued goals, or success—defined in our society in terms of wealth and material objects—they may discover that the culturally prescribed means are denied. This particular form of adaptation—Merton's typology describes five—was characterized as *innovation.* He saw the poverty segment of society as being especially subject to this disassociation, because the poor are more apt to be blocked from access to the popularly promoted success goals. It is in the lower class that the disassociation between such goals and the means of realizing them is the greatest.[47]

Merton assumed that the goal of success was shared more or less evenly throughout our society. He did not make any clear-cut distinctions between those more mobile, organized, and striving segments of the lower class and the immobile, disorganized unstable segments. Consequently, he failed to specify which section of the lower class was vulnerable to the dissociative conditions he stressed.[48]

Criticism has focused on two of Merton's major assumptions: that success goals and pressures to achieve are shared equally across social lines in our society, and that the perception of opportunity does not vary by class. One critical study by Bernard Rosenberg and Harvey Silverstein concluded that to the extent *anomie* is present among lower-status juveniles, it may not differ in quality from the moral *anomie* present in the larger society.[49]

Affiliation and Subcultural Theories

Affiliation theories seek to explain delinquency in terms of the process by which individuals become "converted" and through conscious intention take on behavior that is new or novel for them but established behavior for the group. The emphasis is on the acquisition of behavior that is already a part of the patterned behavior of the group, though sometimes it appears to beg the issue of where did the group get its behavior system or conduct in the first place? Affiliation theories focus on how individual actors become delinquent.[50]

Affiliation was only implicit in the work of the writers of the Chicago school, but it was explicitly used as an explanation in Edwin H. Sutherland's work. Building on his study of the professional thief, Sutherland rejected the idea that we are essentially constrained by affinity or circumstances to become criminal or delinquent. His theory of *differential association* rested on the assumption that delinquency was learned in the context of groups. But it also re-

A pattern of conventional and delinquent subcultures.

lied on *differential social organization,* where learning took place in the context of competition between conflicting cultural beliefs and action systems.[51] The nine interrelated principles of differential association that follow purport to explain how an individual learns the techniques, values, attitudes, and action system of the subculture of delinquency:[52]

1. Criminal behavior is learned.
2. Criminal behavior is learned in interaction with other persons in a process of communication.
3. The principal part of the learning of criminal behavior occurs within intimate personal groups.
4. When criminal behavior is learned, the learning includes: (a) techniques of committing the crime, which are sometimes very complicated, sometimes very simple, and (b) the specific direction of motives, drives, rationalizations, and attitudes.
5. The specific direction of motives and drives is learned from definitions of legal codes as favorable or unfavorable.
6. A person becomes delinquent because of an excess of definitions favorable to violation of law over definitions unfavorable to violation of law (this is the principle of differential association that is the crux of the theory).
7. Differential associations may vary in frequency, duration, priority, and intensity.
8. The process of learning criminal behavior by association with criminal and anticriminal patterns involves all of the mechanisms that are involved in any other learning.
9. While criminal behavior is an expression of general needs and values, it is not explained by those general needs and values, since noncriminal behavior is an expression of the same needs and values.

In the years after Sutherland first published his theory (1939), numerous writers formulated explanations for criminal behavior that combined elements of both affinity and affiliation. These focused upon lower-class culture, blocked opportunity, low achievement, gangs, deviant subcultures, and delinquency.

Albert Cohen, in *Delinquent Boys* (1955), depicts the delinquent subculture as essentially a *contraculture* that emerges out of a lower-class reaction to middle-class morality and expectations. Cohen argues that lower-class boys adjust to their circumstances by repudiating unattainable middle-class standards. They take on group commitments that are expressed in negative, malicious, hedonistic, hostile, and destructive behavior. This delinquent behavior is the predictable result of the oppositional relationship between the delinquent subculture and conventional society. He portrays delinquency as behavior that is radically different from that of "normal" juveniles and determined by forces outside the individual.[53] In a later article Cohen considered a variety of delinquent subcultures, including those of the conflict-oriented drug addict, the semiprofessional thief, and the middle-class delinquent.[54]

Youth Gangs: One Member of a Bronx Youth Gang Tells Why It's So Important

BOX 1

He stands amid a moonscape of decay. Beyond where eyes can see, building after building burnt, empty, filled with rubble, crushed brick, warped tin, maybe one intact wall scratched with graffiti that speaks of living.

A rain-softened cardboard box moves over the rubble as if propelled by a steady wind. Nato lifts a sharpened broom handle above his head. He screams and sends the spear flying through the air. The box is still. He motions to me with his hand as he kicks the box over. Its heart still faintly pumping, the cat-sized rat jerks its head one last time. Nato's laugh starts in his belly, spilling out of his throat, ending in a scream.

We walk over to Chisholm Street, a street with no buildings, no people. Against the boarded, blue, empty Lirico Cultural Hijos de Quisequeya building I load another cassette in my tape recorder.

"If you write what is true, why don't things change?" he asks me. "Why do people want to know about us? Why do you want to know about us?"

We walk over to Jefferson Place where his mother lives. Two small children, barefoot, play in two burned-out cars that sit in the middle of the street. The children stop play as we pass, calling out, "What are you doing? You TV mens? Huh, lady, you TV?"

Nato laughs at them, shaking his head, "I'm TV and I'm making her a star."

We walk into the doorless hallway of his mother's building. The first floor is empty. All apartments stripped of doors, windows, floorboards, fixtures.

Inside his mother's apartment it's hot, dark, airless. A tin pail full of human excrement sits in a bathtub in the kitchen. Nato takes the pail and dumps it out a bedroom window.

"That's why I stay at the clubhouse," he tells me, as he straightens the covers of the one bed that fills the front room. "My mother don't have water here and my sister leave her kids off. Mama can't run them outside every time they got to s____t."

I ask him if he wants to do the taping there.

"Where can we go? Downtown? Where you live. I don't like it too much down there, so I stay up here. Right?"

He flips the tape machine on, rewinding the tape and playing back my words. I hear myself telling him to say anything he wants. We hear the background noises of children shouting, firetrucks, screaming police sirens, the stillness of the empty, deserted blocks we walked down. Fifteen minutes of breathing ends the tape. Nato leans back on the bed, his boots resting on the paisley coverlet. He closes his eyes and puts the mike on his chest. He clears his throat and sings "Do re mi . . . testing, testing."

Outside a dog barks and a woman screams at a child in Spanish. Nato speaks.

"My name is Nato. I am 15 years old. I am a member of the Savage Nomads. We are cold-blooded and we don't take no s____t from nobody. Today I'm talking to the world. I am just talking what I want to talk.

"I been raised in the gangs. Like my brothers were, only they're in jail now and one got on junk so my mother said he's dead. Gangs are families. Like brothers and sisters all together. We rumble cause you have to show blood. Blood is strength. In the Bronx, there's lots of blood.

"People say gangs is bad. Not to me. Gangs help each other, but we fight if there's static. This is just how we live. School don't mean nothing. They don't teach your head for jobs and living. Eating too. Schools don't teach your head to eat.

"You ask me who I am. I am somebody. Down East 139th Street they say, 'No trouble in stores.' Then they throw you out. So maybe we burn them. Then they gone. We still here. We still somebody.

"This is our country up here, like a whole world. Everybody took the money and went, but the gangs stay. We own all this land and all these buildings. If we got money like a country we could rule this place like kings.

"They say gangs will die. They say gangs come and go. But the Savage Nomads is forever. Even people, like adults, tip their hats to us. Cause we are like polices.

"Do you remember when we went downtown to your house last winter? There I liked the looks. You know, the prettiness. But I don't feel like me. I feel people don't like me. Like they're smelling me and they don't like how I smell. Up here we are all in this together.

"Some people could leave, but they don't cause people is real and they stick together. I know there's another world like the one on TV. But this is a world, too.

"If you write gang things people will think we just party and rumble. But mostly we make families with real weddings. Some girls get down with every dude, but really we believe in families.

"My mother don't want me in no gang. But here you have to be. Everybody beat on you if you not a member. Gangs is protection. When I wear my colors I get respect. Since I been 11, I been in gangs. First just one small one named the Masked Marauders. Just four of us. We control Tiffany Street. We do crib jobs to make some change. Taking off old ladies and kids. But that's jive time and other gangs would take us off if we step out of our territory.

"Up here everybody packs. I don't carry heavy hardware like a .45. Too much like a rifle. I just carry a .32 automatic. I got my first piece when I was 12. I stole it off a junkie. That's when my friend, Frankie, got hit over on Melrose Avenue. Two dudes just took him off. They said he stole their dog. It weren't true but they pumped him in the face.

"I walked across the George Washington Bridge that day. This white toll man said get off the bridge. I shot at him twice. They never wrote down one word in the papers but I shot at him twice.

"I wanted to get away that day. My mother told me my father lives in Jersey. I was going to see him. Maybe he had some money for me. I didn't find him, so I just walked around in those big parks over there.

"That's when I joined the Savage Nomads. Big Man took me in. He speaks like a law thinker does cause he done heavy time. He don't want the gangs to fight and he don't let no cliques fight. He says that white people want us to fight each other, then they don't have to deal with us.

"You talk with Big Man and he scares you like something bad. That's the prison eyes he has. He's a cool nigger with dead eyes like the devil. Even cops respect him cause they say he took off three guys at once.

"What else can I say? Maybe what I'd like to be if I get to be someone important. I would buy my mother a house and build a real clubhouse with apartments. Sometimes you have to turn your heart cold because it's too much here. I like it cause we own it. It's ours. But it ain't much. It ain't nothing.

"Sometimes I think this is wrong. That's it. It's just wrong. Not for me, cause I'm a man. But for little children growing up here. They see nothing and then they feel nothing. I know that some people have money and cars and food. Then you think 'Why can't I have that?' But what good does thinking do.

"I been raised here from the time when buildings were more pretty and parks had trees. Now we don't have anything. But you get with your clique and you talk and party and get high. You can feel good. Like somebody.

"This here, what you been hearing, is me. The life and times of Nato. N-A-T-O in the year of the Lord, 1978. The End."

Nato's clubhouse, in the basement of an abandoned building, is like a thousand other gang clubhouses in the South East Bronx, the Lower East Side, Chicago, Roxbury, St. Louis, along the routes of urban Armageddon, placed where people who have power cannot see.

They give themselves names that speak of isolation, power, anarchy. Young Nomads, Tomahawks, Mortar Girls, Savage Nomads, Roman Kings, Black Stone Nations. The membership transcends age and sex. Young babies sit on mattresses next to automatic pistols, never crying for food because their inner timing dictates that stick-ups occur in the late afternoon and that's when the food comes.

Source: *Boston Globe*, Feb. 25, 1979. © 1979 Pacific News Service, San Francisco, Calif. Reprinted by permission.

Walter Miller, in his study of street gangs, took issue with Cohen, arguing that among street gangs delinquent behavior is customary and there is no rejection of middle-class values as such. Rather, these boys act on the basis of focal concerns (values) and in emphasizing trouble, toughness, smartness, excitement, fate, and autonomy, commit acts that are consistent with the traditions of their group. In other words, delinquency results from conformity to the group.[55]

Table 4.3. Focal Concerns of Lower-Class Culture

Area	Perceived Alternatives (state, quality, condition)	
1. Trouble:	law-abiding behavior	law-violating behavior
2. Toughness:	physical prowess, skill; "masculinity"; fearlessness, bravery, daring	weakness, ineptitude; effeminacy; timidity, cowardice, caution
3. Smartness:	ability to outsmart, dupe, "con"; gaining money by "wits"; shrewdness, adroitness in repartee	gullibility, "con-ability"; gaining money by hard work; slowness, dull-wittedness, verbal maladroitness
4. Excitement:	thrill; risk, danger; change, activity	boredom; "deadness," safeness; sameness, passivity
5. Fate:	favored by fortune, being "lucky"	ill-omened, being "unlucky"
6. Autonomy:	freedom from external constraint; freedom from superordinate authority; independence	presence of external constraint; presence of strong authority; dependency, being "cared for"

Source: Walter B. Miller, "Lower Class Culture as a Generating Milieu of Gang Delinquency," *The Journal of Social Issues,* vol. 14, no. 3 (1958), p. 6.

The *theory of blocked opportunity* was developed by Richard Cloward and Lloyd Ohlin, primarily as a reformulation of Merton's anomie theory, but it also contains elements of differential association theory. They argue that when youths find legitimate avenues to success blocked and are unable to lower their aspirations, they may explore nonconformist alternatives. As a result, three types of subculture may evolve. These are the criminal, the conflict, and the retreatist subcultures.[56]

Hirschi, in a study of nearly 5,000 boys in California, demonstrated that as long as juveniles have bonds to conventional parents, the school, and conforming peers, they will not be predisposed to become delinquent. Those who were identified as delinquents—through self-reports and official records—were less attached to parents, schools, and conventional peers than nondelinquents.[57] More recently, Michael Hindelang conducted a partial replication of Hirschi's study with similar results.[58]

In an article written for the Crime Commission, Kenneth Polk contends that delinquency is related to lack of success in school. To fail in school is to be excluded from the "success" that education holds out to its participants as a goal. Lack of achievement means that a youth may find it necessary to become involved in the deviant youth culture.[59] A later study by Schafer, Olexa, and Polk found that being on a lower track (noncollege prep) in high school had a high relationship to delinquency.[60]

LaMar Empey and Steven Lubeck, after summarizing a number of studies emphasizing the importance of school achievement and social class, note that poor school performance is highly correlated with delinquency. But many recent studies (Nye and Short, Gold, and others) fail to show a statistically significant relationship between social class status and delinquent behavior.[61] They conclude: "The fact that delinquency is not limited to the lower class(es) suggests that we might discover as many differences within classes as we discover between them." [62] Further, they suggest that we focus upon other influences for which social class alone might be a poor clue. As Greenberg has observed in a recent article:

> In modern capitalist societies, children of all classes share for a limited period, a common relationship . . . which is distinct from that of most adults, and they respond to their common structural position in fairly similar ways. Although there are class differences in the extent and nature of delinquency, especially violent delinquency, these are less pronounced than for adults, for whom occupational differentiation is much sharper.[63]

Greenberg attributes the high level of delinquency in contemporary society to the structural position of juveniles in advanced industrial economies. He notes, however, that delinquency is not unique to capitalism, for some of the processes he describes are evident in the Soviet Union, where delinquency is associated with "leisure-time consumption activities on the part of juveniles who do not study or work or prepare for work." [64]

Basing their analyses on Durkheimian rather than Marxist assumptions, Paul Friday and Jerold Hage arrive at a similar conclusion. They theorize that such conditions thwart the development of an integrated role pattern. For as societies become more affluent, "adolescents must spend longer and longer periods in isolation or in dependent relationships with the family, school, or 'forced' unemployment. Juveniles so isolated from relationships that could promote integration and commitment face a greater probability of delinquency." [65]

Unless affinity perspectives are linked to an explanation of social processes, they are too limited in their explanations of delinquency. Together with affiliation, they provide insights into the process by which the individual actor becomes linked to deviant subcultures. However, the issue of why some juveniles get "tagged" and labeled as delinquents when others do not demands an understanding of the role of social control agents, who in exercising their authority as rule enforcers, identify and process the delinquent.

SIGNIFYING AGENTS AND ORGANIZATIONS: SOCIETAL REACTION AND BECOMING DELINQUENT

It has been suggested that youthful misbehavior may be a response by the young to the way our society and its institutions are organized. For even much of juvenile law-violating behavior, including status offenses, may be facilitated and supported by conventional societal organization (patterns) and institutions.[66] Given the complex interrelationship between the conventional and deviant in the youth phase of the life cycle, we should look critically at the popular and positivistic assumption that delinquency is essentially a different and pathological aspect of juvenile lifestyles.

Up until now, we have made a number of references to the relation between the organized authority of the state and the role of agents of such authority in the process of becoming delinquent. "But," you may object, "the juvenile is already a delinquent." In reality, a person only becomes a delinquent when legal definitions are applied to behavior, although being involved in delinquent behavior implies that a juvenile's activities risk intervention and efforts at correction by control agents. The labeling perspective focuses upon the interconnection between the delinquent act and official reaction to it.

The term *signification* is used by Matza to designate the process of being labeled, defined, and assigned to a legal classification or category. It also refers to being "signified," "pointed out," and coming to represent or exemplify the category of delinquent.[67]

The agents of two official organizations of the state are crucial in the official processing, or signifying, of juveniles as delinquents: the police and the juvenile courts. For example, a report for the Crime Commission noted that the chance that an American male might be arrested during his lifetime was 52 percent, while for a female it was 13 percent.[68] Richard Perlman in 1964 estimated that about one out of six boys would appear in court charged with delinquency before turning eighteen; for girls the figure was one in twenty-three. More recent estimates are one out of five for both sexes.[69]

Signifying Agents of Delinquency: The Police

We have suggested that the manner in which a youth is processed will influence the degree to which he or she may be defined as a delinquent. The police play a pivotal role in apprehending delinquents and in their entry into the juvenile justice system.

Generally, the first thing police do after taking juvenile offenders into custody is to screen them and decide on a course of action. One youth may be given a reprimand and released without the offense being recorded. Another may be released after the offense is recorded. On the other hand, the youth may be referred to an agency outside the juvenile system, or he or she may be referred to juvenile or family court, an occurrence that takes place in about 50 percent of the cases. If referred to court, the intake staff decides whether the youth is to be released to parental custody or held in detention until the court acts on the case. In 1975, approximately 500,000 juveniles were detained for some period of time to await court action. The model juvenile sentencing law recommends that no juvenile should be held in an adult jail. But fully 93 percent of the juvenile courts report that they have no secure facilities except the county jail in which to hold juveniles pending a hearing.

Studies of social factors that influence the police in their decisions about the disposition of juveniles vary in their conclusions. Empey and Lubeck suggest that there are four types of variables that contribute to the decision as to whether the juvenile offender is released or processed into the system.[70]

1. *Community patterns and police organization.* Police action toward juveniles generally reflects community beliefs, biases, and discrimination. In Pennsylvania, for example, juvenile arrests referred to court range from about 9 percent to 71 percent in different communities. In California, the range is from 2 to 82 percent.[71]

In James Q. Wilson's study of "Eastern City" and "Western City," he contrasted two different police methods for dealing with juvenile misconduct. The highly professionalized police department in Western City had twice the arrest rate of Eastern City. The police in Western City treated juveniles impersonally, strictly according to rules, which resulted in a greater number of court referrals. In Eastern City, police handled juveniles more individually, though blacks were three times more likely to end up in court than whites. Thus police action is affected both by community sentiment and by the type of organization that characterizes the department.[72]

2. *Situational factors.* The nature of the situation in which police make contact with youths and the manner in which juveniles relate to police officers are important. Whether the youth is defined as delinquent may be influenced as much by his demeanor as by the kind of offense committed. Also, situational factors, such as whether the action against the youths was *reactive* (citizen initiated) or *proactive* (police initiated), make a difference. Police usually followed through with arrests when citizens demanded them. Interestingly, they were less likely to make arrests, and if they did were more likely to release juveniles when not under pressure from citizens.[73]

3. *Type of law-violating behavior.* Studies by Robert Terry (1967) and Nathan Goldman (1969) suggest that the more serious offenses are likely to be dealt with by custody and referral to court. Goldman found that robbery, larceny, auto theft, and sex offenses are most likely to be referred to court. Gambling, mischief, property damage, and drinking are less likely to be referred.[74]

4. *Personal attributes of juveniles and signifying agents.* Studies by Irving Piliavin and Scott Briar (1964), Nathan Goldman, as well as Donald Black and Albert Reiss (1970), provide conflicting evidence regarding the importance of personal attributes. Although the first two studies reported that young blacks are more likely than whites to be arrested as well as referred to court, the latter did not find racial discrimination to be a factor. Rather they found

that black complainants were apt to be less tolerant toward juvenile suspects than whites and more likely to demand an arrest. The differences could be due to variation in community attitudes. Attributes related to age, sex, arrest records, and family status were also found to be relevant to the manner and rate of police processing in these and other studies.[75]

In sum, a number of factors—community patterns, situations, nature of offense, and personal attributes—are brought to bear in decisions affecting why some juveniles may be defined as delinquent while others are not.

Police Diversion Programs. In recent years, especially during the 1970s, an explosion of diversion programs has encouraged police departments to direct juveniles out of the system. The programs, funded by grants from the Federal Law Enforcement Assistance Administration (LEAA), were stimulated by recommendations of the President's Commission. As Malcolm Klein et al. have suggested, the programs have reached almost "epidemic" proportions, with over two hundred in California alone. These programs operate under a number of rationales. In some, diversion is directed at curtailing inherent biases in the system by providing standards for mitigating factors. Others decrease the volume of cases processed into the system by directing status-type and other less serious offenders away from the system. Often the programs are less expensive than the formal system, and they tend to avoid stigmatizing the juvenile as "delinquent" or "bad."

Klein and his associates found, ironically, that those juveniles directed into the diversion programs by the police were the very ones who, without such programs, might not have been arrested, or who, if taken into custody, probably would have been released. The result is *increased intervention*, rather than *diversion* from the juvenile system. Of course, though the juveniles avoid being labeled delinquent, they are not called "divertees" and they become "encapsulated" in yet another system.[76]

The Juvenile Court and the Processing of Delinquents

The juvenile court plays an important role in the processing of delinquents, serving in a general sense as the means by which the status or label "juvenile delinquent" is conferred by authoritative agents of social control. The juvenile participates in what Harold Garfinkle has appropriately termed a "status degradation ceremony."[77] And the transformation of the juvenile to a delinquent career is complete if he admits to being a delinquent. Kai Erickson points out that there is no comparable ceremony returning the juvenile to conventional status. When delinquents do return, as most do, it is usually seen as resulting from "maturational reform," rather than intervention by the court.[78] Erickson was referring to the processing of the adult offender. But as Richard Lemert has noted, the official processing of juveniles is even more problematic since children who come to the attention of the court are not apt to be people who have the insight to manage such social stigma.[79]

The transformation into a juvenile delinquent career.

Fortunately, only a relatively small number of the youths arrested in any given year end up in the juvenile court. Still, about 1.5 million juvenile cases are processed by the court each year.[80] And although research suggests that delinquency is distributed across all social strata, children from poverty and minority groups are disproportionately represented among those dealt with by the court.[81]

The Supreme Court, in the *Gault* case, referred to the juvenile court as a "peculiar system for juveniles." As one writer notes, it is peculiar in two respects. First, its procedures do not rely on "due process" to the degree that adult criminal courts do. Second, the court not only administers punishment (treatment) for the violation of laws, which if committed by an adult would be a crime, but it also is charged with deciding whether a child is immoral, wayward, in need of supervision, incorrigible, neglected, or in an unfit home.[82]

The juvenile court exemplifies the *medical or therapeutic model* of positive criminology, with its emphasis on case workers and clinicians to diagnose the individual's difficulty and recommend treatment that may be incorporated into the juvenile court's disposition. In informal processing, which occurred in over half of the cases in 1973, the juvenile may not have a formal court hearing of fact. Consequently, as Kittrie has noted, the courts must guard against excessive "therapeutic zeal."[83]

Criticism of the juvenile court's lack of procedural guarantees developed early in its history and had become quite pervasive by the 1960s. A California commission noted in 1960: "Basic legal rights are neither being uniformly nor adequately protected under present juvenile court procedures." [84] During the last half of the 1960s, the Supreme Court issued three landmark decisions intended to infuse a greater degree of legal safeguards into the processing of juveniles.

In *Kent* (1966) the Court held that procedures for the waiver of the juvenile court's jurisdiction to a criminal court must fulfill "essentials of due process and fair treatment." The Court ruled in *Gault* (1967) that a child has legal rights, including an official hearing of charges, advice of counsel, the right to confront and question witnesses, and protection against self-incrimination. The Court's third decision, *Winship* (1970), ruled that when courts held disposition hearings for minors charged with offenses which would be crimes if committed by an adult, they must require proof beyond reasonable doubt.[85]

These decisions, however, provide only minimal safeguards for juveniles. Studies have suggested that the decisions did not reverse the broadly conceived paternalistic juvenile court powers to the extent that is sometimes claimed. Courts that comply with these decisions were found to commit about as many juveniles to institutions as those that used more informal procedures. Moreover, informal supervision and probation are used widely even in courts that rely on formal legal procedures.[86]

In his recent study, Robert Emerson notes that a basic problem with which the juvenile court must deal is the demand by control agents to "do something"—to take some action against the youths who represent "trouble" for them. The court must resolve such cases in a manner that satisfies, or at least acknowledges, the demands of complainants. The court, however, cannot merely accept these complaints, for not all cases are seen as "trouble" by the court. Consequently, it may make its own assessment of the case and of the need to "do something." This assessment invariably reflects the court's own organizational priorities and its definitions of the relevance of the youth's problems to its own defined task.

In this latter regard, there are two basic considerations the court must take into account in defining delinquency. First, court actions are limited by available personnel, resources, and time. Second, since the court encounters a wide range of youthful misbehavior, it tends to hold a more narrow definition of delinquency than most complainants. This means that in seeking a practical solution to cases involving "trouble," the court asks the question, What kind of a juvenile are we dealing with? The answer involves, as Emerson notes, an investigation into the juvenile's *moral* character.

Characteristically, the court identifies at least three categories of *moral* character: (1) the *normal youth,* who acts according to basic, normal patterns, despite episodic delinquency; (2) the *hard-core delinquent,* who is seen as hostile and pursuing criminal goals; and (3) the *disturbed youth,* impelled to delinquent behavior by irrational motives or compulsions. In the first instance the court may react routinely, meting out formal probation or informal supervision; with the second type the disposition may involve commitment to a training school or other institution; the third type may be referred for special care or psychiatric treatment.

These three types, their dispositions by the court, and the considerations that surround the "solution" of a given case may determine whether a youth is labeled as "normal," a "criminally inclined delinquent," or "mentally ill."[87]

As juvenile delinquency rates have increased in recent years the court has processed and defined a greater number of juveniles as "delinquent." As a result, society reaps a whirlwind of consequences due to the "secondary deviation" that is a product of this process. After being identified as delinquent, and after having this identity reinforced, some youths go on to criminal careers in adulthood.

Juvenile Corrections and Noninstitutional Alternatives

In general, the problems of the juvenile court are reflected in juvenile corrections. The lack of due process, the broad mandate of the juvenile court, and the individualized approach to treating the offender—under the assumption that those identified and defined as delinquent are somehow different from the general population of juveniles—have, in recent decades, led to criticism of the overloading of institutions with members of lower SES and minority group delinquents.[88] The criticism has awakened a new mood of reform.

The juvenile correctional institutions of the twentieth century predate the establishment of the juvenile court. The first institution for children convicted of criminal offenses was the New York City House of Refuge, established in 1824. By 1900, there were about sixty-five reformatories for juveniles in the United States established with the intent of providing special care for juvenile offenders. These institutions were created to isolate children from the horrors of prison life. But they also cared for orphans and neglected children. Over a century after this supposed reform, juveniles committed to institutions for status offenses—those who have violated no laws but are persons, children, or minors "in need of supervision" (PINS, CINS, MINS)—are mingled with those convicted of serious offenses. These juvenile training schools provide "training," but it is the wrong kind of training for neglected and incorrigible children who need something more than custodial care. These training schools have educational programs, for example, but for the most part they are inadequate for the needs of many of their charges. In the state of New York, a state audit in 1975 disclosed that the average youth in such institutions was in school only about seven to fifteen hours a week. Yet invariably these youths had educational deficiencies.

Attempts to reform such correctional programs have involved numerous experiments in residential group homes. The group home concept is now used widely in Florida, in an attempt to avoid the use of custodial-oriented training schools. New York and California, as well as a number of other states, have similar programs on a lesser scale. Numerous other community programs, which rely upon local resources, have developed throughout the country.[89]

Nationally, Youth Service Bureaus, sponsored in part by the National Council of Crime and Delinquency, have been introduced; California has made wide use of them. These organizations seek to provide services for delinquents in their home communities.

During the 1960s, the trend toward controlling and caring for juveniles in the community resulted in greater reliance on probation supervision, with the youth residing at home, or in the case of those from neglectful families, in foster homes. In 1965, there were 62,733 juveniles in institutions and four times as many under community supervision, probation, or after-care (parole), non-residential treatment centers. By 1969, the number held in public institutions had decreased to 43,000, and by 1974, to only 28,000. At the same time, youths enrolled in community programs increased dramatically.

In the midst of a clamor for "law and order" and pressure to lock up more juveniles, Massachusetts closed its training schools between 1970 and 1972. Juveniles were transferred to privately run programs in the community under contract to the state, which also drew federal funding through the LEAA. The movement to deinstitutionalize juvenile corrections is growing, against some opposition from vested interest groups and perhaps also from those who interpret the change too literally. For deinstitutionalization does not mean merely tear down the walls. Rather, it aims to remove children and juveniles from large institutions that emphasize custodial care and reassign them to smaller group-type homes that offer an opportunity for them to participate in supervised situations—both residential and nonresidential, but within the community.[90]

Community corrections can only be effective to the extent that they involve local organizations and policymakers. The reduction and control of delinquency can no longer be left to juvenile justice personnel. New patterns need to be developed so all youths can participate in community activities, including those defined as delinquents. Community programs should not, however, be seen as a total solution. They must be part of a program to regenerate the community, eliminate racism, and provide adequate incomes and living conditions for all. One impressive example of a total program involves "The Renegades," a street gang in East Harlem that is rebuilding deteriorated tenements or slum dwellings as part of a federally funded Urban Homesteaders project.

Suggested Reforms: "Radical Nonintervention"

In his report to the Crime Commission in 1967, Lemert stated: "If there is a defensible philosophy for the juvenile court, it is one of 'judicious nonintervention.'" For, he argued, the court "is properly an agency of last resort for children . . . analogous to [an] appeals courts which require that all remedies be exhausted before a case will be considered."[91]

More recently, Empey has stated that it has become a truism among observers and critics of the juvenile court to argue that healthy and conformist self-concepts among the young are shaped outside rather than within the legal system. He lists the following needed reforms:[92]

1. *Diversion.* The legal mandate of the court should be narrowed, and those juveniles who have educational, familial, moral, and social problems should be diverted to community agencies that are more capable of dealing with these problems. Thus it would be possible for the juvenile justice system to focus more effectively on those youths involved in criminal behavior, including serious predatory violations that have aroused public concern.

2. *Due process.* Steps should be taken to correct legal deficiencies and to provide legal safeguards for juveniles. While the juvenile justice system should retain some of its informal aspects, precautions should be established so that juveniles are not held accountable for actions that would not be criminal if committed by adults; they should be afforded safeguards against self-incrimination, improper legal procedures, and harsh penalties as a result of unconstitutional processing.

3. *Deinstitutionalization.* Confinement of youths has not proven to be a successful means of reforming young offenders. Rather, provision for a wide range of community alternatives appears to have greater potential and would also be less expensive. Such a reallocation of efforts and resources will require that we focus on the community as the basic root of the juvenile's problem. Community structures must be changed and institutions made more responsible and viable; otherwise efforts to change the offender will be futile.

Some general guidelines for public policy that might promote these recommended reforms and thus avoid the negative effects of the overreach of the juvenile justice system have been outlined by Edwin Schur. He concludes his book *Radical Nonintervention* (1973) with the following suggested "new priorities" which buttress and reinforce some of Empey's recommendations.[93]

1. *A reevaluation of the principal ways in which we think about "youth" behavior problems.* We must recognize that behavior patterns seen as delinquent are interwoven into the fabric of society. Therefore, we should accept some of this behavior instead of attempting to "solve" it legally.
2. The most effective delinquency program might be indirect *political changes toward a more just society,* otherwise a just system is a contradiction in terms.
3. *Take the young more seriously.* This would involve promoting meaningful participation of youth in our communities to build bonds of attachment to conventional society.
4. *The juvenile justice system should concern itself* more with dispensing "justice" and less with treating the problems of the "so-called delinquents." This would not constitute a "get tough" policy so much as a *consistently competent* policy of equity.

5. *Utilize a variety of approaches.* Until new approaches are developed we should stress noninstitutional, community alternatives and eliminate bureaucratic, impersonal aspects of existing institutions.

SUMMARY

We have summarized some of the theories and perspectives that shed light on the process by which juveniles are defined, labeled, and processed as delinquents. Some of those theories emphasize *affinities* or predispositions related to biological, psychological, and social factors. Each seeks to answer the question, Why do juveniles commit delinquent acts?

As a context for understanding the interrelationship between conforming and delinquent behavior, we described the socialization process in which youths acquire the goals, values, and behaviors valued by society.

Group processes were described as the affiliations in which the individual juvenile takes on behavior patterns novel for him or her, but established for the group. The *interactionist or labeling perspective* was introduced as a means of analyzing the manner in which behavior perceived as delinquent is responded to by agents of social control.

The relatively powerless position that youth occupy in modern society was emphasized. The emergence of gangs and a subculture of delinquency often appears to be the natural response of youths who develop lifestyles in response to their powerless status in society. The process of social typing and labeling was noted as a critical aspect of becoming delinquent.

The development of the juvenile delinquency "system" and the role of diffuse juvenile delinquency laws in defining juvenile delinquents were discussed. The police and the courts are major organizations involved in identifying and defining delinquency. Criticisms of the court and recent reform efforts of court and juvenile corrections were summarized.

Diversion, due process, and *deinstitutionalization* were suggested as specific reforms we might adopt to provide more effective programs for young people. Both *community development* and *self-development* are required to get at the problem of delinquency. A juvenile justice system with programs that provide a transition to responsible adulthood may involve a reexamination of social priorities.

ADDITIONAL READINGS

Empey, LaMar T. and Steven Lubeck. *Explaining Delinquency.* Lexington, Mass.: Lexington Books, D. C. Heath, 1971.
> An analysis of theories of delinquency that assumes lower socioeconomic status is a causal variable and proposes further investigations stressing patterns of behavior and consequent societal reaction. A sophisticated statistical analysis of several major theories.

Hirschi, Travis. *Causes of Delinquency.* Berkeley: University of California Press, 1969.

> Hirschi provides a cogent summary of three basic theories of delinquency and tests them through research conducted on a large sample of boys in which he compares self-reports with official records.

Klein, Malcolm W., ed. *The Juvenile Justice System.* Beverly Hills: Sage Publications, 1976.

> A collection of recent, original articles dealing with the juvenile justice system, its problems, and recent reform efforts and their evaluation.

Matza, David. *Delinquency and Drift.* New York: John Wiley & Sons, 1964.

> A cogent critique of positivist criminology as it pertains to delinquency. Matza opts for a position between hard determinism and open choice — "soft determinism."

Schur, Edwin H. *Radical Non-Intervention: Rethinking the Delinquency Problem.* Englewood Cliffs, N.J.: Prentice-Hall, 1973.

> Schur points out the ineffectiveness of theories, programs, and current policies for dealing with delinquency that disguise punishment as treatment. He suggests social policies based on the interactionist perspective.

Wolfgang, Marvin E., Robert M. Figlio, and Thorsten Sellin. *Delinquency in a Birth Cohort.* Chicago: University of Chicago Press, 1972.

> An analysis of delinquency in a cohort of nearly 10,000 youths who were not identified through their contact with the juvenile justice system. The findings should stimulate further research and reexaminations of public policy.

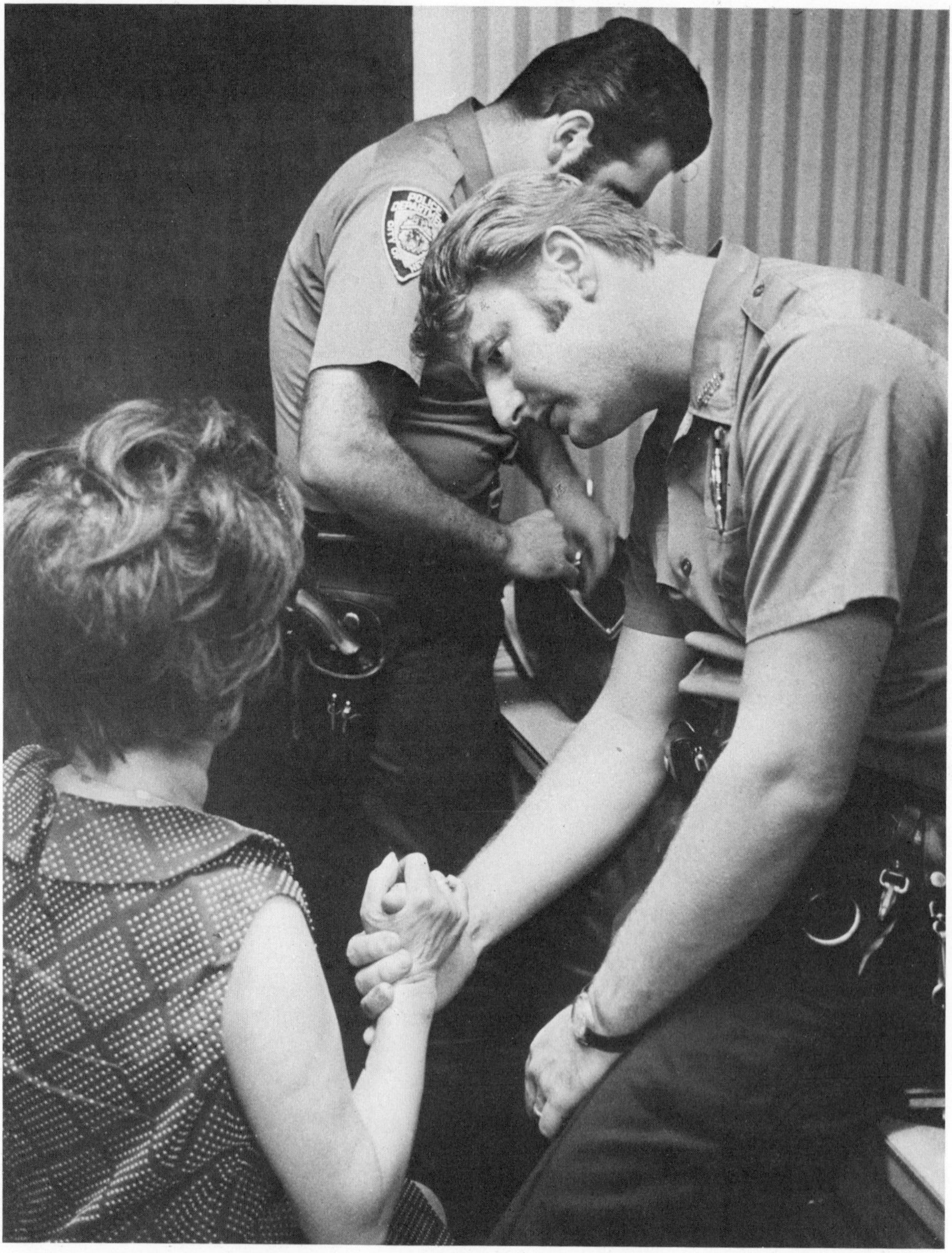

> But for her sex, a woman is a man; she has the same organs, the same needs, the same faculties. The machine is the same in its construction, its parts, its working, and its appearance are similar. Regard it as you will, the difference is only in degree.
> —J. J. Rousseau, Emile

5

FEMALE STATUS: WOMEN'S CRIME AND SOCIETAL REACTION

Is there a new type of female criminal? That impression has certainly been communicated over recent years as a procession of notorious women have popped up on the news pages. Many people have been startled to see women filling the role of the heinous criminal, and the violence of some of the crimes has added to the shocking image. Women seem increasingly to be involved in everything from terrorist bombings to bank robberies to vicious thrill killings.

Partly because it has been so unprecedented, the emergence of the woman criminal has been the object of vast media attention and some misleading interpretations. It is true that women's crime statistics are on the rise. But most of the change has been in the range of property crimes, a natural development as women approach equality in the world of work and the larger society.

The changing nature of women's position in society, both in the family and the work force, has been signaled by the women's liberation movement. At the same time, the women's movement has simplistically been called a *cause* of such social changes as the reported increase and fluctuations in the patterns of women's criminal offenses. These developments, together with the attention that the media have focused on the exploits of women like Lynette Fromme, Emily Harris, Patty Hearst, Sara Moore, Susan Saxe, and others, have stimulated speculation about the emergence of a new "violent" woman criminal type by some criminologists and journalists.

There have been few theoretical or research sources that have focused on female criminality. This lack has been reflected in the general absence of this issue in most criminology textbooks. The oversight is due in part to the lack of attention scholars have given to women's behavior. The same sexist bias is also reflected in official crime statistics that portray crime as the dominion of males.[1]

Much of the limited available material advances positivistic assumptions that focus on the idea that female crime is the result of individual traits of the offender. The "new woman criminal" is regarded as an abnormal person who must be seen as a psychological, physiological, or social anomaly in order to correct or rehabilitate her. Those writers who attempt to relate the apparent rise in female crime to the women's movement argue that an increasing masculinization of women has led to their greater involvement in crime. At least one woman criminologist has written recently about the "thousands" of women criminals who have crossed the "boundary line" that she imagines to exist between male and female categories of crime.[2]

In this chapter we will discuss some of the traditional explanations of female crime and relate how these ideas are reflected in the sexism and discrimination evident in society's reaction to female law-violating behavior. Second, we will describe two major models, or orientations, that currently are used to account for the phenomenon of women's crime: the *role reversal model*, which assumes that females who exhibit more masculine traits have a greater predisposition or affinity for such behavior; and the *role validation* or the *opportunity model*, which seeks to account for such behavior in terms of the sexism implicit in the social structure. This model sees female crime as a natural result of the subordinate social, economic, and political position that women occupy in society. To the degree that the status of women is changing—and the women's liberation movement is evidence of such change—we might expect that change will be reflected in fluctuations in the patterns of female crime. This does not mean that sex gender rates are an adequate basis for explaining such changes in behavior. But social change and conflict, together with socioeconomic factors and sexism in everyday life, may put such phenomena in perspective. Therefore, it is necessary to describe briefly the changing status of women in our society.[3] Third, we will analyze official estimates of female crime and show that contrary to the popular image of a "new female criminal," women offenders typically continue to be nonviolent property offenders rather than violent criminals.

CHANGING PERSPECTIVES ON FEMALE CRIME AND DELINQUENCY

Early Explanations of Female Crime

Although criminology has tended to neglect the female offender, there have been more attempts to account for the unique patterns of women's crime than an analysis of past and present criminology texts might suggest. Early explanations, such as those of Lombroso, saw female criminality as the result of innate biological traits, while Freudian psychoanalytic theories attributed such behavior to the female's feelings of inferiority related to penis envy.[4]

In the 1930s, Eleanor and Sheldon Glueck portrayed women, both adult and juvenile offenders, as pathetic creatures whose major problem was the lack of control over their sexual impulses. In a study of five hundred female offenders, they noted that 80 percent had been involved in status offenses—acts of personal or sexual immorality, or running away—while only 12.4 percent had committed property offenses or crimes not related to immorality.[5] The Gluecks recommended policies to cure, correct, and rehabilitate women who displayed "pathological" patterns of immoral and antisocial behavior. These included voluntary sterilization and the extension of juvenile court functions to social workers and psychiatrists who would diagnose and treat maladjusted females during sentences of indeterminate length.[6]

In 1950, Otto Pollak published *The Criminality of Women,* which challenged the assumptions underlying interpretations of both the low rates and kinds of female offenses. He was the first writer to argue that the incidence of crime among women corresponds with their numbers in the population and that the idea that women are more conforming in their behavior than men is a myth. Pollak's perceptions foreshadowed some of the insights of the women's movement of the 1970s and 1980s. He contended that the attitudes and behavior of men would have to change in order to shatter the myth of female conformity and make visible the actual extent of female involvement in crime.[7]

There have been only a few studies about women's offenses in the decades since Pollak's book. Those that have been published have tended either to describe social interactions among women in institutions or prisons or have been case studies of notorious female offenders—in-depth studies of women who have made the headlines.

Female Criminality: Contemporary Perspectives

Two contemporary efforts to account for female criminality might be seen as emerging from some of the earlier efforts to explain law-violating behavior by women. The first views female criminal behavior as related to role reversal, or, more recently, as an outgrowth of the women's movement. The second, also building upon earlier formulations, seeks to explain female criminal behavior as a natural social phenomenon, considering the societally defined sex-role expectations and patterns of sexism in the social structure.

The first perspective relies on assumptions relevant to the positivistic stress on "kinds of people" discussed in chapters 1 and 6.[8] The second emphasizes women's responses to social factors, social change, and conflict; in its more radical, or "critical" manifestations, women's crime is seen as evidence of the "class structure of sexism." [9]

Role Reversal Perspectives: The Liberation Model. The role reversal perspective began with the biological determinism of Lombroso and expanded under the influence of Freud's psychodynamic theory. In its modern version it takes the form of relating the supposed rising rate of female crime to the women's movement. To put it simply, this perspective asserts that women's crime is the result of the "masculinization" of female activity. Female criminals are said to be biologically, psychologically, and socially more "masculine" than women who are not involved in crime.

Have the forces behind women's liberation eroded the social differences between men and women?

A century ago, Cesare Lombroso argued that women were involved in fewer crimes than men because they lacked intelligence. However, those who were involved were more masculine than those who were not. He held that the woman criminal had a "virile cranium," various physiological anomalies such as an abundance of body hair, and a brain capacity resembling that of a man rather than a normal woman.[10]

Freud psychologized that the female personality was related to her organic makeup; that anatomy was destiny. Since Freud saw all women as experiencing penis envy, it was only those who could not "adjust" to their longing for this lack through sexual fulfillment and motherhood who rebelled against their nature and became "unadjusted." They participated in conventional deviance and criminal behavior to compensate for their lack of maleness—that is, the woman criminal was seeking, both symbolically and through actual behavior, to be a man.[11]

With the revival of the women's movement in the late sixties, sociological variations on the role-reversal perspective emerged. A popular work that presents what has been termed a "liberation model" version of role reversal is Freda Adler's recent book, *Sisters in Crime* (1975). Adler refers to "the social revolution of the sixties which has virilized... previously or presumably docile females" and asserts that "the increasing 'masculinization' of female social and criminal behavior forces us to reexamine the bases of her previous feminine limitations."[12] She concludes that "the forces behind equal employment opportunity [and] women's liberation movements... have been causing and reflecting a steady erosion of the social and psychological differences which have traditionally separated men and women."[13] From this perspective it is logical to conclude that as the position of women becomes more like that of men, the more similar they will become in criminal behavior, particularly in the commission of violent crimes. Adler also sees this new equality as being related to the increased number of female delinquents. She argues that the rising number of girls involved in drinking, fighting, stealing, and gang activity is related to the adoption of male behavior by girls and suggests that even adolescents and juveniles are becoming masculinized.[14]

A variation of this perspective focuses on the *human liberation,* or *role convergence,* explanation of female criminal behavior. This explanation is predicated on the assumption that sex-role expectations, especially among the middle class, are converging. Female roles are being masculinized and male roles feminized, especially among the middle class. Middle-class delinquency, as Nancy Wise has suggested, is becoming more similar for both boys and girls. Both sexes are more influenced by a convergence of male and female definitions than are their lower-class peers. This rather peculiar focus sees middle-class boys, because they are becoming more like middle-class girls, as involved in petty and nonviolent delinquency, as contrasted with the more serious violations of lower-class boys.[15]

In a summary of his recent research on middle-class delinquency, Joseph G. Weis reports that although the pattern of involvement for boys and girls was similar, there were significant sex differences in the relative prevalence, incidence, and seriousness of criminal involvement.[16] His data, based upon a two-year community study of over 550 middle-class boys and girls, utilized a variety of research techniques, including anonymous self-reports.[17] They suggest the following conclusions:[18]

1. Although there is considerable "hidden" delinquency among both sexes, the ratio of female to male involvement is about *half* that reported by official arrest statistics (1 to 2.56, as contrasted with the 1 to 6 ratio of female to male delinquency in official statistics).
2. The most frequent offenses reported by both sexes are petty status offenses such as curfew violations, drinking, smoking "pot," and truancy.
3. Boys are more often involved in more serious offenses, while girls report greater involvement in petty property and school-related offenses.
4. While patterns of delinquency for social and property offenses are similar, the girls in Weis's sample were almost completely nonviolent; most of the fighting seemed to be generated by a small group of boys.

If we look closely at the same official statistics Adler uses to support the role-reversal perspective in her argument that there is a "new woman criminal," we will discover that there has been an increase of female property crimes, but *not* violent crimes. Yet in the prologue of her work, Adler asserts flatly that women are committing more crimes than ever before, especially crimes that involve a greater degree of violence. In the following chapter, she refers to *Uniform Crime Report* data she alleges indicate female crimes are increasing at a faster rate than those of males for nearly every index crime, although she notes that men still commit the largest volume of offenses.[19] As noted in Table 5.1, our summary of these same UCR data indicates that the proportion of women arrested for crimes of violence has remained relatively stable since 1953. Moreover, the rate of increase for violent crimes was nearly five times greater among men than women (see Table 5.3). By contrast, the rate of increase in property crimes was considerably greater for women than for men, with the increase largest for larceny.

In 1964, Mary Cameron estimated that 80 percent of women apprehended for larceny were involved in shoplifting.[20] Other types of crime committed by women showing considerable increases since 1953 are fraud and embezzlement, and forgery and counterfeiting (see Table 5.4). As Dorie Klein and June Kress have suggested, these offenses fall in the area of "consumerism" and reflect women's traditional role in "straight" society. This view sees a basic similarity in the roles of shopper and shoplifter, in the use of legal and illicit drugs, and in writing checks and forgery.[21]

Now it should be remembered that official statistics are of questionable validity. The fact that women are underrepresented in crime statistics may be due to several factors. Their behavior may well be different from that of men since they generally occupy different positions in the social structure; law enforcement officials—primarily men—may show greater discretion in dealing with women.[22] Still, since unofficial self-report studies have identified differences as well as similarities in the criminal behavior of males and females, we maintain that the role-reversal or liberation model is too simplistic and lacks support from available data. It fails to offer a logical explanation of female crime.

The Sexism Perspective: Opportunity Models. The sexism role validation or opportunity perspective seeks to explain women's criminality not in terms of malelike behavior, but as an illegitimate expression of femininity. As early as 1923, W. I. Thomas suggested that rather than denying their femininity through becoming more malelike, teenage female delinquents validate their "femininity" in an illegitimate manner. He saw criminal behavior such as shoplifting and prostitution, traditional women's offenses, as behaviors that are role expressive and supportive—thus extensions of the female role.[23] Pollak argued that female offenses may go undetected because they are appendages to traditional roles—for instance, those of teacher, clerk, secretary, or domestic housewife. Thus, typical women's crimes have a low visibility.[24] Kingsley Davis points out the irony between conventional sex exchanges, such as occur in marriage, and the commercial exchange that accompanies the illegal extension of such exchanges in prostitution.[25] And Klein and Kress have argued that women's lack of participation in organized crime suggests that the structure of sexism is reflected even in the underworld. Thus, women are not involved as "big-time" dope dealers any more than they are involved in high finance.[26] In sum, the sexism perspective views female criminality as the behavior of women who take advantage of opportunities, or their lack, as an illegitimate means of fulfilling legitimate roles as defined by a sexist social structure. This, however, does not mean that changing opportunities for women will necessarily bring a change in crime rates. For as Rita Simon has argued:

> As a function both of expanded consciousness, as well as occupational opportunities, women's participation, roles and involvement in crime are expected to change and increase. But the increase will not be uniform or stable across the entire spectrum of crimes. Women's participation in financial and white-collar offenses...should increase as their opportunities...expand.... crimes of violence...are not expected to increase.[27]

This is a far cry, however, from saying that the women's movement is criminogenic. Nor is it the simplistic kind of social determinism that argues that since the 1960s, women have been impelled by blind forces, regardless as to whether their behavior is conventional or illegal. This latter view is illustrated in Adler's statement:

> Women—criminals and legitimate workers alike—are caught up in the gears of a society which is skidding in a drastic turn, and inevitably some of those gears—and their cogs—are going to be broken before the turn is completed and a steady course is once again established. Increasing numbers of broken gears and bits of flying debris will be found leaping from bridges,... and entering banks with pistols in their pockets. If our society is going to protect itself from them...it must make an effort to understand what makes female criminals.[28]

This kind of determinism not only denigrates the human capacities of women to create and adapt to social change, but it also reinforces sexist stereotypes.

If women have lost their restraints, along with their chains, what keeps most women within the law? The choice may be influenced by several factors, including psychological and economic states, which relate to the individual's consciousness of herself as a "woman" within a sexist society. Yet if female crime is basically a reaction to emancipation, what about the nonliberated, or sex-role-constrained woman's criminal behavior? There are data that suggest that women criminals are more oppressed by socioeconomic circumstances, such as the high rate of unemployment among the poorer groups in society, exploitation by males—for instance the manipulation of street prostitutes by pimps—and even physical abuse, than are noncriminal women.[29] To understand the basis of women's crime and its unique patterns, we need insights that go beyond sex-role theories. Unfortunately, these theories seem to persist, as does the popular notion that there is a relationship between women's liberation and crime.

The Women's Movement and Female Offenders. A brief description of what has come to be referred to as "women's liberation" will further diminish the idea of a presumed relationship between the "raised consciousness" of women and female crime, on which Adler's and similar arguments seem to rely. The current women's movement includes under its umbrella a wide range of political philosophies. It includes relatively moderate organizations such as the National Organization for Women (NOW), which stresses reform, as well as more radical groups like Female Liberation First (FLF), which advocates revolution. The historical roots of the movement can be traced to pre–Civil War women's suffrage organizations that remained active through the 1920s. The revival of feminism during the 1960s came about as a result of a number of influences, not least of which was the struggle for civil rights.[30]

Moderate groups within the women's movement emphasize job equality and working within the system to change laws and bring about the passage of the Equal Rights Amendment to the Constitution.[31] More radical groups see the entire system as based upon a sexist ideology that defines the "economic and social position of women in terms of sexual and maternal aspects of female life."[32] As Klein and Kress have argued recently:

> Within each class, women find themselves in defined female roles with a sex-determined lack of opportunity and control. For most women, "class privilege" is fundamentally a male prerogative that a woman marries for and loses if she loses her man. Thus a feminist analysis must be integrated within a class analysis of women's position in order to understand women's oppression and their particular treatment within the different stages of criminal justice.[33]

Despite these obvious differences and conflicts in the movement, the leadership of the various groups tends to be drawn almost exclusively from white, college educated women with middle- or upper middle-class backgrounds. As Rita Simon has suggested, it is too early to tell whether or not the women's movement will alter the activities and lifestyles of those women who have been involved in crime.[34] For example, when a trio of women were asked in an interview by the *Fortune Society News,* a publication put out by ex-offenders,

"If it's equality they want..."

whether or not women in prison relate to the feminist movement, one replied simply "I think so." A second woman responded that "very few of the women relate to what feminists are discussing; few of them are aware." A third replied that "there is very little discussion about women's rights." [35] The statements in Box 1 illustrate the lack of political awareness of some female offenders.

Although female offenders may not relate to the major concerns of the women's movement, some may verbalize such themes to justify their behavior. The double standard has provided a form of legal paternalism at least in such "typical" female offenses as shoplifting and prostitution.[36] However, this lenient treatment by police, prosecutors, and judges may change. As Simon put it, paraphrasing a survey of police respondents: "If it's equality these women want, we'll see that they get it." [37]

The Status of Women: Complexities of the Opportunity Perspective

The question of equality of the sexes has hardly been resolved in American society. Certainly few if any leaders of the women's movement, confronted

> BOX 1
> ### Sisters in Crime
>
> A Florida female parolee: "I don't think women are sitting down and saying, 'Oh, gee, I'll be liberated. I'll rob a bank.' Things are different today. I was living alone for years. It wasn't any real thought of 'liberation' that had to do with what I was doing. I wanted the money. If I was going to put myself out, I intended to aim as high as I could. I got caught, but a lot of others don't. Off the record I'll tell you, they'd never pinch me again because I've learned a lot now. I'd be a lot more careful."
>
> A Pennsylvania female inmate: "I'm not the only one. I know a lot of sisters who got tired of hanging with some dude who took all their money while they took all the heat that was coming down. I know one sister—she cut her pimp up over a five-dollar bill. It wasn't the money, see. It just got to be too much for her. I get out of here and you better believe that no man's going to do a thing on me again. I don't need them. I got it together for myself now. I can handle my own action."
>
> A Chicago female inmate: "It's like what they say, you know, about mountains. You climb them because they're there. Well, that's the way it is with banks and department stores; that's where the money is. It's not a question of whether you're a man or a woman. It's a question of money. That's it. Money."
>
> Source: Freda Adler, *Sisters in Crime* (New York: McGraw-Hill, 1975), pp. 13–14.

with continued opposition to the Equal Rights Amendment to the Constitution, would argue that sexism has been eliminated from our social structure. Still, progress has been made in several areas. The issue is whether or not this progress has been sufficient to provide support for the hypothesis that increased participation by women in the labor force provides increased opportunity for involvement in certain types of offenses. Or, the corollary to this theory: that the "class structure of sexism" is reflected in the marketplace, where both in conventional and nonconforming realms, female behavior is the consequence of a lack of opportunity.[38] An analysis of the limited success of the women's movement suggests plausible support for the sexism or opportunity model. However, this is only one of numerous plausible explanations for recent fluctuations in female crime rates.

Several studies of women and violent crime in the 1960s provide a framework for placing social changes and patterns of female criminality in focus. It has been argued that violent crime is correlated with feelings of alienation and victimization that accompany a lack of social and economic opportunity. Thus, a successful movement providing women with greater participation in the world of work would tend to reduce both feelings of frustration and powerlessness and involvement in crimes of violence. On the other hand, greater participation in the upper realms of the business world would increase the opportunity for women to become involved in nonviolent property crimes and white-collar offenses.[39]

Rita Simon's analysis, however, suggests that the position of women has not changed a great deal since the 1940s. While there has been a continuing trend toward smaller families, and couples may defer having children so the wife may enter or stay in the work force, both marriage and motherhood remain popular. A more recent study by Angus Campbell (1975) provides a slightly different conclusion. Campbell found that child-free marriages are less stressful both among young marrieds and couples over thirty. Further, he found that more women see going to college and working as alternatives to having children.[40]

Simon found, moreover, that even though a majority of working women today are employed in white-collar-type jobs, occupational patterns, as in the 1940s, are based on sex-role definitions. Over twice as many women as men are in the less prestigious and lower paying sales and clerical positions, while the ratio is reversed for managerial and professional positions. In fact, between 1948 and 1971, rather than gaining a greater measure of equality, women actually dropped farther behind in both professional and managerial employment. During those years their numbers in the work force increased by 48 percent, while there was only a 4 percent gain in managerial and professional jobs. At the same time, the number of men in these positions increased by 9 percent.

During those years, the proportion of women completing college increased by 70 percent. Yet only 12 and 14 percent of the women in professional and managerial positions had completed four or more years of college. The comparable figures for men were 61 and 26 percent.

Women have also fallen far behind men in terms of income. In the same occupations, women were shown to receive as little as 37 percent of the annual income of men. In 1968 the median income for women was only 58 percent that of men, while families headed by females subsisted on about 49 percent of the income of male-headed families.[41] The current economic position of women does not seem to be much different than it was before the revival of the women's movement. What changes have occurred lie largely in the less tangible areas of changing consciousness, legal rights, and more positive self-image.[42]

We might tentatively conclude that given the persistence of sexism, the role-validation or opportunity model represents a more viable explanation than the liberation or role-reversal model. However, as a recent study by Stephen Norland and Neal Shover (1977) of the claimed increased involvement of women in aggressive or serious crimes concluded, there is apparently no unambiguous pattern of change in female criminal behavior. They note that if we are to make any progress in understanding the assumed relationship between gender roles and criminality, we will have to clarify two kinds of problems that hinder research and create imprecise theory. These relate first to the lack of clarity used in specifying what makes a given crime aggressive, serious, masculine, or violent, and second to the ambiguity regarding the use of the terms "gender role" or "sex role" as related to such behavior.

With respect to the first point, in an earlier discussion in Chapter 3, we noted that FBI index crimes include both violent and property crimes as "serious." Thus, an act may be classified as serious without being violent or even aggressive in the usual sense of the word. The concept of gender (or sex) role as it relates to criminal involvement suggests (as Norland and Shover note) a cluster of rather imprecise personality traits that are used to differentiate between the sexes. Thus the stereotypical male personality is aggressive and achievement oriented. Those who exhibit such traits may be seen as having a predisposition or affinity for criminal or delinquent behavior. To move beyond the circular reasoning that infers aggressiveness of personality (maleness) from involvement in crimes termed aggressive or serious, calls for more carefully defined theory and systematic research.[43]

HAS THERE BEEN AN INCREASE IN WOMEN'S CRIME?

The UCR data for 1975 show that male arrests outnumbered female arrests by a ratio of 5 to 1. Twenty percent of those arrested for index offenses were women, but only 10 percent of that figure were arrested for violent crimes. As we noted in Chapter 3, reported offenses provide more *reliable* information than arrest rates. However, offenses known or reported to the police do not characteristically indicate the sex of the suspected offender. Furthermore, since arrest rates indicate police activity relative to criminal behavior, the perceptions of women offenders by police may be reflected in some of the increases in the data that we will now discuss.

The bases of the data are the same for both male and female offenders. Tables 5.1 and 5.5 show the average rate of change for Part II offenses, as well as for index or serious crimes from 1953 to 1975. The average rate of change in the percentage of women arrested for all crimes in the entire time span of twenty-three years was .22. In 1975, one out of every 5.4 persons arrested was a woman, as compared with one of 8.2 in 1953. For serious crimes, the ratio in 1975 was one out of 4.1 as contrasted with one in 10 in 1953. The average rate of change for serious crimes was .52 percent per year for the time interval. So

Table 5.1. Percentage of Females Among All Arrests 1953–1975

Year	All Crimes	Serious Crimes[a]
1953	10.84	9.40
1954	10.97	8.89
1955	11.00	9.12
1956	10.91	9.06
1957	10.63	9.29
1958	10.61	9.73
1959	10.68	10.54
1960	11.04	10.95
1961	11.26	11.47
1962	11.47	12.38
1963	11.68	12.65
1964	11.93	13.54
1965	12.12	14.37
1966	12.33	14.80
1967	12.67	15.03
1968	13.08	15.04
1969	13.82	16.58
1970	14.58	18.04
1971	15.07	18.34
1972	15.27	19.25
1973	15.30	21.10
1974	16.10	19.00
1975	15.70	19.50
Average rate of change 1953–1975	0.22% per year	0.50% per year
Average rate of change 1960–1975	0.31	0.64
Average rate of change 1970–1975	0.23	0.78

[a] Serious crimes include six of seven index crimes, excluding rape.

Source: Adapted from Rita Simon, *Women and Crime* (Lexington, Mass.: D. C. Heath, 1975), Table 4–1, p. 37; and FBI *Uniform Crime Reports* (Washington, D.C.: U.S. Government Printing Office, 1973, 1974, 1975), pp. 131, 181, 191.

the rate of increase among women is greater for serious crimes than for all offenses. And the rate of increase was greater for the interval from 1960 to 1970 than it was for the next five years for all crimes.

Table 5.2 shows that the proportion of female arrests for serious crimes compared to the total of females arrested was less than that of males (1 of 12.8 versus 1 of 10.9). However, the average rate of change over the twenty-three years was greater for women than for men.

Table 5.2. Males and Females Arrested for Index Crimes as Percentages of Their Respective Sex Cohorts Arrested for All Crimes, 1953–1975

Year	Females Arrested for Serious Crimes[a] as Percent of All Females Arrested	Males Arrested for Serious Crimes[a] as Percent of All Males Arrested	Difference Column 2 and Column 3
1953	7.8	9.2	−1.4
1954	8.2	10.3	−2.1
1955	8.5	10.4	−1.9
1956	8.2	10.3	−2.1
1957	9.3	10.8	−1.5
1958	9.9	10.9	−1.0
1959	10.6	10.8	−0.2
1960	12.4	12.6	−0.2
1961	13.4	13.2	+0.2
1962	14.6	13.3	+1.3
1963	15.9	14.4	+1.5
1964	18.0	15.6	+2.4
1965	18.9	15.5	+3.4
1966	20.1	16.1	+4.0
1967	20.8	16.9	+3.9
1968	20.7	17.8	+2.9
1969	22.2	17.9	+4.3
1970	23.8	18.4	+5.4
1971	24.2	19.2	+5.0
1972	25.2	19.2	+6.0
1973	25.8	20.3	+5.5
1974	28.2	23.0	+5.2
1975	29.4	22.7	+6.7
Average rate of change 1953–1975	0.96% per year	0.58% per year	
Average rate of change 1960–1975	1.1	0.67	
Average rate of change 1970–1975	1.8	0.68	

[a] Excludes rape

Source: Adapted from Rita Simon, *Women and Crime* (D. C. Heath, 1975), Table 4–2, p. 37; and FBI *Uniform Crime Report* (Washington, D.C.: U.S. Government Printing Office, 1973, 1974, 1975), pp. 131, 181, 191.

We referred previously to the apparent confusion of serious with violent crime both in the popular mind and the FBI data. This conclusion may have helped create the erroneous popular image of the "new female criminal." For instance, UCR data indicate that twice as many females were arrested for property crimes as for violent crimes. And violent crimes made up 10.3 percent of total female offenses in 1975—far less than the high of 13.5 percent in 1956.

In 1975, one out of 3.6 persons arrested for property offenses was a woman, as opposed to one in 12 in 1953. This increase in property offenses since 1953, especially marked since 1967, supports the hypothesis that "a woman's participation in selective crimes will increase as her employment opportunities expand and as her interests, desires, and definitions of self shift from a more traditional to a more liberated view."

Differences between men and women in index, property, and violent crimes are shown in Table 5.3. The increase in violent crimes among men is considerably greater than among women, despite the fact that it leveled off during the last three years of the twenty-three-year period. But for property offenses, the increase among women is twice as great as among men, except for the period from 1970 to 1975.

Table 5.4 presents the percentage of women arrested for Part I offenses. It shows that of the six crimes* included in this category, only larceny/theft shows a decided increase between 1953 and 1975. Beginning in 1960, the proportion of women arrested for this offense has been greater than for any of the other offenses, including the three types of violent crimes. Until 1959 the proportion arrested for aggravated assault, homicide, and larceny was about even. But by 1975 the percentage for larceny had doubled, while the other two categories had declined slightly.

When these same violent offenses are compared for both sexes, the differences are negligible. Robbery and aggravated assault increased more among men than women (see Table 5.5). Yet while arrests of women for larceny increased three to four times as much as arrests of men, auto theft and burglary remained essentially male offenses.

Trends in female arrests for selected Part II offenses are analyzed in Table 5.6. In 1975 the ratio of women to men arrested for forgery was 1 to 2.5, as compared to 1 to 4 in 1972. Similarly, the embezzlement and fraud ratios were 1 to 2 in 1975, compared with the 1 to 3.5 figure found by Simon in her earlier analysis (1972). If these trends continue, the proportions of men and women arrested for these white-collar offenses will be equal by the turn of the century. The same may be true for larceny, while despite the headlines, the proportion of women involved in violent crimes may actually decrease.[44]

Table 5.7 ranks men and women in terms of the twelve offenses for which they were most frequently apprehended in 1972 and 1975. Again, the increase in larceny arrests is greater in women than in men, while drunkenness shows a

---

* We have omitted the seventh Part I offense, rape.

Table 5.3 Females and Males Arrested for Violent and Property Crimes as Percentage of All Arrests in Their Respective Sex Cohorts, 1953–1975

Year	Violent Crimes Female	Violent Crimes Male	Property Crimes Female	Property Crimes Male
1953	2.2	2.0	5.6	7.2
1954	2.2	2.1	6.0	8.2
1955	2.3	2.1	6.2	8.3
1956	2.3	1.9	5.9	8.4
1957	2.2	1.8	7.1	9.0
1958	2.1	1.9	7.8	9.0
1959	2.3	1.9	8.3	8.9
1960	2.5	2.4	9.9	10.2
1961	2.5	2.4	10.9	10.8
1962	2.4	2.4	12.2	10.9
1963	2.5	2.4	14.5	12.0
1964	2.6	2.6	15.4	13.0
1965	2.6	2.7	16.3	12.8
1966	2.8	3.0	17.3	13.1
1967	2.8	3.2	18.0	13.7
1968	2.5	3.5	18.2	14.3
1969	2.6	3.6	19.6	14.3
1970	2.5	3.6	21.3	14.8
1971	2.7	3.2	21.5	15.3
1972	2.9	4.4	22.3	14.8
1973	3.0	4.7	22.8	15.5
1974	3.0	5.1	25.1	17.9
1975	3.0	4.9	26.3	17.7
Average rate of change 1953–1975	+0.04%	+0.14%	+0.94%	+0.48%
Average rate of change 1960–1975	+0.03	+0.17	+1.09	+0.53
Average rate of change 1970–1975	+0.14	+0.26	+1.0	+0.58

Source: Adapted from Rita Simon, *Women and Crime* (D. C. Heath, 1975), Table 4–4, p. 39; and FBI *Uniform Crime Report* (Washington, D.C.: U.S. Government Printing Office, 1973, 1974, 1975), pp. 131, 181, 191.

decrease for both males and females. Disorderly conduct shows only a mild increase for women and a decrease for men, while narcotic and liquor offenses have increased at about the same rate for both sexes during the three-year interval. The changes in drunkenness and disorderly conduct arrests may reflect laws that have decriminalized public intoxication in several jurisdictions.

Recent data suggest that the trends indicated by Simon three years earlier are continuing. Namely, a greater proportion of women are being arrested for serious property crimes than for other Part I and II offenses. Moreover, this in-

Table 5.4 Females Arrested as Percentage of All Arrests for Index Crimes, 1953–1975

Year	Criminal Homicide	Robbery	Aggravated Assault	Burglary	Larceny/ Theft	Auto Theft
1953	14.1	4.3	15.9	2.0	13.9	2.6
1954	14.2	4.2	15.9	2.2	13.0	2.5
1955	14.2	4.2	16.0	2.3	13.3	2.6
1956	14.8	4.3	17.6	2.3	12.6	2.5
1957	14.7	3.9	17.5	2.0	13.2	2.7
1958	16.4	4.5	15.7	2.4	14.3	3.2
1959	16.8	4.6	16.4	2.7	15.4	3.2
1960	16.1	4.6	15.3	2.8	16.8	3.6
1961	15.9	4.9	15.2	3.2	18.0	3.7
1962	17.2	5.1	14.7	3.6	19.6	3.9
1963	15.9	4.9	14.9	3.3	20.1	3.7
1964	16.6	5.3	14.4	3.7	21.4	4.3
1965	16.3	5.3	14.4	3.8	23.2	4.2
1966	15.9	5.1	14.0	3.8	24.0	4.1
1967	15.4	5.2	13.6	4.1	24.8	4.3
1968	15.4	5.5	13.1	4.1	25.2	4.9
1969	14.8	6.3	13.2	4.3	27.2	5.1
1970	14.8	6.2	13.3	4.6	29.0	5.0
1971	16.0	6.4	13.9	4.8	29.1	6.0
1972	15.6	6.6	13.9	5.1	30.8	5.7
1973	15.1	6.8	13.2	5.4	31.5	6.0
1974	14.6	6.8	13.4	5.4	30.7	6.5
1975	15.6	7.0	13.1	5.4	31.2	.7
Average rate of change 1953–1975	+0.07%	+0.12%	−0.13%	+0.15%	+0.79%	−0.09%
Average rate of change 1960–1975	−0.03	+0.16	−0.13	+0.17	+0.96	−0.19
Average rate of change 1970–1975	+0.16	+0.16	+0.08	+0.16	+0.44	−0.86

Source: Adapted from Rita Simon, *Women and Crime* (D. C. Heath, 1975), Table 4–5, p. 40; and FBI, *Uniform Crime Reports* (Washington, D.C.: U.S. Government Printing Office, 1973, 1974, 1975), pp. 131, 181, 191.

crease in arrests for serious offenses by females can be related to their increased involvement in larceny/theft.[45] For while in 1953 one woman was arrested for larceny for every seven men, by 1972 the figure had jumped to 1 to 3, and in 1975 the gap had narrowed to 1 to 2.5. Yet despite media portrayals of a "new woman criminal," the proportion of women charged with violent crimes has remained relatively stable, especially in the category of homicide. Furthermore, although the rate of increase in arrests for property offenses (except burglary) has been greater for women than for men, there still are far fewer women arrested than men.

Table 5.5 Percentage of Total Arrests of Females and Males for Index Crimes and Selected Part II Offenses, 1970–1975

Offense	Males 1970	Males 1975	Males Percent change	Males Average rate change 1970–1975 (percent of total)	Females 1970	Females 1975	Females Percent change	Females Average rate change 1970–1975 (percent of total)
Index Crimes								
Criminal homicide and nonnegligent manslaughter	84.6				15.4			
Robbery	93.9	93.0	−0.90	0.0 +0.04	6.10	7.0	+0.90	0.0 0.0
Aggravated assault	87.4	86.9	−0.50	+0.14	12.60	13.1	+0.50	+0.08
Burglary	95.3	94.6	−0.70	+0.34	4.70	5.4	+0.70	+0.12
Larceny/Theft	72.1	68.8	−3.30	+0.34	27.90	31.2	+3.30	+0.88
Motor vehicle theft	94.9	93.0	−1.90	−0.08	5.10	7.0	+1.90	0.00
Total index offense	83.1	80.5	−2.60	0.68	16.90	19.5	+2.60	1.8
Part II Offenses:								
Embezzlement and fraud	73.0	66.0	−7.0	−0.02	27.0	34.0	+7.0	0.02
Forgery and counterfeiting	76.3	71.1	−5.20	0.02	23.7	28.9	+5.20	0.06
Narcotic drug laws	84.4	86.2	+1.80	0.28	15.6	13.8	−1.80	0.0
Offenses against family and children	91.1	88.3	−2.80	0.0	8.9	11.7	+2.80	0.04
Total all arrests	85.6 (8,013,645)	84.3	−1.3	—	14.4	15.7	+1.3	—

Source: FBI, *Uniform Crime Reports, 1970–1975* (Washington, D.C.: U.S. Government Printing Office, 1971, 1976), pp. 124–91.

Table 5.6 Other Crimes: Percentage of Total Arrests for Various Crimes of Females, 1953–1975

Year	Embezzlement and Fraud	Forgery and Counterfeiting	Offenses Against Family and Children	Narcotic Drug Laws	Prostitution and Commercialized Vice
1953	18.3	14.0	9.3	15.7	73.1
1954	14.4	13.4	9.6	17.5	70.1
1955	15.6	15.2	9.8	17.1	68.8
1956	15.5	16.6	9.1	16.3	62.9
1957	14.4	14.8	9.0	15.6	69.2
1958	14.3	15.1	8.6	16.4	69.0
1959	14.9	16.2	8.9	16.2	65.2
1960	15.7	16.8	9.7	14.6	73.5
1961	15.7	17.5	11.2	15.4	71.8
1962	17.6	18.1	11.0	15.1	76.1
1963	18.3	18.7	11.5	14.2	77.0
1964	19.5	19.3	11.3	14.1	81.2
1965	20.7	19.2	11.0	13.4	77.6
1966	21.8	20.9	12.1	13.8	79.3
1967	23.4	21.4	11.4	13.7	77.2
1968	24.4	22.3	10.9	15.0	78.0
1969	26.3	23.2	11.4	15.5	79.5
1970	27.8	24.4	11.3	15.7	79.1
1971	27.4	24.8	11.6	16.3	77.4
1972	29.7	25.4	12.3	15.7	73.5
1973	27.5	26.7	9.2	14.5	75.5
1974	29.5	28.6	11.9	14.2	75.6
1975	32.7	28.9	11.7	6.2	74.3
Average rate of change 1953–1975	+0.75%	+0.68%	+0.11%	−0.10%	+0.05%
Average rate of change 1960–1975	+1.13	+0.74	+0.15	−0.08	+0.35
Average rate of change 1970–1975	+1.27	+0.70	+0.08	−1.82	+0.76

Source: Adapted from Rita Simon, *Women and Crime* (Lexington, Mass.: D. C. Heath, 1975), p. 43; and FBI *Uniform Crime Reports* (Washington, D.C.: U.S. Government Printing Office, 1973, 1974, 1975), pp. 131, 181, 191.

Looking further at Part II offenses, tables 5.5 and 5.6 show that white-collar-type crimes—such as embezzlement and fraud, and forgery and counterfeiting—displayed the greatest increases, particularly since the 1960s. If these rates of change continue, women may soon commit as many of these offenses as their male counterparts. It should be noted that Norland and Shover, using the same FBI data, suggest that the increase in women arrested for robbery between 1966 and 1975 is of considerable magnitude—about 2 percent for the nine-year period—although they concede that the increase is greater for non-

Table 5.7 Rank Order of Offenses for Which Females and Males Were Most Likely to Be Arrested, 1972 and 1975

Rank	Offense	Percent Total Arrests	Offense	Percent Total Arrests
	Females, 1972		**Males, 1972**	
1.	Larceny/theft	20.2	Drunkenness	22.9
2.	Drunkenness	9.8	Drunken driving	9.0
3.	Disorderly conduct	8.5	Disorderly conduct	8.5
4.	Narcotic drug laws	6.0	Larceny/theft	8.2
5.	Other assaults	4.1	Narcotic drug laws	5.8
6.	Drunken driving	3.8	Burglary	4.7
7.	Prostitution	3.4	Other assaults	4.5
8.	Liquor laws	2.7	Liquor laws	2.9
9.	Embezzlement and fraud	2.4	Aggravated assault	2.2
10.	Aggravated assault	2.0	Robbery	1.8
	All other	37.1	All other	29.5
	Total	100.0	Total	100.0
	Females, 1975		**Males, 1975**	
1.	Larceny/theft	23.7	Drunkenness	16.2
2.	Disorderly conduct	8.8	Drunken driving	12.4
3.	Drunkenness	6.6	Larceny/theft	9.8
4.	Drunken driving	5.8	Disorderly conduct	7.7
5.	Narcotic drug laws	5.6	Narcotic drug laws	6.5
6.	Other assaults	3.9	Burglary	6.3
7.	Liquor laws	3.0	Other assaults	4.5
8.	Prostitution	3.0	Liquor laws	3.4
9.	Embezzlement and fraud	2.1	Aggravated assault	2.6
10.	Aggravated assault	2.1	Vandalism	2.4
	All other	35.4	All other	28.2
	Total	100.0	Total	100.0

Source: Rita Simon, *Women and Crime* (Lexington, Mass.: D. C. Heath, 1975), p. 45; and FBI, *Uniform Crime Reports, 1975* (Washington, D.C.: U.S. Government Printing Office, 1976), p. 191.

violent crimes. The point is that 9,138 females arrested for robbery in 1975 represent a ratio of females to males arrested for this offense of 1 to 13.3 — a notable gap. Certainly a different type of female offender would have to emerge before this difference could be wiped out.[46]

We have inferred criminal activity from these data on arrests. However, if as Pollak has argued, women commit as many offenses as men, but police discretion toward female offenders is influenced by their chivalrous attitudes, distortions may be present in the data.[47] Since the arrest rates for women vary by type of offense, the double standard does not explain the extent of change that has taken place. For there is no reason to assume that women suspected of homicide or assault would be treated more leniently by the police than suspected property offenders.

Consequently, changes in the manner in which police discretion is applied do not explain the consistent increases in property violations by women over the past decade—or the lack of increases in violent offenses. It would seem more prudent to conclude that changing family structures, such as the increase in female-headed households, together with the greater participation of women in the work force, provide more opportunity for women to become involved in types of crime once thought of as male offenses. Acknowledging this fact "assumes that women have no greater store of morality than men. Their propensities to commit crimes do not differ, but in the past their opportunities have been much more limited." [48] To acknowledge that the double standard or sexist social patterns are now less pervasive in property crimes, however, is a far cry from asserting that the women's movement has spawned a "new female criminal."

THE CRIMINAL JUSTICE SYSTEM AND PATTERNS OF SEXISM

Criminologists who have turned their attention from the offender to society's reaction to crime have been slow to focus attention on sexist patterns that prevail in the criminal justice system. The assumption seems to have been that since female crimes were infrequent, those women who were processed in the system were dealt with kindly, even deferentially.

In focusing attention upon institutional sexism, the women's movement has also brought to light discriminatory sexist practices in the criminal justice system. It was not difficult identifying unequal treatment afforded female offenders, for the criminal justice system reflects the sexist structures and patterns of the larger social system.

An analysis of rape laws by Camille Le Grand illustrates the position of American women relative to the law. Le Grand contends that rape laws are intended to protect women as sexual property of males, rather than to protect women from rape. If such laws were actually designed to protect women, she argues, they would protect them against violence and force in all sexual encounters, including sexual assaults by husbands against their wives. Her analysis notes that the rape victim often is treated as though she were the guilty person. When a violation takes place, the police interrogation of the victim and the cross-examination that ensues should a trial occur focus upon her prior sexual history and the nature of her relationship with the alleged offender.[49] The manner with which such offenses have been dealt has led to various proposals for reform both of the legal definition of rape and the way the criminal justice system deals with rape victims. (Rape, along with other crimes of violence, is examined more fully in Chapter 8.)

Will he "throw the book at her" or give her preferential treatment?

The Female Offender in Court

There are two divergent views concerning the manner in which female offenders are processed and legally labeled as criminal in the judicial phase of the system. One is that they are given preferential treatment and are likely to fare better than their male counterparts. The other is that the courts are harsher in their dealings with women. In this latter view, a female defendant runs the risk of getting "the book thrown at her," because the judge might believe that she is acting contrary to women's nature by being involved in criminal behavior.[50]

One indication of preferential treatment of female offenders by trial judges is described by S. S. Nagel and L. J. Weitzman as a double-edged form of paternalism. This paternalistic treatment is likely to have favorable effects with women less likely to be held in jail during the pretrial period than their male counterparts and more apt to receive lighter sentences if they are convicted. On the other hand, they are less likely to be provided defense counsel, a preliminary hearing, or a trial.

In a comparison of the treatment given women versus that accorded poor male offenders, both charged with assault and larceny, Nagel and Weitzman found patterns of paternalism for women charged with both offenses. Women were more likely to be jailed while awaiting trial when charged with assault. The researchers attribute this stricter dealing in assault cases to the judges' perception of such offenses as being malelike. Thus the women were treated as male offenders would be.[51]

In her studies of juvenile court processing of female delinquents, however, Meda Chesney-Lind noted a contrasting form of sexual discrimination. In many states boys are committed only for delinquency—offenses that would be considered crimes if carried out by adults—while girls may be institutionalized for status offenses. And although self-report studies show that girls frequently admit to nonstatus law-violating offenses, there tends to be more concern with their sexual misconduct than their "delinquent" acts.[52]

In her study of juveniles in Honolulu, Chesney-Lind notes that girls were detained longer in juvenile detention than boys, even though their offenses tended to be less serious. The girls were held for an average of 9.3 days in detention in contrast with 8.9 days for boys. The contrast of her findings with the data of Nagel and Weitzman would seem to call for more carefully designed research.[53]

It may be that some new trends are emerging in the treatment of female offenders by the courts. Yet even here, the evidence is ambiguous. In her analysis of men and women convicted in U.S. district courts between 1964 and 1972, Simon found an increase of 62 percent for women, compared with 20.3 percent for men. The highest conviction rates paralleled those crimes where arrest rates were highest—fraud, embezzlement, and forgery.[54]

A similar analysis of California data showed a 31 percent increase in the proportion of women convicted between 1960 and 1972. Although there had been an increase in arrests for property offenses and a decrease in violent index-type offenses, there was an increase of 19 percent in convictions for violent crimes and a decrease of 13 percent in property crimes. However, Simon found that women who pleaded not guilty in California were more likely to be acquitted than males. Furthermore, women charged with typically male offenses, such as robbery or auto theft, were treated as preferentially as those charged with typical female offenses. Evidently, there is little support for the idea that women involved in male-type crimes are treated more harshly.[55]

In her comparisons of the proportion of women committed to California prisons relative to the number convicted, Simon found that the percentage incarcerated was less than half the percentage of men sentenced for property offenses and slightly more than half for violent offenses (see Table 5.8).[56]

The Double Standard and Class and Racial Factors

It has been claimed that equality between the sexes would lead to equal penalties for similar criminal offenses. But the data in Table 5.8 show that the low rate at which adult women are sentenced to prison parallels their low rate

Table 5.8 Percentage of Convicted Persons Sentenced to Prison, by Type of Offense and Sex, 1967, 1968, 1969

	1967 Percent Committed		1968 Percent Committed		1969 Percent Committed		Mean Rates
Offense	Females	Males	Females	Males	Females	Males	Male & Female
Homicide	27.0	44.9	36.8	45.0	34.4	59.1	1.5
Robbery	16.1	36.0	16.7	31.2	28.0	42.1	1.9
Assault	7.6	13.4	5.3	11.5	6.0	11.3	1.9
Burglary	7.5	11.4	3.5	9.5	7.4	11.8	1.6
Theft	8.0	21.1	7.8	50.6	16.6	28.8	3.6
Forgery (checks)	8.3	15.7	5.7	12.8	3.6	10.0	2.3
Narcotics	0.9	7.6	3.3	5.6	2.1	4.6	4.1
All above	7.4	15.0	6.2	13.1	5.1	11.8	2.2
Violent crimes[a]	13.9	27.4	14.1	23.9	14.3	27.3	1.9
Property crimes	8.1	14.6	5.9	14.1	6.2	14.0	2.2

[a] Homicide, robbery and assault
Source: Adapted from Rita Simon, *Women and Crime* (Lexington, Mass.: D. C. Heath, 1975), p. 76.

of conviction. Some states have sentencing statutes that allow the minimum part of a woman's indeterminate sentence to be set by a parole board in a closed hearing without benefit of legal counsel. This procedure is in contrast with an open court hearing conducted by a judge in the presence of counsel that is customary for men.

This dual standard has stimulated one advocate of women's rights to argue for passage of the Equal Rights Amendment on the grounds that it would eliminate longer sentences for females that result from indeterminate sentences. Since the 1920s, a number of state and federal court decisions have held that such discriminatory sentencing laws were constitutional. Upon reviewing such cases in Pennsylvania, New Jersey, Maryland, Maine, Massachusetts, Iowa, and Ohio, L. Temen concluded (1973) that the Equal Rights Amendment, rather than judicial review, would be the most effective way for women to obtain equality under the Fifth and Fourteenth Amendments.[57]

Simon's analysis of conviction rates in Britain contrasts with the generalizations made in popular news stories. She notes that in 1969 to 1971, the percentage of women convicted for violent crimes in that country varied from 5.4 to 5.8 — about one woman for every eighteen men convicted. Furthermore, the rate of convictions and the rate of increase for property crimes were proportionately greater than they were for violent crimes. Yet it is the sensational violent female crimes that are splashed across the headlines and receive special attention on the nightly TV news, even though they are of little significance for identifying trends.[58]

It is too easy to dismiss the differential treatment of girls and women in our courts as evidence of the last vestiges of chivalry in our criminal justice system. However benign or paternalistic the system, it is necessary that this treatment be seen as an example of sexist means of social control that pervades the larger society. As Klein and Kress argue, women are penalized less severely than men, because due to their numbers, economic marginality, and stereotypical passivity, they are not seen as serious threats to the social order. Perhaps if their social position really changes, these patterns of leniency will be strained.

Klein and Kress argue cogently that in the case of crimes defined as sexual—for example, prostitution and juvenile promiscuity—women are dealt with more severely than males involved in such behavior. Female shoplifters must bear a double social stigma, for scholars such as Pollak conceive of such offenses as a sublimation of female sexuality. And while women who may be involved in prostitution for economic motives are defined as sexual deviants, the men who patronize them—the "johns"—generally are not stigmatized at all.[59]

Even in the illegal marketplace there is a hierarchy of status that affects the manner in which a woman may be convicted and further stigmatized. As Giallombardo's study of the Federal Reformatory for Women at Alderson, West Virginia, has shown, poor women from all racial groups are disproportionately represented in prisons. Although we might think of those sentenced to federal prison as representing the more affluent offenders, one-third of the six hundred inmates were from service occupations, such as laundry workers

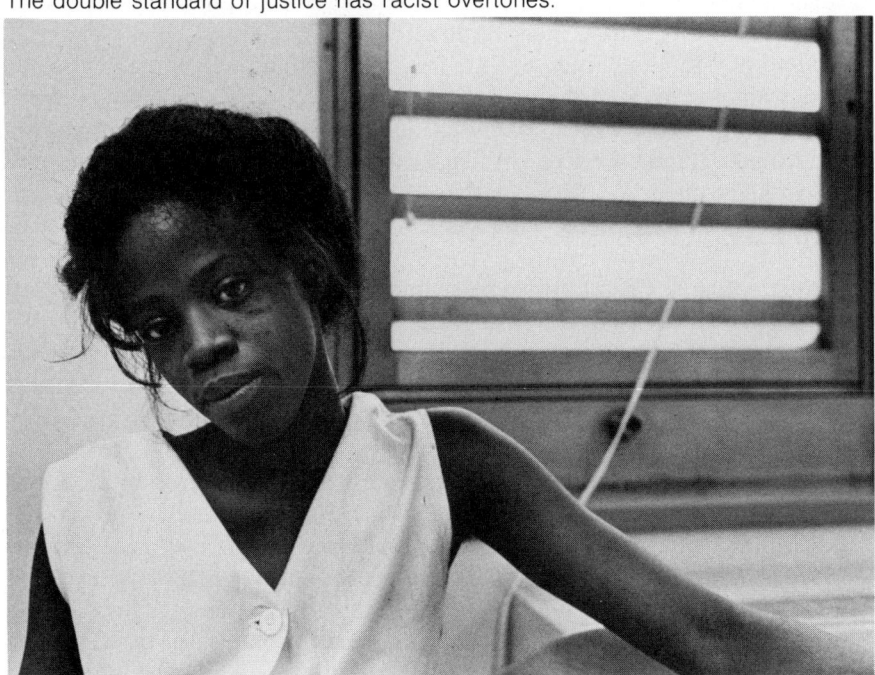

The double standard of justice has racist overtones.

and waitresses, and half had no more than a grade school education.[60]

Among prostitutes, it is the attractive call girls—usually white—who typically earn more money and avoid arrest. The working-class streetwalkers—often blacks—are more vulnerable and often are victimized by "revolving-door" justice, short terms in jail that result from efforts to "clean up" the streets. The treatment of these women, who are at the mercy of police discretion, defense lawyers, bail bondsmen, and politicians, does not qualify as chivalrous.[61]

Women and the Corrections System: Benign Neglect

There are so few women in American prisons that little attention has been focused on the plight of these "forgotten offenders" until recent years. The federal and state prisons are overcrowded with more than 300,000 inmates—more than ever before in our history. But women made up only 4.6 percent of the prison population in 1978, compared with 4.9 percent in 1965. A recent report on prison overcrowding focused almost exclusively on men's prisons, though one crowded women's prison in Arizona was described.[62]

The fact that there are so few women committed to prison usually means that a woman is incarcerated at a greater distance from her home community than most males. Forty-two of the fifty states have only one prison for women; the rest have none. And there are only three federal institutions for women in the entire country.

There is also a wider range of ages and a more heterogeneous population in women's prisons than in men's. And although women may be allowed more social and physical amenities, few job training programs are available. For instance, while the average number of vocational programs available to men is 10, the average number for women is 2.7. The choice is also limited, usually to clerical training, food services, cosmetology, nurse's aide, and keypunch training. So while women are less likely than men to go to prison, if they do go they are less likely to acquire vocational skills that can keep them out of prison in the future.

Preferential treatment does not seem to operate for parole. Statistics show that women are paroled at only a slightly higher percentage than their proportion in the nation's prison population. However, once paroled, women seem to be more successful than men at staying out of prison. Exceptions include those with a history of drug abuse and, as with males, those with prior prison records.[63]

Differential treatment of women in the criminal justice system, although often benign, has been a double-edged sword. Although women are not oppressed in the way that racial and ethnic minorities may be, the paternalistic manner in which they are processed assumes that their gender roles have already predisposed them to fulfill certain docile roles. Not only are they labeled as "criminals," but their unequal position in society is reaffirmed in the process as well.

SUMMARY

Since the 1970s, the mass media and at least one criminologist have painted a common theme regarding women and crime. Women have been pictured as being involved in more violent law violations than at any previous time in our history. This emergence of a "new woman criminal," with her greater proclivity for violence, has been attributed to the women's movement. When four women made the FBI's list of the ten "most wanted" fugitives in 1970, it seemed to support the idea that the image of a "new woman criminal" was accurate.

The analysis we sketched of national crime data over the past several decades, however, results in a different image—one lacking the dramatic impact of the mass media's new woman criminal. Certainly, women's involvement in serious crime has increased, especially since 1967. Nevertheless, the type of offenses in which women's participation has risen has been property crime. Economic crimes such as larceny, embezzlement, fraud, and forgery are attracting women—not assault, homicide, or robbery.

This differential increase in women's crimes may be related to the changing status of women in only a tenuous manner. With more women working outside the home, there are greater opportunities for offenses such as embezzlement or fraud.

Working women may have an enhanced feeling of independence, which is reinforced by the new self-image engendered by the women's movement. And this new felt independence is buttressed by new laws. These factors may relate to the decrease of violent female crime. Women with a more positive self-image may be less likely to strike out against traditional targets, like their husbands or their husband's female friends.

The emerging status of women may provide them with a new social and legal status. Although it will vary by socioeconomic class, women may choose increasingly to live without dependence on a man. Consequently, violent female offenses may decline or remain stable, but there may well be a continued increase in property offenses. There are no firm data on either the national or international level to support the predictions of the mass media that an increasing proportion of younger women will be involved in terrorism and violent crimes. The Susan Saxes, Patty Hearsts, Ulrike Meinhofs, and Emily Harrises will doubtless remain as rare a phenomenon on the contemporary scene as Ma Barker and Bonnie Parker were in earlier decades.

ADDITIONAL READINGS

Adler, Freda. *Sisters in Crime: The Rise of the New Female Criminal.* New York: McGraw-Hill, 1975.
    A popular psycho-social analysis of the roots of women's crime that relates the rise in such behaviors to the women's movement.

Anderson, Etta A. "The 'Chivalrous' Treatment of the Female Offender in the Arms of the Criminal Justice System." *Social Problems* 23, no. 3 (February 1976): 350–68.

> Presents three characterizations of the female offender that have influenced the persistence of the idea that chivalry pervades the criminal justice system's treatment of women.

Giallombardo, Rose. *Society of Women: A Study of Women's Prisons.* New York: John Wiley & Sons, 1966.

> A study of the social organization of women's prisons, with particular emphasis on the informal organization of inmate social relations, including sexual behavior.

Klein, Dorie and June Kress. "Any Woman's Blues: A Critical Overview of Women, Crime and the Criminal Justice System." *Crime and Social Justice* 5 (1976).

> A radical critique of the criminal justice system and the sexism inherent in the laws and their enforcement relative to women offenders.

Simon, Rita James. *Women and Crime.* Lexington, Mass.: D. C. Heath, 1975.

> This book effectively uses statistics and their analysis to portray the extent and nature of female involvement in crime. Simon's careful use of data challenges the idea of a "new female criminal."

PART THREE

Theoretical Perspectives and Crime Patterns as Behavior Systems

6 Theoretical Perspectives on Crime and Criminality
7 Professional and Organized Crime Behavior Systems
8 Patterns of Violent Crime
9 Avocational and Commonplace Crime
10 White-Collar Crime Patterns
11 Victimless Crimes and Public Order Crime Patterns

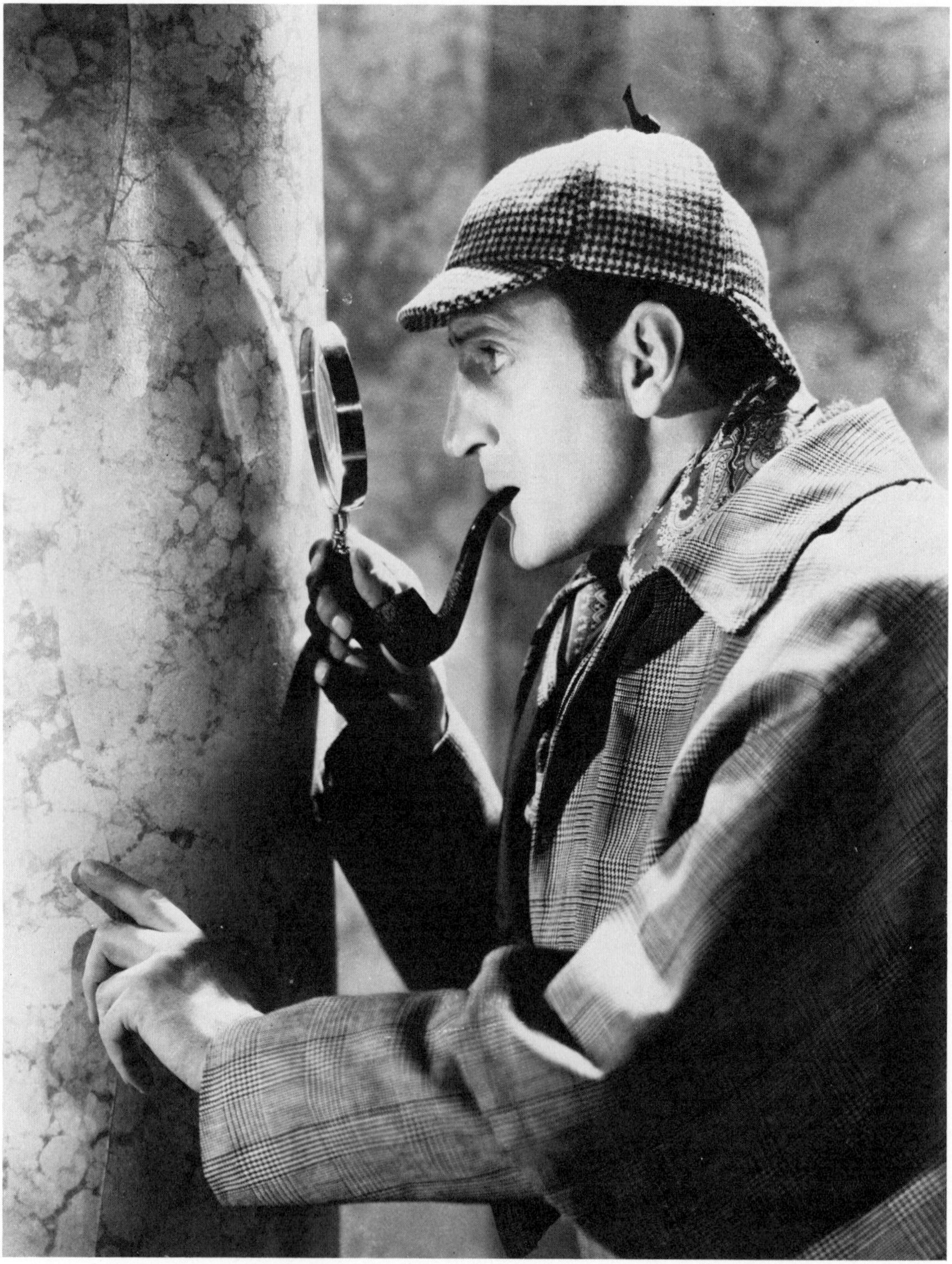

Greed, love of pleasure, lust, idleness, anger, hatred, revenge: these are the chief causes of crime. These passions and desires are shared by rich and poor alike, by the educated and uneducated. They are inherent in human nature; the germ is in every man.
—A French judge, quoted in H. B. Irving, A Book of Remarkable Criminals

THEORETICAL PERSPECTIVES ON CRIME AND CRIMINALITY

This chapter will present the major theories that try to explain criminality and criminal behavior. In Chapter 1 we discussed the persistent influence of the ideas of the *positive school* of criminology, which focused on the "criminal" in seeking to explain crime. Now we will turn our attention to theoretical perspectives that seek to explain criminality as the result of the criminal definitions applied during the process of societal reaction to crime—the enforcement and administration of the criminal law. Although these explanations—one focusing upon the *actor* in seeking to explain the behavior of those who violate the law, the other emphasizing the role of the legal system and the criminal definitions it ascribes to the individual accorded the social status of "criminal"—seem contradictory and even mutually exclusive, this need not be the case. We will attempt to show how the two perspectives are complementary. Since we assume that crime is a phenomenon that includes a diverse range of behaviors, we will suggest an approach involving a convergence of the criminal behavior and societal reaction approaches. In coming to grips with describing both criminal behavior and how certain acts are defined as crimes, it is necessary to show the relationship between those acts legally defined as crimes and relevant social factors. We will use a scheme based on the concept of *criminal careers*, which will incorporate both perspectives in analyzing crime and criminality.[1]

THE QUEST FOR ANSWERS: WHY DO PEOPLE BREAK THE LAW?

In its search for answers to why do some people commit crimes, criminology has become preoccupied with the problem of identifying types of persons—people with special biological, psychological, or social characteristics—who

Prescientific quest for explanations of crime—Devil theories!

become law violators.[2] The stress on why individuals behave in a criminal or delinquent manner relates to the widespread public concern with the correction, reformation, or rehabilitation of those who have broken society's laws.

This correctional impulse as an underlying rationale for the effort to identify criminal types is not the invention of modern thinkers. Before the Age of Reason, various versions of the "demon" theory were accepted as an explanation of crime—"the Devil made me do it!" The causes of deviant behavior were thought to be found in the relationship between an individual and the spiritual world. Criminals were considered sinners. Indeed, there was little distinction made between crime and sin until after the time of Henry VIII in England, when much of the behavior once considered immoral or sinful came to be seen as criminal, and those committing such acts came to be viewed as criminals rather than sinners. Before then, free will was not even an issue, since criminal behavior was thought to be caused by evil spirits, the devil, or by the sinful nature of the individual. As late as 1862, a state supreme court in the United States stated: "To know the right and still the wrong pursue, proceeds from a perverse will brought about by the seduction of the evil one."[3]

With the Age of Reason, demonology was gradually abandoned. Within the framework of naturalist theories, however, contradictory explanations of human behavior developed. From the Enlightenment of the eighteenth century came an emphasis on the criminal law, private morality, and the rational choice of the individual emphasized by the classical school. The focus was on the law as a means of maintaining public order and on a voluntaristic model of human behavior. Yet, as Leon Radzinowicz notes, "the classical school hardened into a bleak and rigid approach to the criminal law." [4]

The second half of the nineteenth century—the Age of Science—witnessed the emergence of theories of crime based on determinism. Crime was seen as a result either of "kinds of environment"—sociocultural forces that predisposed a person toward crime—or "kinds of people"—physical or psychological factors that predisposed a person toward crime. These two approaches are still reflected in current criminological perspectives. They share similar deterministic assumptions relative to why crime exists or why certain individuals become criminals.[5]

As a result of these emphases, American sociologists developed perspectives about crime and its control that assumed individual and social pathology and that improvements in these conditions are guided by scientific principles and laws. Their explanations of criminal behavior focused on biological, personal, and/or environmental factors. In these efforts, positivistic theorists were influenced by *Social Darwinism*—a misapplication of Darwin's theory of natural selection that saw morally defective persons as "losers" due to an inherent lack of "fitness" to compete. This position assumed a consensual model of society since criminal law was viewed as spawned by prevailing moral standards and was to be applied to strengthen social interests and collective morality in dealing with criminals and other antisocial individuals. This criminology was conservative; it was bent on correcting individuals rather than systems. It tended to put its faith in the efficacy of scientific and/or medical treatment and intervention to change social misfits who had been produced by bad social conditions.[6]

Criminology maintained this positivistic bent with its focus on the individual offender during the 1940s and 1950s. At the same time, influenced by the emphasis of the Chicago school on social disorganization (which was seen as a concomitant of the social order of urban communities), a more sophisticated analysis of crime and deviance began to develop. The perspectives that emerged appreciated the complex interrelationship between criminal and conventional worlds. Consequently, they were skeptical whether criminal justice and correctional organizations could make any impact on the crime problem, which they felt would continue to plague us. Still, if the system could be improved here or there, it might be able to keep crime from getting out of hand. Thus, these emerging perspectives have been termed "liberal-cynical" by Don Gibbons and Peter Garabedian and the "new pragmatism" by Radzinowicz.[7]

New emphases included a focus on learning crime patterns in crimogenic subcultures, crime as a natural adaptation to discrepancies between means and ends in the social order, and the view that societal reaction to crime—the process of making and applying definitions of criminality—leads to the assignment of criminal status and the development of a criminal self-concept. Although efforts to explain crime in terms of social processes within the social system continued, new concepts emerged that viewed society as characterized by social conflict between powerful interest groups. The criminal law was seen by this later view as the tool of dominant power groups, and those against whom it was enforced were the powerless—minorities such as the poor, the young, blacks, and others. These perspectives were "cynical" in that they focused on the failure or inability of the criminal justice system to promote their announced and presumed goals of "justice," and in that they lacked faith in the "perfectability" of the system. Rather, law and social control efforts were seen as part of the problem.

Today, although conventional criminology seeks to explain crime in terms of problems inherent in the basic structure of society and its institutions, it maintains its emphasis on reform. Its skepticism about crime control efforts has not resulted in a rejection of the American social order.[8] This is not the case with radical-critical criminology, which views the crime problem as a product of the exploitative political economy of American capitalistic society. This radical-critical perspective rests on a variety of interpretations of Marxist theory and is critical of the assumed "objectivity" and neutral facts of the positivists and the reformism of conventional academic criminology.[9] It endorses a "grand scheme" that calls for a restructuring of society based upon socialist principles as a solution to the crime problem.

Over the past several decades there has been a shift on the part of criminologists and other social scientists away from purely deterministic or mechanistic theories toward a revived interest in theories that see the individual both as a creature with the ability to choose and as a product of social forces. These new insights have been influenced by writers in the areas of phenomenology and symbolic interactionism, as well as the related labeling and conflict theorists. This new "humanism" goes beyond the ideas of Cesare Beccaria, Jeremy Bentham, and the classical school's belief in "free will," as well as the pleasure-versus-pain calculus of nineteenth-century thinkers. It takes into consideration the unique beliefs, goals, and values of the individual and recognizes that they often allow him to define, interpret, reshape, or overcome circumstances.[10] For in criminological theory, as in other academic areas of study where the frame of reference involves political and social issues, the *paradigm,* or explanatory model, chosen to investigate a problem often shapes the kinds of evidence considered and the solutions proposed. We turn our attention now to a summary of some of the specific attempts to explain criminal behavior through biological and psychological positivism.

THE LEGACY OF POSITIVISM: EMPHASIS ON EXPLAINING CRIMINAL BEHAVIOR

The rise of criminological positivism responded to societal concern with the correction of the offender. As a result, the scientific method was reflected in theories of criminology that have attempted to predict, prevent, or intervene in law-violating behavior. Judging by the increase in crime, this quest has not been very successful.

A science consists of a body of knowledge that has been systematically organized. The popularized notion of science that confuses the search for knowledge with the ability to control behavior might better be termed "scientism." Many early attempts at explaining criminal behavior failed to distinguish between facts and theory.[11] For example, Cesare Lombroso's discovery of atavistic abnormalities in the skull of a brigand was doubtless an empirically verified fact. But from this base (although he acknowledged psychological and social forces), he went on to identify other physical anomalies in an effort to hypothesize that inborn factors were the causes of criminal behavior. He later reduced the proportion of "born criminals" to 40 percent of the offenders.[12] This early criminological positivism, as described in Chapter 1, from the beginning was inductive and naive in the manner in which it borrowed from the physical sciences in that it focused on the flawed, personal traits of the individual. Lombroso's ideas have been relegated largely to the status of myth, and should be placed where they were described in the opening chapter—in an historical summary of criminology. Yet, as we shall see, such pseudoscientific ideas linger, and much research in the United States that sought to explain the process of becoming criminal has been influenced and/or misinformed by variations of this affinity.

Biological and Psychological Affinities

Factors such as physical constitution, race, intelligence, lack of education, emotional maladjustments, poverty, and socioeconomic status or class are emphasized in many explanations of crime and delinquency. David Matza used the term "affinity" to describe the assumption that such factors predispose individuals or groups to become criminal or delinquent. When it is assumed that an individual is impelled by forces or circumstances beyond his control, it is said that he has an affinity for that behavior. The underlying idea is borrowed from the idea of attractive force as used in the physical sciences. To be useful in the study of human behavior, however, Matza cautions us that affinity must take into account the social processes in a given set of circumstances that reduce a person's capacity to overcome these factors.[13] In much criminological research, human subjects are portrayed as though they, or their behavior, are controlled by biological, psychological, or social factors. It is assumed that these controlling characteristics can be identified through the use of scientific measurements, thus providing scientific explanations of the behavior of those who violate the laws. As a result, it is assumed, criminal behavior can more effectively be predicted and controlled.

Biological Affinity. Efforts to attribute criminality to innate biological factors influenced policy as well as theory in the United States in the years prior to World War II. Faced with a diversity of immigrants who exhibited cultural and ethnic backgrounds quite different from those of the dominant Anglo-Saxon population, and confronted with the need to justify the relegation of blacks to a subordinate caste, perspectives which focused on hereditary or genetic traits of inferiority found a receptive audience among scholars as well as lay people.

Studies by Richard Dugdale (*The Jukes,* 1877) and Henry Goddard (*The Kallikaks,* 1912) are glaring examples of the so-called "bad-genes" approach to explaining criminality. Goddard's study identified a Revolutionary War soldier whose liaison with a feebleminded woman had resulted in 480 descendants by 1912. Of these, 223 were either mentally defective, illegitimate, prostitutes, keepers of brothels, or criminals (only three were in this latter group). The same soldier later married a woman of equivalent social status, resulting in a line of first-class descendants.[14]

Such studies evidently influenced numerous strategies that attempted to attack crime through eugenics—by sterilizing people who, it was thought, likely would give birth to born criminals or other degenerates and misfits. Little wonder, then, that when the Supreme Court issued a landmark decision allowing the state of Virginia to sterilize a mentally retarded woman, Justice Holmes was to remark: "Three generations of imbeciles are enough." After all, he had scientific evidence, in the work of Dugdale and Goddard, on his side.[15]

Among other attempts to revive this version of affinity was the work of E. A. Hooten, a zoologist-anthropologist at Harvard in the 1930s. He purported to prove that certain physical types were drawn to crime. Hooten compared the body measurements of 14,000 inmates in ten states with those of 3,000 civilians, including state militiamen, firemen, and bathers at public beaches. Assuming incorrectly that all these groups were homogeneous, he drew the dubious conclusion that the physical inferiority of those who were institutionalized was related to their criminal behavior.[16]

William Sheldon's study of *somatotypes* was a more careful attempt to relate physical characteristics to patterns of personality and temperament. In the 1940s he analyzed physical and biographical data on two hundred boys in an institution for delinquents in Boston. He classified the boys according to configurations of three components: *endomorphy* (softness and visceral fat), *ectomorphy* (leanness and fragility), and *mesomorphy* (hardness and muscularity). Sheldon suggested that mesomorphy was the physical constitution most likely to result in delinquency. But his definition of delinquency was vague, for he described his sample as "more or less delinquent," and his statistical treatment, replete with photographs of three views of each of his subjects, did not support his conclusion that delinquents and nondelinquents represent different somatotypes nor that the difference represents inherited inferiority.[17]

Sheldon and Eleanor Glueck's prolific research on crime and delinquency was based on Sheldon's somatotypes. They applied a careful methodology in relating this and other factors to delinquency. In a study of five hundred delinquents, they concluded that although more delinquents than nondelinquents were mesomorphic, 40 percent of the delinquents were not mesomorphs. The Gluecks suggested that mesomorphs have a greater "delinquency potential," but they also referred to psychological factors—especially reactive or compensatory mechanisms—in the shaping of delinquent behavior on the part of nonmesomorphs. A short boy, for example, might try to compensate for his small stature by becoming overly aggressive. However, it may be that the more robust mesomorphs are disproportionately represented among delinquents because the lifestyle of delinquency is an enterprise that rewards and even requires physical prowess and agility. That is, they might be expected to have higher "delinquency potential" for the same reason we would expect them to have a higher "athletic potential."[18]

Another approach used to study the relationship between heredity and criminal behavior was Lange's study of thirty pairs of twins. Thirteen of these were identical twins, and one member of each of the thirty pairs had been identified as a criminal. Lange found that in 77 percent of the pairs of identical twins both were criminal—even though some were raised apart from each other. Only 12 percent of the pairs of fraternal twins were found to be criminal. Although the number of cases of each type was extremely small, and the classification of twins as identical or fraternal is open to question, Lange concluded that criminality was inherited.[19]

These thinkers were dedicated scientists who sought to study criminal behavior in an objective manner. But they attempted to explain behavior by relating it to biological criminal predispositions. Of course, a hundred years after Lombroso, no one would suggest seriously that large ears, long arms, or jutting jaws are signs of inferior heredity. But today, modern biological determinists still seek to identify genetic and chromosomal linkages with criminal behavior.

In recent years, the ideas of atavism and the born criminal gave way to the mesomorphic delinquent, and terms such as "psychopath," "sociopath," and similar, vaguely defined designations that tended to circularity came into vogue. The names were different, but "criminal man" was still some inferior being—a throwback to a lower level of human development.

The rather tragicomic attempt to trace the genetic makeup of the XYY—the "supermale"—exemplifies this recent emphasis on biological affinity. Recent studies, for example, have focused on the supposed link between criminal behavior and the presence in a few males of an extra Y or male-producing chromosome (see Box 1). These studies seek to show that XYY males are not only subnormal, but are also hyperaggressive and appear in greater proportions in prisons and hospitals than in the general population. Once again we see the idea of affinity rearing its head—only now the extra Y chromosome is said to predispose a man carrying it to aggressive, criminal behavior. The fact that the subjects were all in institutions for the criminally insane when tested might be as significant as their genetic makeup in explaining their high incidence of violent behavior.

This relatively inconclusive research, however, had several consequences. First, the British tried to identify XYY carriers by testing a small, longitudinal sample of newborns. The parents of the XYY carriers were informed that the XYY karyotype was believed to be related to crime and violence. It should not surprise anyone who is familiar with the dynamics of the self-fulfilling prophecy to learn that the incidence of crime and violence was higher for the XYY

The XYY Chromosome Carrier

BOX 1

Chromosomes of a human male arranged for accurate count.

Attention was first called to the XYY karyotype and criminal behavior by the publication of the work of Patricia A. Jacobs and her associates in 1965. They had studied 197 mentally abnormal patients in a prison hospital near Edinburgh, Scotland. All of the patients were institutionalized because they were "dangerously violent," although only seven of the men had been found to be XYY karyotypes. This proportion, 3.5 percent, was considered significant since it was theorized that there are only 1.3 XYYs in every 1000 births. Jacobs and her colleagues concluded that the presence of an extra Y chromosome apparently was related to the probability that an individual would be institutionalized for violent behavior.

Normal females have two X chromosomes, males have an X and Y. It was theorized that the X is related to a high component for gentleness while an extra Y doubles the component for aggressiveness. A male with two Y chromosomes thus would have a double dose of aggressiveness and might be inclined to violence and criminality. (Anthropologists would point to this theory as an example of ethnocentrism; there are societies in which females are more aggressive than males.)

The Jacobs study also found that the XYY inmate patients were quite tall—an average of 6 feet 1.1 inches—contrasted with the 5 feet 7 inches for normal institutionalized males. Other studies reported that the XYY males are mentally dull (with IQ between 80 and 95), have abnormal electroencephalographic recordings and exhibit facial acne and a high rate of epilepsy. One writer described characteristics that resemble those of Lombroso's atavistic criminal—long limbs with extremely long arm span, mental illness, and a history of arrests related to aggressive, antisocial behavior that began at an early age.[1]

A major recent study of the XYY phenomenon by a Danish-American team casts considerable doubt on the relationship between an extra Y chromosome and aggressive, violent criminality. Although a significantly higher percentage of XYY men were found to have been convicted of criminal offenses than normal men, the data showed that XYY men were no more likely to commit crimes of violence than men without an extra Y chromosome.[2]

---

[1] P. A. Jacobs, et al., "Aggressive Behavior, Mental Subnormality and the XYY Male," *Nature* (1965): 208–13.

[2] Herman A. Witkin, Donald R. Goodenough and Kurt Hirschhorn, "XYY Men: Are They Criminally Aggressive?" *The Sciences* (Oct. 1977): 10–13.

individuals than would have been predicted from their proportion in the general population. Second, defense attorneys in several countries—Australia, France, and the United States—seized on the existence or presumed existence of the double Y as the basis for pleading "not guilty by reason of insanity" for their clients. One such case was that of Richard Speck who was charged with murdering eight student nurses in Chicago in 1966. His defense attorney argued that Speck was not responsible since he was a double Y. On examination, however, it turned out that Speck was a normal XY after all. In 1970, the National Institute of Mental Health called together a conference of experts to report on the XYY chromosomal abnormality. This body was unable to agree that such a genetic abnormality was definitely associated with abhorrent or abnormal behavior.[20]

The appeal of ideas relating physical and mental traits with criminal potential was noted in 1937 by Alfred Lindesmith and Yale Levin. Their comments remain relevant for us in the 1970s:

> For more than a century before criminal anthropology came into existence, society's responsibility had been recognized and embodied in the legislation of all civilized countries. It may be that the theory of the born criminal offered a convenient rationalization of the failure of preventive effort and an escape from the implications of the dangerous doctrine that crime is an essential product of our social organization. It may well be that a public, which had been nagged for centuries by reformers, welcomed the opportunity to slough off its responsibilities for this vexing problem.[21]

Theories that relied on innate physical traits to explain the offender's behavior appear to be overshadowed by theories that emphasized the offender's emotional health, emotional disorders, and personality configuration. Yet the quest to identify the violent-prone "born criminal" using more sophisticated biological approaches persists. In 1970, Drs. Vernon Mark and Frank Ervin contended that since artificial elective stimulation of the amygdala in the temporal region of the brain results in violent fits of rage and violence in human patients, those with a malfunctioning amygdala have a "low threshold for impulsive violence." They also argued, as did Lombroso, that epilepsy is a cause of crime since it is "causally related to poor impulse control and violent behavior."[22] Now such investigations are generally performed on human subjects who have exhibited aggressive and bizarre behavior. Consequently, we have only a very limited understanding of such aggressive, violent behavior in normal subjects. Thus it would seem premature to announce the demise of biological affinity in the study of criminal behavior. Still, the cruder forms of this perspective have been discredited by empirical studies as well as common sense. Criminals are not inferior beings, doomed by heredity to inflict violence upon society.[23] These dismal ideas have been replaced in recent years with the idea that criminals, especially violent offenders, while not hopeless mental defectives, are "sick" people who need to be treated or rehabilitated.

Psychological Affinity. Unlike the inherited inferiority perspective, psychological affinity assumes that criminals or delinquents possess personality traits or psychogenic factors that cause their behavior. Here again, the roots of the crime are thought to dwell within the individual offenders, the product of their innate impulses, lack of control over those impulses due to emotional instability, mental conflicts, and repression of drives. Both the *diagnostic case study approach,* which has been influenced by the development of psychoanalysis and psychiatry, and the emphasis on *personality tests* by psychologists have stressed the unique characteristics of the individual offender as causes for his or her behavior.

Psychoanalytic theory was largely the contribution of Sigmund Freud (1856–1939). Although Freud's theory did not attempt to explain crime, numerous studies use his approach to analyze crime and delinquency. These theories stress that a person's *ego* (the conscious aspect of the personality) often is unable to control pleasure-seeking biological and psychological drives (the *id*). If a person does not develop a strong *superego,* or conscience, to control the id, the result can be criminal behavior. Here again we have concepts that, while they seek to explain the intrapersonal dynamics of the individual, focus on the inadequate control of the "primitive" aspect of the offender's mental makeup. The offender's behavior, in psychoanalytic terms, is seen as dominated by the id. Through an inability to control criminal impulses, the criminal evidences *ego deficiency.* Consequently, the various versions of the psychoanalytic perspective relate criminal behavior to inner conflicts, emotional maladjustments, unconscious feelings of insecurity, inadequacy, and inferiority.[24]

An important assumption these theories make is that to understand criminal behavior, we must understand the psychodynamics of unconscious motivation. In essence we are all born criminals—at least in respect to the impulses that lurk in our id. As Franz Alexander and Hugo Staub argue, males have a natural hostility toward their fathers and sexual love for their mothers. If the resultant anxiety and guilt feelings go unresolved, the boy will repress them, and these psychic forces will continue in the unconscious. However, this repressed aggression can be displaced, as in the extreme case of homicide. Or, the person may commit a symbolic act against his father, such as wrecking the family car or forging a check in his father's name. The offense of burglary may be displaced unconscious rape—a symbolic act against his mother. Or the person may feel guilty—his superego nags his ego—and he may commit a crime in order to be punished and rid himself of his guilt feelings.[25]

Although the psychoanalytic perspective remains quite popular among forensic psychiatrists and social service personnel who staff correctional programs, criminologists tend to seek a wider social perspective in their attempts to explain criminality.

Among the numerous psychoanalytical studies of crime are those that use lengthy case studies. These studies—including *The Roots of Crime* (1935) by Franz Alexander and William Healy, a study of seven cases; *Rebel Without A Cause* (1944) by Robert Linder; and the popular biography of *The Birdman of Alcatraz* by Thomas Gaddis (1956)—try to explain criminal activity or the criminal personality in terms of the individual's life history. These and other

The Birdman of Alcatraz—a unique life history.

case studies scrutinize the peculiarities of the individual's criminal behavior. As a result, there tend to be as many explanations of criminal behavior as there are individuals who are defined as criminal. Such individual focus tells us little about the behaviors from which we might draw wider generalizations.[26]

Personality Tests and Criminal Behavior. Efforts have been made to develop personality tests that identify emotional characteristics of offenders that distinguish them from nonoffenders. In 1950, Karl Schuessler and Donald Cressey analyzed the results of 113 studies in which the personality scores of offenders were compared with those of control groups. A broad range of traits was covered, and a wide variety of tests was used. These 113 studies did not develop clear evidence that personality traits are associated with criminality.

Only 42 percent of the studies found differences that favored nonoffenders, and the rest were inconclusive.[27]

A recent follow-up study by Gordon Waldo and Simon Dinitz, covering the period 1950 to 1965, came up with more positive results. Their survey of ninety-four studies, twenty-nine of which used the Minnesota Multiphasic Personality Inventory (MMPI), found that 81 percent established differences between the criminal and noncriminal. Among research studies that used other measures, differences were identified in 75 percent of the studies. But the results of these studies are far from conclusive. A number of studies did not control for the effects of the institutional setting upon the subjects, and differences *within* the offender and nonoffender groups sometimes exceeded differences *between* the groups.[28]

Waldo and Dinitz, as does George Vold, point to the subjective nature of the MMPI. The test consists of 550 items to which the individual responds "true" or "false." The questions are designed to diagnose the problems of adults in a clinical setting. It is evaluated according to fourteen scales dealing with habits, marriage and family, sexual attitudes, political attitudes, social attitudes, and so on. Imagine the quandary faced by an institutionalized offender—or, for that matter, by a normal high school freshman—when reflecting on this statement: "My sex life is satisfactory." If the convict plays the "game" and answers "true," he is not responding in terms of the sexual deprivation of most institutional settings. But this answer would indicate a "well-adjusted" subject. Our typical teenager, who may never have had sexual relations, might well respond "false." This response would be seen as evidence of maladjustment. Since each of the scales is scored separately, there is no single score that shows the overall degree of a person's adjustment. Yet the item just referred to, from Scale 4 ("Psychopathic Deviance"), is held to be significantly related to delinquency. Little wonder that Vold concluded that personality diagnosis based on such scales cannot be considered useful in understanding the relationships between personality abnormalities and crime or delinquency.[29] Still, the MMPI is widely used to diagnose the difficulties of offenders who are incarcerated in the United States.

Sociopathic or *psychopathic personality* are terms used to refer to people who are emotionally abnormal or chronically antisocial in their behavior. Although the terms "psychopath" or "psychopathic personality" were once common, the current term for this category is "sociopath" or "sociopathic personality." It has been referred to as a "wastebasket" category because of the ease with which it is applied to explain criminal behavior that does not seem to fit under any other label. The vagueness of the term and the lack of rigor with which it is defined and applied are suggested by the definition attempted in 1952 by the American Psychiatric Association. It defined sociopaths as:

> ...chronically antisocial individuals who are always in trouble, profiting neither from experience nor punishment, and maintaining no real loyalties to other persons, groups or codes. They are frequently callous and hedonistic, showing marked emotional immaturity, with lack of sense of responsibility,

lack of judgment, and an ability to rationalize their behavior so that it appears warranted, reasonable, and justified.[30]

In other words, sociopaths have emotional problems that are not sufficiently severe to be labeled psychotic, although the so-called "neurotic" might fit this definition. When it becomes necessary to explain their behavior, this catch-all label can be applied. The fact that some version of the term is frequently applied to recidivists was impressed upon us recently when we took a class on a field trip to a nearby state prison. The corrections officer (guard) who was briefing the class was asked by a student why the rate of recidivism was so high. "Well," he replied, "you see, most of these men are psychopaths."

Since the term is used so incautiously for a great many types of behaviors, it lacks the explanatory merit it seems to have on the surface. As long as such concepts are buried in the scholarly writings of social scientists, they are of little consequence. But when they are bandied about by agents of social control, we see the potential of the system for stigmatizing those who are labeled. And although a number of studies dating back to the 1940s have shown that terms such as "psychopath" or "sociopath" are as useless as the idea of the *"moral imbecile,"* which they replaced, they continue to be used.

During the 1940s, the media focused attention to what was believed to be a rash of serious sexual attacks across the country. The panic that was created resulted in the passage of sexual psychopathy laws. The laws stipulated that once these offenders were identified, they were to be committed to institutions "until cured." Edwin Sutherland has chronicled the way in which these laws had spread to a number of states by 1950. The absurdity of the statutes was compounded by the fact that "sexual psychopaths" are no more identifiable than other psychopaths. Further, since treatment programs did not exist, these individuals were, in essence, locked up for life.[31] Sexual psychopaths at one state hospital were among those who were unwilling subjects for some of the CIA's drug tests between 1953 and 1963.

The attempt to explain differences between offenders and nonoffenders in terms of personality factors and emotional disorders has not been fruitful. But these theories are often used to explain, through what Edwin Schur terms "retrospective interpretation," some horrible deed committed by an individual who had not previously been identified as deviant. For instance, John Lofland relates how newspapers at first had difficulty in explaining the behavior of Charles Whitman, who shot fourteen people from a tower at the University of Texas in 1966. Whitman had been a Boy Scout, a Marine, and an honor student in college. Eventually, a biography was reconstructed that attributed his acts to an alleged brain tumor.[32]

In the case of David Berkowitz, the notorious "Son of Sam" (see Box 2), we see an example of retrospective interpretation by journalists who were faced with the necessity of writing a biography that would focus on emotional disorders in Berkowitz's past that would be consistent with the murderous acts carried out by this enigmatic, twenty-four-year-old postal clerk. The data provided apparently conform to the symptoms outlined by Kate Friedlander, as

> BOX 2

The "Son of Sam": A Study in Contrasts

By ROBERT D. McFADDEN

The world of David Richard Berkowitz has been full of rigidities yet strangely formless, outwardly friendly but darkly cryptic. It has been touched by drugs and loneliness, love and tragedy.

Some people have known him to be thoughtful and gentle, though shy and seemingly troubled. But according to the police, he is the "Son of Sam," whose reign of terror in New York City claimed the lives of six young people and left others paralyzed, blind and otherwise scarred for life.

As the details of the enigmatic life of the 24-year-old postal clerk emerged, there appeared to have been no single incident or trauma that might explain his abrupt transformation little more than a year ago from the quiet suburbanite that he was to the murderous night stalker that the police say that he became.

Contradictory Impressions

From friends, former Army buddies, neighbors, former teachers and others who have known him, the descriptions seem to suit no theme—he was "sullen," "friendly," "average," "extreme," "sweet," "a loner," "a team player"—all pieces that seem to come from many jigsaw puzzles, not one.

During the hunt for the ".44-caliber killer," the police last May had issued a probable profile that came quite close, in many respects, to describing Mr. Berkowitz, who was seized outside his apartment building in Yonkers Wednesday night . . . .

The police profile had suggested that he might be "neurotic schizophrenic and paranoid, with religious aspects to his thinking process, as well as hintings of demonic possession and compulsion."

"He is probably shy and odd," it added, "a loner inept in establishing personal relationships, especially with young women. There is a strong likelihood that he is a Christian . . . . Educators estimate that he is at least a high school graduate and that he may have some college training."

Religion, by various accounts, has played a major role in shaping Mr. Berkowitz's personality, and there were references to Satan and demons in poison-pen notes he allegedly wrote to a neighbor. His background in recent years had been almost completely that of a loner. He is a graduate of Christopher Columbus High School in the Bronx and he had attended college for a semester.

The contradictions in his life began virtually in his infancy. He was born in Brooklyn on June 1, 1953, the son of Tony and Betty Falco, but he was given up for adoption at the age of 17 months to Nathan and Pearl Berkowitz, a childless couple from the Bronx, who changed his name from Richard David Falco to David Richard Berkowitz.

He was raised in a Jewish household and was bar mitzvahed at the age of 13 years. He attended Public School 77, where he was known as a prankster. A music teacher who had given Mr. Berkowitz saxophone lessons as a boy said that he threw frequent temper tantrums.

"He was the most erratic kid I've ever known," said David Margolies, the saxophone teacher, who is now a stockbroker.

Others who had known David Berkowitz as a boy said that he never knew his natural parents, though he was told he was adopted, and that he was never sure about his nationality.

The elder Mr. Berkowitz ran a hardware store, and, although the family lived modestly in a small apartment, the adoptive parents were said by acquaintances to have been loving toward and sensitive about the needs of young David. Some said David Berkowitz was severely affected by the death of Mrs. Berkowitz. He was 14 at the time.

He Liked Uniforms

His high school years were undistinguished scholastically, though he was said to have enjoyed and excelled in gymnasium classes and in baseball. In 1969, while he was still in high school, he and his father moved to Co-op City.

Bruce Handler, who lived on the floor below, recalled that he and David and two other youths organized a volunteer fire company in Co-op City in 1970, when the Fire Department had had no on-site facility. The youths put out brush fires and turned in alarms, occasionally helping at the scene of apartment fires before regular firemen arrived.

"He was dedicated," Mr. Handler said. "Once in 1970, he ran up 16 flights because he thought someone was still up there during a fire. . . . He liked uniforms."

His father wanted him to go to college after his high school graduation in June 1971, but Mr. Berkowitz instead enlisted in the Army for three years—a step that was to bring dramatic changes in his outlook and his personality.

Gary Corrigan, an engineer with WNEW-TV, had been with Mr. Berkowitz at Fort Dix and recalled that Mr. Berkowitz went absent without leave on the first weekend of basic training, but later came back dejected. . . .

After this incident, Mr. Berkowitz took no more leave, and, when others did, "Berk just stayed in the barracks and spit-shined his combat boots," Mr. Corrigan said.

"I just figured something went wrong," Mr. Corrigan said. "He told me he had smoked grass, but he didn't smoke at all on the post—said he wasn't using it anymore."

Mr. Corrigan said that, inexplicably, Mr. Berkowitz "didn't seem to be the gung-ho type" and "by and large, he was a dove," but at one point signed up for tough airborne training [he failed to get the assignment] and liked to garnish his uniform with optional insignia purchased from the post exchange. He was what soldiers call a "P.X. hero," Mr. Corrigan said.

Mr. Berkowitz received firearms training, but achieved no high rating for marksmanship and no training in sidearms. . . .

From Korea, where he had been sent as a Specialist 4, Mr. Berkowitz sent letters home to friends that suggested his conservative views were turning liberal. There are no Army records indicating that he had used drugs in Korea, but two friends . . . said later that he had bragged about using stimulant and depressant pills and, on occasion, LSD, a hallucinogen. . . .

At Fort Knox, where Mr. Berkowitz was stationed upon returning from Korea, a buddy, a security guard in Saginaw, Mich., said Mr. Berkowitz had bragged about using pills, but not LSD, in Korea. . . .

Seemed to Change

Mr. Billow said Mr. Berkowitz seemed to change drastically in other ways—from gregarious to reclusive, and toward a revivalist form of the Baptist religion. He was baptized, went to revival meetings and, according to Mr. Billow, "tried to convert others."

"He told me that if I did not take Jesus Christ as my personal savior, I'd be damned," Mr. Billow recalled. But two months before leaving Fort Knox, Mr. Berkowitz underwent still another personality change, Mr. Billow said. "He started to swear," he suggested. "Maybe he went back to drugs . . . because somebody doesn't change like that overnight.

Mr. Berkowitz, after being discharged, returned to New York City, took a job as an unarmed guard with I.B.I. Security Services Agency, and moved back for a while with his father at Co-op City. "The Army changed him," said his old Co-op City friend, Mr. Handler. "When he came back he was completely introverted."

Source: *New York Times*, Aug. 13, 1977. © 1977 by The New York Times Company. Reprinted by permission.

well as the classical Freudian interpretations of Alexander and Staub.[33] It seems apparent that the "Son of Sam" represents an atypical case having little in common with the typical homicide offender. His bizarre behavior seems more explainable in psychological terms than by other perspectives. And even though he seemed literally determined by intrapsychic conflicts and forces, we cannot generalize from this atypical case. Berkowitz now says there were no "devils" or "dogs" directing him, but that he simply was using an explanation he considered necessary to rationalize his murderous behavior. Research studies that will be described in Chapter 15 suggest considerable disenchantment with the idea that criminal behavior is a kind of sickness to be cured or treated. Criminological perspectives have, for the time being at least, laid aside the idea that the criminal is a "sick" person who should become a subject for psychiatric "treatment." The factors related to his or her condition are much more complicated than Freud and some of his adherents would have had us believe.

Sociological Affinities

The term "positivism," coined by the nineteenth-century French philosopher, Auguste Comte (1798–1857), has come to be applied to the deterministic perspectives that sought to explain crime and criminal behavior in terms of the new science of that era. Sociological positivism, however, developed in America out of the seminal ideas of Emile Durkheim (1858–1917). In his *Rules of Sociological Method,* he took as his point of departure what he called "social facts." Social facts that can be studied objectively are not subjective, Durkheim argued, since they are imposed upon individuals who are then coerced by these external conditions to behave regardless of individual will. He argued that crime is such a "social fact." However, Durkheim contended that crime was a normal social fact only to the extent that it performed some social function. One of these normal functions of crime is that it marks the boundaries of morality.[34]

Although Durkheim did not explicitly set forth a theory of crime causation, he sensitized us to the complex interrelationship of law-violating and conventional behavior, claiming that "crime is bound up with the fundamental conditions of all social life." For crime may be beneficial since "conditions of which it is a part are themselves indispensable to the normal evolution of morality and law." Furthermore, he argued, "the conditions that make crime possible also make change possible and crime might even directly prepare the way for change.[35]

Durkheim's idea that crime is a normal social fact and that it even performs essential boundary-maintaining functions was to influence attempts to explain crime in terms of social structure. Members of the Chicago school attributed it to the diversity that they saw as an attribute of the social disorganization accompanying urban life. The *functionalist* view—a theory that focuses on the interdependence of institutions—sees society as based on consensus and emphasizes order, shared meanings, and norms within the collective conscience of society. Functionalists see crime as a perspective for accounting for the contradictions and maladjustments in what they assume is an otherwise functioning society.

Sociological affinity was explored in the studies of the Chicago school by sociologists who sought to identify environmental correlates of crime and delinquency. Using an analogy from biology, they studied the interrelationships between social and physical environments and human behavior. They saw crime as part of the social organization of the city, yet not distributed evenly throughout the city. "Why and how does it vary?" they asked. Writers like Clifford Shaw, Robert McKay, and Frederick Thrasher sought answers to these questions in studies in the 1920s and 1930s in which they showed that high delinquency rates were associated with "natural areas" in transition. These areas were different from ideal or "normal" patterns of social organization. They were areas that were changing due to rapid industrialization, urbanization, and the influx of new groups of citizens. This change produced a crisis in the normal social organization, which they termed "social disorganization." Their studies in Chicago were supported by findings in Boston, Cleveland, Philadelphia, and other cities. They contended that areas of social disorganization were supportive of delinquency and crime.[36]

Through their research on delinquency, Shaw and his associates showed how movement into crime was a normal event. The origin of crime, however, was inherent in the values and cultural patterns of the neighborhood, not to individual pathology. Still, they rejected the idea that it was physical deterioration or overcrowded conditions that caused delinquent behavior. Even the gang, Thrasher stated, is not a "cause" of crime, but more accurately a contributing factor. In other words, criminals are made, not born. So the Chicagoans rejected the idea of individual pathology. And in their descriptions of urban society as characterized by social disorganization and change, they paved the way for later ideas of *differential social organization* and *differential association*—theories that were central to Sutherland's theory described in an earlier chapter.[37]

Anomie Theory and Affinity. In a much quoted, influential essay originally published in 1938, but since revised, Robert K. Merton sought to explain the origins of deviance. In this essay, Merton borrowed Durkheim's concept of anomie and modified it. Durkheim's anomie connoted social characteristics of society related to the breakdown of regulatory norms. In his focus on deviance as a result of the disjuncture between cultural goals and institutional means to achieve those goals, he suggested that American culture is universally shared but its structure is relative. Anomie for Durkheim had its source in the deregulation present in society that leads to the dissociation of the individual from collective rules. This state of institutional normlessness in industrialized society leads to egoistic behavior. Merton's version of anomie was both broader and more specific. In his focus on the poor integration between economic goals

"Everyone can make it if he really tries"—a myth.

of success and the existence of jobs and training in society, Merton argued that crime results from the breakdown in the regulatory structure that follows this disjuncture.[38]

Merton seemed to be saying that the ideology of the American Dream—"everyone can make it if he really tries"—is a myth. The American Dream, the idea of material success, is pervasive in our culture through the exhortations of the mass media and the pressure to gain sufficient income to indulge in conspicuous consumption of goods that serve as status symbols. Moreover, this concern with success, measured by money, occurs in the context of a social ideology of equality of opportunity. Those who fail not only forgo the "good things" for which they were striving, but they are held responsible—blamed by others and themselves—for not making it. As a result, society can become a place where the rules lack meaning or force—a situation of anomie where a "cardinal American virtue of success" may lead to a "cardinal American vice," deviance. For in an anomic society, "anything goes," and "any means to an end" describes the prevailing morality.[39]

Merton specified a typology of adaptations that occur in response to differing strains a person in a given social position might experience (see Table 6.1). Four of these—innovation, ritualism, retreatism, and rebellion—are seen as deviant.

Table 6.1 Modes of Individual Adaptation to the Culture of a Society

Modes of Adaptation	Cultural Goals	Institutionalized Means
I Conformity	+	+
II Innovation	+	−
III Ritualism	−	+
IV Retreatism	−	−
V Rebellion	±	±

+ denotes acceptance; − denotes rejection; ± denotes rejection of prevailing values and the substitution of new values.
Source: Robert K. Merton, "Social Structure and Anomie," *American Sociological Review* 3 (1938): 672–82.

Innovation is the most significant. Here, the stress on success goals, combined with rejection or lack of legitimate means, results in the use of illegitimate means to achievement. Merton originally focused on lower-class crime data as evidence of innovation. Even though he revised this emphasis later, many studies still focus on crimes committed by the lower strata for money. Certainly, white-collar crime by corporate executives and embezzlers should be included in this category.

Ritualism can be viewed as a scaling down of unattainable goals of success while abiding by institutional rules in a rigid, overzealous manner; the ritualist plays it safe. This form of adaptation may often be seen among the lower-middle class, for example, lower-level bureaucrats who perform in a ritualistic manner.

Retreatism is the least common type. The retreatist is in society but not a part of it, since he or she rejects both institutional goals and means. This type includes vagrants, chronic drunks, drug users, and artists, as well as others who seek a privatized adaptation of society's demands. The social aspect of retreatism is minimal and unclear, but may be represented by chronic drunkards, drug users, and social isolates whose lifestyles express withdrawal from cultural codes.

Rebellion describes the behavior of those who withhold their support of institutionally approved goals and means in a culture and transfer support to new groups with counter-culture ideologies. This category does not necessarily include criminals, but it does include political activists, nonconformists, heretics, and others who challenge the "system." Such behavior may be functional for the basic goals of the group.[40]

Bernard Rosenberg and Harry Silverstein, in their study of the aspirations of youths in Chicago, New York, and Washington, challenged Merton's hypothesis. Their subjects included white, Puerto Rican, and black youths in circumstances of poverty. They failed to uncover high aspirations for educational or occupational achievement among any of the groups and concluded that to the extent anomie exists, it is not limited to those in lower socioeconomic strata. The anomie they did identify was a reflection of the "moral anomie" that affects the entire society.[41]

In stressing the affinity between segments of the population in poverty and in deviation from the rules, Merton failed to specify which segment of the lower class he was describing. As recent studies have shown, there is considerable segmentation within the lower class.

Subcultural Affinity

During the 1950s and 1960s, a number of theories sought to explain law-violating behavior in terms of what was called the *delinquent subculture.* These writers, including Albert Cohen, Richard Cloward, Lloyd Ohlin, and Walter Miller were influenced, indirectly at least, by Durkheim's idea of anomie as elaborated by Merton. In his work, *Delinquent Boys* (1955), Cohen assumed that delinquency was to be found mainly among lower-class boys. He argued, contrary to Merton, that rather than being innovative and seeking "illicit means" to attain success goals, delinquent behavior was often nonutilitarian, malicious, and negativistic. He agreed with Merton that children in our society are exposed to dominant, middle-class values that only the middle-class children can fulfill. This is especially so in educational institutions, where the lower-class boy faces virtues such as rationality, deferral of gratification, and self-control.

Cohen argues that the delinquent subculture provides a solution to the "status strain" confronted by the lower-class boys. It gives them the means to collectively repudiate middle-class values. In this version, the delinquent subculture represented a "reaction formation," or contraculture, through which lower-class boys could adopt values and behaviors that were the "very antithesis of [those of] the dominant class." For instance, group stealing was pursued not just to get something for nothing, but because it was the antithesis of diligent work. "It expresses contempt for a way of life by making its opposite a standard of status." [42]

The theory of subculture developed by Cloward and Ohlin brought together elements of perspectives from Sutherland, Merton, and Cohen. They argued that differential access exists not only to legitimate means, but also to illegitimate means. These various circumstances of blocked opportunity result in pressures toward the development of three different types of subcultures among lower-class youth. These are the *criminal type*, characterized by racket-oriented activity; the *conflict type*, characterized by street or gang fighting; and the *retreatist* (or drug-oriented) *type*. They suggested that the social structure of a given locality was influential in determining which type of adaptation a youth would make. Cloward and Ohlin are quite specific in delineating the types of neighborhoods that compel youth toward criminal and conflict subcultures, but they are rather vague regarding the third type. They note that retreatist gangs may attract youths who are double failures.[43]

Walter Miller argues that it is lower-class traditions, not a delinquent subculture, that creates gang delinquency. He describes six "focal concerns" that pervade urban lower-class life: (1) *trouble*, as a means to a desired end; (2) *toughness*, a concern with masculinity; (3) *smartness*, being able to con or outsmart others or having a hustle; (4) *excitement*, the search for "kicks," hanging around; (5) *fate*, resignation to forces beyond one's self; and (6) *autonomy*, being free from domination of external authorities.[44] In sum, lower-class boys become involved in law violations in a positive effort to fulfill needs and desires valued within their community.

Hanging out—the search for kicks.

All these perspectives have been criticized for the assumption that delinquency is basically a lower-class phenomenon. Miller's focal concerns have been attacked on the grounds that if his argument were correct, then all lower-class youth would be delinquent.[45] In fact, numerous self-report studies indicate that most boys, lower or middle class, are delinquent at some time. All these theories suggested a causal link between poverty and crime and delinquency. In the process, they shifted the emphasis from "kinds of people" to "kinds of environment," but maintained the idea of affinity. It was, as Matza notes, the favored affinity of sociologists—poverty and social disorganization linked to pathology or crime.[46]

AFFILIATION PERSPECTIVES: SOCIAL PROCESS EXPLANATIONS

Theories stressing affinity attempt to explain crime and criminal behavior in terms of individual or social factors. Although the Chicago sociologists sought to confirm the affinity between poverty and criminal behavior, they also inferred another idea as an explanation for the coexistence of these social factors—*affiliation.* In its original version, affiliation was viewed as another form of affinity and as equally deterministic in that it inferred that social processes in the environment—processes that united or attached to criminal behavior those who were formerly unattached—emerged as a distinctive strategy for explaining the process whereby the individual takes on behavior new to him or her. The process is one whereby the person may be "turned on" or "out." Edwin H. Sutherland's theory of *differential association* provides a more explicit discussion than did the Chicagoans. Sutherland rejects the mechanistic effect of antecedent circumstances (affinity) on the individual's behavior.[47] David Matza contends that Sutherland's theory represents a shift in emphasis toward a perspective that was more suited to the study of human subjects than earlier explanations. In a manner of speaking, he prepared the way for criminologists to use the idea that the process by which the individual is "converted" to crime or deviance involves rational choice. That is, humans are not only able to make commitments, but also to reconsider and renege on them. And we may choose to transcend at least a part of our circumstances and live with and refashion our lives in terms of such choice.[48]

This shift can be perceived in the dual concepts of *differential association* and *social organization,* both central to Sutherland's theory. By itself, the first dimension seems to rely on simple learning theory that may not involve that much choice and little competition among different behaviors. But taken together, the two concepts turn our attention to the conflict and competition among diverse lifestyles in a society characterized by diversity. Sutherland's stress on the "behavior system" of the criminal reflects the influence of the Chicago school. Consequently, as Matza notes, the individual still remained a "creature of affiliational circumstances," but to Sutherland these provided the setting for the individual's "conversion" to crime or deviance. This process involved one's definition of the situation, beliefs, justifications, and learning the techniques. Hence, becoming criminal could now be conceptualized as a process involving choice and meaning. To view this process in such a natural, human context was to acknowledge that becoming a criminal was like becoming anything else, but specifically like nothing else.[49]

The nine principles outlining these two emphases are listed in Box 3. The sixth principle, the crux of the theory, is the principle of differential association. The full text goes on to state that it refers to "both criminal and noncriminal association. The emphasis is on exposure to associations and patterns and definitions of behavior whether or not the patterns are presented by someone who is overtly a criminal." For example, if a father purports to teach his son that it is better to be honest than to steal, yet openly brags that he cheated on his income tax, he may be providing his son with a law-violating behavior pattern. It is possible, as Cressey suggests, to learn criminal behavior patterns from noncriminals, and noncriminal behavior patterns from criminals.[50]

In her succinct summary of Sutherland's perspective, N. J. Davis points out that Sutherland linked three classes of phenomena—subculture, social differences, and differential social organization. However, he moved beyond the Chicago school's idea of subculture by relating the idea of subcultural differences (ethnic diversity) to the law as a device that generates political conflict. He thus provided a premise for the later development of the labeling perspective by stating: "If laws increase and behavior (of some groups) remains the same, crimes necessarily increase." Secondly, in his concept of social differentiation, Sutherland confronted both commonsense and classical ideas that increasing punishment will decrease crime. Due to the variety of groups in society, each with conflicting interests, the individual might readily find a group that would support his or her unconventional behavior. Punishment might promote resentment and drive the individual to seek support for law-violating norms from the in-group. Finally, Sutherland's *differential social organization* concept challenged the idea of lower-class criminality. In his work, *White-Collar Crime*, he argued that by tolerating white-collar offenders, viewing their crimes as technical offenses that do not involve culpability, the stigma and punishment associated with other types of violations would be reduced.[51] More importantly, these are crimes, and they are learned as are other law violations.

Although differential association is one of the major American contributions to criminology, it is not without its critics. In fact, few theories have been the focus of such extensive criticism. Sutherland's co-author and student, Donald Cressey, who, since his mentor's death, has left the nine principles intact in his various revisions of *Criminology*, has summarized and responded to some of the major criticisms in a recent edition. He summarizes them according to five principle types:

First: Some kinds of criminal behavior are exceptions to the theory. Some research studies have found that it does not apply to rural offenders, landlords

Sutherland's Principles of Differential Association

BOX 3

Individuals can readily find a group to support unconventional behavior.

1. Criminal behavior is learned.
2. Criminal behavior is learned in interaction with other persons in a process of communication.
3. The principal part of the learning of criminal behavior occurs within intimate personal groups.
4. When criminal behavior is learned, the learning includes, (a) techniques of committing the crime, which are sometimes very complicated, sometimes very simple; (b) the specific direction of motives, drives, rationalizations, and attitudes.
5. The specific direction of motives and drives is learned from definitions of the legal codes as favorable or unfavorable.
6. A person becomes delinquent because of an excess of definitions favorable to violation of law over definitions unfavorable to violation of law.
7. Differential associations may vary in frequency, duration, priority, and intensity.
8. The process of learning criminal behavior by association with criminal and anticriminal patterns involves all of the mechanisms that are involved in any other learning.
9. While criminal behavior is an explanation of general needs and values, it is not explained by those general needs and values since noncriminal behavior is an explanation of the same needs and values.

Source: Data abridged from pp. 80–82 in *Criminology*, 10th ed., by Edwin H. Sutherland and Donald R. Cressey. Copyright © 1978 by J.B. Lippincott Company. Reprinted by permission of Harper & Row, Publishers, Inc.

who violate rent control regulations, embezzlers, naive check forgers, white-collar criminals, and certain delinquents.

Second: The theory does not take into account psychological variables in criminal behavior.

Third: The theory minimizes the individual process of reception while it emphasizes the social process of transmission, or does not take into account the perceiver's meaning of the different behavior systems.

Fourth: The ratio of learned behavior patterns used to explain criminality cannot be determined accurately in specific cases.

Fifth: It oversimplifies the process by which criminal behavior is learned.[52]

If imitation is a type of compliment, then the many attempts to reformulate, refine, or modify Sutherland's theory suggest the significant impact it has had on American criminology. Among the various efforts at recasting differential association was that of Daniel Glaser, who argued that greater emphasis should be focused on complexities and patterns of organization and the process of *identification* that goes on during social interaction. He used the phrase *differential identification* to draw attention to the manner in which the person pursues criminal behavior by identifying with those persons, real or imaginary, who may see such behavior as acceptable.[53]

More recently, Glaser has refined his modification in a version that uses the idea of *differential anticipation.* This version suggests that:

> A person's crime or restraint from crime is determined by the consequences he anticipates from it; and these expectations are the result of: (1) *social bonds* (both anticriminal and procriminal, which the person may develop in the course of his career); (2) *differential learning* (through which one acquires preferences, skills, and desires which influence whether or not criminal or alternative behaviors will be qualifying); and (3) *perceived opportunities* (which reflect the individual's perception and assessment of circumstances relative to assessed risks in conforming or law-violating behavior).[54]

Another reformulation of Sutherland's theory was developed by Melvin DeFleur and Richard Quinney. They analyzed and rearranged the nine principles in the language of set theory, so their model was amenable to computer analysis. They showed that the "principle" of statement six is implicit in all nine statements. One of their conclusions was that a general theory such as differential association requires the formulation and testing of lower-level theories for specific types of crime.[55] The learning experiences of a professional thief who specializes in stealing cars, for example, would be different from those basic to the behavior of a youth who "borrows" a car for a "joyride."

In their critique of differential association, Ian Taylor et al. argue that Sutherland's passive conception of human nature and his downplaying of differential organization have left his ideas open to revisionist takeovers from behaviorism. They cite the *differential association-reinforcement* theory of Robert Burgess and Ronald Akers as one of the better known behaviorist revisions.[56] This reformulation attempts a revision based on a learning theory which uses operant conditioning—positive and negative reinforcement—as developed by B. F. Skinner and others. This is illustrated in their restatement of Sutherland's sixth principle: "The probability that a person will commit criminal behavior is increased in the presence of normative statements, definitions, and verbalizations which, in the process of differential reinforcement of such overconforming behavior, have acquired discriminative value."[57] According to this view, people engage in criminal behavior because it has been reinforced more frequently in previous experiences than noncriminal behavior.

Taylor and others have decried this adaptation of differential association, claiming it is "a travesty of Sutherland's position," since differential association is concerned with "the acquisition of motives in which a degree of human choice and purpose is a basic aspect." The behaviorist reformulation, they argue, is basically a new form of positivism, contrary to the basic social premises of Sutherland's position. *Operant conditioning* assumes that crime is reinforced in nonsocial situations—for example, that stealing is reinforcing or rewarding whether others know about it or not.[58] In a recent work, Ronald Akers responds to this criticism in his explication of differential association-reinforcement as a "social learning theory." He contends that "social" reinforcement involves not just the reactions of those present during an action, but the entire range of intangible and tangible rewards and their frequency, duration, priority, and intensity which affect whether or not criminal or conventional behavior is reinforced. He notes that the social learning approach has been supported by empirical studies on drug users and delinquents. However, further research designed to collect data for the express purpose of testing differential association-reinforcement theory is needed.[59]

Matza suggests that Sutherland's theory left the individual only "half a man" in that it presumed that humans are overpowered by their environment. Matza notes that had Sutherland appreciated the manner in which different cultural worlds interpenetrate, had he appreciated the pervasive availability of different lifestyles, and more importantly, "had he appreciated the fact that humans, unlike trees or foxes, intentionally move in search of meaning, then the idea of affiliation would have been humanized to mean conversion."[60] Thus, Matza relates the ideas of differential association to a general social psychological framework. He succinctly points out that being exposed to the "causes" of deviant behavior is not the same as doing the deed. Rather, the exposure is part of a process by which one might literally see oneself as the kind of person who might do the act in question. Matza illustrates this process of being converted, of choosing deviance, with a lengthy discussion of Becker's classic essay, "Becoming a Marihuana User" (1963). In the naturalist tradition, he uses the phenomenology (analysis of the subjective process) of the convert to "pot" smoking to illustrate the imagined inner processes of becoming deviant.[61]

The point advanced by Matza is that Sutherland—even though he left intact the idea that we are ordained or determined by associations or social processes (affiliation)—did move our perspectives on criminal behavior closer to the point where the subject was more an active human agent and less a passive creature who merely reacts to personal or social forces. To the degree that the subject was more human, he was seen as living within an associational network that gave him a setting for the "conversion" to criminal behavior in terms of "definitions of the situation, beliefs, reasons, justifications, and techniques." Yet in this view, the person remained, at least to some extent, a captive of his environment. Bereft of real alternatives, the choice of crime became almost inevitable.[62]

Perspectives utilizing social-psychological explanations of crime and delinquency—inherent in differential association and its offshoots—have dominated in recent American criminology. But focusing on the learning process of the offender, the role of the state and its agents, who are part of the social interaction in which the learning, defining, and typing of criminality occurs, often was slighted or overlooked. As Matza points out, it seemed as though "Leviathan (the state) had little bearing on ordinary criminals...." In criminology the process of becoming an ordinary criminal was seen as unrelated to the workings of the state. Matza applied the term *signification* to that aspect of the process during which agents of the state "ban" and "signify" the offender, so that he is viewed by the public and frequently by the offender himself, as exemplifying concretely and symbolically, the "collective representation" of the deviant or criminal act.[63] As long as criminologists took the social order for granted, it was as though the role of the state in the creation of criminality and deviance was irrelevant, even to the lives of those ordinary offenders who fell into its grasp. But the social interaction or labeling perspective was to reverse this emphasis and in the process to focus on political authorities, the bureaucratic apparatus, and its agents of social control.

SIGNIFICATION: THE LABELING PROCESS

The theories described so far have tried to address two questions: Why do some people break the law? and What causes criminal behavior? The focus has been upon crime as behavior and the relationship between certain individual or social factors, social processes, and that behavior. Although certain assumptions were made about the criminal law, the basic stress was upon relating causal factors to a general description of certain types of persons who break the law.

In its quest for scientific explanations and objectivity, criminological theories typically have been developed from a correctional approach. They assume the criminality of certain kinds of behavior and seek to explain it and control or change it.[64] In recent years, several competing theoretical perspectives have developed. These rest upon the assumption of value conflicts in the formulation and application of the law to those who become defined as criminals. The focus of these theories, then, is to show how legal definitions and societal reaction to crime—systems of control and social agents involved in the process—

are implicated in the process of defining criminality. For whether or not a person acquires the status of criminal depends not only on his or her behavior, but also upon the legal, moral, and political evaluation made by officials of the state about that behavior. For crime is "actionable" behavior. It includes the reaction, the reality of warranted correction, and sanction, as well as the act. To be apprehended is to be registered, defined, or classified as a thief, a prostitute, or whatever. This is the meaning of *signification.* Signifying also implies "putting down" or derogation, and as a result comes to stand for or represent a thief, a prostitute, or a criminal type.

Signification Aspects of the Labeling Perspective

Although the labeling perspective did not come into prominence until the 1960s, Frank Tannenbaum had written as early as 1938 about the "dramatization of evil." He was not referring to a one-time episode, but to the "process of tagging, defining, segregating, describing, emphasizing, making conscious and self-conscious, . . . a way of stimulating, suggesting . . . [that] evokes the very traits that are complained of. . . . [and] the person becomes the thing he is described as being." [65] In other words, the process of being arrested and taken to court is a process of public definition, and the labeling signifies to the person arrested and to the public that he or she is a criminal.

Explanations of criminality that stress societal reaction, or labeling, shift the focus from the individual offender and emphasize the extent to which behavior might be the result of the reactions of others, as well as a response by the self to individual or social forces. This perspective assumes a set of social relationships in which "rule enforcers," as Howard Becker terms the authorities, define the subject as a potential law violator and decide whether or not to proceed further with efforts to modify or punish his or her behavior. The question in this perspective is not so much *why* a person commits a criminal act, but rather what social control agents do and in what informal and formal situations does societal reaction occur? For instance, a person may be stigmatized or "cast" as a thief, and thus excluded from society. Subjected to prosecution, sentenced to probation or incarceration, treatment, or preventive detention, it is hoped the chance of his future thievery will be reduced. More symbolically, the person may be excluded from the "normals" in society and be branded with phrases such as, "once a thief always a thief," or "once a convict always a convict." Becker suggests that this process may operate as follows:

> One will be identified as a deviant first, before other identifications are made. The question is raised: "What kind of person would break such an important rule?" And the answer is given: "One who is different from the rest of us, who cannot or will not act as a moral human being and therefore might break other important rules." The deviant identification becomes the controlling one.[66]

A central tenet of this perspective is that crime and deviance are a product of societal reaction or labeling by official or authoritative agents of control.

The focus is on the process by which the "rule breaker" is identified or separated out by social control agents, made the subject of formal degradation ceremonies, institutionalized or incarcerated, and as a consequence takes on a deviant identity.[67]

Becker proposes a relativistic political-conflict model, in which deviance is the result of a specific social context. The differential manner in which society's rules are applied is influenced by class, ethnic, occupational, sex, and age statuses of those labeled and those doing the labeling.

Primary and Secondary Deviation. Edwin Lemert was more systematic in his statement of the labeling perspective than other labeling theorists. He distinguished between *primary deviation* and *secondary deviation.* Primary deviation "is polygenetic, arising out of a variety of social, cultural, psychological, and physiological factors... [which] may be socially recognized and even defined as undesirable... [but] has only marginal implications... for the person concerned." By contrast, *secondary deviation* "refers to a special class of socially defined responses which people make to problems created by the societal reaction to their deviation.... The secondary deviant, as opposed to his actions, is a person whose life and identity are organized around the facts of deviance." [68]

Lemert specified the process by which the individual comes to accept his deviant identity on the way to a deviant career as follows:[69]

1. *Primary deviation:* initial action, such as sexual promiscuity, prompted by various reasons.
2. *Social penalties:* informal sanctions, such as gossip, social ostracism, or rejection.
3. *Further primary deviation:* may be influenced by No. 2, the individual has the name, he may choose the game!
4. *Stronger penalties and rejections.*
5. *Further deviation:* however, now hostility and resentment may be focused upon those who have invoked the penalties.
6. *A crisis point in community tolerance:* formal action is taken and the community stigmatizes the individual.
7. *The deviant conduct is strengthened as a reaction to the penalties and stigma.*
8. *Final acceptance of the deviant social status:* efforts at adjustment to roles associated with it.

The central idea in Lemert's model was a structural emphasis on social control, conflict, and power exchanges. Some of Lemert's followers, however, have slighted this stress on social control. As a result, the state's role in creating and perpetuating deviants has not received the attention that some writers such as Lemert, Matza, and others think it should. Consequently, the actors came to be viewed more as acted upon than acting.[70] For instance, Becker has suggested that "treating a person as though he were generally rather than specifically deviant produces a self-fulfilling prophecy. It sets in motion several mechanisms which conspire to shape the person in the image people have of him."[71] As a result, the person may be labeled deviant when he or she may not have broken any rule at all. Lemert describes the defensive strategies of women labeled as prostitutes, who develop closer relationships with pimps and other prostitutes and a stronger identity of themselves as prostitutes.[72]

The Building of Identity. A basic idea of the labeling perspective is that behavior alone does not create the offender. Societal reaction and processing organizations—such as the family, peer groups, and official bureaucracies, including courts, prisons, welfare agencies, mental hospitals, and others—are involved in different ways in the "status transformation." This perspective has, in recent years, sensitized policymakers as well as theorists to the potential negative effects of efforts to correct or rehabilitate those tagged as criminals or deviants. Evidence based on several studies supports contentions regarding the arbitrary and dehumanizing aspects of official control efforts.

In a study by Egon Bittner of the *Police on Skid Row* (1967), it was found that ad hoc decisions were geared more to the special problems of law enforcement rather than to legal offense categories.[73] In *Justice Without Trial* (1966), Jerome Skolnick described how judges and court officials impose plea bargaining on the accused to hide from view violations of the criminal law by the police and, as a result, systematically circumvent the law.[74] Studies by Marvin Wolfgang and Irvin Piliavin and Scott Briar detailed discretionary and arbitrary practices of the police in their dealings with more vulnerable lower-status offenders such as the poor, the black, the young, and other marginal groups.[75] These groups were found to be the most likely to be reported, charged with an offense, arrested, sent to trial, processed, and sentenced to prison. And studies of welfare agencies, such as Robert Scott's *The Making of Blind Men* (1969), point to the preferential selection of clients, such as younger blind persons or the more resourceful, in order to promote agency programs and goals rather than provide services for clients.[76]

In an earlier chapter, we noted that when juveniles fail to receive approval from parents or do not achieve in school, they often come to see themselves as failures. As Tannenbaum has stated, "the young delinquent becomes bad because he is defined as bad and because he is not believed if he is good."[77] Aaron Cicourel has described similar findings regarding interactions between probation officers and juveniles, where he points to the importance placed on the demeanor of juveniles. He emphasizes that the interpretation of the juvenile's facial expressions and physical appearance by officials has a considerable effect on his classification as a delinquent. Cicourel, as well as some other writers, uses a mode of investigation that takes the perspective of the everyday actors in the social scene and describes their routine interpretative methods—*ethnomethodology*. Ethnomethodologists reject the usual social interactionist concepts. They seek to describe the natural process by which good and evil, or conformity and deviance, emerge from such ordinary conduct and stress their provisional and changing nature.

In order to understand both the public and private ideologies of agencies that deal with law violators, we must gather insights into the ways in which they organize subjective data into formal reports. Thus, it is not only the factual details concerning an individual's deviation from the law that have significance for his future, but also the probation officer's interpretation of and reaction to the manner in which the individual presents himself. For instance, we have had probation officers inform us that "body English"—i.e., whether or not the person sits up straight or slouches—was very important to them in analyzing juveniles. The labeling process, then, is not simply a reaction to criminal or delinquent behavior. It primarily reflects the interaction that occurs between the offender and the officials who process him.[78]

In discussing the organizational processing of delinquents, Schur describes what occurs as negotiated outcomes.[79] Similarly, Robert Emerson's study of the juvenile court points out that the court represents one of the major areas of involvement for helping professions like social work and psychiatry in the criminal law. "These [helping professionals]... provide the... focal point for ... the analysis of the conflicting ideologies and purposes built into the court and the ways in which they are worked out in the practical matters of judging and dealing with delinquents." [80] His study demonstrates how the legal system defines, reacts to, and deals with those who are brought to its attention. It is this process, he maintains, that results in some offenders emerging from the encounter in court "tagged" as potential or future criminals, while others, as a consequence of differential court negotiation, escape without being defined as "really" delinquent, even though they had been adjudicated. According to Emerson, these latter cases represent those who, in the process of negotiation, are characterized by the court as "normal children," who have been influenced by relevant contingencies such as their home situation.[81]

It has become conventional wisdom in the last several decades for criminologists to cite these studies to illustrate the usefulness of the labeling perspective. It probably is not just a coincidence that the studies have focused on illegal behaviors such as juvenile delinquency, substance use (alcohol and other drugs), sex-related offenses, and status offenses. These offenses lend themselves to what Becker has termed the "unconventional sentimental" approach, and they reflect areas of disagreement and uncertainty among various segments of public opinion, which in turn are reflected in official reaction.[82] As Schur has pointed out, these phenomena may more appropriately be studied in terms of the negotiation of deviant identity and the resulting "role engulfment." However, he also notes that some types of nonconformity are not as well suited to labeling analysis as these. Atypical acts, such as an episodic homicide, for example, do not lend themselves readily to analysis by the labeling perspective.[83] But as our discussion of capital punishment in a later chapter will note, arbitrary sentencing procedures for homicide offenders were so widespread, that the Supreme Court ruled in *Furman* v. *Georgia* (1972) that laws which allowed the "uncontrolled discretion" of judges or juries were unconstitutional.

Criticisms of Labeling

Several cautions should be noted about the labeling perspective. First, the idea that societal reaction that labels or stigmatizes the offender leads to an altered identity or self-concept has not been fully proved through empirical research. Among the few exceptions is Lindesmith's careful research on heroin addicts, a study that focuses on the negotiated effects of law enforcement.[84] Adherents of the labeling perspective who claim that societal reaction is the only causal factor in the creation of criminality provide only a partial view of a complex process. The public label may have little impact in many areas of life, since many "normals" who are not sanctioned are also involved in illegal or nonconforming behavior. Labeling then is neither necessary nor sufficient for deviant identity.

A second difficulty derives from the fact that those who use this perspective find themselves dealing with two types of processes. One is the process of official typing, the informal official and unofficial responses to behavior. The other is the process of becoming deviant itself, which recognizes the existence of secret or otherwise nondefined offenses. This difficulty arises when deviance or crime is defined relative to social norms, yet behavior contrary to such rules is not actually defined as such until a specific societal reaction is invoked against it. Davis suggests that one way out of this impasse is to adopt the distinction made by Cicourel between "natural deviance"—the commonsense idea of deviants as clear-cut social types—and "official deviance"—behaviors defined and processed by official agencies of social control.[85]

The labeling perspective, then, in its emphasis on the negative impact of societal reaction, including official processing, provides valuable insights into criminality. It would be presumptuous, however, to expect this perspective to provide an answer to the question that apparently concerns John Q. Citizen: Why do they do it? And confronted with recent research findings that seem to conclude that the variety of rehabilitation or treatment programs based on positivistic assumptions have little or no impact on the likelihood of future criminal behavior, we are inclined to agree with a contention of Edwin Lemert, an early proponent of the labeling perspective. He has argued that this perspective inadequately accounts for the complexities of societal reaction in contemporary society, for it overlooks the great variety of laws that influence the choices of both official agents of social control and offenders when confronted with alternative courses of action. And it also fails to analyze the complex interplay of the numerous interest groups that are involved in the creation of new categories of social control.[86] It is our intention to apply those elements of this perspective that have applicability to an understanding of the criminal career, however, in our description of criminal behavior systems later on in this chapter. For now we will turn our attention to further insights that might be gained by utilizing perspectives that link the crime problem and its control to conflicts between interest and power groups in the social structure.

CONFLICT PERSPECTIVES: POWER RELATIONSHIPS AND THE "SIGNIFICATION" OF CRIMINALITY

Although the labeling perspective focused attention on societal reaction to criminality and on the role of those who do society's "dirty work"—the police, courts, and other officials—in defining criminality, its view was too limited. It slighted what has come to be acknowledged as an important facet of the study of the interrelationship between crime and the social structure. Although it did much to debunk and demystify authority, it did not adequately confront the power and authority arrangements in society that are involved in the formulation and application of the criminal laws. It was left to the several emerging versions of conflict theory to probe more deeply into the question: *Why is it that those without affluence, prestige, or political power are more apt to be defined, convicted, and punished as criminals than those who are not so disadvantaged?*

In its efforts to provide answers to questions such as these, the conflict perspective has enhanced our understanding of the crime problem. This perspective was influenced by the ideas of two earlier thinkers, Karl Marx and Georg Simmel. The ideas of the former, at least reformulations of them, are more apparent in the critical or "radical" version of this perspective noted below. Simmel's notions of conflict were influential in the more moderate version.

The first criminological textbook to give a significant emphasis to crime as a product of social conflict was George Vold's *Theoretical Criminology* (1958). Vold was influenced in his writing by Georg Simmel, the German social thinker who held that interaction between and within groups is affected by opposing individual and group interests, while a continuous struggle takes place between and within groups to improve or maintain status. Simmel saw political activity as an arena for mediating between conflicting groups. Those groups that win out in the political struggle can influence legislation that defines criminal behavior.[87] As Thorsten Sellin has noted, the kind of behavior prohibited often may depend upon the interests of the dominant groups.[88]

Crime may be seen, then, as minority group behavior. Vold suggests that the phenomenon of delinquent gangs may be initiated by a need of those who cannot rely on the legally constituted authorities to band together for protection and strength. Media accounts of "turf" wars between various urban gangs in both the 1950s and the 1970s illustrate this argument.

These ideas also reflected some of the notions of the German sociologist, Rolf Dahrendorf, a contemporary of Vold. He saw conflict as extending beyond the class conflict of Marxist theory to conflict in associations that were basic to the social organization. His ideas were also influential in the writings of Austin Turk and Richard Quinney in the 1960s, although the latter has more recently moved toward a clear-cut Marxist orientation. Dahrendorf's non-Marxist ideas were concerned more with developing a model of society explaining conflict that results from the distribution of scarce resources—as these relate to power and prestige—than with the Marxist notion of conflicts deriving from the struggle to do away with divisions imposed by the system of production. His contention that it is not economic factors that lead to class differences, but rather conflicts that center around authority, was explored in Turk's stress on the differences in the status and role of legal authorities and their subjects.[89] Since Turk views these statuses as present in all societies, he argues that they are felt to be necessary to preserve the social order. He argues that law violation is an indication of a breakdown in authority, a symptom of the absence of a stable authority relationship between the "rulers and the ruled."[90]

Since criminality is a status imposed by those in authority, Turk argues, the focus of criminological study should be the criminalization process that imposes the status. In order to understand the acquisition of the criminal status, he suggests that we study the conflict that results from the status and role differences between legal authorities and their subjects, since we relate to social rules according to our status. Turk's work underscores the idea that the definition of criminality results from differences in power, values, and beliefs that characterize the interaction between political authorities and their subjects. The controversy over decriminalization of marijuana illustrates this conflict. As long as those who made the law were of a higher status than those who smoked the weed, there was little reason to change the law. However, when middle-class children began using the drug, their parents—most of whom did not approve of their children's activity—began to argue that penalties for marijuana use were too harsh. As a result, the movement to decriminalize marijuana use has gained considerable momentum.[91]

In an attempt to identify patterns of conflict, Turk argues that the individual's age, sex, and race will determine the extent to which he or she is able to relate to the norms of the authorities who dominate society. For example, a middle-aged or older white woman will be less likely to have conflicts with authority than a young black of any class. The reason, he argues, is that the youth has not been conditioned to arrangements that exist in the authority structure. For much the same reason, conflict is almost inevitable between juveniles and authorities, since juveniles are apt to be unsophisticated about a given set of norms.

In another middle-range conflict approach, Lofland has suggested that crime and deviance are analogous to certain kinds of power games. Crime is defined as a conflict game in which individuals or small, loosely organized groups are feared by a well-organized group or a powerful minority or majority. Table 6.2 depicts the different degrees of fear, size, organization, and power between groups in conflict that produce changes in public definitions of a situation. The imputation of deviance to an act, or to feared persons, depends less upon the nature of the behavior than it does upon the size and de-

Table 6.2 Conflict Situations: Dimensions of the Character and Relations of Parties in Conflict

Resulting Popular Definition of the Conflict Situation	Size and Organization of Party Feared	Economic and Political Power of Party Feared Relative to Party Fearing	Degree to Which the Well-organized Opposing Large Minority or Majority Feels Fearful or Threatened
Deviance ("crime," etc.)	Individual or small, loosely organized groups	Almost none	Very high
Civil uprising or disorder	Small, loosely organized minority	Relatively low	Very high
Social movement	Sizable organized minority	Relatively low	Mild
Civil War	Large, well-organized minority	Relatively high or almost equal	Very high
Mainstream party politics in the United States	Large, organized minority	About equal	Mild

Source: John Lofland, Lyn H. Lofland, *Deviance and Identity,* © 1969, p. 15. Reprinted by permission of Prentice-Hall, Inc., Englewood Cliffs, New Jersey.

gree of power and the extent of organization of those involved. For example, arson, assault, murder, and torture are ordinary, simple crimes. But when carried out by a small group—even though loosely organized—they can be given political connotations as rebellion or terrorism. On the other hand, if they occur in the course of international conflict—as in war—they may be seen as patriotism or heroism.[92]

Lofland's argument is essentially that crime or deviance is attributed to a weak party when an opposing powerful party sponsors the idea that the weak party is breaking the rules of society. This expresses ideas implicit in the thinking of both Vold and Turk. However, although Lofland uses concrete terms, his rather abstract social psychological analysis, along with his emphasis on the individual, represents a tie with the social interactionist or labeling perspective, rather than an analysis of structural conflict.

In his earlier writings, Richard Quinney, who has since become one of the better known proponents of the Marxist or critical version of the conflict perspective, expressed more middle-range or moderate ideas. His earlier contributions were criticized by Taylor et al. (1973) for their "uncritical subjectivism" that cast doubt on the force of laws in society. However, they note with approval his attempt to maintain a dialectic between the subjective world and external reality.[93] In his work, *The Social Reality of Crime* (1970), Quinney states: "Because man engages in social action, a social reality is created .... Having constructed a social reality, man finds a world of meanings and events that is real to him as a conscious human being." [94] Building on this insight as well as a number of explicit assumptions regarding the nature of the individual and society, Quinney sets forth six propositions that together comprise his theory of the social reality of crime. Proposition 1, the starting point for his theory, begins with a definition of crime: "Crime is a definition of human conduct that is created by authorized agents in a politically organized society." [95] The sixth proposition, a composite of the first five, states: "The social reality of crime is constructed by the *formulation* and *application* of criminal definitions, the development of *behavior patterns* related to criminal definitions, and the construction of *criminal conceptions.*" [96]

The interrelationships between these propositions is shown in the model in Figure 6.1. Quinney argues that "the phenomena specified in these propositions and their relationships account for the extent and nature of crime at any given time, that they constitute the social reality of crime." [97]

It is useful here to note some of the basic assumptions shared by both moderate and radical conflict perspectives.[98]

1. Conflict is the product of disequilibrium and contradictions in the social structure, related to values, economics, or politics.
2. Conflict results from a scarcity of wealth, status, and power; inequality stems from differentials in the distribution of wealth, status, authority, and power among different groups in society.
3. Conflicts are inherent between those who rule and those who are ruled, and the criminal law embodies the interests and ideologies of the ruling groups or classes.

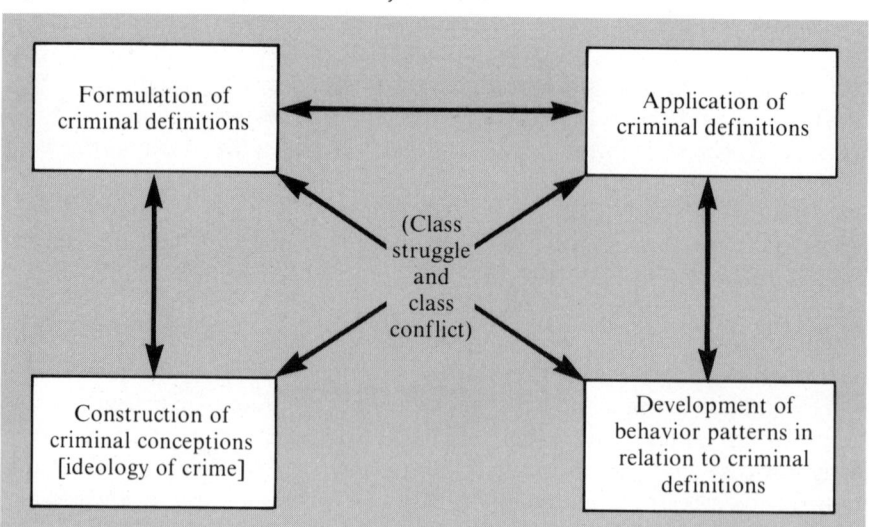

Figure 6.1. Model of the Social Reality of Crime

Source: Richard Quinney, *The Social Reality of Crime*, p. 40. Copyright © 1970 by Little, Brown and Company (Inc.). Reprinted by permission.

This structural analysis describes contradictions in a system more pointedly than anomie theory. In a society that professes to place a high value on equality of opportunity, inequality represents a basic contradiction. The conflicts thus created have been noted by many writers and social critics other than criminologists. Journalist Tom Wicker, for example, has stated:

> Inequality is a major source of social instability and unrest.... Inequality gives rise to feelings of inferiority, which in turn generate inadequacy and self-hate or anger... anger results in crime, delinquency, senseless violence—and, of course, in political protests as well.[99]

Conflict Perspectives and Critical or Radical Criminology

The basic assumptions of the conflict perspective are apparent in the writings of a new version of that perspective, which at various times has been termed "critical criminology," "progressive criminology," "new criminology," "Marxist criminology," or "radical criminology" by both proponents and critics. However, several critics have pointed out that Marx did not develop any theories to explain crime or deviance.[100]

One of the early proponents of this "radical" rendering of the conflict perspective, William Chambliss, has contrasted this perspective with the functional (order) perspective. He points out that they have quite different emphases:

> The functionalist paradigm emphasizes the social psychological experiences of individuals (or groups), which lead some to accept and live by the customs of the society. The conflict perspective places primacy on the role of criminal law and asks how laws emerge and are enforced. Functionalists seek the explanation of crime in the behavior of those labeled criminal. Conflict theorists seek the explanation of crime in the institutions that define criminal acts and in the social relations created by a society's structure, especially its mode of production.[101]

The basic differences between the order perspective, which has characterized mainstream criminology, and the conflict perspective, the emerging radical departure from that view, are contrasted in Table 6.3. This figure highlights the central contention of the conflict perspective, that crime and criminal definitions are the result of a power struggle in which the ruling class succeeds in having its values and norms incorporated into the law. This perspective sees crime as a result of the class struggle.

Chambliss documents his arguments with one of the few empirical studies that the critical perspective has produced. He cites data from his observations in Ibadan, Nigeria, and Seattle to show that in both of these cities crimes are committed by citizens from all classes. He found that laws such as those against bribery, prostitution, and gambling were not enforced. Laws against public drunkenness were enforced. In other words, laws are enforced against the lower classes but not against the ruling classes.[102]

Economist David Gordon provides an analysis of crime that suggests that crime in America is characterized by a rational response to the conditions of

Table 6.3 Contrasts Between Order and Conflict Perspectives on Crime Causes and Consequences

	Criminal Law		Criminal Behavior	
	Cause	**Consequence**	**Cause**	**Consequence**
Conflict Paradigm	Ruling class interests:	Provide state coercive force to repress the class struggle and to legitimize the use of this force.	Class divisions which lead to class struggle:	Crime serves the interests of the ruling class by reducing strains inherent in the capitalist mode of production.
Functional Paradigm (Order)	Customary beliefs that are codified in state law:	To establish procedures for controlling those who do not comply with customs.	Inadequate socialization:	To establish the moral boundaries of the community.

Source: William J. Chambliss, *Functional and Conflict Theories of Crime* (New York: MSS Modular Publications, 1974), p. 8.

competition and inequality fostered by the structure of capitalistic economic and social institutions. He cites as examples, white-collar, organized, and ghetto crime. He argues:

> First, ... that many of the important differences among crimes ... derive quite directly from the different economic classes to which individuals belong.... Second ... that the biases of our police, courts, and prisons explain the relative violence of many crimes—that many of the differences in the degree of violence among different crimes do not cause the selectivity of public concern but *are* in fact *caused* by that selectivity.[103]

Gordon contends that it is implausible to reform our system to eradicate the causes of crime. For one thing, capitalism depends on competition and inequality. Given the fact that capitalists control our policy-making apparatus, we cannot expect the state to change a system that serves the interests of the ruling class.[104]

Quinney has echoed similar arguments in a work that marked his move away from ideas he had formulated earlier, concepts he now terms *"bourgeois academic activity."* His 1975 revision of his model of the social reality of crime now focuses upon *class struggle* and *class conflict* as the links for understanding how the four principles are interrelated (see Figure 6.1).[105] The sixth proposition, however, now has a corollary, first published in his *Critique of the Legal Order* (1974), in which, like Gordon, he asserts: "Only with the collapse of capitalist society and the creation of a new society based on socialist principles will there be a solution to the crime problem."[106]

Criticisms of the Critical Conflict Perspective

This radical version of the conflict perspective has created considerable debate and aroused much criticism. There are, however, variations even of this version, and some of them merge with more moderate views. Critics point out that much of the critical conflict perspectives's critique of earlier criminologists focuses on their neglect of the economic and social conflicts inherent in the development of criminal law. For example, it is one thing to describe the "importance of interest group activity" as a critical variable in influencing legislation of the law, as William Chambliss and Robert Seidman have done. But to specify the varieties of interest groups and the dynamics of their involvement in the process of creating laws involves more than asserting, as Quinney has, that "criminal law is an instrument of the state and ruling class to maintain and perpetuate the existing social and economic order."[107] To attribute single motives to an assumed monolithic ruling class is to simplify a complex process. The complexity of this process is argued in Peter Manning's analysis of England's Metropolitan Police Act of 1829. To attribute this act, which created the first full-time police force, to the protection of the upper classes from the "dangerous classes" is far too simplistic. Manning explains:

> The origins of the civil police in England can be attributed to a variety of factors or causes, some in combination with each other.... there are at least five distinct arguments with supporting evidence which can be formulated to explain the interests which lay behind the conceptualization and passage of the Metropolitan Police Act of 1829.... Each of these is defensible... but none adopts the rigid simplicity of the cruder interest theory implied by Quinney and others.[108]

Another area for which this Marxist-oriented perspective is criticized for presenting an oversimplified view of reality is its accounting of the exercise of power by the ruling class. Much is made by Quinney and others about the "ruling class," who seem to be a small group of people who are the "real criminals" that run society. But we are never told who comprises this small group of ruling elites.

Gresham Sykes accords this perspective's theorists their due for directing our attention to the relationship between the political economy and nonconformity, and thus focusing our attention on the relationships between the individual and the state. But he notes that they have a penchant for uncovering latent functions and turning these into the intended functions of crime control. The fact that racism is very much alive in our society should be explanation enough for the fact that a disproportionate number of minority citizens are incarcerated. It does not necessarily follow that the criminal justice apparatus *deliberately* represses blacks or other minority groups.[109]

Stanton Wheeler suggests that although critical perspective theorists have stimulated an awareness of the political dimensions of crime, they have not generated new empirical findings that support their doctrinaire assertions. Their efforts seem to produce more rhetoric than careful research.[110] Gibbons concurs with this conclusion when he points out that the question, How valid is Marxist criminology? cannot be answered since "there is as yet no comprehensive, rigorously stated radical theory of criminality and responses to crime which can be subjected to empirical test."[111] Critical criminology, then, is still an emerging perspective, holding out greater promise than its proponents have yet produced.

One other major criticism of conflict theory has been advanced by Taylor, et al., whose ideas, it might be noted, are informed by this perspective. They contend that its view of the individual is of a person who is determined by the defining power of the state. This conception of the criminal, they argue, is a "pathological" one—though not to the extent argued by the early positivists. For to explain behavior solely as the result of powerful forces is to deny the individual's integrity and purpose and to suggest that "crime is a nonpurposive (pathological) reaction to external circumstances."[112]

SOCIOLOGICAL THEORIES AND THE STUDY OF CRIME AND CRIMINALITY: CRIMINAL BEHAVIOR SYSTEMS

The prime concern of early criminological theories was the origin of criminal—as contrasted with noncriminal—behavior. More recent theories, however, have sought to explain societal reaction to crime, or why and how specific behavior comes to be labeled "criminal."[113] We have noted that many of these perspectives rest on models of society that assume consensus or order and stability, accept official definitions of behavior, and view the criminal or delinquent as compelled by circumstances to law-violating behavior. We have characterized these positivistic perspectives as *affinities,* since they stress predisposing biological, psychological, or environmental factors that are linked to the person's involvement in crime.

We have also noted that Sutherland's emphasis on *differential association* and *organization* and reformulations of this theory that stressed not only the pluralistic nature of society but also social successes in the development of criminal behavior, might be characterized as *affiliational,* since they sought to describe the group context in which individuals took on or learned law-violating behavior in the same way noncriminal behavior is learned. The labeling perspective, as set forth by Lemert, Becker, and others, has emphasized social reaction to crime, and the manner in which the action of agents of social control affect the subsequent role-career of the offender through secondary deviation. This process—in which agents of the state designate and finally "cast" the labeled person into the category of those who come to "collectively represent" evil, crime, or deviance, as contrasted with noncriminal behavior or conformity—has been related to Matza's third concept, *signification.*[114] This perspective also rejected the search for the causes of criminal behavior in its assumption that crime and deviance grow out of value conflicts in society.

The conflict perspective also linked crime and deviance to conflict be-

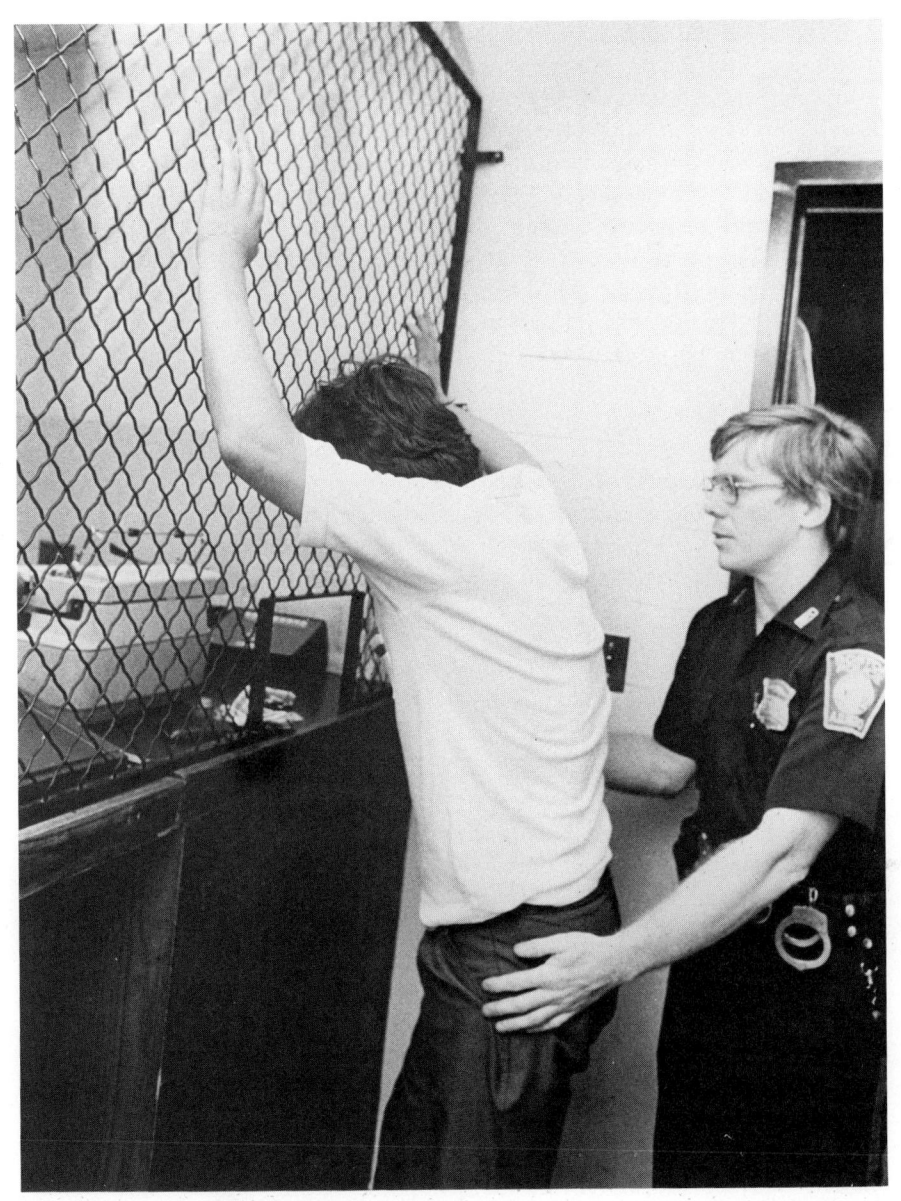

The process of signification and labeling begins.

tween interests and groups. It emphasized that the reality of crime grows out of conflicts in which the ideas of right and wrong held by the most powerful are translated into law. When these definitions are applied to conduct contrary to such laws, the "social reality" of crime is created. A corollary of this premise is that the less powerful, including minorities and the young, are the ones against whom such laws are disproportionately applied. The conflict view has been extended into a radical or critical conflict perspective, based on a Marxist orientation. It links crime to conflicts that emerge from contradictions inherent in the political economy of capitalist societies. It describes crime as behavior that is inimical with the interests of the dominant class in such societies.[115]

This melange of theories illustrates our observation that crime is a diverse phenomenon encompassing an incredibly wide range of behaviors. It is a political, ethical, and moral, as well as a legal problem. Obviously it is beyond the scope of an introductory text in criminology to reformulate and synthesize the many perspectives on crime and criminality into a single grand theory—even if that were possible. But it is incumbent upon the authors to suggest how a student might organize data about crime to better be able to (1) understand the formulation and administration of criminal law, which is the basis for the application of the criminal label; (2) describe and conceptualize the career development of persons and conducts that come to be defined as criminal; and (3) understand the process of societal reaction to crime during which the criminal label is conferred and its subsequent effects on criminal or noncriminal identity.[116]

The behavior, or action system, approach that is described below will provide a perspective for conceptualizing, describing, and interrelating these three subclasses of events or processes encompassed in the study of crime and criminality.

Criminal Behavior or Action Systems: The Typological Approach

The use of criminal typologies to focus on variations between and among types of offenders—rather than analyzing the vast range of traits involved in crime—has become a trend among criminologists. Textbooks by Bloch and Geis, Gibbons, and Sutherland and Cressey use organizing schemes which acknowledge that crime and delinquency are heterogeneous phenomena not lending themselves to analysis by perspectives that explain such behavior either in terms of a single theory or through an accumulation of facts in a shotgun approach.[117]

Other than the fact that they make an unnecessary distinction between criminal and noncriminal behavior, the use of legal definitions such as "misdemeanor" or "felony" has little theoretical significance, since these classifications vary from one jurisdiction to another. A crime classified as a felony in one state may be a misdemeanor in another. Legal categories are also used to relate the criminal to his or her act. For instance, criminals may be identified as burglars, embezzlers, murderers, rapists, robbers, and so on. But as Marshall Clinard and Richard Quinney indicate, these categories present distinct disadvantages. They tell little about the offender or the circumstances or context of the act. They create the false idea that criminals specialize in the type of offense for which they are arrested. And they overlook completely the process of plea bargaining (pleading guilty to a reduced charge). More importantly, these categories imply that those within a given category—burglars, robbers, rapists—basically are all similar. But legal categories are still useful in understanding the process by which behavior is defined as criminal. Since criminality is a status conferred on individuals by agents of social control, the legal definition of crime and its application is an important manifestation of how a category of crime becomes part of the policy of social reaction to crime.

The Criminal Behavior or Action System. A typology is not intended to provide a one-to-one correspondence with reality. Rather, it is a *model* that seeks to assist in the practical, comparative analysis of activity that takes place in the "real" world. Such a model relies on certain assumptions and distinctions inherent in what is to be studied—in this case, criminal behavior as a social process. A criminal typology provides a means for applying several converging perspectives to the analysis of various criminal behavior systems.[118]

Individual and social factors are both significant and interdependent in the shaping of all behavior—criminal or conventional. The individual develops his or her meaning and action systems in terms of interactions with others. In a sense, the individual's beliefs and actions, his or her lifestyle, are the result of comparing, sharing, negotiating, and transmitting such belief and action patterns.[119] As Glaser has suggested in his concept of *differential identification*, a person pursues criminal behavior to the extent that he or she identifies with real or imaginary persons from whose perspective criminal behavior seems acceptable.[120] Consequently, those involved in criminally defined behavior come to identify and interact with those who share their common interest or activity.

The typology of behavior systems that we will use to describe and analyze various criminal action patterns relies on interrelated elements in the social process. For example, we view the concept of *subculture* as a "concrete action system" involving the shared group perspectives, beliefs, or world view of the members. Although a behavior or action system may be relatively stable, the membership of a group may change over time, and a particular actor might move in or out of the "scene" and share the perspectives and identities of other groups, both criminal and noncriminal.[121] Were it not for the pervasiveness and persistence of society's reaction to crime, many criminal careers might well be episodic and intermittent. In other words, social control efforts are viewed as a major contributing factor in shaping the career of the criminal.

A number of assumptions are implied about the nature of crime and society when we set forth and use criminal typologies, and they influence our selection of specific characteristics included in the typology. Since the typology to be used is that of criminal behavior (action) systems, it is necessary to distinguish between the three subclasses of phenomena encompassed in the study of crime. These include (1) the formulation of criminal definitions in the law and its administration; (2) the developing and changing self-images of persons and behaviors that become defined as criminal; and (3) those societal control efforts that influence whether or not an individual is "cast" as an offender.[122]

In setting forth a typology of crime, emphasizing behavior systems is

Table 6.4. Typology of Criminal Behavior Systems

Classification Characteristics	1 Violent Personal Crime	2 Occasional Property Crime	3 Occupational Crime	4 Political Crime
Criminal career of the offender	Low Crime not part of offender's career, usually does not conceive of self as criminal	Low Little or no criminal self-concept; does not identify with crime	Low No criminal self-concept; occasionally violates the law; part of one's legitimate work; accepts conventional values of society	Low Usually no criminal self-concept; violates the law out of conscience; attempts to change society or correct perceived injustices; desire for a better society
Group support of criminal behavior	Low Little or no group support, offenses committed for personal reasons; some support in subcultural norms	Low Little group support; individual offenses	Medium Some groups may tolerate offenses; offender integrated in groups	High Group support; association with persons of same values; behavior reinforced by group
Correspondence between criminal behavior and legitimate behavior patterns	Low Violation of values on life and personal safety	Low Violation of value on private property	High Behavior corresponds to pursuit of business activity; "sharp" practices respected; "buyer beware" philosophy; hands-off policy	Medium Some toleration of protest and dissent, short of revolution; dissent periodically regarded as a threat (in times of national unrest)
Societal reaction	High Capital punishment; long imprisonment	Medium Arrest; jail; short imprisonment, probation	Low Indifference; monetary penalties, revocation of license to practice, seizure of product or injunction	High Strong disapproval; regarded as threat to society; prison
Legal categories of crime	Murder, assault, forcible rape, child molesting	Some auto theft, shoplifting, check forgery, vandalism	Embezzlement, fraudulent sales, false advertising, fee splitting, violation of labor practice laws, antitrust violations, black market activity, prescription violation	Treason, sedition, espionage, sabotage, radicalism, military draft violations, war collaboration, various protests defined as criminal

Classification Characteristics	5 Public Order Crime	6 Conventional Crime	7 Organized Crime	8 Professional Crime
Criminal career of the offender	Medium Confused self-concept; vacillation in identification with crime	Medium Income supplemented through crimes of gain; often a youthful activity; vacillation in self-concept; partial commitment to a criminal subculture	High Crime pursued as a livelihood; criminal self-concept; progression in crime; isolation from larger society	High Crime pursued as a livelihood; criminal self-concept; status in the world of crime; commitment to world of professional criminals
Group support of criminal behavior	Medium Partial support for behavior from some groups; considerable association with other offenders	High Behavior supported by group norms; status achieved in groups; principal association with other offenders	High Business associations in crime; behavior prescribed by the groups; integration of the person into the group	High Associations primarily with other offenders; status gained in criminal offenses; behavior prescribed by group norms
Correspondence between criminal behavior and legitimate behavior patterns	Medium Some forms required by legitimate society; some are economic activities	Medium Consistent with goals on economic success; inconsistent with sanctity of private property; behavior not consistent with expectations of adolescence and young adulthood	Medium Illegal services received by legitimate society; economic risk values; large-scale control also employed in legitimate society	Medium Engaged in an occupation; skill respected; survival because of cooperation from legitimate society; law-abiding persons often accomplices
Societal reaction	Medium Arrest; jail; prison; probation	High Arrest; jail; probation; institutionalization; parole; rehabilitation	Medium Considerable public toleration; arrest and sentence when detected; often not visible to society; immunity through politicians and law officers	Medium Rarely strong societal reaction, most cases "fixed"
Legal categories of crime	Drunkenness, vagrancy, disorderly conduct, prostitution, homosexuality, gambling, traffic violation, drug addiction	Robbery, larceny, burglary, gang theft	Racketeering, organized prostitution and commercialized vice, control of drug traffic, organized gambling	Confidence games, shoplifting, pickpocketing, forgery, counterfeiting

Source: From *Criminal Behavior Systems: A Typology*, 2nd ed., by Marshall B. Clinard and Richard Quinney. Copyright © 1973, 1967 by Holt, Rinehart and Winston, Inc. Reprinted and adapted by permission of Holt, Rinehart and Winston.

useful, since it relates the personal career of the individual who has a probability of being defined as criminal to the degree to which he or she comes to share the perspectives and identities of the group against which social control efforts have been taken. It suggests the extent of group support that might be expected subsequent to such societal reaction.

One of the more comprehensive, albeit eclectic, criminal typologies is that outlined by Clinard and Quinney (1973). In our discussion of *criminal career* patterns in the following five chapters, we will use a modified version of their formulation of a typology of criminal behavior, since it adapts readily to the six types on which we will focus.

The Clinard-Quinney model is based upon four characteristics related to the career development of the criminal. These four defining elements, as we will apply them in our description and analysis of criminal *action* or *behavior systems* are: [123]

1. *The criminal career and criminal self-concept of the offender.* To what degree is criminal behavior a part of the identity and lifestyles of the person or group?
2. *Affiliation forces or group support for the offender.* To what extent is the individual a part of the "concrete action system" of the group? Has he or she come to share the perspectives and identities of this or other groups that might promote affiliation with criminal or noncriminal behavior?
3. *Convergence between criminal and legitimate behavior patterns.* To what extent does the behavior system manifest the complexity of interrelationships between interests, goals, and means as defined by the dominant group? Is there an apparent disjuncture between illegitimate and conventional behavior patterns?
4. *Societal Reaction.* What forms of informal and formal social control efforts are brought into play, such as rejection, arrest, prosecution, conviction, or sentencing, and what are their consequences for the person's subsequent criminal career development and identity?

Legal categories of crime are used to link these four elements or characteristics into a typology of criminal behavior or action systems (see Table 6.4). In subsequent chapters we will explain seven types of criminal behavior systems in terms of these four elements. These include Professional and Organized Crime Behavior Systems (Chapter 7); Patterns of Violent Crime (Chapter 8); Avocational and Commonplace Crime (Chapter 9); White-Collar Crime Patterns (Chapter 10); and Victimless Crime and Public Order Crime Patterns (Chapter 11). The survey of these behavior systems relies on ideas outlined in this and previous chapters. Since criminal behavior is human behavior, it can best be described in terms of the same social processes used to describe noncriminal behavior. It is important that the variety of behavior systems be seen as action systems that change and vary as the concrete circumstances and individual actors change within the context of changing social structures.

SUMMARY

This chapter has recounted some of the major criminological perspectives that have been advanced to account for crime, criminal behavior, and criminality. David Matza's concepts—*affinity, affiliation,* and *signification*—have been utilized, as in two earlier chapters, as a frame of reference that is suggestive of the interrelationships inherent in the development of these various perspectives. The reader should be reminded of a subtle criticism implicit in this discussion; namely, that no one of the bodies of theories referred to by and of itself provides an adequate accounting for the diverse phenomena encompassed in the study of criminology. Yet we do not throw *affinity* out because its explanatory powers are limited. Rather, we build upon it by placing it in the context of the ideas of *affiliation* and *signification*.[124]

The concept of *affinity*—used out of context by early positivists—focused on the assumed relationship between biological and psychological factors and criminal behavior. More recently it has been used to infer "kinds of environments"—social, economic, and cultural factors—that were seen as related to crime and criminal behavior. Such factors may describe the circumstances in which crime occurs, but they are inadequate explanations unless related to social processes (affiliation), social control efforts, and/or societal reaction (signification).

Affiliation perspectives described included those that focus on social processes that are also present in conditions of affinity. Perspectives in this mode have shown a shift toward those that emphasize the manner in which the individual actor learns such behavior in a social context of diverse cultures that present a diversity of choice in which they are learned. *Affiliation* describes the process and social context through which individuals may be "turned on" or "out," and thus affiliate with behavior novel to them. Sutherland's theory of *differential association* was examined as one which represented this shift in emphasis while building upon the earlier ideas of social disorganization of the Chicago school (affinity). While Sutherland's has been the single most influential American theory, it has been widely criticized, and several significant reformulations have been attempted. Among those detailed were the *differential anticipation theory* of Glaser and the reformulation of Akers' *differential association reinforcement*. This version focuses more explicitly on social learning principles that were not specified in Sutherland's theory.

Signification perspectives included the societal reaction or labeling perspective and conflict theories, both moderate and radical or critical versions. The *labeling* perspective stresses the process of the creation of criminality and emphasizes the extent to which behavior results from social reaction and the response by the individual to that social reaction. The labeling perspective views criminality as a status conferred upon a person. This perspective distinguishes between *primary* and *secondary* deviation. Through the labeling process, roles and relationships made available to the person become part of his or her identity.

Conflict theories view crime as conflict over power, status, and wealth between and within various groups in society. More recent conflict theories are, in essence, modifications of the Marxist theory of conflict. For instance, Turk argued in a moderate version that lawbreaking illustrates the lack of a stable relationship between the rulers and the ruled. But Quinney's Marxist-oriented version views crime as the result of the imposition of the interests of the ruling class in a capitalist society. Conflict theorists in both their moderate and critical versions stimulated an awareness of the political dimensions of the crime problem, but have not yet generated new empirical studies of crime.

Typologies of criminal behavior or action systems provide a means for using theoretical perspectives to analyze variations between and within criminal behavior systems. In setting forth a typology of crime, the idea of *behavior systems* is used since it relates criminal definitions to crime career roles, to the degree to which the individual offender comes to share the perspectives and identities of the group, and to societal reaction by the criminal justice system. If the crime problem is to be understood, we must be able to describe why certain groups and behaviors come to be labeled criminal and how individuals and groups come to affiliate with such activities.

Since crime is not a unitary phenomenon, the use of a *criminal behavior system* typology enables us to describe both behavior and the process of assigning criminal status. We are able then to make distinctions between various levels of phenomena—that is, between persons who share certain social characteristics and behaviors—and the definitions that may be applied in the process of social reaction to such behaviors. Such a typology provides a perspective for organizing the study of crime on a multidimensional level, related to the various types of offenders. We also avoid thereby the mechanistic use of numerous individual and social traits which infer "primitive" pathological causes of crime.

ADDITIONAL READINGS

Henshel, Richard L. and Robert A. Silverman, eds. *Perception in Criminology.* New York: Columbia University Press, 1975.

> A collection of sources from the emerging area of perception in criminological research and theory. The introductory essay by the editors is a cogent discussion of this perspective.

Matza, David. *Becoming Deviant.* Englewood Cliffs, New Jersey: Prentice-Hall, 1969.

> The major theme of this work is naturalism, the need to describe deviants as they really are. Part I traces the development of naturalism and outlines some of its main themes, while Part II discusses becoming deviant as viewed from this perspective.

Radzinowicz, Leon and Joan King. *The Growth of Crime.* New York: Basic Books, 1977.

> The authors place the study of crime and their analysis of responses to it in a comparative, international context. Part II, "Explaining Crime," surveys major perspectives, relates these to their ideological assumptions, and suggests some implications to consider in the continuing search for causes.

Reasons, Charles E., ed. *The Criminologists: Crime and the Criminal.* Pacific Palisades, Calif.: Goodyear, 1974.

> This reader provides critiques by criminologists who focus on nontraditional issues and topics that complement traditional concepts. It includes topics such as political crime, corporate crime, and police and correctional crime.

Taylor, Ian, Paul Walton and Jock Young. *The New Criminology: For a Social Theory of Deviance.* New York: Harper and Row, 1973.

> A cogent, comprehensive critique of past and present studies of crime and deviance. The authors relate such explanations to relevant general social theories.

Vold, George B. *Theoretical Criminology.* New York: Oxford University Press, 1958.

> The first textbook to place a significant emphasis on social conflict in explaining crime. Also provides a comprehensive comparative historical description of the traditional schools of criminology.

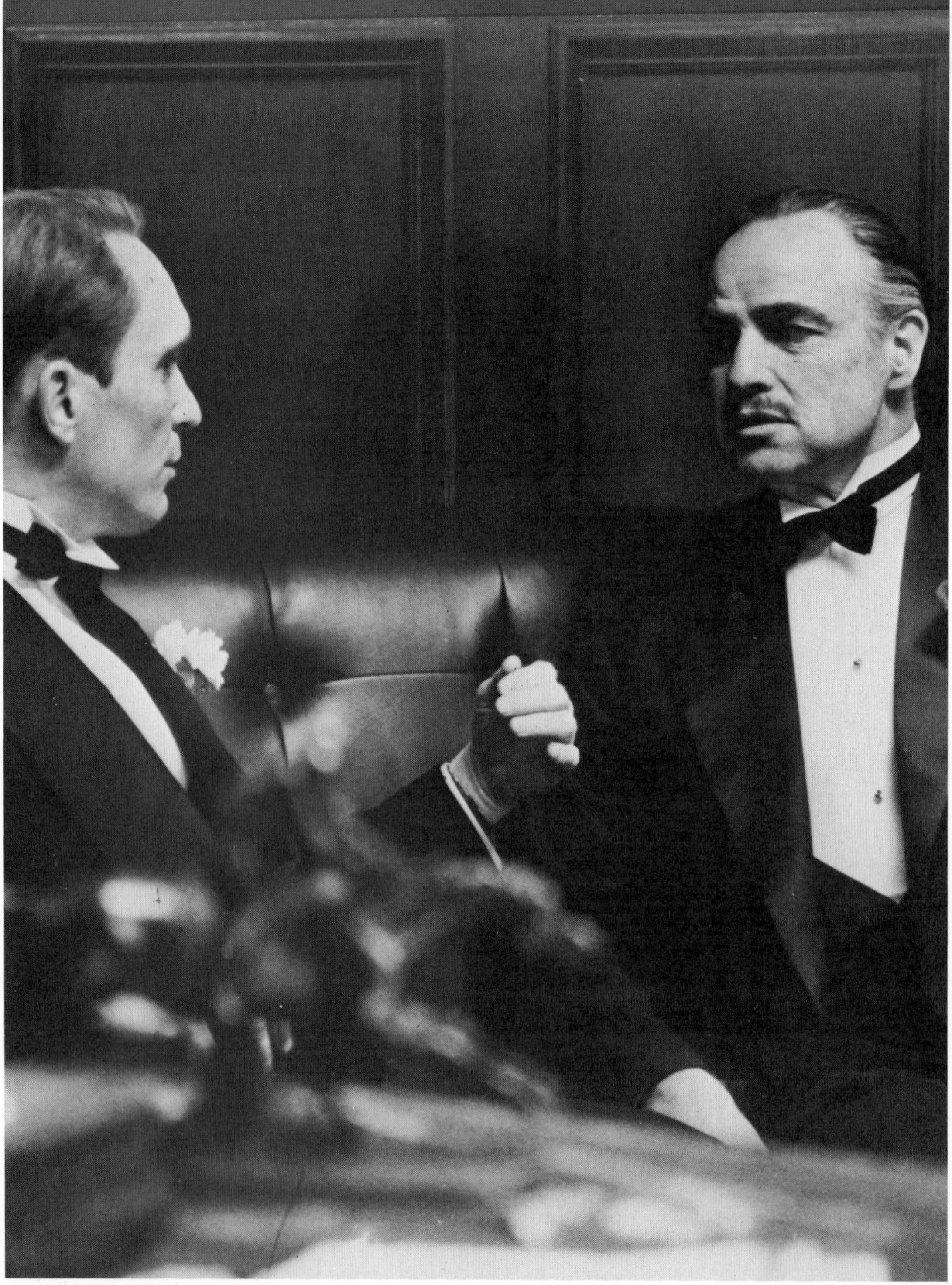

I hate this "crime doesn't pay" stuff. Crime in the United States is perhaps one of the biggest businesses in the world today.
—Paul Kirk, Wall Street Journal, Feb. 26, 1960

7

PROFESSIONAL AND ORGANIZED CRIME BEHAVIOR SYSTEMS

"Organized crime." The phrase conjures up undeniably romantic images of Don Corleone as "the Godfather" (played by Marlon Brando, of course), running his fiefdom of crime, dispensing Mafia "justice" without flinching, helping widows and orphans. The fear of being mugged or having one's home burglarized has left few Americans indifferent to the "crime problem." But few of us who waited in long lines to see Al Pacino pick up the mantle from his fallen "father" and become "Godfather II" lost much sleep that night worrying about organized crime.

Just what is the reality of organized crime in America? Does it really consist only of activities—gambling, prostitution, loansharking and dope pushing—for which there is a public demand and which hurt no one, except, perhaps, the tax collector? In this chapter we shall explore the reality of professional and organized crime and its effects on American society.

Professional and organized crime activities are explicit examples of crime as an action or behavior system. These "vocational" crimes clearly bring together a set of beliefs, perspectives, identities, and self-concepts among their practitioners through a variety of fairly stable behavior patterns or action systems. Vocational crime and criminal activity become a basic dimension of the actor's lifestyle, or action system, within his or her social world. Crime is pursued as a livelihood in both professional and organized crime careers through specialized kinds of offenses or illegal business activities. This kind of criminal activity involves a commitment to shared understandings and behaviors in a long-term, continuing pattern. Edwin Lemert would call these criminals *secondary deviants*, since the behavior defined as criminal encompasses self-concept (self-definitions), a reference group (shared meanings), and a progression into activities defined as criminal.[1]

While general knowledge about criminal activity is sparse, the history of the systematic study of crime reflects a preoccupation with describing and analyzing vocational crime and criminals. Cesare Lombroso located the career criminal, or criminoloid, between the "born" criminal and the ordinary conforming human. Contemporary descriptions of career crime focus on the manner in which perspectives and identity related to the actor's career patterns are brought together and are shared in a relatively stable action, or behavior system. Such an approach enables us to describe the process by which the individual comes to identify and affiliate with relevant lifestyles.[2]

James Inciardi defines career crime as law-violating behavior that is pursued in an occupational context for the purpose of obtaining a steady flow of income. The development of the criminal career begins with initiation into the world of crime, followed by a maturation process involving the acquisition of skills, knowledge, and associations appropriate for maintaining the desired occupation.[3] Inciardi delineates three categories within this general type: (1) *professional crime,* (2) *professional "heavy" crime,* and (3) *organized crime.*

PROFESSIONAL CRIME

Professional crime is the name given to those kinds of law-violating behaviors that involve considerable skill, are nonviolent, and seek to maximize economic gain and minimize the chance of being detected or arrested. The term "professional" is used to imply specialization, a degree of training, an occupational hierarchy, and a status system. Professional thieves look down upon amateurs. The range of illegal activities subsumed under the professional crime label usually includes *pickpocketing, burglary, shoplifting, confidence swindling, forgery* and *counterfeiting,* and *extortion.*[4]

History of Professional Crime

The emergence of career crime in England was traced in one study to economic and social dislocations in the postfeudal period of the fourteenth, fifteenth, and sixteenth centuries. Masses of peasants forced off the land by the enclosure movement were joined by lawless elements, and a tradition of lawlessness developed. A similar process took place in the cities during the Elizabethan era, when urbanization attracted large numbers of people who had been left landless and destitute during the earlier upheavals. Shakespeare immortalized professional criminals of this era in works such as *The Winter's Tale,* which provides a literary reference to a pickpocket as a "snapper upper of unconsidered trifles." Thomas Wright describes a school in London in 1585 that trained pickpockets by attaching bells to dummies to test the inept novice. And Frank Aydelotte's work on *Elizabethan Rogues and Vagabonds* (1913) tells how pickpockets in the 1600s would greet a stranger as though he were a long lost relative. While the victim's eyes were covered with one hand, he would be asked, "Who am I?" and his pocket would be picked by the cutpurse. Aydelotte also describes the *esprit de corps* of the seventeenth-century professional criminal, which closely resembles that of his counterpart today.[5]

Elizabethan professional criminals come to life for us in pamphlets and ballads of that era, which were collected in Arthur Judge's *The Elizabethan Underworld* (1939). These documents include descriptions of the way of life of vagabond *cozeners* and *conny-catchers.* Originally "conny-catching" was slang for a method used to cheat at cards. But it came to mean any method used to carry off a swindle. The methods for cheating are described in Judge's work in the following terms:[6]

1. *Highlaw:* the art of highway robbery
2. *Sacking law:* brothel keeping
3. *Cheating law:* swindling with dice
4. *Crossbiting law:* swindling and extortion by prostitutes
5. *Conny-catching law:* swindling by card tricks
6. *Versing law:* swindling with false gold
7. *Figging law:* the out of the cut-purse (pickpocket)
8. *Bernard's law:* cheating a drunk with cards
9. *Block art:* picking locks
10. *Curbing law:* looking from open windows
11. *Vincent's law:* swindling at bowling games
12. *Priggin law:* house stealing
13. *Lifting law:* shoplifting and general stealing

These methods, as well as accompanying status systems, still survive. Among pickpockets, for instance, the *foist* who used his fingers had higher status than the *nip,* who used a knife to obtain the purse. Also, city *nips* were of a higher order than country *nips,* as were other city types. Although punishment was harsh for these crimes, it did not seem to deter the criminals. Even at the public hangings of pickpockets, we are told, spectators were relieved of their purses. These criminal patterns were not limited to England. They existed on the Continent as well, and eventually spread to the United States, where they flourished, especially on the frontier.[7]

Patterns of professional crime were not studied systematically by social scientists until the 1930s, when Edwin H. Sutherland's *The Professional Thief* was published (1937). This work detailed the characteristics and complexity of the career of a professional thief. The man who described his "profession" was a confidence man and thief named Chic Conwell. Sutherland's work is not just a study of one thief, but of the lifestyle, action system and activities, social institutions, and relationships of this way of life.[8]

Professional Burglary: Behavior System

The activities of direct participants in career crime typically include burglary (house or personal burglary and safecracking), sneak theft (includes shoplifting and pickpocketing), confidence swindling (the "short" and "big con"), forgery, counterfeiting, and extortion.[9] Neal Shover also includes the "connections," who constitute the external organization of the professional. These are the required contacts with those in the straight world who help the professional cope with a variety of problems. Those identified by Shover and others include the *tipster,* the *fence,* the *bondsman,* and *attorneys.*[10]

It is important to keep in mind that we rely on the use of a social-psychological, phenomenological typology to better describe the process by which individuals who share certain characteristics and behaviors take on patterns of behavior—lifestyles—or action systems that may result in their being defined as a criminal. These types are not as clear-cut as they may seem when viewing them through the narrow perspective of official crime statistics. For a burglar may not specialize in "breaking and entering," or "safecracking." As both Bruce Jackson's case study of "Sam," and Sutherland's earlier description show, burglars may be involved in other kinds of theft, forgery, confidence games, and in Sam's career, even pimping. Not all burglary is committed by one type of offender.[11]

Therefore, our references to official statistics are used only to illustrate an aspect of legal reaction to professional crime. Such data are more an indication of police activity than of the reality of crime. While they tell us the incidence of a particular "kind of crime," as defined and recorded by the police, they tell us little about the offender type—the "kind of person"—who commits the crime. A given offender type may be arrested for this or a variety of other offenses. Consequently, his or her activities may appear in official statistics a number of times. As Harry King, narrator of *The Box Man* (1972) notes, one arrest may result in a number of charges. "In the old days, we used to...make a deal with the police....they would have a lot of unsolved crimes....They'd say, I got fifteen capers here we haven't been able to solve, will you clean them up for us?...we'd just sign a confession, I mean it wasn't really a confession."[12]

When official data show that burglary offenses increased by 47 percent between 1970 and 1975 (see Figure 7.1), this does not mean that the number of offenders who identify with the perspectives and lifestyles of burglars has increased proportionately. In fact, since many burglaries occurred in noncommercial situations (see Figure 7.2), it is likely that nonprofessionals (amateurs, "punks," or drug addicts), rather than career burglars, could account for much of the increases. In other words, the considerable cost of burglary—$1.226 billion as estimated by the Joint Economic Committee in 1976—is the result of burglary by amateurs as well as career criminals.[13]

The crime of bank burglary, when it flourished in earlier times, demanded considerable skill in the use of explosives. This technique has faded, due both to regulations on the sale of nitroglycerine and the development of acetylene torches that are effective for cutting through metal in safecracking. Also, safecracking in banks has largely gone out of vogue, after the development of sophisticated timed locks and alarm systems.

Figure 7.1. Percent Change in Burglary, 1970–1975

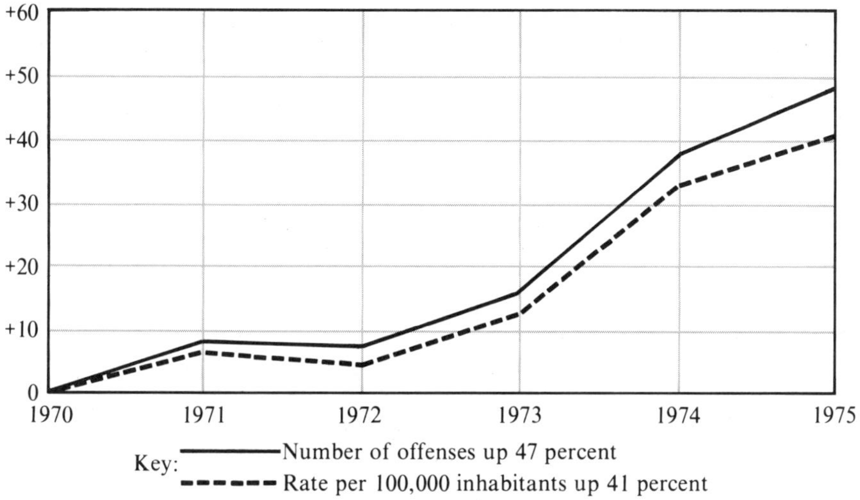

Key: ——— Number of offenses up 47 percent
‑ ‑ ‑ ‑ Rate per 100,000 inhabitants up 41 percent

Source: FBI, *Uniform Crime Reports, 1975* (Washington, D.C.: U.S. Government Printing Office, 1975), p. 25.

Jackson's study of a professional safecracker and forger, *A Thief's Primer* (1969), details action against smaller firms that seldom involved explosives, but rather featured the use of acetylene torches, drilling, or straight lockpicking as the modus operandi.[14] (See Box 1.)

Professional Theft: Behavior System

Shoplifting. Shoplifting is a time-honored variant of career crime, along with pickpocketing. Both fall under the category of "sneak theft" in Inciardi's classification. Official data (see Figure 7.3) suggest that recorded incidents of shoplifting have increased while pickpocketing apparently has declined. In *The Professional Thief,* Sutherland described two types of career shoplifters, the *booster* and the less skillful *heel.*[15] In a more recent work, Mary O. Cameron uses a slightly different typology. She calls the professional shoplifters *boosters,* and those who shoplift for their own use, *snitches.* The professionals, the boosters, prefer small stores in large cities such as Chicago or New York (Cameron's study was centered on a description of activities in Chicago with comparisons to other large cities). The large department stores are protected by store detectives and antitheft techniques that make action more risky.[16]

Although Cameron found that about 10 percent of the shoplifters arrested in department stores were professionals, this estimate does not provide an accurate index of the proportion involved in career shoplifting. The exact extent of shoplifting is difficult to determine. Many thieves go undetected and store managers are reluctant to risk arresting those who appear to be respectable customers. The booster, or career thief, dresses carefully. Thus, it is often the

Figure 7.2. Percent Change in Residential and Nonresidential Burglary, 1970–1975

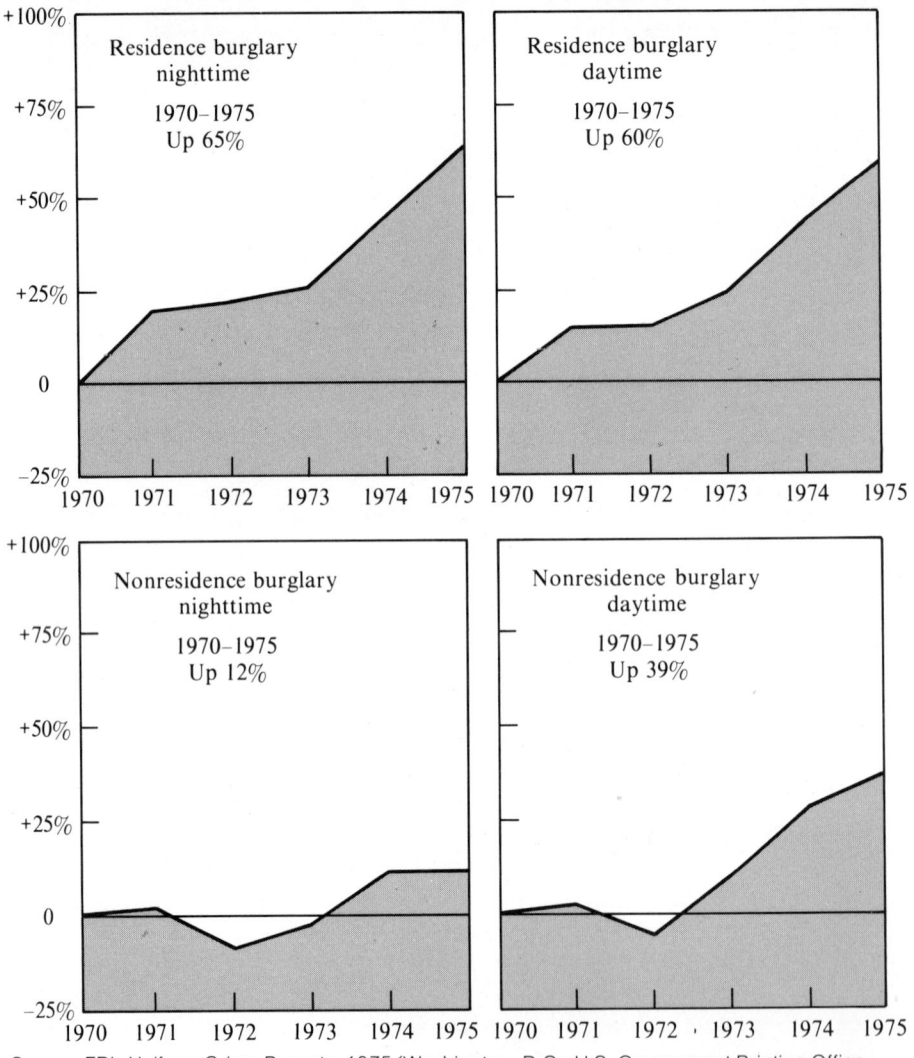

Residence burglary nighttime
1970–1975
Up 65%

Residence burglary daytime
1970–1975
Up 60%

Nonresidence burglary nighttime
1970–1975
Up 12%

Nonresidence burglary daytime
1970–1975
Up 39%

Source: FBI, *Uniform Crime Reports, 1975* (Washington, D.C.: U.S. Government Printing Office, 1975), p. 36.

poor or minority group members who are arrested and prosecuted, rather than the career offender who gives the appearance of being middle class. Women comprise a majority among both boosters and amateur shoplifters (over 60 percent). They often use "booster skirts" and other women's apparel, such as undergarments with hooks, to conceal goods. As one of Inciardi's informants stated, "women always make better shoplifts. Their sex gives them the advantage. They have more places to hide the stuff and they can always dangle a

The Thief's Work

BOX 1

Safecracking is hard work; it is goddamned hard, man. You don't know. You're cooped up in a little office.... I tell you, I have seen the floor in an office where I was working so wet with sweat it looked like it rained in there....

I have worked so hard on a safe I have had to lay down and rest before I could get out of the building. You work until you're completely exhausted....

It's hard work. There's climbing fences and roofs and going through those roofs and chipping that cement out and all that. And you're working under a strain and you're looking over your shoulder all the time.

But there's one thing about safes: I think it actually *charges* you.

There's only two danger points in burglarizing: your entrance and your exit. Your entrance is the most dangerous, and the reason for that is that if they see you go in, you're inside, and they've got you. But exiting, if they see you coming out, you don't have too much to worry about because you're on your way....

Now after I get inside, all my fear more or less is gone, ... and you concentrate on the safe. Of course you always know what kind of safe it is before you make your entrance. You go in, you've got your tools, and you can estimate what's in the safe. If it's a place that has delivery trucks, you can figure a couple of hundred per truck....

But still and all, that jewel *might* be the one (the big score).

It might be the guy that's beating the income tax, or it might be the guy that's booking all the big football payoff or layoff.

And there is no charge in the world like when you see that smoke. For instance, if you're punching it and you hear that pin hit the back of the safe—clinggg—you know you're home free. If you're peeling it whenever you pop the door and see that smoke, you know that you've cracked the rivets and it's all yours. And when you pull that safe door open: it is a *charge!*

Source: Excerpted from Bruce Jackson, *A Thief's Primer* (New York: Macmillan Co., 1972), pp. 114–16. Copyright © 1969 by Bruce Jackson.

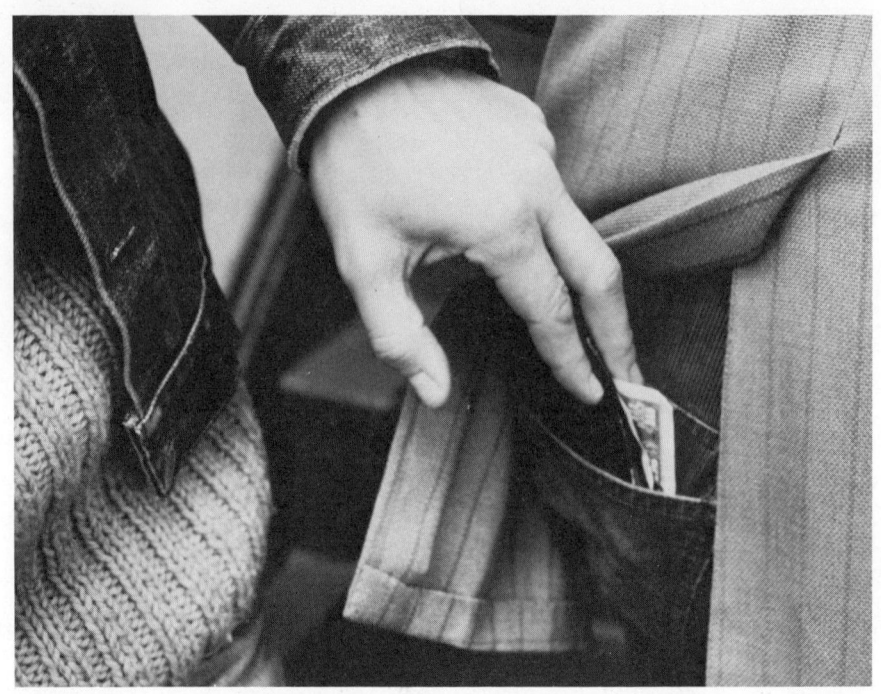

The professional "snitch" or pickpocket.

bag between their legs. They also get more sympathy or holler louder if they are caught."[17]

Cameron relates the case of one woman, who upon being arrested by the store detective, maintained that she was a novice, although the detective was certain that she had a record. When he persisted in bringing charges, she entered a plea of guilty as a first offender through her attorney and received probation. After some discrete inquiries, Cameron discovered that her attorney was hired on a steady retainer's fee, and the woman had a record of numerous offenses. Cameron concluded that snitches are neither compulsive kleptomaniacs nor uncontrolled thieves. Furthermore, once apprehended, the amateur seems unable to accept being branded a thief. She relates how one woman reacted: "Yes, I took the dress, but that doesn't mean I'm a thief."[18] Often the distress over being arrested, together with the prospect of being held in jail and required to appear in court, seems sufficient to deter such people from continuing their activities. This is not the case with the "professionals."

Pickpocketing. Although the behavior system of picking pockets has deep historic roots, it has been declining as a career in recent years, apparently because of the lack of new recruits. It is estimated that the number of expert pickpockets or *class cannons* declined from 6,000 to 1,000 between 1945 and 1955. According to one of Inciardi's informants, who was himself an expert pickpocket in the Times Square area of New York, there were no more than

BOX 2

The Ins and Outs of Pickpocketing

Every December, thousands of tourists fill their wallets and fly to Florida for a sunny vacation. Right behind them come a flock of professional thieves who consider the Miami area a pickpocket mecca. Sociologist James A. Inciardi of the University of Delaware interviewed 20 of these sticky-fingered criminals while they were in Miami for the winter season.

Professional pickpockets, or "class cannons" as they call themselves, ply their trade in amusement centers, transportation depots and other areas brimming with tourists. Resorts make particularly easy pickings, says Inciardi, because they cater to carefree people with a lot of cash. "Their pockets are full and their heads empty," observes one veteran cannon. "You can pull down their drawers and they might not notice."

Smooth Operation. Usually the pickpocket works in a "mob" of three or four members, Inciardi explains, each with a specific part in the theft. First, they select a "mark" on the basis of tourist-type dress and behavior, besides an occupational intuition that the victim has money. Although the mark may be followed for a long time, the theft itself takes less than a second. Cannons snatch a wallet without bumping, jostling or otherwise disturbing the victim, which are sure signs of an amateur. Once the loot is in hand, the cannon quickly passes it to another mob member and immediately leaves the area.

Women are rarely targets, Inciardi reports. In fact, "moll-buzzers" are considered low class by the pickpocket fraternity. One possible reason for this snobbery among thieves is that men usually carry the money, the sociologist suggests. Also, pickpockets seem to feel that robbing a woman lacks courage. And they point out that many women carefully guard their purses, so stealing a wallet can be awkward and obvious.

The class cannons reported average incomes of $23,000 per year; the seasonal take in Miami alone was about $9,200. A hard-working mob will track 10 to 15 marks a day and will "score" five dollars or more in only half its thefts. The average take for each victim is $10 to $25.

Getting Uncaught. Pickpockets claim they get caught by their marks only once in a hundred times. Even then, they can usually talk the victim out of pressing charges. "Just give 'em his money back and then some," said one experienced pro. "Tell him he's gonna have to go to court, give up the loot as evidence." Few marks are willing to spoil their vacations with such legal hassles.

Inciardi found that pickpockets work in a detached manner without hatred or contempt for their victims. They rationalize their thievery by comparing it to the practices of dishonest business persons and corrupt cops. And they argue that the victims—often living in high style—can easily afford the loss.

To avoid becoming a mark, use a money belt or put your wallet in your boot, the pickpockets suggest. Tight trousers make it hard to remove the loot, they add. Most important of all, don't use your wallet as a "portable safety deposit box," advised one class cannon. "You can't get beat if you don't have much."

Source: *Human Behavior*, July 1977. Copyright © 1977 *Human Behavior Magazine*. Reprinted by permission.

600 or 700 in the country in 1965.[19] Doubtless, the increased use of credit cards and checks has contributed to this demise.

Greater reliance on television viewing and the use of private vehicles rather than mass transit in many urban regions have also resulted in fewer opportunities for pickpockets. The American tourist visiting places such as London, however, may hear repeated warnings from the police in crowded areas about the hazards of encountering this type of thief.

Confidence Swindling. Confidence swindling or the confidence game has been aptly described by Chic Conwell: "The con, or confidence game, has many angles, but the central principle in all true con rackets is to show a sucker how he can make some money by dishonest methods and beat him in his attempted dishonesty. For this it is necessary to be a good actor, a good salesman, and have good manners and a good appearance." [20]

In general, there are two basic con rackets: the *short con* and the *big con*. In the short con, the intent is to get the money that the *mark*, or sucker, may have on his person. Among the types of short cons described by Conwell are the money machine, diamond smuggling, dropping the poke or the pigeon drop, the duke (cheating at cards), and selling worthless property as stolen goods of greater value.

In his linguistic analysis of the argot, or specialized slang, employed in confidence games, David Maurer has provided an illustration of how technical skill in the use of words is an intricate aspect of the action system of the con artist. In his recent work, *The American Confidence Man* (1974), Maurer differentiates ten steps in which language is skillfully used to inveigle a victim (the mark) into betting a large amount of money—in this case on a horse race which the mark has been duped into thinking is rigged. The language and pattern depicted are characteristic of the more complicated, classic forms of the confidence game. Of course, all ten of the following steps are not necessary in every scheme:[21]

1. *Putting the mark up.* This may require newspaper advertisements, attendance at conventions or resorts in order to attract and investigate a gullible, well-to-do victim.
2. *Playing the con for him.* In order to gain the victim's confidence and interest, the "outside" man exhibits characteristics of affluence, and provides information on how to make money through investments which gains the respect of the victim, who may also feel flattered by the attention he receives.
3. *Roping the mark.* The victim is "steered" or introduced to the "inside" man. The "roper's" or "outside" man's information may be confirmed by meeting an accomplice who seems to have benefited from similar information; alternatively, this task is left to the "inside" man.
4. *Telling him the tale.* The insider verifies that the "mark" can indeed make a large amount of money through a wise but dishonest investment. This illusion is enhanced, as is the mark's confidence.

5. *Giving him the convincer.* The mark is allowed to make a sizable profit on a small investment.
6. *Giving him the breakdown.* In view of this easy gain, the mark and the con man discuss how much money they might raise from various sources to really make a "killing." While appearing to share in the mark's intended investment, the con men find out how much the victim will invest.
7. *Putting him on the send.* Confident that he has an opportunity to make a quick return on his money, the victim goes to get the amount agreed upon for his share of the investment.
8. *Taking off the touch.* Acting on the assumption that the con men are also investing in the scheme, the "mark" makes a large investment, but is *fleeced*—he loses it.
9. *Blowing him off.* The mark must be gotten rid of. The con men might disappear quickly, or to prevent him causing too much trouble, too quickly, they might "cool the mark out" by giving him the impression that they, too, have lost a considerable amount. They attempt to lessen the hazard of his calling the police by emphasizing the illegal aspects of what has taken place.
10. *Putting in the fix.* The con men seek to protect themselves from legal action. They might pay off police (the fix) in order to insure their gain and continue their "game" on other "marks."

In the big con, the sucker or mark may be kept on the hook for several days. The "wire" (horse race) and the stock market are the main big con rackets and are referred to as the "pay off." Confidence games depend upon the overlap of the values of the person to be swindled with those of the crime professional. As Chic Conwell suggests, you cannot beat an honest person in a confidence game. Sutherland also argues that there is little logical difference between the confidence game and "shady" or "sharp" business practices, except perhaps that shady real estate schemes and consumer fraud rely on the victim's stupidity. Confidence games rely on the cupidity of the victim, who thinks he has an opportunity to show how smart he is. In reality an appeal is being made to the mark's "sense of larceny." Conwell also observed that confidence games do not work well in England because of the "basic honesty" of the English. Yet in America, there have been numerous instances where prominent people have gone so far as to embezzle money to attempt a quick killing in a confidence game.[22]

Forgery and Counterfeiting. Forgery and counterfeiting are defined in the FBI's *Uniform Crime Reports* as "making, altering, uttering or possessing, with intent to defraud, anything false which is made to appear true." They differ from other forms of fraud in that the victim is not involved in the scheme.[23]

Sutherland points out that counterfeiters and forgers have never been considered part of professional thieving. However, professional thieves frequently obtain traveler's checks or counterfeit currency and pass it, or "lay the paper."

In recent years, check forging has become a more or less solitary career, as Lemert suggested in "The Behavior of the Systematic Check Forger" (1958). Although forgery may not be a shared group activity, solitary professionals often buy counterfeit checks and identification from thieves who produce or steal them during their burglary activities.[24]

The Joint Economic Committee estimated the combined cost of check and credit card fraud to be about $1.6 billion in 1976, with check frauds alone accounting for about $1.1 billion. This seems to be a conservative estimate, since a decade earlier one authority put it at $800 million per year. In forgery, as in shoplifting, the total volume of offenses is augmented by numerous amateurs who become involved due to a web of unfortunate personal circumstances.[25]

As banks and other organizations institute various techniques for guarding against fraudulent checks, professional forgers also work on improving their methods. Among incarcerated offenders, forgers generally have been found to be more intelligent than other prisoners. They also are older and have a recidivism rate twice that of others.[26]

Extortion. Known as the *shakedown,* or in its more blatant form, blackmail, extortion is another well-known professional crime with a variety of action patterns. It generally involves taking money from a victim by using fear or an illegal threat. Extortion may occur when the victim is caught in some illegal or immoral act. More often than not, the act is sexual in nature. In Elizabethan England, the accomplice or husband of a prostitute would "catch a couple in the act" and threaten to expose the "respectable gentleman" as a lecher unless he paid a sum of money. This was termed "cross-biting," after the name of Lawrence Crossbiter, who is alleged to have practiced it in the fifteenth century.[27]

Chic Conwell describes two other variants of the shakedown that are still found today. The *muzzle* is a means of blackmailing male homosexuals caught in a compromising sex transaction. They are threatened with being exposed publicly unless they pay up. Other versions of this form of extortion involve methods of entrapment, in which youthful members of a gang lure unsuspecting victims to a public toilet where others, impersonating police officers, interrupt them and demand a bribe. The income tax shakedown involves the impersonation of an IRS agent, who accuses the victim, usually a businessman, of filing a falsified income tax return. The frightened person might pay off to stay out of trouble.[28] This racket has seen some recent variations involving members of vice-squads or other law enforcement officials who extort monies through similar schemes.

The Professional Criminal's Self-Concept

Among the distinguishing characteristics of vocational criminals is their image of themselves as "professionals." They hold amateurs and those involved in violent crime in low esteem. Jackson's thief collaborator, Sam, states:

> A character is a professional thief.... The rest of them are on-again, off-again, hooligans-mulligans.... They're just not professional. I guess we frown on them as much as a doctor would a chiropractor. It's the same thing. A doctor, he's got his profession, and anything short of that... is not enough. It's the same thing with us.... Stealing is a full-time business.[29]

Those involved in professional crime often harbor an elaborate set of rationalizations that apparently serve to neutralize disapproval they might feel from the dominant society. They may, for instance, compare their behavior to "sharp" business practices, or point the finger at dishonest policemen or other law enforcement personnel. It is also typical for them to romanticize themselves as modern-day Robin Hoods who steal ill-gotten wealth from the exploitative rich.

Professional criminals also tend to look down upon their victims. Con men point out that their *marks,* or victims, want to gain at the expense of others. The victim is seen as a sucker; if they didn't take advantage of him, someone else surely would. Con men also sometimes say they only steal from dishonest or large firms that can absorb the damage. In this respect, they reflect attitudes expressed by the general public in a number of surveys of public attitudes—that is, it is less culpable to shoplift or steal from large firms than from small stores or businesses.

The professional criminal tends to view police and other agents of control as occupational hazards more than as enemies. They are not as concerned with justice as with their ability to have a case fixed or take a lesser "rap."[30] Once in prison they "do their time," avoid trouble, and start to "program" how to get out as soon as possible. They have learned in their way of life that prison is one of the calculated risks. As John Irwin and Donald Cressey have pointed out:

> Long before the thief has come to prison, his subculture has defined proper prison conduct as behavior rationally calculated to "do time" in the easiest possible way. This means that he wants... the best possible combination of a maximum amount of leisure time and maximum number of privileges.... The thief wants things that will make prison life a little easier.[31]

Prison is a time for the thief to reflect on past capers and talk about "big scores" that will be carefully planned and sufficiently rewarding to permit him either to turn legitimate or leave the country. When a television reporter for a major network interviewed some professionals in a California prison, he talked with several who told of previous exploits and stated that they made a good living at crime. The reporter seemed amazed at their unrepentant attitude and cited it as evidence of the complexity of the crime problem. His conclusion was accurate, but for the wrong reason. The identity of the career criminal is such that only a few "straighten up their hand" in prison, though many go through the necessary motions to "make points" with the parole board.[32]

The professional criminal's career is not usually a happy-go-lucky life of ease. He is ambitious and success-oriented and strives to be proficient, develop skills, and receive recognition from his peers. He must be calculating and not take unnecessary risks. He must constantly deal with tensions relevant to planning and executing a crime, avoiding arrest, and disposing of stolen goods. He faces concerns over profit and loss. If a rule of life in America is to make as much money as possible, then the professional thief may be thought of as a stereotypical American.

Perhaps the image of the pleasure-seeking professional criminal derives from the fact that the habitat of those involved in crime provides access to a variety of pleasure-seeking activities. Some may resort to narcotic drugs. But professionals who use drugs are seen as unreliable, and drug use may lead to ostracism and movement out of the career.

There are other ways of leaving the criminal career. Old age or a succession of long prison terms may incapacitate the individual. Being deterred by fear of prison is perhaps the least likely means of leaving. Yet Chic Conwell "straightened up his hand," or turned to legitimate occupations, after his third prison term. Many more apparently end up as skid-row drifters. As one burglar noted, "the Bowery (the former name for the skid-row area of New York City) has always been a resting place, and a burial ground." [33]

Affiliational Networks: The Support System of Professional Offenders

Professional underworld crimes rely on a support system or "external organization" composed of a variety of individuals only marginally involved in crime. These "service personnel" include "hangers-on" such as tipsters, who are given various labels to refer to their particular skill—for example, *feelers-out* for those who locate suitable places for theft, and *finger men* who identify potential victims. These marginal individuals often occupy quasilegitimate positions, maintaining connections with both legitimate and illicit social organizations. One such man described his job in the following manner: "I act in the capacity of a 'go-between' for big-time thieves and small-time racketeers. Many of my activities have included pimping for pimps, watching for cops, and even working for cops." [34]

In his description of the lawyer-fix, "box man" Harry King observed that "the only people that really profit from theft is the fix, the judge, and district attorney. They're the guys who make the money, not the guy who stole it." However, he noted that sometimes, if the "heat is on," you cannot get the fix.[35] Sam, a professional thief, also maintained a working relationship with the police. His account emphasizes the role of the attorney in the support system. "When you want a lawyer, you don't want a trial lawyer, you want a fixer.... You're hiring him not to go to trial. And if you have to go to trial ... you're hiring him so—whenever you walk into the courtroom you already know what you're going to get because he's already dealt out what." [36]

Buying or possessing stolen property is a crime. *Fences,* or receivers of stolen goods, are businessmen who carry out their illicit activities by disposing of the thief's stolen goods. They think of themselves, not as criminals, but as businessmen who avail themselves of the opportunities provided by their connections with thieves.

Duncan Chappell and Marilyn Walsh, in describing the activities of Jonathan Wild, provide a good account of the history of criminal receiving. The remarkable empire Wild developed around such activity in the early eighteenth century shows the possible extent of power of such an operation. His exploits, related by Gerald Howson in *Thief-Taker General: The Rise and Fall of Jonathan Wild* (1970), provide a perspective on the sociology of the laws of criminal receiving.

Wild was introduced to the lucrative aspects of crime as a way of life while sentenced to jail as a debtor. When pardoned in 1712, he became involved with a London marshal in recovering stolen property. In 1714, he established his own business and advertised in London newspapers for the return of stolen property, using in each notice the phrase "No Questions Asked." Wild's case illustrates how the receiver dominates thieves and makes their life in crime practicable.[37]

Although successive laws have been passed to control or eliminate receiving—one was effective in bringing about the hanging of Jonathan Wild—criminal receiving still persists. But after more than two centuries of legal efforts, the President's Crime Commission wrote in 1967:

> Little research has been done on fencing, despite its central role in professional crime. More information is needed about the nature of the market for illicit goods and the extent to which demand for various types of goods affects the incidence of theft. More should be learned about the relationship of legitimate and illegitimate markets.... It would be desirable to have more information about the organization and operation of large-scale fencing operations, to aid in the development of better methods of law enforcement.[38]

In the decade since the Crime Commission made its plea for more research, there have been two types of studies of the fence. In addition to the historical analysis of Gerald Howson, there is the recent in-depth, analytical study of Vincent Swaggi, the modern counterpart of Jonathan Wild. This study by Carl Klockars (1974) notes that the term "fence" has historical meaning, which though it has been misused is quite accepted by insiders.

Klockars suggests three criteria that set the fence off from others who trade in stolen goods. First, the fence is a dealer in stolen goods, both a buyer and seller, who has direct contact with the thieves who provide them. Second, the fence is someone who has successfully bought and sold stolen property for profit on a regular basis for a number of years. Third, the fence must be a person who has acquired a public reputation among lawbreakers, law enforcers, and those aware of the criminal world. He must manage that reputation among these various groups. The word "professional" is added by Klockars to underline the characteristics of career, occupation, skills, and ability that relate to the distinctive behavior system of the fence.[39]

Convergences in Belief and Status Systems

A subculture has been characterized as a group's shared patterns of beliefs, perspectives, and behaviors that set it off from the dominant collectivity. There are some values and behaviors that are shared by the conventional and the criminal worlds. But the beliefs and behaviors in the action system of career criminals have developed in isolation from or in conflict with those of the larger society. Although there has been a relationship between the two worlds, it is symbiotic—each feeds on the other and sometimes develops as a result of the crime control efforts of the larger society. Both the insularity of the underworld and its solidarity have developed out of conflict with the legitimate world's attempts to enact laws and policies to repress and control it.

Professional crime represents a complexity of autonomous yet interrelated systems of criminal behavior. It has its own meetingplaces or hangouts, communications network or grapevine, and stylized vernacular or argot. It represents a system of association based on face-to-face interaction and specialized interaction through which activities and exploits are shared in various locations or "scenes."

There also has emerged through the years a status system, which observers suggest might represent a five-level class system. The top level is comprised of bank burglars, bank sneak thieves, and "big con" operators. The next level includes forgers and counterfeiters. The third level consists of house and store burglars and "short con" operators. The fourth level includes hotel and residential sneak thieves, shakedown artists, and shoplifters. On the bottom are the pickpockets and lush workers ("jack rollers," who steal from drunks). More structured types of status levels are found within certain categories of thieves —for example, among pickpockets and confidence men.[40]

But we should remember that there exists in the belief system of the professional thief, values that receive support in the value system of the culture of our society. For it would seem that there are underlying values of contemporary American life that support such behavior. That is, for the "professional" thief to survive, let alone make a living, he or she must have more than personal skills or techniques. This behavior system apparently finds support from certain dominant, as well as subterranean, values and beliefs in our society that reward the ability to manipulate people for personal gain. This is especially apropos of the "big con" artist. As Maurer suggests, they carry to "an ultimate and logical conclusion trends which are often inherent in various forms of business." He also notes that the American belief in rugged individualism and emphasis on self-made success and risk-taking may provide a supply of marks, or victims, for the con man. For in the confidence games both offender and victim are after the same thing—something for nothing, or a quick gain.[41] The confidence game, at least, illustrates an overlap between professional criminal and conventional behavior patterns. This behavior system, then, confronts the usual commonsense distinction between the "bad guys" and the "good guys" in our society. For the professional criminal is as much a product of the social structure as are other criminals. Indeed, he may well share more behavioral similarities with conventional behavior patterns than John Q. Citizen is inclined to admit.

Societal Reaction and Social Change

In the previous discussion of this action system, it was noted that due to their status and informal arrangements with official agencies of control, professional criminals may avoid conviction, although not necessarily arrest. In other words, this criminal action system has operated throughout recent history with a degree of connivance from the law. Yet even this connivance would not be possible were it not for a public tolerance and apathy regarding such offenders. Moreover, because professional crime is relatively invisible, it does not evoke the strong social reaction that street crime does.

Furthermore, even though hard data are lacking, it seems that such offenses are waning. The "big con" schemes apparently have declined with changes in banking procedures and the establishment of bankers' associations and consumer protection groups. Con games or grifts (bribes) associated with carnivals may be declining as well, as the increasing urbanization of society has brought the decline of carnivals. Still, there are accounts that document continued activity among pickpockets, boosters (shoplifters), burglars, sneak thieves, and forgers. And the systematic, or professional check forger may be less visible as he may no longer need to maintain contact with the underworld, since he can take advantage of the increased reliance on checks by businesses and individuals. And so it seems that the number of professionals has declined since the 1940s. Social changes may have brought even more drastic adjustments among career criminals than three hundred years of law enforcement efforts.

PROFESSIONAL HEAVY CRIME

In contrast to professional theft, "professional heavy crime" relies upon the skillful use of coercion, the threat of violence, or force. In legal terms, professional crimes involve taking property without consent, knowledge, or awareness, while professional "heavy" crime, like armed robbery, involves intimidating the victim and taking the property under duress. Sociologically, the basic difference is that robbery involves direct, overt interaction between victim and thief, but burglary does not. This distinction has resulted in some confusion regarding the arbitrary categories of violent and property crimes in the FBI's *Uniform Crime Reports*. Although both involve the taking of property, robberies are summarized under "crimes against persons" and are at times classified as "property crimes." The fact that both burglary, or "sneak thievery," and robbery are illegal should not obscure important behavioral differences between the two types.[42] As with other career crimes, heavy criminals are motivated by the desire for financial gain, but they rely upon careful planning and organization along with force to reduce the risk of arrest.

The category, "heavy professional crime," was coined by criminologists who sought to focus upon the career aspects of violent crime. Yet this kind of activity fills the legend and folklore of the American frontier. Following the Civil War, there were numerous ex-soldiers who became soldiers of fortune in the western territories, where they could prey successfully upon stage coaches, trains, and banks and find legal as well as physical sanctuary on the wild frontier. The developing frontier was the scene of economic conflict and exploitation by absentee economic interest groups. And criminal gangs such as the James-Younger Gang, the Dalton brothers, and Black Bart took advantage of the terrain and lack of legal systems. Amid turbulence and conflict, they operated with a degree of public tolerance. In fact, some were folk heroes in their own time.[43]

The troubled Depression days marked a revival of heavy crime gangs. People such as John Dillinger, "Pretty Boy" Floyd, Bonnie Parker, Clyde Barrow, "Machine Gun" Kelley, "Ma" Barker, and "Baby Face" Nelson were the "heavy" actors in the crime wave of the 1930s. Their primary targets were banks. This surge of heavy crime was short-lived, in part due to the vigorous efforts of the fledgling FBI and legislation making bank robbery a federal offense. In 1943, there were only twenty-four bank robberies. But in the post–World War II years, bank robbery began to increase. The number grew from 346 in 1959 to 2,000 in 1970—an increase of nearly 500 percent. And as Figure 7.3 indicates, the rate of increase according to official data between 1970 and 1975 was almost as great.[44]

Apparently the newer heavy crimes do not involve as many professionals as amateurs who act out of impulse and need rather than as a result of carefully laid plans. The high rate of clearance by law enforcement agents suggests a decline in professional heavy crime.[45] (Clearance refers to "solving" a given offense or series of crimes by the arrest or charging of persons alleged to have committed them. Alternately, a crime may be "cleared" by some record-keeping procedure, such as reporting a car theft as "joyriding" or a petty theft as "purse snatching," when it could be written up as robbery.)

Contemporary, career heavy crime focuses on targets where sizable sums of money tend to change hands. Targets include loan companies, supermarkets, liquor stores, and gas stations. As with the professional thief, the heavy professional rationalizes that the victims can stand the loss or that they are insured. Although these crimes make splashy headlines, they were estimated to total only about 4 percent of the cost of crime in 1976.

The recruitment of heavy crime careers can begin with socialization into petty theft in juvenile gangs. The next move is into activities like auto theft, burglary, and robbery. Along the way, sophistication is developed in dealing with police and other officials. Robbery is seen as a means of quick gain, a way to make the "big score."[46]

The term "hijacking" received prominence in media accounts in the early 1970s. It came to refer to the seizure of a commercial airplane and forcing the

Bonnie Parker—a legendary professional heavy female criminal.

crew to fly the hijackers to some country where they could avoid prosecution. Frequently, the plane and crew were held hostage in order for the hijackers to exact a larger ransom from the airline or bargain for concessions from a government. However, hijackings are episodic, political acts, and generally do not involve traditional career criminals.

Figure 7.3. Trends in Theft by Type of Offense, 1970–1975

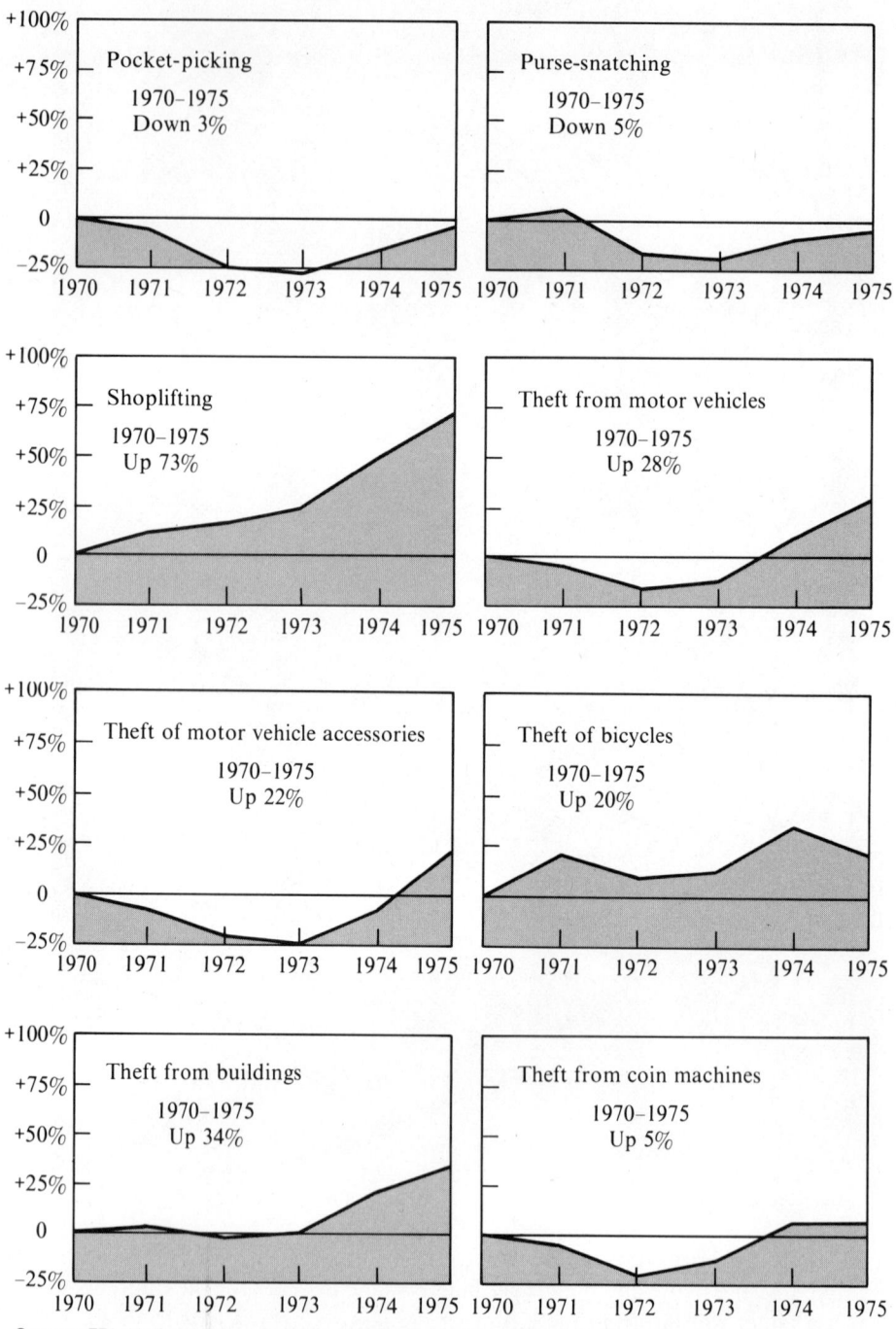

Pocket-picking
1970–1975
Down 3%

Purse-snatching
1970–1975
Down 5%

Shoplifting
1970–1975
Up 73%

Theft from motor vehicles
1970–1975
Up 28%

Theft of motor vehicle accessories
1970–1975
Up 22%

Theft of bicycles
1970–1975
Up 20%

Theft from buildings
1970–1975
Up 34%

Theft from coin machines
1970–1975
Up 5%

Source: FBI, *Uniform Crime Reports, 1975* (Washington, D.C.: U.S. Government Printing Office, 1975), p. 33.

BOX 3

Hijacking: A Major American Industry

By DOUGLAS S. CROCKET

In a recent 17 month period in Massachusetts:

—A trailer truckload of scallops worth $50,000 disappeared from a warehouse parking lot in South Boston.

—A trailer truck containing Revlon cosmetics worth $225,000 was hijacked and abandoned empty in Walpole.

—Another truck with $25,000 worth of plastic trash bags was hijacked in Walpole.

—A truck with $150,000 worth of coffee was hijacked on the Massachusetts Turnpike near Charlton.

And police are convinced that every one of the hijacked items found its way to the shelves of legitimate stores within weeks after the robberies.

Hijacking—the stopping, stealing and looting of commercial cargo trucks—made up more than $7 million of an estimated $50 million in stolen merchandise fenced in Massachusetts last year.

A man known as Bill is a hijacker. He's 34 years old and has already served eight years in prison for various offenses.

Today he's on the streets again, still hijacking and "moving" stolen merchandise.

"You can move (sell) anything if you know how," he said. "Anything.

"I've either stolen or know guys who stole truckloads of golf balls, Polaroid film, razor blades, meat, potatoes and artificial flowers.

"You name it, we've scored (stolen) it. And we've moved everything we ever stole.

"We don't just grab a truck and run around the streets trying to sell the stuff. What we do is go to someone in organized crime before we even hit the truck.

"We go to this somebody and say, 'We're going to score this truckload of cigarettes Thursday. What'll you give us?'

"Say it's $100,000 worth. He says he'll give us $10,000 cash. We say $20,000. He says $15,000. Finally we agree on the figure and the deal's set.

"Thursday, we grab the truck and bring it to a prearranged drop (garage). He gives us the dough and we screw. What he does with it after that is his business.

"What they usually do," Bill said, "is break the entire load up and put it into smaller trucks. The cops, see, are looking for the big trailer. They're not going to be able to spot four smaller trucks all going different directions.

"Then, they might move it out of the city, out of the state even. Sometimes they bring it to a so-called legit distributor who is working for them.

"From him it gets shipped out with legit bills of lading, vouchers and all that stuff.

"Bingo. It goes to the stores. Half the time the store doesn't even know it's stolen goods. The other half knows but don't care. Why should they? They bought the shipment for half what they usually pay and are more than doubling their profit."

Robert Murphy is a 27-year-old state trooper assigned to the criminal investigative unit of the Massachusetts State Police.

He and his partner, Trooper John Allen, devote most of their working hours to slowing down hijacking in Massachusetts.

They've arrested hijackers in the act, arrested them at their "drops," arrested them after the hijacking.

"But it's like fighting the tide," Murphy said. "There's more involved than any private citizen knows.

"When you're talking organized crime, you are talking efficiency.

"If members of organized crime get involved in the load, they can move it through different states. They can get it into the hands of a distributor in Denver who can then ship it back in another truck as part of a legitimate delivery.

"This time, there are bills of sale, bills of lading, vouchers. The store that gets it doesn't even know it's stolen.

"But that's only one part.

"Think about the purely local operation. Local thieves take a truck and bring it to friends who specialize in fencing stolen merchandise.

"The fence might have friends working in warehouses or distributorships.

"The stolen stuff ends up in the same warehouse with nonstolen goods. The people in the warehouse salt the stolen items into deliveries of nonstolen items.

"Then, when they get an order, they ship out the merchandise, half of which might be stolen goods, and get payment for the entire delivery. The store doesn't even know the difference.

"And finally, there's the so-called honest store owner who sees a chance to make a big profit. He knows the stuff is stolen but he doesn't care. If a guy sells him a golf ball for a quarter and he knows he can sell it in his store for a dollar, he's going to jump at the chance."

Professional thieves, hijackers and fences have their own list of priorities when it comes to stealing.

And one of the most desirable items is razor blades.

"Razor blades are a gold mine," Bill said.

"They don't perish. They're small, but the shipments contain millions of blades and you can move them a bit at a time through small stores anywhere in the country."

Polaroid film is another item high on the list of wanted stolen merchandise. "Same thing," Bill said. "You can move it anywhere.

"Appliances are good only at Christmas," he said. "You know—how many times a year is a guy going to give his wife a blender?"

Coin collections, stamp collections, works of art can be "moved" but "only if you know how," Bill said.

Least wanted is perishable foods. "You need a refrigerated truck in the drop," Bill said. "Who the hell is going to buy a load of rotten meat?"

Liquor is difficult to fence because of the federal stamps, he said. "But you can get rid of it locally. Once we had a guy pouring hijacked bottles of CC (Canadian Club) into empty bottles of OT (Old Thompson) and selling it in his tavern for 50 cents a shot."

Hijacking and fencing the merchandise through organized crime, of course, are big business.

Source: *The Boston Globe,* September 25, 1978. Reprinted courtesy of the Boston Globe.

The hijacking of trucks, on the other hand, is a more apt example of heavy professional crime. With the increased use of heavy transport on the highways, virtually all commodities of value are transported at some time in huge trailer trucks. Truck hijacking has replaced the train robberies of years ago. Such action requires pre-event planning that involves knowledge, skills, and connections. The hijackers must be able to remove goods from the truck quickly, with the forced compliance of the driver, or move the truck to a location where the goods can be removed and the truck abandoned after having disposed of the driver by force or cunning. Either method requires arrangements for selling the goods to a "receiver" or "fence." Hijacking operations also occur with the contrivance of inside help in major airport or trucking terminals, where the method of transport may be a part of the planning operation. Or, a driver may use fake invoices or orders for goods. However, in this case, the behavior lies in the realm of avocational crime. Vincent Swaggi, Klockars' "professional fence" points out: "A driver's a working man . . . . He makes a few bucks so he can go out . . . or maybe buy his wife a new coat, . . . to me a thief an' a driver is two entirely different things." [47]

According to official reports, the number of robbery offenses increased by 79 percent between 1966 and 1970 and by 33 percent between 1970 and 1975. The reported robbery rate rose from 78 to 171 percent between 1966 and 1970 and by 29 percent over the next five years (see Figure 7.4). So the incidence of heavy crime, which decreased nearly 10 percent between 1975 and 1977, has leveled off. But it is interrelated in a complex manner with our economic institutions of distribution and the demand for consumer goods.

Robbers may be thought of as a subtype of the professional heavy criminal type, and as such they share certain patterns with other professionals. They endeavor to avoid arrest or conviction and seek to reduce these risks by working with known associates and by using lawyers to arrange the "fix." Both share certain skills, such as casing and planning an event. But the safecracker or other burglar relies on his physical abilities and techniques, whereas the robber must use force or the threat of violence to manage and manipulate those at the scene of the action. This is not the case with the confused "rum," or inept, inexperienced criminal who may brutalize his or her victims for small amounts. The behavior described in robbery statistics relates to activities and crime patterns of more than one type.[48]

ORGANIZED CRIME

In spite of being celebrated in films of the "Godfather" genre and scrutinized by congressional committees, presidential crime commissions, and the media, organized crime has relatively low visibility. Furthermore, there is some public tolerance of organized crime, due to the fact that the illegal goods and services it provides—such as gambling, loansharking, commercialized vice, and narcotics—are in demand by the "upperworld." With the growing investment of

Figure 7.4. Trends in Robbery by Type, 1970–1975.

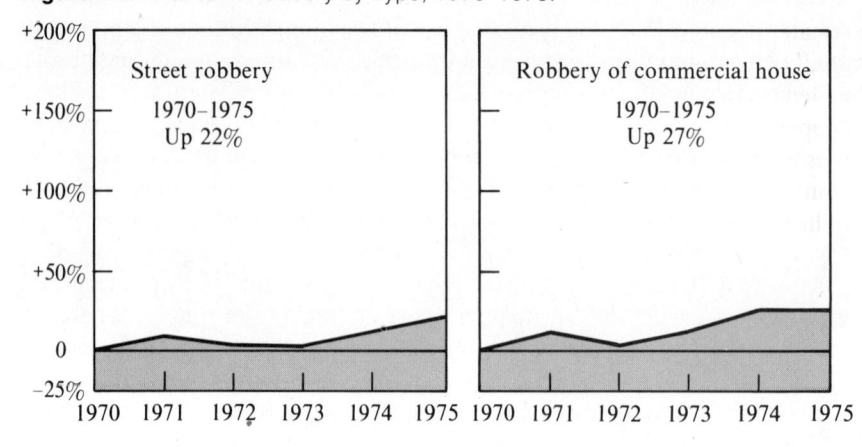

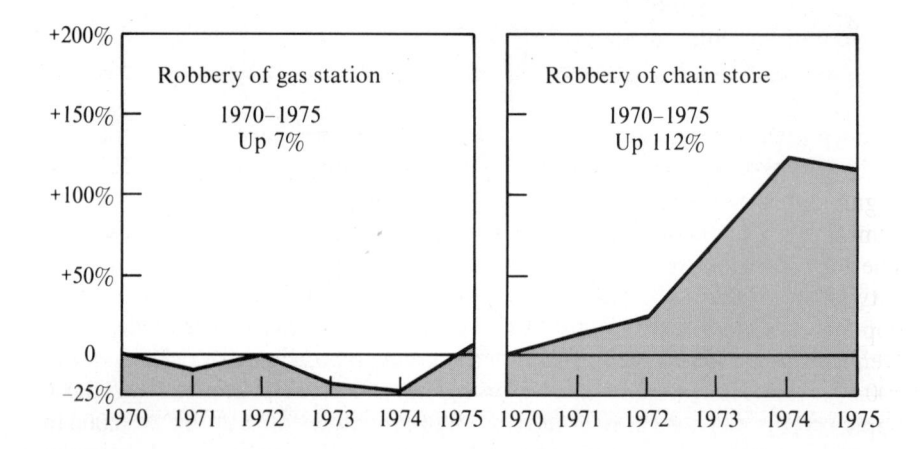

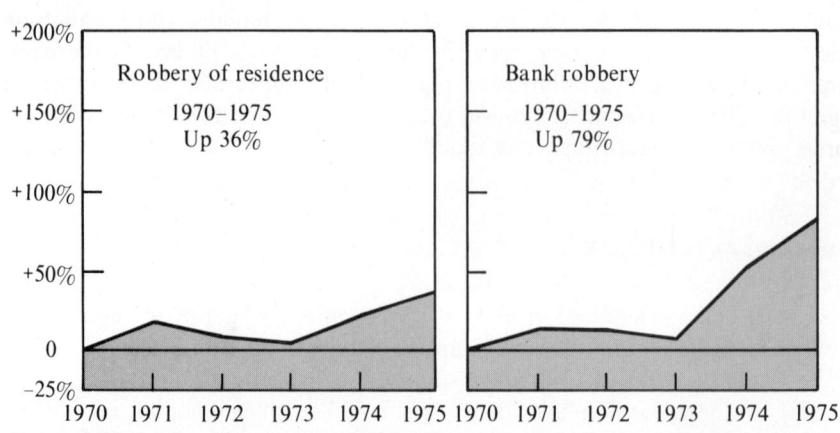

Street robbery
1970–1975
Up 22%

Robbery of commercial house
1970–1975
Up 27%

Robbery of gas station
1970–1975
Up 7%

Robbery of chain store
1970–1975
Up 112%

Robbery of residence
1970–1975
Up 36%

Bank robbery
1970–1975
Up 79%

Source: FBI, *Uniform Crime Reports, 1975* (Washington, D.C.: U.S. Government Printing Office, 1975), p. 27.

profits from organized crime in legitimate activities, it has become difficult to delineate the exact boundaries separating the "underworld" from the "upperworld."

Generally the term "organized" or "syndicated" crime refers to those business operations organized for the purpose of realizing profit through illegal activities or enterprises. Although all types of career crime exhibit a social organization and a pattern of roles and rules, organized crime is frequently thought to exhibit these unique characteristics:[49]

1. A hierarchical structure involving a set of clearly defined relationships specifying mutual obligations and privileges.
2. The monopolistic control of relatively stable and defined areas of influence between different organizations within specified geographical spheres.
3. Coercion, the use of threatened force or violence to maintain such monopoly, as well as discipline and cooperation.
4. A high degree of immunity from intervention and interference by criminal justice and other agencies.
5. Considerable gain through specializing in one or more lucrative enterprises.

It is generally assumed that organized crime operates through a national alignment of criminal organizations believed to control a large share of the gambling, loansharking, narcotics, rackets, and organized vice in America. The Presidential Crime Commission survey of the police departments of seventy-one cities in 1967 elicited the following response: Eighty percent with a population over one million indicated the existence of organized crime elements, as did 20 percent of those with a population between one million and 500,000. Likewise, 20 percent of the cities with between 500,000 and 250,000 population, and over 50 percent of those cities between 250,000 and 100,000 in population, acknowledged such groups. It is doubtful that the situation changed much during the past decade, since all the police departments in cities that noted such activity felt that the criminal group would not be hampered by the death or imprisonment of a top leader. But the greedy network of organized crime is not only a big-city problem. Many smaller towns have reported gambling setups based on race tracks, numbers, or dice games that are tied into organized crime groups in nearby cities.[50]

A limited amount of analysis has been conducted by criminologists of organized crime. This "information gap" has been narrowed somewhat in writings since the Crime Commission's report in 1967. But there is still great difficulty in gaining accurate information. The problems suggest not only something about the limitations of social science, but also about preconceptions regarding the nature of crime that social scientists share with the rest of society. They also provide insights into some of the complex interrelationships between organized crime and conventional society.

First, there is the tendency to see criminality as an individual act rather than an organizational one. We are more likely to focus upon the individual's maladjustments and character than to relate these to broad social and cultural forces in society. Consequently, law enforcement and correctional agencies are designed for controlling or intervening in the lives of individual offenders. This emphasis on the individual offender is quite useless in an analysis of organized crime. The biographies of organized criminals can more clearly be understood when compared with those of others who have emerged from similar backgrounds to successful careers in other areas of endeavor. For example, one writer noted that Al Capone was a man with "administrative capacities which might, if his path and instincts had been different, have made him the head of one of our biggest legitimate corporations." [51]

Several decades ago, George Vold referred to the inclination of criminologists to avoid analyzing crime as an aspect of the power conflict between different political segments of the community. Such a perspective implies that the cause of criminal behavior might be found in the basic structure of the community. He argued that it is apt to be less disconcerting to focus on the personal traits of those involved in ordinary crime than to explore aspects of the struggle for economic and political power in the community. Yet criminological research of the future must confront the problem of how to describe and analyze pertinent aspects of social and economic conflict that are relevant to the pervasive phenomenon of organized crime and corruption.[52] In the same work, Vold pointed to the parallel between legitimate and illegitimate structures when he noted:

> ... organized crime must be thought of as a natural growth, or ... developmental adjunct to our ... private profit economy.... But there is also an area of genuine economic demand for things and services not permitted under our legal and social codes. Organized crime is the system of business ... in this area. It, too, is competitive and ... must organize for its self-protection and for control of the market.[53]

We face some of the same difficulties in studying organized crime when we stress individual factors rather than analysis of competition within the underworld. If we better understood this pattern of competition and interdependence with the upperworld, there might have been less surprise and indignation over the exposé in 1977 that the CIA had contracted with underworld leaders to carry out some of its "dirty work" and plan the assassination of at least one foreign head of state.

Secondly, the media have tended to present organized crime activities in a sensational manner, emphasizing the spectacular activities of gangsters preying on one another, rather than the corrupting influence of such activities in the economic community. Mickey Cohen, a former racketeer, told of asking a newspaper editor why he allowed sensational "untruths" to be printed in the editor's paper about organized crime. The editor's response, according to Cohen, was "When are you going to wise up, Mick? Don't you know when we ain't got news, we're going to use something that's going to sell papers, even if we have to use your name?" [54]

Al Capone—an infamous underworld figure of the 1930s.

A third reason for the limited amount of data about organized crime is the operation of the rule of silence. This is one of the characteristics that sets organized criminals off from professional thieves, who have been known to describe their lifestyles in great detail. The system of mutual obligations in the feudallike structure of organized crime gangs places the highest priority upon loyalty and dependability—which means rigid adherence to a code of silence. This code takes precedence over what are commonly thought to be basic ideas of self-interest and perservation. For instance, a victim of a gangland killing who lived for two days after the attack refused to divulge the identity of his assailant. Other gang members have been known to maintain their silence and refuse to cooperate in naming those involved with them even when promised leniency by prosecutors.[55]

The Task Force on Organized Crime of the Crime Commission pointed out that the code on which this rule of silence is based is similar to the Omerta code of the Mafia of Italian-Sicilian origin. The Task Force also suggested that this code is similar to that of other secret societies or organizations, such as the Irish Republican Army, organized to overthrow established authority. Other experts compare the code to the unwritten "convict code," which operates to maintain the social organization of inmates in our prisons. So, the unwritten code of the underworld is similar to codes required by any underground organization to maintain control over its members and secrecy regarding its means of operation.[56]

Social scientists confront obvious methodological problems in gathering data about organized crime. Although Ned Polsky has suggested that social scientists are mistaken in assuming that research in this area is not feasible, he notes that those gathering data about organized crime do confront unique problems. These include the possibility of facing criminal charges for withholding their information from authorities and the related problem of securing voluntary cooperation of their subjects without losing the right to release such information against the subject's will. Yet a carefully conducted participant-observation approach can be developed, Polsky argues, so that more accurate data might be collected without the researcher having to pass as a criminal or become involved in criminal activity. As Polsky's examples of data that have been gathered from professional burglars and numbers operators show, we can learn much about criminals' lifestyles through their verbal statements, rather than having to observe their illegal action.[57]

Although social science research related to organized crime has not become a common endeavor, there are a few recent efforts that have been able to obtain data in spite of the code of secrecy and other constraints. Included among such studies are the interviews conducted by William Chambliss (1971) to study organized vice and bureaucratic efforts to control it.[58] Another is Joseph Albini's study of the Mafia in America, based upon an analysis of documents combined with interviews (1971).[59] Ianni has provided us with the first detailed, in-depth study of an Italian-American criminal (Mafia) "family," in which he supplemented participant observation by interviews with key members of the organization.[60] However, as Albini has noted, much of the material available in the area of organized crime is more sensational than scholarly in its style and content. They are value laden and often lead to distortion of facts. Some examples of such questionable data will be noted below.[61]

An early New York City street gang—precursors of organized crime.

History of Organized Crime

Organized crime on a large scale is a twentieth-century phenomenon in the United States. The genesis of syndicated crime is usually tied to the passage of the Volstead Act (1919), which provided for the enforcement of the Eighteenth Amendment and launched the Prohibition era. However, prototypes of organized crime can be traced to street gangs that had their beginnings in illegal activities in major cities like Chicago, New York, New Orleans, and other metropolitan centers during the 1800s.

In New York, various gangs operated within their own geographical areas during the nineteenth century. These included the Eastman Gang in the area of the Bowery, 14th and Monroe Streets, and the East River; the Five Points Gang between the Bowery and Broadway; the Gas House Gang along 3rd Avenue between 11th and 18th Streets; the Hell's Kitchen Gang, on the middle West Side during the post–Civil War years; and other more militant groups. These gangs struggled for control over a given area and reaped profits from gambling rooms, brothels, saloons, and tribute levied from merchants. Chicago had undergone tremendous population growth during the post–Civil War era. In this climate of social change and disorganization, criminal gangs found an environment of political corruption, city bossism, and graft in which they could flourish. Similar conditions were also present in Boston, Cleveland, Philadelphia, New Orleans, San Francisco, and St. Louis.[62]

The Prohibition era provided both the context and opportunity for the consolidation of petty gangsterism into a criminal organization within urban centers in American society. The former city gangs were less organized and sophisticated, but they had provided training for individuals who had become reasonably well known for their efforts in the illegal manufacture and distribution of liquor. Among these were Torrio, Capone, Aiello, Moran, Diamond, O'Banion, Schultz, Buchalter, Shapiro, Lansky, and Luciano.[63]

By the early 1920s, a criminal syndicate began to emerge in connection with Johnny Torrio's activities in Chicago. He had received his start as the leader of a waterfront gang in New York before 1908. When he was convicted of bootlegging in 1924, he turned his organization over to Al Capone, one of his lieutenants. Capone's gross "take" from bootlegging and related rackets was estimated at $100 million by 1927. Capone's rivalry with the Moran-Aiello Gang attracted nationwide interest when it ended with the St. Valentine's Day Massacre in 1929, but it also earned him the contempt of other underworld leaders. His career was effectively ended two years later when he received an eleven-year sentence for income tax evasion.[64]

There were numerous other gangland leaders who grew in prominence from the system of distillation and distribution of "outlawed" alcoholic beverages, which became one of the country's largest industries in the 1920s. The success of this business enterprise was aided by the utter failure of efforts to enforce the Prohibition laws. One chronicler of the bootleggers stated:

> ...in a single year of Prohibition, the United States consumed 200 million gallons of hard liquor, 684 million gallons of malt liquor and 118 million gallons of wine, and in that twelve months the income of professional bootleggers was assessed at 4 billion dollars.[65]

It seems obvious that Prohibition as a "noble experiment in appetite control" was a failure, for the Volstead Act, which did not receive widespread popular support, defined as criminal activities those that were related to the lifestyles of high social status individuals. As one former judge noted, "juries turned everyone loose, regardless of the evidence and then went home to their illegal highballs before dinner."

Furthermore, enforcement was a costly activity. The federal government alone spent $375 million, and local and state governments another $3 billion, yet the number of illegal saloons or bars exceeded the number of saloons of pre-Prohibition days. The desire of government leaders as well as "legal" business interests to regain control and access to this considerable revenue resulted in the Twenty-first Amendment. Its passage meant that syndicated crime would find it necessary to turn to other illegitimate as well as legitimate profitable activities.

During the postrepeal period, organized crime groups apparently used their position in the alcohol manufacture and distribution system to gain advantageous positions in legal operations. In some instances they corrupted officials to obtain licenses for which they were ineligible due to their criminal records, or they became silent partners in front operations. They were also identified in bookie operations in conjunction with race tracks, numbers lotteries, and loansharking, and were involved in providing other types of illegal goods and services. A number of men reputed to be leaders in such illegal enterprises were arrested at the home of Joseph Barbera in November 1957. Although the number varies from one report to another—from 50 to 100—those caught in this raid were mainly from the Northeast, although the fact that they were arrested together is often cited as evidence of the existence of a national crime organization.[66]

The Structure and Function of Organized Crime: The "Mafia," Reality or Myth?

Organized crime, as it developed during and since the Prohibition era, might best be understood as a corollary to our private enterprise system. It is basically designed in similar fashion to other large-scale business enterprises. But its intent is to provide goods and services that have been proscribed or prohibited by laws that have been supported and sponsored by well-intended citizens and lawmakers. In the course of providing such illicit goods and services as drugs, gambling, bookmaking for horse races and numbers games, high interest loans (loansharking), and pornographic books and films, it seeks to accrue sizable profits while minimizing risks. The enormous profits pay for support personnel including accountants and lawyers.

Information on the nature of syndicated crime is fragmentary and subject to a variety of interpretations. On the one hand, Norval Morris and Gordon Hawkins argue that the idea of a nationwide monolithic crime syndicate controlled by one commission is a myth that serves as a "scapegoat" for our fears. On the other hand, Donald Cressey, who served as a consultant for the Task Force on Organized Crime of the Crime Commission, suggests that there is considerable unity in the national as well as the regional operation of organized crime.[67] It may be that the organized crime action system is national in scale, yet made up of a loose-knit confederation or alliance. As Thomas Schelling indicates in his "Economic Analysis of Organized Crime," not all businesses lend themselves to centralized organization. He states that "the inducements to expansion and the advantages of large-scale over small are especially present in some markets rather than others." He also suggests that "a good many economic and business principles that operate in the 'upper-world' must, with suitable modification for change in environment, operate in the underworld as well, just as . . . principles that operate in an advanced competitive economy operate as well in a Socialist . . . economy."[68]

Both journalistic and scholarly studies assume that syndicate crime is sufficiently large to have considerable impact on our economic and political institutions. More research is needed, however, to provide sufficient data to make a firm conclusion. The method of organization and operation of the underworld is usually couched in the terms "Mafia," or "Cosa Nostra." The designation of organized crime as the "Mafia" apparently is inaccurate, because to the extent that "syndicated" crime exists, it does not use the term "Mafia," nor does it seem to represent an extension of the Old World "Sicilian Mafia."

Inciardi notes that references to the term "Mafia" grew out of the hysterical reaction to the murder of the New Orleans Superintendent of Police in 1890. His death was attributed to Italian criminals, and the word "Mafia" was used in press reports referring to Italian criminals held responsible for the slaying. At about the same time, the term "Black Hand" came into vogue in the press to describe crimes of extortion within Italian communities. This practice was unique to the New World, though patterned after certain traditions of the Old World *Mafiosi*. It was limited to specific localities and individual groups and dwindled during the Prohibition era, when those who had carried on extortionist activities joined the developing liquor syndicates. Some evidence suggests that *L'Unione Siciliana*—an organization opposed to the Black Hand criminal groups—in its focus on Sicilian cultural traditions, may have provided the organizational basis for criminal groups during the 1920s.

Historical studies have documented the activities of numerous non-Italian gangs in New York and other cities that produced an organized underworld years before Italian immigrants were settled in these cities. The gangs were tied in with political bosses, vice, and rackets, including labor racketeering. Reform efforts in the 1890s tended to force these gangs—who had been more or less segregated in criminal districts—into alternative activities such as extortion, predatory crimes, gambling, and other vice operations. The growth of non-Italian gangland organizations in the 1930s is confirmed by the activities of Dutch Schultz's 20 million-dollar numbers operation, Lepke Buchalter's powerful hold in the New York garment industry, and the existence of Irish, Jewish and Polish-Americans involved in gangster organizations in dozens of urban centers. To the extent that "organized crime" exists, it includes numerous non-Italian bosses as well as workers. The multiethnic character of the underworld has been glossed over by journalists. At the same time, the criminal code has been translated into the Sicilian code of *Omerta*, which means a code of silence, but also includes other behavior patterns, such as authority and loyalty to the oldest generation of the kinship group.[69]

Some writers on organized crime, including those who were influential in writing the Crime Commission report, have argued that its organization embodies a hierarchical bureaucratic scheme similar to that of large complex corporations. The characteristics of this organization have been summarized as follows:[70]

1. A national alliance of twenty-four syndicates or "families" of criminals. Even though there is little empirical evidence that an all-encompassing criminal organization controls the underworld, there undoubtedly is a loose organization of criminal groups involved in selling illicit goods and services. The profits from such enterprises are sufficient to provide funds for penetration into legitimate business enterprises.

2. Members of these "families" are of Italian (or Italian-Sicilian) extraction.
3. The activities of each "family" are directed by one man, the "Boss" (see Figure 7.5).
4. La Cosa Nostra, the largest organization in the underworld, is the means by which these "families" are linked.
5. The bosses of the more powerful "families" serve as a "commission" that seeks to coordinate the activities of the various syndicates in La Cosa Nostra.
6. Non–Cosa Nostra syndicates are linked to these "families" through an informal, elaborate set of "understandings" or "treaties."

As Ianni has pointed out recently, organized crime is not just a criminal way of life, it is "an American way of life, a viable and persistent institution within American society with its own symbols, belief, logic, and its own means of transmitting these systematically from one generation to the next." Seen in its complex interrelationship with the legitimate world, he argues, "organized crime is a functional part of the American social system, and while successive moves of immigrants and migrants have found it an available means of economic and social mobility it persists and transcends the involvement of any particular group...."[71] This is a far different image than the one promulgated by the Senate Crime Investigating Committees headed by Senator Estes Kefauver in 1951, and later by Senator John McClellan, following the arrests of the reputed syndicate leaders at Appalachia, New York, in 1957. The image of a secret, sinister, nationally organized underworld was also reflected in the Crime Commission's final report, as evidenced by its graphic model of this organization (see Figure 7.5).

Crime hearings have not only provided drama for television viewers and a popular audience for such films as *The Godfather*, but they have helped create a folk myth of a powerful criminal organization within our society on which we can blame the crime problem.

In his book, *The Theft of a Nation* (1969), based on materials gathered while serving as a consultant for the Crime Commission, Donald R. Cressey states:

> Upon being invited to work for the Commission, I was not at all sure that a nationwide organization of criminals exists.... I changed my mind. I am certain that no rational man could read the evidence that I have read and still come to the conclusion that an organization variously called "the Mafia," "Cosa Nostra," and "the syndicate" does not exist....[72]

Cressey describes a national alliance of at least twenty-four tightly knit crime "families" in the United States. Members of these "families," he notes, are Italians, Sicilians, or their descendants. In the East, the alliance is referred to as "Cosa Nostra" rather than "Mafia."[73]

A few writers have questioned such interpretations and conclusions. These include Daniel Bell, as early as 1960, Albini (1971), Hawkins (1969), and Ianni

Figure 7.5. An Organized Crime Family

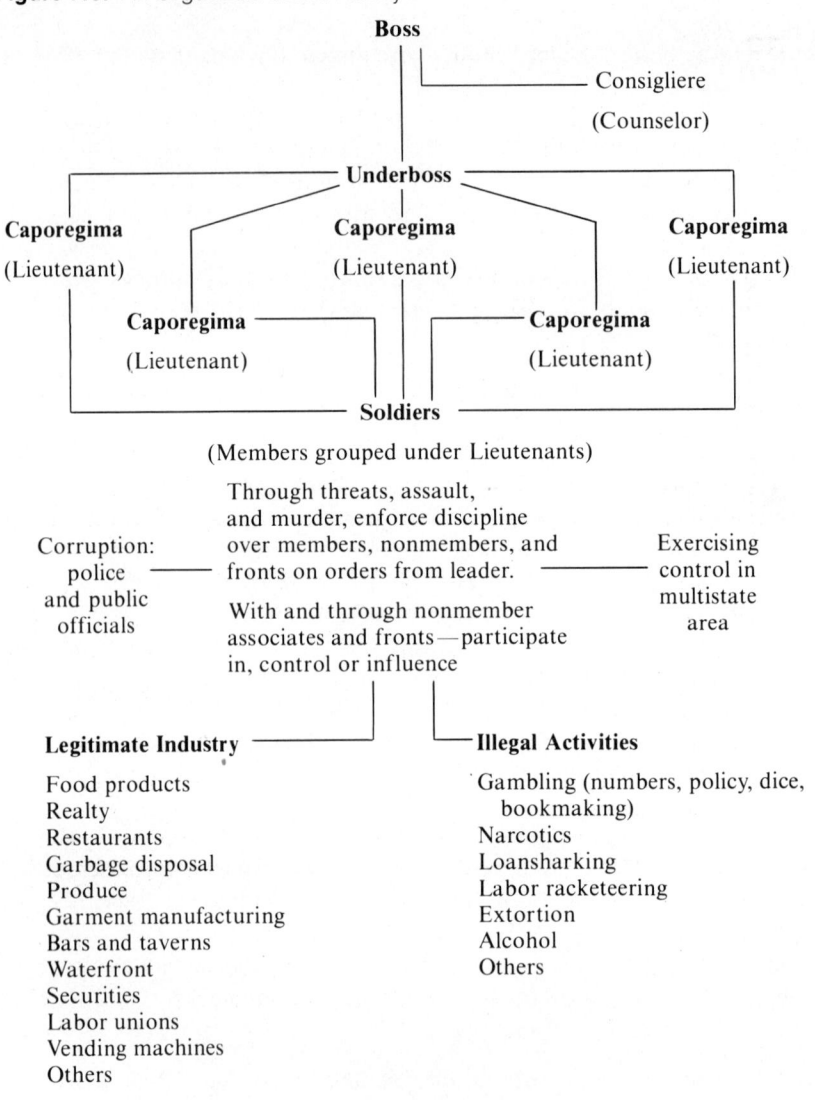

```
                        Boss
                         |
                         |———— Consigliere
                         |     (Counselor)
                         |
                     Underboss
   ┌─────────────────────┼─────────────────────┐
Caporegima           Caporegima            Caporegima
(Lieutenant)        (Lieutenant)          (Lieutenant)
        ┌────── Caporegima ──────┬────── Caporegima ──────┐
        │       (Lieutenant)     │      (Lieutenant)      │
        └─────────────────────Soldiers─────────────────────┘
```

(Members grouped under Lieutenants)

	Through threats, assault, and murder, enforce discipline over members, nonmembers, and fronts on orders from leader.	
Corruption: police and public officials	With and through nonmember associates and fronts—participate in, control or influence	Exercising control in multistate area

Legitimate Industry

Food products
Realty
Restaurants
Garbage disposal
Produce
Garment manufacturing
Bars and taverns
Waterfront
Securities
Labor unions
Vending machines
Others

Illegal Activities

Gambling (numbers, policy, dice, bookmaking)
Narcotics
Loansharking
Labor racketeering
Extortion
Alcohol
Others

Source: President's Commission on Law Enforcement and Administration of Justice, *The Challenge of Crime in a Free Society* (Washington, D.C.: U.S. Government Printing Office, 1967), p. 194.

(1972), among others.[74] Hawkins, in his work *God and the Mafia* (1969), ironically suggests that a belief in the Mafia is like a belief in God, in that it necessitates an act of faith. He notes that once we assume the uniqueness of the "code of secrecy," it is not possible to deny a national conspiracy. He argues that the dominant contemporary view of a national Mafia rests largely on the Senate testimony of Joseph Valachi—a common "soldier" in organized crime

The Career of Joseph Valachi: A "Soldier" in Organized Crime

BOX 4

Joe Valachi testifying before U.S. Subcommittee on Organized Crime.

The testimony of Joseph Valachi before a U.S. Senate subcommittee provides insight into the career patterns of a member of a crime syndicate. It also casts light on the behavior patterns of organized crime, including its perspectives, mutual obligations, and reciprocal relations with conventional society. Valachi was born in 1903. His career in crime began with burglary in 1921. Prior to 1930, his activities as a burglar led to prison terms totaling about five years. He was initiated into La Cosa Nostra in 1930.

After 1930, Valachi turned to more typical organized crime ventures, especially gambling and narcotics. On occasion he carried out a "contract" for a gangland killing. He was able to avoid any further convictions until 1959, when he was sentenced to fifteen years for a narcotics violation. The next year he was again convicted and sentenced to twenty years. He testified that he did not feel that the "things" he did as a soldier for the syndicate were crimes. Although he had been arrested several times over a thirty-year period, Valachi had virtual immunity from conviction or criminal sanction until his 1959 conviction. In 1961, he was convicted of second-degree murder for killing another inmate. After that episode, he agreed to testify before the Permanent Subcommittee on Investigations of the Government Operations Committee of the United States Senate in 1963. These hearings, the five-volume published reports they produced, and the film, *The Valachi Papers*, did much to strip La Cosa Nostra of its mantle of secrecy, though organized crime was glamorized in the process.

Valachi died in prison in April 1971, but these brief excerpts from his testimony might give insight into the career of a soldier in organized crime, who with little education and a rather mediocre career, not only briefly held the limelight, but also furthered the public's awareness of some of the little-known aspects of the social organization of syndicate crime.

Organizational Structure of Cosa Nostra
Question: . . . When did you become a member of this organization?
Valachi: In 1930.
Question: What is the name of it?
Valachi: Cosa Nostra.
Question: That is in Italian?
Valachi: That is "Our Thing" or "Our Family" in English.
Question: . . . What are the different positions, or ratings, or rank in that organization? Starting at the top, what do you have?
Valachi: Well, we have what we call *griemeson*, that is sort of like, in English, would express it as a commission.

* * *

They used to have the boss of all bosses ... and then we had the individual bosses of the individual families, and then we had an underboss, and then we had what we call a *caporegima*, which is a lieutenant, and then we have what we call soldiers.

* * *

Question: You say, now, however, there is a commission. Does it now have a boss of all bosses?
Valachi: No. No more boss over all bosses, they have what you call a *concerti*, a *consiglio*.
Question: ... Do all of the soldiers know each other? Do you know who the rest of the army is?
Valachi: I wouldn't say all of us know the soldiers, know each other.
Question: Do these families meet, as such, or do these 450 members, for example, of one family, ever meet for the purpose of doing family business?
Valachi: Well, my family, I am there 30 years and they never met, not as a whole.
Question: You belonged to Cosa Nostra for about 30 years?
Valachi: Since 1930.
Question: What was your average income from your criminal contacts during those 30 years, your average annual income?
Valachi: Senator, I wouldn't be able to tell you. Sometimes I was doing bad, sometimes I was doing good.
Question: What would be a good year? How much?
Valachi: The days of the ration stamps I would say I made about $150,000.
Question: These fellows at the top made a lot of money? Are they pretty wealthy? Are they up in the hundreds of thousands, the millionaire class? Take the Genovese family.
Valachi: There is lots of wealthy ones there. I would say, I was looking it over. There is about 40 to 50 wealthy ones.
Question: When you use the word *wealthy*, how many dollars are you talking about?
Valachi: Close to the million dollar or past the million dollar or half the million dollars.

* * *

Question: How many in the Genovese family are up in this millionaire class?
Valachi: You have about 40 to 50 wealthy ones [of 119 he identified].

Initiation

Question: Now, what happened after you got there and how many were with you, to become members, to be "made"? ...
Valachi: They excluded the three of us out of the room; I, Nick Padovona, and Sally Shields. ... Then they called us in one at a time. ... When I came in, I sat down and they were at the edge of the table, it was a long table, and there was a gun and a knife on the table.
Question: How many were at the table?
Valachi: About 35 or 40. ...
Question: In other words, when you took that oath, you expected someday to die either by the gun or by the knife.
Valachi: That is right.
Question: That is what you were dedicating yourself to?
Valachi: That is right.
Question: For what purpose?
Valachi: Well, I guess the purpose, that is what the rules were, of Cosa Nostra.
Question: ... What kind of ceremony did you go through in taking that oath?
Valachi: Well, then he gave me a piece of paper, and I was to burn it. ... That is the way I burn if I expose this organization.
Question: What else did you do in that ceremony?
Valachi: After that, they got around the table and they drew numbers. [A ritual method was described for choosing a Godfather—the man responsible for the new soldier.]

* * *

Question: Now, who was, in that method? Who was chosen, or who became your Godfather?
Valachi: Joe Bananas. ...
Question: That is the highest oath you took? In other words, that was the most sacred in this organization?
Valachi: That is right.
Question: ... You became there a soldier or a button man. I see. Were any of the rules explained to you there, or were they explained to you later?
Valachi: Just two rules at this time.
Question: What were they?
Valachi: One was the secret I was just telling you about [not to expose the organization], and the other rule was for instance, a wife, if you violate the law of another member's wife,

or sister, or daughter, these two rules were told; in other words, you had no defense . . . and after the war I learned the rules. For instance, you can't hit another member with your fist. That is a serious charge, not that you die for it, but you have a chance for a trial, which I was involved in one of those. . . . Well, the defense was that we had a business together and he was stealing.
Question: He was stealing?
Valachi: He was stealing most of the profit.
Question: Was that against your code, to steal from each other?
Valachi: Well, yes; against my code it was.

Obligations

Question: Doing these things came as naturally as breathing?
Valachi: That is right; yes.
Question: If you were ordered to carry out an assignment, supposing it was just a plain robbery, and it did not involve any of the rival families, did you have any instructions regarding shoot to kill in the course of that robbery or did you try to avoid it if they were nonrivals?
Valachi: Senator, you would not get any help if you got arrested for robbery. You were on your own. In fact, they didn't allow that.
Question: I mean, were you instructed to avoid killing other than your own, that is what I am getting at?
Valachi: If they don't allow it, how can they instruct you? . . . I ain't supposed to steal.
Question: . . . This making him Man of the Year, was that by the Cosa Nostra government or by the city of Buffalo?
Valachi: Not Cosa Nostra. That was how you put it — newspapers.
Question: A civic honor?
Valachi: Cosa Nostra had nothing to do with what they make him.
Question: Did any of the members of Cosa Nostra go into politics. . . . Did they contribute to political campaigns?
Valachi: Yes, that they did.
Question: For what office?
Valachi: I am not acquainted with that, Senator, you know what I mean. But I know they helped. But how it goes, I never was interested in political affairs.
Question: In what offices were they interested, in judges, prosecutors, or governors, or was the emphasis generally in national activities in their political contributions?
Valachi: I would say national, like president. . . .
Question: You know that they did make contributions?
Valachi: Yes.
Question: May I clear up one other thing? Yesterday the witness was testifying about John Montana or something was in the record about his having been presented an award, the Man of the Year Award by Buffalo, or somebody in the city of Buffalo, is that correct? You said something yesterday about the newspapers presenting him an award. You meant you saw something in the newspapers about him getting an award?
Valachi: Yes, but yesterday I was trying to tell you that Cosa Nostra had nothing to do with that, Senator.
Question: Anyway, when you referred to the newspapers, you didn't mean to imply that the newspapers of Buffalo presented him with the award?
Valachi: No, Senator. . . . It is not that I mean to say the newspapers are doing anything wrong. I feel they have been misled, that is all.
Question: You feel they have been misled. Well, my purpose in asking you this, my understanding is that it was the Fraternal Organization of the Buffalo Police Department that actually presented the award to Montana, and not the newspapers. . . .
Valachi: I didn't know who presented it at all, Senator.

Arrest Record of a Cosa Nostra Family

Question: How many families are there in the New York area?
Valachi: In the New York area there are five, but Newark is six. [Valachi identified the Vito Genovese family, the Tommy Luchese family, the Carlo Gambino family, the Giuseppe Magliocco family, and the Joe Bonanno family.]

Source: Government Operations Committee, U.S. Senate, Organized Crime and Illicit Traffic in Narcotics, Hearings before the Permanent Subcommittee on Investigation, 88th Congress, Parts 1 and 5 (Washington D.C.: U.S. Government Printing Office, 1964). These excerpts selected from Martin R. Haskell and Lewis Yablonsky, *Criminology: Crime and Criminality* (Chicago: Rand McNally, 1974), pp. 114–21, 123–24.

who briefly held the limelight before a Senate committee in 1963. This testimony was uncorroborated and full of contradictions, but it was given credibility by the desire and need of Americans to have a scapegoat who could be blamed for society's crime problem.[75]

In an article describing the manner in which citations in criminology texts lend support to the "Mafia Myth," John Galliher and James Cain (1974) point out that the reliance on official documents is similar to the way in which criminologists rely on official crime statistics. The limitations and the data contained in documents such as Senate hearings reports are duly noted, but they still are used.[76]

Although the state of criminological knowledge concerning organized crime is uncertain and characterized by factual and theoretical disputes, the existence of types of criminal behavior involving illicit activities such as gambling, labor racketeering, loansharking, and drug traffic are, as Ianni has noted, "an integral part of economic life" in our society. Daniel Bell had pointed out earlier that organized crime has "provided a ladder of social mobility out of the slums of our cities." In Ianni's view, however, organized crime is undergoing a period of transition. Blacks and Hispanics, like previous poor minority groups, are discovering anew this means of social and economic mobility within our social system.[77]

While citizens generally condemn organized crime and succumb to the promises of political reformers and crime control organizations to wipe out this "evil" force, the types of activities described below apparently are more influenced by economic factors, such as supply and demand for goods and services, than by laws or episodic efforts at control.

Gambling. Millions of Americans take advantage of the gambling services provided by organized crime. Gambling touches upon a basic contradiction in the American work ethic, which embraces both hard work and a "little bit of luck" as the road to success. Gambling, in the form of public lotteries, was sponsored by state governments prior to the 1830s. But a combination of numerous scandals and moral reaction led to reform efforts, and by 1894 they were discontinued.[78]

Law enforcement officials generally agree that gambling is one of the more lucrative sources of income for organized crime. Illegal gambling includes the "numbers" or policy games, sometimes called "bolita"; bookmaking (the taking of bets on horse or dog races and professional and college sport events); and gambling in illegal casinos (as well as considerable involvement in legitimate casinos). As state governments became involved in lotteries and off-track pari-mutuel betting in the 1970s, it was thought that it would serve not only as a means of generating needed revenues, but would divert profits from organized crime. However, it evidently has resulted in a dividing of "spoils" from increased activity. Recent data provided by the Public Gaming Research Institute disclosed that all major forms of gambling increased between 1970 and 1975. The Institute also found a correlation between gambling activity and public exposure to and availability of both legal and illegal gambling activities.[79]

Now that state-run lotteries flourish and off-track betting parlors appear at various locations throughout our major cities, it appears that the white middle classes have had their preferred forms of gambling legalized. Understandably, this is viewed as another example of the hypocrisy of the "white establishment," for the numbers game, largely a black "thing," remains illegal in most states.

Studies of the role of the numbers game have noted that many residents of black communities defend its importance to the economic life of the community, since it provides jobs as well as a way of life. The numbers runner has a unique relationship with the slum dweller, and subsidiary enterprises such as the publication and sale of "dream-books" are sold to give the bettor clues as to how to place bets based on one's dreams. As one source notes, it "is not only a business—it's a cult." [80]

An illustration of this double standard was provided by the New Jersey edition of the *New York Times* on March 6, 1973. The *Times* reported a vice-squad raid on a Puerto Rican numbers game. Just below the article, the newspaper printed the winning New Jersey lottery number.[81]

There is no accurate estimate of the amount of gross income generated by illegal gambling, but the number of people involved and amount of money involved are considerable. The Crime Commission estimated the number of people who gamble on horse racing at about 4.5 million and the total bets at over $4.5 billion. The commission estimated that illegal gambling grossed about $20 billion a year, and concluded that between $6 billion and $7 billion of this was profit for organized crime groups. In 1976 the Joint Economic Committee estimated that illegal gambling represented $5.9 billion in possible lost revenue.[82]

The fact remains that despite all the laws against gambling in America, people continue to disregard them. And even while the media from time to time attack gambling and its supposed ties with organized crime, they provide information that is essential to such activities, such as race track results. Other citizens inveigh against gambling while they frequent church bingo games, play one-armed bandits (slot machines), and poker. In view of such contradictions, Gilbert Geis has suggested that the prohibition of gambling is among those activities that are "not the law's business." He suggests that we might discover more effective techniques than the present approaches that keep gambling flourishing undercover.[83]

Loansharking. The lending of money at higher rates than prescribed by law, or "loansharking," is considered the second main source of income for organized crime. The profits from gambling provide the capital for such "shylocking."

The types of persons who require this service include gamblers who must cover losses and small business persons who find regular sources of credit closed. Sometimes the same people who take bets from employees in large businesses also serve as "loan sharks" in order to make money to pay debts or take care of living expenses. A few years ago, the New York State Commission of Investigation reported that each of 121 loan sharks who were affiliated with that city's five crime families had at least $1 million out on loan.[84]

Loan sharks are crucial, especially in hard times when other sources of fluid cash dry up, and they can provide access to underworld monies. Loan-sharking is important to syndicate crime as a means for moving underworld monies into legitimate businesses.

The loan shark's interest rates are high—the correct term for this action is *usury*—with the usual interest set at *20 percent per week!* In the case of long-term loans, interest may more commonly be set at 1.5 percent a week. For instance, if you needed $200,000 quickly for your business and your bank refused to extend credit, you might turn to a loan shark. You would get the loan, but you would have to pay $3,000 interest a week until the principal was repaid. In earlier days, you might have experienced an encounter of the worst kind with an enforcer-collector, if you failed to keep up your payments. Nowadays, the loan shark might exchange the promisory note for a forced partnership in the business. This step follows the pattern of legitimate banking systems that seize collateral when debtors default on loans.

It is impossible to obtain a reliable estimate of the gross national income from loansharking. Yet it is known that profit margins are higher than for gambling, and the total is thought to be in the multibillion dollar range. Thomas Plate estimates that the annual income for a successful loan shark in New York City is about $125,000—all tax free![85]

Narcotics Trafficking. Traffic in narcotics is by necessity highly organized, much like any conventional import-wholesale-retail enterprise. The importing of heroin, for instance, requires the coordination of a complex of complementary and competing groups. The importing and distribution of cocaine and marijuana are less organized, but both are international businesses. Those involved in hard drugs, such as heroin, tend to be part of a stable smuggling network or crime syndicate. However, La Cosa Nostra, contrary to popular belief, does not have a monopoly on this activity.

The assertion that "organized crime" groups monopolize heroin distribution was shown by Mark Moore (1977) to be imprecise conventional wisdom. He suggests that the considerable resources required—money, personnel, and connections—result in "economies of scale." Also, a capacity for violence to provide security from other criminals and the police may mean that a dealer who meets the requirements to enter the drug traffic can also control a large share of the market. This results in various forms of "centralization." Moore's evidence suggests that it is the Federal Drug Enforcement Agency's system of classifying those arrested with 2.2 pounds (1 kilogram) or more of heroin or cocaine, among other factors, that results in the offender being identified as the head of a criminal organization. It is the action of the control agents in defining such activity, together with the networks to which they must be tied, that leads to news stories that relate such offenses to organized crime.[86]

The laws against the marketing of some drugs provided the impetus for this profitable business just as the Eighteenth Amendment led to bootlegging. This does not mean that legalizing or decriminalizing drugs would eliminate the drug problem. But illicit drug importers, wholesalers, and dealers would find it difficult to compete against the organizational and business skills of the large pharmaceutical companies in an "open" market. It seems obvious that legalization would not take the profit out of the drug business any more than the repeal of Prohibition took the profit out of the alcohol business. But organized crime would stand to lose an important source of revenue.

The organized approach for providing heroin to street addicts is focused on realizing immense profit at little risk to the importers, wholesalers, and suppliers before the narcotic gets down to street dealers and addict pushers. The amount of ready money needed to maintain international connections and move the supply of narcotics from the overseas source of supply to the street is considerable. The profits also are considerable but so are the risks.

The distribution of drugs downward from the importer is a complicated transaction.[87] Here is one simplified model of how the drug market might operate: Once heroin reaches the suppliers in the city where it is consumed, they cut it—usually with quinine and sugar—and sell it to street dealers who distribute it to the addict pushers. A supplier is usually a member of the local organized crime apparatus, but the dealers and pushers are the ones most often arrested. It is probable that organized criminals operate mainly at the upper levels, where they turn monies gained in other illicit activities into still greater amounts. Nationally, thousands are employed as lower-level suppliers and dealers. The pushers, or drug peddlers, are "small fry." They sell to addicts whose second habit—petty street crime—is the only means by which they can obtain the $50 to $100 a day needed to support their addiction.

The illegal trade in narcotics is a multibillion dollar international business. It is a protected market, for regardless of the intentions of the drug laws, their effect is a kind of monopolistic franchise to underworld entrepreneurs who are willing to break the law in order to profit from the demand for illegal drugs.

This description of the drug traffic should not be interpreted as an endorsement for the legalization of hard drugs. But whatever one's attitude toward the legal structure, it should be recognized that the essential elements of the drug traffic that most citizens find abhorrent are not a function of the drugs themselves. Rather, they are the result, indirect or direct, of a market system similar in many ways to the legal market system, yet one which is affected in various ways by enforcement efforts.[88]

Other Illegal Goods and Services. With the end of Prohibition came the demise of bootlegging. Although the production of illegal liquor continues, it is largely localized within a few southern states. Its risks are too great and costs too high to be attractive to organized crime.

Prostitution is also too risky. Since the convictions of "Lucky" Luciano and other underworld figures in the 1930s and 1940s, crime syndicates have been wary of such activities. The extent of organized crime involvement in street prostitution seems to be left to black and Puerto Rican criminal groups.[89] The emergence of massage parlors and "topless" bars in New York City and other metropolitan and suburban areas has been tied into the network of organized crime operations. A reputed underworld leader, Matthew Ianniello, was identified by law enforcement officials as having hidden financial interests in at least a dozen of the fifty topless bars in New York City. Agents from the Internal Revenue Service have been investigating records of these topless bars and massage parlors, as well as "peep shops," which show pornographic films (see Figure 7.6). Even though these "businesses" gross large amounts of money—as much as $500,000 a year for a topless bar—it is very difficult to find records, since they deal in cash transactions.[90] As one IRS investigator stated: "They pile holding company upon holding company to camouflage what's happening to the money and who's in charge. You get tired and frustrated about ever unraveling the books." [91]

Organized Crime Goes "Legit"

The infiltration of legitimate businesses is both a means of translating illegitimate monies into legitimate—a process popularized since the Watergate episode as "laundering" money—and a means of gaining social respectability. Organized criminals, like many other Americans, are concerned with social prestige and vertical mobility. As Daniel Bell has suggested, crime has a functional role in society, and organized crime serves as one of the "queer ladders" of vertical mobility.[92] It is not at all unusual to find successful leaders of syndicated crime living in exclusive suburban communities.

Organized crime seems to thrive within social structures of poverty and powerlessness. As one writer observed recently about the movement of blacks and Hispanics into organized crime:

> Blacks and Puerto Ricans, like other ethnics before them, see organized crime as one of the few available routes to success, to financial and thus psychological security.... How do you escape poverty through socially approved routes when such are closed off from the ghetto? Organized crime resolves the dilemma because it provides a quick if perilous route out.[93]

This is not to suggest that criminals who seek social respectability are any less criminal because they share the Horatio Alger myth of success with other Americans. But it does place their efforts to move into legitimate businesses in a broader context than just the accumulation of financial gain. Matters of power and prestige are also involved.

The profits that organized crime accrues from illegal activities are invested in a number of legitimate enterprises throughout the country. They rely on accountants, attorneys, business, and tax consultants to help do their business.

Figure 7.6. The Involvement of Three Organized Crime Families in Distribution of Pornography

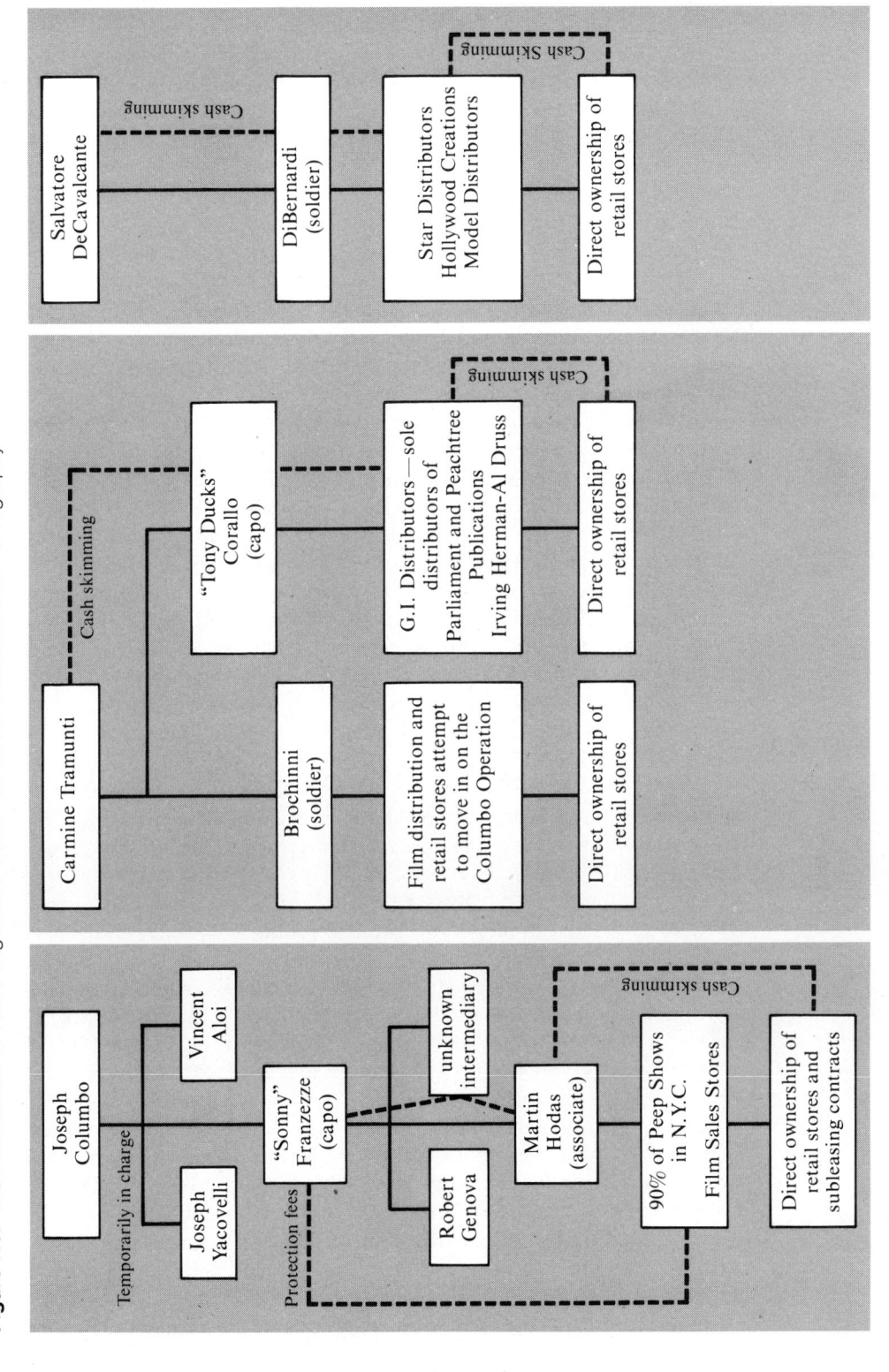

Source: Thomas Plate, *Crime Pays* (New York: Ballantine Books, 1975), pp. 140–41. Copyright © 1975 by, Thomas Platt. Reprinted by permission of Simon & Schuster, a Division of Gulf + Western Corporation.

There are reciprocal benefits and trade-offs for the legitimate business and political institutions. The career of Frank Costello exemplifies such political reciprocity. Costello moved from bootlegging into slot machines and then into real estate. When Tammany Hall needed financial support in the 1930s and 1940s—it was left out by the New Deal reforms—he provided funds. In the same era, Italians began to move into urban politics. The Kefauver Congressional Committee saw this as proof that the "omnipotent Mafia," under the leadership of the despotic Costello, was seeking to take over urban politics. The committee failed to understand what Bell suggests is a salient sociological fact regarding the political life of large urban communities in America, namely that given the power and prestige that organized crime leaders may have within the Italian (or other ethnic) community, they inevitably will have political influence among their large constituencies.[94] A more recent example of a reputed gang leader exerting leadership is Joseph Columbo, Sr., who was left helpless after being shot in the head in an assassination attempt at an Italian Protection League rally in New York City on Columbus Day, 1971.

An example of the reciprocal benefits between industrial racketeers and the "legitimate" business sector was the service provided by organized crime in the 1930s in regulating unstable businesses that were involved in cutthroat competition. Bell suggests that this was a "blessing in disguise." In Robert Merton's terms, the infiltration of business by the crime syndicates paradoxically played a stabilizing latent function by regulating competition and fixing prices. Admittedly, the manifest function was control of such businesses. A case in point was the way in which Lepke Buchalter and Gurrah Shapiro came to dominate sections of the clothing, painting, furrier, and flour-trucking industries in the early 1930s. However, what began as a quasieconomic service soon became an extortion scheme. And these businesses called for government action against organized crime once the New Deal and the NRA took over this stabilizing role.[95]

The manifest or intended function of organized crime's infiltration of business is to turn illicit profits into legitimate profits—in other words, to make crime pay even more. This necessitates the control of businesses. According to the Task Force on Organized Crime, control comes about through one of the following methods: (1) investments of profits from illegal activities; (2) acceptance of a partnership in the business as payment for a gambling debt; (3) foreclosure on shylocking or usurious loans; or (4) takeovers involving some form of extortion.[96]

Once organized crime takes over a business, one available option to a quick profit is planned bankruptcy, or the "scam." This technique was perfected in the 1950s by an underworld leader in Chicago named Alan Robert Rosenberg. The volume of planned bankruptcies in the United States is considerable. The United States Chamber of Commerce states that more than 1,000 uninvestigated scams occur each year. About 250 of these involve leading underworld crime figures. The losers are the creditors. Usually several hundred creditors are involved in each scam, and the amount of money and merchandise involved ranges between $100,000 and $250,000.[97]

The "quick" or "one-step" scam is illustrated by the following examples, reported by the Task Force on Organized Crime. A meat-packing firm was taken over in payment of a gambling debt. The firm overpurchased numerous items, which were sold below market prices. The receipts were skimmed off by the syndicate criminals. The firm then filed a bankruptcy petition, and the creditors were defrauded of their money through a legal device designed to protect honest businesses.[98]

Arson is another device for turning a quick profit. Organized criminals may arrange to have a business's merchandise sold to a fence, then hire a professional arsonist to set fire to the building. Then they collect fire insurance on the building and its (former) contents. It is estimated that about 28 percent of the $4 billion lost to fires in 1976 was due to arson. Professional arsonists are also hired by legitimate business people.[99]

Moving into control of legitimate business has become a highly developed technique of organized crime. An Internal Revenue Service study concluded that 98 of 113 leading crime figures in the United States were involved in 159 legitimate businesses. One underworld group was thought to own real estate valued at $300 million. According to the Crime Commission, organized crime groups control national manufacturing and service industries with well-known brand names. In one midwestern city, it was found that such groups controlled or had shares in eighty-nine businesses whose assets exceeded $800 million.[100]

In New York City, crime syndicates apparently control the pornography business. Three Cosa Nostra families (see Figure 7.6) allegedly have secret ties in pornography shops and peep shows in the Times Square area of the city. The power structure of these three families has changed somewhat since the Columbo assassination attempt in 1971. Box 5 describes the attempt by the Gambino family to take over a private garbage-collecting business in the Bronx. The newspaper account refers to Joseph Gambino as a "reputed key Mafia figure," not as a leader of the Cosa Nostra. In this instance, extortion was used. Similar strong-arm tactics are reported in the pornography business.[101]

These activities are illegal under a U.S. law passed in 1970. Title 18 of the U.S. Code, Sections 1961–1964, is the "Racketeering Influence and Corrupt Organizations" statute. It states that:

> It shall be unlawful for *any income* derived, directly or indirectly, from a pattern of racketeering activity or through a *collection of an unlawful* debt . . . *to use or invest,* directly or indirectly, any part of such income, or *the proceeds,* of such . . . in acquisition of *any enterprise* which is engaged in, or the activities of which affect, interstate or foreign commerce.[102]

In other words, the reinvestment of money gained illegally is prohibited. This law also prohibits attempts to control or seek to acquire any legitimate enterprise through conspiracy, and it prescribes penalties of up to twenty years imprisonment and a maximum fine of $25,000. The act also allows civil action to

BOX 5

Takeover of a Garbage Collector Charged to Two Reputed Mafia Men

By ARNOLD H. LUBASCH

Two reputed Mafia associates were arrested yesterday and charged with using extortion and violence to extend their control of private garbage collecting in the Bronx.

Joseph Gambino, the main defendant, is a reputed key Mafia figure in the Bronx and the owner of several restaurants. He has been identified as a cousin of Carlo Gambino, who was widely regarded as "the boss of all bosses" in the Mafia until his death last year.

The second defendant is Carlo Conti, owner of two private carting companies in the Bronx, who was described as Joseph Gambino's "right-hand man." Both men were charged with "racketeering activity."

The United States Attorney, Robert B. Fiske Jr., announced the unsealing of a 22-count Federal indictment in Manhattan, charging the two defendants with having illegally taken over a Bronx sanitation company from two brothers who allegedly had been threatened and beaten.

Peter D. Sudler, a Federal prosecutor, alleged that Joseph Gambino "has interests in virtually the entire private sanitation industry in the Bronx."

Mr. Sudler also alleged that Mr. Conti "administered vicious beatings" at the behest of Mr. Gambino to collect extortionate loans. The prosecutor added that the case involved a "classic example" of the takeover of a private business in violation of laws against organized crime.

The prosecutor said that Mr. Gambino, who is 47 years old and lives at 1566 Dwight Place in the Bronx, was a citizen of Italy who was appealing an order to deport him for having entered the United States illegally 20 years ago. Mr. Conti, a United States citizen, is 38 and lives at 2426 Seymour Avenue, the Bronx.

According to the indictment, Mr. Gambino and Mr. Conti acquired control of Terminal Sanitation, a private garbage collecting company in the Bronx, by engaging in "a pattern of racketeering activity" that included extortion and violence.

The two defendants allegedly forced Peter and Anthony Darminio, two brothers who owned Terminal Sanitation, to collect garbage from commercial customers in the Co-op City area of the Bronx and to give one-third of the proceeds to a Gambino-controlled company. The Darminio brothers were allegedly forced to pay more than $4,000 a month from 1972 to 1975.

When the brothers were unable to make payments, they were compelled to sell portions of their garbage-collection business to companies controlled by the defendants, the indictment said. It added that "these forced sales" had eventually resulted in "the demise of Terminal Sanitation as a business entity."

The indictment also said the defendants had used "physical violence" against the Darminio brothers to collect an extortionate loan of $75,000.

Mr. Sudler, the prosecutor, added that the brothers had been assaulted, that shots had been fired at their trucks and that they had been subjected to such fear that "they had to hide on New York City subways for days at a time." The defendants were described as a "grave threat" to the lives of the two brothers, who remain important witnesses in the case.

Mr. Sudler recommended bail of $2 million for Mr. Gambino and $200,000 for Mr. Conti. Magistrate Harold J. Raby set the bail at $500,000 for Mr. Gambino and $50,000 for Mr. Conti in Federal District Court in Manhattan.

If convicted, each defendant could face up to 20 years in prison on each of several charges involving racketeering and extortion. Mr. Gambino could also face up to five years each on additional charges alleging he evaded taxes on more than $400,000 from 1970 to 1975.

The defendants were arrested at their homes by agents of the Federal Bureau of Investigation and the Internal Revenue Service.

Source: *New York Times*, March 3, 1977. © 1977 by The New York Times Company. Reprinted by permission.

stop such takeovers of businesses without having to prove criminal violations first. However, this section was challenged in the courts in 1974 and was appealed to the Supreme Court.

Organized Crime and the Corruption of Criminal Justice

Organized crime could hardly be successful without the cooperation of some corrupt officials as well as the benign support of the business sector. The invisibility of organized crime is paralleled by the invisible corruption it encourages. Corruption is difficult to trace and combat. And the potential for corruption is greater today than ever before, due to growing governmental regulation of business and private areas of activity. The success of organized crime depends upon immunity to the law. Throughout its history, organized crime, as the Crime Commission points out, has corrupted law enforcement officials, legislators, regulatory agencies, and others who neglect their legal responsibility.[103]

The way organized crime "captures" public officials is well illustrated by the case of James L. Marcus, New York's commissioner of Water Supply, Gas, and Electricity, during Mayor John Lindsay's administration. Marcus was in debt from bad investments in business ventures and Wall Street speculation. He became indebted to a loan shark, Anthony Corallo, who was reputedly a lieutenant in the Thomas Lucchese Cosa Nostra "family." When he was unable to maintain interest payments, he became involved in fixing contracts, eventually taking $16,000 in bribes or kickbacks for awarding a contract to a company tied into the syndicate. As a result he was sentenced to a prison term.[104]

The Knapp Commission investigation in New York City in the early 1970s illustrates the extent to which "grifting," or taking of bribes, had corrupted the police department of our nation's largest city. The police who came forward with evidence were frequently those who had taken bribes. They were known to the rest of the police force as "renegade cops." The commission made public information that was commonly known among street gangs and other types of criminals and noncriminals who were a part of the street scene in various parts of the city. A colleague of ours, for instance, was informed by some of his respondents in a juvenile delinquency study in East Harlem that the precinct police captain went to the "numbers" headquarters in the area to pick up his "grift" every Wednesday afternoon.

Organized crime seeks immunity by corrupting such middle-level police officials. The efforts of idealistic police officers who seek to enforce legal prohibitions against gambling and related activities can lead to their reassignment to the traffic control division. The officer may learn that it is futile to attempt to enforce the law against such criminals and will turn his attention to other forms of crime not protected by the syndicate. This selective enforcement of the laws against such activities as gambling, when focused upon members of minority groups, results in a kind of monopoly for those crime syndicates with the most effective organization, money, and power.[105]

BOX 6

Organized Crime and Police Corruption: A Cop Tells Why He Blew the Whistle

By JACK THOMAS

Prince of the City is a seamy story, a true tragedy set in the streets and back alleys of New York City, where cops and dope peddlers play the parts of the hunter and the hunted, sometimes chasing one another, sometimes cooperating in a weird, merry-go-round world where morality blinks on and off like a flashing neon light.

The principal character is Bob Leuci, good Catholic boy, handsome and shrewd, who never cut classes in high school, and always went to confession. Leuci becomes a New York City detective, one of the best. But somehow, without realizing it, he crosses an invisible line and begins to engage in criminal activity.

It is a thread that weaves an inevitable web so great it entangles Leuci himself, mobsters, and more than 50 police officers, shaking the New York department from rookie to commissioner.

Det. Robert Leuci and his partner established a lookout post on 116th street across from a drugstore where they suspected heroin was sold.

One day, while monitoring the druggist's telephone, they heard a man tell the owner to close the drugstore for a few days so the Mafia could use it to hide 300 color television sets that had been hijacked.

As the detectives watched and filmed, three well-dressed men carried the television sets in daylight from the truck to the store, assisted by neighborhood children.

Later, however, the locked door aroused the suspicions of a police officer, who peeked through the blinds and saw television sets stacked to the ceiling. Immediately, he telephoned his police station with a 10-13, code that means an officer needs help.

The first police to arrive kicked in the door of the drugstore and arrested several men.

"Within 10 minutes," writes Leuci in *Prince of the City*, "there were 50 cops in the drugstore. After that, more cars began to pull up. Not police cars, but Volkswagens, station wagons. Nearly every cop in the precinct pulled up in his own car, and they started lugging television sets out of the store.

"They were tying television sets onto the roofs of the Volkswagens, they were shoving television sets into the station wagons. Up and down the street, television sets were being carried to their cars. There must have been 15 private cars with cops in uniform behind the wheel. They were waiting in line to get the TV sets."

The situation got worse. Leuci and his partners hurried around the corner to their recording machine, and listened horrified as one cop after another spoke into the tapped telephone. "They were spreading the word about the TV sets," Leuci says in the book.

"A squad commander called his division commander: 'Hey, I've got a television set for the office.' There were 20 or more calls on the tape of cops phoning friends and relatives: 'Get over here fast. I got a television set for you.'"

Knowing such a tape could convict 25 or so police officers of stealing television sets, the three narcotics detectives rushed to the station house to warn the commander to return the 150 sets that had been stolen, to keep the rest of his police officers away from the remaining sets, and to keep them off the tapped telephone.

They had to be subtle, though, in order to preserve their narcotics case against the druggist. If the details of their investigation became known at the station, someone surely would tip off the druggist.

The first narcotics detective entered the station and told the lieutenant, "Get those TV sets back. The walls have ears."

In conversation with his partners back in the car, though, they decided that because the lieutenant was a "big Irish (expletive) jerk," he might not have understood the message. And so, a second narcotics detective went into the station to deliver the message in stronger language to the same lieutenant. "He understands now," the detective reported to his partners.

But when they returned to the tape recorder, they were astonished to hear yet another cop telephoning from the store, this one asking, "How much do you think a 20-inch RCA is worth? What if I can get you one for $100?"

Back the detectives went to the station house, and a third partner went in, came out, and reported to his partners, "I drew him a picture. I told him to get those TV sets back. I told him the goddamn phone was tapped. I told him enough. Don't use the phone. We are watching the place, Lieutenant. Keep the cops out of there, and don't use the phone there."

A patrolman was assigned to stand guard at the drugstore. That night, though, with the detectives listening and recording, the patrolman telephoned the station house to ask the desk officer's advice about $2000 he found in a desk in the drugstore.

According to Leuci's book, the advice the desk officer gave him was to put it in his pocket. The patrolman pointed out that he was still on probation, that he didn't want trouble.

" 'That money is your money,' the old timer interrupted harshly, and for the next few minutes, he pressured the rookie to steal it. 'Nobody will know you took it. Any of the people who work in the store could have taken it. There were narcotics cops in the place today, weren't there? The narcotics guys took the money. Those are the (expletive) guys who took it. Put it in your pocket. Is it in your pocket yet?'

" 'Okay, it's in my pocket, but . . .' "

Leuci and his partners rushed from the recorder to the store, tapped on the glass, and showed their badges to the rookie, who hung up the telephone and opened the door. When the detectives told him to take the money out of his pocket, he wet his pants.

"Every word you just said was recorded, you (expletive) moron," Leuci said. "How many times do we have to tell you (expletive) guys? Now take that money and put it back."

For the third time that day, the detectives drove to the station house to confront the lieutenant, who had remained several hours after his tour of duty, waiting for transportation for himself and his new television set.

"If we had a pair of handcuffs big enough to put around this whole (expletive) station house, we'd take the whole bunch of you," said one of the detectives. "You know we are watching that place. We're taking pictures. We've got a wiretap on the phone. I suppose you never heard of wiretaps? It never occurred to any of you that the phone was wired? Every one of you jerkos used that phone. You guys are a disgrace. You guys are so (expletive) bad, you should all go to jail."

But they did not go to jail. The four Mafia hoods involved in the hijacking pleaded guilty to a misdemeanor. Although only 170 of the 300 television sets were recovered, no investigation ensued.

The narcotics detectives erased whatever portions of the tape incriminated fellow police officers, and they agreed that if they were confronted with the erasure in court, they would lie.

ACT 1, Scene 1: Transferred to narcotics, Leuci joins his partners in illegal wiretapping.

Rationale: "We'd be tapping dope dealers, the bad guys who were in a separate and targeted world. If you don't use illegal wiretapping, you're not going to catch the dope pushers, the killers and the guys who plan to blow up buildings."

Scene 2: Leuci is uneasy that his partners exchange heroin for information. Then one day, while he's questioning an addict, the man begins to cry and becomes sick to his stomach in need of a fix, which Leuci provides.

Rationale: "How can anyone sit and speak to a guy for a long period of time when he's moaning and groaning and beggin' you to put him out of his misery?"

Scene 3: Leuci takes a long weekend, and his informer pleads for two bags to get him through Monday. Leuci goes on a 10-day vacation, and his informer pleads for 10 bags to keep him sane. In both cases, Leuci provides the heroin.

Rationale: "I thought of it as medication. I knew it was illegal, but it was so available to us, and once I'd done it, I mean, when I thought of *why* I was doing it, to help catch the big pushers, well, it seemed like there was nothing wrong with it."

Scene 4: Leuci steals money, a few hundred dollars at first, then a few thousand, always sharing it with partners, mostly from Hispanic drug dealers, in amounts that over the years totalled more than $20,000.

Rationale: "Well, my partner made the point, he said, 'Every time you give a bag of junk to somebody, it's a felony. Now how many felonies have you already committed in the last six months? 500?' Now these guys were making a lot of money, and if you seize it, you're supposed to turn it in to who, the IRS? What do they do with it? They give it to welfare people. They make bombs for Vietnam. We can use the money on the street to buy information, and whatever's left over, you use at home. Hey, we're out there six, seven days a week, and we get $40 expense money, and between us, my partner and myself, how much money, you got in your pocket, $4? How much you got, $3? Awright, we're going to be working all night. You got to eat. And here's this guy with $2000, so if we take $200, it's gonna help pay our bills."

ACT 2, Scene 1: The guilt over his misdeeds builds in Leuci. The years of importuning by his father and the church about honesty fester in him, along with the memory of his brother, who was a heroin addict.

Anxious for penance, Leuci agrees to act as an undercover agent for the federal government's Knapp Commission.

Rationale: "Sure, I knew that some cops might get caught, and it bothered me that I would be violating the code of loyalty cops have to each other. But I figured it would be a way to get at the lawyers, the district attorneys, and the judges who were far more corrupt and a lot less harassed than police officers."

Scene 2: For 16 months in 1971 and 1972, Leuci wired himself with a transmitter around his chest, and arranged meetings with mobsters, detectives, lawyers and bail bondsmen, recording more than 100 tape recordings of 40 people.

At times, he arouses suspicions. He stops wearing the wires whenever he suspects he might be searched, but the guessing game becomes a bizarre version of Russian roulette. At one point, a corrupt detective and a bail bondsman decide to kill Leuci but, ironically, he is saved by a mobster for whom he once did a small favor. "If you think he's a rat, then you should kill him," says the mobster to the would-be killers, "but you better be sure because he's a friend of ours."

Thus, in the mad world of cops and dope peddlers the bad guys save Leuci from murder by the good guys.

Scene 3: Torn by his role as an undercover agent, Leuci hides his own corrupt past from the investigators, popping Valium to remain calm. On two occasions, he considers suicide.

ACT 3, Scene 1: Finally, faced with indictment, Leuci purges himself, although in the process he implicates dozens of police officers.

As a result, the narcotics unit is disbanded. Fifty-two of its 70 members are indicted. Two, unable to face arrest as police officers, commit suicide. Another is committed to a mental hospital.

Leuci's story is told in detail in *Prince of the City*, written by Robert Daley, former New York deputy police commissioner for public affairs, and published in 1979 by Houghton Mifflin.

Source: *The Boston Globe*, Jan. 26, 1979. Reprinted courtesy of the Boston Globe.

The virtual monopoly granted by police and politicians to certain crime groups is a means of limiting open competition and violence that would make the work of the police more difficult. They are able to limit activities like gambling to certain areas of the city so they are available for those who want to engage in them. During periods of reform and municipal elections, agitation for a cleanup may result in raids on illicit gambling establishments. But after the flurry of publicity dies down, the former relationships between police and organized criminals generally are reestablished.

In his anonymous but nonfictional account of the politics of vice and corruption in "Wincanton," John A. Gardiner documents the manner in which an eastern industrial city was controlled by a crime syndicate for many years. In this enlightening essay, the author describes Wincanton's gambling syndicate and the corruption that allowed it to operate. He considers these two factors, gambling and corruption, as social forces and political issues. The ambivalence of the citizens toward the alliance between syndicated crime and corruption is seen when a mob-controlled mayor loses his reelection bid. At the same time, however, any reform mayor who attempts to close up the city to the gambling syndicate will also be voted out. Wincanton city officials would enhance their syndicate payoffs by taking bribes from those doing business with the city. Law enforcement in the city was effectively controlled by such groups, and numerous city, state, and federal laws were violated by official malfeasance, and nonfeasance. In effect, the city had a ruling elite that was involved with and dependent on organized crime.[106]

This association between city officials and organized crime interests is not limited to the East Coast. William Chambliss found similar ties in a study of a western city. He concluded that:

> It is clear from this study that corruption of political-legal organizations is a critical part of the life-blood of the crime cabal. The study of organized crime is thus a misnomer; the study should consider corruption, bureaucracy, and power. By relying on governmental agencies for their information on vice and the rackets, social scientists and lawyers have inadvertently contributed to the miscasting of the issues in terms that are descriptively biased and theoretically sterile . . . . they have been diverted from sociologically . . . important issues raised by the persistence of the crime cabals . . . . the real significance of the existence of syndicates has been overlooked, for instead of seeing these . . . as intimately tied to, and in symbiosis with the legal and political bureaucracies of the state, they have emphasized the criminality of only a portion of those involved.[107]

The existence of crime and corruption in politics at the national level was highlighted by a number of sensational events during the 1970s. The resignation of Vice-President Spiro Agnew was a shocking reminder of the way in which corruption followed the former governor of Maryland to the second highest office in the land. Agnew was allowed to plead "no contest" to a charge of income tax evasion. He had not reported as income money received as bribes over a period of years. The term "plea bargaining" was apt in this case, for Agnew bargained for a mere three years of unsupervised probation and a $10,000 fine. Subsequently, a federal judge stated that he received hundreds of letters from offenders he had sentenced to prison terms who asked essentially the same question: "Are you going to reconsider my case in view of the treatment given former Vice-President Agnew?" Other offenders, upon being confronted with a plea-bargaining situation in which they were about to receive a prison sentence, were reported to have said, "Why didn't I have Agnew's lawyer plea bargaining my case?"

Four years later, Marvin Mandel, the man who succeeded Agnew as Governor of Maryland, was convicted of mail fraud and racketeering. He could have received a maximum of 105 years in prison under the various charges against him, but the punishment was a relatively light prison sentence. Five Maryland businessmen were co-defendants with Governor Mandel. They were involved while they were secret owners of the Marlboro Race Track in bribing the governor to obtain a favored racing schedule. Assistant U.S. District Attorney Skolnik, who prosecuted the case, stated: "There's a lot of corruption in other states and nobody's doing anything about it." [108]

During 1975 to 1977, the public witnessed a series of revelations concerning the collusion that existed during the administrations of several presidents between the CIA and organized crime figures. Organized crime figures, whose gambling casinos in Havana had been closed down by Fidel Castro, had made arrangements with the CIA to plan Castro's assassination. Several attempts were made between 1959 and 1965. Two of the three underworld figures reputedly involved in the plot were killed in 1975 after testifying before Congressional committees. The third, Santos Trafficante, Jr., refused to testify before the House Committee investigating the assassinations of President John F. Kennedy and Dr. Martin Luther King, Jr.[109]

At the same time that these men plotted with the CIA, the director of the FBI was under orders from the attorney general to investigate the relationship between organized crime and business and government. Obviously, such a web of interrelations between the underworld and government officials should not end with the scrutiny of reputed leaders of the Cosa Nostra or Mafia. The exercise of power and its misuse by official bureaucracies must also be analyzed.

Organized crime is more than a criminal behavior pattern. It is part of the American way of life. Its tentacles reach into the highest as well as the lowest levels of power in our society. It is often argued that decriminalizing laws that seek to regulate private morality will make organized crime fade away. This may be true of drug traffic and pornography. However, we can hardly legalize contract killing—even by the CIA. Nor can we legalize the corruption of government officials.[110]

Organized crime, in its many facets, can be seen as a behavior system that overlaps at many points with economic, political, legal, and social institutions in any social system. It may be, as Merton has suggested, that the existence of such sinister "evil" organizations serves a "latent" function—for we should all expect persistent social patterns and social structures to perform positive functions which are not fulfilled adequately by "existing patterns and structures."[111] However, we should see the double irony in such latent functions. It is not only a matter of who benefits, but at whose expense.

Organized crime still flourishes—in fact, a large proportion of the "crime tax," or cost of crime, can be attributed to organized crime. Efforts to combat it are costly. It should be obvious that strategies based upon the assumption of a national conspiracy by a few evil leaders are not effective. We need a new perspective, one that looks at the patterns of American life rather than sensational myths about Italian-Americans and the syndicate. It may be that our society has the kind of organized crime patterns that we desire and deserve.

SUMMARY

In this chapter we have described three types of vocational behavior systems: the professional, "heavy" professional, and organized crime action systems. These three types were considered in the "vocational" or "career" category since they all relate to the pursuit of crime not only as a livelihood, but also because each type involves a greater degree of commitment to a criminal self-concept and to crime as a career than do the other types of criminal behavior systems that will be described in chapters 9 to 11.

The three types of vocational crime differ in their criminal behavior orientation, but all demand commitment to lifestyles that are different from those of conventional society. Professional crime might involve some commonplace offenses such as burglary, but the category of "heavy professional" crime was used to refer to offenses that involve repeated predatory personal and property crimes such as robbery, which involves direct contact and threats against victims. Professional crime typically is limited to nonviolent offenses such as picking pockets, shoplifting, confidence games, and miscellaneous rackets. Since they are isolated from conventional society, and to an extent from other types of criminals, the professionals enjoy a relatively high status in the criminal world and they make their living from full-time illegal activities.

The professional's behavior system not only includes well-developed skills and techniques but also relies on support from legitimate members of society as well as public indifference. This is especially the case in professional offenses involving con games and fraud. In con games, the "mark" is apparently an "honest" member of society who is looking for a "fast buck" and gets taken in. We must look not only at the criminal career of the professional, but also at patterns of fraud in legitimate areas as an important aspect of professional crime. Professionals also seek to manipulate the system of arranging or attempting to "fix" their cases if they are apprehended.

Organized crime is a major area of criminal activity in our society which, though almost invisible, results in considerable economic gain. It differs from commonplace crime in that much of the risk is reduced, since it flourishes with the complicity, if not the protection, of the legal system. Through its hierarchical structure, organized crime is able to influence or exert control over different groups involved in providing illegal goods and services to satisfy demands that legitimate organizations are legally prohibited from providing. Its overlap with the legitimate world and its maximization of profit illustrate how societal values can operate for illegitimate as well as legitimate ends. Its ties to the "upperworld" not only minimize risks but ensure the continued existence of organized crime, barring basic reforms in the legal-political system that result in an effective means of control.

Career crimes, then, involve not only unique behavior systems with roles relevant to criminal activity, an identification with crime, a criminal self-concept, and association with other criminals, but two of the types rely upon support from conventional society.

ADDITIONAL READINGS

Ianni, Francis. *Black Mafia: Ethnic Succession in Organized Crime.* New York: Simon and Schuster, 1974.

>The author presents a description of organized crime in terms of its function in providing a means of mobility for new migrants to our urban centers as it did for former waves of immigrants.

Inciardi, James, A. *Careers in Crime.* Chicago: Rand McNally, 1975.

>This book uses the writings of Edwin H. Sutherland as a framework for the author's research into the careers of the professional, "heavy" professional, and organized criminal. He relates organized crime to the political economy of society. Includes excellent appendix essays on the future of organized crime, Elizabethan cant and argot, and methodological and research suggestions.

Jackson, Bruce. *Outside the Law: A Thief's Primer.* New Brunswick, N.J.: Transaction Books, 1975.

>This book, written with the collaboration of a "career" thief, provides insight into the education, work, and lifestyle of this criminal behavior system. It is a first-person narrative, and also includes an extensive sociological analysis of the career criminal in prison as well as in various "scenes."

Plate, Thomas. *Crime Pays.* New York: Ballantine Books, 1977.

>Although somewhat sensational, this book is an excellent example of the type of investigative reporting that is needed to provide the public with a greater sensitivity of the manner in which organized crime is tied into the fabric of society. Plate focuses on the profits involved in "professional" and organized crime.

President's Commission on Law Enforcement and Administration of Justice. *Task Force Report: Organized Crime.* Washington D.C.: U.S. Government Printing Office, 1967.

> This report is dated, yet provides timeless data and perspectives on organized crime. Its footnotes are replete with references to Congressional investigations that imply some foreign menace. The consultants' papers in the appendix provide sociological and economic analysis of organized crime.

Sutherland, Edwin H., ed. *The Professional Thief.* Chicago: University of Chicago Press, 1937.

> A narrative of the perspectives and social organization of the professional thief, as told by Chic Conwell to Professor Sutherland. Part II includes an analysis of the narrative by the editor. This much-emulated book is a classic among such works.

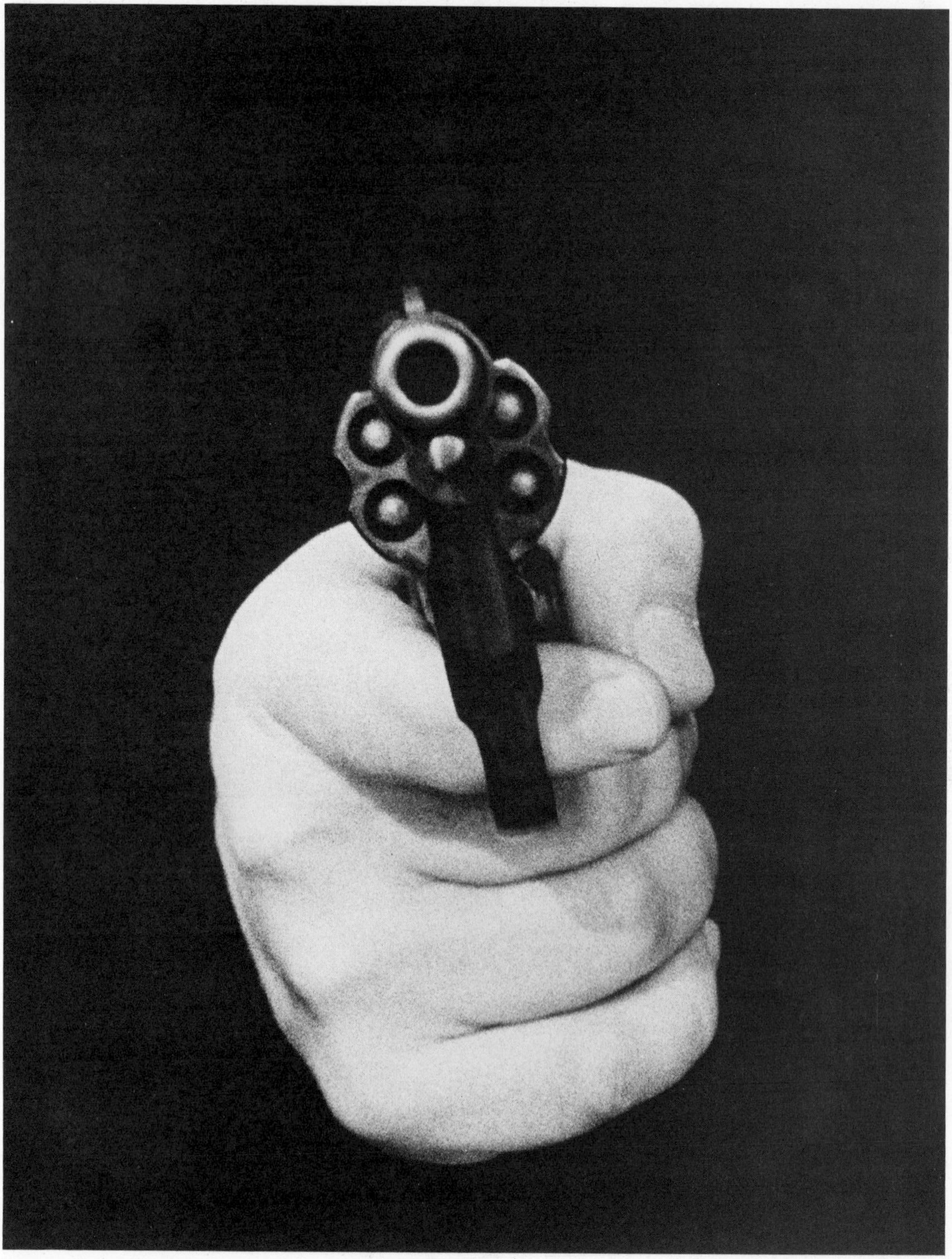

Violence has been pursued in the defense of order by the satisfied, in the name of justice by the oppressed, and in fear of displacement by the threatened.
— National Commission on the Causes and Prevention of Violence, to Establish Justice, to Insure Domestic Tranquility

8

PATTERNS OF VIOLENT CRIME

Public concern over violence in our society is not new. American history is filled with examples of public outrage and reaction against violence. However, the examples of violence in our history that have most often stirred demands for stern measures of control have been riots, mob violence, and vigilantism, not illegitimate criminal violence.

After some especially shocking violent act, such as the assassination of a public figure, one often hears the charge that we are a violent society. But violence in the American past has most often been collective in nature. In the decade following the Revolution, federal troops were called out to put down the Whiskey Rebellion, a protest against taxes. Slavery uprisings in the pre–Civil War South were subdued with considerable violence. Similar treatment was meted out to Civil War antidraft demonstrators in the North. Mob violence and vigilante groups flourished in the South and on the Western Frontier in the latter part of the nineteenth century. Troops were also employed against striking railroad and mine workers in the 1870s and 1880s. During and following World War I, race riots occurred in a number of our major cities, and numerous lives were lost. Urban race riots broke out again in the 1930s and 1940s. And massive race riots swept Watts, Newark, Detroit, and other cities in the 1960s.[1]

American society is not alone in the celebration of a violent history. Machiavelli described the violence of an angry mob that turned on the followers of the dictatorial Duke of Athens in Florence in 1343:

> Those who could not wound them while alive wounded them after they were dead and not satisfied with tearing them to pieces, they hewed their bodies with swords, tore them with their hands and even with their teeth, and that every sense might be satiated with vengeance having first heard their moans, seen their wounds and touched their lacerated bodies, they wished even the stomach to be satisfied — that having glutted the external sense the one within might also have its share.[2]

269

Early concern with violence was not with one-on-one offenses.

Violence and the use of force are prominent in the annals of human history. Consequently, violence is a much-studied problem, although scholars might disagree as to its origins, with men such as Konrad Lorenz contending that it is an innate human trait, while others, including these authors, hold that it is a learned response to social circumstances. The staff report to the National Commission on the Causes and Prevention of Violence defined crimes of violence as "the use or threatened use of force to secure one's own end against the will of another that results or can result in the destruction or harm of person or property or in the deprivation of individual freedom."[3] This definition fits those acts usually thought of as crimes of violence. But it does not provide standards for evaluating many kinds of violence that concern citizens outside the realm of homicides, assaults, and rapes. Citizens are also concerned with collective violence such as riots, conflicts between student demonstrators and police, the assassination of national leaders, violence in the media, and uprisings in our prisons. And it was the growing public concern over the violence of the war in "far off" Southeast Asia that was a crucial factor in our disengagement from Vietnam. More recently, the looting in New York City during the blackout of 1977 was seen as "barbaric" violence. But the violence that most often grips the public imagination seems to be the apparent rising tide of individual violence.

FOCUS ON INTERPERSONAL VIOLENCE

Only a fraction of crime reported in official crime statistics is violent crime. Major crimes of violence—homicide, rape, robbery, and assault—comprised only about 9 percent (1,026,284) of the total of serious or index crimes (11,256,566) reported by the FBI in 1975. Death and personal injury from violent crime amounts to only a fraction of the violence and suffering that occurs in our society. The probability of death by motor vehicle accident is nearly three times that of death due to homicide. Many more people are injured in the home than as the result of a criminal assault.

Yet it is obvious that deliberate violence perpetrated by one human upon another is different and more threatening than injury or even death due to an accident or personal misfortune. Violent crime of the street variety, whether experienced directly or vicariously, seems to touch a deep-seated reservoir of fear. (See Box 1.) Public opinion polls have consistently reported since 1960 that nearly half of the residents of our cities are afraid to walk home at night. Today, those who ride buses in most cities must carry the exact change for bus fare because drivers do not want to run the risk of being robbed.

Certainly there is some justification for this climate of fear. Violent crime is an urban phenomenon that is especially pervasive in our inner cities. Its victims, as well as the offenders, are most often from the lower class and minority groups. Fear is a demoralizing influence in any society. But is there a factual basis for such fear in our society?

Recent official figures from the FBI tell us that violent crimes increased by 39 percent between 1970 and 1975, while the crime rate (number of crimes per 100,000 people) increased by 32 percent. The crime rate increase was 22 percent for murder, 41 percent for rape, and 38 percent for aggravated assault. But it should be mentioned that in the last several years, these same official rates (except for rape) have shown a slight decrease, perhaps as a reflection of changing demographic characteristics of society in general and offenders in particular. Still, the fears of urban residents appear justified when we note that the violent crime rate in cities of at least 250,000 is three and a half times that reported for rural areas, and twice the rate for smaller cities.[4] Yet the idea of a high rate of violent crime in our cities is not unique to our times. Historical records document the fact that violent crime was at its highest level in the first half of the nineteenth century.[5]

In this chapter we will describe variations within interpersonal crime patterns. We will deal not only with homicide, aggravated assault, and forcible rape, which have generally been studied in criminological literature, but also with several other forms of interpersonal violence, including those patterns that involve "battered" children and spouses. These forms of violence share several common characteristics. They are typically viewed by the layperson as bizarre deviations or pathological behaviors as contrasted with conventional conduct, or even conventional criminal activities like stealing and illegal gambling. The behavior of those who are murderers, rapists, assaultists, and

Public Concern Over Violent Crime

BOX 1

Citizen involvement to mobilize a crusade against violent crime.

There is no place to hide, in city, suburb or town. Violent crime is everywhere, and we are all potential victims. With a murder, robbery, assault or rape in the United States every 31 seconds, the shocking thing is that we have almost lost our capacity to be shocked by this. Our TV and movie screens make violence fashionable; public disrespect for law enforcement agencies is growing. What can we do to save society, our children, ourselves? Violent crime is a complex problem, and there are no easy solutions. But because the *Journal* feels this issue is perhaps the most important one in American life today, we ask our readers to join us in a search for answers. Citizen involvement can accomplish two things: it can focus the attention of the government on the problem, and it can furnish the womanpower and manpower needed to people a crusade.

Please read this section—a small first step—and, if you care, fill out the coupon at the end of it; it will be forwarded by the *Journal* to President Carter and/or his designate. America can no longer countenance the kind of spiritual death that violent crime is forcing on us all. Something must be done. You can help.

Source: "How Women Can Fight Back Against Violent Crime," The Editors, *Ladies Home Journal*, March 1977, p. 65.

spouse or child beaters is often explained in lay terms as resulting from some form of personal pathology.

Closer scrutiny, however, will show that interpersonal crime more often than not involves the use of physical force against other individuals—adults or children—in some interactional situation in which both the offender and victim belong to the same social group, such as family, friendship, gang, or some other associational network.[6] Furthermore, though these crime patterns may appear to be impulsive, they can usually be related to a pattern of events or social processes of which the individual is a part. Interpersonal offenders also typically lack a criminal self-concept. It is not unusual for the offender, in the case of homicide, to report his or her act to the police—an action often attributed to the offender's sense of guilt or remorse. Obviously, this is not the case with the well-publicized, atypical cases of interpersonal assaultive behaviors that appear strange, fiendish, and pathological.[7]

The more mundane patterns of interpersonal violent behaviors we will consider are an integral part of violence in American society. These patterns appear to be a complex part of everyday life for many of our citizens and are not as inexplicable as the bizarre violent behaviors portrayed in widely acclaimed reports such as Truman Capote's *In Cold Blood* (1966).[8] Although robbery is officially reported as a violent crime, it will not be dealt with fully here, since it relates to the criminal career of the thief, which will be described in the following chapter. Neither will we describe collective forms of violence such as war, riots, terrorism, and other violent demonstrations, because these generally differ in social organization and quality from forms of interpersonal violence.

To the degree that patterns of interpersonal violence are learned, they are part of the adaptative system that social scientists refer to as *culture*. And to assert that violent behavior between individuals is a cultural pattern in our society is to argue that it is behavior that is learned and transmitted from generation to generation as a part of the individual's or group's social inheritance. Culture, it should be noted, is not behavior; but it provides the tradition and framework for behavior.

Just as societies differ in many forms of behavior, so too do they vary in their patterns of violent behavior. Recent research efforts exploring variations in violent conduct between different parts of our society have led to the use of the concept, "subculture of violence," to describe such variations.[9]

A SUBCULTURE OF VIOLENCE OR A VIOLENT CULTURE?

Groups that are identified with patterns of violent and assaultive behavior are frequently referred to as forming a subculture of violence. This subculture is seen as an adaptive response to the normlessness of conditions of social disorganization. Such a subculture develops when certain groups are excluded from full participation in a society. As a result, the group is forced to develop an alternative behavior system of shared meanings and roles. The subculture that results and its belief system and norms exhibit social processes and patterns similar to those in the dominant culture of which it is a subordinate part. The basic proposition of this perspective is that violence is learned through the definitions individuals receive from their reference groups, for both conforming and nonconforming behaviors are the products of social processes that occur in the individual's social environment.[10]

One of the more widely accepted formulations of the subculture of violence was the attempt by Marvin E. Wolfgang and Franco Ferracuti to explain the frequency of violence and homicide among black lower classes. In the *Subculture of Violence* (1967), they argued that the excessive reliance on aggression by members of the lower social classes reflects the existence of a social subsystem in which violence is expected, or even encouraged, as a means of solving interpersonal problems.[11]

Social Economic Status, Race, and Violent Crime

Violence and a high rate of assaultive crimes are most often associated with the low socioeconomic strata of our society. In fact, with the exception of the white-collar variety, most crime is attributed to the lower economic classes. Studies of rape and robbery in Philadelphia have found that 90 percent of the rapes involved lower SES individuals, as did about 94 percent of the robberies. In a St. Louis study assaultive crimes were also found among predominately lower SES persons.[12]

Crimes of violence seem to be associated with race as well as SES. Official FBI data have shown consistently higher arrest rates of blacks for violent crimes since 1964, when the data were first broken down by race. It has often been observed that police are more likely to arrest blacks than whites. The cohort study by Wolfgang et al. (1972) found a disparity between black and white arrest rates for violent crime. But that study does not eliminate the possibility of some discrimination in police reaction to violence. However, the cohort study of 2,912 nonwhite and 7,043 white youths suggests that in Philadelphia, at least, official statistics were reliable. The FBI data indicate that the ratio of black to white arrests for forcible rape was 12 to 1, robbery 20 to 1, and assault 8 to 1. Wolfgang et al. identified ratios of 13 to 1, 20 to 1, and 10 to 1, respectively.[13] Earlier studies based on arrest rates in the South suggest that racist and discriminatory patterns were operating. For instance, fewer indictments were handed down when whites killed blacks than when blacks killed whites, and Gunnar Myrdal's classic study found that 54 percent of the 497 blacks killed in the South between 1920 and 1932 were slain by police.[14]

In 1967, the Crime Commission found that the rate of assaultive offenses of blacks against blacks was about 3,000 per 100,000. The rate of blacks against whites was only 175 per 100,000.[15] This pattern apparently continued during the 1970s. Until recent years, in fact, homicide was the second leading cause of death for young black men. In 1977, a study of homicides in Cleveland showed that the death rate for young blacks between 1957 and 1974 had increased by 320 percent. During this period the age of most victims dropped from the early forties to the late twenties. According to the National Center for Health Statistics, the increase between 1960 and 1970 in homicide mortality among the population of nonwhite males was 80 percent. By 1974, the startling fact was that homicide was the leading cause of death for nonwhite males between the ages of twenty-five and thirty-four.[16]

But it would be specious to conclude, as some have, either that blacks are biologically prone to violence or that the black subculture is a subculture of violence. Even though rates of violent crime are higher for black youths than for white youths, Clifford Shaw and Henry McKay pointed out some years ago that it cannot be said they are higher than they would be for whites in comparable circumstances.[17] It must be conceded, however, that violent crime in urban settings is largely associated with the economic status and race of both offenders and victims.

Age, Sex, and Violent Crime

Assaultive and violent crimes are offenses committed predominantly by young males in their late teens to early thirties. Violent crime-specific arrest rates for 1975 peak at age seventeen to eighteen and then decline slowly, so that those under twenty-five years include 61.1 percent of all arrests for such offenses. As the report to the Commission on the Causes and Prevention of Violence pointed out, the level of violent crime is disproportionately weighted toward male offenders. In explaining the causes for this high level of young male involvement in violent crime, it has been popular to refer to differences in the socialization of males and females, to the greater physical prowess and toughness of males, or to the masculine protest against maternal domination in female-based households of the lower social economic strata. Studies of youthful crime support these explanations. Adults and middle-aged males are not under the same pressures to prove their maleness. Besides generally being less able physically, they usually have some money, power, and status that help them assert control over their own lives and manipulate others to their ends.[18]

A Subculture of Violence?

The fact that violent crime is apparently related to social factors of low income, racial and ethnic concentration in slum-ghettos, youth, and maleness has led some authorities to argue that a great deal of violence in our urban communities might be explained in terms of subcultural violence. This thesis suggests that the minorities crowded into congested slums share a belief and action system. This "street-corner" male society, it is argued, is characterized by men and boys who victimize their friends, acquaintances, and strangers who share similar beliefs and behaviors.[19]

In his earlier writings, Wolfgang coined the phrase "subcultural violence."

In a more recent article, he points out that this concept refers to the idea that those who live in congested groups in our cities share a belief system that provides them with an orientation and an action system involving the readiness to resort to violence. They live in circumstances where violence may be tolerated, encouraged, or even required. Wolfgang cautions that his thesis does not explain the presence or origin of violence. Even though he suggests that the thesis has definite limitations, it may be a useful paradigm for studying certain kinds of interpersonal violence.[20]

Summarizing the findings of studies of subcultural adaptations to conditions of poverty, Lynn Curtis draws on data from his study *Criminal Violence* (1974). Curtis translates the idea of subcultural violence into an explanation that utilizes the concept of *violent contracultural patterns*. He argues that this violent contraculture has been generated by dominant culture themes and social changes within the larger society, such as demographic movements and racism. Nevertheless, it is the exaggeration of certain expressions of manliness that characterizes the contraculture: an emphasis on macho physical toughness, sexual exploitation, shrewdness, manipulativeness, and thrill seeking.[21] These are values that generally are considered antithetical to the ethos of modern industrialized society. The more affluent upper SES groups, however, frequently become involved in mild forms of risk-taking behavior as leisure time pursuits—everything from mountain climbing, hang gliding, scuba diving, or gambling to participation in the drug or bizarre sex scenes. Apparently they pursue these activities both to escape from the routines of daily life as well as to enhance their social identity. The "swingers" of contemporary society are hardly located only among "street-corner" men. Thus, there are convergences between themes, identified in subcultures of violence and conventional society. David Matza has referred to these as "subterranean convergences."[22] The differences between those who inhabit the so-called subcultures of violence and members of higher SES groups who episodically participate in such behaviors are differences in degree. But they appear to differ in quality, due to differential opportunity for acceptable outlets for their aggression.

The contraculture of violence among young blacks is sustained by the economic marginality of street-corner men. As Curtis suggests, this marginal existence often results in undefined relationships with women. Jealousy over sexual relations can be turned against competing males. The resulting violence between combatants may not only indicate the acceptance of the use of violence, but also a lack of verbal or manipulative options. Often, an individual resorts to force because he has lost a verbal showdown. Street-corner confrontations may also have violent outcomes simply because lethal weapons are sometimes present. Curtis notes that weapons are readily supplied by the white-controlled economy, and that poor blacks can more readily afford them than an automobile—an extension of masculinity accessible to middle-class youth. In other words, violent contracultural patterns emerge, in part, because of institutional racism and economic blockages.[23]

David Greenberg argues that "a compulsive concern with toughness and masculinity" springs neither from a lower-class subculture with an integrity of its own but which is closed off from the dominant culture, nor from "masculine protest" against the maternal domination of the female-headed families of the lower class. Rather, he argues, to the extent that violence occurs among lower-class black males, it is a response to structural constraints imposed by the economic and political order that make it impossible for young blacks to fulfill the expectations for manhood widely held within American society. Men do not need to doubt their identity as males in order to feel anxiety about their ability to work and support their families. Masculine status anxiety may trouble a father who is present but unable to support his family. A youth may grow up in a neighborhood where adult unemployment rates are high for social structural reasons. He might spend much of his time in the company of adult males, who serve as role models and who are experiencing anxiety because they are prevented from fulfilling conventional male roles. This may lead to attempts to ease their anxiety by exaggerating traditional male traits. Within the street-corner context, violence often takes the form of exaggerated attempts to dominate women (including rape) and in patterns of interpersonal violence.[24] This contention is supported by M. Amir's study of rape in Philadelphia, in which all-black rapes made up 77 percent of the 646 cases studied.[25]

Rather than viewing violent subcultures as the cause of violent crimes, we should look to social structural factors that generate such behavior systems. Given the excessively high rates of unemployment among blacks (the Department of Labor reported an unemployment rate of over 40 percent among young blacks in 1979), we might look to status anxiety to explain, at least in part, the high incidence of serious crimes among young, lower-class blacks. Greenberg points out that masculine status anxiety seems to appear and decline most slowly in those segments of the population where male unemployment is especially high. Offenses such as homicide, assault, and rape are offenses that generally are not connected with the drive to acquire material goods. The pattern of arrest rates for such offenses might be evidence of a response to masculine status anxiety.

We should not conclude that since violence is a response to status anxiety, economic forces are irrelevant. For since the ratio of black to white offenses for violent crime was much greater than for serious property crimes in 1975—0.91 compared to 0.43—it might be too easy to conclude that blocked economic opportunity is not a factor. It should be noted that if the subculture-of-violence idea has any merit, it serves to alert us to the social dynamics of violence as a means for the achievement of power for those in positions of powerlessness. Economic factors then, may be crucial, even if the response does not seem as rational as it would if it were reflected in economic crime. That is the point: Violence as mediated by subcultural forces is not rational.[26]

It should also be remembered that while such official data may illustrate trends, they often are highly unreliable. Between 1960 and 1975, arrests for robbery (a violent crime) multiplied 400 percent for males under eighteen. Moreover, such offenses by juveniles are not always reported, and when reported to police they are less likely to be recorded as serious. The victim survey by the National Crime Panel, for example, identified twice as many victims within the twelve to twenty-four-year age group as predicted by official data. And it was twelve to fifteen-year olds who were victimized most often.[27]

In recent years, the growing public concern over violent crime in the streets appears to have been strongly influenced by the growing number of reported muggings. John Conklin's study of robbery indicates that robberies by juveniles tend to be by unarmed assailants. Although 75 percent did not use a weapon, violence or force was used against the victim. Many of the unarmed robberies are apparently muggings committed by several youths.[28] A similar study by Conklin of crimes against the elderly notes that solitary elderly victims usually are robbed by groups of two or more young offenders, who submit them to force that often results in physical injury.[29]

Such offense patterns will be described in the following chapter since they involve a nonspecialized cluster of offense patterns which we will refer to as "commonplace crime." These forms of delinquent conduct might more readily be related to a subculture of stealing, for Conklin found that the juveniles arrested for robbery were more likely to have a record of prior arrests for theft than robbery.[30]

TRADITIONAL PATTERNS OF VIOLENT CRIME

Generally, interpersonal violent criminals are not career criminals. The typical murderer, for instance, is a first offender for this crime, although he or she may have been arrested for other offenses. Evidence from a number of studies shows that a significant number of murderers have never previously been arrested, convicted, or incarcerated. A study by Wolfgang more than two decades ago found that two-thirds of a sample of 588 homicide defendants had prior arrest records, while a more recent study by V. L. Swigert and R. A. Farrell (1977) reported that 60 percent had prior arrest records. However, the largest percentage of these were for status offenses, such as drug violations, public drunkenness, and disorderly behavior.[31] This latter finding is consistent with the report of the National Commission on Causes and Prevention of Violence (1969), which found a positive relationship between the heavy use of alcohol and violent offenses. The ratio of intoxicated to nonintoxicated aggressors was reported to range from 11 to 1 for stabbings to 2 to 1 for murder.[32] Conklin's study of robbers in Boston also noted that a high proportion were chronic drinkers who assaulted their victims while inebriated and then decided to rob them.[33]

Studies of forcible rape generally have found that about 50 percent of offenders had prior records, with no significant difference between black and white offenders. However, only one-fifth had prior arrest records for violent offenses.[34] One study found that while 87 percent of those arrested for forcible rape had prior arrests, less than half had previously been arrested for this offense.[35]

Patterns for spouse and child battering are not clear, since researchers began focusing on these violent crime patterns only recently. The data we have, thus, are more impressionistic than empirical. Wife beating, for example, appears to be related to drunkenness. But this behavior may be a manifestation of general sexist patterns in our society. As women's liberation analysts have suggested, these patterns may provide a rationale for a violent, "machismo subculture" among some males in our society.[36]

In the case of child abusers, there is some evidence suggesting that such individuals, usually parents, have a history of having been treated violently themselves. However, there are other correlates of this form of interpersonal violence that will be noted later in this chapter. The more traditional forms of interpersonal violence are the focus of this section.

Types of Homicide

Homicide is the killing of one person by another. Homicide can be broken down into four legal categories, each of which carries different sanctions.

A victim of violent crime.

1. *Murder is defined by common law as the unlawful killing of another human being with malice aforethought, deliberation, and murderous intent.* The term, "malice aforethought," has several meanings. It is said to be present (express) when the person has made a deliberate intent to cause death or grievous bodily harm; or when she or he willfully acts in such circumstances that there is an obvious, plain, and strong likelihood that death or grievous harm may result; or when she or he is engaged in the commission of a felony; or if she or he obstructs an officer of the law who is either making a lawful arrest or attempting to prevent a riot. In all but ten states there are at least two degrees of murder. *First-degree murder* generally involves the tying together of "premeditation" or prior intent, and "malice aforethought," either express or implied. Since premeditation is difficult to prove, many cases that seem to involve both premeditation and malice aforethought wind up being prosecuted as second-degree murder. This category includes murder where malice aforethought is present but premeditation is not.[37]

Some states, among them California and New York, use the legal category of *felony/murder.* Such laws define felony/murder as a death that occurs in the course of a felony. The California criminal code states that any killing committed in an attempt to perpetrate arson, rape, robbery, burglary, mayhem, or any act punishable as a felony is murder in the first degree.[38] In New York, the felony/murder law also applies to all felonies. In Great Britain, the felony/murder category has been dropped in cases where death is accidental.

2. *Manslaughter is the killing of another person without premeditation, malice, or murderous intent.* It is referred to as *nonnegligent manslaughter* in the category of serious violent crimes in the *Uniform Crime Reports.* Manslaughter is characteristically divided into at least two subcategories: "voluntary" or first-degree manslaughter, and "involuntary" or second-degree manslaughter. First-degree might be charged when death results from a sudden quarrel "in the heat of passion." Second-degree refers to the commission of an unlawful act (not amounting to a felony) or a lawful act that results in death in an unlawful manner. Motor vehicle deaths are often tried under this provision, although in some jurisdictions they may be written up as a third offense subcategory.[39]

3. *Excusable homicide is a killing that results from accident or misfortune and to which no blame is attached.* This category applies to death growing out of lawful acts, done by lawful means, and in which ordinary caution or restraint is employed.[40]

4. *Justifiable homicide is intentional killing sanctioned by law.*[41] An example of this category might be the case of a law enforcement officer killing a suspect in the "line of duty," or the state executioner who electrocutes someone sentenced to capital punishment.

Self-defense murders may be classified either as excusable or justifiable homicide, depending on the circumstances. Justifiable homicide is more widely used when an individual is faced with a reasonable expectation that he or she is clearly in danger of being injured. The person acting in self-defense is required by most states to use no force greater than that required for self-protection. However, the defense of others and the defense of property—under certain conditions—have also been allowed in some jurisdictions. The law does not ordinarily allow provocations such as a verbal or physical threat to serve as extenuating circumstances. It usually holds that if retreat is possible—the "coward's path" to those who live in circumstances of violence—then killing is not justifiable. In some southwestern states, however, frontier mores still persist, and reasonable attempts to retreat before taking to the offense are not required within the law.

The Extent of Homicide

Official data suggest that homicide rates in the United States rose steadily from the turn of the century until the 1930s. They then leveled off, increased at the end of World War II, leveled off again in the early 1960s, then increased until 1974 to 1975. Since then, they appear to be declining again (see Table 8.1), although the number of felony/murders in 1975 was 21 percent higher than it was ten years earlier.

Table 8.1. Murder and Nonnegligent Manslaughter Rate per 100,000, Compared with Rate per 100,000 for all other Violent Crimes.

Year	Homicide	Other Violent Crimes[a]	Year	Homicide	Other Violent Crimes[a]
1960	5.1	155.8	1968	6.9	790.6
1961	4.8	153.4	1969	7.3	321.4
1962	4.6	157.7	1970	7.9	355.6
1963	4.6	163.6	1971	8.6	387.3
1964	4.9	185.6	1972	9.0	392.0
1965	5.1	195.1	1973	9.4	408.1
1966	5.6	214.3	1974	9.8	451.3
1967	6.2	247.0	1975	9.6	471.9

[a] Includes forcible rape, robbery, and assault.
Average Rate of Increase for Homicide: +0.3.
Average Rate of Increase for all other violent offenses: +21.21.
Source: FBI, *Uniform Crime Reports, 1975* (Washington, D.C.: U.S. Government Printing Office, 1975), p. 49.

The persistent rise in other violent offenses reported to the police might in part explain the lower rate of increase for homicide. It may also be that the slower increase in homicide can be attributed to advances in medical science as much as to anything else. Many persons who might formerly have died as victims of violent crimes now are saved through more effective emergency treatment. These become cases of assault with intent to kill, rather than murder or homicide.[42]

Although we might consider our homicide rate high, one study of international crime lists our society among fourteen Western industrialized nations that had a low murder rate but a high larceny rate compared with less developed countries.[43] But the comparative use of national crime statistics is confused by varying definitions. The United States Violence Commission attempted an international comparison in 1968. A recent analysis of these data concluded that the higher rate reported for the United States was due to the fact that U.S. statistics are based on homicide offenses known to police, while Canada and four other nations use only convictions for homicide. When these different definitions were used, the United States had a much higher homicide rate than the other countries. However, when the data were recomputed using homicide convictions as a common denominator, the U.S. rate dropped below that of Canada (see Figure 8.1). The authors of this study reiterated the shortcoming of criminal statistics, citing the hazards of making comparisons between countries. They also stressed the political nature of such data and how they can be exploited by politicians and the media, thereby increasing public alarm about crime.[44]

Another analysis of the commission's data showed that while the United States had an increasing homicide rate between 1955 and 1966, it was half the rate of increase of Norway, about the same as Germany and Denmark, but fully double that of England and Wales.

THE VICTIMS OF HOMICIDE

There were 9.6 murder victims for every 100,000 people in the United States in 1975. The rates were highest in urban areas and were distributed unevenly by geographical region. The murder and nonnegligent homicide rate was highest

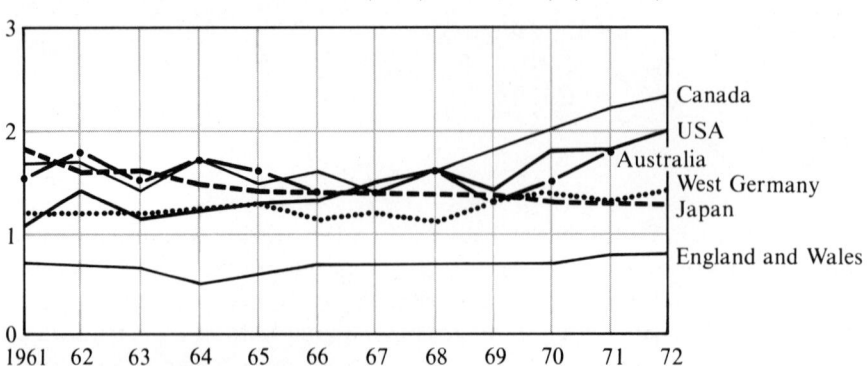

Figure 8.1. Variations in Murder Rates (by Convictions) for Selected Industrialized Countries, 1961–1972 (rate per 100,000 population)

Source: Eduardo Veleri and Graeme Newman, "International Crime Statistics: An Overview from a Comparative Perspective," *Abstracts on Crime and Penology* 2, no. 3 (May/June 1977):260.

Table 8.2. Victim-Offender Relationships in Murder by Percentages, 1970–1975.

Year	Total Number	Spouse Killing Spouse	Parent Killing Child	Other Relative Killings	Romantic Triangle and Lovers' Quarrels	Other Arguments	Known Felony Type	Suspected Felony Type
1970	16,000	12.1	3.1	8.1	7.1	40.8	20.4	8.4
1971	17,780	12.8	3.5	8.4	6.3	41.5	20.4	7.1
1972	18,670	12.5	2.9	8.9	7.1	41.2	22.1	5.3
1973	19,640	12.3	3.2	7.7	7.5	40.3	21.6	7.4
1974	20,710	12.1	2.7	8.0	6.2	43.2	22.2	5.6
1975	20,510	11.5	3.0	7.9	7.3	37.9	23.0	9.4
Average percentages		12.2	3.1	8.2	6.9	40.8	21.6	7.2

Source: FBI, *Uniform Crime Reports, 1975* (Washington, D.C.: U.S. Government Printing Office, 1975), p. 19.

in the southern states—12.7 per 100,000, a decrease of 5 percent compared with 1974. The western states were next with a rate of 9.0, an 8-percent increase over 1974. The north central states had a rate of 8.1, which also represented a decrease of 5 percent. The fewest murders occurred in the northeastern states, where the rate of 7.6 was an increase of 3 percent over 1974.

As we noted earlier, blacks kill blacks and whites kill whites. Furthermore, males tend to kill males, and females tend to kill females. The victims in three out of four of all cases were males, a trend that has persisted over the past several years.

Wolfgang's study of victim-precipitated homicide (1957) found that 37 percent of the homicides grew out of trivial arguments, 13 percent followed domestic quarrels, and 11 percent involved disputes among jealous lovers. This trend seems to be borne out by the victim-offender data for a six-year period from 1970 to 1975 (see Table 8.2). Nearly 25 percent of the murder offenses in 1975 occurred within the family, underscoring the idea that homicide is one aspect of the crime problem that is largely beyond the control of the police. Nearly half of the homicides within the family involved spouse killing spouse. Wolfgang's data for the years 1948 to 1952 also found that 24.7 percent of murders involved members of the same family. Over half of these involved spouse killings. In 54 percent of the cases, the wife was the victim. Wolfgang's study also reported that husbands were the victims in situations they seem to have precipitated. The lethal weapon often was an instrument like a butcher knife available during a domestic quarrel in the kitchen. Wife killings characteristically occurred in the bedroom with a firearm or some other weapon.[45] In 1975, the weapon employed in 66 percent of all killings was a firearm, and about half were handguns (see Figure 8.2).

A 1976 study supports the similarity of the social characteristics of defendants and victims in criminal homicide. An analysis of 444 homicide defendants and 432 victims found that the majority of both were black, lower- and working-class males. The average age was thirty-six for defendants and thirty-eight for victims. This study by Swigert and Farrell found that friends and relatives, rather than strangers, were most often the victims of homicide. Only 20 percent of the homicides involved strangers, and in only four of these cases had there been no prior interaction, such as an argument.[46]

Quarrels between relatives accounted for 34 percent of these deaths, while another 17 percent involved disputes between friends, and 28 percent, disputes between acquaintances. Victims were generally of the same sex and race. Homicides between individuals of the same race occurred in almost nine out of ten cases. Nine percent of the murders were black on white and three percent were white on black. Women were more likely to be involved in the death of relatives than men. Among women, 58 percent were charged with killing a relative, compared with 28 percent of the men. Men were four times as likely as women to be charged with killing a stranger.[47]

An attempt by Swigert and Farrell was made to judge the motives of the defendants by analyzing the situation in which the offense occurred. It was found that 36 percent resulted from quarrels between relatives and lovers that related to finances, alcohol, infidelity, or the desire to end a relationship. This category included cases of child abuse or infanticide 4 percent of the time. An additional 30 percent involved disputes with friends, neighbors, and acquaintances. Felonious homicides that were the result of offenses such as robbery, rape, arson, and drug sales accounted for another 19 percent—as compared

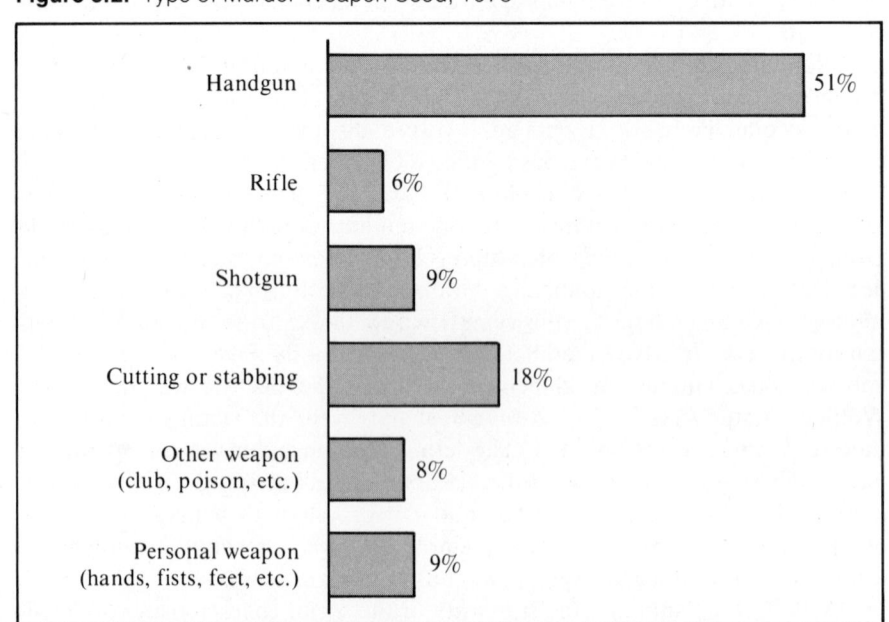

Figure 8.2. Type of Murder Weapon Used, 1975

Weapon	Percent
Handgun	51%
Rifle	6%
Shotgun	9%
Cutting or stabbing	18%
Other weapon (club, poison, etc.)	8%
Personal weapon (hands, fists, feet, etc.)	9%

Source: FBI, *Uniform Crime Reports, 1975* (Washington, D.C.: U.S. Government Printing Office, 1975), p. 17.

Do guns create an affinity for violence?

with 23 to 32 percent in the FBI data. The remainder of the cases were related to arguments with strangers, alleged accidents, or psychotic behavior.[48]

The female incidence of homicides induced by family quarrels was twice that of the males. White homicides were more apt to be in this category or related to felonious offenses, alleged accidents, or psychotic reactions. Blacks were twice as likely to be charged with homicides related to arguments with friends, neighbors, and acquaintances, or the death of strangers.[49]

It was also found that a large proportion of the 444 defendants had previous arrest records. This is consistent with previous research. In addition, nearly half of those convicted of homicide had prior convictions for some other offense. Blacks and males were found to have the greatest incidence of prior arrest for offenses like public drunkenness, disorderly conduct, sexual offenses, gambling, and liquor law violations. One-third of both black and male offenders had previously been charged with violent assaultive offenses.[50]

Studies of those who commit homicides suggest, then, that they are more frequent among the black lower classes. Thus, social scientists, as well as the public, have concluded that the behavior patterns of these groups include violence as an aspect of their lifestyle. Inevitably, this view affects policymakers, judicial officials, and others in their official decisions. And the exclusion of lower-status groups from full participation in society, along with the belief that such groups are predisposed to high levels of violence, reinforces basic cultural differences. Indeed, the societal reaction to and the social control processes aimed at these segments of the population may be important in understanding the patterns that isolate and exclude these groups from equal access to legitimate roles in society.[51]

PATTERNS OF INTERPERSONAL VIOLENCE IN FAMILY SETTINGS

Is the Family a "Violent Subculture"?

In 1892, thirty-two-year-old Lizzie Borden was accused of brutally murdering her father and stepmother. Although the trial ended with a verdict of not guilty, it gave birth to a poem that has become a part of American folklore:

> Elizabeth Borden took an axe
> And gave her father 40 whacks.
> And when the job was neatly done
> She gave her mother 41.

Families are supposed to be the wellspring of love and nurturance for children and parents. But as we noted earlier, 22 percent of criminal homicides occurred within the family in 1975, and over half of these were spouse killings. Even though spouse killings, parent killings, and infanticide constitute a large fraction of our homicides, they are only the "tip of the iceberg." There is much more everyday violence in the American family than is generally conceded. The fact that such violence occurs within *all* social classes raises serious questions about the validity of the concept of a subculture of violence existing only among the poor.[52]

The women's liberation movement has focused attention on the problem of nonlethal physical violence between husband and wife. The phrases "battered wife" and "battered spouse" have become current, and women's centers which include shelters for abused wives have been established across the country. Several state legislatures have enacted laws allowing a battered spouse to bring criminal charges in criminal court rather than in family court.

Research on police activity has shown that police calls involve family conflict as often as they do criminal offenses such as murder, nonfamily assault, robbery, and even rape. Police find these domestic trouble calls both unpredictable and dangerous. About 16 percent of all police fatalities in 1975 were related to the investigation of family quarrels.[53]

Studies of divorce cases have found that 23 percent of middle-class applicants and 40 percent of those who were working class gave "physical abuse" as the major cause for divorce. And this does not tap the incidence of violence among those who do not apply for divorce. Considerable family physical abuse goes unreported, partly out of fear or shame, but also due to the lingering notion that a wife is a man's chattel or possession. Surveys have found that physical abuse against one's spouse is even approved by females under certain conditions. The National Commission on Violence surveyed the amount of violence people might approve. It found that 26 percent of the men and 19 percent of the women would approve of slapping a wife under certain conditions. Several recent studies summarized by Suzanne Steinmetz and Murray Strauss found that 56 percent of the couples in a sample of eighty families had used physical force at some time. Freshman college students reported that 62 percent had used physical force on siblings during the previous year, and 16 percent of their parents had used physical force on each other in the same period.[54]

The legal representative of the Women's Resource and Survival Center in Keyport, New Jersey, reported in August 1977, that a majority of the "battered women" who made contact with the center were white and middle class. Although most researchers on the family concede that conflict in the family is legitimate, many regard physical violence as a sign of psychic abnormality. Research does not support this view. There seems to be evidence that all but a small proportion of those husbands, wives, and children who beat, slap, kick, or otherwise abuse members of their families are "normal" rather than deranged. This does not mean that we should view violence as desirable or acceptable. But it should make us ask why physical violence is so pervasive in what is assumed to be the most intimate of all human groups.[55]

Considerable evidence suggests that violence in the family is learned. Men and women who are husbands and wives, fathers and mothers, fulfill patterns of behavior learned in childhood from their parents and other role models. Among the factors frequently identified in the background of those accused and convicted of both familial and nonfamilial violent offenses is the violent and abusive treatment they received at the hands of parents or foster parents. Furthermore, the family exists within a society in which violence is seen as a legitimate way to solve problems and in which aggression is seen as a normal response to frustration. Consequently, the Supreme Court decisions (October 1975 and April 1977) approving corporal punishment in the schools should not seem surprising. In its 1975 decision, the reasoning was that to forbid corporal punishment "bucks a settled tradition of countenancing such punishments when reasonable." And two years later the High Court ruled that a school child is not entitled to protection under the Eighth Amendment, and suggested that any redress needed was obtainable under existing laws. This decision was heralded by some, including the current president of the National Educational Association, as an effective means of dealing with behavior problems, including delinquency and violence. This "antipermissiveness" mood overlooks the notion that hitting a child might itself contribute to the problem by contributing to the "settled tradition" of violence.

Studies suggest that the willingness to use physical violence may be an attempt to compensate for lack of other resources such as money, knowledge or respect. And the lower the degree of self-direction a man has in his work, the greater his aggressiveness toward his male offspring. Regardless of social class, the lower the job satisfaction, the greater the tendency to punish children harshly. Though intrafamily violence may be more common in lower-class families, some forms of it—for example, hitting children—may be typical of

> BOX 2
>
> ## The Story of a Battered Wife
>
> By NINA McCAIN
>
> The pale green two-story colonial with yellow shutters sits on a dead-end street in one of those comfortable suburban neighborhoods where the houses look a lot alike and there are bicycles and tricycles in every driveway.
>
> The woman who opens the door is blond, blue-eyed and trim in her slacks and sweater. She looks more like the teenage babysitter than the 27-year-old mother of the baby she is holding and a child in the first grade.
>
> What she does not look like is a battered wife.
>
> There are an estimated 28 million battered wives in America. Millions of them live in suburban neighborhoods just like Helen's (not her real name). Most of them, like Helen, think they are all alone.
>
> "We never expected our crisis telephone to ring very often from the homes of the well-educated, prosperous people where we're located," says the director of a program for battered women run by the West Suburban Branch of the YWCA in Natick. "But the phones are ringing."
>
> In the two months since the hot line to the Natick Y has been open, there have been hundreds of calls and the staff of 13 counselors have helped more than 70 women with legal, medical, financial and emotional problems.
>
> The individual stories they tell of fear and frustration are all different from Helen's — and they're all the same.
>
> * * *
>
> "The first time it happened was when I was pregnant with the first baby. He pushed me up the stairs. When the baby was christened, I had a black eye.... When I was pregnant the second time, he kicked me. One time he took me over his knee and spanked me until I was black and blue.
>
> "It didn't happen every Saturday and I never had anything broken. But there was a lot of pushing and shoving and a lot of verbal abuse and fear. It seemed like the big fights always happened on birthdays and holidays, especially his birthdays. I found out from his sister that his mother was always ruining holidays for their family. He just kept repeating the pattern.
>
> "I never hit him back. I was afraid to. Seeing somebody bigger than you standing over you.... It was frightening to see this man go crazy.
>
> "Then, last Easter, he stayed out until five o'clock in the morning. When he came in, I was crying. He took an Easter plant I had and shoved it in the wastebasket. I picked it up and threw it at him and hit him right in the head.
>
> "I felt terrible. I thought, 'What have I done? I've hit the person I care about.' Then I thought, 'Oh brother, I'll get it now.' He slapped me and gave me a black eye. When my daughter woke up looking for her Easter eggs, she saw my face all red and puffy. I felt awful.
>
> "Then on Mother's Day, we were going to visit my parents. He thought I was driving too fast and he started yelling and screaming and pulled me out of the car. I thought, 'That's it. I'm not going to be beaten up on Mother's Day.' That's when I decided to start doing something about it."
>
> * * *
>
> "When I listened to the other women's stories in the support group at the Y, I wanted to say, 'Why don't you leave him?' You could have asked me the same question.
>
> "He was always full of remorse afterwards. He is an extremely sensitive man and he was abused, verbally, by his mother. She was always putting him and his father down. I kept thinking that with enough love and support from me, he could work out his problems.
>
> "Last year, I decided if he wasn't going to do anything about his problems, I wanted out. The biggest mistake is to think you can control someone else. You can't.
>
> "Then, too, I thought it was partly my fault. I thought I was boring. I thought I wasn't fixed up nicely enough when he came home at night. I was always trying to please him, but I never could.
>
> "I thought I had to be a married woman. I thought I couldn't support myself and the children. My mother was the epitome of that — stay with him because you need the money, the social status, the protection of being married.
>
> "My father had a drinking problem. He was a corporate executive and it never affected his

job. But they couldn't go out socially. He'd have one drink and he couldn't stop. I think she knew way down deep she should have left this man who couldn't face his own problems, but she didn't. We never talked about any of this. My parents thought psychiatrists were for crazy people. Maybe that's why I let my own problems go on so long."

* * *

"It's important not to ask 'Why don't you leave him?'" says one of the counselors. "The woman's self-esteem is already so low, that just hurts it further."

"Often she's staying because of economic pressure," adds another. "If she has children, she thinks twice before leaving. She fears she can't provide for them as well as the husband can."

"Some stay because the beatings only happen on weekends. During the week things are OK. There's a real hope that he's going to change, that this is the last time. They often refer to their husbands as Dr. Jekyll and Mr. Hyde. They stay for the good times."

* * *

"My family wasn't rich, but I'd say we were upper-middle class. We belonged to the country club and my brother and I went to private Catholic schools.

"I dated a lot as a teenager — the captain of the football team and boys from the country club. I wanted to be a teacher. But when I met Paul, I threw it all out. I was 20, I was a junior in college and I thought I had seen it all. I thought I was ready to get married.

"I had gone first to a junior college outside of Boston and I loved it. Then, at the beginning of my junior year, I transferred to a university in the city. I got an apartment with two other girls. I liked the freedom of apartment living, but I got kind of lonely.

"Then I met Paul. He lived in our building and my roommate kept saying how cute he was. When we started going together, we'd drive up to New Hampshire and take long walks and sit by the fire, mellow things. He seemed quiet and mature to me.

"We got involved very quickly and all of a sudden I was pregnant. I had always been a good Catholic girl, didn't take the pill or anything like that. I told him and he said, 'We'll get married.' I thought I loved him. I never thought I was making the wrong decision.

"I didn't pick up on his drinking or the fact that he never had any money.

"My roommates noticed he always came to our apartment for food because he was out of money before the end of the week.

"The first time I saw his temper was when he came to pick me up at a job I had downtown. He couldn't find me and they told him to leave the store with his dog. He started screaming and yelling at me. It was insane.

"After we got married, we lived in a little town and I hated it. When the baby came, I was home all day alone with her. He always took the car and he'd get furious if I asked where he was going. I remember crying most of the time. But we did have some good times. We'd go to the beach and we'd garden.

"Then he got laid off. He had seven jobs in the seven years we were married. It wasn't always his fault. Sometimes the companies went out of business or went bankrupt.

"I finally got a job with a real estate agency. I still have it, but I work part time now. The pay is not all that great, but they're super people. When I got the job, he complained, 'You make more than I do. You think you're a hot deal.'

"Still, I was really in love with him. He was into going out with the guys and drinking all the time. His mother was part of the problem, too. She'd come to visit us and tell him I was no good, a bitch, low-class, an alcoholic's daughter. He'd just sit there and let her talk like that.

"I never told anyone about the beatings, except his sister. I never even told my girlfriends. I wanted everyone to think we had a good marriage. I tried to tell my parents once, but they got so upset I dropped it. They were never able to face their problems. Why should they be able to face mine?

"The neighbors never knew, either. I used to pull the shades down so no one would know. Once he cornered me in the kitchen and tried to take our savings account book. I wouldn't let him have it because I knew he'd take out every penny. He started hitting me and I ran out of the house and went to the neighbor's. It was the first time anyone knew. My neighbor was really surprised. She said, 'You and Paul look like the perfect couple.'"

* * *

"If you live in the suburbs, you feel you're the

only one, that it doesn't happen to the neighbors," a counselor says. "You feel you're a real oddity.

"The woman is embarrassed, guilty. She feels maybe she caused this. Often her family is no help. They say, 'There's never been a divorce in our family.' "

* * *

"Once, when we lived in an apartment, the neighbors heard all the noise and called the police. I denied that he was beating me. I felt like I was in with it, too, like we were doing something against the rules and I was part of it.

"I called the police once when we were living in this house. He had thrown a wrench at me and I was really scared. The policeman said he couldn't do anything unless my husband was hitting me in his presence. Then he took Paul outside and talked to him. Paul told me later that he (the policeman) said that he had gone through a divorce and that we women were all the same. He told me I could get a restraining order or something. He didn't seem that sympathetic."

* * *

"The police hate domestic violence calls," a counselor says. "There are more police fatalities on those calls than on any other kind. The police are often sympathetic, but their hands are tied. It's a civil matter. They can't arrest the husband unless they see him hit her.

"The women are often afraid to press charges. The guy may give her a bunch of roses and promise never to do it again, or he may threaten her life. The police and the courts get upset at the amount of time they've wasted if a woman drops charges."

* * *

"I knew I had to do something when I saw that the fighting was beginning to affect my daughter. He never hit the kids, but that temper of his came out at them, too. My daughter was terrified of him. Once, I remember, he was screaming at her for not brushing her teeth properly. I thought there is no way I'm going to have this man in the house upsetting everyone. I'd rather live by myself. My mother couldn't make that decision. But things have changed. We know now that we don't have to take that.

"I went into therapy last May. We had gone together a couple of times to a counselor. But we didn't understand what therapy was all about. We thought you went a couple of times and everything was all right. He went for a few sessions and then quit, but I went back by myself. It's really helped me understand why I put up with everything for so long. I had never realized I was so angry. I had to get that out before I could do anything with myself or my life. Now that it's all out, I've seen a lot of things I had never seen before. It's like lifting a curtain.

"Paul finally moved out in August. But we made a mistake. We kept on seeing each other. He'd say he wanted to see the children, and I'd let him come over. Then he'd want to talk. I finally said, 'Paul, I can't help you. I'm too emotionally involved. You've got to get professional help.' I told him we should stop seeing each other.

"He took off and I didn't hear from him for awhile.

"He called a few days ago and came over and we had a good talk. We're going to get a legal separation.

"He may get a new job in another state and he wanted us to go with him. But I said no. I've come so far, I can't go back now. He doesn't understand that I've come a long way and he's just starting.

"I still have my part-time job and I'm going back to school. I've got a cooperative baby-sitting group going now and it's saving me lots of money. My husband isn't working now, so he can't support us. I finally had to apply for welfare. I get the ADC and the food stamps. I hate using those stamps. I'm embarrassed about it. But my kids need the food. I've learned to budget and to cut corners. I can't afford this house and I'm looking for a cheaper one to rent.

"About two months ago, I read about the Natick Y program. I called and they said to come on in. I went to one of the support groups and I went through the counseling training. I'm going to start helping with the hot line soon. I think I can help other women who are going through this. I keep telling myself that something good has to come out of all this."

Source: *The Boston Globe*, Feb., 26, 1978. Reprinted courtesy of the Boston Globe.

all social classes. Other kinds of intrafamily violence—for example, severe wife beating—may not be typical of any classes.[56]

Child Abuse: Violent Crime or Individual Pathology?

Corporal punishment of children has been legitimated through the centuries by the belief that it was a requisite for disciplinary, educational, or religious obedience. Parents or guardians had limitless power over their children in both the Roman legal code and English common law. Children had a chattellike status with few legal rights. While conventionally it has been considered bad parenting to spare either the "rod or the child," killing a child, whether intentionally or by negligence, is defined as murder or manslaughter in our criminal laws. However, during the greater part of our history—even though children supposedly are highly valued in our culture—the laws have been much less clear and certain regarding the protection of children from serious, nonmortal assault from parents.[57]

The deliberate, violent abuse of children by parents or other child caretakers no doubt is seen by many as unnatural, pathological, and socially inappropriate. Several studies have found that large numbers of people in our society do not even realize that child abuse exists. Apparently, child battering—at least in its less dramatic and nonlethal forms—is supported by implicit cultural patterns in our society.[58] Most people apparently assume that children in contemporary society are protected from exploitation and receive love, nurture, and protection from their families. For example, college students serving as "peer models" for juveniles adjudicated as delinquents often express amazement that a juvenile to whom they are assigned has been disowned for some years by his or her parents. Our presumption of progress and our relative affluence seem to have obscured the ironic fact that many children are the victims of physical, as well as psychological damage, as the result of the violence done to them by parents and other child caretakers.[59]

The number of reported victims of child abuse has increased dramatically in the last decade due to increased efforts at intervention and control. But whether this represents an actual rise in child battering is difficult to say. Accurate statistics are unavailable for either effective intervention or research purposes, because most cases are not reported; because those that are reported generally are not handled by the legal system; and because definitions of child abuse and neglect are often not clear in the law. This confusion carries over in efforts to prosecute. The alleged child abuser may be charged under several laws, or the case may be dismissed if it cannot be proved to be an intentional act, or if the accused agrees to seek counseling. The parents' rights apparently predominate over children's rights.[60]

One early effort by Henry C. Kempe (1962) to study what he termed the "battered child syndrome" involved a survey of hospitals and district attorneys. In the responses from these two groups (consisting of 71 hospitals and 77 DAs) Kempe identified 78 deaths and 114 cases of permanent brain damage.[61] A more ambitious series of studies by David Gil estimated that there were about 6,617 cases of serious child abuse in 1968.[62] A study by public health professionals in New York City between 1966 and 1970 estimated about 2,700 cases for that city. When a "hotline" was set up in Florida from 1967 to 1968, the number of cases reported increased from 39 for that two-year period to 17,662 cases that required intervention from November 1971 through September 1973.[63] The American Medical Association has suggested that battering might be a more frequent cause of death among children than diseases such as leukemia and muscular dystrophy and may rank with motor vehicle accidents as a major cause of damage to the central nervous system.[64]

Violent Patterns of Child Abusers. Generally, child abusers are not considered criminals, and abusing parents do not have criminal self-concepts. In fact, these parents may regard their violence as justified and resent official intervention as unwarranted. Abusing parents are rarely prosecuted; more often, they undergo psychiatric treatment.[65]

Studies of child abuse have focused upon the behavioral patterns of abusing parents and the characteristics of the abused children. Typically, abusing parents are provoked when the child does not perform such tasks as toilet training or eating correctly at an early age. Even when the parents' expectations are beyond the physical or mental capabilities of the child, they administer punishment and abuse the child. This has been called "disciplinary abuse."[66] In the case of teenagers, parents are provoked when the child is defiant, willful, or associating with unacceptable peers; an adolescent girl may provoke abuse if her parents believe her to be promiscuous.[67]

It is often assumed that the reliance on physical force to control children occurs primarily among poor families. However, recent reports indicate that these same patterns also exist in middle-class segments of society. Data presented by Steinmetz suggest that patterns of child discipline are related more to the specific occupation of the parent than simply to a distinction between manual, skilled, or professional occupations. For example, parents who are salespersons, managers, dentists, or truck drivers appear to rely more on physical punishment than those in such supportive occupations as education, social work, and related professions. She suggests that this pattern is related to the status deprivation of those in such occupations. Thwarted by their relative powerlessness or blocked-in occupational mobility, they take out their status anxiety on those who are even more powerless than they are.[68]

Lack of stability in the family—both in terms of mobility and interpersonal relations—also appears to be related to patterns of child abuse. Families in which children are battered generally have been shown to move or relocate more often than other families of the same socioeconomic status. As a consequence, they also are less apt to have community ties. Further, it appears that abusive patterns tend to appear in families in which there is a stepparent or foster parents.[69]

The frequency of child-abuse cases among the poor may be influenced by such factors as the greater sensitivity of the staff in public hospitals about iden-

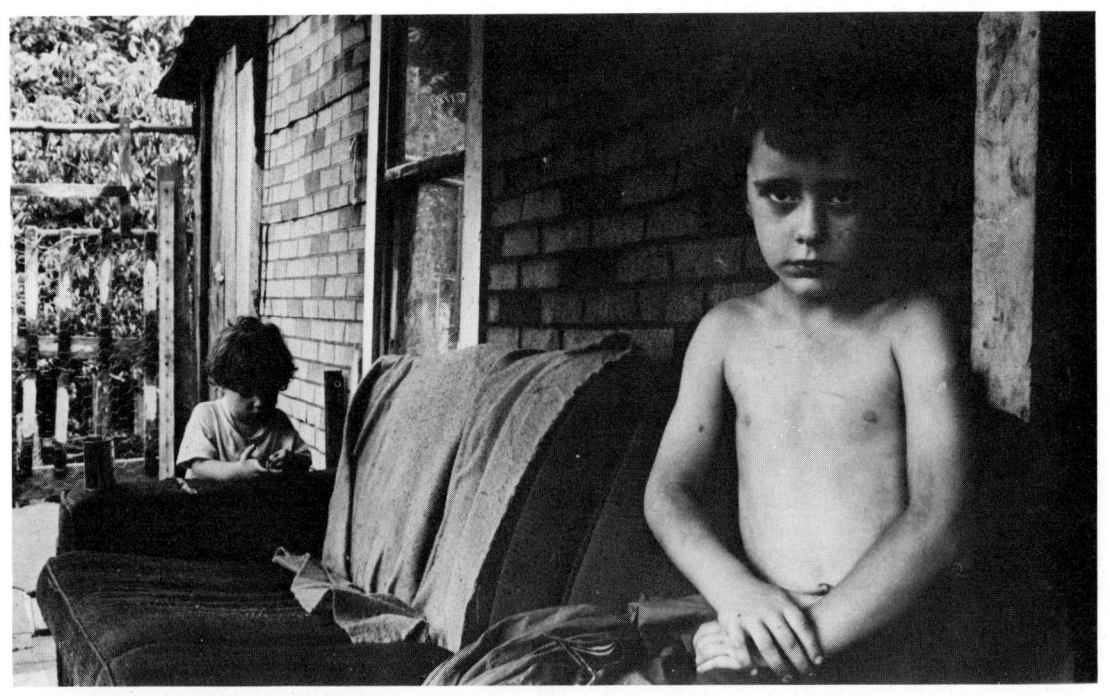

Is the family a violent subculture?

tifying the battered child. The children of affluent parents usually are treated by private doctors who tend to be both less sensitive to symptoms of battering and more sensitive to the fact that the child's parents are their clients.

The pattern of interpersonal violence typical in child-abuse cases is not something that can readily be described in terms of its etiology. An important theme, however, is the manner in which parents are socialized, for it seems quite conclusive that violence is learned behavior. One study found that abusive mothers have a history of deprivation. Another study described the case of a nine-year-old boy who battered his infant siblings; it was found that he modeled his behavior on that of his violent stepfather. Studies of male juvenile delinquents consistently have identified large numbers who had been treated violently at home by parents or older siblings.[70] There is some evidence that both child and spouse abusers share common childhood experiences. Many grew up in situations in which violence and force were used to control their behavior.

Social Reaction to Child Abuse. The social movement that first made officials responsible for the behavior and care of children was the "House of Refuge" reform of the Jacksonian era. This movement focused attention on the need to prevent the abuse of children by their caretakers. The House of Refuge reforms in New York in 1825 resulted in the first laws to intervene in the lives of neglected children. Even though these laws established the state's right to intervene under the principle of *parens patriae*, the underlying rationale was to protect society from delinquency, not to protect the child.[71]

Public interest was again drawn to child abuse in 1875, when the Society for the Prevention of Cruelty to Animals intervened in the case of Mary Ellen, who had been viciously abused by her foster parents. The sensational treatment of the young girl's case by the newspapers probably influenced the formation of the New York Society for the Prevention of Cruelty to Children. In the 1930s, a "Childrens Charter" was issued promising every child a home with love, security, and protection from abuse and neglect. But it was not until 1962 that New York passed a law against the caretaker's abuse of children. Similar statutes were passed in other states over the next four years.

Throughout this period of some ninety years, despite accumulating evidence of widespread physical violence in the family, the abuse was attributed to psychosis or emotional disturbance of parents. Child abuse was not seen as a major social problem—at least not one requiring interference with the power of the parent over the child.[72] In fact, a national survey conducted between 1965 and 1967, when some states were still passing child-abuse laws, indicated considerable tolerance for child abuse. Three percent of the national sample reported personal knowledge of one or more incidents during a one-year period, or about 13.3 to 21.4 incidents per 1,000 persons in a given year. Another 58.3 percent of the respondents agreed that "almost anybody at some time could injure a child." The high degree of empathy with suspected child abusers was shown by the 53.3 percent who felt that the child should be removed from such a home only as a last resort. Only 27.1 percent of the respondents agreed that child abusers "should be jailed or punished in some other way." And 66.4 percent thought that caretakers who abused children "must be closely supervised and treated rather than punished."[73]

The media increasingly began to focus on child abuse in the mid-1960s. These accounts tended to treat child abuse as a "syndrome" rather than as a variant of violent crime. The result was a shift in state laws regarding the reporting of child abuse. Rather than being reported to law enforcement agencies, these offenses now tend to be reported to child protection agencies. Dealing with child abusers within the "medical model" means that the "sick" label is applied and the extent of the problem has become obscured. Though the 1970s witnessed a renewed concern with this social issue, the rate of reported child-neglect offenses has remained about 210 per 100,000 from 1960 to 1974. Even when prosecution does occur, convictions are obtained in only 5 to 10 percent of the cases, and sentences are shorter for child abusers than for offenders convicted under aggravated assault.[74]

This reluctance to confront child abuse as a law violation, and to view the problem as the result of ill-prepared or "sick" parents, means that many children live in situations in which they are objects of violent abuse by adults who express their hostile feelings against the less powerful.[75] The perception of child abuse as a social problem may have increased in recent decades, but our ability to cope with the problem has not advanced significantly.

FORCIBLE RAPE AS A VIOLENT CRIME PATTERN

The offense of forcible rape, along with the types of offenders and criminal careers of individuals who commit this act of violence, is another crime pattern that has been dealt with rather ineptly by both researchers and the criminal justice system. For it was not until recent years that the relationship between rape and a number of other social issues was even acknowledged. In recent years, rape has been viewed within the context of the subordinate position of women in a male-dominated society, an example of what Hans Toch referred to as males expressing their uncontrollable violence against a "safe" victim.[76] Rape is increasingly coming to be seen as a political act as well as a legally defined offense. But this was not always the case. Sir James Fitzjames Stephen, the nineteenth-century jurist, dismissed rape with these words: "I pass over many sections punishing particular acts of violence..., in particular the... offenses relating to... rape and other such crimes. Their history possesses no special interest and does not illustrate either our political or social history." [77]

In 1971, Kate Millet described the traditional view of rape "as an offense one male commits upon another—a matter of abusing 'his woman.' " [78] And the political component of inter-racial forcible rape was stated by Eldridge Cleaver in his *Soul on Ice:* "Rape was an insurrectionary act.... I was defying and tramping upon the white man's law, upon his system of values,... I was defiling his women—and this point... was the most satisfying to me because I was very resentful over the historical fact of how the white man had used the black woman. I felt I was getting revenge." [79] Rape is put in the context of violent crime by Susan Brownmiller, who states that:

> When rape is placed where it belongs, within the context of modern criminal violence and not within the purview of ancient masculine codes, the crime retains its unique dimensions, falling midway between robbery and assault. It is, in one act, both a blow to the body and... to the mind.... Yet the differences between rape, and an assault or robbery are distinctive.... In rape the... intent is not merely to "take," but to humiliate and degrade.[80]

The Extent of Rape

More than any other violent crime, forcible rape has been influenced by social and political changes that affect our beliefs and social structure as well as the societal reaction by criminal justice agencies. The woman's movement has focused attention on this crime through "speak-outs" and conferences on rape. Public concern was increased both by these events and by the sudden increase in reported rapes in the late 1960s and early 1970s. Though the forcible rape rate has consistently remained at only about 1 percent of the total of all index crimes and 6 percent of the total rate for serious crimes, its rapid increase in rate since the mid-1960s has attracted much concern.

The victimization studies in 1967 showed an actual rate four times as great as reported in the FBI data. The "Eight Cities" studies in 1972 and 1974 showed rates that were eight and ten times as great as the official rates.[81] In a comparative study of rape in Boston and Los Angeles, Chappell et al. used a sample of police records from 1967, when Boston reported one of the lowest rates, while Los Angeles had the highest rate in the country. They found comparisons difficult because of differences in the definition of the offense.[82] The FBI defines forcible rape as "the carnal knowledge of a female, forcibly and against her will" in the categories of rape by force, assault to rape, and attempted rape. Statutory offenses (where no force is used—victim under the age of consent) are excluded. This definition is more general than the laws of many states including California, which states that "any sexual penetration however slight is sufficient" (Section 263).[83]

In Los Angeles, the researchers found that a more comprehensive definition was applied than in Boston. For instance, a police officer happened to see a man sidle up to two girls on a busy street and pinch one of them "on the bottom." The officer arrested him. The miscreant admitted to what he had done, and said he got his kicks from frightening the girls. This case was classified by the Los Angeles Police Department as attempted forcible rape. In Boston, the FBI guidelines were strictly adhered to, and consequently the city had a lower incidence of rape. With such disparity in definitions, it is hard to determine accurately the actual extent of forcible rape.[84] What is certain is that despite the fact that the women's movement has made some women less reticent to report the crime, unreported rapes still far outnumber the official figures.

Patterns of Forcible Rape

Data suggest that no more than half of the rapes that are reported involve strangers. Victims are more likely to report offenses involving a stranger than a rape resulting from a sexual encounter with a known person. But there are emotional constraints against reporting either type. The degrading manner in which victims have often been treated by the police has deterred reporting of the crime in the past. A victim asked recently: "Why should a woman report a rape to a cop when their typical responses are known to be: Unless a woman is a virgin, what's the big deal? Why didn't you just lie back and enjoy it? Tell me the truth: Don't all women secretly want to get raped?"[85] To deal with such insensitivity, a number of police departments have conducted special training courses for officers. Other cities have established special "rape squads," staffed and headed by female officers, to help cope with these kinds of problems.

Not much is known about the male offender who as a stranger initiates a forcible sexual contact with his victim. One study suggests four subclasses of males involved in such offenses. The most common category (about one-third of the cases studied) included men with a history of violent conduct whose sexual contacts with women tended to include threats or violence. They seem to be more committed to violence than to sex. The second largest group consisted of juvenile delinquents whose offenses were against female adolescents. Their general lifestyles involved aggressive self-seeking, and they applied the same

> BOX 3
>
> ## Rape: Verdict Was Guilty on All Counts
>
> By MIKE BARNICLE
>
> The charge was rape, and Bill Codinha, the prosecutor, was on his feet in front of the jury, choosing his words with some care, hoping that they would paint a picture of guilt. In back of Codinha, sitting in a straight chair directly ahead of Judge Alan Dimond on the 11th floor of the Middlesex County Courthouse, David Tucceri, the 26-year-old defendant in the case, wore absolutely no expression on his face as the state asked that he be sent to jail for life.
>
> "I submit that there is overwhelming evidence of the guilt of that man," Codinha said, turning, his arm stretched out and his finger pointing right at the defendant, David W. Tucceri.
>
> "I submit to you that David W. Tucceri is guilty of oral rape, of manual rape, of kidnaping, of assault and battery, of maiming a woman."
>
> As always, the case began months ago—June 12—and it started with good, old-fashioned police work.... Close to 10 o'clock on the night of June 12, Frank Burns and Teddy Carlin, two Cambridge cops, were walking their beat in Harvard Square. A call reporting a woman screaming in Longfellow Park, just off Mount Auburn street, came over the radio....
>
> The two men hailed a Harvard police cruiser and not more than two minutes later, joined by Harvard University policeman Jack Stanton, the three cops were edging slowly into the park from the Brattle street side.... Carlin spotted Tucceri coming out of the underbrush and wrestled him to the ground. Burns held a gun on the man while Carlin searched him.
>
> The work was slow and methodical and all by the book, with the police being careful not to disturb any of the rules of law that might end up getting a good case tossed out of court. While Tucceri was lying on his stomach, Burns and Carlin over him, the woman had been picked up by a Cambridge police car over on Memorial Drive.
>
> When she was attacked, the woman had been walking down Mount Auburn street from the hospital, coming from an Alcoholics Anonymous meeting. Her attacker dragged her off the street and into the bushes, beat her, forced her into sex, tried to gouge her eye out with his fingers and choke her with the dirt off the ground.
>
> After nearly a half hour, she ran out toward Memorial Drive away from the rapist. The attacker ran across Mount Auburn and into the upper half of the park, running past an eyewitness as he made his escape.
>
> "I would rather have run into a car than have him get me again," the victim said on the witness stand. "I begged him not to rape me. I told him that I had been raped once before. I begged him not to. Not again."
>
> Before they took her to the hospital that night, Frank Burns asked that she be brought around to where Tucceri was in custody. Sitting in the back seat of the police car, she nodded, "That's the guy."
>
> Tucceri posted $50,000 bail and walked free. After going through one attorney, his new lawyer, Ralph Champa, took a look at the evidence, at the case, and at his client and suggested he cop a plea. Tucceri decided to take his chances in a trial....
>
> "From the back seat of the car, you were able to recognize the defendant?" Champa asked the girl on the stand.
>
> "The eyes," the girl said, in a flat tone betraying no emotion. "He had the coldest eyes I've ever seen. I'll never forget his eyes."
>
> After the first three days of the trial, Tucceri bolted. He didn't show up in court a week ago Friday, and the feeling was that, after hearing the evidence, anyone with any brains would either run or jump out the window.
>
> "When he called me over the weekend," Champa said, "I told him that if he didn't come back, his chances were a million to one of winning. And if he came back, I told him, they were 999,000 to 1. What do you expect? I'm not going to lie to him."
>
> He returned Monday morning, in handcuffs. He sat there, with the eyes of an ice man, staring straight ahead and showing nothing, as Frank Burns and Teddy Carlin and Jack Stanton and Det. Tim McCusker threaded the pieces of evidence together for the jury of seven women and five men.
>
> "I can't stand him. He's just awful," the victim had told Frank Burns as she talked about being

cross-examined by Ralph Champa.

"Ralph is just doing his job," Burns said. "He's a good lawyer just doing his job."

Champa was giving his client his money's worth. The lawyer was dealing with what he had: No evidence of innocence and a defendant who gave even Ralph Champa the chills.

Champa was also dealing with time and politics. In 1974, as a result of the pressures of the women's movement and the dictates of common sense, the charges Tucceri faced had their penalties changed—four years ago they could have meant 15 to 20. Today they can mean life.

"There are a few cases during the year where you really put a little extra into it," Bill Codinha was saying outside the courtroom. "This is one of them. I'd hate to see this guy walk."

"There was no question in the girl's mind on the night of June 12 when she identified David W. Tucceri," Codinha told the jury in his summation. "And there was no question in her mind when she took the stand last week that it was David W. Tucceri."

On Wednesday, just after noon, the jury began to deliberate. They were told to think about the evidence.

What they could not weigh was the inner damage that came with the crime: The rape of the spirit, the assault on a girl's mind and her emotions, the manhandling of someone's sexual integrity, treating a life like it was an ashcan to be tipped over and dumped around in public at random.

At 2:45 that afternoon, after an hour for lunch, Phil Ewell, the clerk of the court, came out into the hallway where Burns and Carlin were talking with Ralph Champa and said, "verdict."

"This is not a good sign," Champa told Tucceri's mother and his wife. "When they're out a short time like this, it is not good."

Guilty on all counts. That was the verdict.

On Thursday, at 10 o'clock in the morning, three court officers brought David Tucceri back to the courtroom for sentencing. . . .

Bill Codinha asked Judge Dimond to give Tucceri 45 to 60 years on the two counts of rape and life on the kidnaping. Champa asked for 20 to 25 and psychiatric care at Bridgewater.

You look at two things in a defendant during the seconds before sentencing: The hands—whether they tremble, whether they reach out for the rail to brace the legs that might be buckling. And the adam's apple—to measure the gulp for breath that comes with the announcement of prison time.

Tucceri showed nothing. No emotion. No tears. No eyes darting around the courtroom, looking for family or friends. Nothing. Not revenge. And not remorse.

"This is a crime of great magnitude," Judge Dimond began. "I am satisfied that Mr. Tucceri is a dangerous person. The counts of the indictment are part of a simple outrage.

"On each count of rape it is the sentence of this court that David Tucceri serve concurrent terms at MCI Walpole of not less that 35 or more than 45 years.

"On the kidnap charge, it is the sentence of this court that David Tucceri serve a term of not less than nine or more than 10 years at MCI Walpole.

"I will place the assault and battery charge on file," Judge Dimond said quietly. "And on the mayhem charge, it is the sentence of this court that David Tucceri serve a term of not less than 18 and not more than 20 years at MCI Walpole. To be served from and after.

"On the unarmed robbery, we'll make it 18 to 20 years at MCI Walpole to be served concurrently."

The court officers led Tucceri from the room. His mother, heaving with grief, had left during Codinha's request for life.

With the case over, Frank Burns walked out of the courtroom feeling good about the job he'd done. Ralph Champa had eyes that read "no appeal." And Bill Codinha remained seated in his chair, preparing himself for a murder one trial just getting under way.

"He's going to be a very old man before he even begins to think about getting out of jail," Ralph Champa said as he headed for an elevator.

"Ralph," said Bill Codinha, with no malice in his voice. "This makes my October."

Source: *The Boston Globe,* Oct. 24, 1978. Reprinted courtesy of the Boston Globe.

approach to sex as to other situations. The third group included those whose judgment apparently was blunted by drunkenness or who lacked the ability to cope with a sexual situation. The last group were those whose behavior was unpredictable, but was termed explosive. Such persons were captivated by their own internal state and seemed unable to interpret whether assent from the female was present. The significance of these categories, developed by P. H. Gebhard et al. (1965), is that the sexual aspects of rape were considered within the context of other behavior. Sexual behavior was seen as shaped by factors such as general aggressiveness, hedonistic lifestyles, confusion due to alcohol, and repressed sexuality. In sum, the profile of the "typical rapist" is not very clear. But more often than not he has a criminal offense record and a known predisposition toward violence. Other factors—aggression, drinking, and sexual ignorance—are present in many sexual encounters. But only some end in violence or rape.[86]

Perhaps an earlier study by Richard Jenkins comes closer to the point we wish to make. Jenkins contends that offenders in cases of this type of interpersonal violence are not very different from law-abiding men. The difference resides not in the sexual content or impulse, but in the differential lack of "inhibition and consideration for the personality" of another person.[87] To extend this perspective, we might suggest the source of the problem may lie in differential gender socialization in a sexist society. For in expressing a caricature of the macho male character, the rapist uses those of inferior status as objects for the venting of an impulse for which he has not learned appropriate forms of control. Rapists, spouse batters, and child offenders are different types of violent criminals. But they appear to share in common differential socialization regarding the appropriate means for dealing with human interaction.

Thanks to the women's movement, the crime of rape has lost some of its mystery and can be seen more clearly in its subtle human or social context. However, if our ability to cope with forcible rape as a violent crime is to catch up with our awareness, it would appear that more consideration be given to the proposal by some in the women's movement that rape be reclassified as a form of aggravated assault, rather than a sexual offense. Redefining this offense would help modify traditional attitudes toward it and aid society to better respond to the problem of assaultive sexual attacks upon women and men.

THE IDENTIFICATION, CONTROL, AND PREDICTION OF VIOLENCE

Though violent crime constitutes barely 10 percent of all serious index crimes, the variety and volume of such offenses in American society is considerable, as is their physical and psychological impact upon society. Public concern over violence has led naturally to an interest in controlling those persons who in the future might become violent. What problems are there in identifying, predicting, and controlling violent behavior? Consider the following cases:

Item: July 1966. Eight student nurses were slain in a town house in Chicago. Richard Speck was charged and convicted. Initially it appeared that he had no criminal record. However, it was later discovered that he had a prior arrest record for a number of public order offenses.

Item: August 1966. Charles Whitman, a student at the University of Texas, ascended the tower on the university campus and began methodically to shoot forty-one people, killing thirteen, before being shot himself by the police. The night before he had killed his mother and his wife. The previous March, Whitman had had an interview with a university psychiatrist who recalled that he said that he was going to go up the tower and start shooting people. An autopsy showed that Whitman had a small tumor in the hypothalamus region of his brain, but it was thought to be unrelated to his behavior.

Item: March 16, 1968. Reports began to circulate in the media in 1969 that Company C of the American Division in Vietnam had entered the village of Song My (My Lai) and systematically shot at least 347 old men, women, and children. At least three of the soldiers had been formally charged with rape by the Army, but the charges had been dropped. Subsequently, Lt. William Calley, a platoon leader, was court-martialed and convicted for killing over 100 civilians in this violent event.

Item: 1972. Juan Corona, a farm labor contractor, was convicted of killing twenty-five itinerant farm workers whose bodies had been uncovered on his property near Yuba, California, the previous year. This was described as the largest mass murder in American history.

Item: August, 1973. Elmer Henley, a seventeen-year old, told Houston Police that he had just shot and killed Dean Corll, and that the two of them together with another youth had assaulted and killed at least twenty-three young males over the past three years. By August 20, the police had uncovered twenty-seven bodies of youths allegedly murdered by this trio.

Item: July 4, 1977. Two well-dressed men walked into the sheriff's office in Riverside, California, and gave themselves up. They were David Hill, a high school dropout who worked at odd jobs, and Patrick Kearney, an engineer. Both were charged with two of the trash bag murders and were thought responsible for killings in five southern California counties since 1964.

Item: July 8, 1977. A twenty-year-old Yale senior was fatally bludgeoned with a claw hammer in a bedroom in her family's home in Scarsdale, New York. Accused of the killing was Richard Herrin, her boyfriend, a Yale graduate who had been staying at her home.

Item: August 15, 1977. David Berkowitz was indicted in Brooklyn in the murder of a young woman and the attempted murder of her escort. The shootings of the two youths were the last attributed to the man known as the "Son of Sam," who is thought to have killed six people and wounded seven others over a thirteen-month period.

Item: January, 1979. John Gacy, Jr., a well-respected local businessman in the Chicago suburb of Des Plaines, Illinois, confessed to having abused and murdered thirty-two teenage boys and young men. The remains of twenty-seven individuals were found in the house of the thirty-six-year-old construction company owner. In 1968 Gacy was convicted of sodomy with a sixteen-year-old boy and sentenced to ten years in prison. He was paroled in 1970.[88]

These violent killings all evoked strong emotional reaction when they were reported in the media. In each case, the murders were not only horrible, but senseless as well. It might seem that if the criminal justice system meted out sterner punishments, or if psychiatrists made fewer mistakes, violent crimes such as these would not occur. Yet of all the offenders in this group, only Richard Speck and John Gacy, Jr. had prior records, and psychiatrists usually err in the direction of caution. They tend to overpredict violence and detain many who may not be dangerous. (Of course, when they underpredict and err by releasing "false negatives," the error will be headlined in the media.) Actually, in eight of these nine cases there was no way that the people who committed the offenses could have been identified in advance.

An approach frequently used to identify the violence-prone offender is to assume that anyone previously convicted of a violent crime is dangerous. In addition, crimes of violence frequently result in lengthier prison terms than nonviolent crimes.

In one study of 342 first-degree murderers paroled in California between 1945 and 1955, it was found that 10.8 percent had violated their parole, but only one parolee killed a second time.[89] Assuming that release on parole is based upon predicting that those released will not become recidivists (repeaters), the success in this group was exceedingly high. However, murderers generally have been found to be good parole risks. Prediction becomes more difficult when we are trying to predict the likelihood of violent behavior among a number of offenders arrested or convicted for the first time.

A recent study by E. Wenk et al., based upon an analysis of 4,146 youths released from the California Youth Authority, concluded that if a history of violent crime were used to predict future violent offenses, then the parole board "would have nineteen false positives out of every twenty predictions." They added that there is no simple means of classification available that would promise improvement of this awful record.[90]

In recent years, a major judicial decision has provided an excellent opportunity to analyze our inability to predict dangerousness. In 1966, in the case of *Baxstrom* v. *Herold* (383 US 107), the Supreme Court held that Johnnie Baxstrom, who had been confined in an institution for the "criminally insane" at Dannemora, New York, had been denied equal protection of the law. He and other prisoners had been incarcerated at two institutions in the New York prison system beyond the maximum sentence without benefit of a civil commitment trial. The immediate effect of the decision was the release to civil hospitals of 967 "dangerous" mental patients (inmates), including Johnnie Baxstrom. This decision provided the opportunity to study the "Baxstrom patients" to ascertain whether or not the lengthy incarcerations of these inmates—thirteen years on the average—was justified.[91]

Henry Steadman and Joseph Cocozza studied the behavior of these men and women in the civil hospitals and subsequently in the community. The Baxstrom patients were older than average—over fifty. Nevertheless, they had been kept in the institutions because psychiatrists were reluctant to release or transfer them. But the Baxstrom patients proved to be less violent than had been predicted. Only 2 percent were returned to the institutions for the criminally insane between 1966 and 1970, and only 19.6 percent of the males and 25.5 percent of the females showed any assaultive behavior in civil hospitals. Their rate of release from the civil hospitals was higher than that of comparable civilly committed patients. Their community adjustment was also positive. Fifty-six percent of the males and 43 percent of the females did not need to be readmitted to mental hospitals during the follow-up period. An intensive study of eighty-four former inmates showed a total of only eighteen criminal contacts with the police. In other words, the findings raise serious questions regarding the legal and psychiatric decisions that had detained these 967 people for such excessive terms in institutions for the criminally insane.[92]

Numerous other studies support the conclusion of Steadman and Cocozza that violence is greatly overpredicted. The populations studied included convicted offenders, such as sexual psychopaths and adjudicated delinquents. John Monahan points out that in these various groups, violence was overpredicted by 65 to 99 percent. Even among those groups we would expect to be more prone to violence than the general population, violence cannot be predicted with any degree of validity. Our ability to predict violence among those who have never committed a criminal act is virtually nil.[93]

The civil rights denied to the approximately 50,000 persons involuntarily detained each year for society's protection raises a crucial moral issue: How many innocent men and women can a free society lock up in order to protect itself from one violent individual? What would be considered an acceptable trade-off between the ends of public safety and individual liberty? Since we require only proof "beyond a reasonable doubt" for conviction and not absolute certainty, we doubtless convict some innocent persons in our need to detain a larger number of guilty ones. Yet we must seek to keep to a minimum those imprisoned through error. Unless we advocate locking up all criminals and "throwing the key away," we must recognize that our inability to predict dangerousness does not square with our principles of jurisprudence and justice.[94] Public policy regarding the control of violence in society must move beyond attempts to identify, predict, and control or incapacitate individuals. Violence is related to other forms of criminal behavior as well as to structures within our social institutions, including relations within the family and sexist traditions. Acts of senseless, raw violence, such as those perpetrated by individuals like the "Son of Sam," are atypical and evidently the result of intrapersonal psychodynamics rather than social patterns. Nevertheless, they too require a rational societal response rather than community paranoia.

SUMMARY

American society has been characterized by patterns of interpersonal conflict on the frontier, but in the nineteenth century our cities were known for their slums, which were virtually under the control of violent gangs. This violent past, with its traditions of direct confrontation, seems to be overlooked in the current concern about the apparent increased level of violence in our society.

The applicability of the four elements of criminal action or behavior systems has not been explicit in this chapter. Some generalizations relative to the difficulty in applying this typology should be noted.

First, violent offenders are not typically *career criminals,* nor do they have a criminal self-concept. As has been noted in this chapter, those arrested for homicide may never have been arrested before, or if they have been, it was for a lesser offense, more often a property or status offense than a violent crime.

Second, *affiliational forces or group support for the offender* may be related to the notion of the *subculture of violence.* There are considerable data that point to the conclusion that the majority of those apprehended for violent offenses come from the lower classes, and especially lower-class minority status. Yet even in these so-called cultures of violence, the incidence of violence is frequently victim-precipitated and turned inward against family or friends. And even in those groups considered prone to violent behavior, the patterns of violence vary by age, class, and sex.

Third, *convergence between criminal and violent behavior patterns* may be seen in the patterns of violence that exist in the larger society. Not only does our society, for instance, sanction violence in times of war, but racial violence and vigilantism have been an integral aspect of our history. Violence may well be seen by some members of society as a means of dealing with their status anxiety. When families—spouses and siblings—resort to violence, it may be because violence is seen as a means of achieving power or status or compensating for lessened self-esteem.

Fourth, *societal reaction to violence* is a factor. Those groups and individuals that are seen as prone to violence—for example, lower-class groups—are generally excluded from full participation in the larger society. This means that they have little to do with the codification or enforcement of rules to regulate their conduct. This exclusion may serve to confirm the assumption that lower-status groups are prone to a high level of violent behavior, and original cultural differences may be reinforced. Thus, the vicious cycle is perpetuated.[95] Consequently, concepts such as the *culture of violence* must be used with parsimony, or else in our haste to explain violence, we may in fact be "blaming the victim."

It seems apparent, then, that violent behavior is learned behavior, but not a unique individual phenomenon. It can be related to social factors and processes in the structure of society, and variations and trends have been identified. For instance, there has been an increase in interpersonal violent crimes among juveniles, some of which is reflected in street crimes such as muggings, which are a form of theft. Robbery, however, is a unique form of violent crime that is motivated by economic gain. Some violent offenses apparently are related to the use of drugs such as alcohol.

Battered spouses and abused children were described as crime phenomena that have been increasingly recognized as social problems in recent years. They may be linked with *differential socialization* regarding the appropriate manner with which to dispel anger and frustration. Many spouse and child abusers were themselves abused as children. Unfortunately, our means of coping with these violent crimes have not kept up with our insights into their origins.

The women's movement has focused on the political and moral aspects of violent crime patterns of forcible rape. As a result, some of the mystery surrounding this crime and its explanation as being related to an uncontrollable sexual impulse have been dispelled. Most rapes are between persons of similar social status and may be a result of differential gender socialization. Research and societal intervention in this violent crime pattern have yet to catch up to our apparent heightened insights. And rape is still not fully recognized as an act of violence—both against the individual woman and against the social order.

In developing a policy to deal with violent crime patterns, hindsight often seems to replace foresight. We typically overpredict dangerousness in individuals. Those arrested for violent offenses are more apt to have a record for other offenses—property and public order offenses—than for violence. The case of *Baxstrom* v. *Herold* is a classic example of overprediction.

The overprediction of violent crime patterns suggests something about the subtle complexity of these crime patterns. Furthermore, the prevalence of such offenses suggests something about the nature of our society. Patterns of violence apparently are an integral part of our social arrangements and traditions. But such patterns do not explain bizarre and atypical murderers, such as those described in Truman Capote's nonfiction novel, *In Cold Blood*. The behavior of such offenders may well be the result of serious personal conflicts and intrapsychic problems.

The more mundane patterns of violent crime can accurately be viewed in the context of everyday social relations. Patterns of violence doubtless are harmful to the social order, but they cannot generally be understood in terms of individual or social pathology. As F. Scott Fitzgerald said, "When the world changes from the good and the bad to the sick and the well, I'd rather be dead."

ADDITIONAL READINGS

Chappell, Duncan and John Monahan, eds. *Violence and Criminal Justice.* Lexington, Mass.: D. C. Heath, 1975.
> This collection of original articles discusses the nature of violent crime, problems of controlling and predicting violent crime, violence in the criminal justice system, and policy implications. A good source for analysis of recent research on violent crime.

Curtis, Lynn A. *Violence, Race and Culture.* Lexington, Mass.: D. C. Heath, 1975.
> This study brings together data from a pioneering work on a national survey of homicide, assault, rape, and robbery with insights from participant observation studies. Curtis reinterprets the subculture of violence in terms of blocked opportunities for blacks and racism in our society.

Ferracuti, Franco and Graeme Newman. "Assaultive Offenses." In *Handbook of Criminology*, edited by Daniel Glaser. Chicago: Rand McNally, 1974.

An excellent discussion of the staff report to the National Commission on the Causes and Prevention of Violence as well as cross-national studies of assaultive and homicidal offenses.

Gil, David G. *Violence Against Children.* Cambridge, Mass.: Harvard University Press, 1970.

An analysis of the national survey by NORC relative to attitudes toward child abuse and child abusers in 1967. Includes appendices on research instruments.

Silberman, Charles E. *Criminal Violence, Criminal Justice.* New York: Random House, 1979.

This is one of the most thorough and provocative studies ever made of violent crime in America. Written for the lay reader by a respected, liberal author, the book takes an iconoclastic view of crime, criminal justice, and the relation between race and crime. Though many will disagree with Silberman's analyses and policy recommendation, his book should be read by all who are concerned with violent crime and the criminal courts.

Steadman, Henry and Joseph Cocozza. *Careers of the Criminally Insane.* Lexington, Mass.: D. C. Heath, 1974.

This is an excellent follow-up report and naturalistic study of the 967 "Baxstrom patients" released to civil hospitals from prison hospitals for the criminally insane following the landmark Baxstrom decision. The inadequacy of our means of predicting violence-prone individuals is well documented.

Swigert, Lynn V. and Ronald A. Farrell. *Differential Treatment and the Legal Process.* Lexington, Mass.: D. C. Heath, 1976.

This recent analysis of offenders and victims in homicides updates earlier studies by Wolfgang. The social and legal history of defendants and the social relationships and social status levels which defendants share with victims are explored. The victim-precipitated aspects of homicide are verified, and the differential treatment of the stereotypical "primitive criminal" types is analyzed and interrelationships explored.

CALIFORNIA
LEMONS
5¢
EACH
MICHIGAN
CHOCOLATE
PEPPERS
5¢
EACH

> The more featureless and commonplace a crime is, the more difficult it is to bring it home.
> —Sir Arthur Conan Doyle, "The Boscombe Valley Mystery"

AVOCATIONAL AND COMMONPLACE CRIME

The criminal behavior systems described in this chapter encompass the greatest number of offenders and potential offenders—individuals whom we will categorize as *avocational* and *commonplace* criminals. These two categories include the one-time losers, habitual losers, novices, outcasts, social misfits, and disorganized types, who account for most of the arrests each year and who jam our court calendars and crowd our jails and prisons. The contrast between avocational and commonplace criminals on the one hand and the career criminals described in Chapter 7 should be apparent. Career criminals relate to criminal lifestyles that involve a more or less persistent criminal perspective and an identity revolving around the pursuit of crime as a livelihood.[1] Professional, heavy professional, and organized criminals seldom go to prison; if they do, generally they do not stay long.[2] For these types the idea of crime as a career is useful, for it focuses our attention on the creation of social roles in everyday interaction; thus criminal behavior may be seen as related to short-term or long-term commitments, or episodic, rather than as a persistent aspect of criminal identity.[3]

The avocational, or occasional, criminal and the commonplace, or traditional, criminal—both noncareer types—have certain characteristics. First, they tend not to think of themselves as criminal, and they lack a full commitment to a criminal career. Second, criminal activity is not their sole source of income or social status, although the commonplace criminal may seek to gain money to use for recreational activities such as the purchase of drugs. Third, both types are thought to be deterrable and amenable to rehabilitation by punishing, correcting, or incapacitating the offender. And fourth, both are involved primarily in property offenses, although they differ to the extent that the avocational criminal's activities are more episodic.[4] In our attempt to describe the action systems of these two criminal types, we will organize data from various research findings within the framework of the four dimensions of criminal behavior systems described in Chapter 6.

AVOCATIONAL CRIMINAL BEHAVIOR SYSTEMS

The "action system" of avocational criminals is at the opposite end of the continuum from that of career criminals. Though their offenses may be similar, they lack the frequency and regularity attributed to career criminal types. Avocational types are inexperienced and unskilled; they may be "naive check forgers," amateur car thieves, or shoplifters. Their offenses tend to be sporadic, based upon needs of the moment, or irrational and impulsive behavior. A significant proportion of check forgers and shoplifters apparently are noncareer offenders. One shoplifter made this distinction between his skillful techniques and those used by alcoholics: "All those rubby-dubs lift socks. Socks is nothing—like a balloon. I take a few pair but socks is nothing."[5]

Selected Avocational Offense Patterns

The individual who occasionally steals, forges a check, or damages property that belongs to another can be thought of as an avocational or occasional property offender. The word "rip-off" has been used in recent years to refer to these types of offenses. The "rip-off" illustrates a concept that David Matza calls "neutralization," in that it provides a means of violating the norms against stealing "without surrendering allegiance to them."[6] It has become a euphemism for the notion that the behavior is *naughty* but not really criminal. Two million cases of shoplifting were reported to the police in 1975, but those statistics hardly measure the real extent of such crime. Many department stores, supermarkets, and clothing shops attribute as much as 50 percent of their profit losses to "inventory shrinkage" that is unaccounted for and assumed to be the result of both customer and employee theft.[7]

Some of the increasing rate of business theft relates to the manner in which business is conducted. As early as 1967, the President's Crime Commission stated:

> In retail establishments, managers choose to tolerate a high percentage of shoplifting rather than pay for additional clerks. Discount stores .... experience an inventory loss almost double that of the conventional department store. Studies indicate that there is in general more public tolerance for theft of property and goods from large organizations than from small ones, from big corporations or utilities than from small neighborhood establishments. Restraints on conduct that were effective in a more personal rural society do not seem as effective in an impersonal society of large organizations.[8]

Mary Cameron's study found that housewives rationalized the "pilfering" of modestly priced objects, generally small luxuries for personal use, on the grounds that the losses could easily be borne by the large department stores. She also found that 92 percent of the women shoplifters had no previous record for such offenses.[9]

A recent experimental study by Erhard Blankenburg (1976) was conducted in a university town in Germany, using youthful experimenters who committed forty acts of shoplifting. The "thieves" reported that they felt safer and that it was simpler to steal in smaller stores, where fewer persons might observe them. It might be that criminal statistics showing a higher incidence of shoplifting in large department and self-service stores reflect the greater likelihood of detection and prosecution rather than a higher rate of theft. The data in this study indicate that less than 10 percent of all shoplifting is detected. It was concluded that official statistics on shoplifting hardly describe actual patterns since the number of undetected and unreported cases is so high.[10]

The total shoplifting losses for department stores in the United States in 1971 were estimated at $4 billion. That comes to over $10 million a day. Obviously, the "average" citizen pays a heavy cost in terms of higher prices to cover these losses. In addition, shoplifting cannot be attributed to the "crime-prone" lower classes. Though lower-status persons are more often detected, charged, and sanctioned, shoplifting is an offense committed by affluent middle- and upper-middle-income young adults as well as by the poor.[11]

Check forgery, which is estimated to cost over $1 billion a year, is another crime in which a majority of the offenders have no prior criminal record. Forgery can take many forms, but it is defined as "making, altering, uttering, or possessing, with intent to defraud, anything false which is made to appear true." [12] So the wage earner who blatantly writes a check knowing there are not sufficient monies to cover it could be charged with such an offense.

Vandalism is the willful or malicious destruction or disfigurement of property. It is usually committed by juveniles or youths. In 1975, 66 percent of those arrested for vandalism were under eighteen, and 86 percent were under twenty-five.

Harrison Salisbury, in *The Shook-Up Generation* (1958), described how a wave of vandalism seemed to spread across the country in the 1950s. Gangs of youths attacked suburban schools, first on the West Coast and then in New Jersey and New York. The Crime Commission summarized some of the reports of the vandalism of buildings and equipment of public organizations and utilities in the 1960s. Telephone and electric companies, schools, libraries, parks, and public housing were among the targets. Estimates of damages ranged up to hundreds of thousands of dollars. In 1965 the public schools in Washington, D.C., reported that 26,500 window panes were broken at a replacement cost of $118,000; Boston schools reported similar damage.[13]

Vandalism is a property offense generally committed by those without a criminal record, although some of the groups involved in such destructive pranks may be seen as delinquents. In the 1970s, vandalism came to include the widespread painting of graffiti on public buildings and on the sides of subway cars.

Joyriding—an avocational crime pattern.

The theft of automobiles is a serious property crime when the intent is to keep the vehicle, sell it, or strip it and dispose of the parts. When a car is borrowed and eventually abandoned or returned, it is "joyriding," a misdemeanor defined as operating a vehicle without the owner's permission. Joyriding is seen by many youths as a way of creating excitement and tension. It is a risk-taking adventure that provides "kicks" for the participants. Asked whether he had done much joyriding, one gang member replied: "Yeah. When I was about thirteen, I didn't do nothing but steal cars. The guy that I always stole with, both of us liked to drive so we'd steal a car. And then he'd steal another car, and we'd chase each other."[14] For gang boys from the lower classes, joyriding represents the creation of an "action" situation from materials available on the street.[15]

We have applied the term *avocational criminal* to those property offenders who commit occasional offenses using amateurish methods and whose behavior is only incidental to their lifestyle. They fail to make a living out of their infrequent offenses, and they do not identify with criminal identities and perspectives.

Criminal Careers and Self-Concept

Many of those involved in shoplifting, like young adults and college students who "rip off" stores, fit into Cameron's category of "snitches" and do not consider themselves criminals. A recent study of young adults in Hawaii found that 28 percent admitted to having shoplifted during the previous year. The director of security of a large Chicago department store was quoted recently as stating that shoplifting has become "a sport of the rich."[16]

Naive check forgers, according to Edwin Lemert's study, generally lack both a previous record or a criminal self-concept. This kind of individual may be caught in a web of circumstances leading up to the forgery. Since forgery often is seen as a relatively minor offense—or no offense at all in some cases—it becomes acceptable behavior for the person who needs money.[17]

Vandalism involves behavior that destroys property but usually does not involve stealing. Often the offenders do not perceive of themselves as criminals or delinquents. The acts of vandalism seem to provide a source of excitement and risk taking for groups of youth who find their leisure time activities dull or boring. Sometimes the vandals' targets are specifically selected. For instance, a merchant who "hassled" a group of street-corner boys may have his property victimized. Walter Miller's study of gang violence found that:

> Little of the deliberately inflicted property damage represented .... hostility against arbitrary objects; in most cases the gang members injured the properties of ... persons who had angered them .... There was little evidence of "senseless" destruction. Most property damage was directed and repressive.[18]

Borrowing someone's car to go joyriding is considered a prank by teenagers and even by some college students in college or university towns. It is not a behavior engaged in for money, and the offenders do not see themselves as criminals.

The neutralization of legal norms evidently has wide applicability to avocational offenders. The amateur shoplifter or "snitch," the novice check forger, the vandal, and the joyrider can all find ways to apply the principles of mitigation found in the criminal law to their particular cases. Although they may not be opposed to the substance of the law—for example, they would not advocate stealing—they do not feel that it applies to their particular case. They negate their responsibility for violating the law and avoid a criminal self-concept in the process.

Affiliational Aspects in Avocational Crime Patterns

Criminality usually can be discussed in terms of subcultural groups or action systems with which the offender associates and identifies and from which he or she receives group support. Since avocational crimes are committed by the inexperienced and involve little or no skill, criminal associations may seem to be of little importance. Becoming affiliated or associated with a group involved in criminal or delinquent activity may not be a prerequisite for learning the skills for naive check forgery. Everyday economics provides experience for most Americans in the use of checks. Lemert's study of naive check forgers found one-third were first offenders.[19] However, activities such as vandalism, joyriding, and shoplifting are typically quite group oriented. Cohen has noted that the malicious and nonutilitarian behavior patterns of lower-class gang boys express their resentment of dominant middle-class values.[20]

The modern day ethos of mass advertising, mass marketing, and self-service selling provides a ripe situation for today's shoplifter. A list of reasons cited by young shoplifters most frequently includes a search for thrills, followed by high prices, poor service, and a philosophy of "ripping off" the establishment. In some cases, offenders did not realize that shoplifting can result in criminal sanctions.[21] Similar behavior patterns were identified by Cameron's earlier study of adult shoplifters. These individuals had little knowledge of arrest procedures, and although they evidently had thought about being detected, they apparently had not considered arrest as a consequence.[22] However, shoplifting by youths differs from that by adults in that it may involve group activity. The relationship between group association and shoplifting is evidenced in the fact that high rates of shoplifting occur in high delinquency areas. The act may take place for nonutilitarian reasons, for "kicks," or it may be a means of compensating, consciously or not, for exploitative circumstances and depressed economic opportunities.

Vandalism typically occurs as spontaneous, collective behavior in a group setting. Andrew Wade has delineated and documented the following five stages in the sequence and patterns that often occur in this miniature form of collective or "crowd" behavior:

Stage I: Waiting for Something to Happen: . . . . the situation from which the suggestion or innovating behavior develops. . . . "An opportunity structure" is present . . . . The play situation is [a] general . . . context out of which vandalism may develop. . . . Vandalism as play generally takes the shape of a game of skill . . . .

Stage II: Removal of Uncertainty (the Exploratory Gesture): The unstructured situation . . . undergoes a significant change when an action-provoking suggestion is made. . . . The exploratory gesture may be in the form of an overt act . . . .

Stage III: Mutual Conversion: . . . . A number of pressures operate . . . . these challenge or threaten the person's self-concept as an acceptable peer . . . .

Stage IV: Joint Elaboration of the Act: . . . . there is a spontaneous eruption of wholesale vandalism once the spirit of the activity takes hold . . . . Contributing to the elaboration . . . is the element of mutual excitation . . . . One participant's behavior serves as the model for another's. . . . A primary function of this element is the tendency of the individual to lose his feeling of self-identity . . . . The peer group inadvertently furnishes a sense of security in numbers which functions to reduce feelings of individuality and responsibility . . . . This feeling of security is enhanced by the . . . belief that vandalism is one of the less serious delinquencies . . . . An impression of universality is created, giving the appearance of group solidarity.

Stage V: Aftermath and Retrospect: . . . . Whatever guilt may be felt is usually neutralized by . . . rationalizations motivating the behavior . . . . In his retrospective view of the act, the participant sometimes redefines his behavior from the original definition of "fun" to a negative one. . . . This re-evaluation in terms of guilt or shame is probably more true in the case of the boy who has never been arrested before . . . . Obviously, much depends on how significantly the actor has identified . . . with the normative reference groups in question.[23]

Convergence of Criminal and Conventional Behavior Patterns

If we assume that normal values concerning the ownership and sanctity of private property are shared more or less equally by all members of society, it makes the task of explaining avocational criminality very difficult. Certainly there is little support for such law-violating behavior in the general norms that place high value on private property.

Indeed, if there is one value upon which most observers would agree, it is that the ownership and protection of property has high priority in our economic and legal practices. The avocational offender acts contrary to these basic values, seeking possessions or material objects that belong to another, which they are unable to obtain legitimately.

However, most avocational criminals are at least consciously committed to the deeply ingrained values of private property as well as other common beliefs and values of our society. Lemert found, for instance, that naive check forgers seem to hold the same attitudes about observing the law as nonforgers.[24] Cameron found that amateur shoplifters tend to come from respected groups in society and have virtually no contact with criminal associates.[25] Youths who take cars for joyrides are also likely to come from conventional, respected middle-class families and generally have no previous arrest record—except for similar offenses.[26]

So there is some ambiguity in attempts to explain the degree to which avocational crime patterns represent a rejection of the conventional norms of the dominant middle-class groups in our society. These offenses pose for us an intriguing dilemma in human nature: namely, why do people violate the very laws in which they profess to believe?[27] Vandalism, at least, appears to involve a direct challenge to those core values in our society that place a high value on private property. But in many cases such behavior emerges from what has come to be termed a "search for kicks" or fun.

Accumulating evidence questions whether conventional middle-class behavior patterns are as deeply ingrained in the self-concepts of even middle-class citizens as we have assumed. Many avocational offenders may be relatively isolated from those dominant group values and patterns that are esteemed in our society.[28] Gresham Sykes and David Matza have suggested that such offenders may "neutralize" their deviance and "deflect blame" by *"denying responsibility."* In this process, deviant persons reduce the effectiveness of the restraint of others that results from social disapproval. They see themselves acting because of forces beyond their control—as more "acted upon than acting"—and thus do not see their behavior as a frontal assault on society's values. For example, in the case of the naive check forger, the individual is faced with a crisis, real or imaginary, and the sense of urgency allows him or her to disassociate legal controls from the act of forgery. The tendency following first forgeries is for the naive forger to give himself or herself up, while expressing puzzlement as to how he or she could have done it, sometimes attributing the behavior to "another me."[29]

The *denial of injury* is another neutralization technique by which offenders may claim commitments to societal norms but still qualify their applicability to their cases. Vandalism, for instance, not only becomes defined as fun or mischief, but the offenders may rationalize that the personal property destroyed was owned by someone who was affluent and thus would not be hurt by its destruction. Joyriding becomes qualified as simply borrowing a car, and shoplifting in large department stores comes to be viewed as a game that would not be played in small, locally owned stores.[30]

A third technique for neutralizing responsibility is the *denial of the victim*. This technique involves the assertion that any damage done is justified due to circumstances. The offender may view his or her act as punishment for some alleged unfair or unjust practice. A school may be vandalized because of actions of a school official, or a large department store might be seen as fair game for a rip-off. Certain stores have also been vandalized by college students who ostensibly were protesting some unrelated problem. In the case of the rip-off of a department store, the owner is also absent. This factor accounts in part for the increased number of shoplifting offenses reported by franchise dealers — the franchise company rather than the franchise holder is physically absent. The lessened awareness of the victim may neutralize the effects of social norms and the fear of consequences.[31]

Condemnation of the condemners is a fourth technique that may provide insight into the manner in which shoplifting is justified as a rip-off of the establishment. For example, the storeowner, it may be said, is corrupt or undeserving of material success. However, Kraut found that this motivation was listed thirteenth in a list of reasons cited by both shoplifting and nonshoplifting college students.[32]

Although Sykes and Matza were trying to explain delinquency, their fifth technique for "neutralizing" or justifying law violations — *the appeal to higher loyalties* — appears to be applicable to both naive check forgers and first-time embezzlers. The check forger may get caught in a financial crisis and argue that the action is justified by the claims the family had on him or her to support them. Or the bank embezzler who needs money for an impending crisis may place loyalty to family over loyalty to the bank and its clients.[33]

In the various forms of avocational crime, behaviors that come to be defined as criminal may be carried out for a number of reasons — some verbalized after the act and some before or during the event. It is important, however, that we do not try to explain such behavior in terms of our values. We can avoid this pitfall as we become more aware of the convergence of conventional and nonconventional norms that characterizes avocational crime.

Societal Reaction to Avocational Crime Patterns

Since the avocational criminal usually does not have a prior record, societal reaction may be mild. The charge may be dismissed if the check forger makes the check good or the "snitch" returns the merchandise and pledges to sin no more. In fact, just being detected without being charged is sometimes an effective deterrent for first offenders.

When first offenders are charged, they often realize that what was done as a "prank" or to satisfy a whim is actually a criminal act. Consequently, such offenders tend to be treated leniently by police and the courts. It has been established that legal sanctions against shoplifters are quite selective and seem to operate mainly against those of low status and members of minority groups. In an analysis of records of shoplifters in Freiburg, West Germany, it was found that adults from blue-collar occupations, foreigners, and college students were overrepresented among those sanctioned.[34] In America, blacks and "hippie" offenders are more often sanctioned. Traditionally, juveniles who shoplift have not been sanctioned.

Vandals may be dealt with informally or given probation. Usually their parents must pay for damages. Joyriders often come to the attention of law enforcement agencies when there is an accident. They may receive probation when apprehended in repeated offenses. However, they do not typically graduate to a career of auto theft. Generally, such offenses end when the youth settles down with a job and a family and assumes conventional adult status.

However as Matza has cogently argued, being apprehended by formal agents of control links the legal reaction with the *actionable* behavior. The person becomes "tagged" or registered and risks "being cast" or moved, even if gradually, toward becoming a thief. Even if the authorities intend for a sanction to be only a "slap on the wrist," this action might itself promote a process of secondary deviation that escalates the process of criminalization.[35]

COMMONPLACE OR TRADITIONAL CRIMINAL BEHAVIOR PATTERNS

Commonplace or traditional crime is closer to career crime than avocational crime, but it is still near the bottom of the ladder. These offenders are still considered inexperienced amateurs or "punks" by career criminals, since they lack the skill and techniques that identify organized and professional criminals or "rounders." The "amateur"/"experienced" distinction is apparently more important to criminals than the concept "professional." Criminals are more apt to make a distinction between the "inept" criminal and the skilled than they are to refer to themselves as professionals.[36] Not only are traditional criminals less skillful in committing offenses and more apt to be detected, but they also lack the social organization that can help them avoid arrest and conviction. Since traditional criminals may get involved in illegal acts as juveniles, they may "mature out" and discontinue such criminal careers once they settle down. A few, however, may continue their criminal careers.

Types of Offense Patterns

Those who commit traditional crimes such as burglary, larceny, and robbery may be regarded as *commonplace criminals.* It should be noted that there are important differences between skills, techniques, and social organization of the career thieves and professional heavy robbers discussed in Chapter 7 and the commonplace types under discussion here. The emergence of auto theft during this century suggests it should be added to the group. In 1975, these four property offenses accounted for over 95 percent of the 11,256,600 serious index crimes. In order of frequency, they were larceny/theft, 53 percent; burglary, 29 percent; auto theft, 9 percent; and robbery 5 percent.

The term theft includes *all* property offenses. However, the English common law denoted theft as larceny. The definition used by the FBI—"the unlawful taking, carrying, leading, or riding away of property from the possession... of another"—still reflects the general intent of the English law, namely taking or carrying away goods from another without consent.[37]

Burglary and robbery also involve larceny and theft. Under the common law, burglary referred to breaking and entering the house of another by night with the intent to steal. This definition has been expanded to include unlawful entry of nonresidential structures whether during the day or night. Since robbery is theft or stealing from a person by force, violence, or the fear of violence, in its noncareer aspects it may be considered a form of commonplace rather than heavy professional crime.

Commonplace Criminal Careers and Self-Concept

Considerable evidence from official arrest data suggests that the careers of many commonplace criminals are launched in juvenile delinquency activity (and, we might add, in juvenile institutions). Although the risks of using such data are apparent, unofficial data from self-reports and field observations support the idea that property crimes peak at about age fifteen to sixteen and then decline in the next two to four years. Robbery, which apparently peaks at the age of nineteen to twenty-one, does not decline as rapidly.[38] Table 9.1 compares the age-specific arrest rates for those under the ages of fifteen and eighteen in 1970 and 1975. In three of the four serious property offenses, persons under eighteen accounted for about half of the total arrests. How are these youngsters recruited? Where do they begin such activity?[39]

Commonplace criminal careers often begin early. The group nature of many of these offenses suggests that the behavior emerges within the teenage culture, especially in urban areas. The lifestyle of these delinquents involves law-violating behavior. The birth "cohort study" by Marvin Wolfgang et al. of 9,945 boys born in 1945 in Philadelphia illustrates the consistent involvement in crime by a significant minority of such youths. Among the boys studied, 35 percent had had at least one contact with the police by the age of eighteen.

It was also discovered that more than 50 percent of the black youths were delinquent. Of this group, only about 18 percent, or 627 boys, were chronic delinquents. These chronic offenders were responsible for 52 percent of all delinquencies committed by the birth cohort, although they made up only 6 percent of the entire group. They were also responsible for 71 percent of the robberies. Yet 37 percent of the first offenders involved in theft and 32 percent of those apprehended for injury and theft did not have any further arrests.[40]

Another study of gangs in Philadelphia found that 77 percent of 918 black youths in twenty-seven gangs, with a median age of 17.6 years, had police records. They averaged six or more delinquent offenses, while one-fifth had more than ten offenses. Moreover, 41 percent of the adult gang members had acquired criminal records. Not all delinquent offenses are criminal violations; others include habitual truancy, incorrigibility, curfew violations, and other status offenses. But a core of persistent juvenile gang offenders continued on into more serious adult offenses.[41]

Studies of delinquency are full of references to gang members, white as well as black, who progress from delinquent offenses to a career in commonplace crime. Our own experience with juvenile detentions and detached youth workers has identified youths in small towns who have accumulated twenty or more juvenile offenses and later were involved as youthful offenders.

The recently published autobiography of John Allen, who grew up in Washington, D.C., traces this progression. Until John was crippled by a policeman's bullet at the age of twenty-eight, he was a mugger, pimp, dope pusher, and armed robber. The account of his early life makes it seem inevitable that he would become a criminal. Most of his friends, neighbors, and even some members of his family were involved in illegal activities. At the age of eight,

Table 9.1. Arrest Totals for Traditional Property Offenses of Persons Under Fifteen and Eighteen Years of Age, 1970–1975

Offenses Charged	Total Arrests by Offense 1970	1975	Under 15 1970	1975	Percent Change	Under 18 1970	1975	Percent Change
Robbery[a]	87,687	129,788	11	9.6	−1.4	33	34	−1.0
Burglary (breaking or entering)	284,418	449,155	23	20	−3.0	52	52.6	0.4
Larceny/theft	616,099	958,938	25	20	−5.0	51	45	−6.0
Auto theft	129,341	120,224	15	14	−1.0	56	54.5	−1.5
Grand total all arrests, all ages	6,570,473	8,013,645	9.2	8.9	0.3	25.3	25.9	0.6

[a] Robbery is included under property offenses in this table, although it is usually placed under violent crime.

Source: FBI, *Uniform Crime Reports* (Washington, D.C.: U.S. Government Printing Office, 1970, 1975), pp. 127, 190.

Will some of these gang offenders graduate to adult crime?

he was placed in a juvenile detention center after committing a burglary. He was involved in the shooting of a fellow gang member when he was just twelve. By age seventeen, he was a mugger. After shooting another youth in a quarrel over a woman, he served three years in prison. When he was twenty-four, he was convicted of robbery. After serving three more years in prison he returned to crime until a policeman's bullet lodged in his spinal column and paralyzed him. Confined to a wheelchair, he dictated his book *Assault with a Deadly Weapon* (1977).

In looking back on his career in crime, Allen stated: "It seems to me that the kind of neighborhood you come up in may make all the difference in which way you go and where you end up.... I feel like it's survival."[42] John Allen sees his life as being predisposed to crime by the circumstances and social forces that shaped him. But before he could be molded by these criminogenic circumstances to move toward a life of crime, something had to happen to reduce his capacity to resist their influence. As Allen put it: "Some figure they'll work their way out. I say, 'Well, I'll rob my way out.'"[43] What conspired to make him think he had no other choice than to pimp, deal in drugs, and look for the "big score"? There is no doubt that discrimination, poverty, and neglect have helped create a black, criminal subculture. But according to official statistics on rates of crime in the ghetto, most inhabitants lead conventional, law-abiding lives.

Career criminals do not see themselves stealing on impulse or against their will any more than "straight" people see themselves as going to work against their will. As one study on *Crime as Work* (1973) has pointed out, a "true" criminal's method of acquiring money is considered a matter of choice. Crimes committed by career criminals are seen as rational and deliberate, whereas the noncareer, commonplace criminal may lack the stability, skill, and dedication of the "true" criminal.[44]

A commitment to crime as a way of life develops as the youth goes through a progression of repeated offenses, arrests, and convictions. Unlike avocational criminals, commonplace criminals—by virtue of their progression into crime and their continued isolation from conventional society—do develop a criminal self-concept and a strong identification with a criminal lifestyle.[45]

The offenses committed by commonplace criminals and career criminals are similar in that they are related to property crime. In fact, commonplace crimes are virtually synonymous with traditional property crimes. The motivation for such offenses as burglary, larceny, theft, and robbery is usually simply to obtain money or goods. Although there is always the fantasy of a "big score," the typical amount gained is small, hardly sufficient for a livelihood. Furthermore, youths just starting out might be limited in what they steal. They might not have any connections with a fence who can buy "hot" goods, so their stealing may have to be restricted to money. As one accomplished burglar stated about his own start:

> "That was B & E on houses.... I was just a kid and I was looking for money. And I wasn't stealing anything: like some guys would walk in and take furniture and everything. But I was just young and I didn't know much." When asked, "Could you make a living off this kind of thing?" he replied, "Well, I guess you could if you were taking, like radios and TVs and you had a way of getting rid of them. Then I imagine you could, yeh! But just taking money, could you make a living that way? No, as a kid maybe." [46]

With each crime producing only a small gain, offenses must be repeated. In John Conklin's study of robbery, he found that the ratio of juveniles arrested for theft to violent offenses was 4 to 1 in 1964 and 5 to 1 in 1968. National figures show that for robbery suspects under age seventeen, the ratio was 8 to 1 in 1964 and 7 to 1 in 1968.[47] A similar study in Philadelphia of persons arrested for robbery found that prior arrest records were more often for offenses against property than against persons. Only 4 percent had records of assault, 45 percent had a pattern of arrests for robbery, larceny, or burglary. No significant difference was found between blacks and whites or between robbers who had or had not used violence. A recent study by Robert Lejeune, however, casts some doubt upon this apparent conclusion that persistence in crime rather than specialization in violent crime is the pattern. His research differentiated between "muggers," relatively unarmed robbers, and professional "heavy" robbers. He suggests that violence and the experience of power over the victim play an important role in robberies where the victim is physically attacked—"mugged"—rather than just threatened.[48]

Commonplace criminals are justifiably concerned about being detected. On the other hand, career criminals may be detected, but due to their skills often avoid conviction. Commonplace criminals frequently end up in prison and make up the bulk of the prison population. As one career bank robber commented, "In this place you've got only thirty thieves—the rest are misfits, nuisances."[49]

The actual effects of processing by criminal justice agencies often are quite different from the intended effects. Tom, a twenty-four-year-old former gang leader in Chicago describes how processing can make an accomplished criminal of a juvenile delinquent:

> Or, you go to the Audy Home. You're nine years old, ten years old. You're in there for some beefs like ditching school, running away from home, right.... You go to court, and the Audy Home sends you to the I.Y.C., St. Charles, Joliet, camps, Sheridan, you know.... You get there and hear all this bullshit about how much money this cat's made, you're not but ten or eleven years old, and you think you're going to be a big shot. So you come out and start with all that "man" shit. You're a tough guy, see. You came out of St. Charles. The society put you there. Society says why does this cat steal. Right? And they put him in the place to teach him how to steal and they came out and they're thieves and society grabs them again and puts them in a bigger place. Now here he learns how to stick up a place—armed robbery. Then the kid's caught again; he goes to the penitentiary. Then he meets somebody from the organization. Which leaves him an artist to kill. It goes on like that.[50]

Generally, the extent to which the commonplace criminal develops skills and sophistication is limited. Unless he can pull off an unusually successful caper, chances are that he will continue as a "young punk," and his crimes will be unsystematic and irregular. As one bank robber serving a sentence in prison stated, "I'm in for bank robbery, but I'm not a bank robber. At least I'm a miserably poor one—in fact, I'm a poor criminal."[51]

The transition from delinquent gang member to criminal is not a smooth one. It is affected by perceived opportunities—both illegitimate and legitimate—and by the person's view of the future. While some delinquents continue criminal activities into adulthood, most desist by the time they are eighteen or nineteen. If they remain street criminals, they often continue in the pattern of prior offenses and maintain a criminal identity. Yet their lack of skill may lead them from crime to jail to crime, with numerous stretches of incarceration. If legitimate options seem closed, they may not want to trade off their status on the street for a low-status, low-paying job. And so they may choose to continue a criminal career, even with limited success and the risks of apprehension. After all, only about 20 percent of all property crimes are cleared by arrests.[52]

BOX 1

Tales of a Reformed Car Thief

By JACK THOMAS

If you work hard in this country, the theory goes, you can become rich and famous. Look at Rufus Tinker Whittier of Dorchester.

He started at 14, and worked so hard that by the time he was 30, he had earned more than a million dollars and achieved more notoriety than he wanted.

Unfortunately, Whittier's work was stealing cars, 8000 of them over a 15-year period, he says, and while he earned a million dollars, he also lost a million dollars. In addition, he was arrested three times, shot twice, beaten badly once, and spent two and one half years in the slammer.

One night in 1970, Whittier was standing in front of a garage in Cambridge when a competitor stuck a sawed-off shotgun between his eyes. As Whittier pushed the muzzle away, the man pulled the trigger. The shot nearly severed Whittier's wrist, and left more than 200 pellets in his chest.

That's when he began to consider a new line of work.

Now, eight years later, Tinker the car thief is Mr. Whittier, consultant and lecturer on auto theft. Companies trying to develop a device that will make automobiles theft-proof seek Whittier's advice, and police departments, which once sought him with warrants, now seek him as a lecturer on ways to prevent auto theft.

On the Today show, he broke into a car in Rockefeller Center and drove it away within 27 seconds. Last month, he was on the cover of Money magazine. Johnny Carson's Tonight Show has invited him to appear, and he has been interviewed by dozens of newspaper reporters around the country.

He exudes confidence about his ability to break into cars.

"If a thief wants your car," he said, "there's no way to stop him. You can slow him down, but you can't stop him. Last year there were 1.5 million cars stolen in the United States, which works out to about one every 32 seconds. In Massachusetts, in 1976, there were 90,000 cars stolen, and that works out to about one out of every 75 cars in the state."

Whittier got an early start, stealing a bulldozer at age 12 from the city dump. For a while, he stole cars from the streets for joyrides, but then learned he could sell them to junk dealers for $25 or $50. In the next 15 years, says Whittier, he stole approximately 8000 cars, sometimes for parts, sometimes on order.

"The best places are where sporting events are held," he said. "Boston Garden when the Bruins or the Celtics are playing, or Fenway Park during the summer."

Car thieves, like other businessmen, must adapt themselves to the changing times.

"The Federal government is putting the pressure on the auto industry to come up with cars that are theft-proof," Whittier said, "and as a result, professional car thieves are already switching their tactics. I'd say 40 percent of the cars that are stolen today are stolen by tow trucks in broad daylight. Just look around and see how many tow trucks you see with no names on them, no nothing—especially at sports events. I used to tow six cars an hour, right off the street," he said. "People are so gullible. They'd think, oh, that guy probably wasn't supposed to park there."

In its war against car thieves, said Whittier, the automobile industry is at a disadvantage because it must publish a description of its antitheft devices.

"When I was a car thief," said Whittier, "I used to go to the library once a month religiously and read the manuals to learn how to circumvent the new devices. The repair manuals always contain detailed descriptions.

"The main targets," he said, "are the expensive models, Lincolns, Cadillacs, Jaguars, Mercedeses, cars that cost $12,000 or more, but some people steal junk cars for scrap and make $100,000 a year. One guy specializes in Volkswagens, but the safest cars are station wagons. For some reason, they don't sell so well. I don't think I stole five in my life."

Whittier was hired by the state of Massachusetts to advise the insurance commissioner on the effectiveness of auto alarm systems, and one day, he bypassed the alarms on five cars in six minutes.

In another test, he broke into 20 automobiles, averaging 43 seconds apiece, three to get in and 40 to get the ignition out and the engine started.

He said that of 26 devices he evaluated for an insurance company, the most effective was Identicar, and the company now pays him $1000 a month to promote its product.

"It costs between $700 and $1000 to replace the windows in a car," Whittier said, "and that would bite into a thief's profit, so when he sees a car's windows engraved with an Identicar number, he's probably going to look for a different one to steal."

Ironically, Whittier, who says he stole 8000 cars, travels modestly today in a 1971 Chevrolet Vega with 81,000 miles on it. "But I never forget to lock it," he said.

Some Tips to Keep Car Thieves Away

Here is Whittier's advice to discourage car thieves:

—Don't get a factory-installed alarm system. They're all installed the same way, and a thief can learn the intricacies from repair manuals at the public library.

—You need a combination of systems. If you have an alarm system, get something else, too, like an ignition-kill system. It interrupts the voltage you need to start the car. That is, a second switch has to be turned before the car will start. A good one is Sav-Car, which costs $60, but you can buy cheaper ones.

—Take the standard door-lock buttons off your car and install tapered ones. This won't stop the professional, but it will discourage the amateur, and the FBI estimates that 65 percent of the auto thefts are by amateurs.

—In a public lot, don't tell the attendant how long you'll be, and give him only the ignition key.

—If you're leaving your car locked somewhere for several days, take the rotor out of the distributor and lock it in the trunk.

—Some people lean nails against the tires. Once, I got a car almost out of the airport, until both front tires went flat.

—The most difficult car to steal is a Saab. Of the 8000 cars I stole, only one was a Saab. To me, they're the ugliest things, but they're hard to steal. The only way you can lock and unlock the door is with a key. I had to force the window down and crawl in.

—Manufacturers could move buttons from the top of the door where they're accessible to the door handle. Also, they could weld a shield over the latch mechanism inside the door frame so it can't be tripped by someone outside the car.

Source: The *Boston Globe*, Nov. 25, 1978. Reprinted courtesy of the Boston Globe.

Walter C. Reckless has suggested that it is more difficult to understand why some people quit or drop out of their criminal careers than it is to explain why they continue. It may be that illegitimate opportunities are as limited as legitimate ones. Or, it may be that a criminal runs a greater risk of apprehension while on parole, because he may be picked up on suspicion following a serious crime in his vicinity.[53] A family can also be a deterrent. Tom, the ex-gang leader, asked if he'd be thieving were he not on parole, replied: "I wouldn't be thieving because you know I got a family.... The guys you're talking about they ain't got no families, or they don't care, so they're thieves, man."[54]

Most gang boys end their delinquent careers by getting jobs and getting married. However, some go to prison, some get killed, and some hang around on the fringes of the underworld. Apparently, most end up with conventional jobs, at least in "good times"—perhaps not so much by choice, but because illegitimate opportunities are neither that numerous nor that good.[55]

Affiliational Aspects of Commonplace Crime Patterns

Commonplace criminals most often are products of the urban slums and ghettos where juvenile gangs persist. Nearly one-third of the property offenses committed in 1975 occurred in cities with populations over 250,000, and 70 percent took place in cities with over 100,000 people. It has been more than a decade since the President's Crime Commission, writing on crime and the inner city, reported:

> One of the most fully documented facts about crime is that the common serious crimes that worry people most... happen most often in the slums of the large cities. Study after study in city after city, in all regions of the country have traced the variations in the rates for these crimes. The results, with monotonous regularity, show that the offenses, the victims, and the offenders are found most frequently in the poorest, and most deteriorated and socially disorganized areas of cities.[56]

Bernard Rosenberg and Harry Silverstein's study of slum areas in three different cities found:

> Nearly every youngster on the slum block, whether in New York, Washington, or Chicago (with but few conspicuous exceptions) does develop some kind of larceny sense. In all probability, while still quite young, he will learn to steal, and he will learn what the risks are—including when, where and how not to go too far....
>
> The impulse to appropriate things is identical in all three cities; similar factors heighten or dampen it; but specific urgencies and opportunities are at work in each case.[57]

Slums do vary, but as John Allen pointed out, each is a subsystem that operates within itself. Hustling is its ethos—trying to "make it" by numbers running, selling narcotics or stolen goods, prostitution, or any means other than conventional work. He claimed that in his slum, every family had a daughter who was bootlegging or a son who was stealing, an uncle who ran numbers or even a grandmother who wrote numbers.[58] The slum ghetto is a demiworld, a subculture with its own norms and values. Slum dwellers—adults as well as children—often are alienated from the power structure of the "outside" world and from its institutions of education and social control. Although they prey upon each other, the economy of the slum is such that there is not much to steal.[59] Even commonplace criminals prefer to steal from those who have something worth taking. Consequently, burglary is increasing at a faster rate in the suburban fringes of our major cities, an increase of 7 percent between 1974 and 1975, compared with 4 percent in cities of over 250,000 in population.

The commonplace criminal apparently gains support for his or her illegal behavior through interaction with delinquent gangs in the urban slum or in smaller communities with delinquent peers. This delinquent peer group structure provides social rewards. It can confer a reputation for prowess in fighting or delinquent acts and provide a means of fulfilling the need for belonging.

One series of studies used detached street workers to keep records of the day-to-day delinquent and conventional behavior of six hundred gang members in Chicago. These data suggest that most of the boys were involved in a variety of illegal and conventional activities, rather than in a narrow pattern of delinquent acts. Gang delinquency takes a variety of forms, both in types of gang organizations and activities. A greater degree of violence may be more typical of gangs in the slums of larger cities than gangs in small towns or rural areas. The diversity and variations in delinquent peer groups are reflected in the variation and nonspecialized nature of commonplace crime.[60]

Research studies have identified several types of property offenders, which we have grouped here under the term, "commonplace criminal." One study

All slums and slum ghettos are not the same—each is a subsystem.

found that about half of those involved in bank robberies were amateurs. But neither official statistics nor the media make a distinction between a "professional" caper and an "amateur" effort. Here is how one career criminal reacted when asked whether it is true that the number of bank robberies has increased:

> Well, the number... in the sense of going in with a note has certainly increased,... but when you take away all—all those with a note, or who are drunk—there was a drunk convicted yesterday, wasn't there?... yeh—2.5 reading! I mean 2.5—you're in bad shape!... He went in with a note. Here's a—there's a bank robbery, I mean you know, on the sheet.[61]

In other words, those who push notes through a bank teller's window are not considered bank robbers by experienced or career criminals. In Conklin's study of robbers in the Boston area, he identifies three types of noncareer robbers in addition to the professional. These are the opportunist, the addict, and the alcoholic.[62] In an earlier investigation of the social characteristics of "antisocial" inmates—"right guys" in prisoner argot—Clarence Schrag et al. found that they tended to be recidivists whose careers in crime started with truancy and petty theft and that they associated with other delinquents or siblings involved in criminal offenses. Although they might have grown up in intact, stable families, the family was usually at a low socioeconomic level, and its members tended to be involved in illegal activities.[63] But not all noncareer criminals have known delinquent backgrounds. Moreover, most youths who have delinquent records do not become involved in a career of commonplace crime. As mentioned earlier, most juvenile delinquents stop their illegal activity by the time they reach early adulthood.[64]

Convergence of Conventional and Criminal Behavior Patterns

Matza suggests that since teenage culture consists of activities indulged in for fun and "kicks," it may be seen as a conventional version of subcultural delinquency.[65] Literature on the youth phase of the life cycle tends to support this argument. The transition from adolescence to adulthood is a period of increased dependence on and sensitivity to the demands of peers and peer groups along with a diminished responsiveness to parental expectations. A convergence between delinquent and conventional activities can be seen in the changing structural aspects of teenage social life.

One aspect involves the tension created by increased autonomy with continued partial dependence upon adults. Adolescents have become an important consumer market, and they often rely on adult subsidies to buy the many items—clothes, radios, or records—considered so important by teenagers. In the past, when parents were unable or refused to underwrite these expenses, a teenager might turn to part-time or even full-time employment. In recent years, however, the percentage of gainfully employed workers in the ten- to fifteen-year-age bracket has declined. This decline has been especially obvious among black teenagers, whose participation in the labor force declined from

67.8 percent to 34.7 percent between 1951 and 1973. The participation of white teenagers in the labor force has remained at about 63 percent. During the recession of the 1970s, teenage unemployment in the sixteen- to nineteen-year-age group increased to about 20 percent, while the rate for black teenagers in the same age bracket was over twice that figure.[66]

The peer group subculture of teenagers places a high premium on popularity and self-esteem. This may come from school achievement and/or an adequate relationship with family and peers. Strain may be experienced most by those teenagers lacking in popularity and self-esteem. There is considerable evidence that unpopular boys are more prone to delinquent behavior and that delinquents generally have poor relations both with parents and peers. The case of Eric Monroe (see Box 2) shows that even popularity is not enough. He moved from the lifestyle of star athlete into a career of commonplace crime.

It should not be surprising that adolescent theft often is related in an instrumental way to the peer group's leisure time social activities. This finding is supported not only by studies in this country, but also by cross-national studies of urban gangs and individuals in Western Europe, Argentina, Israel, and Taiwan. Unemployed or underemployed male youths were found to steal to provide for their group-centered social life.[67]

As David Greenberg points out, self-report studies of middle-class delinquency confirm this finding. He found that for both boys and girls there was a correlation between status offenses, such as drinking and curfew violations, and property offenses—burglary, shoplifting, robbery, and so forth—all of which were motivated by a need to provide money for peer group social activities. He noted, however, that theft by boys and girls takes different forms. Boys apparently have a greater need for money to spend on dates. They are more apt to burglarize homes seeking money or goods that can be sold. Girls are more likely to steal items for personal use. Both boys and girls steal to maintain their position in their peer-oriented social life.[68]

Status is not only a matter of importance for adolescents in delinquent gangs, it is a felt need of all adolescents. However, youths in higher-status levels of society may have families both able and willing to subsidize their activities. This means that middle-class juveniles who resort to law-violating behavior may be more concerned with peer status than with family acceptance. However, such conduct may also be a means of expressing their discontent with the relatively powerless social position they occupy compared with their aspirations to be seen and treated as "adults." Juveniles from lower socioeconomic status levels may not only yield to pressures to commit illegal acts, but also may be more vulnerable to apprehension and subsequent processing and labeling by agencies of social control.

Societal Reaction and Definition of Criminality

Typical commonplace crimes—crimes against property—cost an estimated $5.11 billion in 1976, or slightly less than one-eighth the cost of professional crime and about one-ninth the cost of white-collar crime. So the severe

BOX 2

Basketball, Drugs, and the Black Schoolboy

Many lower-class youths unrealistically view sports as a means of escaping the ghetto.

By ERIC MONROE

A friend recently sent me Walt Frazier's views on the black athlete, the black child and the media's glamorization of sports. It brought back memories of my boyhood as a black athlete.

When I was a kid I used to play basketball, from sunup to sundown seven days a week, and get high on drugs. Although I wanted to become a lawyer, my family and friends just knew I was going to be the next Walt Frazier or Earl (the Pearl) Monroe.

I could throw the basketball in the hoop at will. As a baseball player, I was offered a tryout with the New York Yankees. During my adolescence, basketball, baseball and drugs were my life.

But I realized at an early age that the black man's ticket out of the ghetto was by entertaining America with his artistic or athletic talents.

As a result, black communities have distorted priorities. Instead of seeing sports as part of education, the black community often considers education subordinate to sports.

Subsequently, when the black child goes to school, sports is a major part of his education. If a black youth sees basketball, for example, as a vehicle for getting out of the ghetto, he's going to try to master the game.

Getting High in High School

Because I saw sports as the primary avenue to black success, my education suffered. I was deeply engrossed in basketball while my classmates were equally engrossed in algebra. After school, I would stay on the basketball court till way past dark.

I won't say I had no interest in academic studies; it was just that I enjoyed playing basketball more than studying. In school, I was labeled as a superb athlete and sharp dresser, and I felt I had to live up to my reputation.

Whenever I stepped on the court for a game, I would razzle-dazzle the fans with my flamboyant moves and majestic touch. The lights, the flashing figures on the electronic scoreboard and the roar of the fans would catapult me into exhilaration.

The effect is climactic when the individual player finds the crowd screaming his name every time he scores or steals the ball. The intensity of the atmosphere is almost maddening.

But I felt distressed because I knew that scholastically I was not where I should be. I also realized that sports and drugs pacify one's consciousness, and so I passed my high school years basking in the glow of my athletic success or blowing my mind on dope.

The school administration considered me a promising black athlete. So when the guidance counselor arranged my school program, I was always steered into nonacademic subjects.

I was always well supplied with gym classes and study periods I could cut to play basketball and get high, but biology, mathematics and language courses were extremely difficult to come by. Fortunately, I was semiconscious of the way athletics were trapping me and periodically maneuvered my way into taking worthwhile subjects.

As graduation neared, I considered the possibility of playing basketball professionally. However, drugs, particularly heroin, and sports eventually became incompatible.

As a youth growing up around black pimps, gangsters, numbers runners and dope pushers, I was infatuated with their way of life—the custom-made Cadillac, finest clothes, the flashy rings, watches and wad of money. A dude in school could not afford this style of life.

So at the age of 18 I tried my luck at life on the street. With the friends I'd grown up with, I began to tote a pistol. Holding up supermarkets, construction firms and small corporations became our means of support.

Robbing and Pushing

Now able to accumulate more money in a few minutes than the average black could earn in a month, we began to experiment with traffic in drugs. By the age of 20 I divided the bulk of my time playing basketball, committing armed robberies, selling or pushing heroin and shooting up.

By then, drugs and money had taken precedence over everything else. But I was still attending school because inside I wanted out of this degenerate way of life.

Eventually, I reached the point where graduation from high school seemed a reality. But there were obstacles to applying to college. Academically, I was in a terrible position. My graduation average was 65.14. Of the 350 students in my graduating class, I was No. 349. At that time, as liberal as higher education was, not too many colleges would take a chance on me. And open enrollment was unheard of.

Another deterrent to a college education was my financial situation. One problem with stealing was that the money went as fast as it came, so I was usually broke. Somehow, I had the audacity to apply to Harvard for admission with an academic scholarship, but my poor high school grades foiled me.

By now, though my basketball game had diminished significantly, I still could have obtained an athletic scholarship to a rinky-dink college, but none appeared appetizing. And I did not relish the image of a brainless jock. Later in life, however, I was classified as something worse— a junkie, a dope fiend.

So, the way it looks from here, Walt Frazier is right. The black community should put achievement first and put athletic achievement in perspective for its youth because, as my life shows, the barriers in a young black athlete's path to a good education are monumental and relentless.

* * *

Eric Monroe grew up in South Jamaica, Queens, and was graduated from Richmond Hill High School. In 1974, while a student at Queens College, he was arrested on charges of attempted murder, assault, robbery and possession of a revolver. He pleaded guilty to two lesser counts and was sentenced to four years in the Auburn (N.Y.) Correctional Facility, where he is now confined.

Source: *New York Times*, Oct. 2, 1977. © 1977 by The New York Times Company. Reprinted by permission.

societal reaction against commonplace criminals cannot be explained in terms of the value Americans place upon private property. The fact that these offenders are punished more severely than white-collar offenders may simply reflect American political reality. The stringent laws protecting property holders against thievery reveal disproportionate power in the formulation and administration of criminal laws.[69] The manner in which the criminal law defines the behavior of the commonplace criminal is significant in understanding how some youthful offenders move into adult crime.

Gang boys face a high probability of apprehension due to their visibility in their neighborhoods. Official response and processing of commonplace offenders may mean recurrent arrests and convictions. The resulting sanctions may mean fines, probation, and imprisonment. Future earning power is affected by increased difficulty in obtaining a conventional job. And the stigma of having "served time," regardless of the severity of the offense, means that the offender is a criminal in the eyes of the law and is now alienated from society. These societal reactions may be a factor in explaining why some youthful offenders move on into adult criminal activity.[70]

Perhaps the low clearance rate for property offenses counters the process of developing a criminal identity. In 1975, according to national data, less than one out of every six auto thefts and burglaries resulted in clearance by arrest. Since most autos are stolen for joyriding, and only about 25 percent for resale or stripping of parts, most are recovered. Slightly less than one-third of reported robberies are cleared by arrests. It is worth noting that 36 percent of those arrested for robbery, 56.5 percent of the arrests for burglary, and 62.5 percent of the arrests for motor vehicle theft were referred to juvenile courts in 1975. The offenders were too young to be charged in the criminal courts.[71]

Since property crimes such as burglary and larceny/theft are crimes involving stealth, it is understandable why the clearance rate is low. Robbery is a different matter. A study of robbery in Boston found that most robbers who are arrested are picked up within a few days of their crime, usually at or near the scene. About 56 percent of those arrested for robbery in 1968 were convicted for that offense, while others were convicted on reduced charges in lower courts. This is a higher percentage than the national conviction rate, which was just above one-fourth (26.7 percent) in 1975. A number of factors determine whether a suspect will be found guilty or innocent. Among these are the type of lawyer (private or public defender), whether he is released on bail, the type of robbery for which he is accused, and the manner of his arrest.

The median amount of money stolen in both 1964 and 1968 in the Boston robberies was less than $50. Median, the reader might recall, is the midpoint in a series of values and is not directly comparable with the mean or average. Obviously, robbery is not a very profitable offense.[72] On a national basis, the average loss was $331 for each robbery.

Burglary, larceny/theft, and motor vehicle—the other three index offenses—according to FBI data accounted for 91 percent of all serious crimes in 1975. They also involved 80 percent of the arrests for all serious crimes that year. Larceny/theft was the most common, representing 53 percent of all offenses and 52 percent of all arrests for index crimes in 1975. The average loss due to larceny/theft was $166. Burglary was involved in 29 percent of all index crimes and 22 percent of all arrests. The average loss was $422. Nationally, 85 percent of those arrested for this crime in 1975 were under twenty-five, and 63 percent were under eighteen. The largest proportion of arrests for larceny/theft is among those who are under twenty-five. This age group accounts for about 76 percent of the arrests for larceny and 85 percent of those for auto theft.

The extent to which commonplace criminals move on to career crime seems to depend on the degree to which they take on the identity and perspective of career criminals. One factor influencing their decision may be societal reaction to their earlier behavior. Fortunately, in spite of society's ineffective intervention programs, more potential criminals emerge from delinquent groups in lower-status urban situations than can be recruited or absorbed into career criminal behavior systems.[73] Although they may be available for criminal careers, limited criminal opportunities and lack of skills prevent most of them from adopting a life of crime. They drop out of crime or move in and out of the criminal justice system as "losers" or "disorganized criminals." They are the types on whom much of the system's control efforts are expended.

SUMMARY

We have described two types of noncareer criminal behavior systems: the *avocational or occasional criminal* and the *commonplace or traditional criminal*. Both are involved in theft or property offenses that include naive check forgery, shoplifting, joyriding, vandalism, robbery, burglary, larceny/theft, and motor vehicle theft.

Avocational crimes typically involve the first four of these offenses. Since the careers of avocational offenders do not require an identification with crime, a criminal self-concept, or group support, this type may be considered at the opposite pole from career criminals. Commonplace or traditional criminals tend to be involved in heavier property crimes—the last four noted above. They identify with crime, but tend to vacillate in their self-concept relative to it, and they lack the skill and organizational techniques of experienced career criminals. This criminal behavior system represents a lower level on the scale of career crime.

Avocational criminals are occasional, episodic offenders whose behavior converges with everyday patterns in contemporary society. They choose criminal behavior either as a result of economic crises, as in the case of naive check forgery, or in a search for "kicks" or excitement, as in the case of joyriding or vandalism. They tend to neutralize their guilt about their criminal or delinquent behavior and often are treated as first offenders when caught. Commonplace criminals are nonspecialized and inexperienced offenders, who often first become involved in deviant acts as members of delinquent gangs.

Although they share this background with some types of career criminals, they frequently stop their criminal activity by the time they reach early adulthood. Many property offenses are age-specific, committed chiefly by youths under eighteen. In the case of robbery, however, withdrawal from criminal activity happens at a later age.

Commonplace criminals tend to become enmeshed in their activity in response to a criminogenic environment. Societal reaction tends to come down hard on these offenders, since they are visible members of groups involved in law-violating activity. They represent a considerable volume both of offenses reported and arrests. Yet only about 20 percent of these offenses are cleared by arrests. Apparently, many commonplace criminals mature out or desist after a series of youthful offenses. Still, they are overrepresented in arrest statistics and comprise the majority of those who jam the courts and crowd jails and prisons. Commonplace criminals are generally those whom society has in mind when references are made to the crime problem. But in terms of the total cost of crime, they represent only a small fraction. It is the commonplace criminals who typically are seen as the "bad guys," rather than the less visible professional and white-collar offenders.

ADDITIONAL READINGS

Clinard, Marshall B. and Richard Quinney. *Criminal Behavior Systems, A Typology.* 2nd ed. New York: Holt, Rinehart and Winston, 1973.

>Chapters 3 and 5 describe the criminal behavior of the occasional and conventional criminal in terms of criminal career, group support, criminal and conventional relationships, and societal reaction.

Conklin, John E. *Robbery and the Criminal Justice System.* Philadelphia: Lippincott, 1972.

>This report of exploratory research on robbery in the Boston area treats robbery as a total behavior system. The author also describes how police, courts, and correctional aspects of the criminal justice system respond to this type of offense.

Denfeld, Duane. *Street-Wise Criminology.* Cambridge, Mass.: Schenkman, 1974.

>This book provides an inside view of criminal behavior systems by having semi-professional and career criminals speak for themselves. The first-person accounts provide insights into the perspectives, methods, and activities of "street-wise" criminals.

Greenberg, David F. "Delinquency and the Age Structure of Society." *Contemporary Crises* 1, no. 2, 1977:189–23.

>This exhaustive article presents an analysis of the age distribution of involvement in crime, and shows the disproportionate number of juveniles in major property offenses. Greenberg relates this involvement to the changing position of juveniles in industrial society.

Letkemann, Peter. *Crime as Work.* Englewood Cliffs, N.J.: Prentice-Hall, 1973.

>This book examines the work habits of experienced criminals not involved in organized crime. The book is based on interviews conducted inside and outside of prison. The author contrasts the work of amateur and experienced criminals and examines their work patterns.

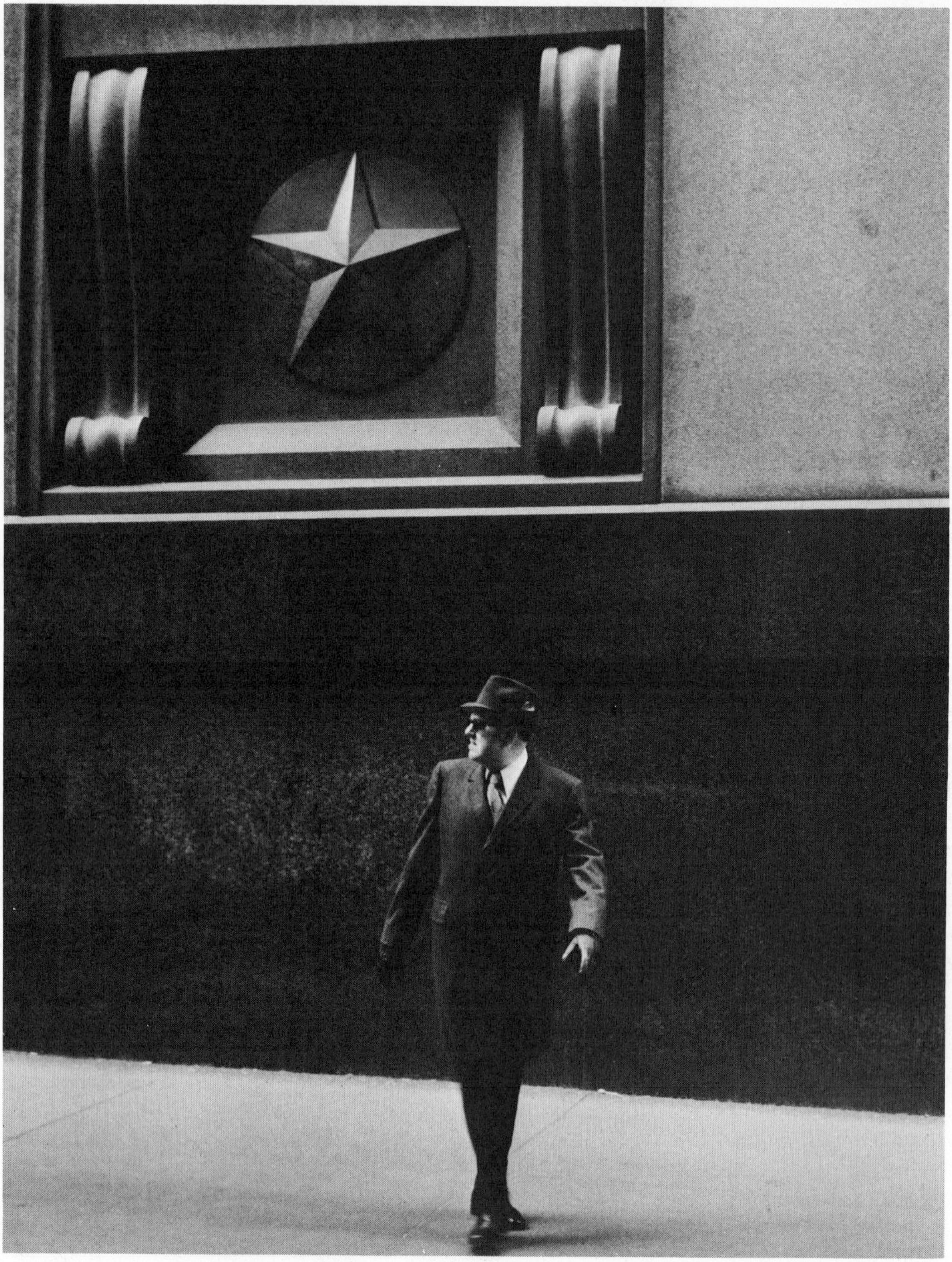

Crime is the logical extension of the sort of behavior that is often considered perfectly respectable in legitimate business.
—Robert Rice, The Business of Crime

10

WHITE-COLLAR CRIME PATTERNS

White-collar crime is the crime committed by "respectable" people—the bankers, the doctors, the corporate executives, and as we learned through the trauma of Watergate, even the men in the White House. White-collar crime represents a major factor in the price society pays for those who choose to break the law.

The white-collar criminal has many faces. He is the doctor or pharmacist who pads medical fees. He is the company president fixing prices with competitors. He is the city employee who takes bribes and the contractor who pays them. He is the FBI agent who installs an illegal wiretap and the manufacturer who installs an illegal smokestack.

Often, those who commit white-collar crimes do not regard their behavior as improper. In the business world, it can be a matter of "everybody doing it." White-collar criminals rationalize away much of their sense of wrongdoing. The slumlord will argue he is just looking for a "fair return" while he violates the law. The bank embezzler will argue she is just "borrowing" the money. The CIA operative will say his illegal actions are in the interest of "national security."

These avocational crimes are committed by persons of "respectability and high social status" in the course of their regular occupation, as Edwin H. Sutherland noted when he coined the phrase.[1] Consequently, such crime patterns are characterized by the lack of an identifiable crime career or acknowledged criminal self-concept, since the offenses are committed by persons who think of themselves as honest and law abiding. These criminals gain most of their income and prestige from association with others of similar respectability and high status with whom they profess to share values such as honesty, accountability, and concern for the public good. Further, the ambivalence with which such crimes are viewed by citizens as well as offenders means that they may be dismissed as trivial. The political, financial, and social importance of those involved, together with the difficulty of securing evidence and the fact that they often are dealt with by special administrative regulatory agencies rather than by criminal courts, makes it difficult to prosecute them or even to ascertain the extent of such offenses.[2] Violent crimes and publicized thefts of private property invariably are condemned by the public. But in the case of white-collar crime, even criminologists lack a consensus on the definition of the term.

THE MEANING AND SCOPE OF WHITE-COLLAR CRIME

The attention now being given to the offenses of conventional, respectable individuals suggests something both about the changing perspectives of criminology and the changing values of society. There has been a move away from a focus solely upon the law violations highlighted in official data to one which views criminal phenomena in relation to the wider social context. The term "white-collar crime" itself is a loosely defined concept attached to a wide range of illegal actions by "respectable" persons, usually of high socioeconomic status. It has been used rather indiscriminately to refer to actions of those who use their positions of trust to embezzle from their employer, who promote illegal corporate actions in restraint of trade, or who engage in illegal unprofessional conduct and misuse of power for personal gain.

The introduction of the concept by Edwin H. Sutherland more than four decades ago was an attempt both to confront the dilemma of definition and broaden the field of study of criminology. Sutherland felt that the field was focused too narrowly upon the personal and social pathologies of the lower classes. In advancing his theory of *differential association,* Sutherland drew some ironic comparisons between the upper-class corporate law violator and the lower-class criminal. He prefaced his presidential address to the American Sociological Society in 1939 with the statement that he was neither "muckraking" nor seeking to reform anything except criminology. Gilbert Geis has suggested that this was a rather disingenuous way of fulfilling his obligation to "scientific sociology," for that professional organization was trying to disaffiliate itself from its prior social pathological or reformist orientation.[3] In his address, Sutherland ambitiously sought to advance a theory that would explain all crime. Nine years later, in yet another address, he was to note with a bit of irony:

> It is very clear that the criminal behavior of businessmen cannot be explained by poverty, in the usual sense, or by bad housing or lack of recreational facilities or feeblemindedness or emotional instability. Business leaders are capable, emotionally balanced, and in no sense pathological. We have no reason to think that General Motors has an inferiority complex or that the Aluminum Company of America has a frustration-aggression complex or that U.S. Steel has an Oedipus complex or that the Armour Company has a

death wish or that the DuPonts desire to return to the womb. The assumption that an offender must have some such pathological distortion . . . seems to me absurd, and if it is absurd regarding the crimes of businessmen, it is equally absurd regarding the crimes of persons in the lower economic class.[4]

Sutherland used a clever rhetorical device, for no serious scholar had suggested that business and corporate officials suffered from inferiority complexes or that traditional criminals are completely pathological. Sutherland's investigations, published in *White-Collar Crime* (1949), sought to advance his concept of "differential association" as a substitute for conventional theories. His theory emphasized that white-collar offenses, professional criminal offenses, and traditional crimes are all learned behaviors. In expanding the scope of criminology by defining white-collar crime as "a crime committed by a person of respectability and high social status in the course of his occupation," he stimulated a flurry of research.

But the term, "white collar crime," remains too vague to be useful, at least in a legal sense.[5] Sutherland's main concern with the sociology of law was to focus upon the differential treatment afforded to such "respectable" offenders by the judicial system. Consequently, it has been argued that he slighted the legal aspects of white-collar crime by emphasizing questions like, Why do certain individuals commit such offenses? In *White-Collar Crime*, for example, how a shoe salesman learned to be an offender through the process of differential association is described in detail.[6] Sutherland was not a radical, but rather he stood in the muckraking tradition, his denial notwithstanding. He was more critical of the white-collar criminal than he was of the political-economic institutions that buttressed the market system that provided the structure within which they operated.

Some interesting parallels have been drawn by Geis between the criticism of American corporate practices by Ralph Nader and his associates over the past decade and the earlier work of Sutherland. Nader feels no obligation to develop theoretical perspectives, scorning such activity by referring to "the leisure of the theory class." But both were opposed to the trend toward "corporate socialism." Nader is also concerned that citizens be informed concerning the misuse of power by business, politicians, and professions.[7] However, unlike Nader, Sutherland's emphasis was on developing a theory to explain all crime, and he took a more detached posture than does Nader in his advocacy of severe penalties for white-collar criminals.

Although the term has been used rather loosely, especially by journalists in the mass media, white-collar crime has come to connote those *offenses committed by offenders acting in their occupational roles.* Namely, these are *offenders who are businessmen or members of the professions who violate trust placed in them or deviate from the legitimate expectations of their everyday occupational activities.* Although in a technical sense the deviation or violation is the crucial aspect of this definition, the type of law violated and the lack of visibility of the offense due to the offender's relative prestige in the community have come to be the focus of much of the controversy in writings about white-collar crime.[8] White-collar offenders typically are in positions of community leadership: attorneys, physicians, business owners or managers, bank officials, and the like.

Some recent writers have expanded the original definition of "respectable" members of the community to include those who deviate from the law in a variety of other occupations. Donald J. Newman, for instance, suggested that dairymen and television repairmen, among others in non-white-collar occupations, might be termed white-collar offenders when they indulge in practices such as diluting milk or doing unneeded repairs on television sets.[9] And Marshall B. Clinard, in his research on black market activities during World War II, included all violators regardless of their occupational level.[10] The concept has been expanded further by Richard Quinney to encompass the idea of "occupational crime," which includes all violations occurring within any legitimate occupational role.[11] In a more recent classification, Clinard and Quinney have used the term "corporate crime."

The concept of white-collar crime used here is the expanded connotation adapted from Clinard and Quinney. It extends to governmental or political crime and includes bribery and corruption among high-ranking government officials as well as actions by government agencies that result in the curtailment of the rights of citizens.[12] These crimes came into recent focus with disclosures of illegal activities by the CIA and FBI in the post-Watergate period.

TYPES OF WHITE-COLLAR CRIME PATTERNS

The ambiguity and multidimensional nature of white-collar crime might be illustrated by the following sampling of newspaper headlines from 1972 to 1978:

> Cotton Mills Resist Cost of Curbing Dust. Ex-CIA Head Pleads No Contest to Charge Linked to Testimony. Ex-Officer Indicted for Cheating Firestone in Funds. Jersey State Senator Is Indicted in Conspiracy to Protect Gambling. Two Jersey Brothers Are Indicted in $8 Million Insurance Fraud. Former Bank Aide and 2 Others Guilty in $1 Million Fraud. 22 Seized in Boston Arson Conspiracy. Illegal Use of Files Laid to Doctor. Ex-Bank Head Admits Fraud. FBI Admits It Opened Mail in 8 Cities in Illegal Program Parallel to that of CIA. Dean Says Nixon Misled the Nation with Watergate Denials. ITT Made Multimillion-Dollar Payoffs Abroad and to Customers, SEC Charges. U.S. Probes Banks' Actions Involving Trading in Dollars. Firestone Recall on Its 500 Tires Will Begin Soon. Westinghouse Agrees to Plead Guilty on Payoffs. Two Firms Accused of Conspiring to Fix Price of Gas Meters.

Unlike conventional crimes, white-collar offenses may not be defined in the criminal codes, for their definitions are in civil laws and in the laws of administrative regulatory agencies. This means that legal processing is frequently

Arson

BOX 1

Arson sometimes involves convergence between upperworld and underworld crime patterns.

By CLIFFORD L. KARCHMER

SEATTLE—Arson is, by all available data, the nation's fastest growing crime problem.

Despite an unprecedented epidemic of arson, there is no national campaign to control a threat to life and property that, in 1976, accounted for $2 billion in property losses, claimed 1,000 lives and continued a 25 percent rate of increase per year. Fewer than one arson in a hundred results in conviction. No other crime problem has been met with such an ineffective response.

Investigators know arson as a collection of disparate motives: pyromania, revenge, vandalism, concealing of crime, and fraud. It is also a barometer of more serious and deeply rooted social and economic ills but, like drug addiction and political terrorism, it is a pernicious symptom that must be confronted in its own right. Although our society has ineffective deterrents for crimes of passion and nihilism, we have seen that crimes of stealth and planning are sensitive to well-planned, selective enforcement. Arson committed for insurance proceeds is one such example. And the deterrent potential of intensive enforcement, in these cases, is still untested.

Police, fire, and insurance investigators who study the insurance motive find that arson is the hub of elaborate schemes involving fraudulent real-estate, bank, and insurance transactions. Arson unites diverse crime specialists. Torches are recruited from the ranks of street criminals. Fences from the underworld of theft arrange the discounted sale of merchandise that will falsely be claimed as destroyed in the fires. Crooked realtors and public insurance adjustors lay the groundwork for intricate insurance frauds. Syndicate hoodlums use arson to collect bad loan-shark debts and get rid of sour mob investments. Arson-for-profit is a curious hybrid—it is the only organized white-collar crime kicked off by a violent offense.

At the core of most arson rings is the fire-broker, a new kind of racketeer. Prosecutions in Detroit, Pittsburgh, Boston and elsewhere confirm his emergence. He searches out financially troubled businesses, then convenes the mix of arson specialists needed for each fire—the chemists, bombers, torches, corrupt investigators, and allied white-collar criminals. For potential clients who need convincing, the fire-broker assembles a package of arson and insurance fraud that he markets aggressively. For his trouble the fire-broker takes a percentage of the insurance settlement.

Most fire-brokers are con artists who advanced from simpler white-collar crimes before discovering the windfall profits in arson fraud, a racket involving similar uses of rigged books, doctored invoices, and hidden ownership.

This nexus of crime often escapes the watchful eye of white-collar and organized-crime task forces, usually concerned with traditional forms of fraud and racketeering. Consequently, arson rings prosper within this law enforcement vacuum.

To officials, investment of scarce resources in arson control produces few results; therefore, it constitutes an imprudent risk.

To the arsonist the risks are negligible and profits enormous. Largely by default, the official response in most communities is one noted for retreat in the face of arson's growing momentum.

Clearly arson-for-profit qualifies as a national crisis. An agenda for action begins with the solid Federal commitment to address a problem far exceeding state and local capabilities. Federal investigative resources could identify and interdict arson rings at their early stages. To break the back of financial arson, legal tools that attack criminal enterprises must be utilized more widely. The Federal Racketeer Influence and Corrupt Organizations Law is one remedy successfully used. This law also provides that racketeering victims such as insurance companies can sue for treble damages. We must remove the insurance incentive that feeds arson. Widespread changes are needed in underwriting and cancellation practices, and in privacy laws now prohibiting information exchanges between insurance industry and law enforcement agencies. Finally, police and fire departments must be trained in all areas of arson enforcement, and primarily in the investigation of arson as white-collar crime.

Source: *New York Times*, Aug. 7, 1978. © 1978 by The New York Times Company. Reprinted by permission.

carried out in civil or administrative rather than criminal courts. In Sutherland's study of 980 violations involving 70 large corporations, only 16 percent were adjudicated by criminal proceedings. Another 43 percent were decided by civil courts, while 41 percent were resolved through administrative actions.[13] Still, it might be well to remember that it is the law, rather than the occupation of the offender, that defines a given behavior as criminal or noncriminal.

A further distinction between white-collar and conventional crime concerns the social status of the offender and the social setting in which white-collar offenses typically occur. The offense often is committed by a person of respectability and high status in the regular conduct of his occupation or profession, but the offense is not a legitimate activity within that occupation or profession. Thus, one writer has suggested that such offenses are "avocational" crimes. These crimes share three common conditions: (1) they are committed by individuals who do not consider themselves criminals; (2) the offenders' livelihood and social status derive from noncriminal activities; and (3) social control efforts which publicly name the offender may deter the continuation of such behavior.[14] The white-collar criminal behavior patterns we shall describe might well be seen as avocational. None of the three types mentioned—occupational, corporate, or official—are activities in which crime is the main concern or central activity of the actors involved.[15]

The first typology is the *occupational* criminal behavior pattern. It includes two general kinds of offenses: (1) crimes committed by persons in the pursuit of their occupational or professional activities, and (2) crimes committed by persons against their corporate employer by virtue of having a position of trust within that organization. The second general typology is the *corporate* criminal behavior pattern. This category comprises a variety of offenses including those committed by (1) corporate officials for their employer, (2) representatives of the corporation against the general welfare, and (3) businesses against the legitimate rights of consumers. The *official* crime behavior pattern constitutes the third typology. It refers to offenses committed by agents of the state by the unwarranted exercise of power or intentional misperformance or neglect of duty in a way that violates the civil rights of citizens. The focus in this typology is on crimes by government officials, not crimes against government.[16]

Occupational White-Collar Crime

Studies of occupational crime patterns have focused on offenses of business and government employees, attorneys, and physicians. Physicians, for example, have been indicted for *fee splitting,* a form of kickback in which one physician pays part of his fee to the doctor who referred the patient to him. Fee splitting is illegal in twenty-three states. Since Medicaid and Medicare came into being as a means of paying for health care for low-income families, there have been new patterns of health-care fraud. Among these patterns are *family ganging,* in which entire families are given assembly-line care, and *ping ponging,* in which the Medicare patient is referred from one specialist to another. Double billing for Medicare, another white-collar crime, cost the state of New York alone some $60 million between 1973 and 1977. Still another white-collar crime is the prescribing of illegal drugs.[17]

Attorneys have been convicted of misappropriating trust funds or becoming involved in fraudulent schemes to collect damages from insurance companies. With the advent of high pay for professional athletes, some agents have misappropriated the earnings of their clients. One agent stole $1.2 million from fifty professional basketball and hockey players between 1974 and 1977. This action was in violation of a trust and was a misappropriation of funds.[18]

These frauds, as well as embezzlement, a form of occupational crime that usually involves officials of banks or politicians, are committed by people in trusted positions or professions. Officials of two different banks in New Jersey were involved in using over $4 million of bank funds for loan-shark operations. The banks closed in early 1977, and the two officials were subsequently indicted. At the same time in Washington, D.C., the Justice Department was investigating charges that the South Korean government attempted to create a favorable climate in the U.S. Congress by dispensing gifts and cash to members of Congress.[19]

Corporate White-Collar Crime

Political pressures to control big business in the United States grew out of the Populist Movement in the last decades of the nineteenth century. The Sherman Anti-Trust Act (1890) made it a criminal offense to combine business in restraint of trade. The original fine was $5,000 and a maximum of one year imprisonment (the fine was later increased to $50,000). Initial efforts at enforcement were ineffective. During the Progressive era, the Federal Trade Commission was established to regulate unfair methods of competition. Additional legislation was passed to protect the "free economic" tenets of capitalism during the New Deal era. It has been suggested by some historians that these efforts of President Franklin D. Roosevelt helped save American capitalism by ridding it of major abuses and forcing the corporate world to accommodate to the public interest.[20]

For the most part, efforts to regulate big business have not been attacks against corporate business. There is considerable evidence that such legislation has been promoted by corporate interests who stood to gain from a free economy. Sutherland's research identified sixty of the nation's seventy largest corporations with a total of 307 decisions against them for acting in restraint of trade. In other words, he found that big businessmen wanted to have it both ways: They supported the elimination of unfair competition in principle, but violated the law when it served their interest to do so.[21]

Since the passage of the Pure Food and Drug Act in 1906, it has been unlawful to manufacture and distribute adulterated food or drugs. However, this legislation was enacted, as a study by Morton Mintz has shown, after 150 separate pure food and drug laws were introduced into Congress and subsequently defeated between 1880 and 1900. These bills were crushed by an alliance of "ruthless crooks, high-priced lobbyists, vested interests, corrupt members of Congress, . . . the apathetic and the duped." [22] In 1933, an attempt to remedy deficiencies of the 1906 law was attacked by the organization of United Medicine Manufacturers of America. This organized group, with a vested interest in the production of patent medicine, attempted to block the bill with "seventeen plans." These included plans to:[23]

1. "Secure cooperation of newspapers in spreading favorable publicity.
2. Secure the pledge of manufacturers, wholesalers, advertising agencies, and all other interested affiliates to address letters to senators to gain their promise to vote against the bill.
3. Line up with other organizations, such as the Drug Institute, Proprietary Association, National Association of Retail Druggists, to make a mass attack on the bill.
4. Enlist the help of carton, tube, bottle and box manufacturers.
5. Ridicule organizations favoring the bill.
6. Convey by every means available—radio, newspaper, mail, and personal contact—the alarming fact that if the bill is adopted the public will be deprived of the right of self-diagnosis, and self-medication."

Despite these efforts, the public interest prevailed. By the 1960s a small number of bills were passed that sought to regulate the manufacture, advertising, and distribution of food, pharmaceuticals, and cosmetics. These included the Food, Drug and Cosmetic Act (1938), which required more effective means for regulating false labeling and advertising, and the Durham-Humphrey Amendment (1951) which tightened regulations on the dispensing of drugs.

Still, corporate interests seem to be overcome only when there is a highly publicized major crisis that confronts legislators with the need to fulfill their obligation to the public welfare. A case in point was the struggle to pass the Kefauver-Hart Drug Act in 1962. The news media had exposed numerous cases of deformed babies born to women who had taken thalidomide while pregnant. Despite heavy opposition by lobbyists of the large pharmaceutical firms, the act was passed and provided for stricter control of drug testing, labeling, and advertising. But it did not achieve one of its original goals, the regulation of drug pricing.[24] And it is clear that the giant food and drug corporations have continued to exert a great deal of influence over the wording of legislation that is passed.

The Air Quality Control Act of 1967 was thought to be a breakthrough for environmentalists. But lobbyists for corporate interests have made certain that standards were not so restrictive that they lowered profits. The act was so ineffective that in 1970 Ralph Nader wrote:

> Smogging in a city or town has taken on the proportions of a massive crime wave, yet federal and state statistical compilations of crime pay attention to

muggers and ignore smoggers. As a nation which purports to apply law for preserving health, safety, and property, there is a curious permissiveness toward passing and enforcing laws against the primary polluters who harm our society's most valued rights. In testament to the power of corporations and their . . . attorneys, enforcement scarcely exists. Violators are openly flouting the laws and an Administration allegedly dedicated to law and order sits on its duties.[25]

The National Air Quality Standards Act of 1970 has been somewhat more effective, but enforcement of this law and other environmental statutes by the Environmental Protection Agency is only on a selective basis.[26]

Official White-Collar Crime

It is generally argued that most official white-collar crimes—violations of laws regulating the conduct of elected and appointed office holders—comprise two different but related types of behavior: (1) activities that result in economic gain by the officeholder and/or special groups; and (2) activities that perpetuate or enhance their power.[27]

Estimating the extent of official criminal activity by federal, state, and local officeholders can only be mere speculation. However, newspaper accounts, past and current, suggest that corrupt government officials are plentiful. Gaining empirical evidence presents almost insurmountable problems, because political scientists and criminologists generally are "outsiders" to any "deals" that might take place. Furthermore, the organizations and laws intended to regulate official acts are designed and enacted by the very people whose behavior is to be regulated. Small wonder that in our country's first two hundred years of existence only seven senators and eighteen members of the House of Representatives had been censured by their colleagues.[28]

Official white-collar crimes for economic gain both on the local and the national level are not new. Since the early part of this century, when Lincoln Steffens wrote *The Shame of the Cities,* we have accumulated a long catalogue of evidence of corruption in the form of nonfeasance, malfeasance, and misfeasance by local officials. In the 1960s, John Gardiner described the relationships that existed between corrupt officials and the underworld in "Wincanton" (Reading, Pennsylvania). The patterns of offenses were similar to those detailed by Steffens in 1904.[29]

A more specific form of official crime—widespread police corruption—was reported by the Knapp Commission in December 1972. Criminal behavior by the police in New York City was considered by many to be the ordinary pattern for over half of the thirty-thousand-man force. The commission rejected the "rotten apple" theory that claims that the corrupt officer is the exception in an otherwise "clean" organization. Rather it is the organization itself and entrenched criminal patterns in the police force that create the corruption.[30] Apparently, corruption is widespread in other big-city police forces. In October 1973, a group of nineteen Chicago police officers was indicted for extortion after action by the U.S. district attorney. In this case, it was the federal government—not the city, as was the case with New York—that carried out the investigation and prosecution of the police.[31]

Sometimes local officials find that after they have gained national prominence, their former careers of official criminal activity are exposed. This happened to former Vice-President Spiro T. Agnew. While holding the nation's second highest office, investigations in his home state of Maryland revealed that when Agnew was serving as county executive and later as governor, he received "kickbacks" from contractors doing business with county and state governments. In the case of former Federal Judge Otto Kerner, it was revealed that while serving as governor of Illinois he had been involved in a scandal, in which race track stock was given to state legislators in return for their votes.[32]

The Watergate "caper"—an unsuccessful attempt to break into Democratic National Committee headquarters in Washington, D.C., in June 1972—has come to epitomize the abuse of official power to extend and enhance political power. The Watergate investigations revealed to what extent official crime patterns can occur at the highest levels in our government. Although official corruption has been the concern of citizens since the emergence of government, Americans found the Watergate revelations especially shocking, once they overcame their initial skepticism toward Watergate as "politics as usual." The violence done to the civil rights of citizens by the CIA, FBI, and the illegal surveillance by the "White-House-plumbers" unit was clearly unconstitutional. Here is what one news commentator wrote about the corruption of power by President Nixon and his administration in the wake of Watergate:

> What is so striking about the arbitrary acts abroad, is that Mr. Nixon and his aides were never called to account for them as they were for the domestic abuses. I think the reason for that distinction is extremely important to understand.
>
> The United States is dependent on law to control the abuse of official power: more so than any other democratic country....
>
> That was the lesson of Watergate. The sense that he had violated a leader's fundamental obligation to obey the law is what brought Richard Nixon down. It was because the idea was so American that foreigners had difficulty understanding Watergate, and still do....
>
> Without the restraints of law, Presidents moved from primacy to the assertion of unlimited authority in foreign affairs. The extreme was reached with Mr. Nixon, who treated disagreement with his policy as a form of subversion to be repressed by any method that he declared necessary. He introduced to the White House the maxim that Boss Frank Hague used to apply in Jersey City: "I am the law."
>
> And men otherwise committed to law did not challenge lawlessness in foreign affairs. Elliot Richardson insisted that Spiro Agnew be held to account for graft, but he excused an act infinitely more contemptuous of our constitutional system: Mr. Nixon's bombing of Cambodia in 1973 without authority in any treaty, statute, resolution or need to protect American lives. To the extent that President Nixon and those around him seemed to act outside the established law, these actions—in foreign affairs as well as domestic—might be seen as official deviance if not crimes.[33]

A wealth of data has been accumulated about what was first referred to contemptuously as the "third-rate burglary" at Watergate. It provides a unique insight into the manner in which positions of political power and trust can be abused to perpetuate criminal behavior. We have selected a sampling from the numerous reports to illustrate the complexities of official crime group affiliations. The Rockefeller Report on CIA activities (see Box 2) documents the pattern of illegal activities by a secret group within the CIA, set up to gather information on American dissenters under the administrations of two presidents. With the secret support of a small number within the CIA, this group carried on illegal domestic surveillance of these citizens.[34]

Abuses of power and infringement of citizens' rights were also a regular aspect of "official crimes" by the FBI. In October 1975, the deputy associate director of that organization stated that FBI agents regularly opened mail for "national security purposes" between 1940 and 1966. By law the FBI may open mail only when issued a warrant by a federal judge.

Careers and Self-Concepts of White-Collar Criminals

In Sutherland's study of seventy corporations, he drew some interesting and ironic parallels between white-collar and professional criminals. These included the following comparisons:[35]

1. Both types are persistent in their criminality and include a high proportion of recidivists—97.1 percent of the white-collar criminals he studied had two or more adverse decisions.
2. Illegal behavior by both types is more extensive than is indicated by prosecutions and complaints.
3. As with professional criminals, the businessman who violates the laws designed to regulate his business does not customarily lose status among his associates.
4. Businessmen are similar to professional thieves in that they customarily express feelings of contempt for law, government, and enforcement personnel. (Sutherland might have added that both are concerned with economic gain.)

It is necessary to make a distinction that Sutherland glossed over in his study. As Geis has pointed out, Sutherland "humanized" the corporations, describing them as though they were persons and failing to differentiate between corporations and those who managed them. Of course, we are familiar with the idea that corporations are legal entities. But while corporations may be subjected to criminal prosecution and penalized through fines, they obviously cannot be incarcerated as criminals. In criminological analysis, we cannot readily personalize corporations as criminals unless we indulge in the fiction that sees inanimate objects as the focus of punishment. Sutherland's assertion that crimes committed by corporations are the crimes of those who manage them certainly has some validity. But we should also be aware of the inaccu-

BOX 2

Operation CHAOS: The CIA's Special Operations Group

Operation CHAOS carried on illegal domestic surveillance of U.S. citizens.

The Director of the CIA responded to President Johnson's request to ascertain the extent of foreign influence on domestic dissidence when he established a Special Operations Group to collect, coordinate, evaluate and report on foreign contacts with American dissidents in August, 1967.

The stated intent of Operation CHAOS was to determine whether foreign contacts existed with American groups. In the course of six years of operation it accumulated a great deal of material on the activities of domestic dissidents. During this time the Operation compiled over 13,000 different files, among them 7,200 on Americans. This data [sic], including the names of over 300,000 persons were placed in a computerized index file.

The staff of the Operation included 52 individuals who were isolated from any review, even by the Counterintelligence Staff to which they technically belonged. The operation recruited a number of agents beginning in late 1969 to collect information from any foreign contacts abroad. In the course of developing ties with domestic groups they inadvertently collected information which was entered in the Operation's files.

When the CIA repeatedly reported that it found no significant connection between domestic disorder and foreign contacts, the White House staff under two presidents—Johnson and Nixon—made further demands on the CIA to commit additional resources to fill any gaps in the Operation's investigation. These demands led to the addition of resources and they also seem to have encouraged the top CIA directorate to stretch, and in some instances, exceed, legal restrictions against domestic activities by the Agency.

In response to President Johnson's concern

regarding revolutionary youth movements, Director Helms commissioned a report, "Restless Youth," which concluded that the cause of unrest was social and political alienation. One version of this report included a section on domestic involvements which raised a question as to the propriety of its preparation by the CIA. Copies delivered to President Johnson and his special assistant for National Security Affairs had a covering memorandum from the director referring to its sensitive nature. When this report was reissued in 1969, and a copy provided Henry Kissinger—the covering memorandum from the director clearly pointed out the impropriety of the CIA's participation in this report.

In the fall of 1969 Operation CHAOS stepped up its recruitment of agents due to White House pressure, lack of success in gathering information from other agencies and the increase in dissident activities. From late 1969 through 1971 three agents were recruited who had entered into antiwar, radical or militant black groups. These were used for surveillance of domestic groups; one infiltrated the "May Day" demonstrations in Washington, D.C., in the spring of 1971. Such activities were illegal and in direct contravention of guidelines laid down by Director Helms in 1968.

The Operation was considered so sensitive that even the staff of the CIA's Inspector General was prevented access to its files during a field check in 1972.

Operation CHAOS was ended on March 15, 1974 when field stations were instructed to turn over any information uncovered abroad on United States citizens to the FBI. The files and computerized indexed data were still intact during the investigation by the Rockefeller Commission.

The Rockefeller Commission concluded that the isolation of Operation CHAOS within the CIA and its independence from the chain of command within the agency allowed it to stray beyond the Agency's legal authority without senior officials' knowledge. No such warrant was needed until recently for a "mail cover," which permits unopened envelopes to be examined. In November 1978, however, a federal district court ruled the practice unconstitutional in *Paton* v. *LaPrade*. In April 1979, the U.S. Postal Service announced it was "resuming mail covers for the protection of national security." This announcement was made in blatant disregard of the judge's ruling in the *Paton* case: "National security as a basis for the mail cover is unconstitutionally vague and overbroad." [1] Actually, mail covers were never terminated. In October 1975, during the height of the public outcry for the chartering of the CIA and FBI and congressional control over their activities, at least seventy-nine mail covers were in operation.[2]

It was also revealed in September 1975, that FBI agents had committed at least 238 break-ins over a twenty-six-year period against "domestic subversive targets." Documents released by the Senate Select Committee on Intelligence Activities indicate that the FBI took steps to hide and destroy records of these break-ins, since it regarded them as "clearly illegal." Former FBI intelligence chief, Charles D. Brennan, stated that under the FBI's "do-not-file" system, officials of the Bureau could testify in court that no records of such break-ins existed. When asked, "Did the FBI ever get caught?" Brennan answered, "I don't think we did, Senator." He went on to say that the FBI was the finest group of individuals he had ever worked with, adding that the Bureau could benefit from better supervision by Congress.[3] The FBI was the law enforcement agency assigned initially to investigate the Watergate episode. Is it any wonder that the concept of the "rule of law" comes to be seen as empty rhetoric when the national law enforcement agency is an acknowledged law violator?

1. Phil Stamford, "Snooping at the Post Office," *Inquiry*, June 11 and 25, 1978, p. 8.
2. Robert L. Jackson, "FBI Admits It Opened Mail in 8 Cities in Illegal Program Parallel to that of the CIA," in Jack D. Douglas and John M. Johnson, *Official Deviance Readings in Malfeasance, Misfeasance, and Other Forms of Corruption* (Philadelphia: J. B. Lippincott, 1977), pp. 140–41.
3. Robert L. Jackson, "Senate Probers Tell of 238 Break-Ins by FBI Against Subversive Targets," in Douglas and Johnson, *Official Deviance Readings in Malfeasance, Misfeasance and Other Forms of Corruption*, pp. 142–44.

Source: Abstracted from an excerpt of the Rockefeller Report to the President, by the Commission on CIA Activities, 1975, from selections in Jack D. Douglas and John M. Johnson, *Official Deviance: Readings in Malfeasance, Misfeasance and Other Forms of Corruption*, (Philadelphia: J. B. Lippincott, 1977), pp. 121–39.

racy and uncertainty that may result from confusing people with corporations.[36] In the following examples, when we discuss criminal careers or self-concepts, we are alluding to the people who make decisions for the corporations, not the corporations themselves.

The three categories of avocational or white-collar criminals—occupational, corporate, and official—share a similar self-concept. But Sutherland has described how this common self-concept differs from that of conventional offenders. The businessman thinks of himself as a respectable citizen and generally is regarded that way by the public. The professional thief, on the other hand, sees himself as a criminal and takes pride in his reputation.[37]

The noncriminal self-concept is confirmed by a statement of a vice-president of General Electric at the time he was convicted in the Heavy Electrical Equipment Conspiracy Case in 1961: "All of you know that next Monday in Philadelphia, I will start serving a thirty-day jail term along with six other businessmen for conduct which has been *interpreted* as being in conflict with the *complex* antitrust laws." [38] Note how adroitly he sidestepped the effects of being signified and defined as a criminal. He did not say "we are not criminals," but rather affirmed that they were "businessmen." He did not say they had been found guilty of violating the law, but rather that their "conduct" had been "interpreted as being in conflict with ... complex ... laws."

The Heavy Electrical Equipment Case, which has been carefully described by Gilbert Geis, ultimately included twenty indictments that touched forty-five individual defendants and twenty-nine corporations. The federal government had apparently initiated grand jury investigations after receiving information from officials of the Tennessee Valley Authority revealing that identical sealed bids had been submitted by manufacturers of heavy electrical equipment. Included in the so-called "conspiracy" were large manufacturers of electrical equipment like General Electric, Westinghouse, and an array of smaller firms. The defendants were portrayed by one reporter as "middle-class men in Ivy League suits—typical businessmen in appearance who would never be taken for lawbreakers." Their defense attorneys pictured them as "pillars of the community—too fine to put behind bars with common embezzlers." And indeed they were men held in high esteem, including church deacons, a president of a local chamber of commerce, a hospital board member, a Community Chest chief fund raiser, and a director of a Boys Club.

The defendants did not plead "ignorance of the law." It was apparent from the testimony of an executive of the Westinghouse Corporation before a Senate committee that the men were well aware of the illegality of their behavior. When asked whether he knew that meetings with his competitors were illegal, the witness replied: "Illegal? Yes, but not criminal. I didn't find that out until I read the indictment. I assumed that criminal action meant damaging someone, and we did not do that." This theme was reiterated by other witnesses. One admitted that "it is against the law," then added, "I did not know it was against public welfare because I am not certain that the consumer was actually injured by this operation." [39]

A noncriminal self-concept reinforced by social status and self-esteem was clearly a factor in the rationalizations these corporate executives used to explain their conduct. This posture of the occupational criminal was described by Donald Cressey in his study of 133 embezzlers who were sent to prison. He found that financial need typically led the offenders to violate their positions of trust. Initially, they rationalized their acts as borrowing, thinking they would repay the money, rather than identifying with a criminal attitude and planning for a "big score." [40]

In Harry Ball's study of rent-control violations by landlords in Honolulu, he identified the focus of the rationalization in attitudes they held about the fairness of the law and the degree to which they felt deprived of a "fair return." Over 90 percent of those who violated the rent ceilings viewed them as unfair, as compared with 55 percent of nonviolators. The idea that the statute was unfair did not explain the offense. But it did provide a rationalization that helped to maintain the offenders' noncriminal self-concept.[41]

In October 1973, Spiro T. Agnew held a press conference to deny charges alleging that he had continued to receive $50,000 in payoffs from benefactors after he became vice-president. A week later he appeared in U.S. District Court and pleaded *nolo contendere*—the practical equivalent to an admission of guilt—to charges of having evaded taxes on funds he had received in 1967. In his farewell statement Agnew stated: "Now I am sure you realize that officials who do not possess large, personal fortunes face the unpleasant but unavoidable necessity of raising substantial sums of money to pay campaign and election expenses." Several months previously, he had labeled the charges against him "damned lies." Yet following his *nolo contendere* plea, he was rationalizing his political style as one that necessitated secret gifts.[42]

Nearly three years after his resignation and subsequent pardon, former President Richard M. Nixon taped a series of interviews with TV personality David Frost. The tapes were then sold to American television stations. Nixon apologized for having "let the American people down" and stated that technically he had not committed "an impeachable offense," but rather had impeached himself through his resignation. A commentator referred to his performance as unapologetic and a "lesson in self-delusion." Nixon's apology and admission of bad judgments have their parallels in utterances of the corporate executives in the Heavy Electrical Equipment Conspiracy Case.[43]

Another example of the way in which official white-collar criminals rationalize their behavior is the plea bargain which former CIA Director Richard Helms negotiated with the Department of Justice in November 1977. Helms pleaded *nolo contendere* to two misdemeanor counts for having lied to a Senate committee about CIA operations in Chile. The alternative was to stand trial on a perjury charge, a felony. After his defense attorney asked for leniency, saying Helms would "bear the scar of conviction the rest of his life," he announced to reporters that his client would "wear this conviction like a badge of honor." Helms candidly admitted, "I don't feel disgraced at all." Then he attended a luncheon in his honor held by former colleagues, at which more than $2000 was collected to pay his fine.[44]

Former President Richard Nixon with TV interviewer David Frost: Nixon's "apology" paralleled statements of corporate white-collar criminals.

This example, and other Watergate-related cases, underlie the notion that Watergate was only the "tip of the iceberg." The former CIA director's case was plea bargained with the authorization of President Carter, who had stated in accepting the Democratic presidential nomination that he saw "no reason why big-shot crooks should go free while the poor ones go to jail." The plea bargain was defended as the most effective way to uphold the "rule of law." Given the public's tendency to accept the need for secrecy, a jury might have been persuaded to acquit Helms on the grounds that he lied to protect national security.[45] Although such rationalizations may, at times, seem valid, lenient punishments for the "high and mighty" perpetuate the idea that high government officials are above full accountability to the law.

WHITE-COLLAR CRIME: BEHAVIOR SYSTEMS AND AFFILIATION

When Sutherland put forth the concept of white-collar crime, he rejected as an explanation the idea of primitive affinity, which assumes that prior pathological circumstances predetermine criminal behavior. He did, however, stress the significance of associations or affiliation as the context and social process through which the individual might possibly become "turned on" to law-violating behavior.[46]

> White-collar criminality, just as other systematic criminality, is learned; ... it is learned in direct or indirect association with those who already practice the behavior; and those who learn this criminal behavior are segregated from frequent and intimate contacts with law abiding behavior. Whether a person becomes a criminal or not is determined largely by his contacts with the two types of behavior. This may be called the 'process of differential association.' It is a generic explanation both of white-collar ... and lower-class criminality.[47]

Although there have been few studies of white-collar crime since the concept was introduced, the behavior patterns of occupational, corporate, and official avocational offenders that have been studied tend to substantiate Sutherland's ideas.

The term "operator" has been coined to refer to those avocational criminals who inhabit the business and professional world in America and make some of their money from fraud and deceit. These sharp business and professional practices create an overlap between the upperworld of legitimacy and the underworld of illegitimacy. Doubtless, they led Daniel Bell to suggest that "crime is an American way of life." [48] No one can remain an "operator" for long—in business or in professional life—without becoming knowledgeable about or involved in fraudulent techniques.

One study of World War II "black market" operations by Clinard estimated that 57 percent of the businessmen in the United States engaged in such illegal activities during the war. He suggests that group support (differential association) for hostile attitudes toward wartime regulations had an important influence on such law-violating behavior. The black market offenders Clinard studied were mainly businessmen who sought to conduct business as they had before the wartime regulations.[49] Another study by Frank Hartung involved violations of wartime regulations in the wholesale meat industry. He found that only 2 out of 122 persons charged with price and related violations had prior records of offenses.[50] Evidently these fraudulent business practices continue, for the Federal Trade Commission reported that more than 30,000 consumers complained that they had been cheated through unfair or deceptive practices in 1975. Though most businessmen do not participate in illegal or questionable practices, they can hardly remain unaware of such behaviors. As Sutherland suggested, one can demonstrate this reality in a casual conversation with a businessman simply by asking him, "What crooked practices are found in your occupation?" [51]

The fact that occupational crimes are not limited to the executive suite is illustrated by Richard Quinney's study of retail pharmacists. Quinney identified four types of role orientations related differentially to prescription violations. The more *professionally oriented* pharmacists were less likely to be involved in occupational offenses—none in his sample. However, *business-oriented* pharmacists were more inclined toward such offenses—75 percent had committed violations—and the *professional/business* and *indifferent* types had 14 and 20 percent offense rates respectively. It seems that a professional orientation provided social controls that inclined pharmacists to obey the law. But fewer controls operated to deter the business-oriented group. Quinney concluded that group support, or the lack of it, may be related to occupational crime in other occupations or professions such as chiropody, dentistry, optometry, osteopathy, accounting, and real estate, since these involve elements of business as well as professional orientations.[52]

The respectable executive who carries out corporate crime receives group support from other officials within and outside the corporation. In fact, these executives may be somewhat isolated from "normal" definitions of law-abiding business practices. Whether padding expense accounts, approving advertising that makes unwarranted claims, or meeting with competitors or politicians, these executives may spend most of their day with other executives involved in similar activities.

Such group support for violation of the antitrust laws was found in the Heavy Electrical Equipment Conspiracy Case. Geis describes how the offenders used fictitious names and codes. The attendance list of the meetings was called the "Christmas card list," and the meetings were referred to as "choir practice." They communicated by way of public telephones and met at trade association meetings or secret locations. While they sometimes filed false travel expense reports to deceive their superiors about the location of their visits, they did not pad expenses. Despite their illegal activity, they chose not to cheat the corporation.[53]

The statement of the judge who sentenced the defendants in this case criticized the corporations as the major culprits. But he characterized those he sentenced as "the organization or company man; the conformist who goes along with his superiors and soothed his conscience with the security and comfort which he found within the corporate organization." [54] Job security and position in the company were assured if one fulfilled the expectations assigned to him by the corporate structure, even if it involved illegal price fixing.

The official or political criminal also receives group support from his associates. But the position from which the official offender operates is unique in that he or she occupies a position of public power and trust. To remain in such a position, at least in a democratic society, requires the continuation of such trust. To those who would violate this trust, a level of secrecy allowing legitimate access to illegitimate behavior is needed. Consequently, a special type of intimate group relationship exists, which, as the Watergate revelations demonstrated, seems to be engendered by the bureaucratic structure of modern government.[55]

The way in which Vice-President Agnew was able to maintain the support of a few close associates in order to bring secret pressure upon the U.S. Department of Justice for a satisfactory bargain was described in "How Agnew Bartered His Office to Keep from Going to Prison" (1973).[56] It is doubtful that Agnew would have been able to "cop a plea" to minor charges related to offenses six years old without the support of the Nixon administration, whose representative acted as broker in the negotiations.

And then there is Watergate, the most dramatic example of official white-collar crime in the history of our nation. For a while, there was a great reluctance to move against the president, out of deference to the office. Those around the president—including participants in the Watergate crimes—conducted an intense campaign to retain their positions of power. As Nixon's most loyal supporters wavered, however, even he began to see that he might face removal from office. His resignation became more advantageous to him than impeachment and probable conviction.[57]

Nixon was pardoned without benefit of a trial or official establishment of guilt. Renata Adler, who served on the legal staff that researched impeachment charges against Nixon, has argued that the Watergate investigation was an evasion of treason and bribery charges that should have been brought against the former president. She argues that unless Nixon did something more than the acts specified in the charges, his forced resignation seems arbitrary—especially in light of the continuing revelations of abuses by the CIA, FBI, and IRS by his predecessors and by numerous corporations and their officials. She concludes that the investigation was at the "tip of the wrong iceberg." The secret that lies hidden in the whole affair, she argues, is corporate America's bribery of officials, parties, and governments abroad.[58]

It may be that in spite of the voluminous amount of information on the Watergate crimes, we still do not comprehend the extent to which it demonstrates the existence of a second government in our nation's capital. This second government can be seen as a complex of "interlocking forces." Pulling the CIA here and organized crime there, using politicians one time and emigré thugs the next, it seems to regard government as a tool for financial enrichment and is to a large extent financed by the newer exploitative businesses.[59]

WHITE-COLLAR CRIME: CRIMINAL AND CONVENTIONAL CONVERGENCES

The study of white-collar crime reflects and illustrates changing values and practices in our socioeconomic life. The nature of our highly industrialized, urbanized, and bureaucratically organized society has created a changing set of relations between (1) the corporate world, business, professions, and government, and (2) consumers, clients, and citizens. Conventional laws defining criminal behavior and antisocial conduct often are inapplicable or ineffective for this new structure of relationships. Consequently, contemporary society has seen the development of new laws of an administrative and regulatory nature to control economic, political, and even professional relationships. Not only do we have new laws defining new forms of law-violating behavior, but these laws run counter to the deeply embedded values of some elements in our society. These individuals and institutions may view new attempts at regulation as antithetical to free enterprise, laissez-faire, and the principle of *caveat emptor* (let the buyer beware!).

Occupational White-Collar Crime

Occupational crime patterns illustrate the interconnections between white-collar crime and the social organization of contemporary society. Frequently there is a conflict between the value system that operates in the marketplace—based on laissez-faire, rugged individualism, and supply and demand—and the value system that demands regulation of some business transactions. As a result, people affiliated with certain occupations often learn methods by which to selectively violate government regulations. As we mentioned earlier, it is often possible to discover the types of white-collar criminality associated with a particular occupation simply by asking, What crooked practices are found in your occupation? [60]

In focusing on the study of such occupational crime, criminology inadvertently has come to emphasize the relationships between these behaviors and the criminal definitions and penal sanctions specified in recent laws. While the laws, influenced by public concern, define these practices as crime, many such occupational practices are not seen as criminal by those who indulge in them. The symbiotic linkage between occupational crime and the action-system or patterns that operate in legitimate society can be illustrated by the brief descriptions that follow.

Medical Fraud. Since 1965, when Medicare and Medicaid became law, inflation in the health-care "business" has been twice that in other segments of the economy. This may stem in part from the fact that Americans often receive more health care than they need from some doctors. A Congressional subcommittee estimated in 1976 that there were about 2.5 million unnecessary operations performed each year, costing some $3.5 billion and claiming 12,000 lives. It may also be a consequence of medical fraud, such as nursing home operators who have been ripping off both patients and the third parties that pay the tab—commercial insurance groups and governmental agencies.

Fees collected by hospitals have soared 56 percent since Medicare and Medicaid were enacted, while physicians' fees have doubled and their income has tripled. Family ganging and ping ponging are illegal techniques that have evolved in poverty areas. Other types of medical fraud are more conventional. These include kickbacks from medical laboratories and billing for services never performed. One doctor billed Medicaid for six tonsillectomies on the same patient.[61] (See Box 3.)

The nursing home business has been the source of some of the more spectacular frauds. Newspaper accounts have detailed numerous cases in recent years. One of the most publicized cases was that of Bernard Bergman, a nursing home tycoon with facilities in Miami, New York City, and New Jersey, who has been convicted of Medicare and Medicaid fraud by both federal and state courts. One writer suggests that large-scale medical fraud began with these programs, which originally were established to provide health care for the elderly.[62]

Internal Revenue Service officials report that one out of three physicians

R$_x$ for Medifraud

BOX 3

By PETER BONVENTRE with NICHOLAS HORROCK and ELAINE SHANNON

At first, Canary Fipps didn't mind the weekly visits to the second-story neighborhood clinic in Chicago's West Side ghetto. She is a 37-year-old mother of seven children whose husband is unemployed, so her medical bills are covered by Medicaid. But when her doctor insisted she bring her whole family along with her for assembly-line examinations, Mrs. Fipps began to get annoyed. What she didn't realize was that every time she or one of her children was examined, it cost Medicaid $10. She did realize, however, that something was fishy when her doctor prescribed 200 pain pills for her husband, had her fill the prescription at a nearby pharmacy and then return all except six pills to him.

Mrs. Fipps's suspicions were confirmed when her doctor told her that six of the children had to have their tonsils removed immediately. It would have cost Medicaid $120 per operation and $60 to $70 per child per day in a hospital. Since the youngsters had rarely suffered even minor colds, Mrs. Fipps and her husband refused to grant permission for the operations.

In medifraud jargon, Mrs. Fipps experienced what is called "family ganging." She was fortunate enough not to get caught in a "Ping Ponging" scam. Ping Ponging is the referral of a Medicaid patient who, for instance, has been treated for stomach cramps to an optometrist, podiatrist or chiropractor—or maybe all three —for additional checkups.

Family ganging and Ping Ponging are only two of the schemes used by unscrupulous health providers to rip off the nation's $18 billion Medicaid program. Medicare, which helps people over 65, is not untouched by scandal, but it is far less ambitious and complex than Medicaid and thus more manageable. The Department of Health, Education and Welfare thinks the cost of fraud and abuse amounts to as much as $1 billion a year.

For years, many prosecutors shunned medifraud investigations because the cases were hard to prove and required knowledge of a highly sophisticated form of white-collar crime.

But Attorney General Griffin Bell has made crimes against Federal programs a top prosecution priority of his Justice Department—and a special team on medifraud has been formed in the criminal divisions. This movement was buoyed by the recent success of lawmen in prosecuting cases against the nursing-home industry.

Beefing Up the Bills

Thanks to the efforts of the Better Government Association (BGA) and the persistence of U.S. Attorney Sam Skinner, Illinois has been one of the most active states in pursuing fraud. The BGA is a privately financed watchdog organization based in Chicago. Its most recent project unearthed how some clinical laboratories make illegal windfall profits. Labs, for example, set up kickback schemes by "renting" office space—sometimes as little as 2 square feet—from clinics that gave them business. Reviewing thousands of bills submitted to the state, the BGA also found that labs charged Medicaid $655,869 for selected tests that would have cost private physicians only $301,700. Further study of twenty of these bills, chosen at random, revealed that in more than 80 percent of the cases, tests never requested by the physician were added to beef up the bill.

Substitution of less-expensive generic drugs for prescribed brand names is a common abuse among pharmacy medifrauders. Some nursing homes even recycle drugs. When a patient gets a prescription of 50 pills and uses only ten, the remaining medicine is later dispensed to other patients—and billed for again. Pressures to keep the Medicaid money flowing can be intense. Three months ago, eleven New York podiatrists were indicted on charges of conspiring to block elimination of podiatry services from the state's Medicaid program. Their alleged method: funneling $100,000 through a pair of high-level mafiosi to an influential legislator.

Prepaying the Costs

Each new scandal that is exposed has pointed up the failure of the government to manage itself and its money. One of the results of such mismanagement has been that doctors often have to wait six months or more for state reimbursements. This creates a cash-flow crisis, especially for inner-city doctors who have a high percentage of Medicaid patients. As a result, many doctors are forced to sell their bills at a discount to "factoring companies," which then process the bills—but usually not before padding them to reflect services that were never performed.

Prepaying health-care costs is regarded by many experts as one answer to medifraud. Under this scheme, doctors get the same monthly fee whether their patients are well or ill. In fact, it is the basis for the Federal Health Maintenance Organization (HMO) legislation, although a similar system has backfired in California. Some California physicians have maximized their profits by screening out the sick and enrolling the healthy, who need less attention. In one case, an administrator forged disenrollment papers on a patient who developed jaw cancer after he joined the plan.

A well-managed, tightly regulated system of HMO's may still offer the best way out of the medifraud morass. In the meantime, Congress is seriously considering an anti-fraud bill that would upgrade medifraud charges from misdemeanors to felonies and give authorities greater access to the books and records of health providers. Along with Bell, HEW Secretary Joseph Califano has promised to make medifraud control a top-priority concern of his department.

The Federal government also has offered to pay 90 percent of the installation costs of the so-called Medicaid Management Information Systems. This state-level program to computerize claims will eventually cost hundreds of millions of dollars. But if it is managed properly, it has the potential to save much more. It should help to pinpoint quickly the doctor who bills for 48 hours of psychotherapy in a single day, or the optometrist who bills for 26 pairs of eyeglasses for the same patient.

Source: *Newsweek*, May 9, 1977. Copyright 1977, by Newsweek, Inc. All rights reserved. Reprinted by permission.

who make a large proportion of their income from Medicare and Medicaid patients is involved in some form of income tax evasion. With the average annual income of doctors now well above $60,000 (after expenses), the amount of tax money lost through such violations is considerable.[63]

Automobile Fraud. The overlap between conventional and criminal behavior patterns is also evident in the market structure that regulates the relations between the auto industry and dealers. A study of fraudulent business practices by new automobile dealers pointed out that it is the pressures placed upon dealers to be "sales-oriented" and to accept the manufacturer's dictum that service is "a necessary evil," which frequently leads to malpractice in servicing motor vehicles. The dealers cut profits on new cars to increase sales and make up for it by overcharging on repairs or increasing margins on used cars.

Are unnecessary repairs blue-collar or white-collar crime?

They also may engage in illegal repair practices, such as phony repairs and the substitution of used parts.[64] In the fall of 1975, the *New York Times* conducted an auto service survey in which a test car was sent to twenty-four garages. Thirteen garages either diagnosed the car's problem incorrectly or made or recommended unnecessary repairs. Little wonder that 15 percent of the complaints received by the President's Office of Consumer Affairs relate to trouble with automobiles.[65] The consumer tends to blame the mechanic or dealer for poor service or for not honoring warranty work. But the unethical and illegal behavior might more accurately be seen as coerced occupational crime resulting from the applied criminogenic power of the auto industry.[66]

Occupational Crime by Computer. With the introduction into the business world of electronic data processing (EDP), a new dimension has been added to occupational economic crime. Computers represent a new and useful tool for business and industry, but laws regulating them have not kept pace with the rapid increase in their use and sophistication. By 1980, there were some 500,000 computers in use in the United States employing nearly three million operators.

In his book, *Crime by Computer* (1976), Donn B. Parker, one of the few researchers to study the problem of computer crime, reports that most computer criminals are young (eighteen to thirty years old), amateur males. They possess the skills required to use computers and have access to computer facilities. These criminals usually plan their crimes carefully with the collusion of other EDP personnel. The nature of their crimes varies. While some steal computer programs, others use computers to cover up overdrafts of sizable sums from banks, while still others instruct computers to make false deposits to personal accounts. It appears that the often talked about cashless money based on EFT (Electronic Funds Transfer) might increase the potential for such activities, even should it reduce the potential for robbery and larceny.

Parker found that while some computer thieves were interested in beating a supposedly foolproof EDP system or in enhancing themselves financially, there were those who, like the naive check forger (see Chapter 9), faced personal financial problems that they attempted to resolve by using the computer to divert funds. While Parker suggests that such crimes may be reduced by better security, screening workers, and separating job functions, his data suggest that a computer specialist with a desire to commit a crime might take advantage of any weakness in the system. Consequently, computer crime is likely to continue rising until a new generation of computers can be developed that can audit the work of those who might want to use the new technology for their own gain.[67]

Corporate White-Collar Crime

As Edwin Schur has argued, business enterprises are regulated on the surface by values such as honesty, reciprocity, public accountability, and concern for the interest of the consumer. Yet underlying values often reinforce deceptive efforts to promote the self-interest of the seller. These subterranean values are conducive to occupational crimes. This is not surprising, notes Schur, who observed that given the pervasive extent of the "business ethic in our society, honesty may be the best policy, but business is business." [68]

Corporations are powerful and pervasive forces in modern society. Phrases such as "the American corporate system" and "the corporate state" represent efforts by social scientists to conceptualize the interrelationships between private and public centers of power. Corporate white-collar practices are both similar to and different from other patterns of white-collar and conventional crime. The similarities should not obscure the distinctive nature and extent of such crime patterns. The underlying motive that corporations share with business-oriented professionals and professional criminals is that of economic gain. Merton has stated in his essay on "Social Structure and Anomie" that certain phases of social structure generate the circumstances in which the infringement of social codes constitutes a "normal response." This is not to suggest, however, that corporate white-collar crime is simply the behavior of greedy individuals constrained by an ethos of greed.[69]

In Sutherland's analysis of 980 violations committed by the seventy largest corporations in the United States, he noted that these violations had injured two classes of persons. The first group included those in the same or related business as the offenders. The second was the general public, which suffered losses as consumers or as constituents of institutions affected by the violations.[70] More recently, *Consumer News* estimated that the extra price of goods due to lack of business competition costs $151 billion a year, while the extra amount paid by consumers because of deceptive selling methods is another $125 billion.[71]

In his study of the Heavy Electrical Equipment Conspiracy Case, Geis describes how corporations respond to external forces in their illegal behavior:

> When the market behaved in a manner the executives thought satisfactory or when enforcement agencies seemed... threatening, the conspiracy desisted. When market conditions deteriorated, while pressures for achieving attractive profit and loss statements remained constant, and enforcement... abated, the price-fixing agreements flourished.[72]

Multinational Corporations and Convergence of Conventional and Criminal Patterns

One way for large corporations to increase their profits and avoid a great deal of the regulation of antitrust laws is to "multinationalize." Whether intentionally or not, going "multinational" is one way of avoiding domestic regulations. For just as we have noted that the laws governing fraudulent advertising are difficult to enforce because of the interstate nature of such activity, so does the conduct of international business allow multinationals to avoid regulation that would occur within the country. A glaring example of the manner in which this absence of regulation in the international economy can be used for activities that would be criminal "at home" is the Investors Overseas Services of Robert Vesco. By working, as it were, in the interstices of the jurisdictions of the various nations, Vesco was able to conduct questionable and shaky investment schemes that would have been illegal in most Western nations. American-based companies constitute a majority of the multinational concerns in the world, and doing business overseas sometimes involves payoffs or kick-backs—commonly known as bribery (see Box 4). Lockheed, which ranked third on a list of corporate bribers compiled in 1977, eventually moved into first place. The Securities and Exchange Commission (SEC) is continuing its investigation into the manner in which that company paid off officials in many countries. Lockheed is not merely a company with some $565 million in defense contracts. It also owes over $80 million in government-guaranteed loans. So the SEC's interest goes far beyond a mere concern with illegal payments.[73]

Both multinationals and intranational corporations are powerful political forces, and they are successful in influencing attempts to regulate their actions. In their continuing efforts to expand and enhance their earning power, corporate businesses are in a more secure position to avoid regulations as well. As Sutherland noted in *White-Collar Crime* (1949), corporations subject to regulation exert a powerful influence in determining the rules by which they are regulated.[74]

Advertising and Mass Appeals as Overlap of Conventional and Criminal Patterns

The overlap between corporate criminal activity and conventional behaviors is striking in the advertising campaigns of modern business. The extent of advertising that actually is illegal is small. But even a casual observer of mass advertising can recognize considerable deception. Mass advertising is basically exploitative and uses information gathered from motivational research to stimulate consumption of ever-increasing quantities of commodities.

The number of fraudulent advertising cases has increased in recent years. The Food and Drug Administration has issued cease and desist orders against the manufacturers of several brands of mouthwash to stop them from making false claims for their products. Legal action has also been taken against the "deceptive and false" advertising for Excedrin, and more recently against the manufacturers of various "cold" remedies. In 1978, pop singer Pat Boone admitted that he had made unsubstantiated claims on behalf of an acne medication and offered to reimburse consumers. The director of the FDA has charged that the manufacturers of prescription drugs have violated laws that proscribe false and misleading advertising. He noted that these companies spend approximately one dollar out of every five on the promotion of their products through advertising.

Similarly, in a suit begun in January 1972, the FTC brought action against the "Big-Four" cereal makers—Kellogg, General Mills, General Foods, and

The Biggest Bribers

BOX 4

In the last several years, a total of 167 American corporations have admitted paying out more than $3 million in bribes overseas. Much of this money has been spent since 1970. The Watergate prosecution first broke open the corporate bribery story; since then, Congress and the Securities and Exchange Commission have gotten into the act. Partly in an effort to avoid the embarrassment of outside investigations, American corporations have been falling all over themselves to disclose past bribery or questionable payments and to promise it won't happen again. Their strategy has been successful: since the government doesn't have the resources for 175 thorough investigations, we mostly have to take the companies' own word about bribe totals. Often this word is highly suspect: Lockheed, which is probably the top banana of them all when it comes to money passed under the table, admits to $25 million, but the SEC is looking into nearly $200 million worth of questionable company payments. At the very least, these confessions do indicate how widespread—and how expensive—international corporate bribery has become. Based only on information supplied by corporations themselves, here are the biggest bribers of the lot:

Company	Total "Questionable Foreign Payments"	
Exxon	$56,862,000	(1963–75)
R. J. Reynolds	$25,170,000	(1970–75)
Lockheed	$25,000,000	(1970–75)
Armco Steel	$18,060,000	(1971–75)
General Telephone & Electronics	$15,000,000	(1971–75)

Source: *Mother Jones* (July 1977), p. 42. Data compiled by Gordon Adams and Sherri Zann Rosenthal of the Council on Economic Priorities.

Quaker Oats—who control 91 percent of the market, for product differentiation by advertising, trade mark proliferation, and "follow-the-leader" pricing. Producers of automobiles, tires, gasoline, soap, television sets, deodorant, and toothpaste also compete in this way. The suit was still pending after seven years of delaying tactics.[75]

Over three decades ago, Sutherland summarized an extensive list of products found in a typical home, which had been promoted through misrepresentation in advertising. The list remains timely, since many of the products still are being featured in media commercials:

> *In the kitchen:* Kelvinator, Quaker Oats, Wheaties, Cream of Wheat, Swans Down Cake Flour, Fleischmann's Yeast, Knox Gelatin, Kraft-Phoenix Cheese, Carnation Milk, Horlick's Malted Milk, Diamond Crystal Salt, Morton's Salt, Welch's Grape Juice, Nehi.
>
> *In the laundry:* Ivory Soap, P. & G. Naptha Soap, Rinso, Palmolive Soap.
>
> *In the bathroom:* Scott's Tissue Toilet Paper, Dr. Lyon's Tooth Powder (or almost any other tooth powder or tooth paste), Schick Dry Shaver, Wildroot Hair Tonic, Ingram's Shaving Cream, Marlin Razor Blades, Drene, Herpicide.
>
> *In the medicine chest:* Phillip's Milk of Magnesia, Absorbine Jr., Pond's Extract, Smith Brothers Cough Drops, Bayer's Aspirin.
>
> *On the dressing table:* Cutex, Peroxide, Ingram's Milkweed Cream, Coty's cosmetics, Mavis Talcum Powder, Elizabeth Arden cosmetics, Murine Eye Wash.[76]

As one retired advertising executive commented about advertising in America a few years ago:

> The American people...are now being had from every...direction.... from trying to persuade us to put dubious drug products and...foods into our stomachs to urging our young men to lay down their lives....The key will-it-sell principle and the employed techniques are the same.
>
> *Caveat emptor* has never had more profound significance than today....Deceit is the accepted order of the hour.[77]

SOCIETAL REACTION: DETERRENCE AND SOCIAL CONTROL OF WHITE-COLLAR CRIME

The legacy of Sutherland's research has not been theoretical disputes over whether or not upper-status offenses really are crimes. Nor has it been whether or not some current business, professional, and political practices should be redefined as culpable. Rather, the challenge he posed was to seek a balance in our study of crime and criminality. He asked us not to focus solely upon lower classes in our explanations of personal or social pathologies.[78] Sutherland did not arrive at a single explanation for all crime—or even for all white-collar crime. Since Sutherland argued that white-collar crime is a result of cultural conflict, which makes the law less effective, he was asserting in effect that such crime—indeed all crime—in modern society is the natural result of social processes characterized by an ambiguity of values.[79]

The Norwegian sociologist, Vilhelm Aubert, called our attention over twenty-five years ago to the ambiguous nature of white-collar crimes. He suggested that rather than debate whether or not we should define such phenomena as "crimes," we should profit by using them as a means of identifying ambivalence on the part of citizens, businesses, legal authorities, and even criminologists regarding such activities.[80]

An analysis of both societal reaction and official efforts to regulate and control white-collar crime cannot ignore the moral uncertainty inherent in Sutherland's theory of differential association as applied to white-collar crime. In arguing that law violations are normative in certain businesses and occupations, and in focusing on the trend away from punishment, the "kid-gloves" treatment of corporate white-collar criminals and the relative lack of organized public resentment against white-collar criminals, he described, inadvertently perhaps, another manifestation of overlap. Sutherland made much of the unequal enforcement of the law against white-collar criminals.[81] But he did not relate this unequal treatment to analyses of white-collar crime as natural consequences of conflicts within the class structure of our political economy. He was intent upon reforming theory and perhaps business practices, but he was not a revolutionary.

It remained for other writers to stress the exploitative nature of our society and to view white-collar crime as a behavioral variation stemming from common motives within the class structure. This view is not merely vulgar Marxism. Rather, it focuses on the social values and relations that vary across and within classes. As Donald R. Taft argues, the businessman might not be a burglar, but he might violate the Labor Relations Act. His group might approve such behavior and the public would not strongly condemn it. The burglar might violate the Sherman Act, but since he lacks the opportunity he cannot do so. His group might be ambivalent about antitrust violations, but they would approve of burglary as a more straightforward act. Some businessmen might exploit without law violations; others might succeed without exploiting. And the noncriminal exploiter in our society accepts basically the same values as the white-collar criminal. Both the noncriminal and the burglar tend to accept the values of individualistic materialism and competition epitomized by the white-collar criminal. The nonexploiter hardly exists in our system—a system which virtually forces us to exploit if we would achieve social status.[82]

Social Control of White-Collar Crime: Regulatory Agencies

If we accept that white-collar crime is inherent within the normative structure of our profit-oriented social structure, then no system of social control or legal sanctions will really work unless there is a drastic alteration of the system. It is doubtful that most Americans would contemplate or support such drastic change. Nevertheless, the last three or four decades have witnessed the growth of numerous regulatory agencies as a part of the government's effort to control white-collar crime. Given what is known about the relationship between rule making and rule enforcing and the incidence of rule-breaking behavior, we need to study this relationship while remaining sensitive to the regulatory process as it reacts and interacts with potential white-collar offenders. However, unlike most traditional crimes, the information required to confirm the illegal behavior of white-collar criminals is often in the possession of those under suspicion.[83]

The intimate relationship between white-collar offenders and regulations affecting them was pointed out by Sutherland some years ago, when he described how businessmen organize for the control of legislation. The enforcement of such regulations depends upon special regulatory agencies, such as the FTC, EPA, SEC, or IRS, rather than on police, prosecutors, and the criminal courts. More attention needs to be focused on this regulatory process in order to assess whether or not it is effective.[84] Those laws that sanction white-collar offenders are often in conflict with prevailing mores. A gap exists between the ideal and real norms of our society; inconsistent and haphazard enforcement of regulatory laws against white-collar offenses may serve to widen this disparity between real and ideal norms. There is a timeworn truth in criminological theory that "certainty" of punishment is a more effective deterrent than severity. However, as Sutherland pointed out, white-collar crime is similar to juvenile delinquency when it comes to differential implementation of penal sanctions. Procedures are modified, and often the trial takes place in an administrative court, so that the stigma of "criminal" is not attached to the offender. Since white-collar criminals have avoided most stigma, the consideration of their offenses has not been included within the purview of criminological theories of crime.[85]

The Deterrent Effect of Punishment

In Sutherland's attempt to show that white-collar crime was really crime, he delineated two ingredients needed to define it: (1) the legal description of an act as socially injurious; and (2) the legal provision of a penalty for the offense. He concluded that laws regarding white-collar crime have been less than effective because the criminality of the behavior was concealed.[86] Though lawmakers and regulatory agencies have been disinclined to deal with our high-status offenders in a punitive manner, there is evidence that such offenders are responsive to criminal sanctions. Clinard's study of violators of wartime price regulations indicates that imprisonment—even for short terms—was most feared. In contrast, lesser criminal sanctions, such as fines or suspended sentences, had very little deterrent effect.[87] Geis reports that the General Electric executives who served thirty days in jail testified to a Congressional committee that they would starve before they would do it again.[88]

But street criminals, who have less to lose, leave prison more alienated and less adjusted. Some argue that there ought to be less punishment of street crimes and that we ought to decriminalize status crimes. To argue for stiffer punishments of criminals from the executive suites, while advocating decriminalization for "street criminals," seems contradictory. In fact, the whole question has received little serious discussion in the decade since the President's Crime Commission argued: "Derelictions by corporations and their managers who usually occupy leadership positions in their communities, establish an example which tends to erode the moral base of the law." [89]

Few people want to see while-collar criminals in Congress or the White House, but should they go to prison? Allen Dershowitz, professor of law at Harvard University states:

> We are really stuck between two modes of irrationality. On the one hand it makes no sense at all to imprison white-collar criminals because they don't need walls around them. On the other hand it's unthinkable to let them go free and simply subject them to fines as a license fee for criminality. Fines are not a stigmatizing event in our society.[90]

Dershowitz thinks that we need more imaginative punishments that would remove the protective trappings from the white-collar criminal. He recommends steep fines proportional to a person's income as one punishment. Another sanction was suggested by Watergate defendant John Ehrlichman, who requested that he be allowed to use his legal skill on behalf of the Indians of the Southwest. But under existing law it seems essential that white-collar criminals go to prison. The paradox of the deterrence theory is that it works best with those who are the most affluent, best educated, and most able to assess punishment rationally as a legal consequence of their crime.[91]

Controlling Occupational White-Collar Crime

Regulation of occupations that have become professionalized takes place through licensing boards. The medical profession, for example, is regulated in most states by the state board of medical examiners. In the case of New York State, and until recently California, this board was composed of physicians appointed by the governor. The governor of California created an uproar when his new appointments in 1977 included several nonpractitioners. These medical boards license doctors and have the obligation to discipline violators, even to the extent of revoking a license to practice.

Other professionals, such as pharmacists, realtors, and morticians have sought to professionalize and regulate their members in a similar manner. Their professional associations and licensing boards are able to administer sanctions with practical immunity from public scrutiny. One result is that occupational white-collar crimes ordinarily do not create the negative public reaction that other white-collar offenses may attract. Even in the case of conventional violations, such as drug addiction by physicians, the professional associations often act as buffers. Unlike the addict who may be sentenced for "treatment," the doctor may only lose his authority to write prescriptions.[92]

Malpractice suits against physicians have been increasing so fast recently that medical practitioners have been faced with sky-rocketing costs of liability insurance. In New York, insurance underwriters threatened to cease writing such insurance. Still, the plaintiff who brings a malpractice suit is at an obvious disadvantage, since he must rely upon the testimony of other doctors. Unless there is an extremely gross violation of medical practice, their sympathy generally is with their fellow professional. Professions such as medicine are also able to protect themselves from public scrutiny, since most malpractice suits are settled out of court by the insurance carriers. Thus, the professional and social standing of members is protected.[93]

Employee theft is another form of occupational crime. The risk of being apprehended or punished is also slight in these violations. One writer has suggested that the employer's desire to avoid publicity is a main reason for lack of prosecution. Unless a sizable amount of money or goods is involved, the employer is reluctant to prosecute; the employee is merely asked to resign.[94]

A recent historical critique of litigation brought under the Sherman Anti-Trust Act, from its enactment in 1890 through 1969, points up the consequences of the failure of enforcement. The author argues that the most critical time to implement a new law as a device for effective social control is during the period immediately following its enactment. This did not occur with the Sherman Anti-Trust Act. The author suggests that the failure of enforcement agencies to reinforce the public indignation that led to the act's passage, neutralized public resentment and allowed the illegal behavior to be redefined. The writer, Albert McCormick, notes that while the Sherman Anti-Trust Act contained civil remedies, it and later antitrust laws classify such activities as crimes. Yet as Figure 10.1 indicates, only 47.7 percent of the antitrust suits set in motion by the government in this period were criminal cases. While 35 percent of all cases led to criminal convictions, only 9 percent of these were litigated. In about 73 percent of the criminal convictions, the corporations pleaded *nolo contendere*.

Corporations can be fined, but they cannot, of course, be sent to prison. The difficulty with *nolo contendere* pleas by corporations is that corporate executives who may be charged do not admit any criminal guilt. Rather, they refuse to contest the charges and accept whatever punishment the court hands down. Consequently, the defendants are not formally defined as criminals. Among the 2 percent of corporate executives who served prison terms in McCormick's study, most were for labor violations.[95]

Controlling Corporate White-Collar Crime

In recent years a more aggressive approach has been attempted in legal actions against corporate white-collar criminals. Although there is a tradition of antagonism toward big business in America, most of the critical attention focused upon the actions of corporate business has come from academic social scientists.

Figure 10.1. Criminal Conviction and Sentencing Patterns in Antitrust Cases Brought by the Department of Justice, 1890–1969, by Five-Year Periods

Period Case Instituted	Total	Criminal Cases	All Convictions	Litigated Convictions	Sentences Imposed and Length	Characteristics of Case
1890–1894	9	4	0	0	0	
1895–1899	7	1	0	0	0	
1900–1904	6	1	1	1	0	
1905–1909	39	26	11	11	0	
1910–1914	91	37	21	12	1–4 hrs.	labor (union misconduct)
1915–1919	43	25	13	8	3–4 hrs.	labor
					1 yr.	labor-sabotage
					1 yr.	labor
1920–1924	66	25	15	14	5–NA	price fixing-labor
					10 days	labor
					10 mos.	labor
					8 mos.	labor
					1 yr.	labor
1925–1929	59	16	14	10	3–6 mos.	labor
					NA	price fixing-labor
					10 days	price fixing-violence
1930–1934	30	11	8	6	6–3 mos.	monopolization-violence
					6 mos.	monopolization-violence
					6 mos.	price fixing-violence
					2 yrs.	
					2 yrs.	price fixing-violence
					2–5 mos.	price fixing-labor-violence
					3–6 mos.	labor-violence
1935–1939	57	27	19	6	1–1 yr.	labor-violence
1940–1944	223	163	123	13	0	
1945–1949	157	58	50	9	0	
1950–1954	159	73	65	10	2–6 mos.	price fixing-labor
					9 mos.	price fixing-labor
1955–1959	195	97	86	21	2–90 days	price fixing-labor
					1 yr.	price fixing-labor
1960–1964	215	78	64	17	2–30 days	price fixing
					NA	price fixing
1965–1969	195	52	46	6	1–24 hrs.	price fixing
					60 days	
Total	1551	694	536	144	26 days (average)	

Source: Albert E. McCormick, "Rule Enforcement and Moral Indignations: Some Observations of the Effects of Criminal Antitrust Convictions Upon Societal Reaction Processes," *Social Problems* 25, no. 1 (October 1977):33.

A Harris poll has found that the portion of the population expressing confidence in business dropped from 55 to 15 percent in the decade after 1965. White-collar crimes by corporate businesses apparently create more public concern than occupational white-collar offenses. The activities in the 1960s and 1970s of consumer advocates, such as Ralph Nader, are supported by such attitudes. Government agencies have begun to show more interest in corporate white-collar crime, although enforcement still lags and appears to be selective. This selectivity in part is because the Justice Department budgets only 15 percent of its funds for investigating such offenses, and these legal actions are often lengthy and expensive.[96]

The Security and Exchange Commission is the regulatory agency that seeks to control our banking and securities activities. Interestingly, no violator of the SEC's regulations has ever received a prison sentence. Like other regulatory agencies, the SEC issues *consent decrees* against violating businesses. This means that the company agrees not to continue the activity, but admits no guilt for previous action.[97] Corporations that have been involved in polluting the environment sign consent decrees with the EPA and announce that they are working on the problem.[98] Imagine the public reaction if a common street criminal were to be dealt with in this fashion. Here's the scene: Joe Thug is apprehended by an alert patrolman after mugging an eighty-five-year-old woman in broad daylight on the streets of Patterson, New Jersey. Brought down to police headquarters, he holds a press conference with the assistant police chief. While not admitting his guilt, he promises not to commit any future muggings and announces that he is working on the problem of crime in the streets.

Controlling Official White-Collar Crime

It has often been said that the Watergate offenses were somehow different from traditional white-collar crimes that involve efforts at personal enrichment motivated by greed. Those involved in Watergate, on the other hand, were supposedly trying to protect their power base. This characterization is supported by the subsequent rationalizations by ex-President Nixon that spying, break-ins, and a general mood of vengeance against critics and political opponents was "paranoia for peace." The business executives who were convicted for underwriting the affair were simply doing business as usual. For them Watergate is only a memory (see Box 5). But the world of corporate and political interrelations that made Watergate possible still continues.[99]

It is within this world that we can observe the complexities of official white-collar crime. These offenses cannot be separated from other illegal and semilegal activities by those in positions of power and responsibility. As a staff member of the Judiciary Committee of the House of Representatives who helped write the articles of impeachment against President Nixon has written:

> When too many scandals have gone on for too long, uninterrupted and inadequately investigated, they tend to merge. What began as isolated instances of corruption grow toward each other and finally interlock. The nursing home operators, and private garbage collectors, and parking lot owners, and film industry executives, and cable television interests, and vending machine distributors, and recording companies, . . . the teamsters, the Mafia, and defense contractors, and finally the investigative agencies of government and

For Convicted Businessmen, Watergate Is Only a Memory

BOX 5

Watergate—the tip of the wrong iceberg?

Not since the Kefauver hearings on the Mafia have so many wealthy criminals exploded so suddenly on the American consciousness. The list of illegal corporate contributors to the Republican 1972 campaign grew longer as the Watergate special prosecutor delved deeper. Now that the headline type has faded, most of us might assume that these convicts have suffered for their crimes. Right? Wrong. A recent *New York Times* survey of 21 business executives who admitted making illegal political contributions revealed that most had retained their jobs. The biggest executives of the biggest companies fared best. Harding L. Lawrence, chairman of Braniff, renewed his contract until 1980 at no less than $250,000 a year—an annual raise of $30,000. He will also, as in the past, be receiving $80,000 a year in Braniff consulting fees, and he can count on $85,000 a year in retirement benefits. Thomas V. Jones, although stripped of his title of chairman of Northrop, remains the corporation's chief executive officer, earning $286,000 a year. Harry Heltzer, who retired as chairman of the Minnesota Mining and Manufacturing Company, received $428,000 in compensation in 1974. His retirement benefits will total about $125,000 a year. Meanwhile, he is making an annual $100,000 doing special assignments for 3M. Another man who stepped down—William W. Keeler, former chairman and chief executive officer of Phillips Petroleum—will be taking home a pension of over $200,000 a year. His stock holdings in Phillips are estimated at today's prices to surpass $3.4 million.

Two of these men paid $1,000 fines. Jones paid $5,000 and Heltzer paid $500. For some, these would be prohibitive amounts; to these folks, obviously, it was pocket change. The exposure of their illegal activities gave corporate criminals some unpleasant publicity. For a few months, they were asked questions or heard comments about nothing else. But most of the questions were friendly, few of the comments were nasty and, now that the hubbub has hushed, they are back at their desks, making their fortunes.

Source: Blake Fleetwood and Arthur Lubow, "America's Most Coddled Criminals," *New Times* (September 1975). © 1975 by New Times Publishing Co.

elected officials up to the highest level begin to have in common not just a general corruption but joint ventures and even personnel. That is an extremely dangerous moment in public life.[100]

In other words, we should realize that when government officials misuse their trust for financial gain or power and when regulatory agencies designed to police business practices allow such powerful groups to operate contrary to the public interest, the law ceases to be an effective means for social control.

Government regulation of business procedures continues to be uncertain and ambiguous. Apparently, vested interests in the political economy are more powerful than the political means available to control them. Only basic changes in the structure of American society can bring about the means to control this imbalance of power that is basic to the problem of white-collar crime.

The extent of official and corporate white-collar crime has become better understood with the abuses and misuses of power revealed by recent scandals. Even as this text was being prepared, the *New York Times* carried a follow-up to an earlier story in which a federal judge had revealed that the CIA had opened 215,000 pieces of mail between 1953 and 1973. He had ordered the government to pay $1,000 to three plaintiffs and to provide them with a written apology. The three, including a sociologist, have received apologies, which they have characterized as "mealy mouthed"—the CIA won't concede that what it did was wrong. But they still have not collected a cent. President Carter's assistant attorney general, Barbara A. Babcock, is fearful of potential liability that may amount to over $215 million.[101]

White-collar crimes, then, provide social indications of the increasing centralization of political and economic power in our society. They also provide insights into the manner in which power is distributed, used, and misused in our society. An analysis of the defined and detected offenses of high-status criminals and of those behaviors that go undefined or undetected even though they may represent considerable social injury, reveals something about the double standard of many who legislate and enforce our laws.[102]

If criminology is to avoid a similar hypocrisy, it must develop perspectives for value-conscious description and analysis of the behavior of the more affluent as well as the traditional "street criminals." Simple explanations, such as poverty or personal pathologies, do not account for the illegal behavior of the affluent and powerful members of society.

SUMMARY

This chapter has focused on an analysis of various types of illegal behavior by affluent, "respectable" citizens. The study of crimes committed by those of high status underscores the pervasive extent and political nature of crime.

White-collar crime is commonplace in our society, although often somewhat invisible. Such behavior cannot be explained in the same manner in which we seek to explain conventional street crime. Pathological, social, and personal factors fail to explain crimes of the affluent and powerful.

The concept of white-collar crime was first defined (rather loosely) by Edwin H. Sutherland. In general, the concept has referred to a wide range of diverse behaviors with few common characteristics. We suggested three categories: *occupational, corporate,* and *official* white-collar crimes. These types have distinct characteristics, yet they share important areas of overlap with conventional behavior. For instance, they represent goals of competitiveness and acquisitiveness basic to core values in our society.

The avocational nature of these crime patterns tends to protect the conventional self-concept of the offenders. The offenses also take place within the conventional associational network of everyday activity, but they are somewhat insulated from public scrutiny.

Occupational white-collar crime covers a variety of offenses including embezzlement from one's employer and fraudulent professional practices. Corporate offenses, such as fraudulent advertising and polluting the environment, are behaviors defined as illegal by an evolving socioeconomic system that regulates corporate giants. Official white-collar crimes involve abuses of power by public officials. Societal reaction to these various types of white-collar criminals is influenced by the social esteem with which the public views them. There is more public indignation over corporate than occupational white-collar crime. And once aroused, as in the Watergate affair, official offenses evoke considerable public indignation.

The militant consumer advocacy of Nader and others, together with a renewed interest in laws regulating business malpractice and governmental malfeasance, has focused interest on white-collar crime. By 1975, the Department of Justice had directed the FBI to become involved in the investigation of these offenses.[103] And in a recent survey, fifty-one writers in the field of criminal justice were asked which new crimes they thought might be added through legislative enactment within three years. More than 60 percent mentioned some form of white-collar offenses. Nevertheless, white-collar crime remains one of the most neglected topics of research. It is even more difficult to study the avocational offenses of the corporate and professional upperworld than those of the largely invisible underworld. But as citizens or criminologists, we cannot overlook the significance of such offenses. Although it is impossible to estimate its economic costs—estimates range from $40 billion to $200 billion a year—the damage to the social order is great. White-collar crime illustrates the hypocrisy in the moral order—what C. Wright Mills termed the problem of "structural immorality"—and the inequality of power and the means by which justice is administered. The social consequences—cynicism, distrust, and contempt for authority—have become even more pronounced since the events of the Watergate episode.

ADDITIONAL READINGS

Clinard, Marshall B. *The Black Market: A Study of White Collar Crime.* New York: Holt, Rinehart and Winston, 1952.

> This study of violations of wartime OPA regulations during World War II provides a timeless study of the flaunting of government regulations intended to serve the objectives of the nation's war effort. Professor Clinard analyzes his data against Sutherland's theory of differential association.

Douglas, Jack D. and John M. Johnson, eds. *Official Deviance: Readings in Malfeasance, Misfeasance and Other Forms of Corruption.* Philadelphia: J. B. Lippincott, 1977.

> The editors present theoretical analyses and proposed solutions of official white-collar crime. They have broadened the scope of their study to include official deviance, thus these selections encompass a wider spectrum than that of corruption per se.

Geis, Gilbert. "Avocational Crime." In *Handbook of Criminology.* Edited by Daniel Glaser. Chicago: Rand McNally, 1974, pp. 273–98.

> Professor Geis analyzes white-collar crime in relation to other avocational crimes, such as nonprofessional shoplifting. He compares such offenses in terms of the offender's self-concept, source of income, and prospect for deterrence. Includes an excellent bibliography.

Geis, Gilbert and Robert F. Meier, eds. *White-Collar Crime: Offenses in Business, Politics and the Professions.* Rev. ed. New York: Free Press, 1977.

> This volume is intended to convey the state of our knowledge about white-collar crime. It includes selections from the first sociological statements on white-collar crime — including Sutherland's seminar paper that introduced the concept — to accounts of the Watergate affair. Less than a third of the material represents work published since the first edition, but the editors suggest that in the future there will be more research on the subject.

Ostermann, Peter, Esther L. Williams and Kevin O'Brien. *White Collar Crime; A Selected Bibliography.* Washington, D.C.: National Institute of Law Enforcement and Criminal Justice, U.S. Department of Justice, 1977.

> This pertinent bibliography, available from the National Criminal Justice Reference Service, provides reference data for researchers, citizens, and law enforcement personnel who might desire to increase their understanding of white-collar crime. It includes general works, material on prosecution, case studies of specific types, and foreign selections.

Sutherland, Edwin H. *White-Collar Crime.* New York: Holt, Rinehart and Winston, 1961.

> The student will profit greatly from a careful reading of this classic. The benefits will include an understanding of Sutherland's criticism of the reliance upon psychological and social pathologies in explaining crime, and his argument that white-collar crime is indeed "crime." The foreword by Donald R. Cressey in this edition is of value in that it confronts many of the criticisms of his mentor's position while he acknowledges the validity of some.

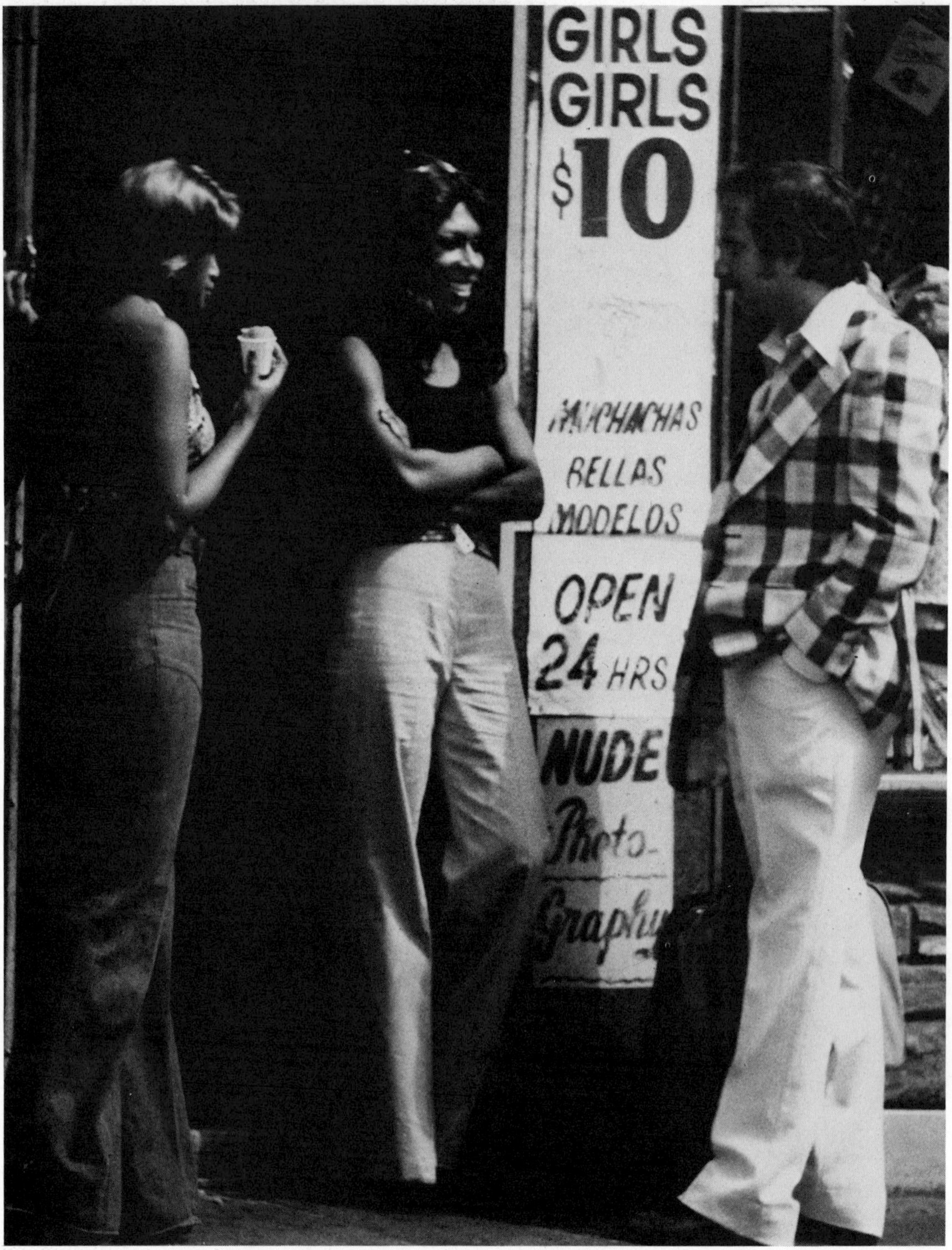
GIRLS
GIRLS
$10
BELLAS
MODELOS
OPEN
24 HRS
NUDE
Photo-

> It is clear that the criminal law is being used to attempt to regulate the private moral conduct of citizens and to coerce them into virtue, although this is done in an arbitrary and haphazard fashion.
> —Norval Morris and Gordon Hawkins, Letter to the President on Crime Control

11

VICTIMLESS CRIMES AND PUBLIC ORDER CRIME PATTERNS

So who gets hurt? This is the question that separates a certain group of illegal activities from all the others. Bluntly speaking, we are talking about some of the behavior connected with drugs, sex, and booze.

All three categories have their socially sensible side. Modern medicine has been grounded in the discovery of beneficial drugs. Sex for procreation and pleasure provides a foundation for all human life. And drinking alcohol for recreation and relaxation is one of this society's most prevailing social habits.

But an illicit aura also is attached to each activity. Narcotics, marijuana, and cocaine traffic are the basis for a gigantic, illegal business world, and where addictive narcotics are concerned, there is the accompanying tragic health factor. Society still places prostitution, and to some extent homosexual activity, in a seedy netherworld with criminal sanctions. And when the heavy drinker becomes the bum on skid row, he is both a social problem and a legal problem.

Because no one is likely to be hurt by these specific activities except the person who engages in them, they have come to be called victimless crimes. And there has been considerable movement toward decriminalizing many of these behaviors to greater or lesser degrees. Although great ambivalence still exists toward them, there is a slow shift in the direction of more enlightened attitudes that may gradually reduce the stigma assigned to the pot smoker, the prostitute, the homosexual, or the public alcoholic. Inherent in this gradual trend is a growing understanding of the impossibility of controlling behavior through the law when you can't even find people complaining that they have been victims.

ARE PUBLIC ORDER CRIMES VICTIMLESS?

Until the 1970s, among the three major classifications of crime—those against the person, against property, and against public decency or public order—crimes against public order were the most numerous. At the time of the President's Crime Commission report in 1967, it was reported that public drunkenness alone accounted for one out of every three arrests.[1]

A behavior prohibited by the criminal code generally is assumed to involve both an offender and a victim. The victim can be a person who suffers injury or loss of property, or it can be a legal entity, such as a corporation, that is deprived of property or legal rights. Ordinarily, the victim is readily identifiable and may institute charges or legal proceedings against the offender. But public order crimes, at least in a number of categories, are borderline cases in which harmful effects are difficult to define. Such borderline behaviors include sex offenses, public intoxication or drunkenness, narcotics and drug use, sexual activities, gambling, and until recently, abortion.

Not all criminologists or legal scholars agree that such behaviors are victimless. Some argue that the drug addict is victimized by his addiction, the prostitute by the exploitative system that "turns her out," the drunk by profit-hungry, alcohol beverage interests, and the gambler by the compulsion to "get rich quick." In one sense, Richard Quinney has argued, all crimes must have victims, for "acts in fact are defined as criminal because someone or something is conceived of as a victim." [2] Edwin Schur concedes that it is as much a value judgment to define a given crime as "victimless," as it is to argue that in a particular situation there is a victim.[3]

Crimes against public order have in common the fact that they are the result of criminal statutes that seek to regulate or coerce morality, or to protect individuals and society from the consequences of conduct that is seen as immoral. As our society has become more diverse, complex, and heterogeneous, criminal laws have been enacted to proscribe or control the conduct of men and women—in private as well as public—so it will conform to the moral values of the dominant interest groups in society. These "borderline" crimes, as Schur has termed them, are symptomatic of inconsistencies and conflicts of interest underlying our legal system. In this respect, they resemble other criminal laws, for few criminal laws are based upon a universal acceptance of norms. As Sutherland has noted, "When the mores are adequate, laws are unnecessary; when the mores are inadequate, the laws are ineffective." [4]

Criminological concern with public order offenses seems to focus on both public and legal definitions and on the lack of consensus concerning the criminalization of such behaviors. The problem is not merely an abstract dilemma about whether or not we can legislate morality. As Schur has argued, victimless crimes involve the combination of consensual exchange transactions with an apparent lack of harm to others. These transactions generally are quite resistant to legal control efforts, especially when the laws designed to proscribe them focus on behaviors that are apt to take place in relatively private situations.[5] Troy Duster has noted that the effectiveness of enforcement is weakest when an offense is without an apparent victim and is hidden from public view. It is maximized when public visibility is heightened, and the offense is reported by a complainant.[6]

The scrutiny of victimless crimes casts light on the manner in which the values and definitions of right and wrong of those who make the laws are instituted and enforced. In the process of administering "no-victim" laws, the methods of enforcement can become objectionable on constitutional grounds, since they frequently involve self-incrimination, illegal search and seizure, and invasion of privacy. In the early 1970s, narcotics enforcement activity led to publicized incidents in which agents broke into private homes and frightened citizens who turned out to be innocent of any involvement in drug violations.[7]

The reliance on decoys, spies, and raids is widespread in vice as well as narcotics.[8] While the professed aim of legislation against such transactional or exchange offenses is to eliminate the behavior in question, the effect of the enforcement is to regulate it. Although social approval is withheld from such transactions, these efforts at regulation in effect represent decisions on how the various goods and services, proscribed by the law, are to be allocated and made available. Moreover, the impact of such laws on those defined, processed, or kept under surveillance escalates the development of criminalistic skills, argot, and lifestyles that facilitate the person's movement from a conventional to a deviant status in society. A number of recent writers have emphasized the manner in which the imputation of deviant status comes to take on aspects of an all-encompassing "master status."[9]

In describing the behavior system of the no-victim offender, we will focus on these aspects as we differentiate and define the various types of victimless crimes. Since the anomalous category of crimes-without-victims relates to violations or norms defined by dominant groups, we will also see how the criminal career, ambiguous self-concepts, and group affiliations develop and overlap with conventional behaviors as these are related to the process of differential and selective societal reaction.

SELECTED PATTERNS OF PUBLIC ORDER CRIME

Offenses in the victimless crime category differ considerably from traditional offenses against persons and property that usually involve both an offender and a victim and in which it is easy to discern the injured person. However, the matter of injury in no-victim crimes is not readily apparent, although the state or political authorities may feel that public order is threatened. But many sections of the criminal law are concerned with behaviors that are criminal largely because at a given point in history "moral entrepreneurs" in the society have declared them so. Homosexual activity between consenting adults, prostitution, narcotic and drug use, drunkenness, and gambling do not involve injury to other individuals, but the fact that they are proscribed indicates society's disapproval.[10]

Sexual Offenses: Prostitution and Homosexual Behavior

The long debate over the use of the criminal law to prohibit immoral behavior by adults came to a head in England in 1957 when Parliament published the Wolfenden Report, which dealt with the problems of homosexuality and prostitution in Great Britain. Lord Devlin urged that the laws continue to intervene in such behaviors because "society cannot ignore the morality of the individual any more than it can his loyalty; it flourishes on both and without either it dies."[11] The opposing view, represented in the eloquent words of John Stuart Mill, was reflected in the Wolfenden Report:

> Unless a deliberate attempt is to be made by society, acting through the agency of the law, to equate the sphere of crime with that of sin, there must remain a realm of private morality and immorality which is in brief and crude terms, not the law's business.[12]

This continuing debate touches the conflicts and controversy over the decriminalization of legal codes restricting and defining sexual offenses in America in the 1980s. The moralistic overtones of the criminal law are most apparent when directed toward sexual behavior. Norval Morris and Gordon Hawkins, both legal scholars, observed some years ago in reference to laws in this area, that "with the possible exception of sixteenth-century Geneva under John Calvin, America has the most moralistic criminal law that the world has yet witnessed."[13] Most laws restricting sexual behavior are intended to regulate one or more of the following aspects of sexual relationships:[14]

Legitimate sex objects in legal codes are adult humans of the opposite sex.

1. *The degree of consent in the relationship.* The most severe legal sanctions are focused here, with some states still defining forcible rape as a capital offense.
2. *Nature of the object.* Sections of the penal code in most states define legitimate sex objects as humans of the opposite sex, of approximately the same age, and separated by a given distance in kinship. Sodomy statutes prohibit relations with members of the same sex, define statutory rape, child molestation, and prohibit relations with close blood relatives.
3. *Nature of the sexual act.* These restrictions usually mean that only heterosexual intercourse is accorded legitimacy. Even then, the act may be subject to narrow definitions of what is legally proscribed. For instance, digital manipulation and oral-genital contact are often defined as illegal, even when occurring by consent between married partners.
4. *The setting in which the act occurs.* Where no other restrictions apply, the behavior may come under the law if it occurs in public or if there is an obvious exhibition of indecency. These statutes may be in force, even where sanctions are not levied against adultery or fornication. Public solicitation and indecent exposure laws often focus on efforts to control the setting rather than the act itself.

These laws illustrate the manner in which the criminal law seeks to enforce a given set of moral standards. No wonder Kinsey speculated that about 95 percent of the population is potentially criminalized by such statutes. The laws also lack the effective threat of legal sanctions that are required for deterrence. As Thurman Arnold noted, "These laws are unenforced because we want to continue our conduct and unrepealed because we want to preserve our morals." [15]

Prostitution is defined legally as the indiscriminate offer by a female of her body for sexual intercourse or other lewdness for the purpose of gain. Prostitution is legally proscribed in all states but Nevada, where it is regulated and licensed in a number of counties.

Commonly called the "world's oldest profession," prostitution has existed in all civilizations. It was a basic part of religious practice in some Eastern religions, and ancient Greeks sometimes considered copulation an act of worship. It was also regarded by medieval thinkers, among them Thomas Aquinas, as a necessary evil that prevented rape and seduction. However, the Protestant Revolution introduced a reaction against such behavior, branding prostitution a "sin of the flesh." [16]

In seventeenth-century England, prostitution was regarded as a public nuisance rather than a crime. In colonial America it was relatively common, although Puritans found it necessary to pass laws against "fornicators, bawdyhouses, and nightwalkers." Prostitutes made their way to the colonies ostensibly to get married. Since wealthy slave owners had access to sexual partners, it was lower-class males in the South who required prostitutes. Over time, there developed a variety of prostitution that appealed to middle-class and upper-class males. The last half of the nineteenth century and the early part of the twentieth century has been termed the "golden age of the brothel" in America. It was also the Victorian era, when a sexual double standard prevailed.[17]

As used here, prostitution refers to a more specific "granting of nonmarital sexual access, established by mutual agreement of the woman, her client, and/or employer, for remuneration which provides part or all of her livelihood."[18] We do not refer to the exchange of social rewards or popularity for sexual intercourse. Nor do we describe male prostitutes, such as those who frequent "gay" bars, although there is some evidence that there may be more male than female prostitutes. However, more research and social control efforts have focused on female prostitution.[19]

In the United States today, most houses of prostitution have disappeared, due to efforts at legal prohibition. But there are still two general categories of prostitutes. The first is the "streetwalker," or common street or bar prostitute. These women usually solicit their customers directly in the streets or other public places. In Los Angeles, a car-oriented city, clients, or "johns," cruise by and ask how much; and the women state their price.[20]

The second type of prostitute is the "call girl," who is considered to be of higher status. She usually makes her contacts with a customer by telephone or by referral from a pimp or other call girl. The distinctions between the two types are not always clear. Streetwalkers sometimes have pimps bring "johns" to them. Sometimes a call girl will work from a cocktail lounge, where the bartender will pimp for her. Some work hotels, but the more successful make their arrangements by telephone. The call girl is more likely to have middle- and upper-class clients, and may charge from $50 to $100 or more a night for her services.[21]

Homosexual behavior between consenting adults is another facet of private morality that the criminal statutes of virtually every state seek to restrict. Homosexuality—sexual behavior directed toward persons of one's own sex—is not against the law. Rather, certain homosexual acts such as anal intercourse (sodomy in the common law), fellatio, and mutual masturbation between members of the same sex are illegal.

Homosexual behavior was practiced in antiquity. The ancient Greeks, for example, often took young men as homosexual consorts and extended to them an elaborate social role. In our society, taboos against homosexual behavior grew out of ancient Judaic laws. These were formalized during the Middle Ages, when the homosexual was seen as a person possessed of evil spirits. This attitude was transmitted into English common law, though there was no special definition of homosexual behavior until the latter part of the seventeenth century. By the early 1700s, the idea of exclusive homosexuality became well established; but it was often confused with transvestism (dressing up in the clothing of the opposite sex).[22] In general, homosexuality developed as a complex social role related to homosexual behavior. Today, homosexual behavior between consenting adults is not proscribed in European countries, except for West Germany.

The absence of laws against homosexuality on the continent of Europe reflects the liberalizing effects of the French Revolution. However, early American laws regarding sexual behavior were influenced by English common law, and they included harsh punishments for sodomy—the original term for homosexual acts. Until recent years, all fifty states had statutes applicable to homosexual behaviors between consenting adults. These varied from those condemning vagrancy to sodomy and fellatio. Several states have repealed their antihomosexual laws, while others have reduced the offense from felony to misdemeanor status. Among those sixteen states that have repealed antihomosexual statutes are Colorado, Connecticut, Hawaii, Idaho, Illinois, and Oregon.[23] Laws defining homosexual behavior as a felony exist in many states except California, Connecticut and Illinois, where it is legal between consenting adults (twenty-one years of age) and the other thirteen states, where it is defined as a misdemeanor.

Laws prohibiting homosexual behavior are meant to apply equally to males and females, but generally they are not enforced against lesbians. Twenty states have sodomy laws, which have been expanded in practice to include fellatio and often mutual masturbation. Other states prohibit vaguely defined acts such as "crimes against nature," "unnatural crimes," "any unnatural copulation," and the "abominable crime against nature with man or beast." Since in most cases, unless force has been used, there is no victim or complainant and there has been a willing exchange of services, homosexual acts are victimless crimes.[24]

Drunkenness: Patterns of Blaming the Victim

Although the volume and the proportion of arrests for drunkenness have decreased slightly due to its decriminalization in some states, it still accounted for about one of six arrests in 1975, compared with one of four in 1970. Strictly speaking, drunkenness does not have the features of a victimless crime, since it does not involve the exchange between willing partners of goods or services emphasized by Schur. But it does involve both personal harm and social disapproval and is a borderline offense relating to the control of personal conduct in public.[25]

Many societies have social controls relating to drinking behavior that are included in their penal codes. In the United States these laws were largely a consequence of the temperance crusade of the nineteenth century. The temperance movement had considerable impact on Great Britain and the Nordic countries as well. Today, the regulation of such behavior, especially in the area of drunk driving, is severely sanctioned in those countries. Joseph Gusfield has written an excellent study of the temperance movement in America, which he termed the "symbolic crusade." He argues that prohibition laws served symbolic functions, since they did not depend on successful enforcement for their effect. Rather, they enhanced the social status and values of small-town, rural, Protestant, middle-class groups at the expense of urban and lower-class groups that practiced lifestyles that allowed drinking.[26] The laws against public drunkenness are most often enforced against lower-class persons. The way in which arrests for drunkenness are related to efforts to enforce community values has been demonstrated in cross-cultural studies. A comparative study of arrests for drunkenness in Helsinki, Finland, and Copenhagen, Denmark, for instance, noted that while the frequency of drunkenness was about the same in the two cities, the rate of arrests in Helsinki was seven to fourteen times as high. It was found that the small number of restaurants serving lower-class persons largely accounted for the discrepancy in arrests.[27]

In the United States, state laws as well as local ordinances prohibit public drunkenness in most jurisdictions. These laws are supplemented by those which prohibit drinking in a public place. Some college towns enforce so-called "open container" laws largely against students. Variations of these laws make disorderly conduct or conduct that is a breach of the peace while intoxicated subject to public drunkenness laws. The laws provide jail sentences ranging from five days to six months, but typically the maximum sentence is thirty days. Habitual drunkenness is punished in some jurisdictions as a felony. Frequently, decisions on whether or not to make an arrest are based upon the discernible affluence of the drunk person. Obviously, the intent of the drunkenness laws is to clear the streets of inebriates who might annoy the citizens, rather than to control criminal behavior.[28] In recent years there has been a shift toward decriminalization of public drunkenness and the removal of drunks from public streets to detoxification units. Some of the implications of this reform will be noted.

DRUG USE AND VICTIMLESS CRIME PATTERNS

Drugs have been used widely in many societies for centuries. Only in recent years has societal concern over the misuse of these substances led to attempts to control them. American society has been termed by some observers as "drug oriented." Many drugs are manufactured, distributed, and used through both legal and illegal channels. Our focus here is on the legal definition of narcotics and drugs and the efforts to proscribe them, since the laws regulating substance use have had the overall effect of defining many users as criminals.

Drug Types and Definitions

It is necessary to clarify definitions and distinctions that will be useful in our discussion of proscribed or controlled drugs. First, an important caveat: all narcotics are drugs, but not all drugs are narcotics. Second, while in law and custom "narcotics" has come to connote more than opium and its derivatives, we will use "narcotics" to refer only to addictive, or "hard," drugs or substances.[29]

The following are classifications of some of the more important drugs (see Table 11.1):

1. *Depressants.* These include *barbiturates,* which encompass over twenty varieties such as barbital and secobarbital. Barbiturates can be obtained by prescription, but they also are available in illicit trade, where they are known as "barbs," "nimbies," or "seccies." *Tranquilizers,* nonbarbituric depressants such as Miltown and Librium, are often termed "downers." Physical dependence or addiction may develop from using barbiturates.[30]

2. *Stimulants.* These include amphetamines, or "uppers," such as Benzedrine, "bennies," dexedrine, Melhedrine, and other pep pills, or "speed." While tolerance to stimulants develops quickly so that larger doses are required, addiction, or physiological dependence, does not develop. *Cocaine* also is a stimulant and has effects similar to those of amphetamines, but it differs in chemical substance and is derived from the leaves of the coca plant. Although tolerance develops to cocaine, there is no addiction. Once used by lower-class slum dwellers, in recent years cocaine has come to be used by "swingers," the "jet set," and even professional athletes and entertainers.[31]

3. *Opiates.* Opium generally is smoked to reach a high. It has also been used for centuries as a pain killer; though only in the late nineteenth century did it become an important ingredient in patent medicines. *Paregoric* contains opium tinctured with alcohol, as does *Laudanum.*

The most potent opiate, *heroin,* is extracted from *morphine,* which in turn is derived from but is more potent than pure opium. *Codeine* is also a derivative of opium. Heroin has been the opiate of choice for the last several decades, although morphine has been used by physician addicts due to its availability. Since passage of the Harrison Act in 1914, heroin has not been used for medicinal purposes. Thus, any heroin now used in the United States has been smuggled into the country. Methadone is a modern synthetic drug, developed in search for an opiate substitute. Although withdrawal symptoms are less severe, methadone is also addictive. Opiates set the standard for "hard" narcotics, and the addictive properties of other drugs are often evaluated against them.[32]

4. *Marijuana.* This is a generic term that refers to a wide range of psychoactive substances derived from *Cannabis sativa,* or the Indian hemp plant. The top parts of the cannabis plant become coated with a resin that contains most of the THC (tetrahydrocannibol) in the plant. The resin from the flowerheads is referred to as "hashish" or "hash." The effects of marijuana can be related to, but are different from, those of alcohol; there is usually no "hang-over." [33]

5. *Hallucinogens and Psychedelics.* These include lysergic acid (LSD-25), *psilocybin, psilocin,* and *mescaline.* LSD is synthesized from the ergot fungus found in rye and wheat; psilocybin and psilocin are derived from Latin American mushrooms, and mescaline is the active ingredient in peyote cactus buttons. Neither the hallucinogenic substances nor marijuana results in dependence or addiction, although some researchers argue that the user may become habituated to them. Numerous studies have suggested, for instance, that tolerance to marijuana may decrease with usage, and it may require less to gain the effect of a "high." [34]

Table 11.1. Drug Types Classified in Semitechnical Terms

1. *Opiates*
   A. Opium
      pure opium
      laudanum
      paregoric
   B. Opium derivatives
      codeine
      morphine
      narcotine
      papaverine
      thebaine
   C. Morphine derivatives
      diluadid
      heroin
   D. Synthetic opiates
      meperidine (Demerol and Nesentil)
      methadone (Dolophine)
      isomethadone
      percodan

2. *Hallucinogens*
   A. Indian hemp
      marihuana (marijuana, mariguana)
      bhang
      ganja
      hashish
      charas
      THC (tetrahydrocannibol)
   B. Other natural hallucinogens
      morning glory seeds
      nutmeg
      peyote
      psilocybe mushroom
      others—epena, jimson weed, fly agaric (central agent probably belladonna)
   C. Chemicals—modifications or derivatives
      LSD (lysergic acid diethylamide)
      DMT (dimethyltryptamine)
      mescaline (peyote)
      psilocybin (mushroom)
      psilocin (mushroom)
      STP (dimethoxy-methylamphetamine)

3. *Depressants, Sedatives, and Tranquilizers*
   A. Barbiturates
      amobarbital (Amytal)
      butabarbital
      pentobarbital (Nembutal)
      phenobarbital (Luminal)
      secobarbital (Seconal)
   B. Tranquilizers
      chlordiazepoxide (Librium)
      chlorpromazine
      diazepam (Valium)
      meprobamate (Miltown)
   C. Other: bromides—chloral-hydrate

4. *Stimulants*
   A. Amphetamines
      amphetamine (Benzedrine)
      dextroamphetamine (Dexedrine)
   B. Nonamine stimulants
      cocaine

5. *Solvents and Deliriants*
   aerosol sprays
   airplane glues
   cleaning fluids
   ether
   gasoline
   paint thinners

Note: There are corresponding argot or street slang for each drug type.
Source: From *Deviant Behavior: A Social Learning Approach*, 2nd ed., by Ronald L. Akers. © 1977 by Wadsworth Publishing Company, Inc., Belmont, CA 94002. Reprinted by permission of the publisher.

These definitions provide a framework for our description of law enforcement and public policy relative to both "hard," addictive drugs, and other proscribed substances. We should note, however, that efforts to regulate the use of these substances have reflected public opinion and public perceptions of the drugs and their users, rather than the actual degree of dangerousness of the substances.

Until recent years, many citizens as well as experts assumed that most laws concerning drugs were enacted to protect the individual and society from antisocial behavior that might result from their use. But Erich Goode has argued cogently that as we examine the laws regulating drug use more closely, this assumption seems less plausible. If the premise were valid, then the more dangerous a drug, the more vigorous would be the legal efforts to proscribe its use. The less dangerous drugs would be less apt to be legally forbidden. Yet his studies uncovered little or no relationship between the harmful nature of drugs and their proscription.[35]

Goode utilized a scheme developed by Joel Fort for establishing the dimensions of actual or potential damage that might result from drug use. The dimensions used related to hazards for brain or organic damage, mental damage, addiction hazards, and potential for violence, motor vehicle accidents, or death. Since these are harmful effects about which there is considerable agreement, he suggests the following three groupings of drugs:[36]

1. *Most dangerous drugs currently in use.* Alcohol, barbiturates, amphetamines, cocaine, and nicotine (in cigarettes). Chronic, heavy use of any of these results in a high probability of physical and mental damage.
2. *Moderately dangerous drugs* (relative to those in the first category). All narcotics (heroin, opium, morphine), due to the hazard of overdosing and the high probability of addiction; and hallucinogens, due to the possibility of psychotic reactions.
3. *Least dangerous drugs.* Aspirin, caffeine, and marijuana, according to current medical and pharmacological knowledge, seem to cause infrequent, relatively superficial damage.

Although former secretary of Health, Education and Welfare, Joe Califano —a former, three-pack-a-day smoker—launched a national antismoking campaign in 1978, and the surgeon general issued a report in 1979 emphasizing the many dangers of smoking, two of the most dangerous drugs, nicotine and alcohol, are readily available to all except youngsters. While cocaine is criminalized, billions of amphetamines and barbiturates are made available by prescription to Americans each year. The moderately dangerous drugs, on the other hand, are illegal except for morphine and its derivatives, which are strictly regulated. The fact that most people do not realize that aspirin and caffeine are about as dangerous as marijuana suggests that it is naive to assume that drug laws are passed by an informed citizenry concerned about public health and safety.[37]

The Marijuana Tax Act of 1937 placed a tax upon the drug and, in effect, created a whole new class of "crimes." This law influenced the passage of similar legislation by most of the states. The laws made possession of even a small amount of marijuana, its sale, or transfer—including giving or handing a joint to a friend—a felony, punishable by lengthy prison terms.

Howard Becker's study of the part that the Federal Bureau of Narcotics played as an organized political interest group in the passage of this law is instructive. The bill, passed as the Marijuana Tax Act of 1937, was written by FBN staff who also lobbied for it in Congress. The law banned possession of marijuana by levying a heavy tax on it. The bill was virtually unopposed, except by birdfeed manufacturers who used hempseed in their products, and by a representative of the American Medical Association whose testimony was ignored. In effect, the law classified marijuana as a narcotic and provided penalties similar to those under the Harrison Act. Subsequently, marijuana was dealt with, in state as well as federal laws, under the assumption that it was a dangerous narcotic.[38] In Rhode Island, for instance, the penalty for selling marijuana to a minor is thirty years in prison—a more severe sanction than for cases of rape or second-degree murder. Whether these sanctions are enforced is another question. When the current movement to decriminalize marijuana began in 1971, the penalties ranged from five to twenty years in Alabama and Minnesota; up to twenty years in Missouri; up to fifteen years in New Jersey and Ohio; and up to ten years in California, Idaho, Indiana, Kentucky, Michigan, and Oregon. Other states had sentences of six months to six years on the books. In 1971, Nebraska was the only state in which simple possession of less than eight ounces was only a misdemeanor, punishable by up to seven days in jail.[39] These draconian laws led to the arrests of thousands of youths. In California alone, there were more than 50,000 arrests in 1968, costing the state some $72 million. The costs of administering control efforts helped spur the move to decriminalize the various antimarijuana laws. By 1979, eight states, including New York, had followed Nebraska's example (see map in Box 1). But none of the laws has yet legalized the possession or sale of marijuana.

The federal and state laws seeking to regulate marijuana were patterned on the Harrison Act of 1914, which outlawed the sale of narcotics like opium and heroin. This act, as Alfred Lindesmith notes, is the basic antinarcotic act of the United States. Passed as a revenue measure, it gave no indication of any apparent legislative intent to deny heroin addicts access to legal drugs or to interfere in medical treatment of addicts. However, subsequent Supreme Court decisions ruled that possession of smuggled drugs by an addict was a violation of the law.[40]

In a series of decisions from 1915 to 1922, the Court ruled that there was no acceptable legal or medical way for addicts to obtain drugs. For the most part, these decisions related to physicians who had provided drugs to addicts indiscriminately. However, in the case of Dr. Charles Linder of Seattle, a female addict-informer was given only four tablets to ease her withdrawal pains. After a prolonged and costly litigation, the case reached the Supreme Court,

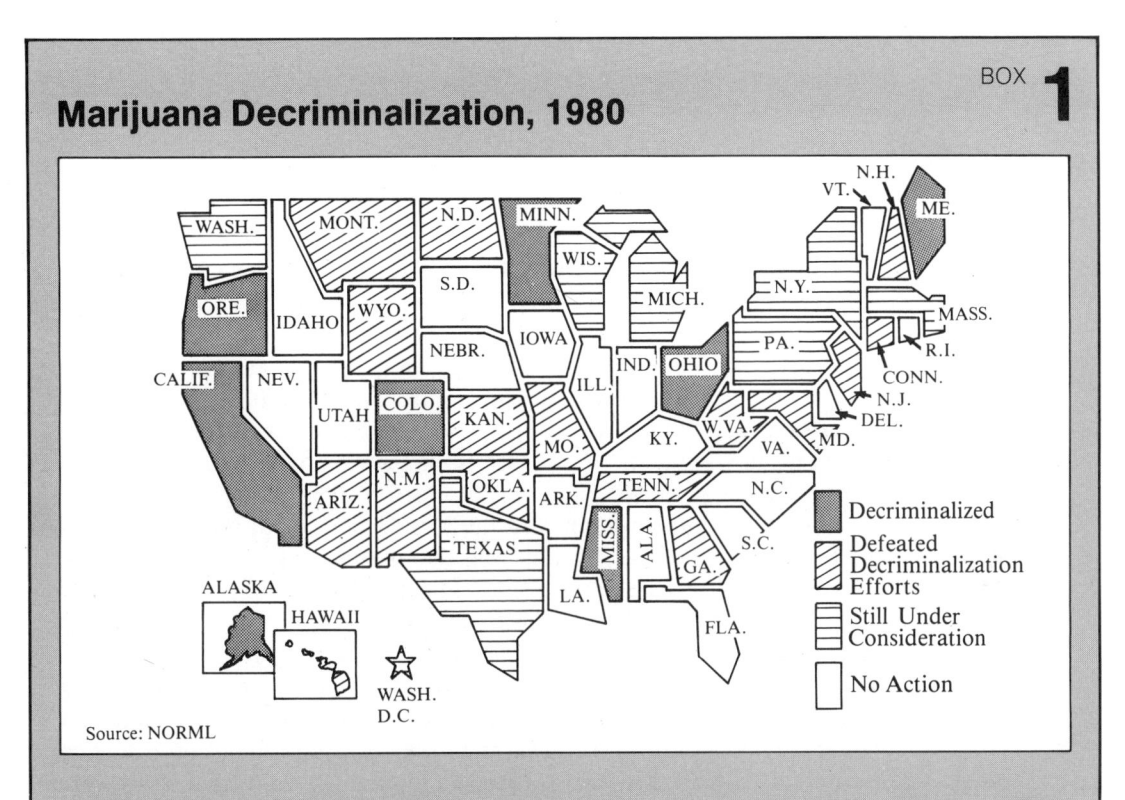

Victimless Crimes and Public Order Crime Patterns

BOX 1

Marijuana Decriminalization, 1980

Source: NORML

- Decriminalized
- Defeated Decriminalization Efforts
- Still Under Consideration
- No Action

(UPI) Eight states have "decriminalized" possession of small amounts of marijuana—that is, they have removed the threat of jail terms and substituted a system of fines, at least for first offenders (second offenders in some states still face imprisonment). Seven other states as well as the District of Columbia are presently considering such action, while similar proposals in 16 more states have been defeated. Decriminalization, experts point out, is not legalization and no one in a responsible government position advocates making marijuana as readily available as, say, alcohol. Use of the drug has jumped dramatically in the past decade; 36 million Americans are said to have at least tried marijuana.

Source: National Organization for the Reform of Marijuana Laws. Appeared in the *Boston Globe*, May 10, 1977. Updated by authors, 1980.

which ruled (1) that addiction is a disease; and (2) that acting in good faith and following appropriate standards, a physician may provide drugs to relieve such distress without being in violation of the law.[41]

The Linder case had no apparent effect as far as enforcement was concerned, for the Federal Bureau of Narcotics ignored it in its efforts to prevent the treatment of addicts by medical practitioners. Through its enforcement efforts, the FBN effectively thwarted efforts of medical practitioners to provide their addict patients with drugs. From 1925 to 1938, the Bureau interfered with thousands of doctors involved in legitimate medical practice; many were prosecuted and convicted.[42]

Policies pursued under the Harrison Act and its successor, the Comprehensive Drug Abuse Prevention and Control Act of 1970, stigmatized the addicted user as a "junkie" or a dope fiend. Unable to get treatment for his addiction legally, the addict must turn to illegal suppliers. The resultant illegal drug traffic has provided enormous profits for organized criminals.[43]

The major difference between the United States' approach to drug users and that of most European countries is that we deal with them as a legal problem, while they see the problem as medical. The British system is one of the better known examples. Until the 1960s, Great Britain was able to control its drug problem by allowing physicians to prescribe drugs for registered addicts who could obtain them inexpensively under the National Health Service.[44] Britain was able to control the illegal traffic in opiates until American and Canadian addicts began to travel there in the 1960s and found ways to exploit the system. In 1968, the British began to replace the individual treatment approach with drug clinics. Recent reports indicate that Britain is having difficulty with an expanding illicit opiate drug market.[45] But in Britain and other European countries, programs for drug users still are essentially directed by medical rather than legal authorities.

STATUS OFFENDER CAREERS: SELF-CONCEPT, GROUP SUPPORT, AND CONVERGENCES

Three of the lifestyles related to public order crime patterns involve traits that have often been referred to as "crimes without victims." They represent action systems that come about through attempts to proscribe or ban through criminal laws an exchange or transaction of goods or services between willing partners. The criminal offense defined in laws regulating prostitution, homosexual acts, and the sale of illegal drugs all share the situational element of a consensual exchange. Public drunkenness does not have this exchange aspect, although some refer to it as a victimless crime. It is very difficult to enforce laws against these behaviors, usually because there is no complainant.[46]

The attempts to ban such activities does not mean that those involved in victimless crimes accept or share the criminal self-concept ascribed to them. Yet all share or tend to develop a deviant self-image, largely as a result of the antisocial definition of their behavior. Still, the ambivalence of societal norms toward such behavior and its overlap with conventional aspects of social life result in the absence of clear-cut criminal careers for victimless offenders.

Sex Offender Careers

Prostitution. In American society, prostitution is an activity whose visibility depends upon the level of law enforcement activity to control it. In the nineteenth and early twentieth centuries, when prostitution was at a high level, it thrived in the red-light districts in which brothels were located. Prostitutes set themselves apart from "good," middle-class women by their lifestyles. The "bad" or "loose" woman displayed flamboyant clothes and hair styles and indulged freely in the use of cigarettes, alcohol, and obscenity.[47]

Even though such overt status distinctions are less obvious today, the individual prostitute still must deal with the discrepancies between the behavior of her social world and the dominant society's values. Even the highest status call girl cannot avoid living partly within a lifestyle that is defined as deviant, if not criminal. By participating in the "life" of the prostitute, she receives emotional and group support for activities that involve selling what society views as a nonpurchasable service. This is not to suggest, however, that prostitutes go through life concerned with guilt feelings about their sexual morality.[48]

A study of the prostitute's self-concept by Norman Jackman, et al., explored two questions. First, since the pervasive, dominant social values reject prostitution, how are women recruited to this career? Second, how does the prostitute rationalize the violation of these dominant social norms?

The authors set forth three propositions regarding the formation and maintenance of the self-concept of the prostitute:[49]

1. *The more isolated woman in an urban situation arrives at a definition of patterns of behavior censured by dominant societal values with less difficulty than the less isolated.* The data suggest that the respondents were alienated from their parents due to hostile feeling toward their fathers, although they later were reconciled with their mothers, from whom they kept their activities secret. "I would go through hell for my mother, but... my father went out with other women." "My father... always treated me like I was strictly from age two. But I got along good with my mother." The subjects also indicated their alienation at the time of their entrance into the "life." They all seemed to feel that they faced an indifferent, hostile world. "I was hanging round bars in Tulsa just looking for kicks. I had no place to go, like. It was strictly from hunger, man."

2. *Since the dominant social values still had some meaning for these isolated women, they found it necessary to rationalize their violation of them.* They justified their violation of sex norms in several ways: "Everyone is rotten; so prostitutes are no worse than others. At least we are less hypocritical." Or they took a defensive attitude toward social disapproval: "Little chippies in bars give it away for a couple of beers." "This business doesn't keep you from having

good children.... What we do doesn't affect religious feelings."

3. *In their rationalizations they exaggerated other values—especially those of financial success.* Some emphasized the unselfish manner in which they provided for those dependent upon them. Given the group norms with which they identified, this was quite normal. Their reference worlds were of two types: the contraculture world and the "straight" world. However, six of those interviewed had no identification at all and expressed feelings of alienation. This latter group (40 percent) were comprised in part of beginners in the "life" who evidently lacked or had not yet developed a network of interaction with significant others, or who lacked a fantasy world to sustain a positive self-image. It is apparent that self-denigration is only one of several self-images available to the prostitute.

It may be that such rationalizations serve as a means of neutralizing social disapproval, and the prostitutes use the neutralization technique of "condemning the condemnors." The straight world is seen as immoral, and they see themselves as no more immoral, and even less hypocritical, than the "squares." At least they are "up front" and honest about what they do, while other women, wives and girlfriends, do the same thing but call it something else: "The only difference between me and some of these wives is that they don't keep the bargain and I do." [50] Such expressions indicate that prostitutes tend to share a common subculture and behavior system, although there appears to be considerable variation within general parameters. This perspective not only helps to provide an identity, but also helps overcome social reproach, especially in the beginning. Once in the "life," economic factors, closing out of other options, and a network of interpersonal affiliations sustain the self-concept and behavior, even if the prostitute comes to doubt the folklore and myths of her profession.[51]

The folklore includes success stories of women who have made it through financial "scores" or who married well. The legends variously portray the prostitute as a woman with a "heart of gold"; or quite the opposite, as a "cold-blooded businesswoman who hates men." Another belief supported by news accounts and impressionistic data is that most prostitutes are heavy users of drugs. Yet Paul Gebhard's study in 1969 identified only 4 percent who were addicted and another 5 percent that he classified as "experimenters." [52]

Information concerning recruitment includes some persistent myths. There is the "white slave" theory, which seeks to explain how innocent girls are lured through false pretense, force, or drugs to enter the life. As recently as November 1977, the *New York Times* and network TV news reports carried news items describing how hundreds of girls from the Midwest—Minneapolis in particular—were lured to New York to work as prostitutes. Two Minneapolis police officers came east to search for teenage runaways on New York City's sleazy "Minnesota Strip," but did not have much success.[53]

Some studies suggest that women are recruited for careers in the "life" in two modal age groups. The first, eighteen to twenty-two years, is the age range in which most streetwalkers enter the "life." "Call girls" are more likely to enter the profession after age twenty-five and generally are better educated.

Streetwalkers generally become prostitutes by drifting from amateur to semiprofessional to professional occupational positions. The call girl, however, becomes trained in the ways of the behavior system through three stages. First, she enters the world of the "life" through a relationship with a woman friend or a male pimp who may have been her lover. Second, she serves an apprenticeship period under the direction of an experienced call girl or pimp for two to eight months. This involves learning interpersonal and sexual techniques, telephone "pitches," and certain rules of the "life." Third, she develops contacts, so that she will have her own clientele.[54]

The behavior system of the prostitute includes several other major roles and meaning systems. Among these is the manner of relating to the clients or "johns" in economic rather than sexual terms. This way of relating to males, including pimps, replaces the dating and courtship patterns learned earlier and often becomes part of the self-image, helping to justify participation in the behavior. Thus, the rules that help justify exploitation—men are immoral and cheat on their wives—serve to lessen the social stigma, real or potential, which the woman may feel.[55]

Homosexual Behavior. In our society, an individual, male or female, who is known to have been involved in a homosexual act becomes labeled as a homosexual. Along with the label comes the stigma of social disapproval from much of the heterosexual world. Similar negative labeling does not occur in the case of those who participate in heterosexual behavior. For them, sex is regarded as merely one facet of their personal behavior and does not ordinarily become the focus of their identity.

The extent of the social stigma accorded homosexuals almost inevitably has resulted in an organized protest movement by numerous homophile organizations. The emerging Gay Liberation Movement has social, as well as legal and political, consequences. Today, there is still considerable controversy regarding the legal status of those who are defined, or identify themselves, as homosexuals.

A sociologist who has published extensively in the field, John Gagnon, traces the current controversy and debate regarding the status of both male and female homosexuals to the report by Alfred Kinsey on sexual behavior in the human male (1948).[56] Although Kinsey's figures may be somewhat inflated due to the self-selection process involved in gathering his data, generally it is conceded that the Kinsey Report is still a valuable source of information on homosexuality in America. Kinsey found that about 10 percent of the males in America had experimented extensively with exclusive homosexuality, although most of these experiences were during adolescence. Further, he found that 4 percent of the total male population and 2 percent of the female population were exclusively homosexual.[57] If this proportion has not changed, we would have about four million men and two million women who are exclusively homosexual today.

The Kinsey findings and later research cast doubt on traditional myths concerning homosexuals. For example, there is no evidence that children exposed to homosexual role models will be induced to accept a homosexual orientation. Nor is there evidence supporting the idea that homosexuals are more likely to molest children than heterosexuals. (The contrary appears to be the case, since in reality most child molesters are males who violate young girls.) In other words, like heterosexuals, most homosexuals most of the time conduct their sexual activities in private and with discretion. The fact that homosexual behavior remains proscribed by the criminal codes in most states means that this aspect of their lifestyle still stirs considerable anxiety in the larger society.

These studies have also challenged the simplistic pathological explanations that had traditionally been advanced by psychological and medical theories. The idea that the homosexual was "sick" had come to be shared by many homosexuals and even some homophile organizations. The new body of knowledge has, in recent years, lessened the social stigma that had been affiliated with such behavior. But discriminatory laws and the underlying social rejection have not disappeared.

The homosexual's changing self-concept has contributed to the evolving social view of the homosexual. Homosexual organizations have united under the Gay Liberation Front. Nationally, members of these organizations have held public demonstrations demanding an end to job discrimination and the right to serve in the armed services. On the local level, they have demonstrated for the right to be employed as policemen and teachers, and they have sought acceptance for homosexual marriages and the right to adopt children.[58]

With the successes of this militant movement, gay confidence has grown. As the Gay Activist Alliance noted:

> There are Hollywood sex goddesses who are lesbians. There are professional football players who are homosexuals. There are weak, limp-wristed heterosexual men and tough swaggering heterosexual women.... The great majority of gay people are "typical" males and females in the pattern of our erotic responses.[59]

It seemed as though the public was coming to realize that gays not only looked like "straight" people, but might actually be like them (except in sexual preference). But a heterosexual moralistic reaction was aroused, as the Gay Liberation Front began to make claims to equal civil and human rights.

This counter reform became most visible in the spring of 1977, with the crusade launched against the Dade County (Miami) antidiscrimination ordinance. Homosexual teachers bore the brunt of Anita Bryant's "Save Our Children Campaign," which forced a referendum rescinding the ordinance. Then in the fall of 1977, the Supreme Court declined to review two separate cases that had been appealed from courts in New Jersey and Washington. The Washington state court decision involved the case of a high school teacher in Tacoma who had been dismissed on grounds of "immorality" when it was learned that he was a homosexual. In New Jersey, a teacher had been ordered by the Paramus Board of Education to undergo psychiatric tests after he became president of the New Jersey Gay Activist Alliance. The teacher refused on the grounds that such a request violated his rights to "privacy and equal protection under the law."[60]

The old myths die slowly. But the gap between attitudes that approve and disapprove of homosexuality appears to be narrowing. As conventional male and female roles become modified, it may be that society will become less inclined to condemn the homosexual to the status of a social pariah.

Careers of Substance Users

Alcohol Use. The use of alcoholic beverages has created controversy throughout human history. The question usually has not been whether or not alcohol should be used, but rather who should be approved to use it and under what social conditions. Even in colonial America, drinking was not seen as a social problem. But though the Puritans did not proscribe its use, they were opposed to drunkenness. The antidrinking movement really began in the nineteenth century, culminating in the "noble experiment" of Prohibition.[61]

There is a persistent myth that alcohol stimulates the drinker. However, as alcohol is ingested into the body, it serves to *depress* the central nervous system. In large quantities, it can even lead to unconsciousness. Researchers believe that alcohol exerts its depressing effects initially on those parts of the brain responsible for the integration of the activities of the various parts of the nervous system. Thus, the higher centers are released from control. With drunkenness, there is a slowing down of motor and sensory functions, and judgments regarding one's actions and self are dulled.

Users of alcohol may be classified in three groups: *the social or controlled drinker, the heavy or problem drinker, and the alcoholic.*[62] One national study located heavy drinkers among the following social groups: males, those with a college education, the next to the highest and the third from the lowest occupational statuses, unmarried people, and urban dwellers.[63]

The drinking problem in our society does not concern *whether* one should drink, but *how much* a person should drink. Since about half the adult population drinks alcoholic beverages for pleasure, the individual addicted to alcohol is not stigmatized to the same degree as the drug addict. But the heavy drinker—especially the chronic drinker—is stigmatized by his behavior and is labeled as an alcoholic.

The available evidence indicates that a significant proportion of those arrested in 1975 for drunkenness were chronic alcoholics or those with a history of previous repeated arrests for drunkenness. This "revolving door" effect can place an extreme burden on the criminal justice system. The more permissive sociomedical orientation of the police has lessened the burden upon the system and also diminished the effects of criminalization upon the individuals apprehended.[64] Yet, if we attribute the problem of alcoholism to alcoholics, we not only "blame the victim" but we obscure the fact that alcohol is the most abused drug in our society.

Indirectly, drinking is assumed to be related to a variety of serious offenses.

There are legal precedents in court decisions that allow involuntary treatment for chronic drinkers, so long as they are not treated as criminals. In 1966, the U.S. Fourth Circuit Court of Appeals found in favor of a man who had been arrested over two hundred times for public intoxication. The court ruled that a chronic alcoholic could not be "stamped" as a criminal if his drinking behavior was the result of a disease and thus was involuntary (*Driver* v. *Hinnant*, 356F, 2nd 761). Another decision held that chronic alcoholism is a defense against the charge of public intoxication and therefore not a crime (*Easter* v. *Dist. of Columbia*, 361, 2nd 50, 1966). The following year, the Supreme Court held by a narrow decision that a chronic alcoholic could be convicted under a state law against public intoxication. But this decision did not invalidate state and local laws that allow such mitigating defenses, since the majority of the Court did not agree on the reasons for its decision.[65] Although the individual arrested for drunkenness need not view himself as a criminal, the ambiguity of his status, even in medical treatment, may still make him feel identified as a wrongdoer.

The concern with keeping homeless, skid row inebriates off the streets considerably augments arrest statistics for drunkenness. The group aspects of these skid row "bottle gangs" are well documented in sociological studies.[66]

The group defines drinking patterns and affords means and methods for obtaining the bottle. The group also provides support for the control of aggressive behavior within the group—behavior that might attract the attention of the police. However, association with these "bottle gangs" can lead to an arrest even if the person is not drunk. One offender recalls:

> One day just after I got out of here [The House of Corrections], I hopped off a streetcar.... A couple of fellows I know were standing at the corner.... I stopped to pass the time of day.... the Wagon comes around and I'm picked up. "I'm just back from the Workhouse," I says. "Aw you're drunk," they tells me, and I'm back in again—without even a drink! [67]

There are at least two ways in which the use of alcohol may overlap and converge with criminal behavior. The first includes public drunkenness, drunk driving, and violations of liquor laws regulating the use of alcohol. Those offenses directly related to the use of beverage alcohol constituted 24 percent of all arrests in 1975. If we add an additional 9 percent for disorderly conduct and vagrancy—usually attributed to heavy drinking—then we have accounted for about one-third of all arrests. Indirectly, it is assumed that drinking is related to a variety of serious offenses. It is known that a high proportion of those who are sentenced for felonies are drinkers. One study in the California prison system found that 29 percent of those incarcerated claimed that they were drunk at the time of their current offense.[68] These men, of course, might have been seeking to neutralize or rationalize their behavior. Though there is little evidence linking alcohol to serious crime, the economic and social effects of chronic drinking may be related to other criminogenic factors. It is generally agreed that the vocational or professional criminal avoids excessive drinking except as a leisure time activity.

Drug Use. The problem of drug use, particularly addictive opiates, is small compared to alcoholism. But society's strong suppression of the behavior tends to push the heavy drug user toward the deviant drug subculture. This affiliation with the drug subculture may be seen, in part at least, as a consequence of the user's exclusion from society. The user's antisocial attitudes and lack of commitment to the dominant society's values may, in turn, be related to the initial movement into the illegal behavior. The response by law enforcement agencies to the illicit activity may escalate the user's criminal career development. This occurs not only through the act of defining the drug as illegal, but also because the illegal substance must be obtained from illegal sources, which usually means through organized crime sources. Should the user become addicted, efforts to maintain a daily supply of the substance—a habit may cost from $10 to $150 a day—involve more and more time, and other interests fade away as the scramble for the fix becomes a lifestyle. As Goode aptly noted, one need not advocate legalization to recognize that nearly all the features of the heroin scene that are viewed as repugnant (except for the act itself) are the result of the present legal and social organization that surrounds addiction and not a function of the drug itself.[69]

Heroin use and addiction is learned behavior, and it usually is learned in association with others. Most users were first "turned on" by friends rather than by "pushers." Because drug use, whether heroin or marijuana, is initiated and maintained through affiliational networks, it is nearly impossible to control.[70]

The fact that users become addicted to opiates, especially heroin, does not necessarily mean that they were naive about the addictive aspects of the substance any more than they were about its illicit aspects. But those who become "junkies" tend to have a naive belief that *they* will not be the ones who get "hooked." Addiction occurs when the user becomes physically as well as psychologically dependent on the drug after the body's system has developed a high tolerance to the substance. Unlike marijuana, tolerance to heroin usually develops quickly. Once dependent upon the drug, the individual suffers withdrawal symptoms that can only be relieved by more use of the drug. If the user suffers such symptoms, realizes that they are the result of interrupted use of the substance, recognizes that heroin will relieve the pain, and then uses the drug to relieve the pain, he or she is addicted.[71]

The marijuana user says that he or she is "straight" when not under the influence of that drug. The heroin user is "straight" when he has used the substance to avoid the pain of withdrawal. Heroin use thus becomes the focus of his or her way of life, while marijuana is just an activity outside of the "straight" scene.[72]

We might view the heroin addict, except for the brief moment of euphoria after he has taken the substance, as an actor who is aggressively pursuing a career that requires resourcefulness, for a heroin user is hustling—robbing or stealing, seeking to avoid the police, and looking for a dealer. The best way to identify the heroin user in a slum neighborhood is to note the person who walks as though he were late for an appointment. From the addict's viewpoint he or she might well ask, "Can a square survive . . . in the kind of jungle we live in? It takes brains, man, to keep up a habit that costs $35 to $40 a day—every day in the year."[73]

The amount of crime committed by addicts is not known, although the general impression is that it is considerable. The proportion of property crimes committed by addicts may range from 25 to 67 percent. There are, of course, drug addicts who are not involved in crime. These include physicians, artists, musicians, and others who become addicted. They may never be defined as criminals, since as long as they can function and have the money to purchase the drug, they seldom come in contact with the criminal justice system. It is not commonly realized, although the U.S. Bureau of Narcotics records substantiate the figures, that the rate of addiction among physicians is thirty times as great as among the general population.[74]

The characteristics, changes, and extent of use of marijuana are so varied that we have neither space nor inclination to attempt to explore its realities or explode the many myths surrounding its use. A 1977 Gallup poll indicated that one out of four adult Americans, and over half of those under thirty, had tried marijuana. This and earlier surveys consistently suggest that from twenty-five to fifty million adult Americans have "smoked" at least once. At the same time the press was reporting the Gallup poll results, it reported that President Carter's nominee to head the Office of Drug Abuse Policy told the Senate committee at his confirmation hearings that he had smoked marijuana and urged the removal of criminal sanctions.[75]

Enough is known about the social factors associated with drug use to support several generalizations. First, the idea that illegal drug use is "pathological" behavior related to deprivation, ignorance, and poverty is wrong. The higher the educational, income, and occupational level of a youth's parents, the greater is the likelihood he or she will use marijuana. There is also a high statistical relationship between the use of alcohol and tobacco and smoking marijuana. The fact that marijuana use has spread since the late 1960s is doubtless due to friendship networks and group associations among youths. Young people are turned on by their friends in the same way that they fashion other social behaviors after the values, opinions, and behaviors of friends (see Figure 11.1).

Our society's ambivalence toward marijuana is reflected both in public opinion and policy. At about the same time that the Gallup poll reported that 59 percent of the respondents agreed that marijuana was both physically addictive and led to the use of hard drugs (which is false), the Mississippi state legislature voted to end criminal penalties for possession of small quantities. Mississippi, often maligned for its social backwardness and the last state to legalize alcohol, decriminalized marijuana before New York and before the question was even being considered in a number of other states. The states that have led the movement to decriminalize marijuana tend to be less urbanized. Their politicians may be influenced more directly by their small-town supporters to lessen the penalties, while politicians from more urban states may be more influenced by general public opinion.

Laws criminalizing marijuana use have begun to change since 1972 as the drug has lost some of its subcultural connotations of social rebellion. No longer confined to college radicals or to politically powerless minority groups such as blacks and Chicanos, its use has reached a "critical mass." Millions have tried it without the predicted dire results.[76]

SIGNIFICATION: SOCIETAL REACTION TO VICTIMLESS CRIMES

Arrests for victimless crimes comprised about one-third of total arrests in 1975. These attempts to regulate standards of conduct and morality through criminal codes do not necessarily represent public opinion, but rather reflect the definitions of morality of vociferous groups and "moral entrepreneurs." In some ways they resemble the heritage of sixteenth-century English law, when sin became crime and immoral behavior was defined as illegal by the state.[77]

Because enforcement of laws against victimless criminals takes up a disproportionate amount of law enforcement resources and effort, there has been some movement to modify such laws. Norval Morris detailed some of the implications of victimless crime laws for law enforcement when he wrote:

> Police work is almost by definition more difficult in cases of victimless crime; the best evidence is lacking, no injured citizen complains to the police and serves as a witness. The police must therefore develop cases with unreliable informers, undercover work, tapping and bugging, entrapment and decoy methods, swift seizure of evidence and forceful interrogation. Drug cases account for most of our constitutional difficulties with search and seizure. Attempting to balance, in these tilted scales, constitutional concerns for privacy and due process with a concern for police effectiveness has lessened for the rest of us the protection of our constitutional rights. In the long run, this enervation of the powers of the Constitution may not be the least of the harms flowing from the overreach of the criminal law.[78]

Signifying Sex Offenders

Prostitution. The issue of prostitution poses a dilemma for lawmakers and law enforcement officials. While they readily admit the futility of controlling street prostitution, they continue to maintain laws and efforts to proscribe it. The hypocrisy of these efforts reflects the nineteenth-century patterns of limiting the public visibility of illicit sex, while allowing it to be available for clients through call-girl operations. Police typically afford protection to the johns, even though these clients are involved in behavior that is illegal.[79]

The methods by which prostitutes gain access to clients require involvement in a network of referrals; in many instances they inadvertently come to the attention of the police or organized crime in certain areas of the country, especially in resort or vacation areas. Frequently, police purposely arrest prostitutes to give them criminal records. Then they can intimidate them to act as informants or even use them for sexual purposes.[80]

A call girl may be able to ply her trade in a nonpublic manner and thus avoid the notice and control of the police, but this rarely happens. On the other hand, nearly all street prostitutes have criminal records, either as a result of a token arrest during a cleanup drive or because the police make it a practice to "signify" all new women by arresting them.[81]

Public opinion regarding prostitution has vacillated considerably over the past fifty years, from a mood of repression in the 1920s to the present, when changing sexual values have resulted in a general decline in the rate at which men seek the services of prostitutes.[82] Today, many clients are reluctant to visit the former red-light districts in our big cities, which generally are located in slum areas. Consequently, the women seek out the men. Thus, we have the phenomenon of the highly visible prostitute in places like New York's Times Square and downtown San Francisco.

As long as the prostitute worked in a less visible part of the city, she was not the focus of public contempt. Now that she has moved downtown, she is seen not only as a "bad woman," but as a public nuisance. Customers formerly were readily identifiable; now she may accost uninterested or even rejecting conventional males, not to mention hostile conventional females. Thus there is more potential for aggression and even violence. There is also the phenomenon of an increased number of recruits to the "life" from highly visible minority groups. This trend continues a historical pattern, but in the past, these women were recruited from white ethnic groups. Additionally, the use of hard drugs has increased, a factor that leads to greater potential for aggression among those who might not have realized enough money from their trade to support their daily needs. As a result of these changes, prostitution has come to be associated with the increase in crimes of violence — a direction that has led to demands for strong reaction by the authorities.[83]

Homosexual Behavior. With the shift toward decriminalization of homosexuality, which began in 1961 with an Illinois law that decriminalized homosexual acts between adults in private, law enforcement attitudes toward homosexuality have started to change, even though much uncertainty remains. In New York, the state appellate court overruled a lower court decision that had denied a certificate of incorporation to the Gay Activist Alliance in New York City. The court declared that the word "gay" is not obscene or vulgar, even though it may be synonymous with homosexual. Since the purposes of the alliance are not unlawful, the organization was allowed to use the word in its legal incorporation.[84]

The American Law Institute, through its Model Penal Code, has worked to repeal laws forbidding sexual acts between persons of the same sex. The American Civil Liberties Union and other groups have joined the movement for reform. In addition, a number of states have repealed or revised their codes to decriminalize homosexual acts. Yet, in some states statutes remain on the books that conceivably could result in the sentencing of a fifteen-year-old boy to fifty years in prison for one homosexual act. Even in states where laws have been changed, police continue their activities of harassment and entrapment.[85]

A study of homosexuals arrested in Los Angeles County revealed that of 493 felony arrests, only 24 involved acts in private. Of the others, 274 were in restrooms, 108 in autos, 18 in jails, 17 in parks, 15 in baths, and 11 on public beaches. Ninety-three percent of these felony arrests were for fellatio. Only 11 of the 493 men arrested requested a jury trial; the rest sought instead to avoid publicity. Only 6 out of 475 misdemeanor arrests took place in private; the remainder were located in restrooms, autos, parks, theaters, bars, in the street, and public baths.[86]

While studies by Laud Humphreys and others have documented that even though police departments rarely note complaints about homosexual activity, the police in many cities continue to harass homosexuals through the use of decoys, two-way mirrors, surveillance with cameras, and radios. Moreover, all of Humphreys' respondents over the age of thirty told at least one story of having paid blackmail or payoff money to police officers. He notes that it is the law itself, and not the law enforcement officer, that must bear the blame for such crimes of blackmail, for the prohibition of homosexual behavior creates a minority group that cannot turn to the law for protection. It is the public disapproval attached to homosexuality and the reluctance of victims to report such exploitation, especially at the hands of police, that serve as an inducement to patterns of blackmail.[87]

The homosexual tends to be fearful of arrest and public knowledge of his behavior that could lead to the loss of employment and disqualification from civil or military service. For example, if he is a member of the military, he receives a discharge without honor, forfeiting any rights he may have gained.

Homosexuality has been decriminalized in most Western European countries for some time. In 1967, Great Britain finally adopted the substance of the Wolfenden Report after ten years of delay. Reforms in Scandinavia and West Germany have been more thorough.[88]

Signifying Substance Use Offenders

Drunkenness. In 1967 the President's Crime Commission made a number of important recommendations for dealing with the offense of drunkenness. These included:[89]

1. Drunkenness should not by itself be an offense, but disorderly conduct and other offenses should be punishable as separate crimes.
2. Civil detoxification procedures should be developed.
3. Communities should set up comprehensive treatment programs including such detoxification units.
4. Communities should maintain and coordinate aftercare resources and residential houses.
5. Research should be expanded by private and public agencies into the problem of alcoholism.
6. Federal laws for the development and coordination of treatment programs should be promoted.

In the decade following this report, half of the states have decriminalized public drunkenness, and the emphasis is now on treating drunks rather than sentencing them to jail. The police department in St. Louis was among the first to institute such a policy. That city set up a forty-bed detoxification center in 1968. Instead of taking drunks to the "drunk tank," they are taken to the center. The program saves the police department the time and money formerly spent on booking, jailing, and holding mass productionlike trials against inebriates. Since 1974 when Massachusetts decriminalized drunkenness, the handling of drunks by police has decreased by 40 to 65 percent. Illinois followed suit in 1976; the Chicago police department reports that it has provided detoxification services to doctors, lawyers, and businessmen, as well as to the "street" type of drunk.[90]

Not all programs have worked well. For example, when a new program was set up in Washington, D.C., in the late 1960s, following the court order forbidding the arrest of chronic drunks, the men were placed in a dormitory previously used for drunk offenders. They still saw this as incarceration. And since they had fewer privileges than when they had been prisoners, they said they preferred the former system.[91]

Some programs attempted to provide voluntary treatment. The most effective were those in New York City set up by the Vera Institute with federal funding. Under this program, police who patrol skid row are accompanied by a civilian, a former chronic drinker. The inebriated individual is invited to go to the detoxification center. If needed, medical attention is provided. After a drying out process, the person is urged to continue treatment. Still, the focus is upon skid row chronic drinkers and not upon middle-class men and women who may have serious drinking problems.[92]

Czechoslovakia, Poland, Great Britain, and Sweden all have made significant advances in dealing with chronic drunkenness in a nonpunitive manner. In Sweden, a person may seek voluntary treatment and receive unemployment pay while in the hospital. However, should the individual fail to take advantage of a program, he or she may be faced with involuntary treatment.[93]

Drugs and Narcotics. Beginning in the late 1960s, there has been an explosion in the incidence of arrests for drug violations. In 1975, 4217 agencies representing a population of over 130 million, reported 334,528 arrests for narcotic drug law violations. This total contrasted with 43,550 arrests in 1965, an increase of 688 percent over a decade.

The *Uniform Crime Reports* statistics underscore general public confusion about drug abuse, as arrests for both narcotics and "soft" drug offenses are lumped together. However, it is a reasonable assumption that the majority of the arrests are for marijuana use. Arrests for marijuana offenses in California exceeded 50,000 a year in 1970—over 25 percent of all felony arrests. On the other hand, a fraction of drug arrests are related to heroin and hard drug use.[94]

According to many criminologists, the rigid social policy of repression and control which began with the passage of the Harrison Act in 1914 had the following results:[95]

1. Since legal sources for these drugs did not exist, a thriving illegal traffic developed.
2. The organized criminal underworld developed a commerce in these illicit drugs and sold them through illegal means for huge profits.
3. An addict subculture developed, particularly in the poorer ghetto slums of our cities. This subculture has perpetuated itself as a means of coping with society's antiaddiction policies and as a circulatory system for securing illegal drugs.

The federal laws against drugs served as a model for the passage of similar harsh laws in many states. California and Missouri even made addiction a criminal offense. The landmark Supreme Court decision of *Robinson* v. *California* (1962) declared these laws unconstitutional.[96] Some states have even instituted the death penalty for drug pushers, and as recently as 1971, New York enacted a series of mandatory sentences, including life imprisonment for pushers and dealers. These statutes were enacted over the opposition of the District Attorneys Association and law enforcement officials, both of whom were convinced they would make the apprehension and conviction of drug dealers more difficult.

Overall, the social control policies pursued by the Federal Bureau of Narcotics and the various states have exacerbated the problem and raised the specter of a dope-fiend menace in America. The dope fiend, or "junkie," came to be seen as a pariah: a degenerate crime-prone person who engages in violent crimes while under the influence of drugs. At least one study of addiction treatment programs has concluded that one of the major problems in treating addicts is that they tend to have incorporated society's negative feelings regarding addicts into their self-image.[97]

National surveys indicate that the number of marijuana users has increased substantially over the past decade (see Figure 11.1). Lawmakers seem to be responding to changing public opinion that penalties for marijuana use are too severe. And while medical experts still debate conflicting evidence on the harmful effects of chronic use, an increasing number of policymakers have come to accept the arguments of the National Organization for the Reform of Marijuana Laws (NORML).

These social, legal, and political forces of change are apparent in the successful efforts to decriminalize the possession of small amounts of marijuana for personal use in Mississippi in 1977. The director of that state's Bureau of Narcotics and the head of the prison system both backed the bill. The head of the prison system supported decriminalization because he knew of a number of youths sentenced to prison for marijuana use who subsequently were brutalized by the violence in those institutions. The new law was a recognition that control under the old law was not working, that police resources were being wasted, and that lives were being ruined. The fact that several children of state legislators were among the three to four thousand people arrested each year, also helped passage of the bill.[98]

When Oregon decriminalized in 1973, it was predicted by some that the state would be deluged with "potheads." The number of arrests for simple possession did increase, but the number arrested for trafficking dropped significantly in the first year. A survey showed that the percentage of adult Oregonians who had ever used marijuana increased slightly from 19 to 20 percent, while those reporting current usage declined from 9 to 8 percent. Police save time for more pressing matters, since they now issue citations—similar to those for traffic offenses—rather than making arrests.[99]

As young adults move into positions as legislators and policymakers, decriminalization probably will continue. But acceptance is far from complete, as the map in Box 1 (p. 385) indicates. In 1974 a young black man in Virginia

Figure 11.1. Increasing Use of Marijuana (percentage of people who have tried marijuana, 1973–1977)

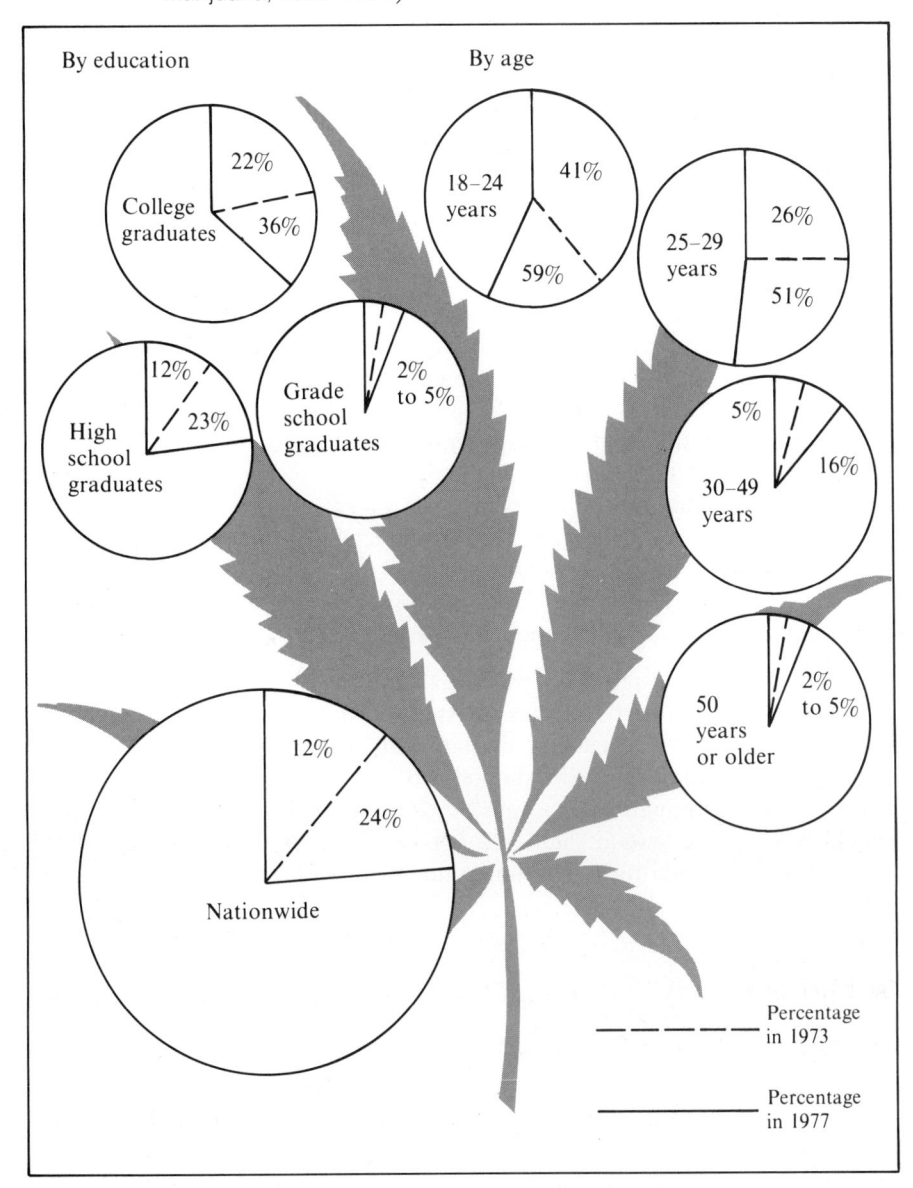

By education

- College graduates: 22% / 36%
- High school graduates: 12% / 23%
- Grade school graduates: 2% to 5%
- Nationwide: 12% / 24%

By age

- 18–24 years: 41% / 59%
- 25–29 years: 26% / 51%
- 30–49 years: 5% / 16%
- 50 years or older: 2% to 5%

- - - - - Percentage in 1973
———— Percentage in 1977

Source: *New York Times*, May 23, 1977, p. M29. Data from Gallup poll.

was sentenced to forty years in prison for selling a small amount of marijuana. He was released by a federal court order several years later on grounds that this punishment was "cruel and unusual."[100] It is extremely doubtful, however, that marijuana will be legalized and controlled like alcohol any time in the near future.

Problems in Regulating Victimless Crimes

The difficulties inherent in the regulation of victimless crimes have been summed up as follows:[101]

1. Victimless crime laws function as a "crime tariff" that makes the supply of such goods and services profitable for criminal operations.
2. This atmosphere contributes to the creation and financing of "large-scale criminal groups" and promotes "commercialized" crime in the organized underworld.
3. The "secondary criminogenic effect" that is set in motion results in crimes *with* victims committed by some of those who must pay the high prices for these goods and services.
4. The way addicts and prostitutes associate with those involved in other criminal behaviors results in the development of an extensive criminal subculture.
5. The "diversion and overextension" of law enforcement resources results in a failure to deal adequately with serious crime, a factor which may contribute to its increase.
6. Since there is no victim to ask for protection of the law, it is difficult to enforce such laws without the use of entrapment and illegal police methods. Paid informers are used, bribery tends to flourish, and political corruption of the police may result.

These arguments relate to the social and economic costs of victimless crimes. Recently, Gilbert Geis has questioned whether we should be content with countering the overreach of the law with such cost-benefit tactics. After estimating the national bill for such efforts at $3.4 billion, he has suggested that even if decriminalization should create more problems, our basic goal should be a justice system that does not deprive individuals of their liberty when they do not harm the legitimate interests of other citizens.[102]

SUMMARY

This chapter described patterns of public order offenses, or victimless crimes, in American society. Initially we commented upon the use of the criminal law to regulate the private moral conduct of our citizens. It was noted that reliance upon the criminal law poses problems in the administration and enforcement of such laws. It has placed a heavy burden upon the official bureaucracy, since more than a third of all arrests are for such offenses. Aside from the cost, this treatment of victimless crimes has also created a criminal subculture—or at least contributed to its expansion.

Four major types of victimless crimes were described within the two categories of *sexual offenses* and *substance use*. We described the impact of efforts to regulate such behaviors, and more significantly, the negative effects of this process upon those defined as "criminal."

In the realm of sexual behavior, the self-concept, affiliational nature, and overlap of prostitutes and homosexuals with conventional behavior were related. Traditional views and myths about these victimless criminals tend to persist. Still, changing policies toward such sexual offenders have contributed to more positive self-images, though some citizens view a freer attitude toward sexuality as destructive of traditional morals.

The use of alcohol is legal. Yet the chronic drinker and alcoholic are stigmatized by laws prohibiting public drunkenness. It was indicated that those who are arrested for chronic drunkenness tend to be street or "skid row" types of low status, although there are millions of middle-class chronic drinkers. The overlap in the use of illegal and legal drugs was noted. The dope fiend myth persists and has a negative effect on efforts to reform the addict. The high cost of illicit narcotics frequently results in addict involvement in criminal activity, or "hustling." The dope fiend myth was applied to marijuana users for a time, but with the increasing acceptance of marijuana some of these attitudes are eroding.

By 1979, eight states had decriminalized marijuana and over half had decriminalized public intoxication. A handful of states has removed the punishment of consensual homosexual behavior, but prostitution is still illegal in all states except for some counties in Nevada.

It is our belief that the continued decriminalization of victimless crimes will have a positive impact on our society. Certainly we would argue that the elimination of no-victim crimes (with reasonable regulation related to the damage a given act might do to others) could lessen specific undesirable consequences currently related to their existence and enforcement. We should not imagine or assume, however, that there is clear and convincing evidence that decriminalization will greatly decrease any undesired negative consequences or avoid any behaviors that might be judged as tawdry. This claim has not been advanced by the more careful advocates of such changes.

In noting the various advantages flowing from decriminalization—such as the saving of money, the advancement of decency and fairness, and a system of justice less biased by racism and sexism—Gilbert Geis suggests that we tend to fall back on evidence of the derivative effects of criminalization, like the costs citizens must pay to enforce no-victim laws. He argues that sociological studies should seek to identify more carefully the various issues related to decriminalization. Until more evidence is available, we should not allow the absence of complete data on the impact of decriminalization to deprive persons of their right to the "pursuit of happiness" when they do not directly interfere with the legitimate interests of others.[103]

There are "moral crusaders" who hold quite different views. These moralistic opponents of decriminalization tend to fear consequences such as moral decay, a Communist takeover, an increased involvement in proscribed behaviors, or secondary effects such as the seduction of the young and naive. Their refusal to acknowledge the obvious class and racial biases in policies toward marijuana use, for example, suggests that they have not pondered why it is that after a history of almost exclusive enforcement against blacks and others in marginal social status, this substance suddenly was seen as overpunished by the law after youths from middle-status groups began to use it.[104]

We concur with Geis that the final decision about the decriminalization of victimless crimes does not rest fundamentally with social science knowledge. Social science cannot determine what a sensible price might be to achieve a given goal; it only is able to suggest what might be involved in such a price. It is not known, nor can it be tested, whether it is politically more beneficial to have fewer guilt-stricken and fearful homosexuals who are unlikely to be arrested than vice versa.

Still, we would opt for the repeal of victimless offenses from criminal law in the hope that this act would advance basic concepts of human dignity and freedom. But let us avoid any self-deceptive assertions that decriminalization will automatically result in a social order that will reflect in an overwhelming manner these social values. This may occur or it may not. We cannot simply substitute our version of utopia for the unfulfilled promise of the "moral crusaders." Historian Jacob Burkhardt summed it up when he wrote, "The essence of tyranny is the denial of complexity." [105]

ADDITIONAL READINGS

Gagnon, John H. "Sexual Conduct and Crime." In *Handbook of Criminology.* Edited by Daniel Glaser. Chicago: Rand McNally, 1974.

Provides a perspective on the learning of sexual scripts in the process of conventional development and relates this complex process to deviant and criminal as well as conforming behavior.

Goode, Erich. *Drugs in American Society.* New York: Knopf, 1972.

This book provides a sociological perspective on drugs and their use, including both marijuana and "hard" drugs. It also provides a cogent description of the relationship between legal and illegal drug use and an overview of drugs and the law.

Morris, Norval and Gordon Hawkins. *The Honest Politician's Guide to Crime Control.* Chicago: The University of Chicago Press, 1970.

A cogent, readable analysis of our moralistic criminal law by two law professors. They are advocates as well as analysts.

Pittman, David J. "Drugs, Addiction and Crime." In *Handbook of Criminology.* Edited by Daniel Glaser. Chicago: Rand McNally, 1974.

A concise summary of the history and terminology of drug use as well as a description of problem substances including alcohol. These substances are also described in relation to crime and criminality.

Schur, Edwin M. and Hugo A. Bedau. *Victimless Crimes: Two Sides of a Controversy.* Englewood Cliffs, N.J.: Prentice-Hall, 1974.

A criminologist and a philosopher discuss the adequacy of the concept "victimless crimes." Their cross-disciplinary analysis zeroes in on this major policy issue, and although they do not agree on terms, they do agree on the moral inconsistency involved in criminal laws that seek to legislate morality.

PART FOUR

Crime Control and Societal Reaction: Criminal Justice, Intervention, and Prevention

12 Law Enforcement: Police, Crime, and the Community
13 The Courts and the Administration of Justice
14 Jails: Their Function in Detention and Confinement
15 The Dilemma of Corrections: Treatment, Punishment, or Justice?
16 Public Policy: Crime and Social Priorities

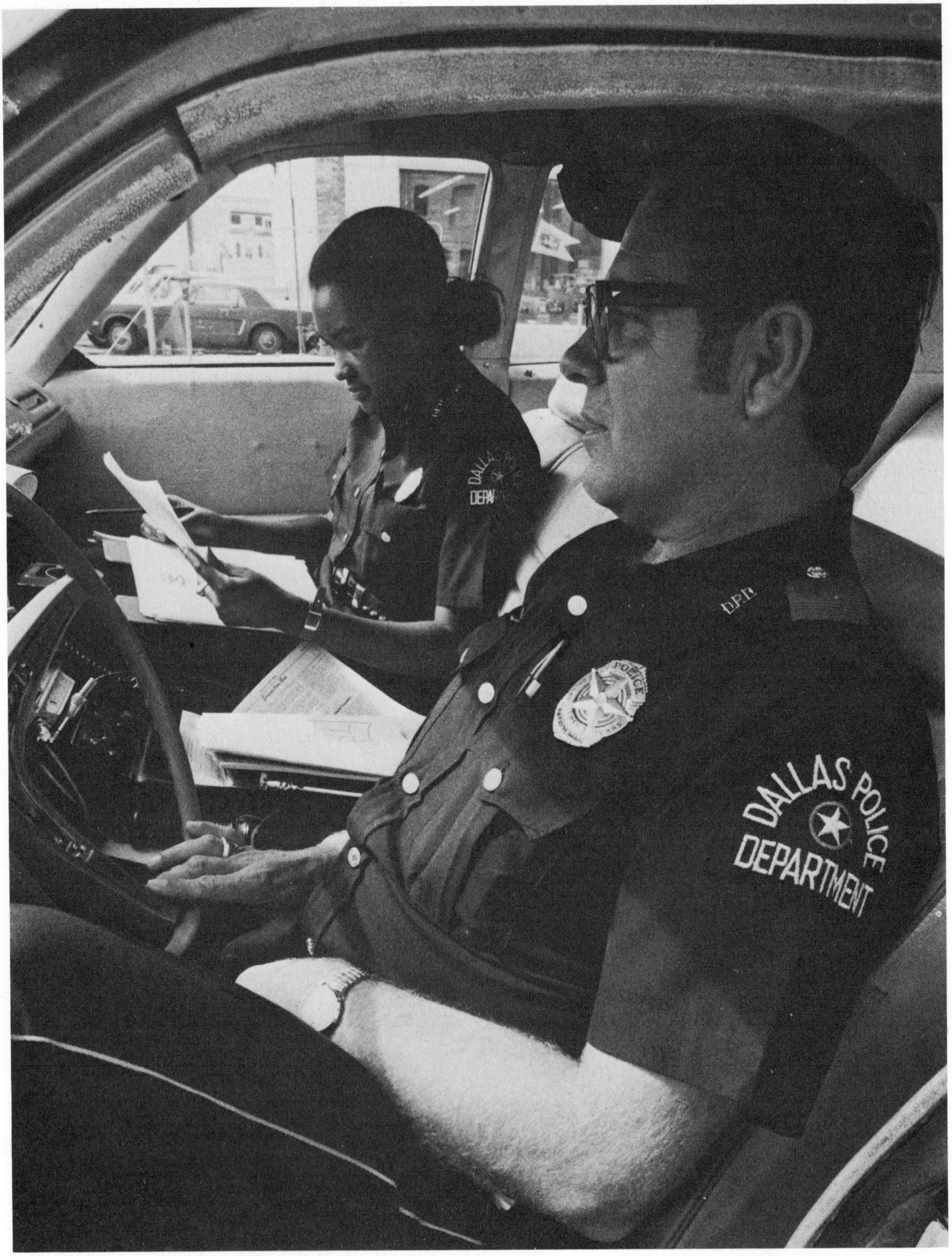
DALLAS POLICE
DEPARTMENT
D.P.D.
POLICE

Every society gets the kind of criminal it deserves. What is equally true is that every community gets the kind of law enforcement it insists on.
—Robert F. Kennedy, "Free Enterprise in Organized Crime," The Pursuit of Justice (1964)

LAW ENFORCEMENT: POLICE, CRIME, AND THE COMMUNITY

They have been respected as British "bobbies" and deplored as "pigs," bashing heads on Chicago streets during the Democratic National Convention in 1968. The police today stand as the most visible symbol of law enforcement. Yet they have a confusing role. Regarded as crime fighters, they spend most of their time on social services or traffic control. Despite their being called on to enforce laws, some of their most effective work is done exercising their discretion *not* to enforce the law.

The modern police department has a relatively short history. Only since 1829 has "the buffer in blue" been given the heavy responsibility of maintaining civil order. In urban areas, especially in recent years, the police have increasingly come into conflict with black and other minority groups and have seemed more isolated and insulated from the public they serve. And in coming years, the role of the police is sure to remain controversial as they grapple with issues like professionalism and community relations. While service functions and peace-keeping functions will dominate, the myth that the police serve primarily as a crime-fighting and controlling agency will continue, since it is deeply inbedded in the public consciousness.[1]

THE POLICE: A VISIBLE SYMBOL

The police are the most numerous, expensive, and visible element of the criminal justice system. They share responsibility for maintaining order and enforcing the law with the courts and the corrections system. The average citizen views the police as an organization involved in doing something about the crime problem, and the great number of crime programs on television seems to reinforce this notion. When crime rates increase—as they generally have since the early 1960s—the public demands more effective police work. In bureaucratic terms this usually means that the number of police increases. It should not surprise us that the number of police in our society increased by 75 percent between 1965 and 1975. But crime increased even more dramatically during this period, with serious crime going up by about 120 percent. Still, the public's faith in the effectiveness of police as "crime fighters" seems to continue.[2]

In contrast to the average citizen's perspective, criminologists who study the police have come to realize that the typical citizen's image of the police function is misleading. About 85 percent of police department activity falls into the categories of peace keeping and public service—settling family disputes and rescuing cats from trees—rather than law enforcement that involves solving or preventing crimes.[3]

The social control function of the police is what comes to mind when citizens think of the "buffer in blue" who stands between disorder and anarchy and domestic tranquility. Because the police represent the authority of the state, they also represent a means of constraint and are sometimes looked on with mistrust and suspicion rather than respect.[4] Moreover, the police have a significant function in defining certain behaviors as criminal and in designating and labeling individuals as criminals.

In a complex society, there tends to be more reliance upon formal means of social control than upon the family, school, or religious organizations. However, the most effective means of social control result from the kinds of social relations that exist between individuals. British criminologist Michael Banton illustrated this principle by contrasting the rates of murder and rape in Edinburgh in 1962 (a city with a population of half a million people) with that of a comparable American city. The American city had thirty-six homicides and sixty reported incidents of forcible rape as contrasted with only four homicides and eight rape cases for Edinburgh over the same period. The difference was not due to Edinburgh's more efficient police, but rather to the informal means of social control that resulted from the orderly nature of that city's human relations. Recent attention has also been focused on the comparatively low crime rates in Japan, which apparently are related to Japan's continued reliance on traditional forms of informal control through communal or neighborhood associations—even though that country is highly urbanized. Japanese traditions, however, also reinforce patterns of cooperation between police and the immediate community in which the officer is assigned.[5]

The substantial role filled by the police in our heterogeneous society suggests something about the nature of relationships in this culture. Police departments, in urban jurisdictions at least, are highly bureaucratized organizations. The laws that the police are sworn to uphold are designed to protect and maintain the interests of the dominant power groups in the community who have the highest stake in stability and order. Less powerful and influential members of the community recognize a need to be protected from intra-community disorder, disruption, and violence, even though their economic stake might not be as significant. Their interest in a police force adequate to exercise effective social control and maintain the social order coincides with, and at times complements, that of the dominant groups.

The interests and values of the less favored groups, however, do not always complement middle-class conceptions of the law. It sometimes seems, as Wilbur Miller, Nicholas Alex, and others have indicated, that there is "one law for the rich and one for the poor." Consequently, the law may be viewed as repressive, particularly in situations of overt and intense conflict.

The police are agents who enforce social policies previously established by dominant groups to control threats to the social structure. In meeting demands for "order," the police work within the framework of procedural law which provides for the protection of both individual and property rights. The historical development of the police as formal agents of social control in Anglo-American societies is a reflection of this dilemma of maintaining order in a heterogeneous society within a context of legality.[6]

ORIGINS OF MODERN POLICE: FROM THE "WATCH SYSTEM TO BUREAUCRACY"

Early History

The first police force in the Anglo-American countries was established in London, England, in 1829. Numerous debates in the Parliament had focused on the need to provide for the tranquillity of London without resorting to the army. When Sir Robert Peel introduced the Police Reform Act, he reassured his political opponents that the new police organization would be accountable to the rule of law. He took care to emphasize that the police—"bobbies," as they came to be called after Sir Robert—would be separate and distinguishable from the army. First, no applications were to be accepted from military officers for senior positions in Scotland Yard, police headquarters. Second, since the force was for domestic social control, they would not carry firearms. To this day, firearms are used only in special emergencies by British police. Finally, the police were to be accountable to Parliament for their actions. Since the police were to be recruited from the populace, their public support plus legal accountability would help balance the contrary goals of freedom and order.[7]

The uniforms of the "bobbies" set them off from the rest of the populace. They were trained to be fair, imperturbable, and authoritative, and through their first century they gained the respect of the many who saw them as symbols of the law as well as order. By not carrying firearms, they did not remind citizens of the power of the state to take a life.[8]

Until 1837 in America, as in England prior to 1829, cities were protected by the "watch system." Men patrolled the city streets during the night and at intervals called out the time and announced that "all is well." The night watch

The first Anglo-American force for domestic social control: London, 1829.

was not noted for its efficiency or organization. Underpaid watchmen were known to sleep and even be drunk at their posts.[9]

The first attempt at reform came in Boston in 1837, following an outbreak of anti–Irish-Catholic rioting. A six-man day watch was added to strengthen the night watch system. New York was the first city to create an organized police force by combining day and night watches into a day and night police force. Within the next several decades, Chicago, Boston, New Orleans, Philadelphia, Baltimore, and several other cities set up police systems. By the end of the century almost every major city had an organized police force. Unfortunately, the officers were not as carefully recruited, disciplined, or organized as the English "bobbies." [10]

Along with the watch system, the colonies had adopted the English system of sheriffs, constables, and justices of the peace. The system grew into a parallel and sometimes overlapping and competing means of law enforcement. The sheriff's office still exists in all 3,099 counties in the United States, but in some urbanized areas this office no longer exercises traditional police functions. In Cook County, Illinois, and Nassau County, New York, the sheriff oversees the county jail and detention facility. A number of urbanized counties have county police forces under a separate police commission. Connecticut did away with the county system, but several attempts to abolish the office of sheriff were defeated.

The general concept of American law enforcement was first adapted from the English model. In colonial America and later on the frontier, the sheriff was the chief law enforcement agent. However, he was also responsible for numerous civil duties, and in some western counties served as chief executive. The importance of the sheriff diminished as the country became more urbanized during the latter half of the nineteenth century. During the turbulent 1870s and 1880s, the idea of a professional police force emerged. And as the function of elected sheriffs and constables decreased, the control of the police in the developing cities was shifted away from the voters. In its place, a more centralized type of force developed, one which approximates the military model advocated by Secretary of War McCray in 1877. One aspect of this move toward the creation of a professional police force that would be responsive to the needs and wishes of the rising industrial interests—the new ruling class—was the creation of the state police between 1910 and 1920.[11] Over the past century, as we moved from an agrarian to an industrial political economy, additional levels of law enforcement organizations evolved. The number of police agencies has grown, along with methods of law enforcement. However, while the primary objective of law enforcement tends to remain the same—that is, crime control, the prevention and detection of crime and apprehension of offenders—the primary activities of police agencies pertain more to community service functions.[12]

Federal, State, and Local Police: Fragmentation and Expansion

The variety of levels of police agencies, comprising the more than 40,000 law enforcement organizations in the United States, stretches any reasonable meaning of the term "police system." There are, however, five levels of police organizations that employ about 700,000 officers and civilians:[13]

1. *Federal police agencies,* including the Federal Bureau of Investigation, the Secret Service and the Alcohol Tax Unit of the Department of Treasury, the Bureau of Internal Revenue, Bureau of Customs, the Immigration Border Patrol, Post Office Inspectors, and the Bureau of Narcotics. Within the Justice Department there is also the Office of United States Marshals, which provides assistance to the federal courts.
2. *Various state police departments* and their affiliated criminal investigation units. These had their major development in the 1920s. Pennsylvania organized the first such force in 1905.
3. *County sheriff's organizations and county police* in urbanized counties such as Dade (Fla.) and Nassau and Suffolk (N.Y.).
4. *Municipal police* in more than 13,000 cities and constables or marshals in about 20,000 townships and New England towns.
5. *Police agencies* in the nation's 15,000 incorporated villages and boroughs.

In addition, a growing number of private police or security agencies employ between half a million and a million individuals. These "contract security"—or "rent-a-cops," as they sometimes are disparagingly called—provide

Figure 12.1. Police Employee Data: Average Number of Police Department Employees and Range in Number of Employees, by Population Groups, October, 1975 (per 1,000 inhabitants)

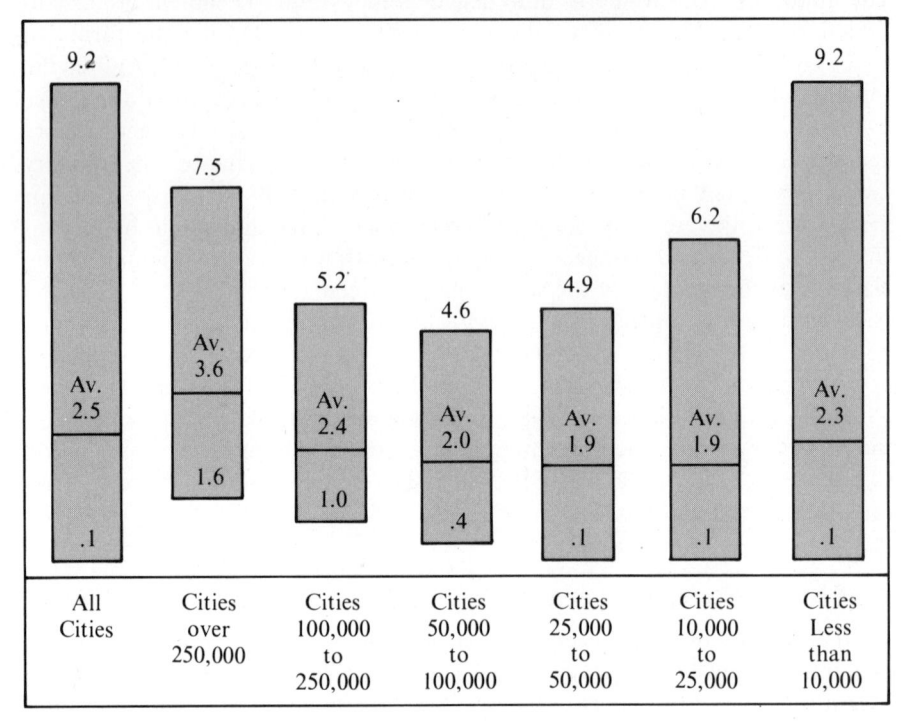

	All Cities	Cities over 250,000	Cities 100,000 to 250,000	Cities 50,000 to 100,000	Cities 25,000 to 50,000	Cities 10,000 to 25,000	Cities Less than 10,000
High	9.2	7.5	5.2	4.6	4.9	6.2	9.2
Average	2.5	3.6	2.4	2.0	1.9	1.9	2.3
Low	.1	1.6	1.0	.4	.1	.1	.1

Source: FBI, *Uniform Crime Reports, 1975* (Washington, D.C.: U.S. Government Printing Office, 1976), p. 222.

security far beyond that of plant protection. They patrol everything from rock concerts to shopping centers to sports events. As a Rand Corporation Report noted, such private police organizations are a "recession-resistant" growth industry, expanding at a rate of 10 to 15 percent annually. The expenditures for such private police more than quadrupled between 1963 and 1978. Several of the larger firms have even become multinational in their operations.[14]

The structure of law enforcement in America is quite fragmented, and police agencies are not part of a national, unified system. In the United States, as in Britain, law enforcement is the responsibility of the local government. Yet in Great Britain, there are 158 separate police agencies for a population of 60 million, and only 13 of these have fewer than 100 members. In contrast, the 225 million people in the United States are served by more than 40,000 organizations. In Britain, Her Majesty's Inspectors of Constabulary inspect the local agencies; if they meet established standards, the national government funds half of the local budget. In the United States, there has been little or no central direction, except that provided through the FBI Police Academy.[15]

Since the passage of the Omnibus Crime Control and Safe Streets Act of

1968, however, local police have been receiving considerable federal support and direction through the Law Enforcement Assistance Administration (LEAA). The method of funding is through federal grants, which usually involves matching grants from the local government. The impact of this federal assistance might be measured by the growth in police employment and police budgets over the past ten years. At first, LEAA monies were concentrated on police activities, and as a result added to the existing emphasis on this aspect of criminal justice. Since 1971, more funds (52 percent) have been allocated to courts and corrections, including probation and parole.[16]

The increase in full-time police employment—both officers and civilians—was 4.7 percent between 1966 and 1969. From 1969 to 1971 the increase was stepped up to 7.1 percent, and the total number of police at all levels increased to 575,000, with local police reaching about 420,000. By 1975, the total number of police in this country had climbed to 653,000, which represents an increase of 49 percent in per capita police employment over 1960 levels or 340,000 employees. During the same period, however, official crime rates increased by 157 percent. The apparent increased crime-related workloads might be deceptive, for there has been an increase in the employment of civilian workers to release sworn officers for line duty. Still, only about 59 percent of all law enforcement employees are directly engaged in patrol or investigative work. And a major portion of patrol time involves noncrime-related activities.[17]

Expenditures for state and local law enforcement from 1969 to 1970 totaled $4.5 billion, a 14 percent increase over the two previous fiscal years that had already reflected a similar rate of increase over previous years. However, while the amount spent for supplies and equipment in 1969 was $276 million, the figure increased by 203 percent over the next two years. This considerable increase underscores the influence of LEAA monies on police technology.[18]

A more equitable distribution among the subsystems of criminal justice has begun in the past few years (see Table 12.1). Whether or not the law enforcement agencies have become more effective in terms of cost-benefit economics remains to be seen. We are spending more money to combat crime, and we have more police employed than in 1970—2.6 per 1,000 inhabitants as

Table 12.1. Federal Aid to State and Local Governments (dollars in millions)

Category	Fiscal Year 1971 Amount	Percent	Fiscal Year 1973 Amount	Percent	Percent Increases 1971–1973
Police activities	$154	60	$279	48	81
Courts	18	7	38	7	111
Correctional programs	85	33	264	45	211
Total	$257	100	$581	100	126

Source: Morris Cobern, "Some Manpower Aspects of the Criminal Justice System," *Crime and Delinquency* 19, no. 2 (April 1973):197.

compared with 2.3 in 1970. However, we cannot attribute the leveling off or slight decrease in crime rates reported in recent data to higher expenditures for policing. On balance, it appears that social and economic forces such as demographic changes account more clearly for crime rate trends than any increase in police staffing levels (see Table 12.2).

The economist who compiled these data added a parenthetical note. He stated that we might know more about how these extensive police resources are allocated if the FBI's *Uniform Crime Reports* devoted as much space to the analysis of how nearly a half million workers in state and local police departments are deployed as it does to the factors related to the killing of one hundred policemen in 1970.[19] The 1975 UCR was no better on this question. It describes the employment of over a half million police employees in about two pages and devotes four times that space to an analysis of the death of 129 police officers killed in the line of duty (see Figure 12.2). This is not to deny the fact that policing is a hazardous occupation, but in terms of mortality rates, miners, construction workers, and even farmers are involved in equally if not more hazardous work.

Table 12.2. Trends in Local Police Department Employment and Associated Costs, 1971–1975

Category	1971	1973	1975
Sworn officers (in thousands)			
Policemen and detectives	360	460	425
Civilian personnel	60	100	135
Total	420	560	560
Expenditures (in millions of current dollars)			
Employee compensation [a]	$3,595	$5,970	$5,640
Other	835	1,050	1,100
Total	$4,430	$7,020	$6,740

[a] Employee compensation includes salaries, pensions, and cost of other fringe benefits.

Source: Adapted from Morris Cobern, "Some Manpower Aspects of the Criminal Justice System," *Crime and Delinquency,* 19, no. 2 (April 1973):199.

POLICE FUNCTIONS IN CONTEMPORARY SOCIETY

Since the large urban police departments are organized along bureaucratic lines, the basic functions of police organizations sometimes are bypassed or lost in the maze of bureaucratic rules and regulations. Also, because they operate within a social milieu, police bureaucracies may be subject to pressures of social change as well as pressures from the political power structure of communities. A former dean of the School of Criminology of the University of

Figure 12.2. Situations in which Law Enforcement Officers Were Killed, 1966–1975

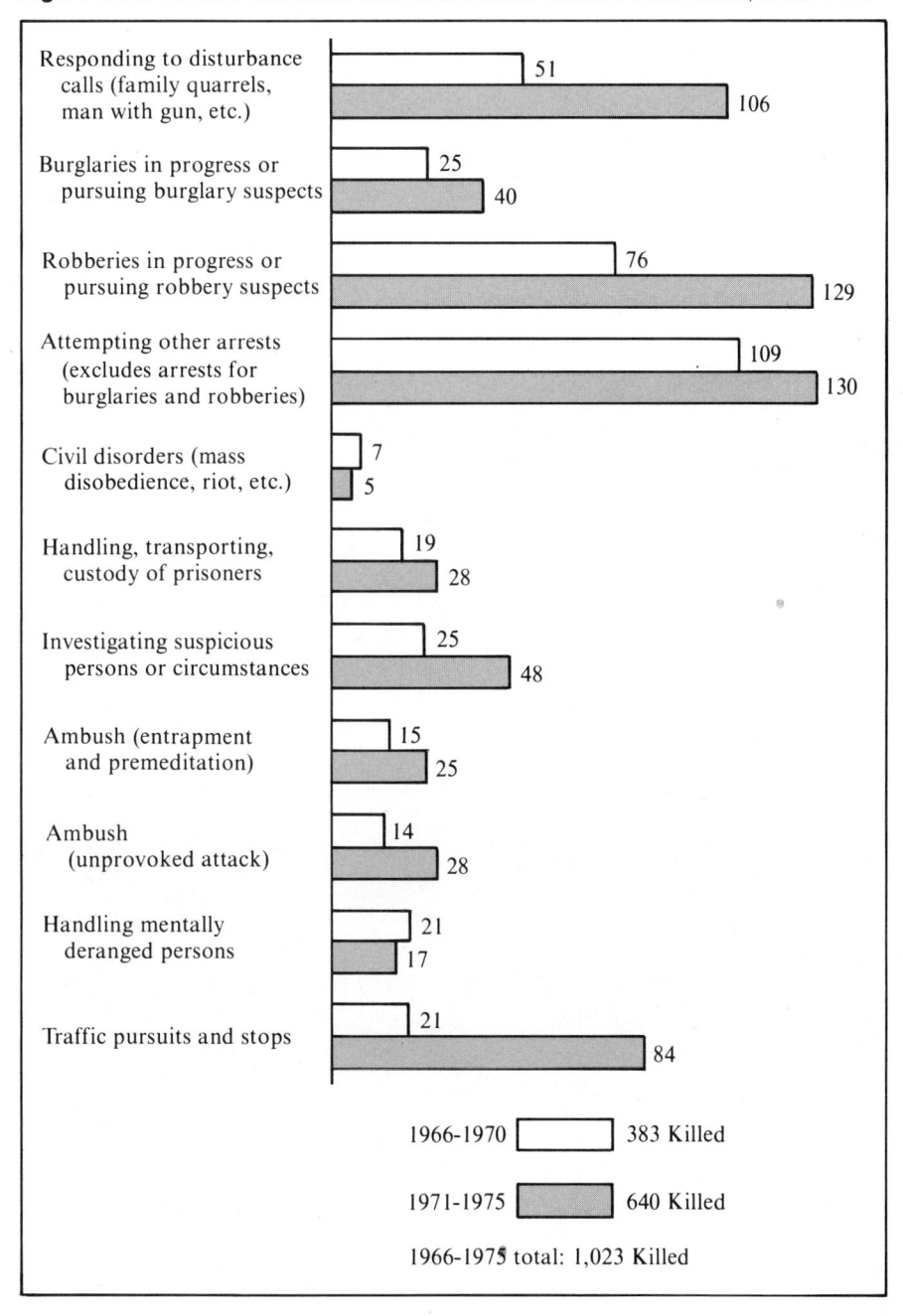

Situation	1966-1970	1971-1975
Responding to disturbance calls (family quarrels, man with gun, etc.)	51	106
Burglaries in progress or pursuing burglary suspects	25	40
Robberies in progress or pursuing robbery suspects	76	129
Attempting other arrests (excludes arrests for burglaries and robberies)	109	130
Civil disorders (mass disobedience, riot, etc.)	7	5
Handling, transporting, custody of prisoners	19	28
Investigating suspicious persons or circumstances	25	48
Ambush (entrapment and premeditation)	15	25
Ambush (unprovoked attack)	14	28
Handling mentally deranged persons	21	17
Traffic pursuits and stops	21	84

1966-1970: 383 Killed
1971-1975: 640 Killed
1966-1975 total: 1,023 Killed

Source: FBI, *Uniform Crime Reports, 1975* (Washington, D.C.: U.S. Government Printing Office, 1976).

California at Berkeley, who once served as a policeman and as sheriff of Cook County, Illinois, has suggested, "The police function is to support and enforce the interests of the dominant political, social, and economic interests of the town, and only incidentally to enforce the law." [20] This statement may sound similar to radical critiques that assert that the police "serve the interests of the ruling classes." But it also underscores the notion that the police can best be understood as an institution that interacts within the total social structure.

The functions of the police outlined many years ago by former FBI Chief J. Edgar Hoover included the protection of life and property, preservation of the peace, prevention of crime, detection and arrest of violators of the law, enforcement of laws and ordinances, and safeguarding the rights of individuals.[21] John Clark and Richard Sykes have outlined four social functions of the police that define and influence their activities as they operate in modern urban society: (1) coercion, (2) team members in the criminal justice system, (3) omnibus public-service agency, and (4) symbolic representative of government.[22] Each of these functions deserves further explanation.

The Police as Primary Agents of Direct Social Control

The police do not have a monopoly on the exercise of social control. *Coercion* to conform is also exercised by the family, schools, welfare agencies, building inspectors, courts, penal institutions, and various rehabilitative agencies. But the coercive power of the police is more pervasive in the community, for by virtue of their greater mobility, the police are often more immediately available in the community than other agencies of control.

The assertion of police power is ubiquitous and occurs at times when individuals are most vulnerable. However, this power is selective in its application and limited both by the norms of the society and by the more specific norms and work rules of the police organization.[23]

Yet police do employ coercive force or violence in a misdirected or excessive manner. This situation may occur, as Peter Manning has noted, in instances when the law is not technically involved and the police officer feels his authority has eroded. In an attempt to regain control, force may be misused. This misuse apparently occurs most often during the process of an arrest. Albert Reiss reported that about 50 percent of all arrests in his study involved the use of physical force, while "gross force" was used in 9 percent. Paul Chevigny's study of selected cases, in which he was able to prove misuse of force by police officers in court, suggests that the New York police tended to respond with violence and a charge such as assaulting an officer when faced with noncompliance to their requests.[24]

The application of police power is limited by the fact that the majority of contacts with the public are citizen initiated. The police limit their exercise of power to those who seek it, those who may be deterred by it, and those directly involved in the situation.[25] They also conform to the rule of law as these regulations are transmitted through organizational rules. For practical reasons, it is

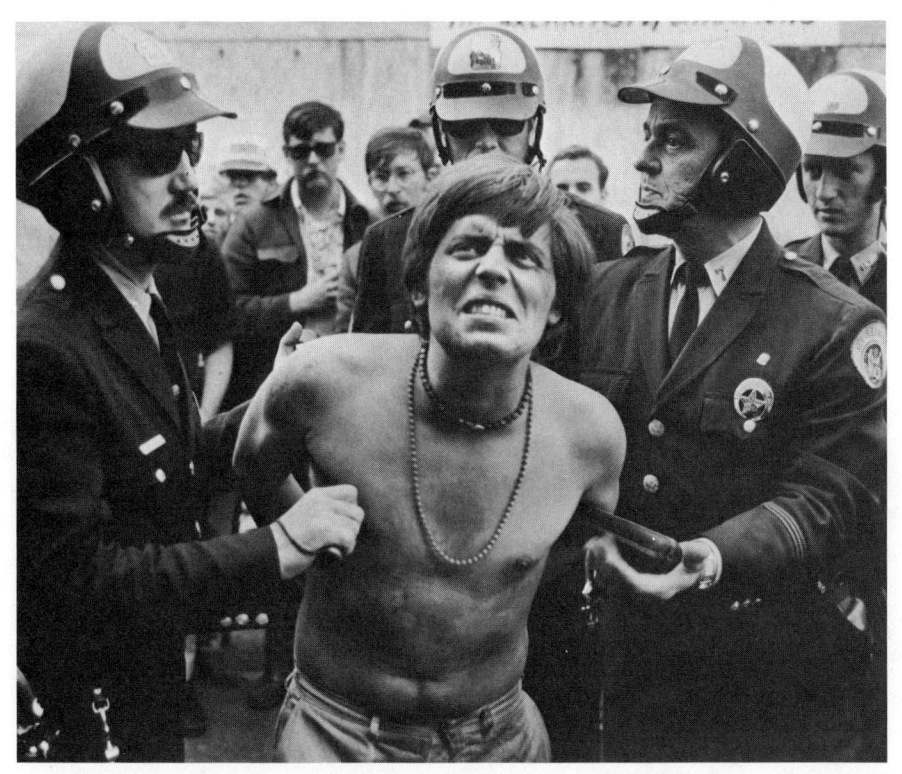

For practical reasons it is foolish to use force when unnecessary.

foolish to use force (applied power) when it is unnecessary. Too much force limits alternatives. It is better to keep the situation "cool" and solve the problem as quickly as possible. The use of force is also affected by those in the encounter, both the alleged violator and bystanders. Sometimes the police use force (implied or real) in an illegal, unjust, unnecessary, unwise, or insensitive manner. Since the police do the "dirty work" for other groups in society who prefer not to use force, they are acting for the vested interests within the collectivity of the structure of a highly diverse society. Yet, as specialists in the maintenance of order and the protection of the general welfare, they must minimize their use of coercion so as to promote the legitimacy of their mandate.[26]

The Police as Buffers and as a Linkage in the Criminal Justice System

The police not only provide the courts, prosecutors, and correctional organizations with clients, they also provide the initial information on the cases to be processed. The extent of action to be taken by these agencies is influenced by the evaluation made by the police, whose early judgments affect later reaction. Police discretion is limited in this process when there is no clear cause

Law Enforcement Code of Ethics

BOX 1

The police are sworn to uphold the law impartially.

As a Law Enforcement Officer, my fundamental duty is to serve mankind; to safeguard lives and property; to protect the innocent against deception, the weak against oppression or intimidation, and the peaceful against violence or disorder; and to respect the Constitutional rights of all men to liberty, equality and justice.

I will keep my private life unsullied as an example to all; maintain courageous calm in the face of danger, scorn, or ridicule; develop self-restraint; and be constantly mindful of the welfare of others. Honest in thought and deed in both my personal and official life, I will be exemplary in obeying the laws of the land and the regulations of my department. Whatever I see or hear of a confidential nature or that is confided to me in my official capacity will be kept ever secret unless revelation is necessary in the performance of my duty.

I will never act officiously or permit personal feelings, prejudices, animosities or friendships to influence my decisions. With no compromise for crime and with relentless prosecution of criminals, I will enforce the law courteously and appropriately without fear or favor, malice or ill will, never employing unnecessary force or violence and never accepting gratuities.

I recognize the badge of my office as a symbol of public faith, and I accept it as a public trust to be held so long as I am true to the ethics of the police service. I will constantly strive to achieve these objectives and ideals, dedicating myself before God to my chosen profession . . . law enforcement.

Source: FBI, *Uniform Crime Report. A-76* (Washington, D.C.: U.S. Government Printing Office, 1976), p. 221.

for arrest and in cases of arrest warrants. The police typically enter a situation after the action and upon the request of an individual complainant or organization, such as a school or business. Police actions initiated by citizens are called *reactive;* those which the police initiate are *proactive.* Most police efforts, according to recent studies, are reactive.[27]

Police initiative in gathering information and locating violations—for example, in watching for vice or morals offenses—are relatively unsuccessful. The police place their emphasis on disruptive and disorganized behavior with identified victims. In terms of time and resources, it is more practical to make a speedy response after a violation than to expend time and energy in prevention. The police, even in their reactive orientation are influenced by the "crime-fighter" or "gang-buster" syndrome, which emphasizes getting to the scene quickly, making an arrest, and obtaining a conviction.[28]

Police officers' arrival on the scene is a sign of official authority and concern. They are more than symbols of authority: they are agents of the state. Since police officers have the right to use a gun if required, they embody the state's monopoly on the use of force. Once on the scene, the police are expected to manage the situation, but they must depend upon interpretations and data provided by the complainants. Once the decision to arrest or not to arrest is made, it is not easily changed by others at a later date, except for oversights or legal technicalities. For this reason, the police often fall back upon the "crime-control" model, which stresses "facts" that must be brought to bear upon legal proof. Their conduct becomes one of interpreting the law to those involved in the situation. They must also be prepared to testify to the facts of the situation. The reports that are filed are also used in processing the case. Thus the police serve as a front-line extension of the criminal justice system in their reaction to social disorder. They are buffers, representatives of the system to society. They make the authority of the state manifest, and the information they convey about the case influences its processing into the system.[29]

Comprehensive Service Function of the Police

A great deal of police activity could best be described as a comprehensive service function. These functions have developed historically in response to the demands and needs of the community with which the police interact. At least some of these services could be performed more efficiently by other service agencies, which could release the police to concentrate on activities more relevant to law enforcement. For example, in many communities the citizens turn to the police when they are in trouble, when garbage is uncollected, housing codes are violated, or consumer fraud has occurred. The police act as information and referral agents for those who are unfamiliar with other urban service agencies. Yet the police argue that through such activities they are better informed about what is going on in their neighborhoods. These and other activities, such as helping the elderly, providing security information, intervening in domestic disputes, and investigating noisy gatherings, may lessen the need for more direct action. Social service functions represent a low-key, low-yield crime prevention emphasis and project a positive image of the police as "friendly helpers."

The police may reap indirect benefits from providing these traditional functions. And public pressure places the police under some obligation to perform such services. Analyses of police calls suggest a high expectancy for such services. James Q. Wilson's sample of calls of citizens to one urban police department over a seven-day period found 22.1 percent were for information, 37.5 percent were requests for services related to accidents, illnesses, lost persons or property, and 30.1 percent were requests to intervene in family, neighborhood, or gang disputes. Law enforcement calls constituted the remaining 10.3 percent.[30] Reiss's analysis of 6,172 calls to the Chicago Police Department's Center of Communications showed a slightly different picture. He found that in one day, the 58 percent of the calls pertaining to criminal matters included disputes or breach of peace, 26 percent; criminal violations against persons and property, 6 and 16 percent respectively; traffic violations,

Often police calls involve intervention in family disputes.

5 percent; suspicious persons, 3 percent; and miscellaneous, 2 percent. Thirty percent of the calls were clearly on noncriminal matters—family or personal issues, traffic hazards or accidents, and medical crises. Reiss concluded that service functions are as much a police function as the exercise of coercive authority.[31]

It would appear that police only rarely deal with crime or those defined as criminals. Rather, they expend considerable time and effort fulfilling requests for services not related to their legally defined function. Yet the fulfillment of demands for public service leads to a feeling that they are not tending to the duties they see as relevant to their crime prevention/criminal catcher role. Consequently, many officers see such service functions as unrelated to "real" police work.[32]

Police as Symbols of Governmental Authority

The fact that the police are the dramatic presence of the legal order and a symbol of governmental authority is perhaps one of the more controversial aspects of their work. In principle, our society is committed to peaceful social relations. Yet we resort to an organization that is given a monopoly on the use of force to maintain the domestic peace. We justify this decision by pointing to the crime control activities of the police and emphasizing the rising crime rate. This aspect of the police function is even used by some to set the police above the legal norms that constrain others in the community.[33]

The controversy grows, in part, from the contention of critics of the police that the government which the police represent and the laws they enforce serve the interests of the propertied classes and perpetuate a social order that is class-based and oppresses a majority of the people. Although we have avoided such ideology, even middle-class "apologists" have asserted that the governments and laws represented and enforced by the police often lack a sensitivity and a responsiveness to the needs of the lower classes. The police and local governments are seen as more responsive to the demands and needs of the dominant groups in the community. Consequently, as Manning has argued, the middle-class property owner becomes the most important audience. He suggests that this relationship is an important aspect of the police ideology. The police believe they represent a segment of the population that shares a consensus regarding the values and standards they enforce, while the criminal elements embody the "evil" in society. Manning argues that they serve as a system that amplifies and increases the importance of the threat of such "evil" forces to the public by their public statements and actions, and by the reaction and attention of the media to their pronouncements and policies.[34]

Consequently it may be argued that the actions and belief systems of the police—of both administrative officers and patrol officers—are important in understanding the manner in which they rationalize their work and its consequences to themselves. These actions and beliefs also come to serve as the public's stereotypical definition of the police role.[35]

The Occupational Culture and Role Definition of the Police

Before we move to a description of the formal organization and function of the police, it will be helpful to discuss briefly the occupational culture of the police that has evolved within the context of their definitions and perceptions of their functions. This occupational culture is important, since police in America define their occupational roles and actions relative to assumptions they hold about the nature of social reality. In other words, as Manning suggests, the police officers' self-esteem is maintained and their self-concept is influenced by the intermingling of the responses they gain from the many audiences before which they perform as social actors. These include their families, peers, and friends (both at work and leisure), and superiors. They develop the criteria from which to evaluate their performance from this ideology within their occupational culture. Thus, their concept of the "good police officer" is compared with the ever-present ideal image purveyed in police literature and traditions. This ideal is more than a definition, for it also includes the belief system, shared perspectives, and identities of their occupational group.[36]

Such an occupational culture, Manning argues, in turn promotes those assumptions about everyday life that come to serve as the basis for the strategies and tactics employed by law enforcement organizations. From the writings of nine scholars, Manning has drawn the following ten assumptions about the occupational culture of the police:[37]

1. People cannot be trusted; they are dangerous.
2. Experience is better than abstract rules.
3. You must make people respect you.
4. Everyone hates a cop.
5. The legal system is untrustworthy; police officers make the best decisions about guilt or innocence.
6. People who are not controlled will break the laws.
7. Police officers must appear respectable and be efficient.
8. Police officers can most accurately identify crime and criminals.
9. The major jobs of the police are to prevent crime and to enforce the laws.
10. Stronger punishment will deter criminals from repeating their errors.

In qualifying these assumptions or postulates, Manning indicates that they are less applicable to those who administer urban police departments and to minority group members in these departments than to the typical line officer who is not college educated. They are also less applicable to the assumptions derived from the occupational culture of nonurban, state, or federal law enforcement personnel.[38]

These assumptions frequently operate in a taken-for-granted manner, as the police seek to fulfill their mandate of preventing and detecting crime and apprehending criminals. Yet to the extent that they operate, they may serve to provide a source of conflict between the formal organizational structure and legal framework of policing and the functional occupational roles that emerge in the context of police encounters.

POLICE ORGANIZATION: MANAGEMENT, OPERATION, AND CONTROL

By virtue of their emphases upon social control and public order, police organizations have a highly developed structure stressing authority and patterned closely after the military model. It is in the police departments of our large cities and urban regions that bureaucratic paramilitary organizational features are most apparent. The cities maintain the larger police organizations, although as Figure 12.1 shows, there is considerable variation in the number of police per 1,000 population. The number varied in 1975 from an average of 1.9 per 1,000 for smaller cities to 3.6 for larger cities. The lowest ratios, according to FBI data, were in the West North Central and West South Central States (2.1 per 1,000), with Omaha, San Diego, and San Antonio having the lowest ratios among cities. The Middle Atlantic and South Atlantic States had ratios of 2.9 and 3.1 per 1,000 in 1975. The highest ratios of police per 1,000 were in Boston, New York, and Washington.

Michael Banton, in his study of American and British police systems, has suggested that the police agency resembles both a professional and a bureaucratic organization. Within a professional organization there is little variation in skills and the professional has considerable discretion in serving his or her various clients. In a bureaucracy there is considerable specialization, and the members are ranked according to the functions they perform.[39]

The emergence of policing as a profession has involved efforts to improve the quality of training and performance as well as public relations and propaganda efforts to transform the police occupation in the eyes of the public. Professional standards involve, among other criteria, the following:[40]

1. High standards of admission.
2. A specialized body of knowledge and skills.
3. A code of professional ethics and dedication to service.
4. A lengthy period of training for new recruits.
5. Autonomy of control in providing service.
6. Pride in the profession and publicly recognized status and prestige.

Professionalism appeals to police officers, who see themselves called upon to assess situations and use their discretion in investigating and resolving them. It also assumes police officers' integrity and their drive for advancement.[41]

James Q. Wilson has classified police departments according to "nonprofessional" and "professional" criteria. The nonprofessional department is run according to the "system." Here, the police are dominated by politicians, although this type of department has gradually given way over the past half century to the independent type. The nonprofessional system may appear corrupt by community standards, but it administers justice in a rough manner understood by the citizens. The professional department, on the other hand, ideally is free of corruption and is impersonal and technically competent.[42] Seldom do these two types exist in pure form, of course. As the *Handbook* of the Municipal Police Administration notes:

> Control of the police force is a tremendous asset to a spoils-minded political machine, for the services which such police can render to a machine are legion. Fixing traffic citations has won many a vote.... Prosecution of serious crimes can sometimes be arranged to suit the convenience of the person charged....
>
> When the police department is controlled by the machine, political influence begins with the appointment of the recruit, helps to secure an unwarranted promotion for him, or gives him a soft job. Politics in the force will gradually undermine the character of the rank and file policemen. [For] most of them have families dependent on them.[43]

Nationally, the level of police organization could hardly be termed professional at the time of the President's Crime Commission's report in 1967. Surveys of 300 departments found 24 percent without any minimum educational requirements, and 72 of the police agencies in the New England states did not even require a high school diploma.[44]

In the course of the past four decades, through reform efforts aimed at eliminating political influence, police departments have become more bureaucratized than professionalized. In the course of this reform the urban police departments have developed their own political power within the structure of the local bureaucracy. Bureaucratic police departments tend to view any attempt to interfere with police department affairs—for instance, through civilian review boards—as political interference. In recent years, critics of urban police have focused upon the growing bureaucratic nature of the organization, which isolates it from a sensitive understanding of community needs. The considerable increase in administrative staff of the larger urban police departments tends also to isolate the rank and file police officers from both the hierarchy of command and the community. Police officers' self-esteem suffers when they realize that they occupy low-status positions in a bureaucracy that society ranks low on the prestige scale.

Arthur Niederhoffer has demonstrated that the low prestige given police officers of the lowest rank tends to reflect upon those in higher echelons. He suggests that this low occupational ranking is a barrier to the police obtaining professional status. He compared the occupational rank given police in six countries. The highest rank was 35 (on a scale of 1 to 100), with the lower the number the higher the rank. The lowest was 69 in Denmark. American police were at about the median, with a rank of 52. Niederhoffer also had American college students rank police captains, lieutenants, sergeants, and patrol officers along with nineteen other occupations. The captain was ranked eighth, seven ranks below the doctor and three below the sociologist; the lieutenant was ninth, the sergeant twelfth, and the patrolman was seventeenth out of the twenty-three occupations.[45]

Niederhoffer pointed out that the move to professionalize the police gained impetus during the Depression years, when middle-class youths chose police work because of the salary and job security. The complexity of modern police work requires a corps of experts, such as radar and computer operators and radio and television technicians.[46] This movement toward professionalism has sought to provide the police with status comparable to that of the legal and medical professions. But the parallel does not exist. Rather there is a distinction between "learned" professions and professionally trained police. The term "professional" has even turned off many poorly educated, tradition-oriented members of the rank and file, who have organized to protect their prerogatives through quasiunions called Policemen's Benevolent Associations.[47]

As political intervention at the top has been curtailed and high ranking police administrators have come to see themselves as professionals, the power of the buraucracy has grown apace. This bureaucracy ensures promotion from within, and through its paramilitary organizational structure it is able to maintain internal loyalty and minimize external control of police activities. Centralization of command is also contrary to professionalism. If the police officer is to be a professional, he or she must have the autonomy and skill to provide the best possible means of meeting challenges to public safety. Professional policing requires more than a well-defined organizational structure. It also requires that authority be defined within the law.

Changing Emphases

In 1966, David Bordua and Albert Reiss noted that there were no careful analyses of how police command organizations actually worked.[48] A more recent review of the literature has indicated that studies of the police had been done primarily by historians, administrators, and muckrakers until William Westley's study of police violence and secrecy in the 1950s. Studies in the 1960s stressed conflict between legal standards and organizational imperatives to control crime, as well as the administrator's control role in defining how a police organization deals with offenders (Banton, 1964; Skolnick, 1966; Wilson, 1968). More recently, there has been a new emphasis on police structure and the economics of policing as related to the capacity of the police to deal with crime (Greenwood et al., 1977; Kelling et al., 1974; Wilson, 1975).[49]

The principles of organization that can be inferred from these studies touch several aspects of police organization. For instance, the formal and ideal aspect views police organization as being characterized by a rigid chain of command, strict subordination, accountability of command, and the lack of formal means for consultation between ranks. This aspect stresses the paramilitary characteristics of an organization responsive to "orders from above" that are seen as "legitimate." However, it would be a mistake to think of large urban police departments only in terms of the classic bureaucratic model. In many ways, police organization and practice rely upon decentralized professional control patterns. Maintaining control by issuing orders from above is difficult, although a minimum of control can be realized through centralized radio communications and record keeping. As O. W. Wilson pointed out in

1950, a decade before he became police commissioner in Chicago, "It is relatively easy to delegate authority by giving a command, but to ascertain the manner in which the order was carried out... is often difficult." [50]

A police organization in a society with democratic values must be accountable to external civil and legal authorities as well as to the organization. But without adequate organizational structure, even the most reform-minded chief or commissioner will not be able to ensure that the police will function efficiently—or even legally. Out of such lack of control over police operations emerge police riots, like that of the Chicago police so convincingly documented by Daniel Walker in *Rights in Conflict* (1968).[51]

The Crime Commission's Task Force Report on the Police (1967) noted that some improvements had occurred in the level of police leadership since the earlier Wickersham Commission's report in 1931. But it concluded that many departments still lacked qualified, well-trained administrators. Only one-third of the nation's top police administrators had ever attended college, and a mere 9.2 percent had earned a college degree. Many of the commanding officers had come up through the ranks without any formal training as professional administrators.[52] Seven years after the Crime Commission's report, the U.S. Census surveyed the *Characteristics of Employees of Criminal Justice Agencies* (1974), and provided data that suggest a relationship between educational background and the rapidity of promotion of police officers. As Table 12.3 shows, the percentages of police officers who had completed one or more years of college were found to be proportionally higher in each of the higher status categories—investigators, supervisors, and managers—than among line officers, except for those with less than six years of service. Among those officers with sixteen or more years of service, nearly half of all supervisors, but only about 20 percent of line officers, had some college education. The fact that the proportion of college educated police officers, at the managerial level—chiefs and deputy chiefs—was smaller than at the supervisory level, is apparently due to the fact that a larger percentage of managerial level officers are employed in smaller, less urban police departments, while supervisors tend to be concentrated in larger departments.[53]

At about the same time, the LEAA reported that after five years of federal grants for police training by that agency, less than half of the police chiefs in cities over 25,000 agreed that police recruits should have a minimum of two years of college training, while 15 percent thought four years of college should be required. Since police administrators are promoted from the ranks, it is little wonder that the level of training has not improved appreciably. Even with the Law Enforcement Educational Program of LEAA, most police officers still are rewarded largely by the seniority system. A number of the departments we surveyed in northern New York were located in college towns, yet only one police chief had obtained a college degree. One respondent reported that he endorsed a requirement of two years of college training for promotion to sergeant, but civil service regulations did not require such training.[54]

Table 12.3. Proportion of Sworn Law Enforcement Personnel with One or More Years of College, Percentage by Occupational Level and Years of Service

	Less Than 6 Years Service	6–18 Years Service	11–15 Years Service	16–20 Years Service	21 or More Years Service
All sworn officers	50.9	47.6	45.4	35.1	31.6
Patrol officers	53.2	44.3	35.1	22.6	20.2
Investigators	70.7	62.9	59.4	52.4	27.2
Supervisors	49.6	70.3	63.1	48.2	50.9
Managers	34.5	46.6	48.7	46.3	39.8

Source: U.S. Bureau of Census, *Criminal Justice Employees Characteristics Survey* (Washington, D.C.: U.S. Government Printing Office, 1974).

With the lack of attention given to adequate training for administrators, it is not surprising that the Crime Commission found that there were serious organizational problems in many of America's city and county police forces. The Crime Commission asserted that most management experts familiar with police organization agreed that departments should evaluate their internal organization to ascertain whether:[55]

1. There is a logical plan for dividing the department's work among the various individuals and groups.
2. Lines of authority and responsibility are direct and clear.
3. Any one police administrator supervises a greater number of subordinates than effectiveness would allow.
4. The organization exhibits a unity of command throughout.
5. Responsibility is accompanied by comparable authority, and once delegated, those who exercise it are accountable for its use.
6. There is coordination of the units and their members that facilitates the harmonious functioning of the organization in accomplishing its purpose as a well-integrated police organization.

A well-organized police force whose structure follows these principles is shown in Figure 12.3.

The Crime Commission made numerous pleas for federal and state funds to encourage and stimulate research, development, and experimentation. In the years since the report, the LEAA has provided about $3 billion in federal grants to state and local governments for criminal justice. A significant proportion of the discretionary grants and specified funds have been spent encouraging education, research, and development of law enforcement. One group of radical critics sees these activities on the part of the LEAA as a "serious attempt to develop a national police apparatus for repression and control."[56] Even if this view were true, it is extremely doubtful that the police could become that effective.

Figure 12.3. One Form of a Well-Organized Municipal Police Department

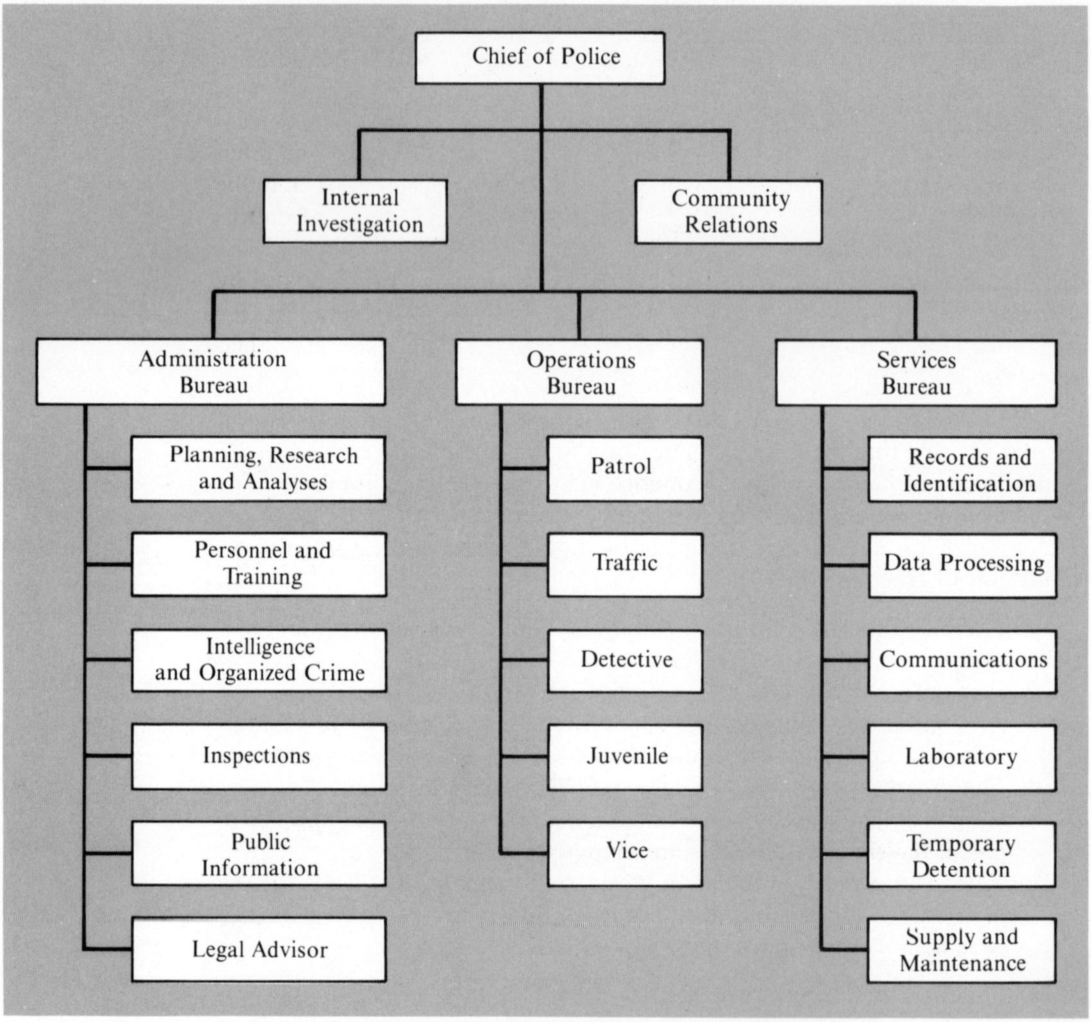

```
                          Chief of Police
                               │
              ┌────────────────┼────────────────┐
         Internal                           Community
       Investigation                        Relations
              │
     ┌────────┼──────────────────┬──────────────────┐
Administration              Operations          Services
   Bureau                     Bureau             Bureau
     │                          │                  │
  Planning, Research         Patrol          Records and
  and Analyses                                Identification
     │                          │                  │
  Personnel and              Traffic         Data Processing
  Training                                        
     │                          │                  │
  Intelligence               Detective        Communications
  and Organized Crime                             
     │                          │                  │
  Inspections                Juvenile          Laboratory
     │                          │                  │
  Public                     Vice             Temporary
  Information                                 Detention
     │                                             │
  Legal Advisor                               Supply and
                                              Maintenance
```

Source: President's Commission of Law Enforcement and Administration of Justice, *Task Force Report: The Police* (Washington, D.C.: U.S. Government Printing Office, 1967), p. 47.

POLICE WORK: PATTERNS AND PROBLEMS

Both the formal and informal aspects of police organization fill the everyday life of the police officer. The diversity of services and multiplicity of demands placed upon them caused the Crime Commission to recommend that police officers involved with law enforcement should have a college degree. The officer's world is influenced both by internal factors within the organization and by the community in which one performs his or her duties.

Patterns of Police Operations

Police Patrol. The most time-honored, and perhaps the least changed, police activity over the past fifty years is that of patrol. Officers on patrol—whether on foot or in a squad car—move from situation to situation, interacting with different constituencies. In a typical day they may investigate suspicious circumstances and suspicious characters on several occasions and listen to or respond to complaints; and although a lot of time may be spent on traffic violations, very little of the officers' time is directly related to crime control.

In his study of police activity in the high crime areas of three cities, Reiss found that 87 percent of the decisions to dispatch a patrol car were initiated by citizens. When an officer arrives on a scene, it may be assumed that some citizen thinks the officer has the duty and right to be there. It was also established that 87 percent of citizen requests were by telephone, 6 percent were made to the officer on patrol, and 7 percent were walk-ins.[57]

Police authority in the form of discretion begins at the point of receiving the call. A decision must be made whether the call is urgent or merely routine. Reiss's three-city observational study found that about 18 percent of calls were of the urgent variety, 73 percent were routine, and the rest unimportant.

The observers used by Reiss in his studies noted that interaction between officers and citizens took place in 70 percent of the reactive incidents. In situations that involved citizen interaction, Reiss classified the participants into *principal actors* (complainants, suspects, and offenders) and *minor roles* (informants and bystanders who might shift into principal roles as the situation changed). However, he suggested that there are many changing scenes and participants, and no tour of duty could be called typical for the patrol officer. Most patrol shifts *do not* involve the arrest of anyone, although traffic citations may be written.[58] Most patrol duties involve events such as directing traffic at the scene of an accident, calling ambulances, protecting drunks from themselves or others, cooling domestic disputes, breaking up fights among gangs or other youths, keeping order at fires, and general peace-keeping functions. These activities are most effective when arrests are not made. Peace keeping is perhaps a police department's most effective function.

Preventing and controlling crime is a more difficult matter. And as George Kelling and others found in the Kansas City Preventive Patrol Experiment, police car patrols organized around the strategy of preventing crime failed to have this effect. Rather, as other studies have shown, the tactic of preventive patrol contributed to the image of the police as an alien force remote from the community. This has been particularly true in minority communities, where police vehicles have come to symbolize the alien representatives of the white establishment. The result has not only been ineffectiveness, but the further alienation of citizens.[59]

Criminal Investigation. Police assigned to patrol do not ordinarily investigate major crimes. If a burglary is reported but is not in progress, the patrol officer makes a preliminary report and turns it over to the detective unit of the precinct. If this task is centralized, the detective bureau will be called in. Should arrests be made, they will be handled by detectives, unless the patrol officer picks up suspects in another action. This is one example of the limitations on the line officer's autonomy. At the same time, Reiss's data indicate that in Washington, D.C., 87 percent of the arrests were made by the patrol division, and patrol accounted for at least 50 percent of the arrests of Part I (index crime) offenses.[60] One writer has summarized well the myths about investigative work:

> Part of the mystique of detective operations is the impression that a detective has difficulty to come by qualifications . . . ; that investigating . . . is a . . . science, . . . that all detective work is exciting; and that a good detective can solve any crime. . . . It is arguable whether special skills . . . are required. . . . It borders on heresy to point out . . . that a considerable amount of detective work is undertaken on a hit-or-miss basis and that the capacity of detectives to solve crimes is greatly exaggerated.[61]

Criminal investigation has traditionally relied on informers. Such individuals are often used by narcotics and vice squads. As Reiss has noted, it takes considerable effort to gather information on an offense. If citizen complainants and direct police methods are unavailable, detectives resort to informers, usually civilians.

Jerome Skolnick concedes that an informer system frequently operates in the apprehension of public order offenses. He counters J. Edgar Hoover's argument that informers in America serve of their own free will to fulfill their obligations as citizens. Skolnick found that informers rarely provide information unless they get money or some personal benefit in return. If narcotic squad police pay money to an addict-informer, are they not indirectly involved in the drug traffic they are supposedly controlling?[62]

The investigation of victimless crimes is expensive in terms of both time and money. It also results in police intruding into an area of private morals. Lacking complainants they may resort to decoys, wiretapping, surveillance, or no-knock raids. Although this activity is usually police initiated, the police frequently are under pressure from interest groups—perhaps businessmen or others who may want a gambling, pornography, or prostitution operation closed down because it offends their moral values or interferes with their businesses.

The investigation of narcotics dealing and vice involves services and commodities that generate very large sums of money. The likelihood of bribery and police corruption is greatest in these areas.[63]

Traffic Control. Violations of the vehicle code and their enforcement outnumber other offenses by about 10 to 1. Traffic control constitutes a justifiably major emphasis of law enforcement, since about 55,000 citizens are killed each year in motor vehicle accidents—three times the number who die each year in homicides.[64]

Traffic divisions are concerned with traffic control, enforcement, and accident investigation. In recent years, highway safety has also been related to energy conservation, with the imposition of a federal speed limit of 55 miles an hour. Although departments usually deny the existence of quotas for traffic citations, informal norms or standards often are maintained as a means of evaluating an officer's level of performance.[65]

Though traffic control is a significant aspect of policing, it is often seen as an incidental facet of law enforcement in smaller departments. State police, however, regard highway patrol as one of their major functions. Banton reports that even the smaller Scottish police departments have special units for traffic control. Other European countries have established specialized forces to handle traffic so that peace officers can concentrate on more serious offenses.[66]

Police Community Relations. The phrase "police community relations" should not be confused with slick public relations efforts at image building. The two ideas are interrelated, however, to the extent that good will and mutual respect flow from police efforts to control crime and maintain order in a legitimate, responsible, respectful manner.[67]

Law enforcement is one function of government that confronts the citizen with coercive power. If the local government and its agencies, such as schools

How might positive police-citizen interaction be maximized?

and social service organizations, are insensitive to the needs of its various community members, then the police—the most visible extension of government—cannot be expected to make up for these deficiencies. Nevertheless, if there are conflict and mistrust between the police and the community, these must be recognized as related not only to social ills of the past and present, but to the current everyday experiences that people have with police or that they hear about through the community "grapevine." Effective use of such community networks, which provide useful information, might mean closer ties with the community from which the officer desires to ferret out secrets than a legalistic view of police duties might allow. As William Whyte suggests in his study of the police role in "Cornerville" (South Boston):

> ... The policeman who develops close ties with local people is unable to act against them with the vigor prescribed by law.... Law enforcement has a direct effect upon Cornerville people, whereas it only indirectly affects the "good people".... the smoothest course for the officer is to conform to the social organization with which he is in direct contact and ... try to give the impression to the outside world that he is enforcing the law. He must play an elaborate role of make-believe, and in so doing he serves as a buffer between divergent social organizations and their conflicting standards of conduct.[68]

Some of the earlier efforts by the police to gain public support and create good will in the communities they serve were clearly public relations efforts. In his book, *Police Administration* (1950), O. W. Wilson referred to public relations, not community relations.[69] Several viable police community relations experiments were in operation in the 1960s. For example, San Francisco's Police Chief Tom Cahill responded to the recommendation of civic groups when he set up a community relations bureau in 1962. Its objective was the creation of better understanding and closer relationships between the police and the community and the promotion of more effective cooperation by the public with the police department.[70]

The urban uprisings of the 1960s created pressures on city governments to reexamine their relations with minority communities. The police also reassessed their role, and numerous police community relations programs had emerged in cities by the late 1960s. Consequently, police community relations became synonymous with police minority, or police black relations.[71]

In 1967, the Crime Commission requested a survey of public attitudes toward the police. Although most of the general public thought the police were doing a good job in a respectful manner, the differences in responses by race startled the commission. Questions on attitudes toward performance, respectfulness, and honesty evoked significantly different perceptions of the police. Minorities other than blacks—as Chicanos, the poor, and the young—consistently expressed attitudes different from those of dominant groups (see Table 12.4).

The commission noted that it seems paradoxical that those who are most often the victims of crime are the most distrustful of and hostile to police. But this attitude is not really surprising, given the history of race relations in this

Table 12.4. Complaints Against Police (in percentages)

	Happened in Area	Saw it Happen	Happened to Someone You Know	Happened to You
Lack respect or use insulting language	85	49	52	28
Roust, frisk, or search people without good reason	85	52	48	25
Stop or search cars for no good reason	83	51	49	25
Search homes for no good reason	63	22	30	7
Use unnecessary force in making arrests	86	47	43	9
Beat up people in custody	85	27	46	5

Note: This study also shows that males below the age of 35 were most critical of the police. For example, 53 percent of young males reported they had been subjected to insulting language; 44 percent to a roust, frisk, or search without good reason; 22 percent to unnecessary force in being arrested; and 10 percent to being beaten up while in custody. Well over 90 percent of young males believed that each of these kinds of incidents occurred in the area, and 45 to 63 percent claimed to have seen at least one of them. There were no substantial differences based on economic levels. Blacks with higher education reported more insults, searches without cause, and stopping of cars without cause.

Source: Arthur Niederhoffer and Alexander B. Smith, *New Directions in Police and Community Relations* (Hinsdale, Ill.: The Dryden Press, 1974), p. 37. Adopted from President's Commission on Law Enforcement and Administration of Justice, *Task Force Report: The Police* (Washington, D.C.: U.S. Government Printing Office, 1967), p. 147.

country and the ghetto conditions in which most minority citizens live. The commission noted that the crux of the police community relations problem was that minority groups had specific grievances against the police. It stated that too many police officers are indifferent to the perspectives of minority groups, and that this insensitivity, together with patterns of physical and verbal abuse, contributes to the resentment of police expressed by many members of minority groups.[72]

The commission submitted that residents of minority communities would not receive the police protection they want and need until the police feel their presence is welcome and their problems are understood. It added, however, that since the police are public servants whose sworn duty is to protect all community members, they must take the initiative in creating such acceptance and understanding. The commission stated that a police community relations program is among the most important functions of departments where there are large minority groups. It suggested that programs be established and operated in terms of the following five principles:[73]

1. A community relations program is a long-range intensive effort to mutually learn about police and community problems and to seek action to resolve them.
2. Community relations should not be left to special units or programs, but should relate to all aspects of police activity: recruitment, training, and deployment of staff; operation of field procedures; staff policy and planning; discipline and control; and the processing of citizen complaints.
3. Requirements of effective community relations and law enforcement will not always coincide. The stress on professionalization and efficiency may have reduced the number of informal contacts between police and citizens. Over the short term, priority may be given to crime control. But in the long run, it should be realized that solid community relations are a prerequisite for effective law enforcement.
4. Community relations involves a reexamination of basic attitudes and behaviors. Since those who are critical and hostile are those with whom relations need to be improved, the police officer must be able to keep his "cool" when denounced or even threatened.
5. The police must be able and willing to work in a constructive manner toward understanding the desire for opportunity, civil rights, and autonomy on the part of the poor, minority groups, and the young.

These lofty principles marked a high point in the movement for police community relations. During the 1960s numerous police community relations programs emerged. Some departments set up separate PCR units, while others argued that "all police officers are involved in community relations." [74]

The apparent success of a few programs has been more than balanced by the failure of many others. Those programs that focus on community leaders and dominant groups, where a residue of good will or at least neutrality exists, evidently succeed in reinforcing good will through public relations activity. Those that try to modify the hostility and distrust of minority community members have been less successful. These attitudes are too complex to respond to "Officer-Friendly" visitation programs in the schools, neighborhood discussion groups, or police boys clubs.[75]

Another approach that has had a measure of success is the cooperation of the police with community development action groups, such as the North City Congress (NCC) that gained a degree of recognition from the Philadelphia police in 1964. But by the time it was funded in 1966, the commissioner had resigned and was later succeeded by the politically ambitious commissioner, Frank Rizzo, who supported community relations on different terms. Rizzo was a traditional career policeman who took police community relations out of the hands of the NCC and set up his own training program. Although minority relations with the police apparently deteriorated in 1968, Rizzo mobilized black community leaders to keep the community "cool" at the time other cities experienced turbulent uprisings following the assassination of Martin Luther

King. But the fact that Philadelphia avoided such disorders cannot be attributed to the efforts of either the commissioner or the NCC project.[76] It seems that something positive had taken place that was lacking in other cities.

Citizen or civilian review boards were advocated and established in some of our larger cities in the 1960s. Those review boards that have continued to operate have done so *within* the police organization. Citizen review boards that were organized to serve as neutral ombudsmen to consider citizen complaints against the police have been discontinued. Civilian review boards on a citywide basis in urban locations such as New York hardly represented the ultimate in citizen control of the police. For one thing, they were too far removed from the community and represented a more general attempt to invoke civilian rather than citizen control. Nevertheless they were successfully resisted by the police through political means and through court decisions in places like New York, Philadelphia, Minneapolis, Rochester, and York, Penn.[77]

The larger urban police departments have built into their organization special personnel or units that investigate complaints against police activity. A comparative study was made in Philadelphia on the concurrent operation of the Police Advisory Board (made up of prominent citizens external to the organization that reviewed complaints regarding alleged misconduct) and the Police Board of Inquiry (an internal disciplinary board that also reviewed citizen complaints). The different focus of the two boards provides a poor comparison, but as Table 12.5 shows, the Police Board of Inquiry was more active than its civilian counterpart.[78]

The American Bar Association's Advisory Committee on the Police Function has argued for vigorous internal controls through the chief administrator's office as the way to answer citizen grievances and discipline police. Failure to provide the means to deal with police misconduct, the committee concluded, is one of the more critical problems facing criminal justice today.[79]

POLICING AND THE RULE OF LAW

The police are empowered to enforce the laws that define crime. In the enforcement of legal rules they are to be guided by procedural law. Under procedural law, the legal and civil rights of those suspected of violating the "law" are to be protected. This may appear quite simple, but in the police officer's daily round of activities, a wide discrepancy can exist between the procedures allowed under the law and actual practice.

Most authorities agree that the scope of the criminal law is such that police officers find it impossible to enforce all laws. However, the law does not provide any guidance about which ones should be enforced. Consequently, officers must use their own discretion in deciding which violations to ignore. The policing procedures we will describe emphasize the tension between pressures for an efficient police that will maintain order and one that is strictly bound by the rule of law.[80]

Table 12.5. Comparison of External Police Advisory Board (PAB) and Internal Police Board of Inquiry (PBI), in percentages

		PBI (1960–1968)	
Recommendations	PAB[a] (1958–1968) (N = 145)	Civilian Complaints (N = 458)	Noncivilian Complaints (N = 2214)
Suspensions	14	52	76
Dismissals	1	14	5
Reprimands	16	6	9
Other negative action	6	—[b]	—
Other action (letter of apology, expungement of record, etc.)	20	—	—
Not guilty	—	28	10
No recommendation	40	—	—
Not ascertained	3	—	—
Totals	100	100	100

[a] Includes only principal complainants to eliminate double counting on recommendations.
[b] No comparable category.

Source: James R. Hudson, "Organizational Aspects of Internal and External Review of the Police," in Jerome H. Skolnick and Thomas C. Gray, eds., *Police in America* (Boston: Little, Brown, 1975), p. 283.

Arrest and Clearance

The power of the police to enforce the law is demonstrated in the authoritative command, "You're under arrest." Although much has been made of the technical right of individuals to make a "citizen's arrest," private citizens lack authority to make arrests in lesser crimes except in cases of breach of the peace. Private police, however, may in certain situations exercise this right.[81] Arrest is a power that the law grants to the police officer along with the special right to carry a weapon or to call upon citizens for assistance.[82]

In strict legal terms, arrest can be defined as taking a person into custody under the law. An arrest deprives a person of liberty through legal authority. In a narrow legal sense, a traffic citation might be considered an arrest since it briefly restricts an individual's liberty. However, it is not commonly thought of that way by either the police or the public. Police officers typically consider an arrest as the completion of "booking" an individual, which is the basis for reporting the offense and holding the offender in jail.

The exact arrest powers of police officers vary in different states. Generally, they typically are empowered to arrest whenever there is "probable cause" that a crime—whether a misdemeanor or felony—has occurred in their presence, or that a felony may have been committed out of their presence by someone who might escape. Arrests can also be made on warrants or written orders of the court. A judge or magistrate may issue a warrant upon application by an officer, or it may be issued when the judge is convinced that there is "probable cause" that a person is guilty of an offense.

Millions of arrests are made each year—9,275,000 in 1975—but these do not indicate clearly the number of people taken into custody or the number of crimes cleared by arrest. An individual may be taken into custody and released without being booked. A single arrest for burglary may clear a number of burglaries, or a group of arrests may clear only one offense.

The decision on whether to arrest may be influenced not only by a citizen's complaint but also by the officer's decision on whether the complaint is of a criminal or noncriminal variety. Police departments are reluctant to acknowledge the use of such discretion because it raises doubts about the image of impartiality that the police want to project. But the fact of the matter is that individual officers have great discretion over the way in which they will enforce the law. Such discretion, of course, opens the door to the possibility of corruption.[83]

The decision to arrest is not always defined strictly by legal means, but is often a matter of personal or professional judgment. Discretion operates in all professional organizations. Although police often are alleged to act beyond their authority, their use of discretion is seen as improper only when it goes beyond the definition of criminal behavior as defined in the law. However, as Banton has suggested, in situations of patrol instances often occur when the police officer may decide not to enforce the law. Such decisions also reflect arbitrary police power. Banton points out that where minor offenses are involved, a decision against enforcement is the rule both in Britain and the United States.

Police often find it necessary to establish priorities in enforcing the law, even though many citizens assume that the police should enforce all criminal laws. For one thing, it is impossible to have a criminal code that clearly encompasses all criminal behavior and that keeps pace with changing social conditions. Further, the police do not have the resources to enforce all the laws effectively. For instance, if police were to monitor all street intersections where there are stop signs, they would be unable to do anything else.

Police Discretionary Power: Use and Misuse

Police have vast discretionary power in deciding whether to arrest or not to arrest, to hassle or overlook what crimes to investigate and how to proceed, and what crimes not to investigate due to economies of time and personnel. In this respect, the police, as Kenneth Davis argues in *Discretionary Justice* (1969), are a most important policy-making agency, despite the widespread assumption that they are not.[84]

In his book *The Rationing of Justice* (1964), Arnold Trebach argues that a combination of police confusion concerning the law and deliberate violations results in numerous invasions of individual rights. One practice that results in a great number of such violations is arrest "on suspicion" or "for investigation." The legal stipulation is that no arrest without a warrant can be made without "probable cause," which means that arrests should not be made on vague suspicion.[85] Yet arrests on suspicion were routinely reported in the FBI *Uniform Crime Reports*' total of estimated arrests as late as 1970. In that year, 83,500 such arrests accounted for about 1 percent of the total. By 1975, the 36,200 arrests on "suspicion" were not included in the total. The apparent decrease—which looms even greater when one considers that 136,325 such arrests were reported in 1960—suggests some tightening of police discretion.[86]

One earlier study of the Detroit Police Department, for instance, found that one out of every three arrests from 1947 to 1956 was in the category of "arrests for investigation." The method for these arrests was sometimes the so-called "dragnet" operation. In such instances, large numbers of police descend on a high crime neighborhood—typically occupied by the poor and racial minorities—and arrest people without due concern for probable cause. Such methods are usually in reaction to crimes that "shock the conscience" of the community. They are justified as desperate measures for difficult situations.[87]

Unfortunately, it is the innocent poor and minorities who suffer most in such cases. For instance, when a series of attacks on women occurred in Detroit in 1960, as many as 1,000 arrests for investigation were made. And in 1961 in Odessa, Texas, when a white woman claimed to have been raped by a black man, the police arrested almost every young black found on the street—eighty-eight initially.[88] Such methods often are seen as one way of reducing crime. But it should be noted that they represent illegal invasions of individual constitutional rights, and any advantage gained is small compared with the social and personal costs. In this regard, one study by a committee of lawyers in Washington, D.C., found that during 1960 and 1961, only 5.7 percent of those arrested were charged with specific crimes. In seventeen out of eighteen cases, the police either lacked evidence of "probable cause," or those arrested were innocent. The committee concluded that the cost to the community was too great, and arrests for investigation were banned by the District Board of Commissioners. Arrests for investigation gave many innocent lower-status persons a police record and present an additional hurdle for future employment.[89]

Police policymaking of this nature is, as Davis has noted, illegal or semi-legal, for it is contrary to the Constitution and statute law or is the result of legislative failure to provide adequate guidelines. Such police illegality usually involves selective enforcement of laws, making deals with offenders in order to gain information, or using the power of arrest when there is insufficient evidence to support a charge. This discretionary power, even when flagrantly misused, is a powerful weapon, for it is difficult to control through effective judicial review.[90]

Legal Restrictions. Considerable evidence supports the argument by Davis, calling for improved police procedures that will close the gap between police manuals and the apparent misuse of police power—the dispensing of "street-corner justice." Traditionally, a "good cop" was expected to use persuasion, threats, and even force to maintain order without having to resort to the courts. It is in street encounters between police and suspects that the gap between administrative command policy and police behavior is the greatest.[91] As noted previously, the arrest and search of a suspect ideally is guided by the legal principle of "probable cause." The police do not have authority to search or arrest just anyone. In his observations of police activity in Boston, Chicago, and Washington, Reiss found that the probability that a suspect would be searched was only one in five. It was much higher in New Orleans. Yet searches of suspects in these three cities, which usually took place when there was reason to think that a crime had been committed, resulted in the discovery of more dangerous weapons than in New Orleans.[92]

Citizens are protected from unlawful searches and seizure of property under the Fourth Amendment to the Constitution. For years the local police operated under the assumption that search and seizure was not regulated by substantive law. In 1961, the Supreme Court overturned Dollree Mapp's conviction, since it was based on evidence seized in clear violation of the Fourth Amendment. Thus the *Mapp* case extended protection against search and seizure by state or federal officers, and it excluded from evidence property seized from a suspect in violation of the Fourth Amendment. As a result, many states had to add an exclusionary rule declaring that such evidence was inadmissible. In other words, police must discover proof of an offense in a lawful manner.[93]

The Fifth Amendment states that "no person...shall be compelled in any case to be a witness against himself." Consistent with this protection, the Court ruled in *Miranda* v. *Arizona* (1966) that police must give a clear warning to a suspect prior to interrogation. This has been a controversial decision, opposed by law-and-order advocates, including former Attorney General John Mitchell. In subsequent cases, the Supreme Court has modified various aspects of this decision. One such decision, removing restrictions relative to Miranda warnings from "voluntary" suspects not under arrest, is described in the document, "Justices Curb Miranda Rights of Suspects Questioned by the Police" (see Box 1, Chapter 2). Overall, *Mapp*, *Miranda*, and other decisions regulating police power have not seemed to impair police efficiency.[94]

The basic principle governing confessions concerns whether or not they are voluntary. The procedures followed by the police must meet constitutional requirements, and no law enforcement officer is supposed to violate these constitutional guidelines of protection of personal rights. The laws are intended to provide fairness and ensure procedural regularity in order to protect the innocent against abuses of power and to provide impartial justice. But the laws do change, and procedures derived from them are in a state of flux. The very ambiguity of the laws may reinforce traditional police procedures and provide justification for violating them. The police conception of the law tends to be instrumental. Laws are seen as a means—not an end in themselves. It would seem evident, though empirical evidence of post-Miranda practices is limited,

The Miranda Warning

BOX 2

Police procedures must meet constitutional requirements.

The U.S. Supreme Court in *Miranda* v. *Arizona* (1966) established as procedural safeguards, that when "a suspect is being questioned in custody—whether under arrest or deprived of his freedom in any way—he must first be warned and advised that:

1. You have the right to remain silent.
2. Any statement you make may be used against you in a court of law.
3. You have the right to consult with an attorney and to have an attorney present during the questioning.
4. If you are unable to afford an attorney one will be appointed to represent you, should you desire, before any questioning."

Source: Adapted from Paul B. Weston and Kenneth M. Wells, *Elements of Criminal Investigation* (Englewood Cliffs, N.J.: Prentice-Hall, 1971), pp. 62–63.

WAIVER

After the warning has been given, the suspect may waive such rights, but the waiver must be made knowingly by the accused. A standard way for the prosecution to manifest to the court that such a waiver was given is to have the suspect sign a card with a copy of the above four statements. The police department provides officers with cards on which the above statements are printed. Opportunity to exercise such rights must be allowed throughout all phases of the interrogation. To ensure that the meaning of the warning is clear, after the warning is given, and in order to secure a waiver, an affirmative reply should be received to the following questions:

1. Do you understand each of the rights explained to you?
2. With these rights in mind, do you now wish to answer our questions?

that the use of the third degree or extended interrogation employing mental or physical force to extract confessions has declined in the years since the Miranda decision prohibited such investigative tactics.

Misuse of Necessary Force; Police Abuses. Although the Crime Commission and earlier studies such as Westley's have documented that unauthorized or illegal violence can occur in police citizen encounters, especially where the officer's authority is challenged, police violence does not occur in the majority of cases for a number of reasons. *First,* many police do abide by legal restrictions against unnecessary violence. *Second,* most people comply with an officer's request. And *third,* arrests usually take place in public situations where there are observers. Still it is the point of arrest where police use force in an excessive, unnecessary manner.[95]

One such case came to the attention of the Philadelphia Police Advisory Board in 1960. When two officers intervened in a family argument in which Eugene Hutchins was alleged to have slashed his wife, he punched one of the officers, who then knocked him down and handcuffed him. Both officers then proceeded to beat him with their nightsticks and a blackjack. Although the officers claimed that their action was "necessary force," the board decided that it was "unnecessary" and that they had indulged in force "past the point of resistance." [96]

The study by Westley of a police force in an Ohio industrial city of 150,000 found that 37 percent of the police interviewed thought that an officer was justified in roughing up a man if he showed disrespect for the police, and 19 percent felt that violence was justified in order to obtain information. Westley related such violence to the occupational self-concept of the police officer.[97]

During the civil rights demonstrations of the early 1960s and the antiwar protests later in that decade and in the early 1970s, the press recorded numerous incidents of police violence against demonstrators. In these situations, special riot police, specially armed for the "mob," were used. In some cases, provocation by demonstrators set in motion excessive use of force by the police. In 1968, police baiting resulted in beatings and bashing of heads in Chicago, in what has been termed a "police riot." [98]

The attitude of individuals is important to police, and youths seen as uncooperative or antagonistic are apt to be dealt with harshly. The Crime Commission's survey reported that 40 percent of the respondents in the Watts area of Los Angeles believed there was police brutality. Among those respondents between the ages of fifteen and twenty-nine, about 50 percent claimed to have witnessed such behavior.[99] The observers who rode in police cars in Reiss's study of three cities witnessed thirty-seven instances involving forty-four citizens in which police used excessive force. Encounters with 643 white suspects and 451 black suspects were observed. Twenty-seven of the white suspects were subjected to undue force, compared with seventeen blacks. Reiss concluded that "the most likely victim of excessive force is a lower-class male of either race." [100]

A study by Paul Chevigny of complaints to review boards in New York City concluded that the police role often forces the police to attempt to establish their authority. Police are recruited from conventional backgrounds, and they adopt the rationale that those who challenge them are troublemakers. In street encounters, when the police see their authority challenged, they seek to assert it by demanding respect from the suspect through force. Chevigny suggests that street situations that evoke the use of force by the police are similar to assaults by private citizens. But in cases of police violence, the illegal aspect includes not only abuse of authority in the use of physical force, but the charges of resisting arrest that often follow such acts to cover them up. In these cases, the legal basis of the justice system is subverted, and the suspect ends up with a criminal record. Police behavior that forces obedience or submission from a citizen by unlawful means is justifiably seen as an act of oppression.[101]

The public wants an efficient police force, and it demands that something be done about crime. But society also has a claim to due process and impartial justice. The public evidently does not thoroughly disapprove of police violence of the kind described by Westley and other students of the police. Nor does it seem wholly unsympathetic toward the police riots at the Democratic National Convention in 1968, the retaking of Attica in 1971, or violence at Kent State and Jackson State in 1970. The tension between the rule of law and the maintenance of order cannot be solved by making police departments even more isolated from the public. When professionalism becomes politicization, the question that is raised is, *Quis custodiet ipsos custodes?* (Who shall guard the guardians?)

Police Corruption: "Bad Apples" or Social Patterns?

Public law enforcement organizations emerged in the period in the history of our cities during which local governments were notoriously corrupt. In his muckraking study of American cities at the turn of the century, Lincoln Steffens documented police corruption. Little wonder that police history, as well as popular fiction, portrays images of "crooked cops" who accept "payoffs," and not only betray public trust but tarnish whole departments. In an earlier chapter, reference was made to the Knapp Commission's report of the involvement in crime and corruption of the New York City police force. The commission found that a large proportion of that city's police force was engaged in some type of corruption. This corruption ranged from the numerous "grass-eaters," who accepted and solicited small sums of money from construction companies, tow-truck operators, and gamblers, or who accepted "perks" (small favors such as free meals and discounts from businessmen) to the "meat-eaters," who accepted large sums of money on a regular basis.

Such corruption, however, is a chronic problem in large city departments, not just in New York City. The question, as with other criminals, is why do they do it? In the case of police corruption, the question refers to individuals who have knowledge of the penal code and whose departmental regulations prohibit such crimes of malfeasance. Since most every police officer faces the temptation to accept a small gift or "payoff," the explanation frequently heard from police officers for such behavior is that there are a few "bad apples" in every organization. And consistent with this bad-apples theory is the recommendation for more careful screening of police recruits.

We find the bad-apples theory too individualistic, for it does not account for the manner in which the individual officer accommodates to the informal police subculture. And it overlooks the widespread corruption in many urban police departments. As the Knapp Commission noted, even those who are not involved in any corrupt activities are engaged in corruption in the sense that they do not do anything about what they know or suspect is going on.[102]

It may be that the police recruit inadvertently moves into taking "payoffs" by first accepting small favors. He or she "mooches," or receives free coffee or lunches, with the implicit understanding or expectation that the favor will be returned. He may "chisel" or demand discounts or free admission to theaters, and so forth. Another form of minor corruption is "favoritism," where immunity from arrest or citations may be granted, particularly if the offender can show membership in a special group, for example, another police force. The "shakedown" is a more clear-cut move toward corruption, for it involves taking expensive goods in the course of an investigation and reporting them as stolen. "Shopping" is similar, only the items are less expensive. And "extortion" may be used to sell tickets or require cash for traffic violations. Once these minor corruptions are practiced, it is relatively easy to become involved in the less prevalent pattern of serious graft or "meat eating." [103]

Thus, the moral career of the "corrupt cop" is that of an officer who may be compromised by the moral ambiguities of the community as well as the law enforcement organization. The officer is corrupted by legitimate businessmen as well as by criminals. And the officer may take the payoff and still see himself as an honest, good police officer. Such police corruption can best be understood as growing out of the pressures of affiliation with the police organization and its relationship to the community—and not just in the individual's character. Yet in whatever form corruption takes, it reduces police morale, diminishes administrative control, creates a perception of hypocrisy among police officers and between police and civilians, and thus increases public cynicism. And most importantly, it tarnishes the social order that the police represent. In short, as Manning reminds us, police corruption underscores the fact that major problems of the police defy technological solutions, for they are social and human problems.[104]

POLITICIZATION OF THE POLICE AND OTHER DILEMMAS FOR THE RULE OF LAW

It has become a cliché to speak of the political polarization between conservative and liberal perspectives in American society during the 1960s. In Jerome Skolnick's epilogue to the second edition of *Justice Without Trial* (1975), he suggests three developments during that period that were concomitants of increased politicization of the police. These were the increased political awareness and militancy of nonwhite communities, uprisings on college campuses and antiwar protests, and the increased use of marijuana and other drugs. He suggests that in this environment the police developed even more of a protective stance than they traditionally had taken regarding police misconduct. This new police solidarity took the guise of police power in our large cities. Police chiefs ran for elective office and were elected as mayors in Philadelphia and Los Angeles.[105]

It might be argued that the police have always been involved in politics. In some cities the chief police administrator is a political appointee. In some departments advancement or promotion is still politically controlled. As recently as 1960, politicians controlled the police department of Chicago. But the "new" politics of police organizations has another dimension. The police emerged from the 1960s as a self-conscious political constituency seeking the power to determine policies that formerly were presumed to be laid down by the representatives of society. This change raises the same issue that might arise were the military to become politicized in a democracy.

Examples of police politicization are well known. Among them are the police job action by the Detroit Police Association, which in 1967 forced the city to give in to wage demands, and the successful efforts by the New York City Police Benevolent Association to force a referendum on the civilian review board in 1966. In Detroit, Indianapolis, New Orleans, and other cities, there have been virtual strikes when the police have called in sick with the "blue flu." The New York City police, however, were unable to follow up on their political victory over civilian review boards. In 1969, the state legislature passed a bill allowing the city to abolish the fifty-eight-year-old, three platoon system. Police have also sought to monitor the conduct of judges they considered too lenient in the sentences they handed out to offenders, and in Detroit the police tried, although unsuccessfully, to remove a judge.

We should be wary of the problems that a politicized and well-financed police force might present regarding the preservation of democratic values and the social order. Our position is that police forces united for political action is a development to be regarded with caution, not because of their conservative bias, but because the nature of their power places them in a situation in which this power might be used against political opponents.

New Technologies: The Police as Technicians

In recent years, developments in electronic listening ("bugging") devices have made it possible for the police to extend their surveillance into the privacy of the citizen's home. Even though the value of such devices for controlling crime has not been demonstrated, many police officers are convinced that they provide needed information on law-violating activity. The invisible nature of electronic eavesdropping makes it open to abuse, though legally the police are required to seek a judicial order before bugging devices may be used.

Another technological breakthrough has been in the use of computers to store and share information on arrests. The federal government has funded many of these expensive systems through the LEAA. By 1971, the hundred largest law enforcement agencies in the United States had installed computer systems that were tied into the FBI National Crime Information Center (NCIC). This technology has provided detectives with the capability to gather and analyze data with speed and accuracy not previously possible. Through communication with other systems, they have access to a mass of data that improves their effectiveness in dealing with crime.[106]

Nevertheless, the data gathered by local, state, and federal police, not to mention the CIA, DIA, and the computerized index systems of many other agencies on millions of our citizens, pose a threat both to privacy and the freedom of dissent. With the post-Watergate revelations of illegal buggings, surveillance, and even "second-story" jobs by the FBI and CIA, the hazards of such an information system have been brought home dramatically to many Americans. Until these revelations, the Department of Justice had resisted any efforts to control or limit the government's power to gather data on or about individual Americans. Fortunately, the Freedom of Information Act has made it possible for citizens to find out whether data on their activities are on file — at least to a degree.

The New York State Identification and Intelligence System (NYSIIS) is a huge computer data bank serving more than 3,000 criminal justice agencies in New York. It has tried to protect privacy by limiting the number of its users. It also restricts the type of data that can be stored, forbids unauthorized disclosure, and allows citizens to examine and correct their files. It also has a "forgiveness" principle written into the program, so that only the names of active or "potential recidivists" are kept "live"; however, it should be noted that the term "potential recidivist" is a vague and inaccurate term which can be misused. Other states are developing comparable systems, all of which interface with the FBI's NCIC system. This merger of technology and the law enforcement bureaucracy looms as a shadow of repression and a hazard to our democratic values. Recently there has been a move to reorganize the various federal statistics in crime and criminal justice agency files. The project has been delayed because the cost will exceed $50 million. Fiscal considerations may for a time have done what Senate Bill 1437 failed to do — slow down the trend toward greater centralization of the computerized crime data system.

Policing and the Community

Once we know what the police should do and can do, then we can address the three critical problems of police recruitment, training and leadership. As matters stand now, we do not know what we are recruiting for, what kind of leadership we ought to be developing.[107]

This statement was written in 1972 by the former chief of police of Miami. It reflects a note of realism required for any improvement of law enforcement within the context of the democratic values of American society. In the past, many have hoped that police reform would come through improved professionalism of personnel. Much attention has been focused by social scientists on studies of the police function and role. This literature has often been critical of police behavior. A broad range of problems has been identified, from abuse of citizens' rights to community relations, police discretion and role definition, and more recently, cost-effectiveness.[108]

Aside from necessary changes in the law, two problems seem most urgently in need of solution: (1) How might police departments and policing be reorganized in terms of a mandate that emphasizes the peace-keeping function rather than law enforcement? and (2) How might the policing function reflect community control, accountability, and needs, rather than alienation from the communities the police are intended to serve?[109]

As has been noted in recent years, police salaries have improved and the number of officers and the use of new technology have increased dramatically. Police benevolent associations have become powerful unions with political clout. And in the past decade, police organizations have been the focus of more research than most other aspects of the criminal justice system. Out of this research have come numerous suggestions—some of them apparently contradictory and confusing—regarding the development of future police roles and tactics. One of the more succinct summaries of these developments has been provided by George Kelling, who serves as evaluation field staff director of the Police Foundation. His theme is that by defining themselves as "crime fighters," the police have concentrated on the development of crime prevention strategies for which they have been rewarded financially and professionally. However, this emphasis not only has failed to achieve its goal of reducing crime, but may very well have increased the alienation of citizens from police and added to the fear of crime.[110]

The Ineffectiveness of Present Strategies

The presumed effects of police strategies such as preventive patrol, rapid response to calls for service, team policing, investigation, and new technology for the reduction of crime that we will now describe, have been at the expense of other important activities. Still, the legend of the police as crime fighters and as an organization involved in detecting and preventing crime is embedded in our traditions and continues to be reinforced by the media.[111]

Presumed Effects of Preventive Patrol. The variations of preventive patrol are all based on the presumed effects of police activity on crime. With the introduction of police cars, police came to see themselves as "in service" or "in action" when cruising, but "out of service" when away from their vehicle interacting with citizens. This increase in police presence was presumed to prevent crime, but numerous studies have challenged its effectiveness.[112]

In the early 1960s, Reiss found that time spent in such activity was unproductive. The Rand Institute's later study found mixed benefits. And in the carefully designed Kansas City Preventive Patrol Experiment, the presumed effects on crime prevention and control were found to be lacking. It has been suggested by the Crime Commission and more recent critics, that such tactics as preventive patrol have augmented the idea that the police are an alien force—especially in minority communities. In retrospect, efforts to establish police community relations programs are now seen as attempts to compensate for some of the negative effects of preventive patrol. Thus, in the long run, the strategy of preventive patrol has resulted in the worst of two worlds: ineffectiveness and citizens alienated from the police.[113]

Rapid Response Time. It has long been assumed that if police could reduce the time interval between the commission of a crime and their arrival at the scene, there would be an increase in arrests, more effective crime prevention, and greater citizen satisfaction, all of which would result in a diminished fear of crime. Quicker response time would complement preventive patrol in promoting police effectiveness, it was thought. However, several studies, using data from the Kansas City Police, have shown that response time has no effect on robbery rates, and that in any event, citizens sometimes called someone else before notifying the police. Moreover, the crucial factor was whether or not the police fulfilled citizen expectations in their response.[114] What occurred was that in linking response time to police effectiveness, the matter of whether or not response time was related to citizens' apprehensions was overlooked. And so this strategy, involving expensive automatic vehicle locator systems, has also been costly in allocating police officers by confining them to their squad cars and has influenced police management systems—all without achieving the beneficial effect that was promised.[115]

Team Policing. One of the most promising concepts introduced in the 1960s to develop closer police citizen interaction was team policing. It recognizes the multifunctional aspects of policing, emphasizes decentralization, and encourages police to identify and cooperate with agencies and resources in their assigned neighborhood. Among cities that have tried team policing are Cincinnati, Detroit, Dallas, and New York. However, it has not been established on a systemwide basis in any large city.[116]

A recent evaluation of Cincinnati's effort found that after one year, crime had decreased, citizen satisfaction had increased, and police enthusiasm was obvious, but these gains had been lost by the end of the second year. Subsequently, team policing simply expired in Cincinnati. Kelling suggests that team policing followed the pattern of enthusiastic beginning, commitment, and promise of many other programs before fading away. This sequence apparently is a general pattern for two reasons. First, such a decentralized operation is threatening to formal and informal entrenched power groups in the organization, as well as to employee organizations who may have influence with politicians and others. Second, the focus of team policing on planning out-of-service programs, such as meetings with community groups, is incompatible with police emphasis on rapid response to calls for service. So this orientation takes priority over a multidimensional approach to community service.[117]

Investigative Tactics and Strategies. Several recent studies have examined investigative effectiveness. An exploratory study by Peter Greenwood, et al., which has been both criticized and praised in the press, underscores the idea that the role of investigators in solving crime is overrated. A study in Rochester looked at problems of case management. The researchers not only found that investigation could be more efficient if detectives focused on solvable cases, it also found that line officers could facilitate this process by identifying such cases. Although these are only preliminary studies, they point to the need for improving coordination between patrol officers and investigators in order to increase effectiveness.[118]

Technology: For What Purpose? Since the introduction of the radio in police work, some have predicted that advanced technology—helicopters, computers, new weaponry, surveillance systems, and the like—would enhance policing, if not eliminate crime altogether. Kelling, however, argues that with the possible exception of personal radios—which have been more useful as management devices than in crime fighting—and new lightweight bulletproof vests, little evidence supports the idea that technology has greatly improved police effectiveness. Technology may have potential for more efficient management, but we have yet to see its impact on multiple police services.[119]

It is not merely that technology—such as radio, computer-aided dispatch, and automatic vehicle locator systems—represents expensive toys, but that in assuming that such devices would result in a "presumed effect," a higher priority has come to be placed on crime fighting than on providing community services. Thus, basic changes in the kinds of services, as well as the manner in which services are delivered, have taken place. As one critic of military technology for police use has noted, money is easily diverted to technology. When people confront problems, the inclination is to show that you are doing something about the problem in a scientific manner. The important question regarding the application of technology to policing that has not as yet been answered adequately is, For what purpose? [120]

Improving Police Citizen Cooperation and Minimizing the Fear of Crime

If policing is to obtain the desired goals of maintaining order in a society emphasizing a diversity of values and behaviors, then the police will have to develop strategies that are multifunctional in scope, and they will have to earn the support of citizens—a necessity for effective social control in the community.

Information Strategies Involving Citizen Interaction. A number of studies have suggested that more effective programs might be developed to gather and manage useful information through the improvement of the kind and degree of police citizen contacts. These programs would run counter to the present emphases on crime fighting and rapid response to requests for service.[121]

Implementing such programs would entail the broadening of police function and organization, so that members of the community might find it easier to report more information to the police. It would also necessitate police training that enhances their ability to understand the community in which they operate. The police reward structure would also have to be modified so that sharing of information would occur.

The organizational aspects relevant to information effectiveness include supervision, training, and rewards that emphasize the collection and distribution of information. The maximization of police citizen interaction to bring about the collection of useful information is a matter of strategy. Arranging for efficient storage and retrieval of information is a matter of effective use of technology.[122]

Police as a Community Service Agency. Research studies over the past several decades have documented the fact that police spend a relatively small proportion of their time (20 to 27 percent) fighting crime. It seems apparent that such information has important implications for the various facets of police organization. If police organization reflected the *reality* of the police role, not only would those attracted to police departments be different, at least in their idea of what is expected of them, but their training would emphasize work in community conflict management and human relations, rather than the current focus on paramilitary organizational control and technology used for rapid response. This would mean that the reward structures would have to be modified, for most people perform best at those kinds of activities that produce rewards — both financial and status rewards.

Although crucial crime problems may demand attention, focusing the total organizational effort routinely on crime control appears to have a limited effect and is not only costly, but detracts from public order maintenance and public service functions.[123]

The crucial focus for future strategies and styles of policing demands a basic improvement in the quality and degree of interaction between citizens and police, not to improve the image of the police, but as a means of enhancing the ongoing social control efforts of a viable community. As Kelling argues, although the police are a basic part of society and should be viewed as promoting the community's solution of its problems, policing is too important a function to be left solely to the police.[124]

The methods used by the police should reflect all aspects of policing. We should note how information is gathered and processed and provide rewards to encourage its being shared. By changing citizens' expectations, the undue emphasis on response time can be lessened. Reducing the fear of crime should also be an important police task, so that citizens will be encouraged to feel comfortable when they use the streets with a degree of caution. As Kelling suggests, the time has come to test the untried hypothesis: that the extent to which police make available all dimensions of services will determine the degree to which citizens utilize and enlist them against crime. Meanwhile, we ought to declare a moratorium on technology and focus intensely on reformulating the police mandate, so that we might discover what it is they should do and are able to do.[125]

SUMMARY

The activities of the police are significant, since the police are the most visible of the three main elements of the criminal justice system, and because they define and apprehend those who are processed through the courts and corrections. With the focus on a rising crime rate over the past decade—up 120 percent between 1955 and 1975—the number of police has increased by 75 percent.

Our early police forces grew out of the *watch system* and were modeled after the British system, which began in 1829. Boston and New York City developed police departments in the 1840s. We still rely upon local government to provide police protection. *Federal funding under LEAA has been influential in the development of police agencies and policies since the late 1960s.*

Four functions of the police were outlined: *coercion, link in the criminal justice system, community service,* and *symbolic representative of governmental authority.* Modern urban police departments are bureaucratic and paramilitary in their organization. As police departments confronted urban unrest in the 1960s, the need to develop effective police community relations with minority communities became obvious, due to the resentment of the police and their methods by minority communities.

Professionalization of police departments has led to a demand for autonomy, while the police have resisted attempts for greater civilian control.

Police activities are restricted by accountability to the rule of the law. Although police are reluctant to acknowledge it, they exercise discretion in decisions over whether or not certain laws will be enforced. This may lead to underenforcement as often as to overenforcement. Ideally, the police are regulated by procedural law in the manner in which they enforce the law. Additional restrictions exist in the substantive law—especially in matters of search and seizure and in obtaining confessions. Recent studies have focused upon conflicts between legal standards of the rule of law and public and organizational pressures for the control of crime. The police riots of 1968 and the early 1970s have evoked concern about the problem of controlling the police. Meanwhile, the police have tended to become more politicized, which limits the development of professionalism.

New technology, such as electronic surveillance devices and computerized data bank files, has provided police with an increased capability not only to investigate crime, but also to invade the privacy and breach the First Amendment rights of private citizens.

In developing strategies that focus mainly on the functions of crime control and prevention, the police have not only failed in their announced objectives, but they have slighted the importance of positive relations with the communities they serve and have too often alienated citizens on whose support they must rely for effective fulfillment of their many functions.

ADDITIONAL READINGS

Banton, Michael. *The Policeman in the Community.* New York: Basic Books, 1964.

> A comparative study of policing in Great Britain and America. Similarities are explored, and differences in definitions of organization, police duty, interpersonal relations, and self-definitions of the officer's role in the two societies are interestingly drawn.

Fogelson, Robert M. *Big-City Police.* Cambridge: Harvard University Press, 1977.

> This historical study of the institution of the police places their development in a sociopolitical context. While tracing the various attempts at reforming the police he demonstrates their corrupt roots and the ironies of this double legacy in contemporary bureaucratic big-city police organizations.

Greenwood, Peter W., Jan M. Chaiken, and Joan Petersilis. *The Criminal Investigation Process.* Lexington, Mass.: D. C. Heath, 1977.

> This study, by the criminal justice research staff of the Rand Corporation, is helpful in laying aside some of the myths regarding criminal investigation. It suggests necessary changes in areas such as follow-up inquiry, special units, and information processing systems.

Kelling, George, et al. *The Kansas City Preventive Patrol Experiment.* Washington, D.C.: Police Foundation, 1974.

> A report of a carefully controlled empirical study of preventive police patrol in Kansas City, which demonstrates the unproductive results of such proactive police efforts in crime prevention or control.

Manning, Peter K. *Police Work: The Social Organization of Policing.* Cambridge, Mass.: MIT Press, 1977.

> Based on the author's extensive fieldwork in England and the United States, this book provides a dramaturgical-interactionist perspective on policing by focusing on policing as an activity, an organization, a set of symbolic repertoires, situated actions, and as a source of myth, drama, and commonsense theories of social behavior.

Muir, William K. Jr. *Police: Street-Corner Politicians.* Chicago: University of Chicago Press, 1977.

> The author, a professor of political science, presents a study of the moral dilemma that confronted twenty-eight policemen in achieving just ends through coercive means. He theorizes that a successful police officer requires two attributes, moral equanimity and an awareness of the universality of human suffering, in order to perceive the limits of his or her role.

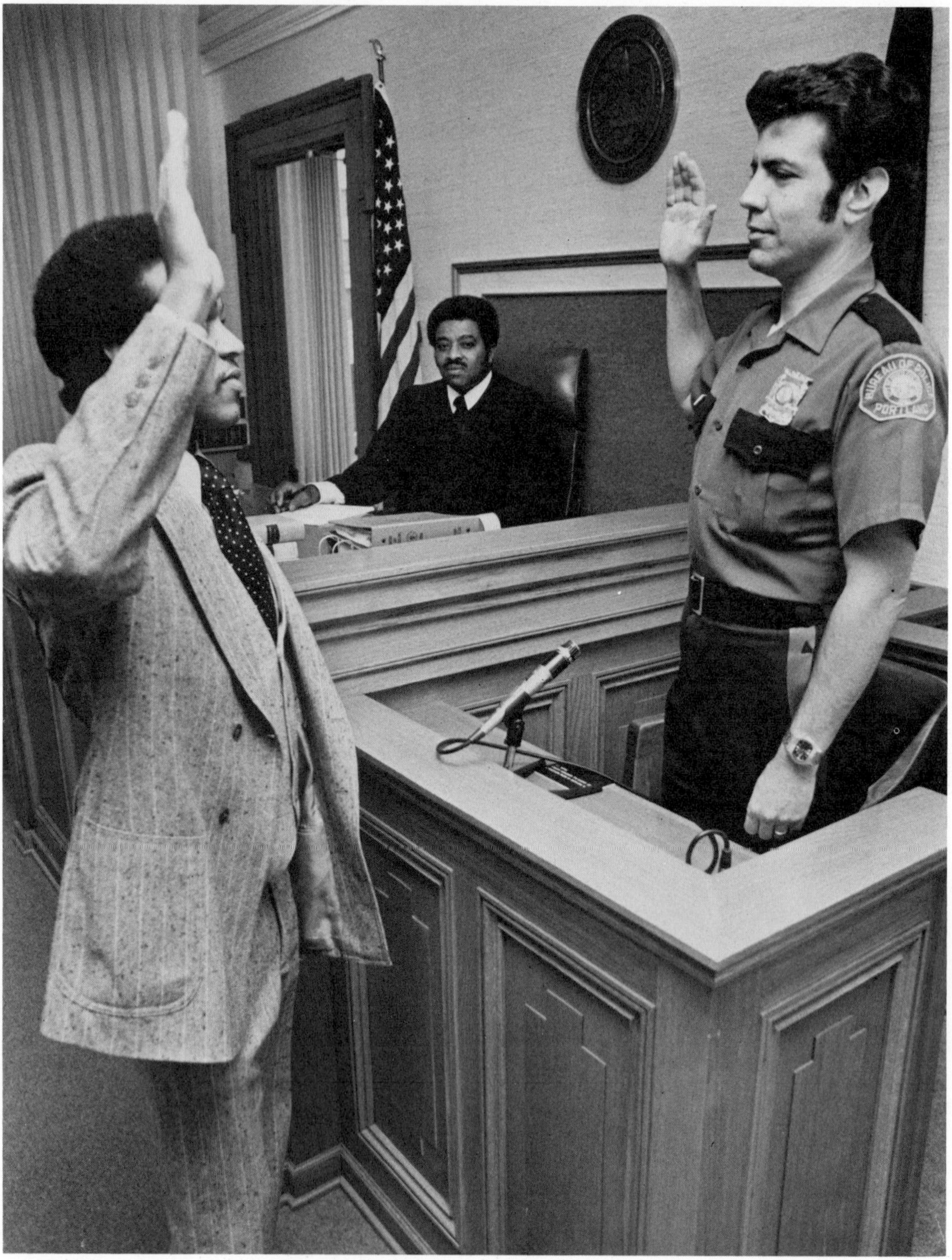

Everywhere there is one principle of justice, which
is the interest of the stronger.
—Plato, The Republic (4th century, BC) 1. tr.
Benjamin Jowett

13

THE COURTS AND THE ADMINISTRATION OF JUSTICE

The courts may not create criminals, but it is through the judicial process that criminal definitions are applied. Once the accused stands before a robed judge, the process of criminalization, begun with arrest, takes on new significance. This process involves a series of decisions by agents of the state that will determine whether or not the label *criminal* will be applied.[1]

If the offender pleads guilty or is found guilty of a crime, he or she becomes subject to punishment that can vary widely, depending on the attitude of the judge or the jurisdiction in which the crime occurs. But the court also has both the right and the power to divert people away from the criminal justice system. Police, attorneys, judges, and juries are interlocked in a delicate network of discretion, all focused on the accused individual. Their deliberations and decisions can lead to freedom or trigger a process that includes the drama of a trial, conviction, sentencing, and incarceration in prison.

For the courts, the continuing struggle is to find ways to further guarantee fairness in the administration of justice, particularly in the sentencing of those who have been convicted. The courts deal with the middle phase of our three-part criminal justice system. At the center of the process between law enforcement and correctional agencies, the courts make two crucial decisions: (1) Is the person apprehended to be legally assigned the status of criminal? and (2) if so, what legal disposition or punishment will be levied?

The court acts as a filtering process regulating the flow of alleged offenders into the system by screening out or diverting some, and continuing legal procedures against others. After the police apprehend offenders and remove them from the community, the courts sort them out, and a few are processed on to correctional agencies. The courts ideally have as their legal mandate the conviction of the guilty and the protection of the rights of the innocent and the guilty. They do not decide upon guilt, punishment, or acquittal in a neutral, mechanical manner. Conflicts are built into the process between the ideals of the law and society's demand for order and conformity.

The courts have had the responsibility in recent years to ensure that the other two components of the system—the police and corrections—protect the rights of those entrusted to their care. The rules of the court limit the activities of the police. In addition, the court increasingly has taken on a supervisory role over the manner in which the correctional agencies carry out sentences.[2]

The intent of this chapter is to show how the processes of the court serve to define an alleged act as a crime and to evaluate the guilt or innocence of the accused. As we focus on this process, which begins with the apprehension of the accused by the police, the complex and nebulous nature of the interrelationships among police, courts, and corrections—referred to as the *criminal justice system*—might become more apparent. Subsequently, we will describe the organizational complexity of the court and the various professional roles associated with it. We will also delve into the problematic aspects of the sentencing process, including judicial discretion, especially as it relates to imprisonment and capital punishment.

PROCESSING THE DEFENDANT: APPLYING CRIMINAL DEFINITIONS

Although we are concerned basically with the courts, it is important to keep in mind that they interface with both police and corrections in the criminal adjudication process. Here, the status of the accused is changed from that of "free citizen" to suspect, and then to a defendant who is either acquitted or convicted. If convicted, he acquires the status of probationer, or inmate, parolee, and ex-offender.

Stages in Processing: Pretrial and No-Trial

In its effort to describe the "system" by which the three main bureaucratic organizations comprising the criminal justice apparatus seek to carry out their separate but interrelated tasks, the Crime Commission presented a simplified model. This schematic model illustrates the various stages in the processing of people through the system, including the points at which the accused may be diverted, dismissed, acquitted, convicted, discharged, or looped back into subsystems (see Figure 13.1). We can note from this scheme how different classes of offenders are routed to different elements of the criminal justice network. In this chapter, we will describe more fully the stages that involve the majority of cases. Since most cases do not go to trial, our discussion will include the stages involved in pretrial or no-trial.[3]

Investigation and/or Arrest. Investigation and arrest have been described in the previous chapter. It should be noted that arrest may follow investigation, or an investigation may continue after the accused is taken into custody.

Figure 13.1. A General View of the Criminal Justice System

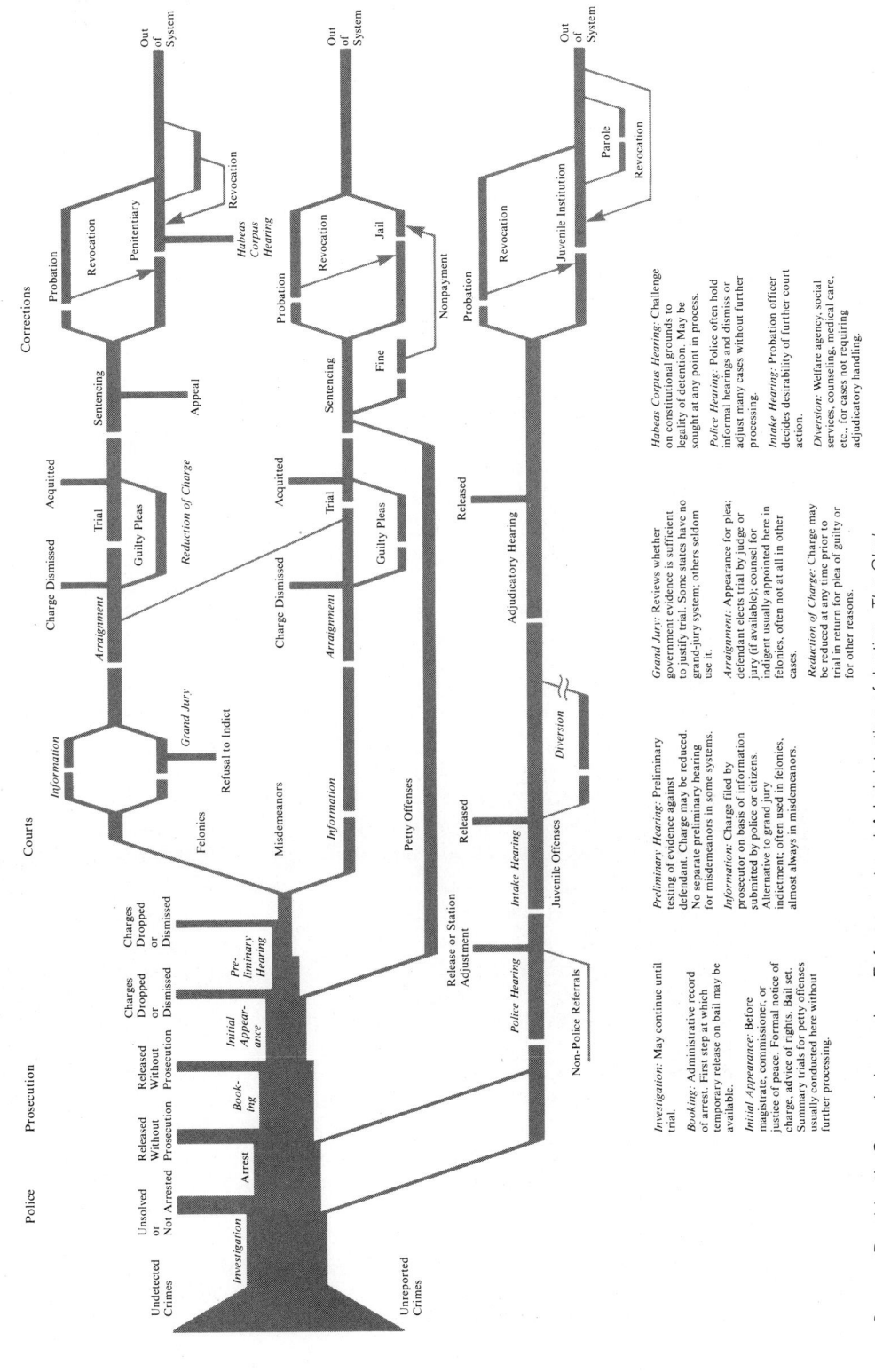

Source: President's Commission on Law Enforcement and Administration of Justice, *The Challenge of Crime in a Free Society* (Washington, D.C.: U.S. Government Printing Office, 1967), pp. 8–9.

Arrests may take place after an arrest warrant has been issued by a judge, but many arrests are made without warrants on the basis of the observation of a crime or a reasonable belief by a police officer that a crime has been committed.

Booking. The process of making an administrative record of an arrest is called *booking*. It may take place either before or after interrogation. The nature of the charge and other data are entered in the police log. If a felony is suspected, the person may be fingerprinted. In certain misdemeanor cases, a citation may be issued by the arresting officer or the citation may be written up in the station. Bail and alternatives to bail are typically dealt with in the next stage.

Initial Appearance. Within a "reasonable" period after arrest (usually twenty-four hours), the accused must be brought before a magistrate (in small or rural jurisdictions, before a justice of the peace). Here he is given formal notice of the charges, advised of his rights, and considered for release on bail or release on recognizance (ROR).

The bail-setting or pretrial-release aspects of this *initial appearance* set it off from the later stage of the *arraignment*, or formal plea to charges, although the initial appearance often is referred to as "first arraignment," or sometimes simply "arraignment."

Preliminary Hearing. In many jurisdictions, the initial hearing has been eliminated in cases involving felony charges. At the *preliminary hearing*, the accused is advised of his or her right to legal counsel and advised of the charges against him or her. The formal charge is then read. This stage does not involve an effort to determine guilt or innocence; the defendant may waive his or her right to this hearing and go directly to the next phase. If the defendant has exercised the right to legal counsel, however, the defense attorney may insist on a preliminary hearing to ascertain the degree of evidence for or against the accused. If this hearing suggests that there is insufficient evidence to support the case, or that a crime for which the accused was arrested did not take place, or if there is a lack of compliance with legal procedures, such as improper warrant, the charges might be reduced or dismissed. This hearing, as well as the initial hearing, permits a possible exit from the system.

Information or Indictment. These are the formal means that process those accused of felonies on toward the point of a guilty plea or a formal trial. A formal *indictment* requires action by a *grand jury*. Grand juries function in about half of the states and on the federal level. The grand jury is a nontrial body composed of twenty-one members. In the pretrial or indictment process its chief function is to approve or reject the prosecutor's request for a specific charge to be levied against a defendant or defendants. If the request is approved, a "true bill" or indictment is issued. If this body rules "no bill," the accused is released. An *information,* used in most western states, is a document similar to an indictment and is a rather common means of bringing formal charges. It is written by the prosecutor, who then presents it for the approval of a magistrate, rather than a grand jury. The evidentiary standards for both documents is "probable cause" that the defendant committed a crime and consequently should be "bound over" for trial. Should the prosecutor find insufficient evidence to continue the case as a felony charge, it may be reduced or even dismissed.[4]

Arraignment. Upon the return of a "true bill," or the filing of an information, the *arraignment*, which is preliminary to a trial, takes place. At this formal hearing, the information or indictment is read and the defendant is asked to enter a plea. The plea may be guilty, not guilty, nolo contendere, or the defendant may stand mute. *Nolo contendere* or "no contest" implies a plea of guilty. If the defendant "stands mute" a plea of not guilty is entered, but this action does not waive his or her right to enter legal protests to any procedural irregularities that may have transpired during the previous legal processes.

Guilty Plea; No-Trial. Most convictions are the result of the accused pleading guilty after the decision has been made to prosecute. In other words, in a majority of cases *plea bargaining* (see discussion below) takes place between the prosecutor and defense attorney. Such negotiated pleas may take place before, during, or after arraignment, or in some cases even during the trial. Those who plead not guilty go on to the trial stage.

Discretionary Aspects of Pretrial and No-Trial Processing

Although the phrase, "stages of processing through the criminal justice system," implies an orderly, almost mechanicallike flow of decision making from investigation and arrest to conviction, this is hardly the case in reality. For even though the Crime Commission referred to this process as "... a continuum—an orderly progression of events—some of which, like arrest and trial, are highly visible and some of which, though of great importance, occur out of public view,"[5] it was describing an ideal, not the reality. In its report the Crime Commission recognized some of the problems inherent in the process. More recently, the American Bar Association referred to the criminal justice "nonsystem."[6] We turn now to some aspects of the criminal justice process that will shed light on the use and misuse of discretion during the process and the extent to which certain practices and procedures often lead to the failure and breakdown of justice.

Jail, Bail, or Release on Recognizance. A suspect may be released in the traditional manner of setting bail—cash bail or a 10 to 20 percent bail bond. Alternatively, the suspect may be released on his or her own recognizance (ROR), which means that he or she promises to appear at a specified time for arraignment or trial. (See Chapter 14 for discussion of bail and ROR under alternatives to pretrial detention.)

The magistrates who decide whether to allow bail, ROR, or to hold in jail are often justices of the peace, who traditionally have been reluctant to use the

ROR procedures. Often, a defendant who is too poor to raise bail will be detained in jail, even though he meets the qualifications for ROR. Although under the laws of our society a person is presumed to be innocent until proven guilty, in many instances a suspect joins convicted criminals in our overcrowded jails. In 1972, for instance, fully 55 percent of the persons being held in local jails were awaiting trial or further adjudication. And about 30 percent of the larger jails were overcrowded.[7]

Formal Criminal Charges: Discretion and Screening Out. If the charge is a misdemeanor, the accused may be tried by the lower court and acquitted, fined, or sentenced to jail or probation. If the charge is a felony, the lower court binds the accused over to the prosecutor. The prosecutor in many jurisdictions must, after a formal hearing or arraignment, bind the defendant over for the grand jury's consideration.

Up to this point, the process might sound systematic and rational. But once the prosecutor gets the case, he may employ "screening" or discretionary procedures. The prosecutor may dismiss the case if he concludes that there is insufficient evidence to prosecute. This "screening," the discretionary decision to stop proceedings against a person who is being processed in the system prior to plea or trial, constitutes one of the major openings in what Harry Allen and Clifford Simonsen have termed the "correctional funnel" (see Figure 13.2). Between 50 and 80 percent of those arrested on felony charges by the police are dismissed at this point.[8]

The fact that discretion operates in a manner that creates inequities was acknowledged in both of the President's Crime Commission reports (1967, 1973). In 1967, the Crime Commission reported that only about 41 percent of those adults arrested for index crimes were formally charged.[9] In 1973, the National Advisory Commission on Criminal Justice Standards and Goals noted that the extensive use of informal processes creates the danger of inefficiency and inequity in crime control. After all, those processed by the system, whether guilty or not, have a right to fair and appropriate treatment. If the accused is guilty, such treatment might enhance the possibility of his or her reintegration into the community with less hindrance to other objectives of the system, such as deterrence. The commission noted that the lack of established standards and procedures for such screening led to abuses. Screening, the commission concluded, is appropriate only when neither conviction nor diversion is desirable.[10]

So the criminal justice system as it now operates acts as a filter to keep a great many out of court. For instance, in 1975 there were 11,256,600 index offenses reported to the police, but only 149,069 persons were committed to our prisons that year, although those incarcerated might account for more than one offense each. The fact remains, however, that out of 2,298,900 people arrested for index crimes, about 2,149,831, or 94 percent, were able to avoid incarceration. Obviously the system is not working very efficiently when we arrest only about 20 percent of the offenders and sentence only about 6 percent of these.[11] Those who are convicted may well feel that someone just as guilty has escaped and is "outside" going about business as usual (see Figure 13.2).

The idea of a criminal justice system might lead us to assume that those accused of law violations will have their cases decided in the courts through a trial. But almost half the cases are screened out before a formal charge or indictment is made. Once a formal charge or indictment is handed down, formal charges are filed, and the defendant hears them in the court that will eventually hear the case if it goes to trial. At this arraignment he or she is asked to plead to the charge. In a majority of cases the defendant pleads guilty. An overwhelming majority of the guilty pleas are negotiated in advance of the arraignment during plea bargaining between the prosecutor and the defense counsel.[12]

Negotiated Pleas: Bargain Justice?

The general public may assume that every convicted person has had the benefit of a trial. Trials occur, however, in only a minority of cases. In many jurisdictions about 90 percent of convictions result from the defendant's own plea of guilty, rather than from the verdict of a jury or judge. Pleading guilty

Figure 13.2. Funneling Effect from Reported Crimes through Prison Sentence

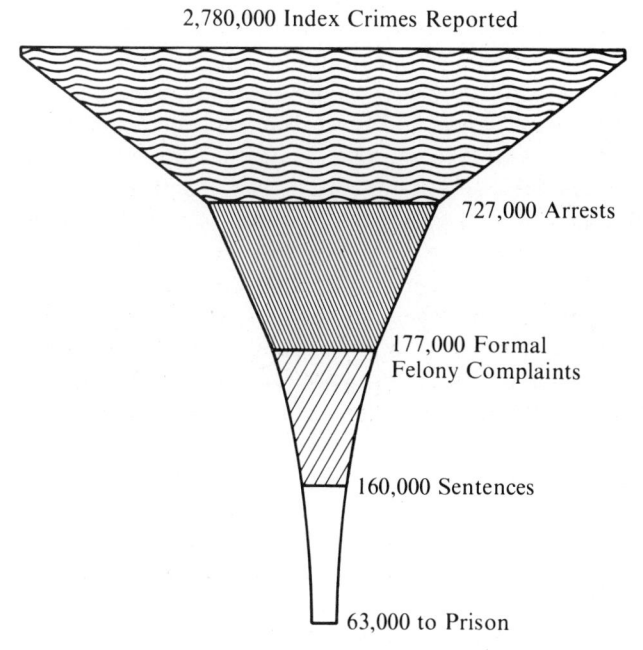

2,780,000 Index Crimes Reported

727,000 Arrests

177,000 Formal Felony Complaints

160,000 Sentences

63,000 to Prison

Source: President's Commission on Law Enforcement and Administration of Justice, *Task Force Report: Science and Technology* (Washington, D.C.: U.S. Government Printing Office, 1967), p. 61.

means that the defendant relinquishes his or her right to trial by jury, where guilt must be proven "beyond a reasonable doubt."

Guilty pleas are generally of two types. There are those that result from specific plea bargaining between the defense attorney and the prosecutor—as each attempts to secure the best settlement possible—and those that result from defendants who decide to admit their guilt. They may want to acknowledge their guilt or they may plead guilty, conscious of the practice of leniency in sentencing in the case of guilty pleas.

In plea bargaining, the defense lawyer may either negotiate a lesser charge—with lower maximum or minimum sentences—or the prosecution may agree to recommend a lighter sentence to the judge. The recommendation of the prosecutor is not binding on the judge in most jurisdictions, but the judge routinely goes along.[13]

The compromises and inequities related to plea bargaining are well known. But they are usually defended in the name of expediency as a means of keeping the overloaded dockets, especially in urban jurisdictions, from jamming up the courts. One recent survey of 3,400 courts in California, Michigan, New Jersey, and Texas indicated that this expedient operates at the expense of the defendant's rights. Of those responding, 61 percent agreed that it was "somewhat probable" or "probable" that defense lawyers—who are supposed to represent their clients' and not the courts' interest—"engaged in plea bargaining so as to expedite the movement of the cases." Another 38 percent of those responding agreed that it was "somewhat probable" or "probable" that most defense lawyers "pressure clients into entering a plea that the client feels is unsatisfactory." The respondents to this survey included police, prosecution and defense attorneys, judges, and probation and correctional personnel.[14]

There have been efforts to improve plea bargaining by making it more visible and more formal by both the President's Crime Commission and the American Bar Association's Project on Minimum Standards. In 1971, the Supreme Court, in the case of *Santobello* v. *New York* (404 U.S. 257), held that due process requires that if a plea of guilty is entered, based upon a prosecutor's promise, the promise must either be kept or the defendant must be given relief, such as an opportunity to retract the guilty plea. The National Advisory Commission on Criminal Justice Standards and Goals, after pointing out that the process works to the benefit of the more experienced defendants and to the disadvantage of young, naive defendants, recommended that it be abolished—a recommendation that evoked considerable opposition.[15]

Norval Morris has pointed out that sentenced prisoners know that what counts is not the attorney who can mount the best defense, but the attorney who can negotiate the best bargain. No wonder some of them have been known to say, "Get me Agnew's lawyers."[16]

Diversion is another means for lessening the pressures on the court. This term refers to the suspension of formal criminal procedures against the defendant on the condition that he will fulfill certain conditions. Diversion programs have been called "the poor person's substitute for plea bargaining" by

Arnold Hopkins of the American Bar Association's Commission on Corrections, since diversion is one way in which the powerless can negotiate their way out of the system into a work-training or similar program. Such programs for chronically unemployed, substance-use-related offenders, and juvenile delinquents have proliferated in the decade since they were recommended by the President's Crime Commission. Strictly speaking, diversion should take place prior to sentencing or trial, since it is intended to avoid the stigma of a criminal conviction. For instance, the defendant may agree to participate in a rehabilitation program for chronic drinkers and receive a suspended sentence for an offense related to his drinking problem. Upon successful completion of the program, the charges may be withdrawn and the record expunged.[17] But it should be noted that when defendants agree to participate in diversion programs, it is as though they are admitting guilt.

The Trial Process: Ideal versus Reality

The court system has nourished the three traditional assumptions of the justice system: the idea that justice is blind or impartial; the idea that the defendant is presumed innocent until he is proved guilty beyond a reasonable doubt, with the burden of proof resting with the state, not the individual; and the idea that we have an adversary system, as opposed to the inquisitorial system that operates in Europe.

Arthur Niederhoffer and Alexander Smith have argued convincingly that these assumptions are more legal fiction than reality. First, justice is neither blind nor impartial, but seems to be influenced by such factors as socioeconomic status, race, religion, and defense attorneys. As one federal judge writing in the *New York Times* more than a decade ago stated, "There is one law for the poor and one law for the rest of us." Second, the prosecutor usually is more interested in obtaining a conviction than in the innocence of the accused; and the judge who accepts guilty pleas in 90 percent of the cases contradicts the operation of the presumption of innocence. The ideal of an adversary system is belied by the fact that the defense and prosecution attorneys, who are the supposed antagonists, are both members of the court structure that is seeking some satisfactory resolution of the case.[18]

The *adversary system* presumes the trial is a contest between two sides—a sociological drama in which the jury listens to evidence provided by witnesses for both sides—presided over by an impartial judge who mediates the contest between the contending prosecutor and defense attorney. (If it is a judge only rather than a jury trial, he or she also decides on the guilt or innocence of the defendant.) Under the *inquisitorial system,* however, the accused is presumed guilty, and the burden of proving one's innocence is emphasized.

Unless the defendant has entered a guilty plea, the trial begins. Although the Sixth Amendment to the Constitution guarantees the defendant the right to a "speedy trial," the crowded dockets and outmoded court administration frequently result in long delays. An interval of ten to twelve months may pass

Is there one law for the poor and one law for the rest of us?

between the arrest of the accused and the beginning of the trial. (See Figure 13.1 for representation of the litigated case.) It should be noted that the defendant can choose a "juried" trial or a "judge only" trial.

The prosecutor faces the burden of proving beyond reasonable doubt to the judge or jury that the defendant is guilty. If the accused exercises his right to a jury trial, the selection of the jury can take considerable time. In one recent well-known trial, jury selection took four months and involved the examination of over one thousand prospective jurors, though the norm is between twenty-five and forty. Defense and prosecution have the right to challenge the choice of a certain number of jurors and reject them without stating their reason. Once the jury has been selected, the trial begins with opening statements by the prosecutor followed by those of the defense attorney. Other delays, such as adjournments and court recesses, may follow.

The prosecution presents its evidence first. The defense counsel then typically moves for a dismissal based on the assertion that insufficient evidence to demonstrate guilt has been presented. If the motion is not sustained by the judge, the trial continues. The defense counsel seeks to cast doubt on the evidence bearing on the accused's guilt. This typically means presenting evidence that is intended to disprove the case or that might support a defense admissible under the law. It is up to the prosecutor to prove the guilt of the accused. After the defense evidence is presented, the defense may again move to dismiss. If this motion is denied, he or she may seek to counter the evidence or raise reasonable doubts concerning it.[19]

Once the evidence is presented and all defense motions are made, the jury is instructed by the judge. These instructions concern their responsibilities relative to issues and the law, under which they will decide whether or not the state has proven guilt beyond a reasonable doubt. After the instructions to the jury are read, or sometimes before, the defense sums up the arguments for acquittal to the jury. The prosecutor, both by tradition and legal standing, has the final summary.

The jury is then sequestered in the jury room to begin its deliberations on whether the state has established guilt beyond a reasonable doubt. The deliberation of the jury is the least visible aspect of the trial process; we have little direct evidence on how juries proceed.[20]

The verdict is typically either guilty or not guilty. About 70 percent of the cases that go to trial end with a guilty finding. Depending on the nature of the instructions to the jury, however, the jury may decide that the defendant is guilty of a lesser offense. For instance, in a case of homicide, first degree, it may find that the accused is guilty of homicide, second degree. Or in a case of attempted homicide, the jury's verdict may be assault. Or in the case of multiple offenses, the verdict may be guilty of one or more and not guilty of the others. A verdict of not guilty does not mean that the jury holds the defendant to be innocent. Rather, it means that the prosecution has not established guilt beyond a reasonable doubt. Although the option is rarely exercised, some jurisdictions allow the judge to refuse to accept a guilty verdict if he feels that the evidence does not support the jury's decision.

The process is greatly simplified if it is a bench trial heard by a judge. Evidence as to whether judges or juries are more or less lenient is inconclusive. The judge may have access to information on the defendant's record not available to the jury. There are judges known and even maligned for their leniency, just as there are some with reputations as "hanging judges."[21]

Sentencing. Sentencing naturally follows a verdict of guilt or the negotiation of a guilty plea. Sentencing is the responsibility of the judge, except in thirteen states that allow jury sentencing in noncapital cases. The Commission on Standards and Goals maintained that since jury sentencing is unprofessional, arbitrary, and likely to be based upon emotional factors, it should be abolished.[22]

Sentencing is the major function of the trial judge. It is one of the major points of discretion in the justice system and is the focus of much criticism and reform effort. The judge often must make his or her judgment within legislative specifications and mandates. As a result, he or she can decide whether fines, probation, or incarceration are levied. But the length of the prison sentence may depend on the prescribed sentencing options of the state. Should the sentence be *mandated* by statute, the judge has no discretion except to reduce the charge or suspend the sentence. There are three general types of sentences: *definite* or mandated, *indeterminate,* and *indefinite.*[23] A fourth type, the *fixed* or *flat* sentence, will be discussed later.

Definite Sentence. The definite sentence is a sentence for a specific period, for example, five years for murder in the second degree, if the penal code so specifies.

Indeterminate Sentence. The indeterminate sentence has come into vogue with the emergence of rehabilitation programs. In this procedure the judge sentences the offender to prison, and the date of his or her release is left up to professionals in the correctional administration, usually the parole board—for example, five years to life imprisonment, as stated in the California penal code. The idea is that the corrections professionals are in a better position than the judge to know when the offender is "cured" and ready for release.

Evidence suggests that there is more custody than cure tied to the indeterminate sentence. California adopted the indeterminate ideal more fully than most other states and saw the average time in prison increase from twenty-four to thirty-six months between 1959 and 1969. The California Adult Authority, the prison administration, argued that an increase in offenders who needed psychiatric treatment led to the longer time in prison.

Indefinite Sentence. A number of states also have indefinite sentences, in which the judge sets a minimum and maximum prison term. The offender gets credit for good behavior and may be released within a shorter period than the maximum term. The flexible minimum is believed to provide an incentive for good behavior and is favored by prison managers. Many versions of this sentence represent a combined form of indefinite-indeterminate sentence in that parole and good time are both possible forms of release.

With all three types of sentence, the judge may be guided in deliberations regarding sentencing by a presentence report that provides relevant facts about the offender. Data relative to the offender's social background and offense history usually are gathered by a probation officer assigned to the court.

Not only is the sentencing stage of crucial significance for offenders, it is also important to the community. For the defendants, the manner in which they perceive the fairness of their sentences will influence the degree to which they inculcate a sense of justice or injustice. This invariably will affect both the manner in which offenders respond to any correctional programs and the way in which they return to the community.

Appeal. Once the sentence has been set, an appeal motion may be entered petitioning for a review by a higher court. If a change of jurisdiction or questions of constitutional legality are involved, the appeal may take place before a final verdict is rendered. At one time, appeals occurred in only a minority of cases. Now appeals are made in as many as 90 percent of the cases in some courts; the result has been a flooding of higher state and federal courts. A time limit is generally placed on appeal petitions, but occasionally they are made successfully after the offender has served a number of years in prison. These are often based on questions of rights under the Constitution. In most states, an appellate court review of trial proceedings for error occurs in nearly all serious cases.

MAJOR ROLES IN THE COURT

The courts serve a pivotal function as a link in the chain of criminalization, as its official agents evaluate the defendant's behavior and determine the criminality of his or her conduct. Thus it is that society seeks to exert external social control over its members and promote conformity to the social order. The trial is the central drama in this process in which guilt or innocence may be established. But other important functions are carried out through a variety of procedures related to the court's position as an intermediary between the police and corrections. These procedures depend not only on legal definitions, but also on the professional and social background of those who carry out such functions.

The Judge

This court official plays a central part in the conduct of the court—both in its informal administrative aspects and in the trial and sentencing proceedings. Sitting at the apex of our criminal justice system, the judge represents the power of the people in the process through which society deals with wrongs.

In modern urban courts, the judge should be an able administrator, although usually there are assistants who give attention to everyday matters. In smaller rural jurisdictions, the smooth functioning of the court may be directly under the judge and the chief clerk of the court.

In cases at law, the judge serves as an umpire over the proceedings and may be subjected to political and social pressures—especially in cases that have generated public concern. Under such pressure, the role of the impartial umpire may be difficult to fulfill. As Niederhoffer and Smith have argued, the judge may respond to such pressure by attacking the defense as well as the jury. Jessica Mitford relates how in the conspiracy trial of Dr. Benjamin Spock, the judge was overheard advising a clerk to tell the prosecutor to desist from a given behavior or else he would "blow the case" and get the court in trouble.[24]

The behavior of Judge Julius Hoffman, who presided over the trial of the "Chicago Seven," typified the interplay of personality, power, and politics at work in the courtroom of an arrogant judge. Judge Hoffman employed sarcasm and rebukes against the defense attorneys again and again. He interrupted the defense and told them not to waste his time. He constantly overruled or denied their protests and notions. He cited four of the defense counsels for contempt of court, and had two of them kept in jail without bond over a weekend.[25]

The most important factor influencing the quality of judges is the method of their selection. Although most are trained in the law, there is no formal training for becoming a judge until after appointment or election. One reform method of selection, the Missouri Plan, developed by the American Bar Association in 1940, has been adopted in many states. Under this plan, the judicial appointee is nominated by a judicial nominating commission. The Commission on Standards and Goals recommends an initial appointment of four to six years. After that, the commission suggests that judges be required to run on their record, without an opponent. If defeated, a successor is appointed. An unpopular judge who is fulfilling his duties in an adequate manner, but who has offended the sentiments of the community, might be removed through such a process. Though not wholly satisfactory, this approach effectively removes the initial appointment of judges from the political arena.[26]

The role of the judge in serving as referee, as legal advisor to the jury, as impartial arbitrator, and as the official who imposes a sentence that deprives the offender of freedom, requires more than a politician seeking a life tenure in a judgeship. A judge should not only represent the community and society, but also the rule of law.

The Prosecutor

The prosecutor may have the most important role in the courts as they now operate when you consider his or her role in screening cases out of the system and in negotiating pleas. The prosecuting attorney represents the people's case against the alleged offender. The job can produce a conflict between the duty to pursue justice, even if it means losing a case, and the need to win a case and maintain a good record. When election time comes around, prosecuting attorneys want to display a strong conviction record or "batting average." The scales of justice can be tilted in their favor by carefully screening and plea bargaining out of the system those cases in which conviction is not assured. While the prosecutor is expected to organize evidence against the accused to show guilt beyond a reasonable doubt, under present practices he or she cannot withhold or suppress evidence from the defendant's counsel that might aid in gaining acquittal. However, prosecutors operate under a compelling desire to win, although restricted by procedural rules. Their prime concern is conviction, rather than justice in the abstract sense.[27]

Defense Counsel

The defendant's lawyer, regardless of skill or reputation, becomes involved in a power conflict with the prosecutor—the legal adversary. In many instances, the defense counsel might also feel in conflict with the judge. Effective trial lawyers serving as defense counsels often run the risk of incurring the wrath of judges and receiving contempt of court penalties for their courtroom behavior.[28]

Defense counsels of successful reputation are also expensive. This means that defendants with financial resources, including professional criminals, usually have access to the best legal counsel. Poor defendants often have assigned

"True—my client did threaten the defendant with a deadly weapon, push her into a dark hallway, remove all of her clothing and forcibly have sexual relations with her—but I will prove to you it was all an accident."

Human Behavior Magazine

legal counsel. They might be members of the local public defender's office, members of the local legal aid agency, or lawyers assigned by the court from a list provided by the local bar association. Public defenders are often overworked, underpaid, and inexperienced. And even though they are required to serve as defense counsel to the best of their abilities, they are members of the legal structure that appointed them and are not adversaries in the true sense of the term.

David Sudnow's analysis of the public defender's office illustrates how such defense attorneys function to create "assembly-line" justice for poor or indigent defendants. He points out that the public defender occupies a position in the court structure as a regular employee. He found that in the county he studied, there were twelve public defenders who in one year represented 3,000 defendants in the lower and superior courts of the urban county. The public defenders depended largely upon scanty information gathered in the courtroom. There is little preparation, and it is often assumed that the public defender will lose the case. They provide adequate legal representation, but raise no questions that might refute the police, narcotic agents, prosecutor, or trial judge. They fulfill their role as though the legal process were not an adversary proceeding.[29]

Any defense lawyer must maintain some kind of effective working relationship with the prosecutor and judge. But even if the typical defense lawyer has almost a symbiotic relationship with the court, from time to time, with the prodding of his fee-paying clients, he ought to challenge the system. But the defense attorney—whether a legal-aid type or on private retainer—is too often involved with impersonal aspects of economics, time, fees, plea-bargaining strategies, and his or her own ties with the court system. This has not been the case with the F. Lee Baileys, Clarence Darrows, William Kunstlers, and others who have made the role of defense attorney more meaningful by rejecting the conventional docile defense role.[30]

The Jury

The jury has its historical roots in English common law. The original intent of the jury was to limit abuses by the government. But Alexis de Tocqueville, commenting on the existence of juries in America, maintained that rather than diminishing the powers of the judge, juries have increased them, for they are a political device by which the judiciary can instill the spirit of the legal process in the minds of the people.[31]

Although "the right to a speedy and public trial by an impartial jury..." is guaranteed by the Seventh Amendment, this right does not apply to many misdemeanor cases tried in the lower courts. Since only a small percentage of those cases processed by the courts are litigated, juries are not as significant as ordinarily assumed. Jury trials sometimes are bypassed upon motion of the defendant's counsel, when the defense feels a jury might be more inclined to decide harshly than the judge. But a series of studies on the American jury system, conducted at the University of Chicago in the 1950s and 1960s, found that juries were more lenient than judges in 19 percent of the cases, while the converse was true in 3 percent of the cases. This study, based upon data from 555 judges throughout the country, concerned itself largely with the extent to which the judges agreed with juries in 3,576 trials. The findings of this research indicate considerable agreement between the view the judge had of the case and jury decisions.

Figure 13.3 illustrates the extent that the hypothetical verdict of the judge matched the actual verdict of the juries. The figure does not make it clear that the jury may acquit, convict, or "hang," while the judge may only acquit or convict.[32] Hypothetically, the verdicts are distributed in six cells. Note that while the judges and jury would have agreed in over 75 percent of the cases, the balance is in favor of a net leniency of 16 percent. This means, the authors point out, that the defendant may fare better 16 percent of the time if he or she decides for a jury trial.

This jury research study also analyzed instances in which the judges might have acquitted those convicted by a jury—the so-called "cross-over phenomenon." Such cases apparently related to social and personal characteristics of the defendant that influenced the "twelve good citizens" on the jury, who supposedly were his or her peers. The judge might overlook such factors. These factors were explored more fully in a later facet of the Chicago jury study.[33]

A variety of criticisms have been noted concerning the use of juries. The methods of selection have been called inadequate and time consuming. The

Figure 13.3. Agreement and Disagreement of Judges and Juries in

	Jury			
	Acquits	Convicts	Hangs	Total Judge
Judge	13.4	2.2	1.1	16.7
	16.9	62.0	4.4	83.3
Total Jury	30.3	64.2	5.5	100.0%

☐ = judge – jury agreement.

Source: Harry Kalven, Jr. and Hans Zeisel, *The American Jury* (Boston: Little, Brown, 1966), p. 56.

fact that a jury often must return a unanimous verdict means that one stubborn or corrupt juror can obstruct the completion of a trial. Juries have also been criticized as unqualified, too easily swayed, or not representative of the social status of the defendant. The Chicago studies found that there was no measurable difference in the ability of jurors of various educational levels to perceive whether substantive data were relevant. But there was a difference in the interpretation of instructions. Higher-status males tended to participate confidently and receive satisfaction from serving on juries.[34]

The Commission on Standards and Goals has proposed a system of jury selection that would curb some of these problems. It suggested that the judge should conduct the questioning of prospective jurors, that the number serving on a jury be reduced to as few as six, and that the number of peremptory challenges be limited to the number in the jury. The idea of a smaller jury may be accepted in the near future. In 1970, the Supreme Court ruled in *Williams* v. *Florida* (399 U.S. 78,100) that the most significant criteria for a jury were that it constitute a representative cross section of the community and that it be "large enough to promote group deliberation which is free from outside intimidation."[35] This lowering of the size restriction would also avoid the delays that occur in some courts when less than twelve jurors are available.

The unanimous verdict is not a constitutional requirement, but it is a practice that is enshrined in tradition. When a deadlocked or "hung" jury occurs, the judge may either declare a mistrial or insist upon further consideration of the case in an effort to break the impasse. In the event of mistrial, the state has the option of beginning new proceedings.

With needed reform, the jury may enable the justice system to fulfill de Tocqueville's analysis that "the jury, which is the most energetic means of making the people rule, is also the most efficacious means of teaching it how to rule well."

THE STRUCTURE OF THE COURT SYSTEM

Federal and State Court Systems: Dual Sovereignty or Fragmentation?

The court structure of the United States is frequently described as a dual system—as though the courts of the fifty states and several territories can be generalized into a system that parallels the federal system. More accurately, the court structure can be described as fifty-one jurisdictions: each of the fifty state jurisdictions, defined and restricted by their state constitutions and operating with the powers reserved to the states under the Tenth Amendment; and the federal system, limited and defined by the federal Constitution, including the first ten Amendments. It should be noted that there are also county courts, city or municipal courts, traffic courts, police courts, and justice of the peace courts, all of which exist with limited power delegated by the states to local governments.[36] Decisions of state courts may be reviewed, upon appeal, by certain appellate federal courts, the highest of which is the U.S. Supreme Court.

Both the state and federal systems have *trial* and *appellate* courts. Trial courts hear evidence and decide whether the accused is guilty or innocent. Appellate courts do not seek to establish the defendant's guilt or innocence, but review the proceedings of the lower court. The *appellant* may find that errors in the trial proceedings warrant a new trial. The *appellee* — the court in which the appellant was the defendant — is, in essence, on trial. It argues that such errors did not occur, or if they did, they were not sufficient to warrant a reversal of the trial court's decision and a new trial.

Appeals from lower courts, or courts of original jurisdiction, occur in both the federal and state systems. The right of the defendant to appeal operates in both federal and state courts, but only a small percentage of cases is ever reviewed by the U.S. Supreme Court.[37]

The Federal Courts. The federal court system has three basic tiers, not including administrative courts and the United States Court of Military Appeals. The first tier is that of the United States *district courts.* There are over one hundred of these federal district courts, which are *trial courts* of original jurisdiction. Districts may be subdivided in populous areas, so the district courts are served by about four hundred federal district court judges.

The second tier is that of the *Circuit Court of Appeals,* to which cases may be appealed from the district courts and the state courts. There are eleven circuit courts, including one designated to review cases coming from the District of Columbia.

The top level is the *Supreme Court,* which can review appeals from lower federal courts or those that may come directly from the highest state courts.[38]

State Court Systems. Since the fifty state systems have varying organizational features and use different names, it is difficult to generalize about them. All states have a level of trial courts that exercises general jurisdiction over criminal and civil cases. In some states (such as California) they are called *district* and *superior courts;* in others (such as New York) they are called *common plea* and *supreme courts.* There may also be lower courts with limited jurisdiction that have been delegated judicial responsibility by the state. These lower courts include *municipal courts, justice of the peace courts, police and traffic courts,* and others. They try such things as misdemeanor and petty offenses and routine traffic cases. But there are exceptions. In New York, the county courts in the rural areas try criminal cases, but the indictment from the grand jury goes to the district supreme court, which transfers the case to the county court. In New York City, criminal cases are tried in the criminal division of the city courts. Cases appealed from these courts are reviewed by the State Court of Appeals, the highest state court. In sum, there are state courts of general jurisdiction over criminal cases. This jurisdiction is shared with county courts in about half the states.

A defendant's initial appearance may be in a lower court—municipal, police, or justice of the peace. If the formal charges specify a misdemeanor, the case may be heard in such a court. If the formal charges specify a felony count—unless the case is screened out or reduced to a misdemeanor—the case will be processed through the state or designated trial court holding general jurisdiction.[39]

Lower Courts. The *lower courts* of our urban centers and their rural counterpart, the *justice of the peace courts,* have been harshly criticized by the Crime Commission, the Commission on Standards and Goals, and as far back as the 1930s, by the Wickersham Commission. These numerous courts handle about 90 percent of criminal cases—all misdemeanors or petty offenses—and the initial phase of felony cases. They are minor not only in name but tend to be inferior in financing, facilities, quality of personnel, and programs.

It is in these courts that a great many defendants receive their first impression of the justice system. Typical defendants may range from those with no criminal record, to those numerous "revolving door" or multiple misdemeanors cases, to those who seem to appear habitually in court for public intoxication and/or vagrancy and similar charges. The crimes of which they are accused may include traffic offenses, petty larceny, prostitution, and public intoxication. One study found that 80 percent of youths who had committed major violent crimes had been convicted of a prior offense in such courts.[40]

In the cities, the lower courts are characterized by great delays. Once brought to court, cases are dealt with in assembly-line fashion. The Crime Commission found that a majority of the thirty-five states with justice of the peace courts in 1967 compensated the justices with fees assessed against the parties. Three of these states provided for fees *only if there was a conviction.* The fee was collected from the defendant, a practice since ruled unconstitutional by the Supreme Court. No wonder someone quipped that the term "J. P." referred to "justice for the plaintiff." [41]

There have been some attempts at reforms, but since these courts are mandated by state constitutions, change is difficult. In some states the justices have been replaced by professional judges, and Iowa, Mississippi, and New York require justices to take regular training.[42]

The Commission on Standards and Goals has recommended that all justice and municipal (lower) courts be replaced by statewide systems of lower courts. These would be staffed by full-time magistrates. In the short run, it also suggested that rural justices of the peace continue to function under the supervision of the district administrative judge. They would continue to issue warrants, set bail, bind defendants over on felony charges, hear small claims, and perform other similar duties.[43]

Juvenile Courts: "The Worst of Both Worlds"?

In expressing the concern of the Supreme Court over the failure of the juvenile courts to fulfill the aims of the reforms that had brought them into existence, Justice Abe Fortas stated, "There may be grounds for concern that the child receives the worst of both worlds: that he gets neither the protections accorded to adults nor the solicitous care and regenerative treatment postulated for children."[44]

The original juvenile court act was passed by the Illinois legislature in 1899. It set up a separate jurisdiction in the state to deal with cases of delinquent, dependent, and neglected children. It was to put an end to the nineteenth-century practice of dealing with juveniles in a way that stigmatized them as criminals. The reformers of this "child-saving" movement hoped that the juvenile court might serve as a means of preventing delinquency by reinforcing the institutions of family, school, and church. It would impose social control by applying newly developed social welfare concepts to the treatment of children of lower-class immigrants whose behavior was seen as leading to misconduct.[45] In the new court, children would be dealt with in closed, informal hearings, and they would be detained apart from adults with their records kept confidential. Rather than emphasizing adjudication, they would be diagnosed for "treatment."

It might be of interest to note briefly that the child welfare boards in Scandinavia developed about the same time as juvenile courts were evolving in America. These are nonlegal entities composed of lay persons appointed by elected city and other local government officials. In these countries, children under the age of fourteen do not come under the jurisdiction of any court, but are the responsibility of the child welfare boards. The boards rely heavily on preventive forms of programs such as warnings, supervision, and various supportive measures. If these seem ineffective, the child welfare board may decide to provide social therapy for the child in a private foster home or a state institution. But when the local boards make such a decision, they must gain the approval of the National Board of Health and Welfare.[46] Such commitments have declined in Sweden in recent years.

The United States sought to combine the welfare concept with the punitive legal model under the common law concept of *parens patriae*. This has come to mean that if parents do not fulfill their obligation as parents, the state assumes the role of providing for the child's welfare. Although delinquency may be defined as an act committed by a juvenile that would be a crime if committed by an adult, the definition in many states also includes status offenses that apply only to children. These typically include curfew violations, swearing, running away from home, hanging around pool halls, being ungovernable, and truancy. About one-third to one-half of those who appear in juvenile court in some states are charged with status offenses such as being incorrigible, or persons in need of supervision (PINS), or children in need of supervision (CINS).[47]

The mix has not worked very well. Years after the juvenile court system was well established, there were many gaps between the ideal goals and "real" practices. And the juvenile court has had to deal with a vast array of children's problems. Cases before it include not only criminal violations, but truancy, curfew violations, incorrigibility, parental neglect, and dependency. The Crime Commission noted that about half of juvenile court judges had not received even an undergraduate degree. It recommended that the juvenile courts limit their cases to behavior that would be considered criminal if committed by an adult.[48]

The same year that the commission submitted its report, the Supreme Court, in the decision *In re Gault*, ruled that some of the civil rights of adult defendants should be extended to children. These included (1) adequate and timely notice of charges, (2) the right to counsel, (3) protection against self-incrimination, and (4) the right to confront and cross-examine one's accusers.[49]

The *Gault* decision required some changes in juvenile court procedures. However, it did not mean the end of this specialized court for children. California had already enacted legislation to protect the legal rights of children and at the same time continue the court's social welfare function.

In another landmark Supreme Court decision, *In re Winship* (1970), the Court ruled that proof beyond a reasonable doubt, required by the due process clause in criminal trials, is required during the adjudicatory stage of the juvenile court when the youth is charged with an offense that would be a crime if committed by an adult. Formerly, the "preponderance of evidence" rule had been used in most juvenile courts. (This is a standard of proof similar to that followed in civil court suits.) These rulings have been implemented unevenly, and so the jurisdiction of juvenile courts continues to extend to children who have not committed any act that would be criminal if performed by an adult. Schools as well as parents turn to these courts to deal with truant and recalcitrant children. While the police refer only about 50 percent of the over two million children arrested to these courts, other agencies refer their problems to the juvenile court as a last resort.[50]

With the continued rise in delinquency rates in the late 1970s, delinquency prevention and diversion programs have expanded the umbrella of social control agencies related to the juvenile court. We cannot help but wonder whether the court is competent to compensate for inadequate and neglectful families and poor educational programs.

PERVASIVE PROBLEMS OF THE COURTS: LIMITING DISCRETION AND CAPITAL PUNISHMENT

Sentencing Disparities

Sentencing patterns in the United States are unique in that they result in the longest prison terms in the Western world. Disparity in sentencing can be attributed to at least two main factors. First, the great variation in sentence schemes that exists *among* the fifty states; and second, the variation between judicial sentences *within* a given jurisdiction. A third controversial factor is disparity due to the widespread use of indeterminate sentences.

Statutory penalties vary in a crazy-quilt manner from state to state. The minimum sentence for rape, for example, varies — often without any distinction between forcible and statutory rape—from a one-year term in six states to the death penalty in four. For armed robbery, the minimum goes from one year in ten states and five years in twelve, to a capital offense in two states. In Nebraska, Oregon, and eleven other states, simple possession of marijuana is a misdemeanor; in the majority of states it remains a felony.[51]

The schemes of sentencing also vary. Some states have both the maximum and minimum fixed by law; others allow these to be set by the court. Some set the minimum, but not the maximum; others do the reverse. Some set legal limits for maximum and minimum, but variations are allowed within the limits. Still others set upper and lower limits for each offense. With this patchwork, common sentencing patterns across jurisdictions are not possible, although Model Penal Codes have advocated uniformity since the 1960s.[52]

Sentencing should be based on the interrelationship of two factors: the nature of the offense and the nature of the offender. The judge should base his decision upon his analysis of these factors and try to balance any mitigating circumstances against the need for just punishment and the protection of society. But numerous studies have shown that in the sentencing decision, the judge possesses more discretion than any other actor in the judicial process. Like anyone else, judges have attitudes regarding law-violating behavior and other human foibles. In the case of the judge, however, his or her biases and personal attitudes are translated into decisions that can be reflected in the sentencing of convicted offenders.

Federal Judge Marvin Frankel, in his book *Criminal Sentences* (1973), has pointed out, "We do not allow each judge to make up the law for himself on other questions. We should not allow it with respect to sentencing."[53] Judicial abuse of this inadequately regulated discretion has been well documented in recent years. One such study of sentencing patterns in a county court in Ohio indicated that while one judge gave probation to 21 percent of those he sentenced, another judge used this option with 51 percent of those he sentenced. While one judge sentenced 62 percent of those convicted of larceny to prison, he imprisoned only 17 percent of those convicted of robbery—a more serious offense.[54]

In 1967, the Crime Commission asked the former head of the Federal Bureau of Prisons about the disparity of sentences among federal prison inmates. One embezzler received 117 days for taking $24,000 while another received a 20-year sentence.[55] A more recent survey of the sentencing variations in federal courts indicated that the sentence for robbery ranged from an average of 39 months in the Northern District of New York to 240 months in West Virginia. The sentence imposed for burglary varied from an average of two months in the Eastern New York District to 167 months in Kentucky. Probation was used 55 percent more frequently than the national average in some districts, but 39 percent less frequently in others. Great variation was also apparent among adjacent districts in the same state.[56]

A well-known experiment involving fifty federal district judges in the U.S. Court of Appeals for the 2nd Circuit highlighted different attitudes as they affect sentencing. The judges were asked to make recommendations on the basis

BOX 1

Making Sure Punishment Fits the Crime

By MIKE BARNICLE

There were two of them and the charge was assault and battery. A glance at the sheet of paper describing the case told you that neither one had yet seen a 17th birthday. But, on a fine September morning, they were found in the middle of the noise and artificial lighting in the corridor of Juvenile Court.

"Is this you?" the taller one, the one in red sneakers and dungarees, was asked as a finger pointed to the name typed on the sheet of paper.

"What's it say?" he asked.

"Is that your name?" he was asked.

The boy stared at the name for a few seconds and his face turned from a blank stare into a look that was half smile, half sneer. "Yeah, that one's me," he answered.

"What's the matter? Can't you see?" the boy was asked.

"I can see okay," he said. "I just can't read so good."

Across the hallway, through the doors leading into the clerk's office, Paul Heffernan, who is in charge of all of the paperwork and many of the people in Juvenile Court, was sought out to discuss the phenomenon of 16-year-olds charged with crimes, unable to read their names printed in English. Heffernan, raised in South Boston with one part school, two parts street as a good educational foundation, has a face of no surprises and a job that would lead a lesser man to jump off the Hancock Building in despair.

"It doesn't surprise me at all," he was saying. "Many of the kids who come through here, too many, can read all right. But they have absolutely no comprehension of what they are reading...."

An added element is the fact that these two kids—and others—are doing apprentice work in one of the few businesses where government cannot get it together. One side wants all of the people involved in crime either in the chair or in jail for 100 years while the other side wants day trips to the beach and extensive psychiatric care for almost everyone caught on the wrong side of the law.

Add an election year to the problem and you have something as difficult as trying to toast marshmallows in a blast furnace at Bethlehem Steel. The talk that comes out of the mouths of candidates in a political year resembles feeding time at the zoo....

Liberals and conservatives get together and iron out differences in order to tax people, to build highways, to save beaches, to clean the air, to come up with codes of ethics. But when it comes to punishing honest-to-goodness bad people—adults or juveniles—or trying to salvage human beings on the verge of going bad within a system of prisons and penalties set out by law, there is only failure or speeches.

Someone gets sentenced to three to five years and ends up back on the street in 15 months. Someone else gets asked to do one to three and walks out the same morning, free.

You have to look far and wide for the candidate or the judge who talks about an absolute mandatory minimum jail sentence, one that requires a defendant to complete at least the bottom line: If it's one to three, 12 months off the street; three to five, 36 months behind bars with the rest of the sentence decided after a look at the inmate's conduct in jail....

The electric chair and 25 years for drug pushers is a wonderful thing to hear in a climate of fear. But the words do not take sharp lawyers, wealth and the stumblings of the judicial process into account.

"Well, that's ridiculous," Paul Heffernan was saying about the idea of mandatory 25-year sentences for drug pushers. "First of all, you have to get the system to start treating druggies involved in violent crime the same way it treats a violent criminal. Let 'em go cold turkey in the slammer instead of in some withdrawal center.

"And, if you want to talk about mandatory 25-year sentences, why not hand out a couple to the drug companies who put the stuff out and the liquor companies who advertise that you'll never get a girl unless you drink their booze. That stuff is addictive too, isn't it?" Paul Heffernan asked.

Source: The *Boston Globe,* Sept. 25, 1976. Reprinted courtesy of the Boston Globe.

of a file of twenty cases. The range of sanctions for bank robbery varied from five years to eighteen years. An extortion and tax evasion case attracted sentences ranging from three years in prison to twenty years and a fine of $65,000.[57]

Numerous studies have tried to relate such factors as race, age, sex, and socioeconomic status to the application of judicial discretion. John Hagen's analysis of twenty studies argues that the conclusion that racial discrimination is related to differential sentencing is not statistically proven and is often the result of faulty interpretation of statistics. He suggests that data regarding such extralegal offender characteristics do not contribute more than about 5 percent to our ability to predict sentencing decisions.[58] Academically this may be the case. But for the black inmate who looks around him in prison and sees a disproportionate number of blacks, the impressionistic evidence suggests the system seems to operate against blacks. The reality is that the racism of the larger society is reflected in the involvement of the system with lower-class and minority groups. Social justice involves wider concerns about distributive justice as well as applying retributive justice to those readily identified by virtue of factors such as income and race.

Indeterminate Sentences and Sentencing Disparity

Discretion plays a major part in the attempt to individualize treatment under indeterminate sentencing procedures. Rubin, in his *Law of Criminal Correction,* points out that 57 percent of those sentenced to indeterminate terms in New York serve two years or less, compared to 70 percent of those serving definite sentences. It seems clear, he concludes, that the indeterminate sentence keeps a greater proportion of offenders in prison for longer terms. The goal of rehabilitation, which is the underlying premise of such sentences, is a significant factor in the use and abuse of discretion.[59] The lack of control of discretion, according to Richard McGee, a former prison administrator who now serves as president of the American Justice Institute, is responsible for the attention focused on both the "hanging judge" and the "softhearted judge." Both are the result of disparities in the system. He concludes:

> A system needs to be devised and put into operation which will (a) protect the public, (b) preserve the rights of individuals, and (c) satisfy reasonable men that it is fair, consistent, intelligent, and incorruptible. Such a system must be capable of adapting to ... the changing social and economic needs of the total society.... Such a system of ... justice does not exist in America today.... This ... is more apparent in sentence determination than in most other phases of our nonsystem....[60]

Limiting Discretion: Fixed Sentences or General Principles?

Numerous proposals in recent years have advocated the removal of as much discretion as possible from the sentencing process—or at the very least make its use conform to formal, established procedures. Norval Morris, Dean of the University of Chicago Law School, notes that discretion is somewhat like matter: it cannot be destroyed, only modified or controlled. In his view, one solution would be to remove the discretion that has come to be used by prosecutors and parole boards, and return it—with appropriate structure and a range of guidelines—to judges.[61]

The flood of recent proposals seeking to limit the well-documented abuse of discretion, which has created disparities in sentencing, has been cogently summarized by David Fogel.[62] They include the following:

1. Sentencing criteria should be required by legislative statutes.[63]
2. Sentencing procedures should be based upon classification of offenders into risk categories, for example, nondangerous, dangerous, professional, and multiple or habitual offenders.[64]
3. Sentences to imprisonment should be more definite—indeterminacy as now used is, in essence, rejected—or fixed and graduated according to the seriousness of the offense.
4. Provision for review should be included in procedures.
5. The reliance on sentences of imprisonment should be materially reduced. Such a sentence should be the court's last available sanction.[65]
6. Sentences of imprisonment should be justified only after an extensive review fails to suggest a viable noninstitutional, less coercive sanction.[66]

In summary, these proposals might be characterized as a neo-Classical consolidation of procedures for sentencing, or what Fogel has referred to as a perspective of "justice as fairness" that relies on a narrowing of discretion by the judicial official as a result of procedural regularity in the criminal law.[67] The challenge is for a consistent, fair means to decide on imprisonment or noninstitutional sanctions such as probation, fines, or suspended sentence.

The legislators of the various states are not unaware of these proposals. Three states—California, Indiana, and Maine—have abolished the indeterminate sentence. The new determinate sentences, sometimes called "fixed" or "flat" sentences, took effect in 1976 in Maine and in 1977 in California and Indiana. Thirteen other states are considering similar legislation. The revised Federal Code, passed by the Senate in 1978 as S.1437 and under consideration by the House, includes sentencing reforms that would control discretion. A sponsor of this bill, Senator Edward M. Kennedy, referred to present practices as a "nonsentencing" policy that is a national disgrace. He said current sentencing practices "bring about a complete disrespect for, and lack of confidence in, the criminal justice system." [68]

CAPITAL PUNISHMENT: DETERRENCE AND RETRIBUTION OR IRREPARABLE CAPRICE?

Sentences involving the death penalty have only rarely been carried out in the United States since 1967. The average number of executions—utilizing a variety of means including electrocution, the gas chamber, hanging, and in one state, the firing squad—declined to only ten per year between 1965 and 1967. Because of efforts to abolish capital punishment, a great number of litigations were under way by 1967. Many of these were based upon the contention that the death penalty violated the protection of the Eighth Amendment against cruel and unusual punishment. As a result, all executions were suspended by the federal courts while these constitutional objections were considered.[69]

By June 1972, there were more than six hundred persons on death rows in thirty-two states. The Supreme Court then ruled by a five to four vote that "the imposition and carrying out of the death penalty . . . constitutes cruel and unusual punishment in violation of the Eighth and Fourteenth Amendments" (*Furman* v. *Georgia,* 408 U.S. 238). The decision reversed the death sentences in all the cases before the Court.[70]

In this 1972 decision, the Supreme Court ruled that any statutory arrangement that allowed arbitrary selection processes to determine whether or not a defendant would receive the death penalty is unconstitutional. It ruled that the death penalty is unconstitutional when it is imposed according to the "uncontrolled discretion of judges or juries" and is "dependent on the whim of one man or twelve." This uncontrolled discretion, the Court stated, enables it to be applied selectively against those who are "poor and despised and lacking in political clout" or those members of "a suspect and unpopular minority." Consequently, it operates in favor of "those who by social position may be in a more protected position."[71]

Three of the five justices in the Furman ruling were not willing to find the death penalty unconstitutional per se. Rather, they based their arguments on the fact that out of those eligible for the death penalty, only a few were selected—seemingly at random. The rest received the lesser sanction of imprisonment.[72]

Proponents of capital punishment were busy in the aftermath of *Furman,* and new capital punishment laws were passed in thirty states in the next four years. These laws were of two kinds: those that prescribed the death penalty as a mandatory sentence, and those that established sentencing procedures in which the jury would decide on prison or the death sanction, guided by certain aggravating circumstances.

By July 1976, under these new laws, 588 people were on death rows in thirty-five states. At this time, the Supreme Court sought to clear up some of the confusion in two separate decisions: *Woodson* v. *North Carolina* and *Gregg* v. *Georgia.* In the first, it ruled that the mandatory death penalty for first-degree murder was unconstitutional under the Eighth and Fourteenth Amendments. Those sentenced under such laws were resentenced to life imprisonment. In the second decision, it ruled that those laws requiring "objective standards to guide, regularize and make rationally reviewable the process for imposing the sentence of death did not violate the Constitution." The decision in *Gregg* v. *Georgia* upheld death penalties enacted in Georgia, Florida, and Texas. These laws are being used as the models for other states now seeking to bring their statutes into line with the Court's ruling.[73] It was under a capital punishment law of this sort that Gary Gilmore on January 17, 1977, gained the dubious distinction of being the first person executed in the United States since 1967.

The two basic arguments usually set forth to support the death penalty are retribution and deterrence. *Retribution* implies the repayment of a debt to society and the expiation of one's offense, as codified in the ancient biblical injunction of "an eye for an eye, a tooth for a tooth." Those who favor retribution might ponder whether the "moral value of sheer retribution is sufficient justification for the infliction of such a penalty in the absence of clear standards or given the possibility of mistakes." [74] The second, and most often used argument, is *deterrence*—that is, the death penalty deters murder and other capital crimes more effectively than do prison sentences. The arguments against the deterrent value of the death penalty generally take the following three forms:

1. *In order for deterrence to be effective, punishment must be both certain and swift.* But even before the recent litigation, from 1930 to 1960 there was only one execution for every seventy homicides. And in the 1970s, with the number of homicides averaging about 20,000 a year, death sentences have averaged only one hundred a year. There was also great delay in carrying out death sentences. The average time a convicted murderer spent on death row rose from 14.4 months to 32.6 months between 1961 and 1970.[75]

2. *Murder and related crimes of violence typically are crimes of passion.* The great majority of capital offenses are committed either during armed robberies, perhaps as the result of fear, tension, or anger of the moment, or they result from the passion of the moment or mental disorder. However, if a potential murderer were to weigh the possibility of capital punishment, he might calculate that he has better than a 98 percent chance of avoiding such a fate.[76]

3. *Evidence does not show that the death penalty is any more effective than lengthy prison terms in deterring crime.* There is no decrease in the homicide rate when the death penalty is used. As Table 13.1 shows, Minnesota and Wisconsin have lower homicide rates than neighboring capital punishment states. Michigan, however, does not.[77]

States that have reinstated the death penalty, such as Delaware, have not experienced a decreased rate of homicide. Thorsten Sellin's investigation found that when Delaware restored capital punishment after having abolished it between 1958 and 1961, it experienced an *increase* of 3.7 homicides per 100,000 population. He compared the criminal homicide rates of some neighboring states—one with and one without the death penalty. The state that had the death penalty did not show a consistently lower rate. Comparing Michigan with Indiana, for instance, he found that Michigan with no such sanction had a homicide rate that averaged 3.49 between 1941 and 1955; Indiana, where nine persons had been executed in that same period, had an average homicide rate of 3.5.[78]

The Case for Capital Punishment

BOX 2

Why should society inflict the death penalty? The answer, says the author, is simple. We want to punish murderers in order to pay them back.

By WALTER BERNS

The criminal law, I am now convinced, must be made *awful*—by which I mean awe-inspiring or commanding "profound respect or reverential fear." It must remind us of the moral order by which alone we can live as human beings, and the only punishment that can do this is capital punishment.

Until recently, my business did not require me to think about the punishment of criminals in general or the legitimacy and efficacy of capital punishment in particular. In a vague way, I was aware of the disagreement among professionals concerning the purpose of punishment—whether it was intended to deter others, to rehabilitate the criminal, or to pay him back—but like most laymen I had no particular reason to decide which purpose was right or to what extent they may all have been right.

I did know that retribution was held in ill repute among criminologists and jurists—to them, retribution was a fancy name for revenge, and revenge was barbaric—and, of course, I knew that capital punishment had the support only of policemen, prison guards, and some local politicians. The intellectual community denounced it as both unnecessary and immoral.

It was the phenomenon of Simon Wiesenthal that allowed me to understand why the intellectuals were wrong and why the police, the politicians, and the majority of the voters were right: We punish criminals principally as retribution, and we execute the worst of them out of moral necessity. Anyone who respects Wiesenthal's mission will be driven to the same conclusion.

Of course, not everyone will respect that mission. It will strike the busy man—I mean the sort of man who sees things only in the light cast by a concern for his own interests—as somewhat bizarre. Why should anyone devote his life—more than 30 years of it—exclusively to the task of hunting down the Nazi war criminals who survived World War II and escaped punishment?

Wiesenthal says his conscience forces him "to bring the guilty ones to trial." But why punish them? What do we hope to accomplish now by punishing SS Obersturmbannfuhrer Adolf Eichmann or SS Obersturmfuhrer Franz Stangl or someday—who knows?—Reichsleiter Martin Bormann? We surely don't expect to rehabilitate them, and it would be foolish to think that by punishing them we might thereby deter others.

The answer, I think, is clear: We want to punish them in order *to pay them back*.

We think they must be made to pay for their crimes with their lives, and we think that we, the survivors of the world they violated, may legitimately exact that payment because we, too, are their victims.

By punishing them, we demonstrate that there are laws that bind men across generations as well as across (and within) nations, that we are not simply isolated individuals, each pursuing his selfish interests and connected with others by a mere contract to live and let live.

To state it simply, Wiesenthal allows us to see that it is right, morally right, to be angry with criminals and to express that anger publicly, officially, and in an appropriate manner, which may require the worst of them to be executed.

Modern civil-libertarian opponents of capital punishment do not understand this.

They say that to execute a criminal is to deny his human dignity; they also say that the death penalty is not useful, that nothing useful is accomplished by executing anyone. Being utilitarians, they are essentially selfish men, distrustful of passion, who do not understand the connection between anger and justice, and between anger and human dignity.

Anger is expressed or manifested on those occasions when someone has acted in a manner that is thought to be unjust, and one of its origins is the opinion that men are responsible, and should be held responsible, for what they do. Thus, as Aristotle teaches us, anger is accompanied not only by the pain caused by the one who is the object of anger, but by the pleasure arising from the expectation of inflicting revenge on someone who is thought to deserve it.

We can become angry with an inanimate object (the door we run into and then kick in return) only by foolishly attributing responsibility to it; and we cannot do that for long, which is why we do not think of returning later to revenge ourselves on the door. For the same reason, we cannot be more than momentarily angry with any one creature other than man; only a fool or worse would dream of taking revenge on a dog. And, finally, we tend to pity rather than to be angry with men who—because they are insane, for example—are not responsible for their acts.

Anger, then, is a very human passion, not only because only a human being can be angry, but also because anger acknowledges the humanity of its objects: It holds them accountable for what they do. And in holding particular men responsible, it pays them the respect that is due them as men.

Anger recognizes that only men have the capacity to be moral beings and, in so doing, acknowledges the dignity of human beings. Anger is somehow connected with justice, and it is this that modern penology has not understood; it tends, on the whole, to regard anger as a selfish indulgence.

If men are not saddened when someone else suffers, or angry when someone else suffers unjustly, the implication is that they do not care for anyone other than themselves or that they lack some quality that befits a man. When we criticize them for this, we acknowledge that they ought to care for others. If men are not angry when a neighbor suffers at the hands of a criminal, the implication is that their moral faculties have been corrupted, that they are not good citizens.

Criminals are properly the objects of anger, and the perpetrators of terrible crimes—for example, Lee Harvey Oswald and James Earl Ray—are properly the objects of great anger. They have done more than inflict an injury on an isolated individual; they have violated the foundations of trust and friendship, the necessary elements of a moral community, the only community worth living in.

A moral community, unlike a hive of bees or a hill of ants, is one whose members are expected freely to obey the laws and, unlike those in a tyranny, are trusted to obey the laws. The criminal has violated that trust, and in so doing has injured not merely his immediate victim but the community as such. He has called into question the very possibility of that community by suggesting that men cannot be trusted to respect freely the property, the person, and the dignity of those with whom they are associated.

If, then, men are not angry when someone else is robbed, raped, or murdered, the implication is that no moral community exists, because those men do not care for anyone other than themselves. Anger is an expression of that caring, and society needs men who care for one another, who share their pleasures and their pains, and do so for the sake of others.

A moral community is not possible without anger and the moral indignation that accompanies it.

Capital punishment serves to remind us of the majesty of the moral order that is embodied in our law, and of the terrible consequences of its breach. The law must not be understood to be merely a statute that we enact or repeal at our will, and obey or disobey at our convenience—especially not the criminal law. Wherever law is regarded as merely statutory, men will soon enough disobey it, and will learn how to do so without any inconvenience to themselves.

The criminal law must possess a dignity far beyond that possessed by mere statutory enactment or utilitarian and self-interested calculations. The most powerful means we have to give it that dignity is to authorize it to impose the ultimate penalty.

The founder of modern criminology, the 18th-century Italian Cesare Beccaria, opposed both banishment and capital punishment because he understood that both were inconsistent with the principle of self-interest, and self-interest was the basis of the political order he favored.

If a man's first or only duty is to himself, of course he will prefer his money to his country; he will also prefer his money to his brother. In fact, he will prefer his brother's money to his brother, and a people of this description, or a country that understands itself in this Beccarian manner, can put the mark of Cain on no one.

For the same reason, such a country can have no legitimate reason to execute its criminals, or, indeed, to punish them in any manner. What would be accomplished by punishment in such a place? Punishment arises out of the demand for justice, and justice is demanded by angry, morally indignant men; its purpose is to satisfy that moral indignation and thereby promote the law-abidingness that, it is assumed, accompanies it. But the principle of self-interest denies the moral basis of that indignation.

Not only will a country based solely on self-interest have no legitimate reason to punish; it may have no need to punish. It may be able to solve what we call the crime problem by substituting a law of contracts for a law of crimes.

According to Beccaria's social contract, men agree to yield their natural freedom to the "sovereign" in exchange for his promise to keep the peace. As it becomes more difficult for the sovereign to fulfill his part of the contract, there is a demand that he be made to pay for his nonperformance. From this comes compensation or insurance schemes embodied in statutes whereby the sovereign (or state), being unable to keep the peace by punishing criminals, agrees to compensate its contractual partners for injuries suffered at the hands of criminals, injuries the police are unable to prevent.

The insurance policy takes the place of law enforcement and the *posse comitatus,* and John Wayne and Gary Cooper, give way to Mutual of Omaha. There is no anger in this kind of law, and none (or no reason for any) in the society.

The principle can be carried further still. If we ignore the victim (and nothing we do can restore his life anyway), there would appear to be no reason why—the worth of a man being his price, as Beccaria's teacher, Thomas Hobbes, put it—coverage should not be extended to the losses incurred in a murder. If we ignore the victim's sensibilities (and what are they but absurd vanities?), there would appear to be no reason why—the worth of a woman being *her* price—coverage should not be extended to the losses incurred in a rape. Other examples will no doubt suggest themselves.

This might appear to be an almost perfect solution to what we persist in calling the crime problem, achieved without risking the terrible things sometimes done by an angry people. A people that is not angry with criminals will not be able to deter crime, but a people fully covered by insurance has no need to deter crime: They will be insured against all the losses they can, in principle, suffer.

What is now called crime can be expected to increase in volume, of course, and this will cause an increase in the premiums paid, directly or in the form of taxes. But it will no longer be necessary to apprehend, try, and punish criminals, which now costs Americans more than $1.5 billion a month (and is increasing at an annual rate of about 15 percent), and one can buy a lot of insurance for $1.5 billion.

There is this difficulty, as Rousseau put it: To exclude anger from the human community is to concentrate all the passions in a "self-interest of the meanest sort," and such a place would not be fit for human habitation.

When, in 1976, the Supreme Court declared death to be a constitutional penalty, it decided that the United States was not that sort of country; most of us, I think, can appreciate that judgment.

We want to live among people who do not value their possessions more than their citizenship, who do not think exclusively or even primarily of their own rights, people whom we can depend on even as they exercise their rights, and whom we can trust, which is to say, people who, even in the absence of a policeman, will not assault our bodies or steal our possessions, and might even come to our assistance when we need it, and who stand ready, when the occasion demands it, to risk their lives in defense of their country.

If we are of the opinion that the United States may rightly ask of its citizens this awful sacrifice, then we are also of the opinion that it may rightly impose the most awful penalty; if it may rightly honor its heroes, it may rightly execute the worst of its criminals. By doing so, it will remind its citizens that it is a country worthy of heroes.

Source: From *For Capital Punishment: Crime and the Morality of the Death Penalty,* by Walter C. Berns, © 1979 by Walter Berns, Basic Books Inc., Publishers, New York.

BOX 3

The Argument Against Capital Punishment

By Rev. RICHARD W. BAUER

Walter Berns's argument in favor of the death penalty has a certain elegance about it. He bypasses completely the shopworn arguments about capital punishment being a deterrent, or a cost-effective way for society to rid itself of its undesirables. Instead, he goes right to the heart of the matter: *"We want to punish them in order to pay them back."*

In Berns's view capital punishment is a rightful exercise of the passion of anger. There is an important connection between anger and justice, and between anger and human dignity. A very straightforward argument.

Berns also avers that the criminal law, especially, must possess what he calls a "dignity," and "the most powerful means we have to give it that dignity is to authorize it to impose the ultimate penalty."

His argument acquires a distinctly religious quality. He claims the law must be "awe-ful," "awe-inspiring," "capable of eliciting a reverential fear." That which inspires awe is, by definition, holy—something out of the ordinary, something from which one shrinks back in dread.

It is at this point that we run into difficulty, it seems to me. Instead of imparting dignity to the law, the death penalty actually has the effect of desecrating it.

Judgment is a double-edged sword. Certainly we judge of necessity to protect the public safety. We also judge with the hope of restoring some percentage of society's mischief-makers back into fair-to-middlin' citizenship. But if, in the process of judging, we ourselves become seduced into committing a violation, the judgment we pronounce tends in one way or another to find its way back home to us.

Even the sternest of us tend to shrink from exercising judgment at certain points, whether we have the law with us or not. Ayatollah Khomeini's supporters are now advocating a return to Sharai law—which requires, among other things, the cutting off of the hands of thieves. I have heard some Westerners speak of the practice with a certain amount of admiration.

But it is interesting that of the three countries which have such laws on the books, Libya doesn't enforce it at all, Pakistan has had trouble finding doctors willing to supervise the execution of the sentence, and in Saudi Arabia only five sentences have been carried out in the last 20 years.

It may well be that there is some wisdom in the Cain and Abel myth worth appropriating. Contrary to some popular misunderstandings, the mark God put on Cain for his murder of Abel was not a curse, a kind of fingering for extinction. To the contrary, it was a tattoo of some sort placed on Cain to *keep others from killing him.*

Did that make God "soft on crime?" Hardly. Cain was condemned to be a fugitive and a wanderer—cast out of community, cut off from the earth, set loose on an aimless, disconnected life. Now there's a truly awesome punishment.

Our popular televised myth, embodied in all the police shows, has it that violence—particularly the death of the bad guy—is the only true solution to our ills. But the mark on Cain says just the opposite: There needs to be a limit on the never-ending skein of violence, revenge, revenge of revenge, that steeps us in a culture of violence. Cain's mark is a sign that even the life of the violence perpetrators is holy, protected by God.

No life, however shabby, however violence-ridden, however vile, is to be irreversibly profaned, made into a subhuman object which can in turn be violated at will by whoever happens by.

Ironically, the plea of Mr. Evans in his Alabama death cell to be put to death turns out to be a pathetic grasping after ersatz dignity: "Confirm my belief that my life is worthless, utterly lacking in dignity," he says to us, "and kill me.

"If I cannot have dignity, let me at least enjoy notoriety. So I profane the society and its standards in the process. I seduce you into buying my world view. Go ahead. Pull the switch."

If killing the likes of Mr. Evans imparts an awesome dignity to the law, it is of an ironic and obscene sort.

Source: The *Boston Globe*, April 1979. Reprinted by permission of Rev. Richard W. Bauer.

In fact, the death penalty may be correlated with a *high* homicide rate, as in the case of California. It was found that homicides in California tended to increase in the days prior to an execution by the state. Daniel Glaser and Max Zeigler sought to explain this correlation by suggesting that a reliance on capital punishment and high rates of murder are the result of the low valuation of life, and both reflect the existence of attitudes that apparently are conducive to killing. They found support for this hypothesis in their analysis of the length of the terms of confinement required for those sentenced to prison for homicide prior to parole. Note that groups II, III, IV, and V in Table 13.1 show an inverse relationship between this variable and the number of executions.[79]

Documented clinical cases indicate that the existence of the death penalty apparently incited the crime it was intended to deter. In the so-called suicide-murder syndrome, those who want to commit suicide but fear taking their own lives apparently commit murder so that society's agents will do it for them through the death penalty. Several recent studies, it should be noted, have provided data and arguments that tend to raise questions on both sides of the deterrence position. Isaac Ehrlich (1975) presents evidence that apparently contradicts the findings, since his data support the hypothesis that capital punishment can result in the prevention of homicides. A more recent study by Gary Kleck (1979), however, failed to identify any consistent evidence of a deterrent effect of the death penalty on homicide rates in the United States for 1947 to 1974. Nor did he find consistent support for the idea that executions by the state increase the rate of homicide by stimulating initiative violence or a diminished respect for human life. He faults Ehrlich's study for relying on UCR data on murder rather than on vital statistics of deaths due to homicide.

Kleck's study is extremely important for another variable omitted from other studies of deterrence—that is, the explanatory factor of gun ownership. For, as Kleck argues, the increase in the U.S. homicide rate attributed to the decline in executions in the 1960s by Ehrlich, may have been caused instead by the rapid increase in the supply of privately owned guns. It appears that homicides may have pushed up gun ownership, and gun ownership, in turn, elevates the homicide rate, in a grisly cycle of death and fear. He also found that imprisonment of offenders had an incapacitative effect as distinct from deterrence effects. Of course, the death penalty may also have an incapacitative result, for obviously the death penalty ensures that those executed for murder will not commit further offenses. But this preventive function can also be served by long-term imprisonment. And strong evidence indicates that few convicted murderers commit additional crimes of violence.[80]

Racial and Social Bias in Capital Punishment

One basic tenet of due process is justice as "fairness." This is especially relevant to a sanction like the death penalty. But there is substantial evidence that many death penalty decisions have been racially biased, arbitrary, and unfair.

Table 13.1. Murder and Nonnegligent Homicide Rates per 100,000 Persons per Year for States with and without Capital Punishment within Selected Regions, 1962, 1967, 1972, and 1976

Region and State	Capital Punishment?	1962	1967	1972	1976
New England					
Vermont	Yes	0.3	3.1	1.7	5.5
New Hampshire	Yes	2.4	2.0	1.7	3.3
Connecticut	Yes	1.3	2.4	3.2	3.1
Massachusetts	Yes	1.8	2.8	3.7	3.3
Rhode Island	No	0.8	2.2	1.3	2.4
Maine	No	1.4	0.4	5.3	2.7
North Central					
South Dakota	Yes	3.3	3.7	1.2	1.7
Nebraska	Yes	1.5	2.7	2.9	2.9
Kansas	Yes	2.8	4.0	4.0	4.5
Indiana	Yes	3.5	3.7	6.0	7.1
Ohio	Yes	3.2	5.2	7.5	7.4
Missouri	Yes	5.5	7.3	8.3	9.3
Illinois	Yes	5.3	7.3	8.8	10.3
North Dakota	No	1.2	0.2	1.3	1.4
Iowa	Yes/No[a]	1.1	1.5	1.7	2.3
Minnesota	No	0.9	1.6	2.4	2.3
Wisconsin	No	0.9	1.9	2.8	3.0
Michigan	No	3.3	6.2	11.0	11.1
Pacific					
Washington	Yes	2.5	3.1	4.2	4.3
California	Yes	3.9	5.4	8.8	10.3
Oregon	Yes/No[b]	2.9	3.1	5.5	4.2
Hawaii	No	2.9	2.4	6.8	6.2
Alaska	No	4.5	9.6	9.5	11.3

[a] Death penalty abolished in 1966.
[b] Death penalty abolished in 1965.

Source: Table adapted and reprinted, with permission of the National Council on Crime and Delinquency, from Daniel Glaser and Max S. Zeigler, "Use of the Death Penalty vs Outrage at Murder," *Crime and Delinquency* 20, no. 4 (October, 1974): 334; FBI, *Uniform Crime Reports* for the years shown.

A recent study by Marc Reidel has concluded that the racial disproportion was greater on death row in 1976 than in 1971, although the Supreme Court decision in *Gregg* v. *Georgia* argued that new laws must protect against such discrimination. Reidel's study also found a relationship between poverty, lack of social roots, and inadequate legal representation as important factors in determining whether a murderer would be sentenced to death or life imprisonment. It was found that 62 percent of the post-Furman death row inmates were unskilled service or domestic workers, and only 3 percent were professional or technical workers. A large majority were unemployed at the time of their offense, and most were represented by court-appointed defense counsels.[81] As Clinton Duffy, the former warden of San Quentin has noted, capital punishment is a "privilege of the poor."

Irreversibility

The death penalty is unlike other criminal sanctions in that once carried out, it cannot be reversed. Even if discretion could be completely controlled, human judgments remain fallible. Since 1900, as one writer points out, there has been an average of one innocent person convicted of murder each year. A number of them were sentenced to death. Fortunately, through the intervention of appellate courts, only a small number were ever executed. Most recently, in 1975, Freddie Pitts and Wilbert Lee, both black, were released from a Florida prison after waging a nine-year legal battle for pardon, even though a white man had confessed to the crime for which they were convicted. That same year, the prison authorities in New Mexico released four men who had spent eighteen months on death row, after the real murderer confessed.[82]

Cost-Benefit Analysis

Although it is assumed that life imprisonment represents a greater financial burden than an electrocution, a hanging, or a gassing, this has not been proved. In fact, the opposite may be true if we consider the costs of appeals as well as trials, which usually are longer than noncapital hearings and are paid for by the public. *Time* magazine calculated that the commutation of the death sentences of fifteen Arkansas inmates in 1971 saved the state about $1.5 million. Richard McGee has pointed out that "the actual costs of operating the maximum security unit, the years spent there by some inmates in condemned status, and a pro rata share of top-level prison officials' time spent in administering the unit, add up to a cost substantially greater than the cost to retain them in prison the rest of their lives."[83]

Capital punishment opponents feared that the death of Gary Gilmore would set off a series of legal executions across the country. By 1978, one year later, there were 409 people on death rows in the United States. As the number climbed to 500 in 1979, the executions began in Florida, while others are slated to die in Georgia and Texas as their appeal processes end (see Box 4). Although the laws in these states were ruled constitutional in *Gregg* v. *Georgia* (1976), two facts established by the majority in *Woodson* (1976) and *Furman* (1971) were not refuted: namely, that capital punishment does not deter crime and that the death penalty in both practice and theory is unfair and inequitable without the provision of approved guidelines.[84] However, the minority argument of the 1972 decision seems to dominate now. It pointed out that "public opinion polls have not shown anything that approximates the universal condemnation of capital punishment that might lead us to suspect that the legislatures in general have lost touch with current social values."[85]

A recent analysis of public attitudes toward capital punishment concludes that the large numbers of citizens who apparently favor the death penalty do so in the belief that it serves a useful purpose and may be capable of deterring potential offenders from involvement in types of violations defined as capital offenses. The authors concluded that the prodeath penalty sentiment exhibited in their survey and perhaps in recent public opinion polls is based on unrealistic expectations. Further, they suggest that to base the constitutionality of capital punishment on such apparently uninformed public opinion—as was argued by the majority in *Gregg* v. *Georgia* (1976)—does not provide necessary support for such laws.[86] Meanwhile, in July 1978, the Supreme Court struck down by a six to two decision the capital punishment statute of Ohio—reprieving one hundred prisoners on death row there—and cast doubt on the constitutionality of such laws in twenty-four other states. The Ohio state law was invalidated because it defined mitigating factors too narrowly[87] (see Box 4).

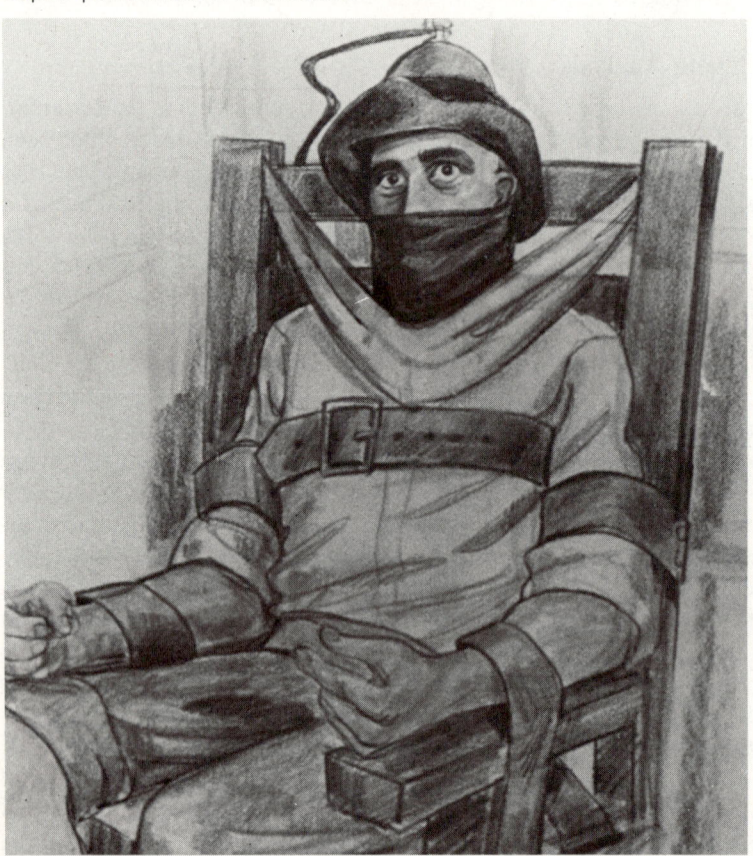

Capital punishment is irreversible.

BOX 4

The Execution of John A. Spenkelink

By THOMAS E. SLAUGHTER

Starke, Fla.—It seemed like an eternity.

The first jolt of 2300 volts of electricity was in his body. He sat there, rigid, his hands clenched.

I wondered if he was dead. Then I saw smoke rising from his leg and knew it was over. . . .

When I entered the witness room, the first two of four rows of folding chairs already were taken by 13 official witnesses, all volunteers. The reporters sat behind them.

I sat in that room, with 31 other people I didn't know, waiting to watch the execution of a man with whom I had never spoken.

Then someone in the death chamber raised the venetian blinds that had blocked out the preparations—leaving until last the central one, the one with the direct view of the chair.

I will never forget what I saw. I was stunned. John Spenkelink already was strapped in his chair. I had thought he would be brought into the death chamber after the blinds were raised.

His eyes met mine. They were open wide and seemed moist, almost imploring. It was the most helpless expression I have ever seen.

John Spenkelink was bound in this manner:

—A leather harness or helmet covered his shaved skull, held closely by a strap that seemed to press his chin into his face. Inside that cap was a fine-grained sponge that had been soaked in salt water to increase its electrical conductivity. On top of the cap there seemed to be a piece of metal resembling a wing nut.

—Wide leather straps bound him tightly to the massive oak chair, holding him across the chest and binding his arms, thighs and calves.

The blinds were raised at 10:11. Less than a minute later, a man wearing heavy gloves lowered a black blindfold from the helmetlike cap that would send the current charging through Spenkelink. The fabric hung like a veil, covering his face.

The eight somber men in the death chamber stood back. Then, without warning, the first jolt surged at 10:13 a.m. At that point I didn't notice the executioner, but I was riveted by what was happening to Spenkelink.

His body lurched. His hands began contracting; the index finger of his left hand pointed toward us as his other fingers curled. Then he clenched his left hand in a fist. Both hands turned blue, especially near the fingertips.

I stood in my chair and saw smoke coming from Spenkelink's calf. A few inches below the rolled-up cuff, there was a three-inch wound. It looked as if his skin had split, but there was no blood. I had expected to smell burning flesh. Thankfully, I didn't.

At 10:14, a minute after Spenkelink received the first of three surges of electricity, another man in the death room removed the chest strap, unbuttoned Spenkelink's shirt and raised his T-shirt.

Then a prison doctor listened to Spenkelink's heart through a stethoscope, backed away and looked toward the prison's warden, David Brierton, who was standing in the death room. No one moved.

Again we waited. Rev. Tom Feamster, who had visited Spenkelink often over the past two years, spoke out in the witness room. Although the individuals in the tableau of the death chamber couldn't hear him, the Episcopal priest said: "I hope you gentlemen are praying that this is a just and merciful punishment."

For the first time, I caught sight of the executioner. He was standing behind a floor-to-ceiling partition in a far corner of the death chamber. Through a slit for him to view the execution, I saw two eyes looking through holes cut in a black hood. His identity is withheld. He receives $150 for his work.

The doctor, whose name was not disclosed, stepped over to Spenkelink's rigid and masked form again. Again he checked for a heart beat. Again he stood back.

At 10:18, the doctor again approached the chair. First he checked for heart beat, then for pulse. Then he lifted the black blindfold and peered into each of the motionless figure's eyes.

He stepped away again and nodded to Brierton. John Spenkelink was dead. The blinds were lowered. I walked outside, into the sunshine.

Source: Associated Press, May 26, 1979. Reprinted by permission.

Still, the problem persists. The majority of the public that favors the death penalty, according to recent public opinion polls, has provided a shaky premise, *vox populi,* for concluding that the Eighth Amendment might not apply to such laws were they appropriately written. Public sentiment, according to some Supreme Court justices, represents "evolving standards of decency of a maturing society," even in the face of a worldwide movement away from a penalty that lacks utilitarian value and defies procedural safeguards. Yet as Associate Justice Thurgood Marshall argued in the recent series of rulings on the death penalty, there is insufficient "due process of law" in our legal system to make capital punishment constitutional. Further, it is irrational and inhuman to impose the death penalty, whatever the aggravating or mitigating circumstances.[88]

SUMMARY

The courts stand at the middle stage in the process of the criminal justice system. The fact that the court system relies heavily upon administrative procedures, rather than upon adversary proceedings, is a major factor explaining the discrepancy between the ideal goals of justice and the reality. The function of discretion to screen or filter out of the system many who are apprehended and the operation of plea bargaining to dismiss or reduce charges make the "correctional funnel" operate more like a sieve.

The trial is at the apex of this middle stage in the criminal justice process, but only about 10 percent of those who enter the system ever come to trial. The rest are screened out, have their charges dismissed, are diverted to noncriminal justice programs, or negotiate a plea of guilty.

In its symbolic representation of the four precepts—justice, impartiality, presumption of innocence, and adversary proceedings—the trial represents high drama.

The structure of the federal and state courts was described in terms of converging jurisdictions based upon dual sovereignty. The juvenile court was described as representing a mix of social welfare and legal goals, in which the welfare function has not been achieved and the legal protections have been inadequate.

The abiding problem of discretion was related to sentence disparity and to efforts to provide individualized sanctions relevant to indeterminate sentences.

The conflict over abolition and retention or reinstatement of capital punishment was related to arguments for retribution and deterrence. It was also pointed out that evidence indicates that the death penalty has more often been invoked against the poor and minority group members, those of powerless social status. This is due to the discretion that exists in the system, which at times is applied arbitrarily. Moreover, the death penalty has been shown to be ineffective as a deterrent, and it may even promote rather than discourage violence. Maintaining the death penalty as the most severe punishment in the continuum of sanctions, given the fallibility and imperfections of our justice system, suggests that there is a simple resolution to violence in society. In fact, there are no simple, easy answers. The death penalty certainly is not an answer; it is a reaction.

ADDITIONAL READINGS

Bedau, Hugo A., ed. *The Death Penalty in America.* 2nd ed. Garden City, N.Y.: Doubleday, 1968.

> This comprehensive collection of sources provides attitudes and perceptions on just about every perspective on capital punishment—including the insights of death row residents. It includes, along with articles pro and con, a fine bibliography.

Blumberg, Abraham S. *Criminal Justice.* Chicago: Quadrangle Books, 1967.

> Professor Blumberg is a criminal lawyer turned criminologist who has experienced first hand the bureaucratic management that has come to emphasize justice by negotiated plea. The role of lawyers in this process as agents of the court structure, rather than adversaries, is described and documented.

Bowers, William J. *Executions in America.* Lexington, Mass.: D. C. Heath, 1974.

> This study of recent research on discrimination and deterrence in capital punishment provides findings not available at the time of the Furman case. The book has added significance in view of subsequent Supreme Court decisions to reinstate revised death penalties.

Frankel, Marvin E. *Criminal Sentences: Law Without Order.* New York: Hill and Wang, 1973.

> Judge Frankel, of the New York Federal District, delivers a heavy assault against the pretensions of fairness and rationality in the sentencing process. The arguments for the need to bring the judicial process within the purview of the law it administers is most cogent.

President's Commission on Law Enforcement and Administration of Justice. *Task Force Report: The Courts.* Washington, D.C.: U.S. Government Printing Office, 1967.

> After more than a decade, this analysis of the need for the courts to rise to the challenge of fairness and seek a proper balance between that objective and an effective system is still timely. This report did much to make visible the nontrial aspects of administrative justice, such as the negotiated plea.

Von Hirsch, Andrew. *Doing Justice: The Choice of Punishments.* New York: Hill and Wang, 1976.

> This report of the Committee for the Study of Incarceration turns its attention to asking hard questions about punishment in general, focusing especially upon incarceration. Does it deter? Does incapacitation serve the ends we assume? Does the system have the ability to predict dangerousness? An effective committee report, much quoted and questioned.

WELCOME
MISSION
CITY JAIL
HEARTBREAK
HOTEL
FOR
POLICE
CALL
747-2266
OR
856-2255

Remote from public view and concern, the jail has evolved more by default than by plan. Perpetuated without major change from the days of Alfred the Great, it has been a disgrace to every generation.
—National Advisory Commission on Criminal Justice Standards and Goals

14

JAILS: THEIR FUNCTION IN DETENTION AND CONFINEMENT

The jail serves as an introduction to our criminal justice system both for those who are accused, though later dismissed from the system, and as the gateway to the corrections system for those convicted and sentenced to imprisonment. Jails are important not only for the dual roles they perform, but also because of their number: there are more jails than any other type of "correctional" facility. In the United States today there are over 4,000 facilities on the county and local level that are called jails. On any given day, the number of convicted and detained people held in such facilities is more than 141,000, a population equivalent to that of a small city. During a typical year, as many as four million citizens are confined in facilities that have remained largely substandard. In other words, jails affect—most probably in a negative manner—more people than can be claimed as citizens by all but fifteen of our fifty states.[1]

Jails serve two basic functions. They serve as a detention or holding facility for accused or convicted persons pending their disposition into or out of the criminal justice system, thus serving as a link between the police, the courts, and correctional programs. Jails also serve as a place of confinement, now often called "correction," for those minor offenders sentenced to short terms, typically less than a year. In recent years, the first category has accounted for an increasing percentage of the jail population. Although those held for trial or "other disposition" are referred to as the "untried," another term, "detainee," is more appropriate, for many of these people may actually have been tried and are waiting for appeal decisions or sentence.[2]

Who are the people who are confined in our numerous jails? Why are they being held or confined there? They are a diverse lot. One study reports:

They are mostly people accused of minor offenses—motor vehicle, vagrancy, disorderly conduct, drunk and disorderly, AWOL (from the military), prostitution, petty thefts, and assaults. Many—(on the day of the census, [in 1970] 7,800) are juveniles. Others are not criminals at all but persons who are being held pending hearings to determine their sanity. Some are material witnesses. The jail also holds alleged felons—persons who are accused of having committed serious crimes—but these are a minority.... In almost every case, people in jail have one thing in common, they are very poor.[3]

The fact that the poor lack political influence may explain why disgraceful conditions persist, hidden from the community's view. The very poor also lack the money or credit to obtain bail, and they often may not have a high enough stability rating to qualify for release on recognizance or other alternatives to bail. And so the poor, unemployed and underemployed, and the friendless are locked up while awaiting trial. Those who are affluent, who have friends, or who have lawyers on retainer, including professional and organized criminals, do not face this prospect.[4]

It is our assumption that jails as they now exist are destructive, dehumanizing environments and that to hold a pretrial detainee not only subjects him to human indignity, it also flies in the face of a basic constitutional presumption—that a person is innocent until proven guilty. Moreover, we assume that the jail is a counterproductive and expensive method of dealing with minor offenders. We must utilize alternatives for jails that are more civilized, less destructive of human potential, and more consistent with basic constitutional principles.

THE FUNCTION OF JAILS IN AMERICA

As distinct from federal or state prisons, jails serve a unique function. In addition to being places of confinement, they serve to insure the accused's appearance for trial; they also are gateways or entry points from which individuals are moved into correctional institutions to serve the sentence invoked by the court.

Reports written about jails have consistently concluded that they are inadequate—a "crucible of crime" (Joseph Fishman, 1923), "dirty, unhealthy, unsanitary" (Wickersham Commission, 1931), and "sick" (Richard McGee, 1971).[5] Although jails have existed for centuries and have been the focus of reform in recent years, they have been relatively resistant to attempts to cure their acknowledged ills.

The first nationwide jail census was taken in 1970 by the U.S. Census Bureau under an arrangement with the LEAA. It identified 4,037 jails that met the definition of "any facility operated by a unit of local government for the detention or correction of adults suspected or convicted of a crime and which has authority to detain longer than 48 hours."[6]

As of March 1970, 160,863 persons were confined in jails. Over half (54 percent) of the 153,063 adults were being held for arraignment, trial, or other judicial disposition. Fifty percent of the adults and 66 percent of the 7,800 juveniles were not yet convicted. The Census Bureau conducted a second census in the summer of 1972 and found that 141,588 persons were being held in 3,921 jails. More than half (55 percent) were awaiting trial or were in some phase of adjudication; the average time spent awaiting action was about three months. About 10 percent were being held or had been sentenced for drunkenness or vagrancy.[7]

The number of people who pass through jail facilities in a given year may, as previously noted, total four million. Some may stay only a few hours, days, or months before the courts process their cases. In many instances, those held have their charges dismissed, are acquitted, or receive some sanction other than incarceration. For those who are later sentenced to prison, the jail and its sordid conditions usually provide the first contact with the penal system. By virtue of sheer numbers and its negative impact, the jail is one of the most significant and problematic institutions in the criminal justice system.[8]

A Historical Perspective on Jails

The antecedents of the jail can be traced to twelfth-century England during the reign of Henry II (1154–1189). These early jails, called *gaols* in Old English, were forerunners of our modern prisons. Although conditions in prisons have undergone relative improvement, jails have remained substandard. In the beginning their only function was to hold the accused until trial. Upon conviction, the offender would be hanged, or some lesser form of corporal punishment would be administered—flogging, mutilation, branding, or being placed on public display in stocks and pillory.

These harsh efforts at public control of crime were assumed justified, since crime had come to be regarded as a revolt against public authority—a threat to the authority of the king. Violations of the law came to be dealt with by public, rather than private, acts of vengeance. Coupled with the idea of revenge was the notion that severe punishments served as deterrents. The more heinous the crime, the more severe the punishment. Consequently, the early gaols, located in dark dungeons and damp cellars, served both to coerce the accused as well as to confine them.

With the breakup of feudalism, there was a shift in England from an agrarian to a commercial economy. The new economy was dependent upon a supply of cheap labor. Poor laws were passed by the English Parliament in the fourteenth century to curtail the movement of vagrants and peasants, who were consigned to gaol if they had no lawful means of livelihood. Consequently, Parliament found it necessary to require the building of houses of correction in addition to the gaols, which were built alongside the jails and used as workhouses for the less lawless vagrants. These parliamentary houses of correction had merged with the jails by the mid-eighteenth century. These institutions performed a combined holding function for paupers, the mentally ill, and those considered morally deviant (drunkards and prostitutes, for example) until the development of penitentiaries and insane asylums during the first half of the nineteenth century.[9]

By the sixteenth century, the county sheriffs and the justices of the peace were held responsible for building and maintaining English jails. The sheriff was not paid for running the jail. Rather, he provided amenities and life's necessities on a fee-for-service basis. These fees varied with the offense and the prisoner's social standing, and there were charges for admission and release even if acquitted. This system was brought to colonial Virginia, where the cost of admission and release was 10 pounds of tobacco, and the cost of "keep" per day was five pounds.[10]

The basic administrative pattern that characterizes our jails today was created by the General Assembly of Virginia in 1642, although ten years earlier the city of Boston had ordered that a "people pen" be built. The six Virginia counties (then shires) were directed to build jails to hold prisoners for the sessions of the General Court, which were held monthly in Jamestown. The legislation set up standards for construction materials and security. This basic model was to be followed for the next three centuries.[11] Massachusetts Bay

Visitors to a debtors jail: curiosity seekers or jail reformers?

Colony followed the Virginia model in 1669 by placing the jail under the sheriff's authority. Later the General Assembly ordered that jails be built in every town where court was held.[12]

The problems of the jail have always existed. John Howard became so appalled at the conditions of jails in England after he was made the governor of one, that he became a prison reformer. After his tour of European jails in the 1770s, he noted that more persons died of gaol distemper or fever than were executed. In this country, the Reverend Timothy Dwight wrote in 1831: "In regard to our county prisons nothing has been done in the way of reform." [13]

As jails evolved, they housed different types of people. But most inmates have shared a common status of poverty and have come from deprived segments of the populations. Throughout the early 1800s, orphans, debtors, and the insane were housed in jails until the development of houses of refuge and orphanages drew off orphans and delinquents. By 1860, about 80 percent of the states had established institutions for the feeble-minded and insane.[14]

The jails were discussed at the national meeting of prison reformers at Cincinnati in 1870. In 1911, the Eighth International Prison Congress received international notoriety when a British critic noted the "startling inconsistency" that was apparent between the conditions in our "common gaols" and the progressive prison reform underway in Europe. The foreign delegates had found unsanitary conditions, a modified fee system, corruption, idleness, insanity, and misuse of pretrial detention. American critics were even more vocal. In 1911, the National Conference of Charities and Corrections was told by one speaker that overthrowing the jail system was the only hope for reform. The rallying cry of the reformers was that the evils inherent in the organization and management of the jails could be corrected only by the state. This theme has continued until the most recent Crime Commission report in 1973.[15]

Louis Robinson reported in 1923 that jails then were about the same as they had been for centuries, except for the introduction of probation, installment fines, and a decrease in juvenile residents.[16] The same year, a former Federal Bureau of Prisons inspector, Joseph Fishman, published *Crucible of Crime*, a book describing 1,500 jails. He noted that conditions were so bad that some of those convicted would ask to be given a year in prison rather than six months in jail. Those awaiting trial were handled in the same way as those sentenced. A defendant might be found innocent after serving as long as three months in jail. Fishman wrote that jails were "a melting pot in which the worst elements of the raw material in the criminal world are brought forth, blended, and turned out in absolute perfection." [17] Of 3,000 jails inspected by the Federal Bureau of Prisons in 1936, 65 percent were deemed unacceptable for federal prisoners, and 480 of the remaining 1,056 were acceptable only in emergencies.

National commissions and national study groups have repeatedly condemned the jails. In 1931, a report to the Wickersham Commission stated that jails were not fit to "produce . . . a beneficial effect on inmates." The report charged that the American jail was "the most notorious correctional institution in the world."[18] In 1934, the Attorney General's Conference on Crime was told that jail conditions were medieval, barbarous, and contrary to common standards of social justice and democracy. The conference condemned the unsanitary, insecure, and inhuman conditions that existed in many local jails. In 1967 the Crime Commission once more emphasized that the great majority of jail facilities were old and did not meet minimum standards for sanitation, space, and segregation for different ages and types of offenders. Six years later, the National Advisory Commission's report on corrections was even more pointed in its indictment. Jails, it noted, reflected attitudes toward the alleged or convicted offender. They were "outmoded, archaic, lacking in basic comfort, inadequate in programs, and perpetuate a destructive rather than an integrative process."[19]

Since the Crime Commission's report in 1967, an increasing number of pretrial alternatives have been attempted in a variety of experiments across the country, aimed at finding ways to avoid committing people to local jails. These programs, however, have not reached the proportions of a concerted national jail reform effort. But the fact that the jail population decreased between the 1970 and 1972 census by over 19,000, when index crimes were on the increase, suggests that the various alternatives to pretrial detention may be having some effect.[20]

ORGANIZATION, ADMINISTRATION, AND CONDITIONS OF JAILS TODAY

Organization and Administration

The jail census of 1972 classified jails in three categories: *small,* less than 21 inmates; *medium,* 21 to 249 inmates; and *large,* 250 or more inmates. These categories represented, respectively, 74, 23, and 3 percent of the 3,921 jails surveyed.[21] Hans Mattick, a well-known authority on jails, has said that the typical jail has about twenty-five cells, was built between sixty and one hundred years ago, and is located in the town that serves as the county seat. At the other extreme are the huge city houses of detention, such as the Cook County Jail and House of Correction complex in Chicago and the Rikers Island Correction complex in New York City. These larger city jails are significant beyond their numbers, for though they represent less than 10 percent of all physical facilities, they process and hold more than half of the jail population and are chronically overcrowded. The 90 percent of those "typical" jails, on the other hand, are often both underused and neglected.

In five states—Alaska, Connecticut, Delaware, Rhode Island, and Vermont—local jails are run by the state government. In the other forty-five states, the jails usually are run by a jailer or warden appointed, like all members of his department, by the sheriff. In recent years, in some states like New York, these positions have become civil service jobs.

City jails are maintained by the municipal government. Typically, they come under the jurisdiction of the city police. In the case of New York, they are administered by the city's Department of Corrections, headed by a commissioner of corrections. The city police maintain the overnight "lockups," though the use of lockups in smaller cities has decreased.

The function of jails is widely variable, but most handle three types of prisoners: (1) detainees held for trial, (2) those misdemeanants serving sentences of a year or less, and (3) inmates of various types being held for other jurisdictions or awaiting transfer. Not all jails contain all three types. In some states, the sheriff handles the detainees in the local jail, and the state manages camps for misdemeanants. This is the case in North Carolina and in Illinois, outside of Cook County, for those serving over sixty days. In Vermont, the State Department of Corrections runs four regional correctional centers, and the local sheriffs have the duty of maintaining the jails as forty-eight-hour "lockups." After that period, the accused is transported to one of the regional jails.[22]

The fact that most jails are controlled by the sheriff, typically an elected local official, is one of the central problems of the American jail. The sheriff may be elected due to local politics or his law enforcement experience, neither of which is directly related to the administration of a correctional facility.

In some states, counties have developed patterns of cooperation in jail use. One county may contract with another for the use of existing jail facilities in the adjacent county. Other counties may have work camps for sentenced prisoners that may be utilized by adjacent counties for their sentenced offenders. More recently, the concept of regionalization has been promoted by the LEAA through the National Clearinghouse for Criminal Justice Planning, located at the University of Illinois in Urbana.[23]

Jail Conditions: Crowding and Neglect

In 1971, Richard A. McGee's article, "Our Sick Jails," suggested that the problem is not only the jail but the aggregate of services related to the management of those arrested—"the services of police, courts, prosecutors ... detention jails, probation ... and parole at the local level." This nonsystem has to deal with the whole range of offenses from traffic violations to felonies. Offenders run the gamut from murderers to beggars. In practical terms, however, the jail holds mainly "drunks, addicts, and petty thieves." And if it were not for the prostitutes, the women's quarters would be empty most of the time.[24]

Jails are not places of final disposition for most residents. Hans Mattick suggests that the national ratio of total daily jail population to total annual commitments is at least 1 to 9 and as much as 1 to 34. If we use these ratios to compute the estimated yearly jail commitments based on the 1972 figure of 141,600, we get an estimated jail population per year between 1.3 million and 4.8 million.[25] Only a minority remain in the jail for any great length of time.

In 1972, the American Civil Liberties Union reported on the conditions that a team of volunteer lawyers and law students observed in a study of the jail in Washington, D.C. They found:

> ... the District of Columbia jail was a filthy example of man's inhumanity to man ... a case study in cruel and unusual punishment, in the denial of due process, in the failure of justice.
>
> The jail is a century old ... overcrowded. It offers inferior medical attention to its inmates when it offers any at all.... It ... forces men to live in crowded cells with rodents and roaches, vomit, and excreta. It is the scene of arbitrary and capricious punishment and discipline ....
>
> The eating and living conditions would not be tolerated anywhere else. The staff seems, at best, indifferent to the horror over which it presides. This they say is the job society wants them to do.[26]

It is a sad but true fact that many of the country's jails are not much better off than the jail serving our nation's capital.

Inadequate Physical Facilities

The poor physical conditions of the jails are not merely due to age. In Scandinavia, we have observed prisons in good repair much older than the typical American jail. Both overuse and underuse suggest an absence of priorities for providing humane facilities in which to house detainees and sentenced offenders. Building new jails—the "Edifice Complex"—will not remedy the problem, for this only "gilds" the "cage" while aspects of repression and human degradation remain intact.[27]

The poor, unemployed, and friendless are locked up while awaiting trial.

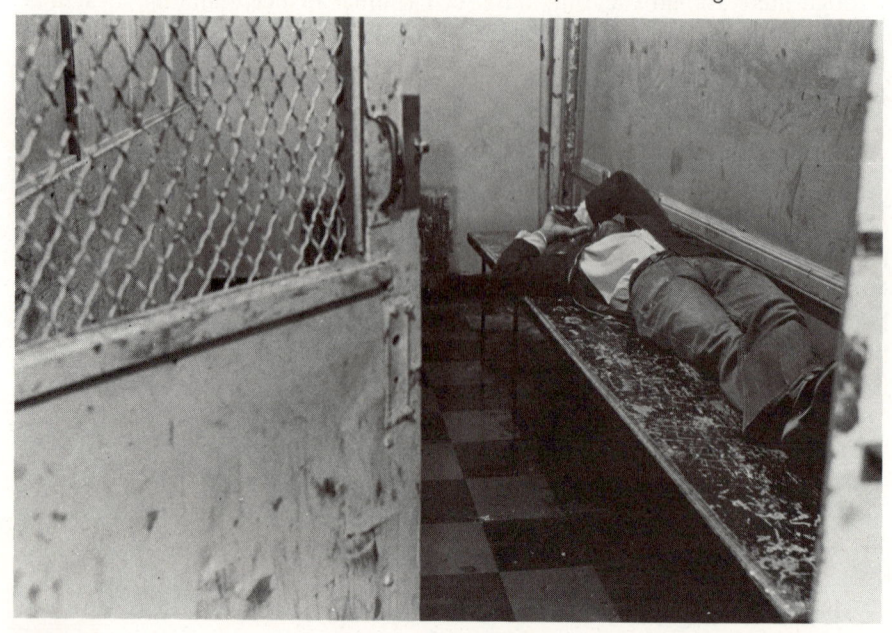

Sanitation is a persistent problem behind jail walls. Cleanliness in personal habits as well as in the physical surroundings is difficult when items we ordinarily take for granted—soap, safety razors, towels, clean bedding, and even toilet tissue—are difficult to obtain. As Hans Mattick notes, "If cleanliness is next to Godliness, most jails are in the province of Hell." [28]

The 1970 jail census noted that forty-seven of the 4,037 jails surveyed did not have flush toilets. Many more lack wash basins or toilets in the cells, and the old-fashioned buckets are still used. Shower facilities generally are insufficient in number or inaccessible, so that inmates are not allowed daily showers. Facilities like classrooms, recreation space, and visitation rooms are also lacking.[29]

Inadequate Staff

The national ratio of inmates to staff in 1972 was 3.2, and it ranged from a high of 5.3 in California to 0.6 in North Dakota (see Table 14.1). It should be noted that the ratio increases from 1 to 3.6 when only full-time employees are included. Remember also that a jail is a 365-day, 24-hour-a-day operation that typically involves three shifts; moreover, jail employees usually work only a five-day week. So instead of 13,209 employees, we have 9,435 per shift, which means about 2.4 full-time workers (not allowing for vacations, illness, or other absences) for each of the 3,921 jails surveyed, containing an average population of 36 persons. Since most of the full-time employees are in the larger urban jails, small town or rural jails have very little supervision by full-time employees, and many jails in smaller jurisdictions employ part-time employees or sheriffs' department personnel to look in on the jail occasionally. Even if a full-time jailer is employed, he may not be on duty at night, or he may spend all his time at the front desk, away from the cell-block area, performing other duties. Consequently, those detained or sentenced to jails spend large portions of the day unsupervised and usually locked in their cells. We have visited small county jails where the average population was two persons—on a typical day there might be one person held in the detention section and one locked in the section for sentenced prisoners. (New York requires that these two categories be separated.) Obviously such arrangements do not lend themselves to flexibility of program. While inmates can be locked in most of the time for security reasons, this confinement does not help them to use their time in jail in a constructive manner.[30]

Very few custodial personnel have any sort of prior training; therefore, the availability of in-service training is important. Training programs are provided on a release-time basis in some states where state academies for corrections officers have been expanded to accommodate the training of jail personnel. The overwhelming majority of employees—96 percent—is still administrative, custodial, clerical, maintenance, and teaching. Whether correctional officers can be transformed into correctional counselors or their equivalent, as one state corrections system has proposed, is very doubtful. The need for effective,

Table 14.1. Number of Jail Inmates and Employees, by State

State	Number of Inmates[a]	Inmates per 100,000 Population[b]	Number of Employees[a] Total	Number of Employees[a] Full-time	Number of Employees[a] Part-time	Ratio of Inmates to Employees Total Employees	Ratio of Inmates to Employees Full-time Employees
Total	141,588	68.0	44,298	39,627	4,671	3.2	3.6
Alabama	2,972	84.4	770	676	93	3.9	4.4
Alaska	87	26.8	53	42	11	1.6	2.1
Arizona	1,754	89.4	351	300	51	5.0	5.9
Arkansas	941	46.9	407	326	81	2.3	2.9
California	25,348	124.2	4,815	4,505	310	5.3	5.6
Colorado	1,427	60.4	532	479	52	2.7	3.0
Connecticut	—[c]	—	—	—	—	—	—
Delaware	—[c]	—	—	—	—	—	—
District of Columbia	4,215	560.5	1,131	1,122	9	3.7	3.8
Florida	8,104	110.3	2,202	2,028	174	3.7	4.0
Georgia	6,243	131.9	1,643	1,446	198	3.8	4.3
Hawaii	124	15.2	88	73	15	1.4	1.7
Idaho	411	54.4	271	202	69	1.5	2.0
Illinois	4,894	43.5	1,772	1,598	174	2.8	3.1
Indiana	2,017	38.2	647	599	48	3.1	3.4
Iowa	537	18.6	416	334	82	1.3	1.6
Kansas	870	38.4	587	454	133	1.5	1.9
Kentucky	1,896	57.4	589	488	101	3.2	3.9
Louisiana	3,340	89.4	839	778	61	4.0	4.3
Maine	247	24.1	110	92	18	2.2	2.7
Maryland	2,218	54.8	714	667	17	3.1	3.3
Massachusetts	1,847	31.9	977	926	50	1.9	2.0
Michigan	4,148	46.0	1,296	1,159	137	3.2	3.6
Minnesota	1,071	27.6	586	489	96	1.8	2.2
Mississippi	1,498	66.4	504	448	56	3.0	3.3
Missouri	2,246	47.3	1,092	1,010	82	2.1	2.2
Montana	281	39.2	231	191	40	1.2	1.5
Nebraska	742	48.6	443	351	92	1.7	2.1
Nevada	656	123.1	272	223	49	2.4	2.9
New Hampshire	283	36.6	160	126	34	1.8	2.3

Jails: Their Function in Detention and Confinement 503

State	Number of Inmates[a]	Inmates per 100,000 Population[b]	Number of Employees[a] Total	Number of Employees[a] Full-time	Number of Employees[a] Part-time	Ratio of Inmates to Employees Total Employees	Ratio of Inmates to Employees Full-time Employees
New Jersey	3,517	47.9	2,043	1,914	129	1.7	1.8
New Mexico	899	83.6	279	255	24	3.2	3.5
New York	15,190	82.7	5,468	5,092	376	2.8	3.0
North Carolina	2,155	47.0	667	603	63	3.7	4.1
North Dakota	125	19.7	213	189	24	0.6	0.7
Ohio	4,804	44.8	1,898	1,592	306	2.5	3.0
Oklahoma	1,808	68.7	625	547	78	2.9	3.3
Oregon	1,185	51.2	486	398	88	2.4	3.0
Pennsylvania	6,274	52.7	2,169	1,932	236	2.9	3.2
Rhode Island	—[c]	—	—	—	—	—	—
South Carolina	2,424	90.2	706	608	97	3.4	4.0
South Dakota	295	43.4	206	168	38	1.4	1.8
Tennessee	3,372	82.8	787	720	67	4.3	4.7
Texas	9,802	84.5	2,112	1,807	305	4.6	5.4
Utah	475	42.1	178	134	44	2.7	3.5
Vermont	4	0.9	21	5	16	0.2	0.8
Virginia	3,119	65.5	949	872	77	3.3	3.6
Washington	2,410	70.5	834	736	98	2.9	3.3
West Virginia	1,054	58.7	271	239	32	3.9	4.4
Wisconsin	1,767	39.0	697	532	165	2.5	3.3
Wyoming	192	55.5	193	150	43	1.0	1.3

Number of jails surveyed: 3,921
Detail may not add to total shown because of rounding.
[a] Rate of inmates per 100,000 population based on Bureau of the Census population estimates as of July 1, 1972.
[b] No locally operated jails.

Source: U.S. Department of Justice, Law Enforcement Assistance Administration, *The Nation's Jails: A Report on the Census of Jails from the 1972 Survey of Inmates of Local Jails* (Washington, D.C.: U.S. Government Printing Office, 1975), pp. 23, 24.

humane managers of people to work in the jails is still the basic personnel problem. It may be that the recession years of the 1970s and early 1980s will provide a pool of well-qualified workers for our jails similar to those who were recruited by the police and prisons during the Great Depression.[31]

Administrative Inadequacies

The great volume of people who are moved in and out of our jails and the reliance on cell blocks built of steel and concrete to restrain the inmates (59 percent ate in their cells in 1972) create problems in administering the jails. Due to insufficient staffing and the lack of screening at intake, virtually all inmates in jails are kept in maximum security. Table 14.2 indicates that detainees, or nonsentenced inmates, drunk traffic offenders, and first offenders are not separated in most jails. This reliance upon security at the expense of meaningful programs is based upon the administrative principle that Mattick termed "custodial convenience." Within this maximum security setting the inmates are often left to their own devices, permitting experienced inmates to assume control. Sometimes this control is formalized with certain inmates given trustee status; they maintain order in return for special privileges.[32]

Those held in jails have even less privacy than prison inmates. Their routine is often a continual round of idleness. The only recreation is of the passive variety—playing cards, watching television, and endless talking. In 1972 only 16 percent of jails had recreation yards, and 33 percent had no programs of any kind (see Table 14.3).[33]

The lack of administrative control permits development of a jailhouse subculture that can be dangerous. In his study of the Philadelphia jails in 1968, Allen Davis noted that the superintendent and three of the wardens admitted that young men who were slightly built were approached sexually within a day or two of their admission. Many were raped repeatedly by gangs of inmates. Attacks even took place in the vans transporting them to jail from the court.[34]

The disgraceful conditions in our jails have been denounced by reformers for generations. More recently, these conditions have been documented by two crime commissions and the Bureau of Census surveys for 1970 and 1972. The crime commissions have lent their support to the need for reform. Some of these recommendations might lead us to conclude that newer facilities, modernized and efficient jail administration, more and better trained staff, and regionalized community corrections would solve the problem of the jail. But the problem of the jail is related to other problems in the "system." Jail administrators have little control over the volume or types of individuals committed to their care, nor do they decide how long they will be incarcerated. Many of the problems that bear on the adequacy of the function of the jail are external. If we are to deal with the dilemma of the jail, it can be most effectively addressed by reforming the pretrial process, that difficult aspect of the criminal justice system that has been relegated to the "role of stepchild." [35]

Table 14.2. Type of Detention Arrangement by Size of Jail Population in United States, 1972 (in percentages)

Type of Arrangement by Inmate Type	All Jails	Small (less than 21)	Medium (21–249)	Large (250 or more)
Total Each Category	3,921	2,901	907	113
Pretrial inmates: detained separately	35.7	3	43.7	57.5
Not detained separately	51.2	55	41.5	30.1
Not available or not applicable	13.1	13	14.8	12.4
Drunk traffic offenders: detained separately	46	45	48.7	38.1
Not detained separately	46	48	40.9	43.4
Not available or not applicable	8	7	10.4	18.5
Mental patients: detained separately from all others	73.2	73	73.3	75.2
Not detained separately	6.1	7	4.7	5.3
Not available or not applicable	20.6	20	22	19.5
Work release inmates separated from all others	18.2	15	27.5	25.7
Not detained separately	15.2	16.6	12.5	7.9
Not available or not applicable	66.6	68.3	60	66.4
First offenders: detained separately from repeaters	23.4	23.8	22.2	23.9
Not detained separately	66.6	66.1	68.4	68.1
Not available or not applicable	9.9	10	9.4	8.0
Juveniles: detained separately from all others	82.4	85.9	74.2	58.4
Not detained separately	2.0	2.2	1.2	2.7
Not available or not applicable	15.6	11.9	24.6	38.9

Note: Figures may not add to total of 100 percent because of rounding.
Source: U.S. Department of Justice, LEAA, *The Nation's Jails* (Washington, D.C.: U.S. Government Printing Office, 1975), p. 28.

DEPOPULATING THE JAIL: ALTERNATIVES TO PRETRIAL DETENTION AND DIVERSION

Interest has revived in recent years, whether out of humanitarian, political, or economic concerns, in coping with the problems of jails. Since 55 percent of the 141,600 persons in jail in 1972 were awaiting trial or other court action, and 10 percent were in jail for drunkenness or vagrancy, any discussion of jail-related problems must focus on the many alternatives to incarceration at the pretrial stage. Decreasing the number of pretrial detainees and diverting those whose behavior is deviant rather than criminal or who are social and welfare problems would ease some of the pressure on the jails, lighten certain administrative problems, and remove some of the excuses that inhibit personnel from working positively with those who remain. Some of the measures recommended by the Commission on Standards and Goals that might reduce the jail

Table 14.3. Number of Jails with Programs by Size of Jail

		Capacity					
		Small (less than 21) Total: 2901		Medium (21–249) Total: 907		Large (250 or more) Total: 113	
Programs	Total: 3921	No.	Percent	No.	Percent	No.	Percent
Federally funded	475	184	6.3	233	25.7	58	51.3
Referral to federally funded	635	394	13.6	191	21.1	50	44.2
Other funding	2646	1722	59.4	816	90.0	108	95.6
Operated from outside	2365	1580	54.5	703	77.5	82	72.6
Operated internally	825	379	13.1	359	39.6	88	77.9
Nonfederal vocational training programs	542	288	9.9	205	22.6	49	43.4
Work-related programs	1665	1182	40.7	434	47.9	49	43.4
Weekend sentences	1821	1256	43.3	498	54.9	67	59.3
Services/Facilities							
Three or more meals	2628	1747	60.2	772	85.1	109	96.5
Medical facility	480	111	3.8	270	29.8	99	87.6
Recreational facility	2422	1592	54.9	720	79.4	110	97.3
Separate pretrial/sentenced	1400	940	32.4	396	43.7	65	57.5

Source: LEAA, *The Nation's Jails,* Tables 6–8, 11, 17–21, and 23–25, cited in Wayson et al., *Local Jails* (Lexington, Mass.: D. C. Heath, 1977), p. 15.

population to the minimum include diversion of noncriminal and sociomedical problem cases and those who can be better provided for outside the system, greater reliance on release on recognizance, citations and summonses in lieu of arrest, and speedy trial procedures.[36]

Detention Reform: Citations or Summonses in Lieu of Arrest

The offender in most jurisdictions enters the criminal justice network by being arrested. Some states have resorted to summonses and citations in lieu of arrests to take the pressure off their jails, a procedure in which the petty offender signs a promise to appear in court. The citations may be given out in the field by a police officer. The Manhattan Summons Project is a precinct house citation program that began in 1964 under the sponsorship of the Vera Institute of Justice and was expanded to all five boroughs of the city in 1967. New York's new Criminal Procedure Law adopted the program throughout the state in 1971. Considerable savings result from this kind of program. Furthermore, defendants have failed to appear in court in only about 5.3 percent of the cases, compared with the more than 6 percent who fail to appear after posting bail, though these are not comparable groups since citations generally are given for less serious offenses.

The Commission on Standards and Goals supports this alternative for bail in its reports on the courts, police, and corrections. The report on the courts recommends that citations or summonses be deemed inappropriate when their use involves a danger to the community, or if the accused lacks ties to the community or has previously failed to appear. Such practices are also supported by the American Bar Association's pretrial release standards and by the National Council on Crime and Delinquency (NCCD).[37]

Depopulating Jails: Bail Reform and Release on Recognizance

Bail. The jail's function as a detention center has only one legitimate basis—to assure the accused person's appearance for trial—that is, unless the courts sustain the practice of preventive detention that has been practiced in the District of Columbia under a recent statute. The idea that bail is a credit transaction may seem surprising since making bail has little to do with the seriousness of the offense. The American Foundation has found, for example, that the offender most unlikely to make bail is the common drunk. William Nagel notes that based on a survey in Florida, only 57 percent of those arrested for drunkenness made bail, while 83 percent of offenders charged with felonies against persons—such as robbery—made bail. He suggests that these figures are typical of the situation throughout the United States. The drunk apparently is a poor credit risk, and jails become overpopulated because drunks are the largest single category of admissions to jail.[38]

The number of persons held in pretrial detention is much larger than the number sentenced. A basic contradiction in the pretrial process is thus suggested. A small number of those in jail on any given day may have just been booked following arrest and may be waiting for their initial appearance before a magistrate. Another small fraction may have been denied bail due to the nature of the charges. The largest number, however, are being held because they have been unable to raise the money for bail, or even the 10 percent premium on a bail bond—that is, 10 percent of the face value of the bail bond.

The purpose of bail is to ensure the defendant's appearance in court. The Eighth Amendment to the Constitution explicitly states that "Excessive bail shall not be required." The amount of cash or bond bail set is related to the severity of the alleged offense and not to the ability of the individual to pay. It is also related to the presumption of innocence. But as the Commission on Standards and Goals noted, the present bail system is in reality a preventive detention system in which judges set excessive bail to ensure that the defendant will be held in detention prior to trial.[39]

Excessive bail was used as preventive detention against protesters during the civil rights movement in the 1960s and more recently against antiwar protesters. Jerome Skolnick's study of bail during riots and protests in Baltimore, Chicago, Detroit, Newark, and Washington, D.C., described the use of preventive detention against blacks in the urban uprisings of the late 1960s. The alleged rioters were presumed guilty rather than innocent and were held in jail for a number of days; high bail was set without regard for circumstances. Yet many of those held could have been released upon the condition of not returning to the riot.[40]

The excessive reliance upon money bail represents an abridgment of the defendant's rights under both the Eighth and the Fifth Amendments (due process). As the Commission on Standards and Goals points out, the status of the defendant, who is presumed to be innocent, is often worse than that of those sentenced to the same jail. The young and first offenders often are detained with hardened criminals and those charged with drunkenness or alcohol-related offenses. Due to their status, they may be denied certain freedoms afforded sentenced prisoners, such as work release and vocational and educational programs. And the longer an accused is held in detention, the greater the chances that he or she will be convicted.[41] It should be noted that pretrial detention may make it more difficult to maintain contact with one's lawyer. An extended stay in jail may also take its toll on one's physical appearance; appearing unkempt at the trial can make a negative impression on the jury.

Several studies growing out of the Manhattan Bail Project in New York City have shown that detention before trial has a negative effect on both conviction rates and sentencing. Yet it may be that the same factors that are relevant to a decision as to whether or not a person should be released awaiting trial may also be related to the type of sentence. Therefore, it could be argued that it follows that those released on bail would naturally fare better. Consequently, the causal link between detention and sentence might be questioned.[42] However, Anne Rankin's study isolated detention as a constant variable and varied other favorable conditions such as lack of a prior record, stable family, and employment—all factors that might mitigate against severity of sentence. But as Table 14.4 indicates, pretrial detention tends to outweigh these favorable characteristics.[43]

Table 14.4. Relationship Between Detention and Unfavorable Disposition When Number of Favorable Characteristics Is Held Constant

Disposition	None Bail	None Jail	One Bail	One Jail	Two Bail	Two Jail	Three Bail	Three Jail
Percent sentenced to prison	[72][a]	82	26	73	17	52	6	—
Percent convicted without prison	[6]	2	42	8	44	24	48	—
Percent not convicted	[22]	16	32	19	39	24	46	—
Number of defendants	(18)	(107)	(68)	(110)	(122)	(62)	(67)	(2)

[a] Brackets indicate the number of cases is small and the percentage should be read with caution.
Source: Anne Rankin, "The Effect of Pretrial Detention," *New York University Law Review* 39 (1964):654, cited in Commission on Standards and Goals, *Corrections* (Washington, D.C.: U.S. Government Printing Office, 1973), p. 100.

Release on Recognizance. Another alternative to bail is release on recognizance (ROR). Under ROR programs, defendants who appear to be good risks give their word that they will appear for trial. ROR differs from the use of citations in that defendants are "RORed" after arrest, usually at the time of their initial appearance, although release may occur after they have been held in jail for a period of time. The criteria that have been applied successfully to determine whether or not ROR will be granted include length of residence in the community, marital status, nature of the offense, and work history. One of the earliest programs was the Manhattan Bail Project. In operation from 1961 through 1964, it resulted in 2,195 RORs out of 10,000 defendants who were interviewed. Only fifteen failed to show at the time of trial or court appearance. By 1964 the ROR investigators were recommending 65 percent for release, and they were obtaining judicial support about 70 percent of the time.[44]

In 1972 the Office of Economic Opportunity surveyed the eighty-eight pretrial release projects then in operation. Paul B. Wice conducted a more comprehensive study of pretrial ROR projects in 1973. He compared cities using traditional bail procedures with those using ROR. The eight reform cities released more defendants and at the same time had a forfeiture and rearrest rate that was lower than the national average for bail.

Opposition to ROR programs often comes from professional bail-bonding agencies. The agents for companies in the bail-bonding business make their money by collecting about 10 percent of the amount of the bail bond. This money is split between the bonding company and the bail bondsman and is not returned to the accused even if he or she is acquitted. These unsavory characters often have the compliance of court officials and further their gain at the expense of the helpless defendant. In Wice's study, 36 percent of the defendants in the reform cities used bondsmen, compared to 46 percent in the traditional cities.

Although release on recognizance is a viable alternative to bail that has saved jurisdictions money and helped to depopulate the jails, the number of persons released has not been as great as bail reformers had anticipated.[45]

Speedy Trial Procedures

Speedy trials are guaranteed in the Constitution. Delay in bringing cases to trial is directly related to the overcrowding of jails in our large cities. Delayed trials have also been the cause of jail riots like the one at the Manhattan House of Corrections in August 1970. The list of grievances drawn up by the inmates of "The Tombs," as the facility was called, began: "We address ourselves to what we feel to be the injustices we suffer in the courtrooms of the criminal court...." The document goes on to list denial of hearings, excessive bail, unanswered writs, and delays of eight months to a year while motions for speedy trials are ignored by the courts.[46]

In 1974 Congress passed a Speedy Trial Act that set up a schedule that became effective in 1979. The act mandates that criminal cases be tried within sixty days of arraignment and allows a maximum of ten days between indictment and arraignment. However, if an arrest precedes an indictment, the grand jury has thirty days in which to act. Beginning in 1979, the maximum time limit between arrest and trial was to be one hundred days. The law, unfortunately, has had little impact on the federal system because the courts have not been given the resources to speed up processing.

Following the riots in The Tombs in 1971 and 1972, the Economic Development Council suggested reforms that reduced case backlogs and time spent in detention. The reforms included a revised calendar system and night, weekend, and holiday court arraignment sessions. Through modern management techniques and a concerted effort on the part of the courts, reduction in trial delays should shorten the time spent in detention and help to depopulate the jails.[47] Yet without increased court personnel, such modern management techniques might very well place added stress on other facets of the criminal justice process, such as increased plea-bargaining demands, more pressure on overworked public defenders, and so forth.

Depopulating the Jails Through Case Screening and Pretrial Diversion

Screening and discretion operate to minimize the movement of persons into the criminal justice network. Screening might be considered an informal diversion process. Diversion is a more drastic, formal alternative of pretrial intervention.

Case Screening and Reducing Jail Populations. Programs such as those recently published by the National Institute of Law Enforcement and Criminal Justice provide a step-by-step description for establishing a means of screening cases in the offices of larger jurisdictions. However, such screening can be formalized in all prosecutors' offices. This method is one way to ensure that discretion is exercised systematically by the prosecutor. Screening programs should be designed to provide early review of cases brought by law enforcement agencies.[48]

The National Center for Prosecution Management has also set forth guidelines intended to formalize case screening practices. The guidelines are just that, for they are designed to be adapted and refined in a given jurisdiction by the prosecutor's office. The following four criteria are suggested as being of fundamental significance in determining whether a charge should be dropped or continued: [49]

1. Does the type of crime make it a serious threat to the community?
2. Is the defendant potentially a serious threat to the community?
3. What are the probabilities of conviction?
4. What alternatives to prosecution are available?

These criteria obviously are interrelated. Each augments the other three, and they are applicable to screening cases into pretrial, noncriminal dispositions as well as to screening cases out of the system.

Diversion. This process refers to formal, organized efforts to utilize alternatives to the initial or continued processing into the justice system. The individual is diverted to a program outside the system prior to adjudication, but after an offense is committed.[50]

In the years since the President's Crime Commission made its report, hundreds of diversion programs have emerged as part of a renewed interest in reforms of the criminal justice system. These early diversion programs have, in a sense, been an acknowledgment that almost any alternative for diverting offenders out of the system is better than processing them further into it. At the same time, "early diversion" has offered what appears to be the best of all worlds: the possibility of saving money, hope for rehabilitation, and more humane treatment.

In 1975, there were several hundred juvenile diversion programs in California alone. There were also about fifty adult programs, but the fragmented nature of the way in which criminal justice operates in local, state, and federal courts makes it impossible to estimate the number of persons diverted out of the system.[51]

Juvenile Diversion in England and the United States

The current focus on diversion should not lead to the hasty conclusion that the United States is a leader in this reform. Police in Great Britain have gone further than in the United States to formalize police diversion practices for juveniles. As early as 1968, the Juvenile Bureau of the London Police changed its procedures so that young offenders would be given summonses instead of facing formal charges. The new system's main feature is the use of the "caution" by the police as a substitute for court proceedings.

In Great Britain, the Advisory Council on the Penal System on Non-Custodial and Semi-Custodial Penalties includes among its recommendations the idea that juvenile offenders be given an opportunity to fulfill a specific amount of community service in lieu of incarceration.[52] In the United States, a recent five-year study by the National Assessment of Juvenile Correction (NAJC) estimates that "up to 500,000 juveniles are processed through adult jails each year." This figure is in addition to the number of juveniles held in detention facilities.[53] In Wisconsin, another study found that the county jail was the facility most frequently used to hold youths awaiting court action. It was also found that the conditions to which youth were subjected prior to any determination of guilt generally were more punitive and restrictive than those they were placed in following disposition.[54] Ronald Goldfarb's study of *Jails: The Ultimate Ghetto* (1975) devotes a lengthy chapter to the jailing and detention of juveniles. He cites numerous cases of misuse and overuse of the jailing of juveniles.

In Massachusetts, where juvenile care was deinstitutionalized between 1970 and 1972, the State Department of Youth Services, rather than county authorities, now has the responsibility for juveniles detained pending court action. The number held in secure facilities has been reduced by using creative community programs as alternatives. This agency purchases services for juveniles held in shelter-detention programs throughout the state. These changes in the Massachusetts system, which suggest some creative, realistic alternatives for training schools as well as detention in jail for juveniles, have been carefully followed by Lloyd Ohlin and his associates. The venture has been both criticized and championed in the media, but its positive implications for the humane care of juveniles suggest that viable diversion opportunities do exist.[55]

Types of Diversion. The Manhattan Employment Project, developed by the Vera Foundation in 1968, has become a model diversion program. One of the most promising types of diversion programs, it intervenes in the court process just after arrest. Accused persons meeting eligibility criteria are asked if they would like to earn a recommendation to the court for dismissal of charges after ninety days. If they agree, they must not be rearrested in order to keep the recommendation. They must also keep all appointments with staff and prospective employers, attend and participate in counseling sessions, and make satisfactory vocational adjustments.

During the initial year of operation, 39 percent of the participants had their charges dismissed. The second year, 46 percent were dismissed; the third year, 61 percent. The unemployment rate was 16 percent for a sample group fourteen months after dismissal, compared with 40 percent for a control group terminated from the program. The rearrest rate was 15.8 percent, as against 30.8 percent for those who failed. A comparison group from the general court population had a rearrest rate of 46.1 percent.[56] In his research on the Manhattan Project, Frank Zimring found that the screening drops four out of five from the project at the first stage. Though more than half who become participants eventually succeed in having their charges dismissed, the rest are referred back to court action. Moreover, as he and other critics have noted, using those who were terminated from the program as a measure of success for those who completed the program is not a valid comparison.[57]

Diversion and pretrial intervention programs are being used to provide alternatives to criminal processing for alcohol and drug-related offenses as well as for those with emotional maladjustment. Cases related to public drunkenness represent the single largest category in the jail population. Programs in St. Louis, New York, and Washington, D.C., provide models that have successfully diverted alcohol-related cases.

The Commission on Standards and Goals has suggested the following seven criteria to be used in deciding whether an offender should be selected for diversion to a noncriminal program and thus diverted from the system: [58]

1. Prosecution may serve to harm the defendant (through criminalization) or exacerbate the social conditions related to his or her offense.
2. Services to meet the defendant's needs are not available in the criminal justice system or they can be more effectively met outside the system.
3. It is apparent that the arrest has already served as a deterrent for any such further behavior.

4. The needs and interests of both victim and the community may be better served by diversion than further processing.
5. The offender does not present any apparent danger to the community.
6. The alternative program to further criminal processing is voluntarily accepted by the offender.
7. Facts of the case seem sufficient to establish that the alleged act was committed by the defendant.

These criteria focus on the safety of the community and the interests of the victim. However, the question of guilt is implicit in the defendant's acceptance of diversion. This may be why such programs are seen as comparable to plea bargaining, especially for first offenders and nonprofessional criminals.

Decriminalization of some categories of drug offenses is another basic form of diversion. Treatment for narcotics use has also diverted alleged offenders from the system. Civil commitments allowing individuals to avoid criminal prosecution by being committed to a drug treatment facility have been tried in a variety of cases. One notorious example was the system adopted for a number of years in New York, until it was discontinued in 1976. The per inmate cost at some institutions had reached the astronomical figure of $29,000 to $44,000 a year.

In the early 1970s, the American Bar Association established the National Pretrial Intervention Service Center to stimulate wider experimentation with diversion. In 1974 the center published a source book detailing ten model programs, and its research unit issued a report on fifteen demonstration programs. These sources provide considerable information on the process of setting up and operating such programs. Although questions have been raised regarding the evaluation of these programs, the criterion of failure is rearrest. Recidivist rates vary from 3 to 23.4 percent.[59]

The basic legal issue of early diversion programs is that the defendant, in effect, waives his or her right to trial. In a legal sense the defendant admits to being guilty of the offense. But these programs do provide a means for the poor who cannot afford a lawyer to negotiate a plea and to manipulate the system both to their own as well as the community's advantage.[60] Diversion substitutes a more humane system of noncriminal controls for the more harsh and stigmatizing criminal justice process. It offers a carrot instead of a stick and provides support and hope for the clients. Adequately funded and staffed, it may hold more promise than the stigma of conviction and time in jail.[61]

ALTERNATIVES FOR THOSE SENTENCED TO JAILS

Over 60,000 of those 141,600 individuals held in local jails in 1972 were serving sentences.[62] Most of these were misdemeanants convicted of petty larceny or nonsupport; others were convicted of victimless crimes. Many states do not allow sentences of more than a year in jail; the result is that those convicted of felonies are not ordinarily sentenced to jails. Usually those sentenced to jail are the less dangerous offenders who would not be a threat to public safety. As the policy statement on nondangerous offenders of the National Council on Crime and Delinquency states:

> Confinement is necessary only for offenders who if not confined, would be a serious danger to the public. For all others, who are not dangerous... the sentence of choice should be one or another of the wide variety of noninstitutional dispositions.[63]

The board of directors of NCCD made this statement in 1973 and directed it at state prisons. When it was reissued in 1975, it was tied to the NCCD's policy statement advocating a moratorium on the construction of new detention or penal facilities.[64]

Suspended Sentences

The suspended sentence is similar to formal probation. It is also an alternative to incarceration. As such, it seems appropriate for many who are so affected by the process of being arrested and convicted that harsher measures, even probation, would be redundant. Sol Rubin advocates greater use of the suspended sentence as a proper sanction for cases such as nonsupport, paternity suits, compulsory education violations, and other minor offenses where either confinement or probation is unnecessary or excessive.[65]

Fines

The fine may be used as a noninstitutional alternative, especially if installment arrangements are available. Fines, however, can be discriminatory, and judges may have little information on an offender's ability to pay. Certainly, fines are not as severe a sanction for the affluent as for the impoverished. Nordic courts have a day-fine system, in which the individual may have to spend a day in jail for each set amount if the fine is not paid. But no one can be sent to jail merely because of inability to pay a fine; it must be shown that the defendant refused to pay. In this country, where the law allows the courts to levy either the sanction of a fine or jail, judges more often resort to jailing.[66]

Probation

Under the probation option, an offender is released to the supervision of the probation department. The probation officer acts as an officer of the court in carrying out its disposition. All states have laws providing for probation as a sanction, and probation services exist in all states. It is usual for this sanction to be used for felony cases and juvenile delinquents.[67]

The Crime Commission reported in 1967 that 82 percent of juveniles under sentence were on probation, while the percentage for adult felons was 63 and for adult misdemeanants, 59. The use of probation varies greatly and certainly could be used more widely as an alternative to jail for misdemeanants. Studies comparing the effectiveness of probation with fines and incarceration have shown varying results. It appears to be as effective as imprisonment when measured by recidivism. Several studies found it significantly more effective for first offenders and about the same for recidivists. However, one study in Great Britain found that both fines and discharges (suspended sentences) were more effective than either probation or imprisonment (see Chapter 15 for further analysis).

Since greater use of probation might help to depopulate our jails, and since many of those sentenced would be good risks for such a sanction, it is hard to understand why it is not used more widely. It has been estimated that probation costs about fifty cents a day, as compared to $15 to $20 a day for holding an offender in an urban jail. As Hans Mattick suggests, it seems that "adequate probation services for misdemeanants would be one of the wisest investments of scarce criminal justice dollars."[68]

Sentence Options Related to the Jail Program

Even short jail sentences result in the loss of employment. In recent years several sentence options have developed to avoid this problem.

Weekend Sentences. These sanctions permit the offender to serve a prescribed number of weekends in jail and maintain regular employment during the week. Jail administrators are not particularly pleased with these sentences because of the security problems involved when an individual is checked in and out of jail.[69]

Work Release and Educational Release. Under work release, the inmate leaves the jail during working hours and returns after work. The first law authorizing this practice was Wisconsin's Huber Law in 1919. Since that time, most states have enacted similar laws. Recently they have been extended to educational programs, both college and vocational training. In the 1972 census, 1,665 jails (42 percent) reported work release programs. The American Justice Institute survey in April 1972, identified 522 counties that used such programs. About 4,600 individuals were released to work on a given day, and 22,000 had participated in the previous year. But over half of the misdemeanant work release programs were found in just five states.

Although work release is often promoted as a rehabilitative program, it is also justified on a cost-benefit basis. The inmate not only provides support for his dependents, but the programs charge the participants for room and board, usually three to five dollars a day.

David Greenberg has summarized some of the evaluations of work release programs in jails in Santa Clara and San Mateo counties, California, and in North Carolina. He found that the three studies reported mixed success. In Santa Clara, for instance, eighteen months after release the arrest rates for those participating in such programs were only half that of the arrest rates for nonparticipants. The two groups were matched for social and personality traits, but the study omitted absolute rearrest rates for either group.[70] In North

Work release is justified on a cost-benefit basis.

Carolina, on the other hand, differences between crudely matched work release participants and nonparticipants were either small or unfavorable to those on work release. However, participants decreased their mean length of sentence, which lowered the population of the jails.[71] A follow-up of 110 work release inmates in San Mateo who were compared with a control group of 94 individuals released two years earlier indicates that those on work release had 10 percent fewer rearrests and 30 percent fewer reconvictions than the matching group. But results were not conclusive, since the two groups were not "at risk" during the same period and since the work release group excluded those with unfavorable social backgrounds.[72]

Educational release has advantages for the inmate without the financial payoff for the jail administrator. But the programs do allow an individual to continue his or her education. Vocational educational release may get the person started in a vocational program that can be completed after leaving jail and may enhance employability.[73]

A CHANGING ROLE FOR THE JAIL

Community Corrections: Fad or Reform?

Efforts at jail reform since 1970 generally have included a recommendation for the regionalization of local jails. At the same time there have been numerous advocates of community correctional facilities at the local level.[74]

The idea of community corrections is not as new as it may seem. Essentially, it means seeking to maintain ties between the offender and the community. It stresses less reliance on incarceration and greater use of dispositions, such as probation, suspended sentences, and fines, that allow the offender to remain in the community. Another facet of community corrections is the utilization of community resources. Certainly, this is much less expensive than attempting to duplicate within the jail programs that already exist in the community. But community corrections can become a reality only if the community and its social control agents stop locking up petty offenders.[75]

Advocates of jail reform have looked into regionalization as a means of overcoming some of the negative effects of local control—mainly the problems of small jails that are underutilized and lacking in adequate programs or staff. As the summary of the 1972 jail census in Table 14.3 shows, these jails have fewer programs for sentenced inmates and are less apt to receive outside funding, including federal monies, for what programs they do have. Even though they are comparable in work release and weekend sentences, the numbers involved are smaller.[76] The move toward regional detention facilities is a way of providing needed detention services in an efficient manner. Among those studies advocating the concept of regionalization is the Report on Corrections of the Commission on Standards and Goals. In Standard 9.1, "Total System Planning," the commission recommends an overall community correctional system design:

> A regionalized service delivery system should be developed for service areas that are sparsely populated and include a number of cities, towns, or villages. Such a system may be city–county or multicounty.[77]

As Billy Wayson et al. have pointed out, advocates of regionalization base their arguments on the lower operating cost of larger units. But cost is related to factors other than day-to-day operation of the jail. To regionalize the jails in a multicounty area and still have the courts operate in the various jurisdictions, would mean the costly transportation of inmates to and from the centralized detention center and the decentralized courts, particularly if the ideal goal of speedy trials is to be sought. And the costs related to capital construction of large jails are not clear. Furthermore, building one big jail for a multicounty region may mean the additional construction of miniprisons that may, for reasons of efficiency, be used to hold offenders and detainees who would be better served through community-based sentences like probation.

Community-based corrections is less expensive and no less effective than caging offenders in overcrowded or underutilized jails. Although as Andrew Scoll has noted in his critique, *Decarceration* (1977), community-based corrections might be better understood as reforms that have developed as a response of the state to the fiscal crisis of contemporary welfare capitalism. A great variety of programs across the country are referred to as community corrections. Some of these programs may provide innovative and realistic means for depopulating our jails. But others are self-deceptive forms of "word magic," in which a new name and perhaps a new wrinkle have been added to an old, counterproductive, substandard, control-oriented jail.[78] Community corrections programs, if they are to be viable, noncoercive alternatives, will have to use different methods from those that have clogged our often outmoded jail system. Further, more concrete and steel jails, whether built by multicounty regions or state-local-federal collaboration, are no panacea for the jail.[79]

Hans Mattick has set forth a five-point scheme for jail reform that sums up some of the difficulties we must confront in dealing with the dilemma of contemporary jails in the United States.[80]

1. A concerted effort should be made to reduce the number who are jailed. This means reform of the criminal codes, strict arrest standards, and pretrial and posttrial release instead of jail. Consistent with public safety, those cases that can be handled in the community should be diverted.
2. More careful records should be kept at the levels of arrest, detention, court, and sentencing to provide systematic and comprehensive data as well as more adequate records on budget and staff.
3. Except in large urban jurisdictions, it is impossible to provide the variety of facilities and services needed in a given county or even city. Therefore, cooperation and cost-sharing means should be explored between city and county and between adjacent counties.
4. State supervision, if not state control, should be invited by way of minimum standards and inspection and compliance procedures.
5. Efforts to increase staff and replace or build new facilities should be preceded by measures for diversion and careful study of the target population. Community-based treatment should be developed not only for economic and humanitarian reasons, but to minimize pressures for more and more detention and jail buildings.

SUMMARY

The jail functions as the "intake" institution for the prisons and as a detention facility for the police and courts. It is the oldest type of penal institution, its roots going back to medieval England. Early jails, like contemporary ones, were under local control of sheriffs. The number that pass through the jail in a given year far exceeds the 140,600 that were counted by the 1972 census. Over half of those held in jail are not under sentence.

The larger jails are overcrowded, while the typical small jail of about twenty-five cells may be underutilized and neglected. Jails are characterized by old, inadequate buildings and are poorly staffed and often administered by sheriffs who are more interested in law enforcement than in correctional programs. Both of the recent crime commissions have advanced proposals for jail reform, including closer state supervision and control. Many jail problems are due to forces beyond the control of jail administrators.

In order to depopulate the jails, a number of reforms will be required to modify judicial and legal procedures that contribute to the difficulties. A careful analysis of possibilities for alternatives that might lessen pressures on jails includes citation, ROR, diversion, and at the sentencing stage greater reliance on less restrictive sanctions than incarceration, such as fines, suspended sentence, probation, weekend sentences, and work release.

The description of these alternative programs and sentences has overlapped and augmented material on the courts in the preceding chapter, as well as some of the discussion which follows on corrections. This should underscore the interrelated function of the jail as a holding facility as well as a correctional facility. Unfortunately, jails might well be one of the weakest links in the criminal justice "nonsystem." They remain, as Mattick has termed them, "the Cloacal Region [cesspool] of American Corrections." [81]

ADDITIONAL READINGS

Flynn, Edith E. "Jails and Criminal Justice." In *Prisoners in America.* Edited by Lloyd E. Ohlin. Englewood Cliffs, New Jersey: Prentice-Hall, 1973.

> Professor Flynn, who served as a member of and consultant to the Task Force on Corrections and Standards, provides a summary of the problems of the jail, goals for its reform, and a description of organization, physical conditions, staffing, and major administrative issues. Her proposals for reform outline means to relieve the pressure on the jail and to achieve closer regulation by the state.

Goldfarb, Ronald. *Jails.* Garden City, N.Y.: Doubleday, 1975.

> This book by a practicing attorney characterizes jails as the poorhouses of the twentieth century. The author draws on historical as well as a wealth of current sources to show how the jail has continued to be a "dumping ground for the sick, alcoholics, addicts and the young." He draws vivid images so that the reader may see jails as instruments of revenge and illegal punishment.

Hickey, William L. "Depopulating the Jails." *Crime and Delinquency Literature*, June 1975.

> Written by a Senior Information Analyst of the Information Center of the National Council on Crime and Delinquency, this article focuses upon criminal justice practices which, if followed, would reduce the size of the jail population. The author documents the need for a moratorium on jail construction until alternatives to incarceration are achieved.

Mattick, Hans W. "The Contemporary Jails of the United States: An Unknown and Neglected Area of Justice." In *Handbook of Criminology.* Edited by Daniel Glaser. Chicago: Rand McNally, 1974.

> Professor Mattick, former associate warden of the Cook County (Ill.) Jail, provides a broad-ranging, well-documented discussion of our nation's most neglected correctional facility. This is a comprehensive analysis of the various facets of jail problems based upon survey research, and it includes a discussion of possible solutions.

National Advisory Commission on Criminal Justice Standards and Goals. *Corrections.* Washington, D.C.: U.S. Government Printing Office, 1973.

> This report of the Task Force on Corrections of the Commission on Standards and Goals provides narrative chapters and proposed standards for pretrial release and detention, diversion, local adult institutions, community corrections, staffing, and suggestions for change. All of these are practical and useful, although more reformist than revolutionary in emphasis.

Wayson, Billy L., Gail S. Funke, Sally F. Familton, and Peter B. Meyer. *Local Jails.* Lexington, Mass.: Lexington Books, D. C. Heath, 1977.

> This book is a straightforward and cogent exploration and analysis of the economic implications of jail reform as influenced by state standards. It provides an extensive case study of Washington state jails as they were influenced by the imposition of state standards.

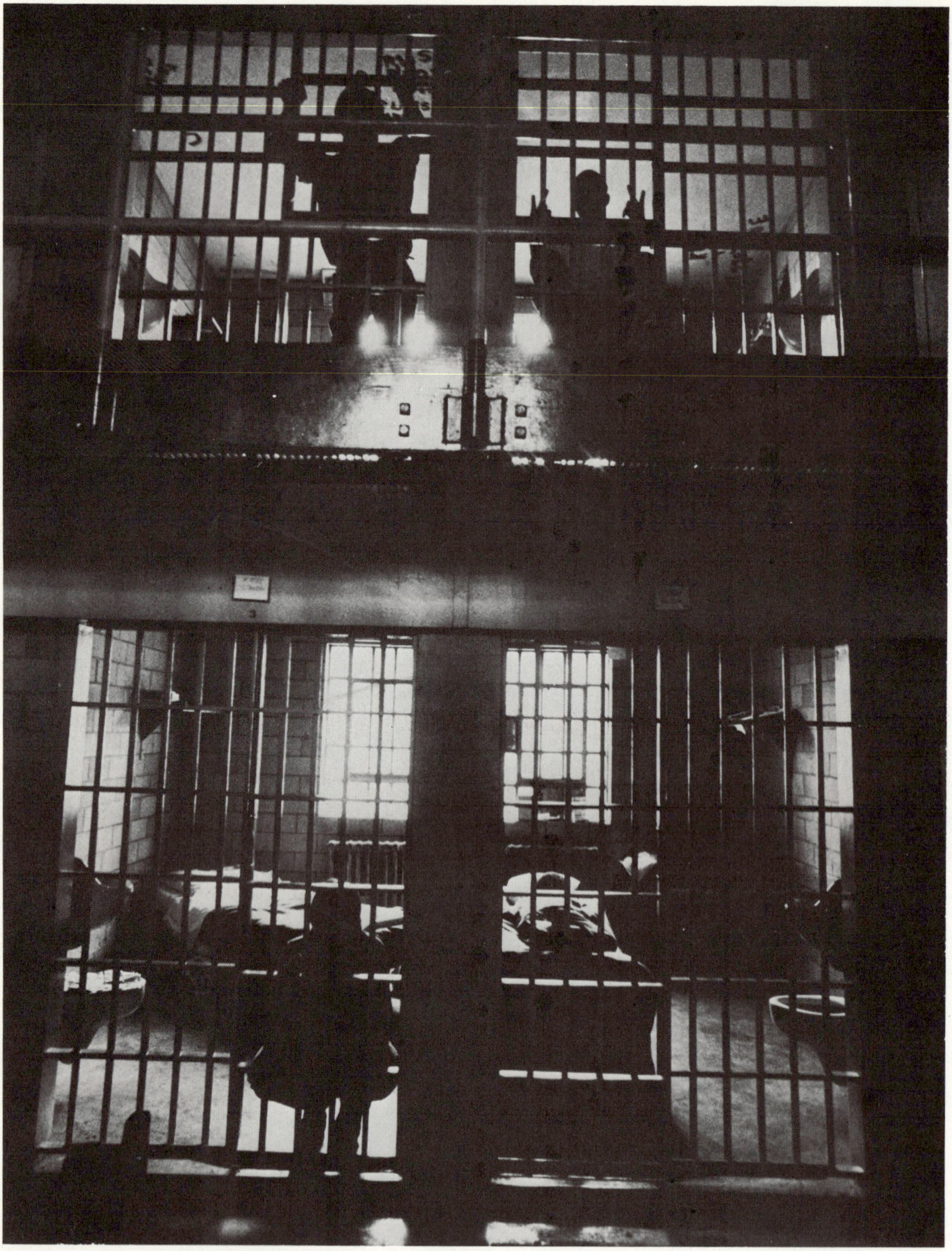

> When we cease to consider what the criminal deserves and consider only what will cure him or deter others, we have tacitly removed him from the sphere of justice altogether; instead of a person, a subject of rights, we now have a mere object, a patient, a "case."
> —C. S. Lewis, "The Humanitarian Theory of Punishment," Res Judicatae, 6 (1953)

15

THE DILEMMA OF CORRECTIONS: TREATMENT, PUNISHMENT, OR JUSTICE?

The fortress prison. The place where nothing works. It is finally sinking in that the rehabilitation function of the prison is and always has been a joke, "a noble lie." Even the best-intended efforts have proven ineffective. In reality, the big prisons are human storehouses where the inmates and their keepers, the guards, are locked into an abnormal and tense world. No one is helped. Furthermore, in the name of reform, more and more prisoners in recent years have been given indeterminate sentences. The result: more lengthy prison stays. Efforts to "cure" criminals have been dismal failures.

Confronted by crises such as recidivism, overcrowding, and protest, the future of prisons seems bleak indeed. But if there is any hope for positive change, it probably should begin with the phasing out of big prisons as we know them today and with the emergence of a range of alternatives for dealing with the convicted criminal.

Once an offender is convicted, he or she becomes subject to legal sanctions and official coercion by the state. This sanctioning process results in a form of deprivation that involves loss of status as the person is defined and stigmatized as a criminal—someone quite different from the great majority of law-abiding citizens. The effect of the label is so powerful that the person is seen as morally inferior and is given a master status that implies that all areas of "self" are afflicted by the "problem." This "status degradation" renders the person subject to being deprived of money through fines, excluded from full participation in society through probation, or confined and taken out of the community and isolated with persons of his own kind.

In the process of arrest, booking, and conviction, the offender comes to realize the power of the state to impose its will and to isolate him or her from former social roles. But the formal process of punishment begins when the offender is given over to the correctional officials who are empowered to carry out the sentence of the court. The study of the correctional subsystem of criminal justice—traditionally termed *penology*—is an important emphasis of criminology that focuses on the various programs employed in the administration of the criminal sanction on those defined as criminals.

THE SCOPE OF CORRECTIONS

The Nature and Extent of Corrections

Corrections encompasses the variety of means used by agents of the state to intervene and carry out legal sanctions or punishments imposed upon those convicted as criminals. This postsentence, postconviction aspect of societal reaction, as Austin Turk has pointed out, is a continuing part of the process by which the individual is made a criminal. The sanctioning process is, in effect, a criminalization process—establishing individuals' criminal identity as they become first convicts and eventually ex-convicts, or ex-offenders.[1] Should these persons refrain from further criminal activity, those who were employed to control them will claim that they have "cured" or reformed them. But in the eyes of conventional members of society, they will remain a symbolic representation of evil.

Corrections refers to both nonpenal and penal means of punishment, including fines, probation, incarceration, parole, or any combination of these. The correctional system of the federal, state, and local governments includes a wide variety of facilities, programs, and institutional and noninstitutional means for classification, custody or control, and treatment of the offender. These facilities include maximum, medium, and minimum security for adults, reformatories for younger offenders, training schools for those defined as delinquents, and separate institutions for women.[2] (Since adult male offenders in institutions outnumber females by about 14 to 1, the focus of this chapter will be mainly on adult male offenders. For a discussion of female offenders, see sources cited in footnote 2.)

More than 275,000 men and women were confined in our prisons in January 1977, an increase of 25,000 over the previous year (see Figure 15.1). If the more than 7,000 sentenced felons awaiting placement in our county jails are included, the figure rises to about 283,000 (see Table 15.1). Another 250,000 adults and juveniles are held in jails, detention centers, and training schools. There are nearly a million more on probation or parole supervision or involved in other community-based correctional programs.[3]

The estimated costs for federal, state, and local prisons in 1975 totaled more than $3.8 billion. This figure includes salaries for more than 200,000 personnel in more than 5,000 facilities. The direct cost was estimated at $8,500 per offender per year. Should administrative costs be included for central staff and administrators who are usually located in state capitals away from prisons, this figure would be higher. And if the cost of lost income and increased taxes for the public support for families of those imprisoned were added, by

Figure 15.1. Total Population of U.S. State and Federal Prisons, 1962–1978 (figures in thousands, as of January 1)

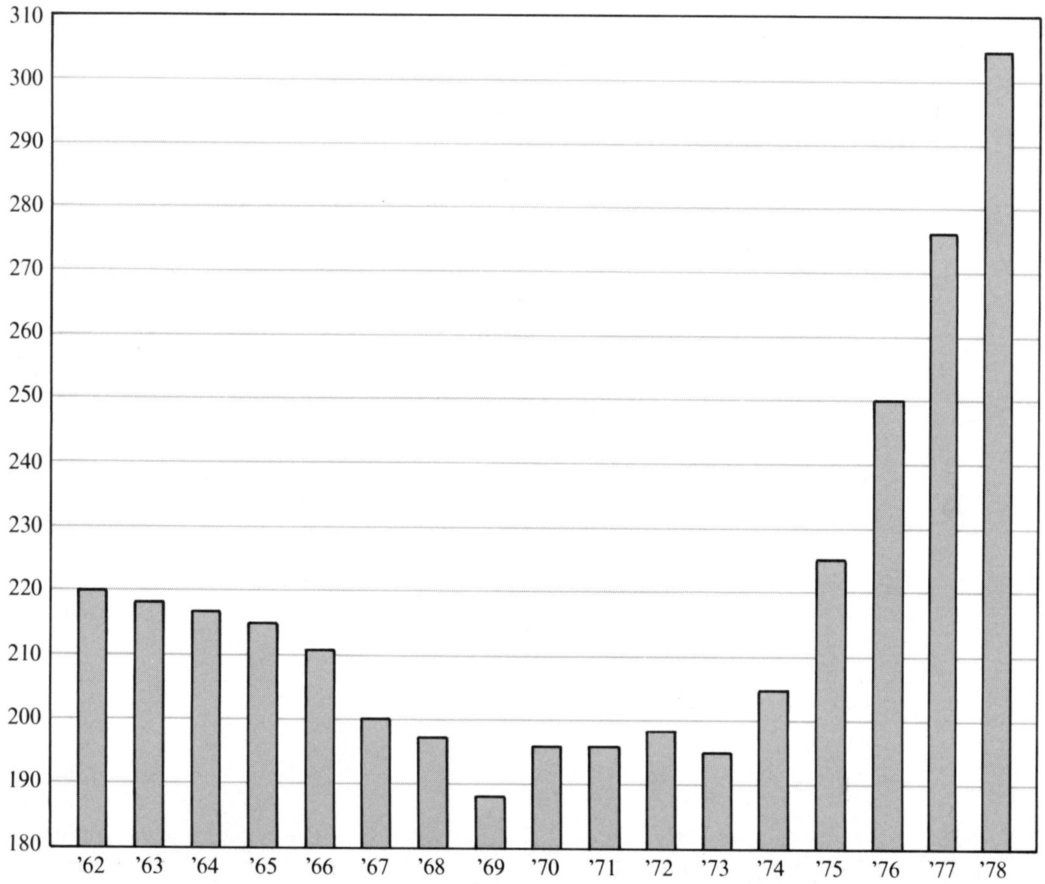

LEAA figures for '69, '70, '71 do not include certain states.
Figures from 1962–1974 from LEAA: 1975–1976 figures from *Corrections Magazine* survey.

Source: Adapted from Steve Gettinger, "U.S. Prison Population Hits All Time High," *Corrections Magazine* 2, no. 3 (March 1976):9.

conservative estimates the direct and indirect cost would be about $11,000 per prisoner.[4]

The offender typically is confined in an institution that is isolated from the community. Prisons are largely out of sight, and their activities are largely unknown to the average citizen. From time to time, a prison riot or a scandal occurs, and citizens become interested or concerned. After the riot "cools" down, there is a tendency to forget about the demands for reform.

In 1862, Dostoevski wrote, "The degree of civilization in a society can be judged by entering its prisons," a statement still worth pondering as we describe and analyze the nature, development, organization, effects, and dilemmas of our correctional system.

Table 15.1. Survey of Inmates in State and Federal Prisons, 1977

State	Number of Inmates 1/1/76	Number of Inmates 1/1/77	Percent Change
Alabama	4,420	3,096 (2,300)[b]	+22[c]
Alaska	349	543	+56
Arizona	2,712[a]	3,072	+13
Arkansas	2,338	2,445	+ 5
California	20,007	20,914	+ 4
Colorado	2,039[a]	2,324	+14
Connecticut	3,060	3,186	+ 4
Delaware	701	953	+36
D.C.	2,330[a]	2,617	+12
Florida	15,709	18,229 (373)[b]	+18[c]
Georgia	11,067	11,423 (533)[b]	+ 8[c]
Hawaii	366	413	+13
Idaho	593	725	+22
Illinois	8,110	10,002	+23
Indiana	4,392	4,430	+ 1
Iowa	1,857	1,956	+ 1
Kansas	1,696	2,126	+25
Kentucky	3,257	3,659	+12
Louisiana	4,774	4,695 (1,714)[b]	+34[c]
Maine	643	622	− 3
Maryland	6,606	6,860 (1,070)[b]	+20[c]
Massachusetts	2,278	2,701	+19
Michigan	10,882	12,462	+25
Minnesota	1,630[a]	1,684	+ 3
Mississippi	2,429	2,135 (125)[b]	− 7[c]
Missouri	4,150	4,748	+14
Montana	377	500	+33
Nebraska	1,259	1,339	+ 6
Nevada	893	953	+ 7
New Hampshire	302	297	− 1
New Jersey	5,277	5,987 (200)[b]	+17[c]
New Mexico	1,118	1,359	+22
New York	16,056	17,791	+11
North Carolina	12,486	13,261	+ 6
North Dakota	205	242	+18
Ohio	11,451	12,626	+10
Oklahoma	3,435	4,106	+19
Oregon	2,442	2,848	+17
Pennsylvania	7,054	7,584	+ 7
Rhode Island	400[a]	544	+36

Table 15.1. (continued)

State	Number of Inmates 1/1/76	1/1/77	Percent Change
South Carolina	6,100	6,985	+14
South Dakota	372	521	+40
Tennessee	4,569	5,350	+17
Texas	18,934	20,708	+ 9
Utah	696	827	+19
Vermont	343[a]	386	+12
Virginia	6,092	7,001 (1,375)[b]	+11[c]
Washington	3,063	3,767	+23
West Virginia	1,213	1,216	—
Wisconsin	2,992[a]	3,340	+12
Wyoming	384	355	− 7
Total states and D.C.	225,908[a]	247,913 (7,690)[b]	+12[c]
U.S. Bureau of Prisons	24,134	27,665	+15
Total U.S.	250,042[a]	275,578 (7,690)[b]	+13[c]

[a] Revised figures based on new state data. Last year's *Correction Magazine* survey showed a total of 249,538 inmates as of 1/1/76.

[b] Figures in parentheses represent inmates sentenced to state prisons, but currently being held in county facilities because of overcrowding.

[c] Includes the inmates sentenced to state prisons but being held in county facilities.

Special Note: Information now available indicates that three states had inmates backed up in county facilities on 1/1/76. They are Alabama, Louisiana and Virginia. But the number of inmates involved cannot be determined. Consequently, the percentage increases noted in the chart for those jurisdictions and the total percentage increase (13%) do not fully reflect the 1976 situation.

Source: Rob Wilson, "U.S. Prison Population Again Hits New High," Report of *Corrections Magazine* Survey, in Peter Wickman and Phillip Whitten, eds., *Readings in Criminology* (Lexington, Mass.: D. C. Heath, 1978), p. 353.

The Goals of Corrections

Corrections has been defined as *the official reaction of a community to a convicted offender.* This definition precludes the pretrial detention of alleged offenders who are presumed innocent and do not fall under the purview of corrections.

Over the past hundred years, it has become popular to maintain that the goals of corrections have changed from retribution to rehabilitation and preventive imprisonment. Thus the stated goals of corrections are to protect the community from the offender and to rehabilitate him or her. As the Crime Commission's report on *Corrections* stated in 1967, "Some jurisdictions have developed strong programs for the control and rehabilitation of offenders but most lack capacity to cope with the problems of preventing recidivism—the commission of further offenses."[5] Several years later, with increasing research critical of recidivism, the Commission on Standards and Goals modified this statement to note that the two "apparent" goals of the correctional system are (1) punishment of individuals who break society's rules, and (2) reduction of crime.[6]

It might be more explicit to refer to goals of *punishment,* although punishment is sometimes confused with revenge and retribution. The use of the term *rehabilitation* confuses the issue still further in that it leads to what David Rothman has called the "noble lie," the assumption that prisons serve to rehabilitate those incarcerated.[7]

At least four goals are characteristically claimed for punishment. The first is *retribution,* or social revenge. This goal is the oldest justification, based upon the concept of *lex talionis*—an eye for an eye, a tooth for a tooth. The second goal is *incapacitation,* the restraint and isolation of convicted offenders and the prevention of criminal activity during their confinement. The third goal of punishment, which has received considerable attention from criminologists, is *rehabilitation,* sometimes referred to as *"specific" deterrence.* The offender is subjected to beneficial treatment that allegedly reduces the probability that he or she will offend again. In this respect, the goal is the reformation of the individual as measured by benefits to society.[8] The most common way of measuring the effectiveness of rehabilitation is to study rates of recidivism. Yet this criterion is viewed by many as inconsistent with the assumptions of the medical model that underlies rehabilitation ideology. As the American Service Committee notes in *Struggle for Justice* (1971), a cogent critique of the medical model, it is ironic that a treatment ideology that claims to look beyond the offender's crime to the "whole personality," focuses on the single factor of whether or not the individual has been reconvicted for a criminal act. Robert Martinson's survey of 231 studies led him to ask, "What works?" He noted that "these studies lead irrevocably to the conclusion that nothing works."[9]

The fourth purpose of punishment is *deterrence,* or the idea of general prevention. "Belief in the deterrent efficacy of penal sanctions," Franklin Zimring and Gordon Hawkins point out in their definitive study (1973), "is as old as the criminal law itself." Yet as the Commission on Standards and Goals has argued:

> There is an illusion relative to the deterrent value of imprisonment. The deterrence of potential offenders has not been supported by evidence. Despite many attempts... no one has ever proved that the threat of severe punishment actually deters crime. Indeed there is evidence that swiftness and certainty have much greater deterrent effect than a long prison sentence....[10]

Herbert Packer has pointed out that deterrence is effective to the extent that it deters those who have been socialized to conform to the influences of the dominant society—the "right-minded." In deterrence the offender is treated, as Justice Holmes noted, as a means to an end, and used as a tool to set an example for the benefit of the general welfare.

Public concern over crime and issues of law and order suggests that even in the absence of evidence supporting the goals of general deterrence, punishment for its own sake may continue to be a major basis for the legitimacy of the correctional aspect of our criminal justice system.[11] The reliance on punishing the criminal offender for moral and symbolic reasons has persisted despite nearly two hundred years of efforts for penal reform.

THE HISTORY OF THE PRISON: INGLORIOUS REFORMS AND PRESENT PATTERNS

Over the past several centuries we have moved from forms of punishments that relied on physical torture, mutilation, consignment to galleys, and banishment to a primary reliance upon imprisonment. Nils Christie, a Norwegian criminologist, suggests that we have achieved a "kindlier" system of criminal punishment. But he notes it is difficult to say which punishment is more humane. Christie points out that in the seventeenth and eighteenth centuries, criminal sanctions in Anglo-Saxon and Scandinavian countries generally involved execution, accompanied by intense physical pain. In 1697, a decree relating to "the punishment of horrible murders" stipulated that the guilty person should be punished without mercy. He was to be pinched by red-hot tongs outside the place where the murder occurred and in the town's public places

"Oh, I suppose I can't complain. Things could be worse."

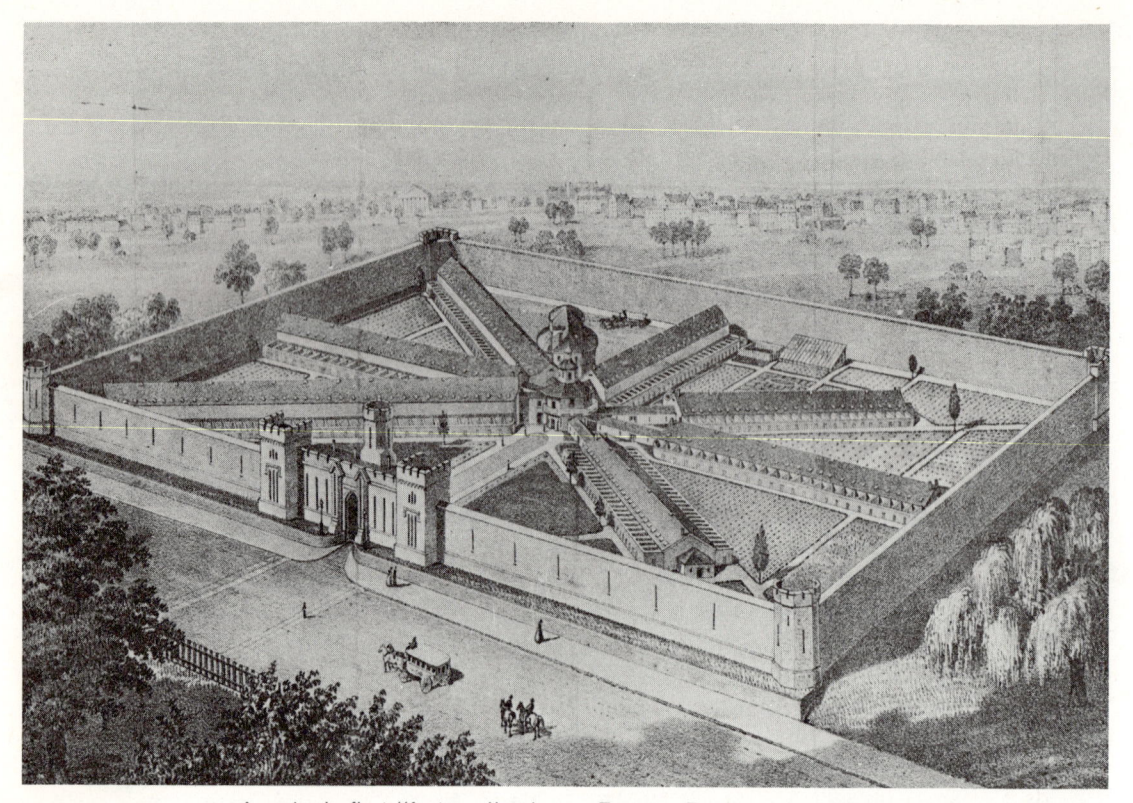

America's first "fortress" prison—Eastern Penitentiary of Philadelphia.

between the scene of the crime and the place of execution. At the execution, first the right hand was to be chopped off and then the head. The death penalty was also inflicted for abortion, incest, robbery, counterfeiting, and arson with intent to kill. When these penalties were abolished in 1815, it became necessary to rely more on imprisonment.[12]

Colonial America operated under English penal standards. In Massachusetts, after the Quakers were banished, anyone who read their books had one ear cut off for the first offense. Nonattendance at church was a capital offense in early Virginia. And branding was employed as a punishment until the end of the eighteenth century. Although the idea of confinement was introduced in the late seventeenth century by William Penn, it did not become a reality until after the Revolution. Because of the Quaker influence, in 1776 the provisional Pennsylvania constitution stated that the penal laws shall be reformed by the legislature and "punishment made in some cases less sanguinary, and in general more *proportionate to the crime*." [13]

Imprisonment was to become a substitute for capital punishment, but the laws establishing prisons were not enforced until after the Revolution. The old Walnut Street Jail in Philadelphia was renovated in 1790 under the influence of Dr. Benjamin Rush's Philadelphia Prison Reform Society, but by the early nineteenth century, that jail was overcrowded and unworkable. The state legislature, responding once again to the reformers' zealous influence, enacted legislation in 1821 that led to construction of America's first massive fortress prison, the Eastern Penitentiary of Philadelphia, known as Cherry Hill. It included four hundred large solitary cells, 8 by 15 feet, each with its own exercise yard. The prisoners were held in solitary confinement during their entire sentence. They worked in isolation with only a Bible for company, if they could read.

Reformers in New York had also been active. Auburn Prison opened in 1819, followed by Sing Sing in 1825. New York introduced a modification of the solitude model—the "congregate" system. In this system, prisoners were locked up at night in small cells, 7 feet long by $3\frac{1}{2}$ feet wide. By day they worked in common workshops, where a "rule of silence" was enforced. Both prisons separated the inmates, one physically, the other psychologically. Both emphasized work, on the assumption that idleness was related to criminal behavior.

A veritable pamphlet war was carried on in the early nineteenth century by reformers advocating the Pennsylvania and New York systems, with both groups zealously proclaiming the virtues of their respective reforms. The Pennsylvania system relied upon penitence and seclusion in separate work cells, while that of New York, which evolved at Auburn, utilized enforced seclusion from the contaminating outside world, congregate work in silence, and separation at night, all of which would hopefully break the offender's spirit.[14] Reformers came from Europe to observe these new experiments in penal methods. One observer was Alexis de Tocqueville, who in commenting on the pervasive effect of the rule of silence at the Auburn prison wrote: "There were a thousand living yet it was as a desert solitude."

The era from 1820 to 1850 was a period in which the rigid model of penal administration was established in the United States. Both the fortress-type prison and the paramilitary program were seen as ways to reform or transform the offender. For a century and a half, any changes in our prisons would have to fit into this rigid mold; the basic premise was strict seclusion of the offender. Any show of individuality was met with a program of coercive, group compliance, enforced with the whip when necessary. At Auburn and Sing Sing, no letters, visits, or communications from the outside world were allowed. The prisoner was taught to think of himself as dead to those outside the walls. New inmates were told by one Sing Sing warden that they were to be "buried from the world."[15]

The "rule of silence," originally a means for providing solitude and penitence, became an obsessive prison practice along with the lock step, a shuffling military march by which the men were moved while looking to the right to prevent verbal communication. Nonverbal communication was also forbidden. This practice persisted until the 1930s.

The attorney general of the United States summed up the fifty years that followed the opening of Auburn Prison when he noted in 1940 that the two contributions of this period were (1) the prison industries program, and (2) the interior cell block. But he noted that both developments had proved to be liabilities, for the indiscriminate caging of prisoners in steel and concrete cells and the imposition of silent labor could not be justified economically or penologically.[16]

A wave of optimism in corrections following the Civil War resulted in a new era of penal reform in the 1870s. The principles of the new penology were embodied in the Declaration of Principles issued at the National Congress on Prison and Reformatory Discipline, which met at Cincinnati in 1870. It stated that:

> Crime is an intentional violation of duties imposed by law.... The aim of prison discipline is the reformation of criminals, not the infliction of vindictive suffering.... The progressive classification of prisoners based on merit ... should be established ... a penal stage ... a reformatory stage ... a probationary stage.... The prisoner's destiny ... should be placed, measurably in his own hands.... Sentences ought to be replaced by those of indeterminate duration ... limited only by the satisfactory proof of reformation....[17]

These grand principles were followed by the establishment of reformatories for younger first offenders. Elmira Reformatory was opened in 1876. But the reformatory idea was grafted onto the concept of the fortresslike prison and was doomed to failure. Although the design of this prison followed that of Auburn, it differed from the typical prison of that time in two respects. First, prisoners were committed on indeterminate sentences. A maximum term was set, but prisoners were released earlier on parole if they showed progress. Second, inmates were assigned to one of three categories, depending on their progress and behavior. Initially, new inmates were assigned to group two for the first six months. They then advanced to group one if they made their "marks"; if not, they were demoted to group three. Similar reformatories were built in seventeen states by 1913. However, the reformatory idea and the moral purpose that accompanied it became lost in the prison system. Now, however, the prison had a new effective disciplinary tool—the indeterminate sentence.[18]

In New York state prisons, "ten days good time" is automatic for each thirty days served, although it can be lost by disciplinary infractions. Good time is now a part of almost every prison system and is generally computed at a ratio of one day credit for two good days served. Parole is tied to the indeterminate sentence and is a dominant aspect of prison life in America. Under this program, first adopted at Elmira in 1877, the offender becomes eligible for release after serving the minimum sentence *if the parole board approves.*

The legacy of nineteenth-century prison architecture, programs, and practices still persists. Out of the 113 state maximum security institutions in operation in 1971, 92 were built prior to 1960, 56 before 1900. The ultimate priority in their design was security. Built in remote areas, both captives and keepers are isolated from the larger community. The structures themselves, designed for the silent, lock-step system of control, do not lend themselves to normal

Isolation from the community and internal security characterize our "monster" prisons.

human relations. Maximum security prisons are characterized by high walls, gun towers, and fences for constant external control. Security dictates the daily round of life on the inside. Rather than having doors, which would allow a measure of privacy, the cell opening is covered by iron grills or bars. Toilets are open to view, and showers are supervised. These prisons encourage reliance upon authoritarian and impersonal means of control.

Relationships with the outside community are still difficult, even in the newer institutions. In his survey of prisons in 1971, William Nagel found that contrary to the recommendation of experts, the twenty-three newest institutions were located an average of 172 miles from the state's largest city. While minorities comprised 45 percent of the population of the prisons, staffs were made up of an average of 8 percent minorities. The inmate population is typically made up of urban offenders. The staff, however, especially the guards, tend to be rural whites who often are unable to understand or communicate with inmates.[19]

In 1870, the number of prisoners in the United States was 32,901 according to the Census Bureau. This figure increased to 45,233 by 1890, and to 53,292 in 1904, an increase of 62 percent. By 1935, the prison population was 140 percent greater than in 1904. There was a slight decline during World War II and again in 1969, followed by an increase of 33 percent between 1969 and 1976 (see Figure 15.1).

THE SOCIAL STRUCTURE OF THE PRISON

Formal Organization of Prisons

As a correctional institution, the prison is a formal organization in the sense that it developed as the result of a conscious effort to mobilize and organize individuals to achieve the goals of punishment: retribution, incapacitation, deterrence, and rehabilitation or reform of the offender. It is organized according to a scheme that seeks to establish patterns and procedures by which the employees will advance these purposes in a legitimate, orderly manner. The management and administration of prisons is similar to many other organizations in society in that they are bureaucratic in nature.

The prison is also similar to other social service organizations such as welfare, mental hospitals, and schools to the extent that it is a "people-processing" organization. Although its intended goals are to punish, control, or change the offender's behavior, it is much more oriented to processing. Formal rules and procedures to achieve the ends of controlling the offender operate within the walls of the prison. The "keepers"—guards and other staff—are expected to conform to formal behavior patterns. A formal inmate organization with rules imposed and enforced by the prison administration also exists.

The goals of the prison are confusing and contradictory, particularly in regard to rehabilitation or treatment. Donald Cressey has suggested that the most severe impediments to treatment are not necessarily the result of inefficient prison administration. Rather, they are due to the conflicting attitudes about crime control shared by the American public, some of which get translated into penal administration policy.[20] Furthermore, as the authors of *Struggle for Justice* (1971) note, the words retribution, revenge, and punishment often are used as though there were no difference in meaning among them. Although the first two imply punishment, it does not follow when we talk of rehabilitation or treatment that punishment is eliminated.[21]

Since the introduction of the treatment model, which grew out of the nineteenth-century positivist school's focus on the criminal rather than the crime, there has been a continuing debate regarding the relative benefits of punitive and nonpunitive prison programs.[22] In 1971, the Director of the California

Department of Corrections told a prisoners' rights conference: "There is no one of any consequence in this field that believes prison is the place to send a person for rehabilitation." But the *Manual of Correctional Standards* of the American Corrections Association (1966) states:

> Today with few exceptions correctional administrators subscribe to the philosophy of rehabilitation as opposed to the old punitive philosophy.... Punishment as retribution belongs to a penal philosophy that is archaic and discredited.... Penologists in the United States today generally agree that the prison serves most effectively for the protection of society against crime when its major emphasis is on rehabilitation.[23]

With the introduction of the treatment ideology, wardens have been expected to operate rehabilitative programs and at the same time meet the punishment goals of retribution, control, and deterrence. The corrections administrator finds it necessary to pay lip service to rehabilitation, keep law-and-order politicians happy, and get pay raises for the custodial staff. The administrator must do some fast talking and be involved in what appears to be "word magic" when dealing with budget committees and prison reform groups. The prison is called a correctional facility, the warden becomes the "superintendent," the guard a "correctional officer," and solitary confinement cells are dubbed "adjustment centers" or "seclusion." [24]

Organizational Structures

The organizational structure of the prison is complicated by the attempt to bring into coexistence the punitive and nonpunitive functions. Since these functions are often in conflict, the work of the prison administrator typically involves the resolution of conflicts between personnel promoting one or another of these functions. Needless to say, custodial needs frequently prevail.

Although no organizational chart can adequately depict the lines of authority that are involved, certain organizational components of prisons can be generalized. An organizational chart for a "typical" adult prison is shown in Figure 15.2. The superintendent is shown at next to the top level. He is the staff person who is directly responsible to the department of corrections for the day-to-day operation of the prison. He is the "outside" contact with the state bureaucracy, responsible to the director of the state prison, sometimes called the commissioner of corrections, and the corps of administrative staff persons located in the state capital. The superintendent depends upon the assistant superintendent in charge of custody as his "inside man."

Prisons have not been known for efficient administration. In some states superintendents are still selected through political patronage, and political appointees often do not have the training or experience to deal with complex prison problems. As a result, they tend to rely upon the "inside man," who may be an old prison staff person, to run the prison. Donald Cressey noted that the chief administrative officers of prisons were under civil service or the merit system in only twenty-three states. He notes that over a fifty-year period the average tenure of American wardens was 5.2 years, while 13 percent held

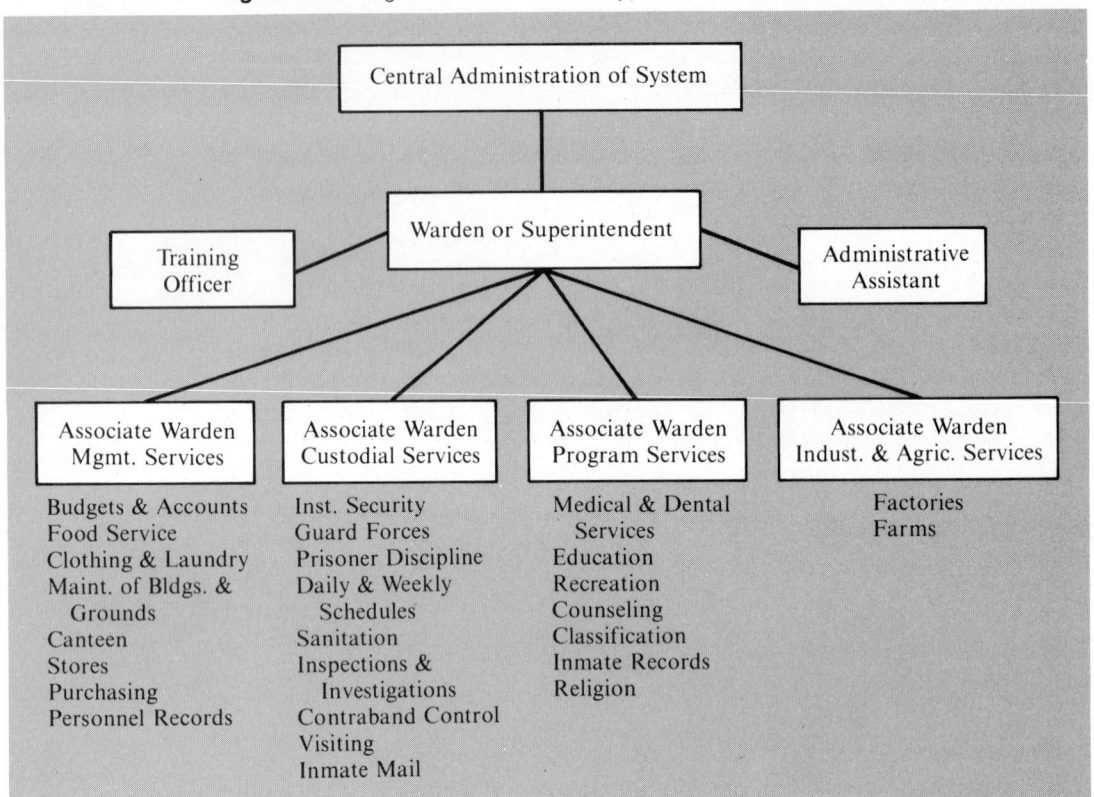

Figure 15.2. Organization Chart of a Typical Prison for Adult Offenders

```
                          Central Administration of System
                                        │
                                        │
                             Warden or Superintendent
          ┌─────────────────┬───────────┼───────────┬─────────────────┐
    Training                                                    Administrative
    Officer                                                       Assistant

  Associate Warden      Associate Warden      Associate Warden      Associate Warden
  Mgmt. Services        Custodial Services    Program Services      Indust. & Agric. Services

Budgets & Accounts    Inst. Security         Medical & Dental       Factories
Food Service          Guard Forces             Services             Farms
Clothing & Laundry    Prisoner Discipline    Education
Maint. of Bldgs. &    Daily & Weekly         Recreation
  Grounds               Schedules            Counseling
Canteen               Sanitation             Classification
Stores                Inspections &          Inmate Records
Purchasing              Investigations       Religion
Personnel Records     Contraband Control
                      Visiting
                      Inmate Mail
```

Source: From *Corrections in America* by Robert M. Carter, Richard A. McGee, and E. Kim Nelson. Copyright © 1975 by J. B. Lippincott Company. Reprinted by permission of Harper & Row, Publishers, Inc.

the position for ten years or more, and 22 percent were in office for one year or less.[25]

The organization of prisons differs in two significant ways from the typical business and industrial organization. First, a prison does not have separate hierarchies of management and workers. The guard is both the lowest status worker and a manager of men. Second, as a result of the attempts to add the treatment function to prisons, new services and roles have been added but not integrated. There is a clear chain of command, but the noncustodial positions such as psychologists, social workers, and academic and vocational teachers are neither part of the custodial chain of command nor are they part of the staff organization in terms of business or industrial models.

In other words, the organizational structure depicted in Figure 15.2 encompasses the three functions of *keeping, using,* and *serving* prison inmates, but does not integrate these divergent and sometimes contradictory functions. The superintendent must balance off competing groups or end up giving one the greater priority. The conflict typically is resolved in favor of the most numerous and highly organized group, the custodial staff, whose priorities relate to *keeping* and *using*.

The professional staff frequently fails to come to grips with the basic totalitarian structure of the prison. As Charles McKendrick, a former Sing Sing warden, has pointed out, they do not accommodate their professional skills to the prison but rather attempt to adapt the prison to their specialty. They may underestimate the intelligence and power of the custodial employees, who in turn often look upon the professional with suspicion. The custodial aspect is as old and basic to the prison environment as are the inmates. Treatment processes are only one of the relationships in the prison. They cannot be separated from custody.[26]

The public seems willing to espouse and even expect the goal of rehabilitation. A Harris poll conducted in 1968 showed that 84 percent of those interviewed agreed that the major emphasis of prisons should be rehabilitation. However, 59 percent were unwilling to have their tax burden increased to finance such programs. Correctional treatment professionals often argue that they have not had a chance to show what they can do, stating that treatment and punishment do not mix in an essentially punitive, custodial-oriented prison. In 1968, a national commission contrasted the clinical staff to inmate ratios with the custodial staff to inmate ratios (see Table 15.2). The meager part that treatment services play in prison budgets is underscored by noting that at Attica Prison, out of a budget of nearly $7 million for the fiscal year 1971 to 1972—the year of the uprising—62 percent went for supervision of inmates, and less than 4 percent was spent for counseling (including parole services) and academic and vocational education. It seems apparent that taxpayers will not invest the money needed for such programs behind the walls.[27]

Prison Guards or Correctional Officers?

The prison is organized as a large, impersonal "people-processing" institution. The guard, who occupies the lowest status rank in the organization, is a

Table 15.2. Comparison of Clinical and Custodial Staff Inmate Ratios in American Corrections, 1968

Position	Number	Ratio of Staff to Inmates
Social workers	167	1:846
Psychologists	33	1:4,282
Psychiatrists	58	1:2,436
Academic teachers	106	1:1,333
Vocational teachers	137	1:1,031
Custodial officers	14,993	1:9

Source: James P. Campbell, et al., Task Force on Law Enforcement, National Commission on Causes and Prevention of Violence, *Law and Order Reconsidered* (Washington, D.C.: U.S. Government Printing Office, 1969), p. 575.

manager as well as a worker. Guards have a low status relative to the prison administration, but they supervise inmates in terms of a set of rules and regulations that govern their relation with those above them in the hierarchy. No comparable parallel exists in the business world. Their supervisory function, though, has an historical analogy in the role of the overseer of slaves. Since most guards do nothing but guard, they do not use inmates productively. Rather, they manage them and their activities. In the prison organization, management is not only a means but basically an end.

Guards are also caught in a conflict between the contradictory goals of the rehabilitative ideal and the need to carry out their primary task of managing large numbers of men. James B. Jacobs and Harold G. Retsky have documented these and other role incompatibilities in their excellent work, *Prison Guard*, an ethnographic study of Statesville Prison, Illinois. They provide an analysis of the rigid supervision and compliance enforced upon the guards by their supervisors and the same coercive tactics they themselves apply to the inmates. Although the wages for guards were above the national average—beginning pay was $9,912 in 1976—the turnover rate in Statesville was nearly 100 percent, and absenteeism was very high.[28]

Jacob and Retsky provide insights into the guards' world, which is filled with frustration and fear of the unexpected. Except for those on the tower, guards are unarmed while inmates often carry homemade weapons. The guards can also serve as convenient scapegoats for the treatment staff's lack of success. They can always be blamed for subverting efforts of modern nonpunitive penology.

Most guards are cynical toward the treatment staff's work inside the prison. They feel that they are in a better position to evaluate the inmates' depth of commitment to such programs, and they tend to believe in a "free-will" theory of human behavior. They hold that a person can be rehabilitated by "outside agents" only when he is self-motivated.

The prison organization seems determined to reduce the inmate to the status of a child. Therapists and guards alike "juvenilize" the convict. The "treater" assumes that the inmate has a psychological or social problem and is lacking in volition. The guards make the inmate dependent through continuously enforced routines of counts. But during all their activities, the guards are expected to contribute to the rehabilitation program while promoting internal security and preventing escapes. Consequently, the world of the prison guard is a confusing one. He is in a sense "locked in," and he shares the fate of the convict while doing society's dirty work. George Jackson, in one of his letters from Soledad Prison, has captured this mutual fate and mutual anger:

> The days and nights that a guard has to spend on the ground (sometimes locked in a wing or a cell block with no gun guard) are what destroy anything at all good, healthy or social about him.... Fear begets fear. And we come out with two groups of schizoids, one guarding the other.[29]

Two relatively recent developments have brought the guards and middle-level custodial staff into positions of greater influence, conflict, and visibility.

The first is the development of occupational and professional identities through the affiliation of guards with professional organizations and unions. The American Correction Association has tried to recruit line officers, though the active participants in conferences and committees of the ACA are drawn largely from top management and upper supervisory staff. David Fogel estimates that only about 10 percent of the 100,000 working guards are active in the ACA.[30] According to a survey of union membership in 1977, at least twenty-five of the forty-nine prison systems reporting had active unions for state custodial officers. The various unions to which guards belong include the American Federation of State, County, and Municipal Employees, the Teamsters, and several state employee associations.[31]

Guard organizations emphasize the traditional collective bargaining goals of better pay benefits and working conditions. Generally, demands are for more punitive controls rather than for correctional innovation. At Walpole Prison (Massachusetts) in 1973, the guards' union called a partial strike and refused to work inside the prison when they felt that the commissioner of corrections had taken away some of their authority to control prisoners. For fourteen days the inmates virtually ran the prison. A similar situation occurred at the same prison in March 1979. In California, the head of the guards' organization and members of the service staff were instrumental in bringing charges against a former prison psychiatrist for complicity in the murder of a guard. The guards felt that he was too sympathetic to militant inmates. This same organization later threatened a strike if the prison administration permitted the establishment of "prisoner organizations" to represent the inmates in disciplinary matters with the administrators.[32]

The influx of younger guards from minority groups and urban backgrounds represents the other significant recent development, and it has tended to make guards a more active and conflict-ridden force in the prison world. Jacobs and Retsky reported emerging conflicts between this new breed of guards and the older guard types. The "old guards" reported that the newer urban-type guards were less loyal to the prison system, lacked discipline, were friendly with inmates, and often smuggled contraband to prisoners. Some of the new guards reported that they identified more with the inmates, with whom they shared more in ethnicity and experience, than with the older guards who were predominately rural and white. At Statesville, Illinois, the old guards often stated that the new breed were more of a problem than the prisoners. The high turnover rate at this prison may have magnified the problem.

Naturally, inmates are aware of and make use of these divisions in manipulating the guards. Since, in some prisons, one division is along racial lines, the newer guards are reminded of shared ethnic backgrounds by the inmates. In other instances, the age and lifestyles of the younger guards are similar to those of younger inmates.

These basic tensions between the "new breed" and "old guards" — reflecting the changes and complexities of the larger society — will have a continuing influence on the prison social world.[33]

> **BOX 1**
>
> ## Jail Guards, Good and Bad
>
> By WILLIAM RECKTENWALD
>
> PONTIAC, Ill.—I was walking the same floor that three other guards had walked before they were stabbed and beaten to death less than three months earlier.
>
> This was the Pontiac prison's north cell house, and all around were eerie reminders of the July 22 riot. Only recently had plastic been put up to cover the broken windows. The four-tier cell house was lit by only a handful of bulbs; there should have been 10 times as many, but no one had replaced the smashed lights or repaired the wiring.
>
> The north cell house is only a backdrop for this story. It's a story about prison guards, one of whom may already be marked for violence by inmates at Pontiac.
>
> It is also a story of contrasts. Most people are aware that the inmate population of a large prison is made up of every type of person and personality imaginable. Yet the prison guards are often portrayed with a sameness that could lead to the conclusion that they all perform the same way.
>
> Nothing could be further from the truth, I learned in two nights' work as a guard in Pontiac's most infamous cell house.
>
> I was paired with a stocky, veteran guard nicknamed Cadillac, about 30, who was soon holding forth on how to survive at Pontiac.
>
> "Remember, they'll kill you in a minute," he warned. "That's all they want. They'll kill anybody in a minute.
>
> "So you treat 'em like dogs. Just like dogs. If you treat 'em like anything other than dogs, they're gonna take advantage of you."
>
> Cadillac and I were assigned to serve dinner. Mealtime in prison is always special; in a prison under deadlock, with men confined to their 9-by-5-foot cells 24 hours a day, it takes on even more significance. It's the only thing to break up the monotony of the day.
>
> That night we were serving what the inmates considered the best meal on the prison menu—fried fish, potatoes, peas and carrots, and chocolate chip cookies. With that on the food cart, we figured to have very little trouble.
>
> But Cadillac seemed determined to start some as he wheeled the cart briskly up the gangways.
>
> The cells in the north cell house have no openings through which a dinner plate can be passed, so paper plates were used. They had to be folded and slipped through the bars.
>
> At each cell, Cadillac threw some food on a plate and folded it carelessly so that everything slid together and oozed out the ends. Then he'd ram it through the bars with maximum spillage, all the time keeping up a monologue of insults and curses aimed at the inmates.
>
> If they asked for more food, he'd curse them and say, "this is all you're getting."
>
> Pretty soon he had the inmates going. "What's the matter, Cadillac? You have too much wine last night, Cadillac? Look at that dirty shirt you're wearing, Cadillac. You drink too much last night, Cadillac?"
>
> There was no affection in their taunts. The inmates were working him over.
>
> Finally, on the fourth tier, a couple of inmates complained that Cadillac had dumped the cookies in with the fish on the food cart. This took on great importance because cookies are highly valued in the prison.
>
> "Cadillac, what you doin' putting those cookies in the fish?" mocked one inmate. "Cadillac, that's just terrible."
>
> Another snaked a hand out of his cell and took some cookies from the tray. Cadillac quickly picked up a serving spoon and began beating on the inmate's hand. The man's cellmate grabbed a broom and began poking the guard. While they battled, the first man raced to the sink to fill a container with water.
>
> Several cookies had fallen on the floor, and Cadillac stamped them into crumbs. Then he scooped up a plate of peas and carrots and was about to throw the food into the cell when I pushed him away.
>
> "Officer," I said. "Be cool. Let's keep going." It seemed absurd that in my first week on the job I was calming a veteran guard. But I kept remembering the only formal instruction I'd received the day I began work: "Whatever happens, don't lose your cool."
>
> I was furious at Cadillac for losing control—and determined not to lose mine. At that moment, Cadillac represented the only real danger

on the tier. He seemed dazed. His body began to tremble.

As we left the last tier, Cadillac told me he was never going to feed those men again, but was going to come back later and beat a few of them up. There's no evidence that he did, but he returned in full riot gear later in the evening to strut around the North Cell House.

Over a few beers later that night, a young guard told me that Cadillac had a reputation as an officer who could walk into a perfectly calm situation and rile it up.

Some inmates told me much the same — Cadillac was trouble. "Some day we're going to get that Cadillac," one of them told me.

My other partner in the North Cell House was named Grant. The night we served dinner together, we were dishing out a beef stew that had the consistency of a thin soup. There was so little meat and so many carrots that it had an orange coloring.

The stew was so watery it was hard to keep on a paper plate. Grant would carefully fold a plate in the middle, then turn up the edge to ensure that the stuff didn't drip on the inmates or in their cells when he passed it through the bars. At each cell, he'd chat amiably with the men, assuring them that the stew would taste better than it looked. I felt like adding, "It would have to."

As we were leaving one cell, an inmate yelled that I had forgotten the cookies for his cellmate. I gave them to him.

Grant stopped the cart and beckoned me to the cell.

"Do you see any 'cellie' (cellmate) in there?" he asked.

All I could see was one man with an ear-to-ear grin. Grant started laughing, and so did I. The inmate had conned me into giving him an extra cookie ration, but it felt good that I was enough of a "fish" to make that prisoner's entire day.

That night's feeding went without a nasty incident. I knew there were other guards like Grant working at Pontiac and quietly doing a good job. I admired them. Under the worst conditions, working for modest pay, they were able to maintain a semblance of humanity.

One who stood out for his unique approach was a soft-spoken, balding guard named Carlile, who presided over Pontiac's Protective Custody Unit.

"I like to treat each man like a gentleman," he said. "Whenever I can, I do what I can for him, as much as I can."

But when an inmate didn't respond in kind, Carlile wasn't above taking care of the problems with what he considered good jailhouse justice. In a conversation with a rookie guard who had been the target of a cup of urine and cleanser, Carlile explained how he would have handled the incident.

Carlile said he'd go home and fill a big jar with the most noxious creation possible. He told with relish how he'd shake it up every day and make sure it had fermented before bringing it to the prison.

"I'd bring the jar here one day and go up to that cell with the top off," he said. "Then I'd say, 'Come here for a minute. I have to talk to you.' And just as he got up to the bars, I'd throw it right in his face."

Carlile saw it as doing to others as they did to him. Too many other guards appeared to have a more indiscriminate response to any inmate trouble. I listened at dinner one night as officers from the segregation unit talked of some trouble they'd had that evening and how they'd used three cans of Mace and a canister of tear gas to knock an inmate out.

I quickly learned that the stories some of the guards cherished and chortled over most were those of inmate abuse. I don't know if the stories were true or not, but some guards obviously enjoyed sitting around and talking about "how it used to be."

There were also stories of the tower guards. One, described as a crack shot, had reportedly said: "We ought to let 'em all loose in the yard. Anybody gets over that fence, I'll serve his time out."

I might have dismissed such tales if I hadn't worked with Cadillac. But he seemed capable of dirty tricks, and it disgusted me.

I had a different perspective, of course. I hadn't been working that Saturday in July when the guards were murdered. I hadn't had a daily dose of hot water and cleanser thrown in my eyes. If I had, perhaps it would be different.

Source: The *Boston Globe*, Nov. 4, 1978. Copyright © 1978, *Chicago Tribune*. Used with permission, all rights reserved.

INFORMAL PRISON ORGANIZATION: THE INMATE'S WORLD

The prison also has its informal "other face." The patterns of the convicts' social world have developed in reaction to the social and psychological deprivation of the closed prison system. The prison, after all, is the ultimate total organization. Earlier systematic studies of prisons attributed the development of this inmate social structure to their adaptation to deprived status. This "adaptation" or "indigenous" model of inmate culture views the prison as a microcosm of society isolated and separated from the larger world. The inmate code is seen as proof of the idea that the prison is a closed, monolithic society, and the inmate population is homogeneous and united against a system organized to reform them.

Recent studies have challenged this analysis of the "adaptation" model and have argued that the inmate subcultures and diverse behavior systems were not indigenous to the prison. Rather they were imported by inmates with ties to professional and organized crime as well as gangs and ethnic groups. This view of the inmate social structure is termed the "importation" model.

Traditional Views of the Convict World: The Prison Culture

Donald Clemmer, a sociologist and prison warden, authored an early analysis (1940) of the convict's world. He identified a number of primary groups or cliques who shared and protected each other. Clemmer saw the prison culture as a cluster of folkways and mores that the new convict took on through the process of "prisonization." The degree of prisonization was determined by the extent to which he was involved in primary groups.

Although the idea of prisonization has been questioned by recent writers, it is useful in the way it describes the process by which the inmate becomes part of the prison world. Clemmer identified seven factors related to this process and the degree to which the inmate is affected: [34]

1. Length of sentence: shorter versus extented.
2. Stable personality versus unstable personality relative to preprison relationships.
3. Positive relationships with those "outside" versus a lack of such relationships.
4. Refusal to integrate into prison primary groups versus a readiness and capacity to integrate with the prison culture.
5. Refusal to accept the prison code and willingness to cooperate with administrators versus a blind acceptance of the prison code.
6. Chance affiliation with cellmates and workmates who are not part of the inmate social organization versus placement with those who are.
7. Noninvolvement in gambling and "abnormal sex behavior" and involvement in recreation and work versus participation in the first two and "doing time" relative to the other two.

The concept of "prisonization" is frequently cited as a reason why rehabilitative programs do not work. Other studies expanded upon Clemmer's ideas and focused on the prison as a relatively self-contained, cohesive system. Some analyzed the prison world in the manner of anthropologists. They identified two inmate types—the *politician* (who pays lip service to the convict code but is involved in a conspiracy with prison administrators), and the *right guy* (who although hostile to the administration is given special consideration because by enforcing the "code" he aids in controlling other convicts)—as the leaders. They also identified the *square johns* (who have ties to the straight world), the *merchants* (who supply scarce goods and services to the convicts), and the *outlaws* (who identify with criminal activities in the prison). These represented the types who were integrated in different ways into the convict world.[35]

In his *Society of Captives* (1958) and his later work with Messinger (1960), Gresham Sykes attempted to analyze these prison types in relation to the prison as a social system confronted with two contradictory roles. The prison consists essentially of two societies: the captives and the administrators. The problems each face are unique. The administrators have the task of maintaining external security and internal order over a potentially rebellious group of inmates who outnumber the custodial staff. The inmates, on the other hand, deal with the deprivation of being in prison with not only a loss of freedom but also with physical discomforts, loss of self-esteem, and fear of harm from other inmates.[36]

The social system that evolved to cope with these two problems was seen as an "accommodative" one. The degree of control exercised formally by prison guards is small compared to the control enforced informally by certain inmate leaders. The inmates quickly learn that it is as important to obey the prisoners' code as it is to conform to the formal controls imposed by the prison administration through the guards.[37]

Certain inmate leaders receive special privileges in return for enforcing an informal social order—an order epitomized in the underlying tenets of the informal prisoner organization, "the code." It includes the following five categories: [38]

1. Be cautious: *don't interfere with inmate interests; don't rat or inform; be loyal to other "cons."*
2. In disputes with fellow prisoners: *don't lose your head; do your own time; play it cool.*
3. Don't take advantage of other inmates through force or fraud; *don't break your word; don't steal from cons; be right!*
4. Maintain self-respect: *don't cop out (admit guilt); be tough!*
5. Keep your mouth shut and never let the staff know that anything is getting you down; *don't be a sucker; never talk to a screw (guard); have a connection.*

The central precept of this inmate code, "do your own time," has been documented as present in many prisons throughout the country and is now seen as being related to the criminal code that provides alternative patterns of adjustment to deprivations imposed by maximum security prisons. Although it seems antagonistic and in opposition to the goals of prison administration, it includes a number of major roles in the inmate social system that may be used by the administration to maintain control of the prison. Thus, relatively privileged types, such as the *right guy,* the *politician* (who has a wide variety of contacts with officials as well as inmates), the *punk* (an inmate who copes with sexual deprivation through homosexual activities), the *merchant,* and the *queen* (who has been involved in homosexual activity in the free world), receive certain privileges and benefits that further the exploitative aspects of the prison world.

The code is a means by which an implicit, accommodative, yet exploitative, arrangement comes to exist between the inmate leaders and the administration. While its central precept, "do your own time," seems antagonistic and in opposition to the administration, it actually furthers the exploitation of the many while benefiting the privileged types like the right guy, the politician, the punk, the merchant and the queen, who receive material rewards and privileges and in a covert way assist the administration in the control of the prison.

The difficulty with this description of the system within the prison—although it provides a rationale for the ineffectiveness or rehabilitation—is that it leaves unexplained what happens to the value and behavior orientation that the offender brought into the prison. The answer is that the process of prisonization acts to transform former roles and identities as prisoners become socialized into the indigenous prison world.

Importation and Interchange Models of Inmate Social Organization

This "indigenous, accommodative" theory was questioned in an essay by John Irwin, an ex-convict trained as a sociologist, and his mentor, Donald Cressey. They noted that the inmate culture was influenced by the behavior system or subculture to which the new inmate, *the fish,* had been committed in the outside world. Irwin and Cressey argued that "the code" was an adaptation of the thieves' code that originated in the criminal subculture. Thus, the behavior of some convicts was not an adaptation to the prison, but an adaptation to the larger criminal subculture that served as their "reference" system while in prison.

In his later work, *The Felon* (1970), Irwin expanded these ideas more fully with data gathered from 116 convicts in California prisons. Irwin was impressed by the variety of influences from the "outside" that affected the social organization of the prison. Since the initial focus of his study had been the parole process, he noted in particular the manner in which the preparation for release on parole was the intersection of social relationships and events from the outside as well as from the prison world.[39]

Irwin contends that both the "indigenous" and th "importation" models have ceased to be useful in analyzing the prison social world. He suggests that the concept of "interchange" is a more effective tool for such analysis. Due to the rapid pace of social change and the related conflict of recent decades, it now appears that the prison social organization is more fluid and even more volatile than ever.[40]

He describes the black nationalists and Muslim movements that developed as the prisons became populated with higher proportions of blacks. Racial pride spread to other minorities, and white prisoners became politicized as a result of an increased sense of injustice growing both out of legal procedures and the conviction of the prisoners that the indeterminate sentence was an arbitrary and capricious means of enforcing custodial goals in the name of rehabilitation.

The Prisoner Labor Union Movement. The 1960s witnessed unity strikes involving all races at San Quentin. In the 1970s there were the killing of three black inmates and the apparent reprisal death of a guard at Soledad Prison. The Folsom Prison strike in 1970 helped launch the prisoners' union movement. Among the lists of demands that followed this nineteen-day strike that centered on inmate dissatisfaction with the indeterminate sentence and the shooting of the three black inmates was one that demanded the right to form a union. This strike demonstrated a heightened political awareness by the inmates, and the movement received support from prison reform and ex-offender groups outside, as well as convicts inside various California prisons. The original constitution of the Prisoners' Union specified that the organization would be controlled by ex-convicts in order to facilitate negotiations.

By 1974, Local 9 of the California Prisoners' Union in San Francisco was apparently well organized, with a staff of twenty employees. This union provided much of the impetus for the formation of similar unions across the country.[41] In following the California model, these prisoners' unions maintained a labor orientation, but their main focus was on civil and human rights for prisoners and the abolition of the indeterminate sentence.[42]

In New York, a union was established at the Greenhaven Correctional Facility in 1972 and affiliated with a labor union, but its request for collective bargaining rights as "public employees" was denied by the state. Unions were also established in Massachusetts, North Carolina, Michigan, Maine, Vermont, Rhode Island, New Hampshire, Kansas, Georgia, Ohio, Minnesota, and Washington.[43]

The most vigorous and successful prisoner unions have been in Scandinavian countries. These organizations have also been aided by outside prison reform groups known as KROM in Norway, KRUM in Sweden, and KRIM in Finland and Denmark. In 1971, the Swedish prisoners organized the United Prisoners' Central Organization (FFCO) and negotiated for all 5,000 prisoners with the National Correctional Administration.[44] This might be seen as an example of Irwin's "interchange" model of prisoner social organization, for Sweden is highly unionized, and unionization inside prisons reflects the patterns of the larger society. Furthermore, unionization inside prisons was not seen as a threat to security. Nevertheless, by 1974 we found more than one Prison

Advisory Council—elected representatives of inmates—disclaiming any identification with either the FFCO or KRUM.[45]

By the late 1970s, the prisoners' union movement in the United States also seemed to be in disarray. After earning apparent judicial approval in some states, the unions were vigorously opposed by prison administrators. One state director of corrections publicly stated in 1973: "These men are convicted felons—convicted of breaking the laws of our society. Under no circumstances will I recognize their so-called union." [46] The apparent death knell of prisoner unions was signaled by the Supreme Court decision, *Jones* v. *North Carolina Prisoners' Labor Union, Inc.,* in 1977. The majority of the court overturned a federal district court decision that had found merit in the union's arguments that under constitutional rights of free speech, rights to association, and equal protection, the inmates could not be prohibited by prison authorities from recruiting members among other prisoners. The district court's ruling that the union had the privilege of bulk mailing into the state prisons was also overruled. As a result, by the end of 1977 the prisoners' union movement was apparently fragmented, and the California Prisoners' Union had effectively ceased operation.[47]

Ordered Segmentation. The prison world might be seen as a network of small cliques formed by prisoners of the same race with ties to the outside world. The social order that has emerged approximates the "order segmentation" that Gerald Suttles noted in his study of a multiracial Chicago slum. Inmates who live in the restricted prison world confine their associations and interact with their own clique and a few others of similar ethnic and social backgrounds.[48] Ex-offenders have verified the operation of Irwin's "interchange" model. One ex-convict student, after reading Gresham Sykes's *Society of Captives,* reported, "The prisons I did time in weren't like that." He described how the various cliques divided the yard up into territories for their activities, including the wheeling and dealing that goes on between the cliques as well as within them.

Implications of the "Interchange" Model

While prisoners were attacking the system from the inside, prisoner rights groups as well as social scientists, influenced by a growing racial and political consciousness, began to challenge the rehabilitative goal of prisons. The "interchange" model suggested by Irwin may provide an impetus to develop a broader perspective on the problem of dealing with crime and criminals. Before a rational, humane role for prisons can be developed and the rehabilitative ideal can be reformed, we must unmask what David Rothman has termed "the noble lie"—that prisons serve rehabilitative purposes. Rothman argues that "the most serious problem is that the concept of rehabilitation legitimates too much in that it expands the sanctioning power in the guise of treatment.[49]

To acknowledge that rehabilitation in prison is a pretense might remove some of the inherent contradictions between this goal and the punitive goals of retribution, incapacitation, and deterrence. Attention would also have to be given to other aspects of the system, such as the reform of plea bargaining and sentencing practices and the overall *just* administration of the criminal justice system. Many critics of rehabilitation have based their criticism on evidence that the criminal justice system in general, not just the prisons, has utilized unacceptable, discriminatory, and even unconstitutional means in the guise of treatment.

THE EFFECTS OF CORRECTIONAL PROGRAMS: DOES ANYTHING WORK?

Rehabilitation and Treatment Assumptions

Throughout the twentieth century, rehabilitation has been assumed to be the major goal of the penal sanction or sentence. In 1963, the American Law Institute's Model Penal Code recommended that the sentencing court might choose prison as a sentence instead of probation if it was ascertained that the offender is "in need of correctional treatment that can be provided most effectively by his commitment to an institution." This recommendation was reiterated in a number of commission reports including the ABA's *Standards for Sentencing* (1969), *The Model Sentencing Act* of the NCCD (1972), and the *Commission on Standards and Goals* (1973).[50]

Rehabilitation has influenced the manner of sentencing as well as the way in which dispositions are carried out. Rehabilitation relies upon an analogy from medicine—the medical model—where the offenders are defined as "sick," and it is assumed that crime is the result of some personal or social pathology. The offenders must be "treated" or reeducated or resocialized. They should be held until they are "cured" and can be safely released. Rehabilitation may be defined as any means employed to change offenders' characters, behavior patterns, or habits to decrease their criminal tendencies. Although much is said about helping offenders with their problems, the effectiveness of treatment generally is evaluated in terms of its effects on recidivism.[51]

Rehabilitation focuses upon a nonmoral approach to the crime problem. In theory at least, it assumes the possibility of punishment and reeducation occurring simultaneously.[52] Sentences are to be designed to fit the offenders' needs for treatment. The courts and corrections officials are given great discretionary power in individualizing sentences and release dates.

In the summary of various treatment strategies that follows, it should be noted that although the assumptions mentioned above underlie such programs, the basic criterion used to evaluate their effectiveness, success, or failure is the recidivism rate. This poses a problem, as the writers of *Struggle for Justice* have pointed out, more basic than the unreliability of statistics. They note that it is the height of irony to measure success against the single factor of reconviction for a criminal act when the treatment ideology bases its claim to success on treating the "sickness" of individual criminals. The average offenders are obviously not sick persons, but the criminal justice system has rested its claims to broad discretionary power over individuals on this rationale. As the American Friends Service Committee suggests, we might be thankful that such treatment programs—which apparently seek to condition inmates to an unthinking conformity to inflexible, externally imposed rules—do not work. For "if such . . . methods really did work, it might be more success than a free society could endure."[53]

Educational Programs: Academic and Vocational

It is generally believed that if a prison could provide effective academic and vocational training, it would reduce the rate of recidivism. Educational programs in many prisons are below standard, but even where high quality, well-staffed programs have been established, the results have been disappointing. A study of a New York program in 1964 found recidivism unaffected by academic achievement except for the 7 percent of the subjects with high IQs who previously had excelled in outside schools.[54]

A study in California in 1962 compared males who had been trained as bakers and auto body workers with those who had no training. Six months to a year after parole, the control group had about as much difficulty as might be expected from its Base Expectancy scores, while the trained group had *more* major problems than predicted.*

In a study of men who received both vocational and basic education at the Draper Correctional Center (Alabama), which relies upon behavior modification techniques, it was found that the number of violations at the end of three years was unrelated to whether or not the released prisoners had such training.[55]

Another more recent California study of women prisoners found that those who had received five months' training in cosmetology, ceramics, or as nurses' aides had the same parole record as those with no training. As a result of these and similar studies, the California Department of Corrections stated in a report on their evaluation that "profiting from these experiences, the department does not claim any particular capability for reducing recidivism for vocational training."[56]

At the Rikers Island facility in New York City, an IBM trainee program for males sixteen to twenty-one years reported a success rate of 52 percent compared to 34 percent for the nontrained group, but the differences were eliminated when dropouts were counted.[57]

---

* Base Expectancy scores are estimates or predictions of an offender's success upon release. The scores are assigned to each offender according to whether his history shows the presence or absence of certain characteristics, such as arrest-free period of five years, no opiate-use history, no commitments for career offenses (e.g., burglary or forgery), no family criminal record, no alcohol-related crimes, positive employment history, no aliases, first imprisonment, favorable living arrangement, and not more than two prior arrests.

After surveying six adult vocational training programs reported between 1948 and 1965, Martinson concluded that they apparently failed because the programs (1) had no relationship to the outside world, (2) taught obsolete skills, (3) were not able to counter the harmful effects of prison life, and (4) may have been unrelated to the offenders' propensity toward criminality.[58]

Individual Therapy (Treatment)

The effects of individual counseling on males averaging 17.4 years of age were reported in a follow-up study fifteen months after release from the Priston School of Industry in California. The rate of parole revocation was higher (58.5 percent) for those who had received such treatment than it was for the untreated youths (47.7 percent).[59] Another California study evaluated teenage females who were compared for success on parole based on whether or not they had been involved in individual, group, or no therapy at all. No statistical differences in rates of revocation were found.[60]

The California Intensive Treatment Program was designed to assist inmates in developing insights regarding their problems. The results of this program in psychodynamics were so disappointing that the corrections department shifted to an emphasis on group methods.[61]

At Walpole Prison in Massachusetts, inmates who had been involved in a twenty-five-week individual psychotherapy program were studied in a four-year follow-up program. The expected rate on Base Expectancy scores was contrasted with the observed rate. The program was considered quite successful, even though the observed rate was 53 percent. The Base Expectancy score was based on only four factors—number of prior arrests, age, education, and number of juvenile incarcerations. This system contrasts with the more sophisticated Base Expectancy scores in California, which use twelve variables. The factors of risk may not have been adequately controlled in the Walpole experiment, and since the study excluded those who had dropped out, the results may have been biased.[62]

Group Therapy (Treatment)

The term "group therapy" encompasses many styles including guided group interaction, milieu therapy, and therapeutic community meetings. Numerous variations have been tried in the prison setting, but results have been inconclusive. One study of group therapy conducted at the California Medical Facility at Vacaville compared 736 group therapy inmates released between 1965 and 1968 with a control group released from other California prisons who had not been involved in groups. Both groups had similar Base Expectancy scores. The difference after six months was not significant. But after one year, 51 percent of those treated had no serious problems as compared with 44 percent for the control group. After two years, the figures were 36 and 30 percent.[63] Another extensive follow-up study on nearly 1,000 California parolees from medium security prisons over a three-year period was conducted by

Group counseling may aid custodial ends.

Gene Kassenbaum and his colleagues. It identified no relationship at all between various group therapy groups and rates of recidivism.[64]

The emphasis upon recidivism in measuring effects has precluded the assessment of whether or not important secondary benefits have been gained from such group techniques. These benefits might include lessened tensions, reduced aggression and violence, and a more docile prison population. In other words, group therapy might have aided the custodial function, even though reformative goals were not achieved.

In her book *Kind and Usual Punishment* (1973), Jessica Mitford applies her journalistic skill to convey the perspectives of prisoners, practitioners, and criminologists in a devastating critique of treatment programs. She cites a comprehensive study for the California Department of Corrections that drew the following pessimistic conclusion:

> Thousands of inmates and hundreds of staff members were participating in this program at a substantial cost . . . in time, effort, and money. Contrary to the expectations of the treatment theory there were no significant differences in outcome for those in the various treatment programs or between treatment groups and the control group.[65]

It was also noted that group counseling had diminished neither the adherence to the *inmate or criminal code* nor the frequency of discipline problems.

The author of this report predicted to Mitford that the "liberal treatment era," with its idea that convicts could be converted to conform to conventional behavior, would be replaced with "behavior modification" experiments—an accurate prediction. As Andrew von Hirsch has suggested, the rationale may be: If Freud cannot cure criminals, why not try Skinner?[66]

Behavior Modification: Treatment or Repression?

Treatment schemes in this category involve three basic strategies: negative reinforcements for undesirable or antisocial behavior, rewards for desirable behavior, and treatment to alter the inmate's basic personality structure.[67]

In 1974, a psychiatrist formerly employed in California prisons revealed that certain black militants, sexual deviants, and other undesirables had been treated with Anectine—a drug which simulates death and had been proscribed for military use in the Vietnam war. He reported that the experiment, although lacking in controls and other safeguards and designed to alter behavior, had degenerated into outright torture at the hands of nonprofessionals.[68]

Legal restrictions have been placed on the use of such chemotherapy when the courts have become apprised of their use. In the case of *Knecht* v. *Gillman* (1973), a federal Court of Appeals enjoined the use of Apomorphine—a drug that causes vomiting for as long as an hour—because appropriate guidelines had not been developed. Other nonchemotherapeutic tactics include neuro or psychosurgical techniques that seek to change behavior directly and operant conditioning combined with tactics similar to the "brainwashing" techniques used on American prisoners of war during the Korean War. The proponents of these techniques claim that they are effective in the control of disruptive behavior and that they may have a "carry-over" effect after release.[69]

Several evaluations of such techniques by David Greenberg suggest that claims regarding their effectiveness may have been premature. One study of fourteen-year-olds in Nevada and another of fifteen- to seventeen-year-olds in California found no effects of "behavior mod" on recidivism rates.[70] Norval Morris, in discussing aversive conditioning, draws a parallel between this technique and the Ludovico technique used on Alex in *A Clockwork Orange*. He notes the increasing use of behavioral modification techniques in our prisons. Experiments with electric shocks, called "Edison Medicine" by the inmates, are used on "volunteers" to change undesirable behavior. Morris states that volunteering for such experiments is "coerced," since participation often is tied to release or parole from prison.[71]

Work Release

Work release programs have been operated out of prisons and jails with mixed success. A small group of inmates was participating in such a program at Attica at the time of the riot in 1971. It is generally agreed that such programs operate most effectively out of minimum security or open institutions.

A summary of Greenberg's analysis of the mixed results of work release programs in jails and prisons is provided in the previous chapter.

Community-Based Treatment

Community-based treatment, in lieu of imprisonment, has been tried since John Augustus asked the court to release certain prisoners to his care in Boston in 1841. In addition to probation and parole, some of the same treatment modalities—such as individual psychotherapy and vocational counseling—have been used with a measure of success in community settings. Joseph Massimo's study of a program using both insight therapy and vocational counseling found a small decline in recidivism rates, which he felt was due partly to the program's small size and the use of enthusiastic therapists. Another program evaluated by Stuart Adams found that individual therapy had little effect on recidivism.[72]

Probation

Experimental programs with adults on probation have revolved around job readiness. Greenberg has summarized three such programs, in which groups who received job counseling and placement were compared with those who did not receive such services. He found no significant differences in rearrest rates between the two groups. In two other programs using volunteer supervisors there were no significant differences, except in the Oakland, Michigan, program where the failure rate for those who had volunteer supervisors was 14 percent, as contrasted with 9 percent for those without volunteers.[73] A study in Saginaw, Michigan (1963), found that the use of probation greatly decreased recidivism rates. However, the groups and programs were not matched for comparability. Although some probation studies have shown that probation may give offenders a better opportunity to avoid future arrest than if they were sent to prison, other studies merely show that their chances will be about the same.[74]

Parole

Parole is defined as "the release of an offender from a penal or correctional institution after he or she has served a portion of the sentence, under the continued custody of the state and under conditions that permit reincarceration in the event of misbehavior."[75]

A number of studies were conducted in California in the 1960s to ascertain whether varying the intensity of parole supervision would affect the recidivist rates of male offenders. Initially the case loads of parole officers contrasted were fifteen and ninety, with some in each group released early and assigned to intensive supervision for ninety days. Some differences were noted, but these were due to selection factors, since the low-risk cases were assigned to the officers with small case loads. Another phase of this experiment compared case loads of thirty to those of ninety men for a six-month period. A year later, there were no significant differences between the groups. The third phase involved comparisons between case loads of thirty-five and seventy-two men. These were carried out for more than a year. There was some evidence that the smaller case loads were more effective, though it appears that the positive effects may have been as much due to changes in the manner in which the parole officers related to the offenders as to the size of the case loads.[76]

A further experiment with drastically reduced supervision found that good risk parolees under minimal supervision—one meeting every three months unless the offender asked for help or evidenced criminal tendencies—had the same failure rate as those assigned to regular supervision.[77]

Half-Way Houses

Programs using the half-way concept have enjoyed a wide acceptance over the past decade. A number of studies, however, suggest that their effectiveness does not match the hope that has attended their development. In Gary, Indiana, a half-way house for males, aged eighteen to twenty-five, who were released from a state reformatory, provided jobs, residence, and available counselors. The failure rate after one year was 21 percent for residents and 16 percent for nonresidents.

Young adult offenders in Washington, D.C., aged seventeen to twenty-three, were assigned at random either to a house in a predominantly black section of the city or to the reformatory at Lorton Prison. Those assigned to the house were involved in school or work programs and a nontherapeutic program of restricted interaction with other residents. They progressed through stages of residential confinement, nonresidential parole, and total release. Those assigned to Lorton participated in therapeutic group sessions with trained psychologists and were paroled to a half-way house prior to final discharge. The rearrest rates for both groups were similar.[78]

Sentencing and the Effectiveness of Punishment

The effectiveness of various types of sentences has been the focus of numerous studies. Roger Hood and Richard Sparks found that the use of fines and discharges both for recidivists and first offenders, for all age groups, was more effective than either incarceration or probation. Studies they describe found no correlation between the frequency of the use of probation and revocation rates. Martinson provides an analysis of four studies which indicates that offenders released on early parole did neither worse nor better than those released on scheduled parole dates. Hood and Sparks analyzed three studies from California with similar conclusions. They also found that while recidivism rates may not decline or increase with early release or the use of probation, there seems to be a hazard of an increasing crime rate when the number of potentially repetitive offenders rises in the community.[79]

Data from Daniel Glaser's study of a federal prison, although criticized for lack of control of the degree of risk within offender categories, are frequently noted as examples of the effects of sentence length. Glaser's data show a rather high success rate of 73 percent for those serving less than a year, 65 percent for those serving two years, and 56 percent for up to three years. Yet the success rate on parole rose to 60 percent for those who had served more than three years in prison.[80]

Martinson cites two British studies and a Danish study that correlated the type offender and its relationship to the effect of length of sentence on recidivism. It was found in all three studies that decreasing the length of sentence did not improve or lower the rate of recidivism for "hardcore" adult "recidivists"; however, one study in Great Britain found the reverse to be true with juveniles.[81]

The Interchangeability of Penal Measures

The inconclusive nature of the studies of correctional treatment is summed up by the British criminologist Nigel Walker, who says we are seeing "the interchangeability of penal measures." He suggests that the common assumption that the right treatment can be discovered by a diagnostic process is the result of thinking in terms of the medical model: once the offender's "sickness" is diagnosed, the remedy becomes apparent.[82]

Walker cautions against the methodological weaknesses he sees in most of the "success rate" studies. He provides the following summary of eight central sequential results in the numerous studies reported:[83]

1. *Fines* generally are followed by fewer reconvictions than other measures.
2. *Heavy fines* are more effective than light fines.
3. Generally the disposition followed by fewer reconvictions other than fines seemed to be *discharge* (absolute or conditional). However, the older "first offender"—aged thirty or more—tends to have an abnormally high reconviction rate following discharge.
4. *Imprisonment* is followed by more reconvictions than fines or discharge.
5. But *imprisonment* compares better with other measures when applied to "first offenders."
6. *Probation* is followed by more reconvictions than imprisonment.
7. Yet *probation*, when it was applied not to "first offenders" but to those with previous convictions, compares a bit more favorably than other sanctions, even though it is still the least effective.
8. For some reason, "first offenders" convicted of burglary have lower reconviction rates than any other type of *probationer* when they receive this disposition.

The interchangeability hypothesis indicates that we do not know whether offenders who desist from criminal activity after a particular type of sentence may also have desisted after most other kinds of sentences. Norval Morris and Gordon Hawkins have concluded that one way to reduce overcrowding in prisons and to deal with the social and economic costs of such institutions without increasing reconviction rates is simply to sentence fewer offenders to prison (see Box 2).

EUROPEAN CORRECTIONAL PERSPECTIVES

Limiting the Use of Prisons in Northern Europe

Eugene Doleschal's comparative review of sentencing practices notes that the rate of incarceration is higher in the United States than in most European countries, with the exception of the Soviet Union. The U.S. rate per 100,000 adults is 131. If the number sentenced to jails and juvenile institutions is included, it might well be over 230 per 100,000 population. Holland has the lowest incarceration rate in the world—18 per 100,000, followed by Denmark, 28; Sweden, 32; and Norway, 37 (estimated) per 100,000 population.[84]

Since the Criminal Law Reform Act of 1969, West Germany has substituted fines or suspended sentences for prison terms under six months in all but exceptional cases. In Austria, the use of fines instead of short prison terms has become the rule since 1970. In Holland, fines are applicable except when the offense is punishable by a prison term of six years or more.

In 1970, the Dutch courts levied one million fines for a revenue of about 45 million guilders. This is about what it would cost to care for 1,250 offenders in prison for a year. In addition to fines, "settlements" are used for property offenses of a minor nature. These fines enable the offender to make an arrangement with the prosecutor, without court intervention, to pay a set amount in settlement of the offense. More than two-thirds of property offenses are dealt with through fines or "settlements" as are half of all morals offenses and traffic violations. A 1970 study of imprisonment for the nonpayment of fines found that sentences were imposed in 0.8 percent of the cases in district courts and 0.5 percent of those in local courts.[85]

In Denmark in 1972, a study group published its report on reducing the reliance on imprisonment. It noted that the number of unsuspended prison sentences had resulted in an increase in the volume of penal sanctions so that by January 1971, Denmark had an incarceration rate of 70 persons per 100,000 population. The study group said that conditional (noninstitutional) sentences could be used to a greater extent, based on the findings of Bengt Borjeson, a Swedish researcher, who concluded that for all risk categories, imprisonment leads to higher recidivism than nonpenal sanctions.[86] The recommendations of this report led not only to a decreasing reliance on prison and an increase in the use of fines and conditional sentences, but also to shorter prison terms in the Danish Penal Law of 1972. As a result, the rate of incarceration dropped to 28 by 1974.

In Sweden, the prison population had dropped considerably below its capacity of 5,100 to 3,700 in 1974, and only about 9 percent were sentenced to

BOX 2

No More Prisons? There Are Alternatives

By COLMAN MCCARTHY

WASHINGTON—Supposedly these were the soft judges. They spoke of their dislike of sending people to prison. They used the word "offender" rather than criminal. They believed punishment and vengeance are separate. They said the courts are isolated from the overcrowding and filth of the nation's prisons and jails.

From this, it would follow that the 30 judges at the recent Conference on Creative Alternatives to Prison were little more than a pack of untamed eastern liberals who sneaked onto the bench when no one was looking and are now intent on stirring a furor. In reality, the judges who came here were from places like Winona, Minn.; Hammond, Ind.; Des Moines, San Antonio, San Diego and other areas where the heartland values of America are said to be secure.

As for being soft, nothing is less true. These judges know the hard truth: Prisons don't work; they produce crime; they destroy the spirits of both the keepers and the kept; they are extravagantly costly; and their operation is often unconstitutional. We have known this for decades, with a sagging shelf of countless studies and commission reports for those who doubt it. The importance of this group of judges meeting in Washington is that for the first time some practical leadership is being offered toward the goal of closing the prisons.

Assuredly, the judges are not calling out for the cellblocks to be emptied instantly. Instead, they tell of modest local successes involving forms of punishment besides incarceration—sentences to community service, requiring thieves to make restitution to their victims, and fashioning sentences to fit the crimes. In most cases, the criminals were first-time and nondangerous offenders.

Within the criminal justice field, alternatives to prison represent a small but growing movement. This particular group of judges is among the enlightened who have seen the results of creative sentencing—low recidivism rates, compensation to victims, benefits to the community and the criminal, and large savings in the penal budget. Whether this philosophy, proven both workable and humane, can spread is an open question. Much of the public angrily believes that the courts already are "coddling" too many criminals. Tougher sentences are needed. Many of the police are boiling, too. They see the courts regularly "turn loose" known criminals. More prisons are needed, not fewer.

Judges at the conference, familiar with these muddled sentiments, know they are bucking the current mood. One trial judge told of punishing a drunk driver convicted of manslaughter by having him volunteer for three years of weekly service in a hospital emergency room, as well as attend Alcoholics Anonymous. "Every minute he was in the emergency room," the judge said, "I wanted him to remember he was responsible for someone else's death."

That was fine, but both the state's attorney and the victim's family protested. The judge recalls that "They were up in arms. They thought the punishment didn't take into account the seriousness of the offense and the life that was destroyed. I tried to explain to the family that I couldn't restore a life, and it is probably a much better memorial that the guy who committed the offense is not going to be driving drunk again."

If the idea of alternative sentencing is going to spread—so that imprisoning people becomes the rare exception, not the standard punishment—the judges at the Washington conference have two obligations: First, stand firm in the rightness of their views and, second, get out among the public to explain the benefits of alternative sentences.

If others can help, it is the national judicial leadership. Unfortunately, Chief Justice Warren Burger has chosen to fritter away his opportunity to speak out forcefully for alternative sentences. Instead, his speeches on prison reform are bland; he grumps about old buildings or bemoans the recidivism rate. Those are the safest issues.

In the absence of daring from on high, judges in the ranks will have to push forward themselves. By meeting in Washington, they are keeping in motion a movement unlikely to be stopped.

Source: The *Boston Globe*, Nov. 17, 1978. © 1978 The Washington Post Writers Group.

terms of over one year. The great majority, 76 percent, were sentenced to terms of less than four months.[87]

Treatment Ideology: Breakthrough and Reevaluation

The treatment ideology made an early breakthrough in European countries several decades ago. This was especially so in the Nordic countries, according to Inkeri Anttila, the former Finnish minister of justice. Treatment was equated with medical treatment, and psychiatrists applied the same classification in determining penal measures and manner of treatment as they used in treating other patients. For a period of years, psychiatrists came into prominence and competed with lawyers as criminal experts.[88] The treatment ideology saw the offender as "sick" or inadequately socialized. In order to provide treatment, specialized institutions for chronic recidivists and psychopathic offenders, which relied upon indeterminate sentences, developed in European prison systems. Since the 1960s, after having been widely accepted, the treatment ideology has come under attack and criticism.[89] (See Box 3 for global perspectives.)

The principal criticisms are similar to those directed against treatment in this country. First, treatment of offenders is different from that usually provided a client, since it is coercive in nature. Second, there is an inherent conflict of interest. The therapist serves the state, not the individual, and treatment often is given without adequate safeguards for the legal rights of the offender. Third, the evidence for the success of such treatment is slight and unreliable. Fourth, treatment ideology is based upon a conception of the offender as abnormal, when in fact, research indicates that offenders are not different, at least not in the way that the treatment model suggests. There is too much crime that goes unpunished, and criminality is too pervasive to accept the idea that it is a basic abnormality. As a result of these criticisms there is a movement, led by lawyers and social scientists in the Nordic countries, to redefine the nature of societal reaction against offenders.[90]

Norman Bishop, a British criminologist who is head of the Research and Development Unit of the Swedish Correctional Administration, has planned and evaluated a number of innovative programs in Swedish prisons. He has said that "no matter what you do it seems that the results—recidivist rates—are about the same."[91] In a recent interview with *Corrections Magazine*, he stated that "the danger of the treatment model to the system is that good programs will be discarded because it cannot be proved that they are effective."[92]

Examples from two Nordic countries illustrate some of the practical results of attempts to curb the excesses that resulted from the treatment ideology. In 1973, Denmark's penal care law was modified to place strict legal restrictions on the use of the indeterminate sentence. Effective in 1973, young offenders would serve definite sentences. Dangerous recidivists, including sex offenders, had for some years received indeterminate penal sanctions.[93] Martinson notes a twenty-year study conducted by Dr. Georg Stuerup, the Danish psychiatrist, who compared the results of chemotherapy and castration on recidivism among sex offenders. Those who had been castrated had a much lower rate of recidivism for sex offenses (3.5 percent)—though amazingly not a rate of zero—than did those who received hormone treatment. As unbelievable as it might seem, castration was seen as voluntary even though the offender traded his loss of manhood for freedom from the prison hospital.[94]

Under the 1973 law, dangerous recidivists could be kept beyond a specified term only if a ruling of the court found the person dangerous to self and others. Danish psychiatrists feel that they have lost some of their authority over their prisoner-patients to the legal authorities. A psychiatrist on the staff of one of the institutions for dangerous recidivists said in 1974, "We have lost a battle (for control) to the lawyers, but the war is not over yet." [95]

In Finland, as the result of reform laws, offenders given suspended sentences or conditional release (parole) will no longer be supervised and given social service help by the same agency. Correctional agencies will be responsible for control measures, and treatment or social service assistance will be provided by regular community agencies. A new type of probation, called "punitive supervision," has been instituted in lieu of six-month prison sentences. Parole supervision is being abandoned to avoid the conflict between control and help. If the released offender desires help, he can get it in the community. The only basis for revoking parole is the commission of a new crime more serious than an offense punishable by a fine.[96] Finland had the highest rate of incarceration of any of the Nordic countries in 1974—101 per 100,000 population. These reforms have already succeeded in reducing the number of dangerous recidivists from twenty-one in 1974 to a mere three by 1976.[97]

The debate over criminal policy in the Nordic countries has also focused on the issues of inmate rights regarding the treatment ideology. Swedish journalist Svante Nycander has written:

> The debate has reflected above all the contradiction between the demand for justice; i.e. fixed, unambiguous rules applied identically to all persons, and the need for individualization from the standpoint of both care and custody. The prisoners and their representatives tend to assign priority to justice rather than treatment, the authorities to treatment rather than justice.[98]

The trend in these European countries is toward justice. (See Box 3 for fuller descriptions.)

THE FUTURE OF CORRECTIONS

Where is corrections heading in this country? Will there be a continuing reliance on enforced treatment and the "coerced cure," perpetuating the myth that prisons rehabilitate? Will we send more offenders to prison in the hope that prisons will protect society from crime and maybe even deter future crime by strict punishment? Should we "destroy the prison root and branch" and

BOX 3

Prisons: A Global Problem

The problems of the prisons are not limited just to the United States. They are universal in scope and afflict almost every nation in the world, especially the industrialized nations. Here are a variety of perspectives on the problems of prisons, as well as brief descriptions of several reforms, from France, Germany, and Spain.

FRANCE — An Obsolescent Philosophy:
Contradictory goals of rehabilitation and revenge

By JACQUES LEYRIE

As one familiar with prisons from the inside, do you believe they should be destroyed?

The prisons of today, yes. The ideal prison, no. What does a hardened criminal have in common with the professor who killed his wife so he could live with his mistress? What would you say if a doctor administered the same medication to all his patients, whether they had the plague or the flu?

If by criminals we mean intelligent people who have antisocial personalities, then prison is the answer. These people are professionals. They never try a job without first weighing the financial and legal consequences. Getting caught is an occupational hazard; getting convicted is part of the game.

There is no possibility of their rehabilitation. When I talk with them they tell me, "Let's not kid around. The only thing I know how to do is burglary. I am here because my technique is not what it should be. My ambition is to improve it." Prison for those criminals is not a punishment, but a quarantine.

What about the other criminals?

Criminals of behavior, unlike criminals for profit, commit crimes of passion, sexual crimes, pathological ones. They constitute the basic problem in prisons, although they represent only about 10 to 12 percent of inmates. Take the child molester. How can we judge his possibilities for rehabilitation? Here, in a tacit way, prison is used as revenge.

The other prisoners tolerate sexual offenders badly. The prison guards say they are "strange." The penal system considers them outsiders, the psychiatric system does not take care of them.

They are the failures of the criminal world. Eight of ten of these criminals get caught — proportionately many more than criminals for profit, and public opinion gives them too much importance. If you journalists wrote according to importance, you would devote eight lines to the criminal for profit as opposed to two for the criminal of behavior. You do the opposite.

Who are the criminals for profit?

There are the "accidental" criminals (something snaps in the balance of an unstable individual), the crafty ones, and the primitives. And today we have ecological crime: the *Amoco Cadiz*, for example. The people responsible for the pollution calculate financially the risk of sanction as opposed to the benefits of breaking the law.

Are crimes of behavior rising?

Contrary to a popular belief, they are decreasing — sexual crimes in particular. On the other hand, crimes of profit are increasing considerably. But in both forms of crime, there is more violence.

What do you recommend for first offenders?

Longer sentences with remission, explaining carefully what that means: "If you slip again. . . ."

Then we still have prison as quarantine and prison as rehabilitation?

With prison as quarantine, you say to an antisocial individual, a professional criminal, "You have gone beyond the group's threshold of tolerance. You are being isolated like a virus. For five years, for ten years, for twenty years."

And afterward?

Life imprisonment would mean a priori that man is incapable of changing. That would appear to me tragic and scientifically wrong. It is more in keeping with both human rights and logic to say, "This time you have five years, or ten years. You know the rules of the game."

But society hasn't the courage to tell the convict that prison is a punishment, that it is a sanction. His sentence is presented to him as a rehabilitation.

You condemn the idea of prison as revenge, but many good people want prison to be revenge.

That is contrary to the evolution of law and of penal science. In ancient times, the group would wreak vengeance. But civilized societies went on to retributive sanction. We drew up a list of infractions and a list of punishments: Then we worked out an equivalence between the two. With modern times, we arrived at theories of "social defense": the sanction varies according to the possibilities for rehabilitation.

Who is in high-security prisons?

Those reputed to be dangerous, or capable of stirring up a revolt within the prison, or likely to organize an escape. The high-security prison has a very small capacity and very tight security. Patrols are far more frequent than in ordinary prisons, and there are systematic cell searches. Visitors must undergo strict checks.

I have been working at Evreux for several years, and even I never enter without the head guard or the warden. During a meeting with a prisoner, we are alone, but we are shut up in a special room. Often the prisoners come to see me in order to see the sky through the window, or part of a tree.

Some of the prisoners are giants in the flower of youth who are being shut between four walls. Every day they tell me, "I am suffocating, I have to ease my nerves in some way." One can say, "It serves them right." But they must be helped to recover their equilibrium.

How do you evaluate the chance of recidivism?

We have a few indications. First, the convict's record. If he repeats his offenses more and more frequently, then he is in a dangerous state. A second important indication is escalation among violent offenders. If a man starts off being tried for assault and battery in slightly doubtful circumstances but gradually commits more serious crimes, we have a certain criminal maturation which is definitely a danger sign. A person who commits a crime of passion and has no previous offenses, will never do it again. The crime of passion—even premeditated murder—involves practically no risk of recidivism.

Don't the accused get maximum or minimum sentences according to your verdict as psychiatrist?

I am not the one who puts them in prison. The system of justice is mistress of its decisions. Clinical criminology is only a technique. No matter how refined it becomes, it will never replace a decision of both a legal, moral, and sociopolitical order. This is basic to individual freedoms.

We always come too late. When we start to care for a family because the father is an alcoholic and hits his kids, because the mother is reputed to be a loose woman, because the children don't go to school, the situation is already marginal.

People ask for help more than you would think. Lots of poor souls realize that they are trapped, that they're going to get into trouble, that they can't make the rent on their tenements, that they are in over their heads financially. But when someone needs help, it is not necessarily from 8 a.m. Monday through Saturday noon. Prevention can be envisaged only as part and parcel of a living environment.

Wouldn't the cost of the prevention you envisage be prohibitive?

It is a budgetary choice. Means for evaluation and assistance do exist. But we wait for a subject to commit a serious act before implementing them.

Source: Paris, *L'Express,* Nov. 18, 1978.

GERMANY — Rehabilitation by Sea

By HERMANN SÜLBERG

There they were, seven men serving prison sentences totaling life plus thirty-four years—thieves, robbers, confidence men, pimps, and even a murderer—all sitting peacefully at a table in a tavery in Kiel-Holtenau, enjoying a meal. When finished they paid in cash.

They had just come ashore after a week-long voyage on the Baltic Sea. As participants in an experiment they had served as crew aboard the Greek schooner *Yachara,* which means "good luck." Now they were headed back to Fuhlsbüttel Prison in Hamburg, which houses 595 hardcore offenders.

The unusual voyage was the idea of prison sociologists Robert Eickmann and Uwe Hagenah and divisional warden Manfred Zimdar. They believed that it might add a new dimension to the familiar prison precept, "We're all in the same boat." Why not have a group of prisoners work on a schooner, performing all duties except those requiring expert nautical skills?

The antagonisms behind bars, they theorized, would be converted to teamwork aboard ship as guards and inmates worked together for a successful trip. Shipboard duties would be related to something useful, as opposed to the busywork in prison. Disagreements would be viewed not as manifestations of prison rivalry but as the ordinary give-and-take of human interaction, and the close quarters would mandate that differences be resolved in a positive way.

For weeks, those selected for the sea voyage practiced tying knots, identifying buoys, and reading the compass. They learned what to do if the ship sprang a leak or caught fire. Improbable as it seems, five of the men thought of providing spending money for two fellow crewmen who had been unable to save anything while in prison.

The first hours aboard the *Yachara* were strained, but as the men plunged into their tasks, they relaxed. They confirmed the trust invested in them by not once straying while on shore—not even to head for a bar. Peter, a confidence man and a prime candidate for escape, according to the authorities, explained his reaction. "It was not just for myself," he said. "I knew if I crapped out all of the others would suffer."

Source: Hamburg, West Germany, *Der Stern,* May 3, 1978 (translated and abridged).

SPAIN—Inmate Participation

Ana María de la Rocha, the first woman director of Yeserías, the women's prison in Madrid, believes that inmates should have a role in running the prison. A moderate feminist, she is forty-two years old, holds degrees in both law and criminology, and during her sixteen years with Spain's corrective institutions has held virtually every kind of job in jails. "To speak of a self-governing prison, though, is premature," she says.

"We work closely with the inmates, but final decisions concerning internal matters are always up to the staff. We do let the prisoners run the cultural and recreational programs by themselves," the director adds.

Yeserías is relatively permissive. Inmates may receive visitors every morning and have the right to unrestricted communication with their families. They can receive food from the outside, and a staff member is available to buy whatever they want—except alcohol, narcotics, or cutting tools. Ana María de la Rocha is aware that any prisoner who wants to smuggle in drugs will manage to do so. "That's a risk we have to accept in our open system," she says.

In effect, Yeserías is a maternity ward, a detention center, a facility for drug addicts and psychiatric patients, and an ordinary prison for women—all in the same building. Ana María de la Rocha believes this causes many problems. "The life of a prisoner who has just given birth is not the same as that of a woman under preventive detention, or of someone mentally ill. It's very difficult to tell a woman who has a baby that she can't watch television as late as the others to allow time for her child."

The abandonment of the old locked cells for a modern system has made necessary a new building with a special entrance to isolate those prisoners who are allowed to leave to work on the outside. "We are ready to expand the program," says Ana María de la Rocha, "once facilities for the open system are ready."

Source: Madrid, *Cambio 16,* Dec. 31, 1978.

"substitute something else" as Tannenbaum advocated over fifty years ago? [99] Or is there a fourth direction that accepts realistically the necessity for prisons, but sets as our task the need to make punishment "just" and "humane"? [100]

An overview of some of the conflict and controversy between treatment supporters and their growing number of critics is offered in the interchange between Ted Palmer of the California Youth Authority and Robert Martinson in recent publications of the National Council on Crime and Delinquency, and also in the response to Donald MacNamara's article "The Medical Model . . . Requiescat in Pace," in *Criminology*.[101] Although treatment may not be a dead issue, we are among those who see it as a facade or disguise for the punitive power of the state. To be sentenced to prison as *punishment* is to be given the status of prisoner. To be further labeled as pathological or "sick" not only compounds the stigma but leaves the offender open to more severe mechanisms of control. We do not conceive of enforced treatment as a nonpunitive penal sanction. The "noble lie" should be exposed as punishment in disguise.

The Abolitionists

As the *Struggle for Justice,* a book reporting the conclusions of the American Friends Service Committee, states:

> If the choice were between prisons as they *now* are and no prisons at all, we would promptly choose the latter. We are convinced that it would be far better to tear down all jails now than to perpetuate the inhumanity and horror being carried on in society's name behind prison walls. Prisons as they exist are more of a burden and disgrace to our society than they are a protection or a solution to the problem of crime.[102]

However, the committee acknowledges that this is not a real choice. It proceeds to critique the treatment model and follows with a recommendation for the virtual elimination of discretion in police arrests, pretrial release, plea bargaining, sentencing, and parole. These advocates of abolition, however, seek alternatives to prisons as they now exist (see Box 2).

There are some who advocate abolition but are skeptical of any possibility of meaningful improvement in the prison system without a total reordering of society. We are among those who hold that a significant transformation of the prison and the criminal justice system can take place without total societal change. We concur with David Rothman who noted that the reform of prisons will not be readily accomplished and that it is not likely to take place by the piecemeal adoption of determinate sentences, the abolition of parole, or the extension of the legal rights of inmates.[103]

The Prison Moratorium Movement. We might begin our transformation by lessening our reliance on the maximum security prison as a means of punishment. Some reformers suggest a moratorium on the construction of any new prisons as a means of achieving this end. William Nagel of the American Foundation Institute on Corrections, one of the leading advocates of this movement, has argued:

> If this country is resolved to do something constructive about the crime problem ... it must call a halt to the building of new prisons, jails, and training schools ... while we plan and develop alternatives. We say this for two reasons. First, so long as we build we will have neither the pressures nor the will to develop more productive answers.... No study that I have ever seen, and there are many, provides any assurance that the prison reduces crime....
>
> And secondly, jails and prisons are so very permanent.... If we were to begin to replace only those ... jails and prisons built more than 50 years ago the price tag would exceed $1.5 billion.... Americans would be saddled with an expensive and counterproductive method of controlling crime. Moreover, additional thousands of offenders would be subjected to new variations of what we euphemistically call correctional treatment, but which is more frequently abject vegetation and sometimes severe brutalization.[104]

The National Council on Crime and Delinquency (NCCD) has lent its influence to the moratorium movement since 1973 through lobbying, public statements, and lawsuits. Another organization with close ties to the NCCD is the National Moratorium on Prison Construction (NMPC), which coordinates regional conferences that seek to involve the participants in action to halt the building of new prisons in their communities. In a recent issue of its newsletter, the NMPC quoted statements from three Watergate offenders that support its perspective on alternatives to prison. Jeb Magruder wrote of the potential benefit of long terms of supervised community service. John Ehrlichman advocated public service for all but the 25 percent of offenders who might be dangerous. Charles Colson expressed the hope that someday soon the nondangerous 80 percent of the prison population will be punished in ways that are "constructive for themselves and others." [105]

The "Realists" or Conservative Neoclassicists

There is also a group who propose more effective and stricter punishment of criminals as a way of reducing crime. These "new conservative criminologists," whose ideas seem to harken back to the pleasure-pain calculus of the early classical school, include Ernst van den Haag, James Q. Wilson, and to the degree that he stresses strict surveillance of certain types of offenders on probation, Robert Martinson.

In his book *Punishing Criminals* (1975), van den Haag argues that a decline in punishment has resulted in a decline of respect for the law. He advocates redressing the balance by returning to swift and certain punishments that vary in degrees of harshness. He proposes fines for minor offenses, short definite terms for more serious offenses, longer indeterminate terms for chronic offenders, and even banishment and the death penalty.[106]

Wilson's *Thinking About Crime* has been widely acclaimed for providing a rationale for a "get tough" policy with criminals, especially street criminals. He admits in the introduction that he does not intend to deal with crime in the executive suites, for most citizens are more concerned with predatory crime.[107] Wilson argues that since most serious crimes are committed by repeaters, much might be gained by simply locking them up and incapacitating them. If such offenders were separated from society, even for short terms in prison, crime rates might be reduced. Swift and certain punishment, he contends, will deter others who might be tempted to commit such offenses. He refers to studies that undercut the myth of treatment and underscore the difficulty of rehabilitating "unwilling subjects under duress." [108]

Martinson's ideas are more reform oriented, since he advocates intensive surveillance of recidivists in the community as an alternative to the use of imprisonment. He suggests that such offenders, whom he calls *restrainees,* would be supervised on a one-to-one basis. He contends that this method would result in a reduction in crime rates. Although Martinson is antiprison, his focus seems to be on controlling predatory street criminals.[109]

Although these "realists" reject the treatment model, their emphasis on incapacitation of the individual offender in order to reduce crime glosses over or ignores the fact that crime is a very complex problem and that justice in the criminal justice system depends on social justice in the larger society. To deal with crime we must also deal with injustices in society. The heavy use of incarceration will not contribute in a significant degree to the reduction of crime. And it certainly will not deal with social injustice.[110] Even though these ideas are inherently repressive in their reliance on an expanded use of the criminal justice apparatus to deal with crime, their stress upon punishment and incapacitation (custody) and the ineffectiveness of treatment may hasten the demise of the "noble lie."

Prison administrators are faced with the task of controlling a growing number of offenders and a rising incidence of prisoner-to-prisoner violence and conflict in the prisons. They must deal with the fact that their guards and other employees are becoming unionized and asserting their own interests. The paramilitary organization of the institution is eroding at the same time that the treatment or rehabilitation philosophy that provided a professional rationale and justification for their penal work is coming under heavy fire. Over the past century, wardens and superintendents have viewed themselves as humanitarian reformers of criminals. They are not likely to accept a punitive prison philosophy.

The Justice Model

The justice model represents a fourth prescription for reordering the goals and functions of corrections. Based on ideas of writers such as David Fogel (1975), Norval Morris (1974), and Andrew von Hirsch (1976), it focuses on the ideas that the prison system as it now exists engenders a sense of injustice rather than justice and that incarceration has been used too widely. Although there is agreement on the need to limit the use of imprisonment, the authors differ in their emphases and approaches to the problem of deincarceration. Their ideas are consistent with Irwin's "interchange model" of the prison. This option acknowledges the existence of social injustice in the larger society, which is reflected in the manner by which offenders are processed into the system—from arrest to sentencing to release.[111]

Morris accepts the punitive goals of prisons—to punish, to deter, to incapacitate—while proposing a "jurisprudential model" which might do away with the "corruptive effects of compulsory rehabilitation" and limit the purposes of the prison and the method of deciding who should be sentenced.[112] Von Hirsch stresses the need to reform both the irrational process by which some offenders end up in prison while others receive lesser sanctions and the haphazard way in which release dates are left to the discretion of parole boards.[113] Both Morris and von Hirsch focus on the "fraudulent link" between participation in prison treatment programs and release from prison.

Fogel, a former commissioner of corrections, also argues for limitations on the discretion that operates in the sentencing and parole process. He advocates that the goals of justice be reached through the consumer perspective. Under this justice model, the penal sanction or sentence would merely represent the deprivation of the offender's liberty. The prison would be responsible for carrying out the sentence, not for rehabilitating the offender. The sentence is simply "one part of the continuum of justice" to be experienced justly, reasonably, and constitutionally. Within the restrictive environment of the prison, the inmate is to be dealt with as a human being. Consequently, he or she may choose programs for his or her own benefit. Those programs that are not chosen by inmates should be discontinued.[114] This assumption of volition and responsibility is directly contrary to the treatment model, which assumes determinism or nonvolition.

Fogel aptly sums up the perspective of the justice model:

Simply stated the prison stay is an enforced deprivation of liberty.... When men are confined against their will... the bottom line of the arrangement of life for both the keeper and kept should be justice as fairness. Opportunities for self-improvement should be offered but not made a condition of freedom.[115]

Under this concept of *justice as fairness*, the prison administrator would seek the development of an organization that would provide a lawful and rational means to structure the relationships between prisoners and staff. It would provide a context of fairness and, it is hoped, a meaningful existence for the shared enterprise of the captives and their keepers during the time of incarceration. Fogel and other writers advocate the phasing out of the fortress prison system. The prison as we know it will survive in the immediate future. This is not to infer that the justice model would be a means of promoting the survival of our "monster" fortress prisons. However, it is intended as an interim strategy during which relations between the "keepers" and "kept" might be more "up-front." In the process, the less dehumanizing, more meaningful alternatives advocated by the abolitionists would be developed more fully.[116]

We return, in conclusion, to the imperative for a "consumer" orientation in corrections. Such a concept involves a concern for the real world of the participants involved in the day-to-day activities of the criminal justice system,

Will new prisons such as this perpetuate the "noble lie"?

although wider concerns of social justice provide the backdrop for its operation. We need to consider the demands and needs of the citizen-taxpayer who seeks accountability and safety for the money being expended, the citizen-victim who seeks restitution and punishment, the offender who has a right to fairness and decency, and to those who staff the system and should be able to believe that they perform worthwhile, productive tasks that have positive benefits for society. But it is difficult to conceive, or concede, that any or all of these needs can be achieved in the setting provided by the fortress prison.[117]

The United States incarcerates offenders at a higher rate than almost any industrialized Western nation—a rate of 230 per 100,000. And with the possible exception of political prisoners in totalitarian states, those in our prisons serve the harshest and longest sentences. In 1974, 98 percent of those in our prisons were serving sentences of one year or more, while by contrast, 91 percent of the inmates in Swedish prisons were serving less than a year. We sentence to prison thieves whose crimes net an average of less than $300. In addition, we expend as much as $26,000 a year per inmate in operation and administrative costs.[118]

In the years since 1973, we have added over 100,000 men and women to our prison population, spent nearly $5 billion a year to maintain our prisons, and plan to spend an estimated $5 billion more for prison expansion—at the same time that other countries have decreased the use of the penal sanction. And confronted with continuing evidence that the widespread use of discretion in sentencing, prison administration, and release on parole amounts to a form of lawlessness in the system, there are scholars and politicians who advocate the use of still tougher sentences as a means of reducing the high rate of street crime.[119]

A recent study of New York's "get tough" laws, which provide mandatory sentences, found that the tough approach did not give the protection it promised. It failed to deter crime and has become a source of dysfunction in the administration of the state's prisons, which are now overcrowded. An empirical study of the effects of mandatory prison sentences by Joan Petersilia and Peter Greenwood (1979) substantiates this conclusion. These researchers conclude that while such mandatory minimum sentences might reduce crime through incapacitation, it is apparent that for even a modest reduction in adult crime to be achieved, a substantial increase in prison populations will be required. For example, analysis indicates that to achieve a 1 percent reduction in crime, prison populations will have to increase by 3 to 10 percent, depending on the target offender population to be sentenced. This conclusion is consistent with other studies that estimate a 5 to 1 ratio for increase of prison population over crime reduction.[120]

Although longer and tougher prison terms are not the solution to the crime problem, it seems that prisons will continue to be used as a sanction for crime for a long time to come. If so, they should be used only as a sanction for those clearly identified as dangerous, career, or repetitive offenders. They do not represent a rational punishment or sanction for the great majority of less serious, nonassaultive offenders who populate our jails and prisons. The minority for whom prisons are a necessary sanction would be provided a humane, safe environment while incapacitated, protected from endemic institutional violence while society is protected from them.

Meaningful, alternative forms of punishment must be developed for the nonassaultive property offenders—for example, day fines, community-based sentences, or less punitive settings.

Sentencing reforms and less dehumanizing prisons and community alternatives may provide short-term improvements in the system, but these kinds of reforms do not confront the problems of social injustice that are related, in a complex manner, to the high rate of street crime. For it is the poor, uneducated, unskilled, and minorities who dominate our prison populations. As von Hirsch notes, "as long as a substantial segment of the population is denied opportunities for a livelihood, any scheme for punishing must be morally flawed." Just desserts are difficult to administer in an unjust society.[121] This does not mean, however, that meaningful reforms in the crucial area of the justice of administering sanctions should be set aside while we strive for long-range goals of social justice.

SUMMARY

The correctional subsystem of the criminal justice system was described with a focus on the various means used by agents of social control to intervene and carry out legal sanctions or punishment imposed upon those convicted and defined as criminals. The corrections system was shown as a continuation of the process by which the individual is made a criminal.

Since prisons are largely invisible institutions for administering sanctions, considerable attention was focused on their development and their historical functions of *retribution, punishment, rehabilitation,* and *incapacitation.*

The prison world was described in terms of the formal organization that carries out the legal sanctions and the conflicts inherent in such institutions. The conflicting goals of rehabilitation and custody placed on this organizational structure have resulted in the emergence of informal organizations by which prisoners and staff relate, often in mutual hostility. The custodial staff are unable to control those incarcerated in our large fortress prisons without the manipulation of the inmates and their exploitation by certain privileged inmate types.

The idea, shared by the public as well as by social scientists, that prisons are indigenous societies, separated and insulated from the larger society, was shown to be false. Rather, there exists an "interchange" between those who reside in prison and the ongoing changes and conflicts in the larger society. Not only are prisons created by societal forces, but the prison experience of the offenders is influenced by their previous careers.

We noted the lack of empirical evidence for the effectiveness of rehabilitative programs in prisons. Treatment programs are contrary to the custodial emphasis of prisons, and treatment goals often are given low priority. Moreover, the prison is not effective as a treatment setting because of its coercive nature. Rehabilitation in prisons should be seen as the "noble lie" that it is. We must acknowledge the punitive goals such as retribution, incapacitation, and deterrence and not rely upon sentencing offenders to indeterminate sentences until "cured." Since prisons are ineffective in reducing recidivism, or rearrest rates, we should seek the least restrictive punishment.

Thus, the large fortress prison system is outmoded and unnecessary. Further, such prisons serve to inculcate a "sense of injustice." Reforming the prison might be effective if we can take a systemwide perspective and develop a means of punishment based upon the *just* administration of *justice* throughout the entire process—from sentencing procedures to the operation of prisons in a *lawful* and *just* manner, to rational release procedures. In the long range, however, this can only be achieved in a society in which social injustice is viewed as intolerable and amenable to change.

ADDITIONAL READINGS

Bagdikian, Ben H. *Caged: Eight Prisoners and Their Keepers.* New York: Harper & Row, 1976.

> This is the dramatic, journalistic description of the longest and most peaceful prison strike in the history of the Federal Bureau of Prisons. In this story of the eight leaders—elected by the inmates who were condemned to solitary—it becomes apparent that the federal prisons are not the model they often are held up to be.

Blom-Cooper, Louis. *Progress in Penal Reform.* Oxford: Clarendon Press, 1974.

> From this collection of papers by nineteen criminologists, only one of whom is an American, we can gain cross-national insights into why and how the treatment model has failed and how the recognition of its failure is stimulating new alternatives for incarceration in Northern European countries.

Fogel, David. *We Are the Living Proof: The Justice Model for Corrections.* Cincinnati: W. H. Anderson Company, 1975.

> Writing from the background of a practitioner, academician, and policy planner, the author provides a cogent analysis of imprisonment and a thoughtful alternative to the dilemma of treatment or punishment.

Ignatieff, Michael. *A Just Measure of Pain: The Penitentiary in the Industrial Revolution.* New York: Pantheon, 1979.

> This is a comprehensive look at the origins of incarceration and the variety of ideas and interests that combined to create the penitentiary. Ignatieff's book is the first systematic account of the development of the English prison, which greatly influenced our own prison development. The book examines the development of the prison in light of its social, economic, and political contexts.

Keve, Paul W. *Prison Life and Human Worth.* Minneapolis: University of Minnesota Press, 1974.

> The author gives a balanced picture of prison problems and prompts an understanding of what happens to both inmates and staff in the process of confinement. He describes problems of management, communication, and training and shows why stress and disturbances are a part of the massive fortress prison.

Morris, Norval. *The Future of Imprisonment.* Chicago: The University of Chicago Press, 1974.

> Morris offers a model of imprisonment to replace the present archaic model, which he contends was inadequate from its inception. He would retain what is valuable in the "treatment model" while eliminating the corrupting aspects of enforced treatment.

von Hirsch, Andrew. *Doing Justice: The Choice of Punishments.* Report of the Committee for the Study of Incarceration. New York: Hill and Wang, 1976.

> This report of a four-year study by the committee attacks the underlying assumptions of rehabilitation and the prediction of dangerousness as a basis of sentencing. Von Hirsch argues that sanctions imposed have very little to do with the severity of criminal behavior, due to the wide use of the indeterminate sentence for various type offenses, while parole boards make judgments about release date based upon assumed prediction of dangerousness.

LAW ENFORCEMENT ASSISTANCE ADMINISTRATION
L E A A
U.S. DEPARTMENT OF JUSTICE

> Justice is the first virtue of social institutions, as truth is of systems of thought. A theory, however elegant and economical, must be rejected or revised, if it is untrue; likewise, laws and institutions, no matter how efficient and well arranged, must be reformed or abolished, if they are unjust.
> —John Rawls, A Theory of Justice (1971)

PUBLIC POLICY: CRIME AND SOCIAL PRIORITIES

What to do? Crime pervades the society. It grows. It disrupts. It instills fear and drains resources. In recent years, money and manpower have been generated to try and curb the rise in crime, but neither seems to have brought results. Almost $5 billion in new federal funds were trickled into the system through the Law Enforcement Assistance Administration (LEAA), only to be absorbed effortlessly into the existing law enforcement establishment without producing an impact on the problems they were meant to solve. Local police authorities lobby for more personnel and still watch crime rates climb.

It is not clear what set of reforms would best set the society on a course toward less crime, but the failures of the current system must be recognized. There is a double standard of justice for rich and poor. Criminals from the lower classes are stigmatized, and many, often from the same lower strata, are victimized. And there is increasing evidence that prisons as they exist serve a rehabilitative function for no more than a small proportion of those incarcerated. For it cannot be said that those who do not get rearrested or sentenced have changed, or if they have that their behavior is the result of anything that was done for them by way of a given "treatment" program.

Only when these realities are accepted will society, through its political structure, be able to move from ineffective controls to an enlightened coping with crime and its causes.

PERSPECTIVES ON CRIME CONTROL

It has been well over a decade since the Crime Commission published its report, *The Challenge of Crime in a Free Society* (1967). This volume was issued against the background of President Lyndon Johnson's message to Congress on February 6, 1967, in which he declared a "war on crime" in the United States and proposed the enactment of the Safe Streets and Crime Control Act. Congress responded by passing the Omnibus Crime Control and Safe Streets Act in 1968. The bill was the lawmakers' response to an apparently alarming increase in crime, particularly violent street crime. Specifically, it created the Law Enforcement Assistance Administration, which, as one writer notes, was the Congress's way of saying in an election year, "support your local police." [1] It should not be surprising that almost immediately, the LEAA became a pork-barrel operation for the police and other criminal justice agencies.

The disbursement of federal funds—$60 million in the initial year, 1968—stimulated a period of unprecedented growth in expenditures for personnel and expansion of criminal justice programs and technology. In the decade 1966 to 1975, the rate of increased expenditures for criminal justice at all levels—federal, state, and local—was about five times that of the previous decade. Between 1971 and 1975, such expenditures increased from $11 billion a year to $17 billion, or about 58 percent. By 1977, outlays for criminal justice were about $22.7 billion, an increase of 34 percent over 1975.[2] Moreover, the number of criminal justice employees spiraled upward by 22 percent, from 802,000 in 1971 to 1,051,000 in 1975.[3] Under the stimulus of LEAA spending, the idea of a criminal justice system described in the Crime Commission's report became more of a reality.

The history of the LEAA constituted an ironic exception to the axiom of Nixon Administration policymakers, who never tired of criticizing President Johnson's ill-fated war on poverty with the dictum: "You can't solve social problems just by throwing money at them." [4] The war on crime promised a total solution, but the crime policymakers focused on what was normal, or traditional, street crime. Neglected somehow was crime in the executive suites, organized crime, and political corruption. Public concern with violent crime—an historical concern—grew, even as the LEAA's interest in violent crime was made manifest.[5] It may even be that the expansion of the institutional apparatus to deal with crime is related to the growth of public concern about crime. For as policymakers (politicians) talked about solutions, crime rates rose and then stabilized. Today, while most of the optimism about controlling crime has dissipated, a sober public concern remains.[6]

Any public policy regarding crime certainly must come to grips with both subjective and objective aspects of the problem. Criminology can be useful in providing a means for viewing crime in its broad social context. This means that we must move beyond the study of crime qua crime. The problem of crime cannot be understood merely as objective, statistical data—as nonpolitical, amoral events. As we have noted often, crime and criminal behavior represent diverse and wide-ranging phenomena—not only the breaking of laws, but the making of laws and societal reaction to lawbreaking.[7] Such a broader view should provide society with a way of coping with crime that transcends any narrow perspective, whether interactionist, positivistic, conflict, or radical. We must expand our analysis to focus on the interaction between *crime* and *social structure.* This means moving beyond attempts at ascertaining the exact amount of "hidden crime" to seeing not only crime, but our reaction to it, as indicators of the kind of society we are and are becoming. In the process, we should focus on discrepancies between the reality and ideals of society and explore the kinds of policy changes needed to move toward the basic human values inherent in the ideals of our society, including the concept of social equality.

Viewing crime as a means of understanding a society's shortcomings is another way of suggesting that crime need not be seen in an entirely negative light. Criminologists and sociologists often refer to Emile Durkheim's argument that crime is "bound up with the fundamental conditions of all social life" and is thus useful, since "these conditions of which it is a part are themselves indispensable to the normal evolution of morality and law." Crime, he argues, has indirect and direct usefulness in the role it plays in the evolution of morality and should not be cast as an evil to "be too much suppressed." [8]

Crime and crime control might be seen in a broader social context by noting some of the Marxist, and non-Marxist, critiques of the positive aspects of crime control efforts for our kind of society. Marx discussed crime only briefly. And although he did not hold it to be either inevitable or normal, he indicated rather ironically that it might be viewed as positive and productive in a modern capitalist society in which criminals produce legitimate work opportunities and professional occupations. As Marx stated:

> The criminal produces the whole apparatus of the police and criminal justice, detectives, judges, executioners, juries, etc., and all these different professions which constitute so many categories of the social division of labor, develop diverse abilities of the human spirit, create new needs and new ways of satisfying them.[9]

One does not have to accept Marxist theory to note the obvious impact of the economic effects of crime in our society. We have noted in Chapter 3 that the Joint Economic Committee of the United States Congress estimated its economic effect at about $125 billion for 1976. However, the Joint Committee's data referred to the negative economic effects of crime. Yet it could be argued that even these figures indicate positive economic benefits, for much of this money is kept in circulation through the transfer of funds in traditional, organized, and white-collar criminal activities. However, a considerable amount is expended for federal and state criminal justice activities.[10] Indeed, as one non-Marxist criminologist noted recently, "Criminal justice is a major American growth industry. It supports millions of people, directly or indirectly, and constitutes much public and private wealth." [11] He might have added that the phenomenon of crime also provides income to criminologists who lecture and write criminology texts.

In addition to providing income for insurance bonding companies and jobs for the controllers—lawyers, prison guards, judges, social workers, criminologists, and other professionals and paraprofessionals—over 300,000 individuals are removed from the labor force each year. These prisoners provide a source of cheap labor, for they produce goods and maintain institutions. They are also a captive pool of subjects for scientific research and volunteer efforts, as well as a safety valve for racial tensions, since a disproportionate number of minority group members are incarcerated.[12]

The classical radical analysis suggests that in these respects, crime contributes to the capitalist system. This same analysis also sees crime as a result of contradictions within the capitalist system.[13] Now it should be obvious that similar contradictions exist in noncapitalist systems since conflicts due to oppressive, authoritarian, and bureaucratically organized states can be readily identified in all modern societies. However, the major focus in this chapter seeks to answer, What kind of a crime policy should we seek in order to make our ideals of equality and the optimum development of human potential and participation square with social realities? Some of those less intent on radical analysis—the "liberal cynics"—view the system simply as "messed up." And some of the new conservatives—the "new realists"—fault both criminology and the criminal justice system for not providing policies and programs for the effective prevention, enforcement, and punishment of crime and criminals.[14]

We need a thoughtful, rational policy to deal with crime. If we begin by narrowly focusing only on reducing the amount of crime, we will end up using our knowledge and power to deal with crime in a limited manner. But we must confront the problem of crime boldly if we are to survive as a society. Criminology must move beyond such narrow concerns to apply criminological research to human problems and confront the basic issue of social justice. This perspective involves "value consciousness," an awareness of political and moral choices. This awareness implies not only a consideration of public attitudes and values, but also a consciousness of consequences and alternatives. In short, it means we must search for genuinely new action alternatives rather than serving as faceless technicians for a system of injustice.[15]

Crime Policy Reform

Public policy concerning crime must be made with the awareness that we are moving into political arenas in which possibilities for reordering social arrangements in society to achieve social justice are constrained and may result in unforeseen consequences.

To argue that reforms in the criminal justice system rest upon critical analysis and intermediate and long-range reforms of the basic social arrangements of society opens us up to criticism from conservatives who would opt to make the system more effective through better management and more sophisticated technology. In the process it would also make the system potentially more repressive. Radical critical criminologists would argue that the only real solution is to be found in a political struggle against the capitalist system. Our assumption is that the criminal justice system exists within the framework of the larger society. We concede that many of its problems grow out of contradictions in the social structure of society, contradictions that lead to inequalities in power, participation, and distribution of opportunity, services, and wealth, even as equality is claimed as a basic value.

The word "reform" as applied to social injustice has come to mean a program of palliatives and "patchwork tinkering," rather than a set of economic, political, and social reforms that attempts to redistribute power and resources more equitably, so that people may become involved in decisions that affect their lives and work in a more meaningful, democratic manner. We do not know, nor are we brash enough to attempt to spell out, the exact nature of the reforms needed to achieve the kind of society that can cope with the reality of the crime problem. We lack adequate knowledge of how the powerful maintain control of the mass media and public agencies of social control and thus shape policies concerning crime. It is also difficult, given the present state of our knowledge, to know how the power to participate in day-to-day decisions might be returned to the victims of social injustice.[16] But we do not believe that it is necessary to accept the radical approach—that the criminal justice system as we know it can be changed only by creating a new socialist society—in order to acknowledge that the kind of crime that has caused so much concern is linked in a complex manner to human deprivation. Understanding that crime is related to social justice means we must turn our attention to the political arena, where decisions about the kind of society we are to live in are made. Unquestionably, structural changes in society that would eradicate racism, sexism, and poverty would require a more fully developed perspective and critique than we have provided.

In his study of *The Politics of Abolition* (1974), Thomas Mathiesen, the Norwegian criminologist, maintains that "any attempt to change the existing order of things into an alternative that is 'completely finished' or 'fully formed' is destined to fail, for a completely finished alternative is apt to return us to the contradictions of the present system." [17]

"Simple justice" is our goal, but it is a starting place, not an end. Still, a beginning that focuses on the need for reform in the direction of moving the larger system—as well as the criminal justice system—toward the fulfillment of society's basic goals of justice and equality must of necessity contradict the present reliance on repressive measures that emphasize "law and order." Our immediate interest is reform—short-range steps leading toward the equalization of opportunity. But long-range reforms must involve citizens in creating a commitment to an ongoing process of change that seeks to eliminate basic structural defects in our social system and its institutions.

DILEMMAS OF CRIME CONTROL EFFORTS

Looking back over the efforts of the past decade or so, the future of crime control seems dismal at best. During this period, we have come to question some time-honored solutions to the crime problem. Any observer of the police over the years since 1965 would tend to be skeptical of claims that the number of law enforcement personnel has much to do with curbing the crime rate. During the decade from 1965 to 1975, the number of police nearly doubled, while the crime rate, as reported by the *Uniform Crime Reports,* increased by about 116 percent, or over 10 percent a year. It may be that the law-and-order mood of Americans during that period did more to stimulate the expansion of our criminal justice organizations than to influence an adequate crime control policy.

The UCR reported over 11.2 million index offenses known to the police in 1975, with a clearance rate of 21 percent representing those identified and charged. Yet the Census Bureau announced in 1976 that its victimization surveys had uncovered nearly four times as much crime as was reported in the UCR in 1974. Assuming that this ratio of unreported crime was relatively constant, it can be estimated that the police arrested or identified only about 5 percent of those involved in the seven index offenses in 1975. Still, criminal justice officials and their supporters call for more police. Edward Davis, former chief of the Los Angeles Police Department, for example, was reported by the *Los Angeles Times* in June 1976, to have requested additional police officers for that city on the basis that the present size of the force had allowed a "resurgence of the rate of crime." [18]

An analysis of the impact of police activity during the previous decade would lead one to regard Chief Davis's request with skepticism. We can readily find evidence that would make us dubious about the positive effect of police activity on the crime rate. Since the Omnibus Crime Control and Safe Streets Act was passed and signed into law in 1968, we have had ample opportunity to observe the ineffective attempt to establish a crime control policy on the national level. As Richard Harris has documented, the Omnibus Crime Control Act was a political reaction to the public fear of crime, rather than a reform. Public fear was generated by backlash and reaction over uprisings in our urban ghettos and by selective reaction to decisions of the Supreme Court, such as *Mallory* and *Miranda,* which some vocal critics felt had placed curbs on the power of police to deal with crime in the streets.[19]

In *Mallory* v. *Hogan* in 1964, the High Court had declared that the right to remain silent rather than incriminate oneself, as guaranteed in the Fifth Amendment, was also binding on state authorities. Two years later in *Miranda* v. *Arizona,* it ruled that this privilege against self-incrimination extended to interrogations by local as well as federal law enforcement officials.

The Crime Control Act sought to reverse the effects of these decisions regarding the way offenders were handled in the federal courts. *Mallory* was reversed by allowing for delay between arrest and charge, and *Miranda* was modified by allowing for "voluntary" confessions in federal courts.

The act also established the LEAA, an agency that became the most heavily funded branch of the Justice Department in the early 1970s, funneling over $5 billion of federal funds into local and state criminal justice programs between 1969 and 1976. The LEAA has been a mixed blessing. It has been criticized—justifiably in our view—for overemphasizing the police. It provided funds for sophisticated hardware and modern technology, such as computerized information systems, at the expense of other agencies. For this reason, and perhaps because of its name, it came to be seen by the press and the public as intended primarily to assist law enforcement. But it also provided a total of $234.7 million to enable law enforcement, court, probation, parole, and corrections personnel to continue their education in colleges and universities through its Law Enforcement Education Program. Under this program, more than 300,000 law enforcement personnel have gone back to college, many obtaining AA or BA degrees. By 1977, the number of baccalaureate degree programs in Criminal Justice had increased nearly tenfold since the establishment of the LEAA.[20]

Criticism of the LEAA has come from persons with widely varying political beliefs. Newspaper columnist Jack Anderson has denounced it. California Governor Jerry Brown labeled one LEAA administrative structure a "Byzantine pretzel palace" and cut back the staff of the State Planning Agency from two hundred to forty. The Texas Department of Corrections opted out of the program because of criticism of its personnel practices.[21] In a report to the Center for National Security Studies in Washington, Sarah Carey called it a "joke" and recommended that it be abolished altogether.[22] And in a sharp critique of LEAA's impact, Richard Quinney has stated that it has resulted in an unprecedentedly coordinated system for repression in an advanced capitalist society. For the first time in our history, he states, all levels of the state and its various legal agencies are linked into a national system of criminal justice. In the name of "criminal justice, the national government is providing a comprehensive, coordinated system of crime control."[23]

We will not quibble over the meaning of the word repression, for without a doubt there is considerable potential for repression in a great many aspects of a bureaucratically organized society such as our own. Given the fact that much of the LEAA's expenditures have gone for hardware, it might be argued that the police do have the technology to annihilate criminals as well as those perceived as threats to the social order. In the 1960s and early 1970s, two presidential administrations launched campaigns against militant blacks and Indians as well as war resisters.[24] And by now, the involvement of the FBI and CIA in domestic spying and illegal surveillance is well documented in the news media and reports of congressional hearings. Certainly, these activities underscore the need for legal control over heavy-handed misuse of power by federal and local law enforcement agencies in our society. They should keep us alert to the modern corporate state's tendencies for repression. The existence of such a potential suggests the need for a countervailing legal means to protect the powerless against exploitation by the powerful. It is also an argument for an alternative decentralized legal system better geared to the complexities of modern society.[25]

It has been noted that LEAA efforts have resulted in making the concept of a criminal justice system more of a reality. One means of promoting this end has been the requirement that each state form State Planning Agencies

(SPAs) to administer the LEAA's block grants to state and local agencies. These SPAs have both the structure and the potential to become strong lobbying groups, both at the state and federal levels, as well as having a direct influence over local agencies to whom they disburse monies. The latter power has resulted in more planning and coordination between and within local agencies, but the political impact of the SPAs on criminal justice policies, which would seem to be considerable, has yet to be assessed.[26]

Since its inception, LEAA has funded many programs other than police "cop-shops" — a term sometimes used to refer to the emphasis on expensive technological innovations rather than on providing needed services and solving difficult social problems relevant to law enforcement. These changes include just about every conceivable type of program related to law enforcement, ranging from providing a few thousand dollars to get volunteers involved in a community's local probation program, to multimillion-dollar projects to redesign an entire state corrections system, as in Hawaii and Oklahoma.

Many community corrections programs, diversion programs, and drug-counseling programs owe their existence to the LEAA. In addition to funding training programs, it has also financed prison reform organizations. In addition, it has provided employment for numerous professional consultants, since many individuals and consulting firms have been the recipients of LEAA grants.[27]

Without LEAA, the Pretrial Services Agency in New York City might not have come into existence, since it has received over $5 million in federal funds. And thousands of New York City residents would not have been able to avail themselves of a free bus ride to visit their relatives in remote upstate prisons — LEAA provided over half a million dollars for this project. The closing of juvenile training schools and their replacement by contracting to nonprofit community programs in Massachusetts was helped by over $6 million in LEAA funds.

Indeed, the public in the various states, counties, and municipalities that receive LEAA monies seldom is aware that this agency's federal funds are included in the budgets of state and local operations. Yet if LEAA had not existed, between 1969 and 1975 New York State might have spent $109.7 million less on its correctional system; California $91 million less; Alabama $17 million less; Colorado $19.5 million less; and Massachusetts $34.7 million less.[28]

Granted, this money has been pumped into programs intended to extend control in the name of "treatment," programs that have not proved effective in the past. Whether or not our correctional programs are more effective is open to question. More alternative community diversion programs exist, even as our prison population has reached a new high and as the population on death row has increased.

On the other hand, the impact of LEAA has been minimal in special target crime-prevention projects. In 1972, LEAA provided $160 million for eight target cities with the intention of reducing serious crime by 20 percent over a five-year period. Six of the cities experienced considerable *increase* in crime rates, at least as reported by the UCR, and two of the target cities showed little significant change.

If we look to the Justice Department's victimization surveys for these cities, generally considered more valid than the UCR data, there was no significant change for crimes of violence in 1973 to 1974 and only a slight increase for property crimes. These were the very years when federal spending was supposed to have had its greatest impact.[29] Congress responded to the critics of LEAA by cutting its budget for fiscal 1977 from the $810 million of the previous year to $753 million. Evidently, Congress, as well as the general public, had taken notice of the official statistics indicating that "serious" index offenses had not decreased while crime control agencies were being funded at a high level.[30]

LEAA funds have been welcomed by local contending, social control agencies such as the police, courts, and corrections. Although the grants were intended to stimulate the development of innovative programming, these agencies frequently have been more imaginative in creating innovative names for old programs and have used funds to augment services already in operation. In New York State, for example, LEAA funds of $1.5 million were used to bolster medical services for inmates in the state prisons. This use of funding is quite removed from a policy that conceivably could be related to the reduction of crime. A total of fifty-five State Planning Agencies were established to devise plans by which the block grants to the fifty states, the District of Columbia, Virgin Islands, Guam, Puerto Rico, and American Samoa would be used on the local level. But the various programs are not highly coordinated within, let alone among, these jurisdictions.[31] Perhaps in addition to providing employment for numerous middle-class college-educated types, the LEAA programs have also provided evidence that more money and personnel alone do not make for an adequate crime control policy.

JUSTICE IN THE MACRO SOCIETY

Criminological data should sensitize us to the fact that the crime problem is rooted deep within the social structure and processes of society. As we become aware of the *interaction between crime and the social structure,* we become increasingly skeptical of the simplistic perspectives that tend to influence social crime policy. It might seem that we are assuming that social processes and structures determine behavior. This is not the case. Rather, we support a voluntaristic model of behavior, in which the individual's actions are the result of intentionality and choice. The individual finds meaning, makes choices, and acts within a social situation shaped by various social forces.

Since crime is linked to the social structure, we might conceive of two broad alternative strategies of prevention. The first might be based on traditional theories that assume that street crime—the "garden variety" that

Is street crime caused by wretched poverty?

evokes so much fear and concern—is linked to wretched poverty, which reduces the human potential of those in the lower classes. Based on this assumption, reform efforts would try to equalize social opportunities by changing the reward system of society to promote a greater degree of conformity among the lower-status segments of society. The second strategy assumes that since crime derives from the basic values of society, if we are serious about wanting to eliminate or reduce it, we must reform those values and alter the social system. Since we simply do not know what transformations are needed to achieve either of these objectives, nor can we calculate what costs might be involved, the answer may lie, as Nils Christie has suggested, not in creating a new social order but in finding ways to reshape our institutions so they might be controlled by ordinary humans, including those who are powerless victims of social injustice.[32]

This solution implies that criminologists will have to evaluate critically the relationship between their field of study and proposed policies directed toward creating a more just society. In this respect, we must reject one of the contentions of James Q. Wilson's popular book, *Thinking About Crime* (1975). Although Wilson has pointed to a crucial tension between academic criminology and policy analysis, his solution is to ignore, or more pointedly, reject, the search for cause; for he argues that "policy analysis asks not what is the cause of the problem, but what is the condition we want to create."[33]

This narrow realism creates a false dilemma between the study of crime as an integral aspect of the social structure and efforts to deal with the phenomenon of crime. This position is contrary to sound logic. For if we are to make decisions or recommend policy, it is imperative that we go beyond asking what are the conditions we want to bring into being? A more basic question is what are the conditions we are seeking to ameliorate? To overlook this question is to set forth a faulty proposition, or premise. Rather, we ask, if these conditions prevail and are found related to crime, what then can be done to achieve the kind of society that the people who live in it desire?

In his penchant for cost-benefit analysis, Wilson proposes a criminal justice system that would be more effective through increasing the cost to those who commit crime. Although justifiably critical of any simple cause-effect relation between poverty, he concedes that the "benefits of work" must also be increased simultaneously. However, he argues that efforts to reduce unemployment (among the young) will not be effective as long as the criminal justice system is ineffective.[34] This view has been perceived as "hard-nosed liberalism," a "new realism," and by some as a "new conservatism." It certainly is a popular view, for Wilson's book is one of the most widely distributed and quoted books dealing with crime policy.

Rather than delve further into a critique of Wilson's book—conservatives, liberals, and radicals have all had a go at that—we will discuss the need to work for social justice as a concomitant of an effective criminal justice system. It is not an either-or situation. To advocate an effective criminal justice system in which swift, certain, and just punishments are meted out is to ignore the fact that social justice can render the laws unjust in a variety of ways.[35] We have noted earlier in this book that radical criminologists contend that we can consider adequate solutions to the crime problem only as we free our society of the contradictions of capitalism and its repressive control directed at protecting the existing order.[36] We have taken exception to the radical claim that any gains in the struggle for justice must await a reordering of society. However, we share some of the assumptions and assessments of the radicals and others, such as Ronald Chester's recent review of evidence, in which he concludes that much property crime represents rational responses to the perceptions of relative deprivation on the part of members of the lower classes. If we are to deal with the crime problem, we must open up the channels of upward mobility by reallocating wealth and power. This equalization should be accompanied by a greater adherence to the "supposed norms" of the middle class by all members of society, including the advantaged.[37]

Crime Control Policy for the Future

A framework for a future crime control policy should be based on the recognition of the *consumer perspective,* rather than on utopian schemes. The interests and needs of three groups should receive special attention in such a policy. As suggested by Paul Tappan, these are (1) *the taxpayer,* who pays the bills; (2) *the real or potential victim,* who bears the direct costs; and (3) *the offender or alleged offender,* who may be convicted and punished with a greater or lesser degree of justice.[38] This policy would presuppose what Scandinavian criminologists have come to term "value-conscious" criminology. The values of these various "consumer" groups must be anticipated in the policy development process, as must the values of the criminologist. Value-consciousness has little meaning if it does not involve flexibility and self-awareness. For instance, Wilson acknowledges the impact of one's values when he refers to the manner in which opinions influence policy recommendations by criminologists. The answers one might expect to requests for advice, he notes, will be colored by political values. Conservatives will say "nothing is possible," while liberals will argue that "everything is possible."[39] Since we are attempting to suggest alternatives, the several proposals offered below do not fit either of these viewpoints. It might be well here to clarify and make explicit an implicit requisite of the consumer orientation. It is that this orientation requires a move toward greater participation in decision-making by an informed and critical-thinking public—the powerless as well as the powerful—admittedly an elusive goal in any bureaucratically organized society.

Some of the ideals and goals basic to an effective consumer-oriented crime control policy would include the following:

1. *A social order that will promote law-abiding behavior throughout all strata of society and still protect individual rights and diversity.* There is considerable evidence of discrepancies between the standards set by the "rulemakers" of the dominant classes of society and the standards that they actually practice. This discrepancy has been made glaringly apparent by Watergate, "Koreagate," and other scandals.

Former President Nixon and many members of his administration, including his attorney general, were vociferous public advocates of law and order. At the same time, they were deeply involved in the cover-up of the Watergate caper as well as in illegal activities of the FBI and CIA. The double standard was evident in the manner in which the Watergate offenders were sentenced and treated after sentencing. Former Attorney General John Mitchell, for instance, received a six-month medical furlough from federal prison, returning shortly before his scheduled release. How many inmates of our federal prisons from among the lower social strata have been afforded comparable care?

The concern with violent, predatory street crime, for which the estimated cost was about $4 billion in 1976, far outweighs our concern with white-collar crimes such as embezzlement, consumer fraud, and bribery, which cost about $44 billion in 1976. Since the criminal law assumes the operation of *retributive justice,* which redefines a wrong done to an individual as a wrong to society, fraud and corruption in business and high places might in the future be more seriously regarded as crimes against society. It would seem reasonable that in applying a uniform standard to all criminal behavior, the relative number of those sentenced for traditional "street" crimes might decrease, while the proportion of persons defined as criminal for "executive suite" crimes—pollution offenses, misuse of public office, tax and business fraud, and endangerment of public welfare—would increase.

2. *Laws defining criminal behavior must be based upon strict rules consistent with a fair distribution of justice.* Our first priority should be the elimination of discrimination against the socially powerless segments of society—minority groups, the poor, females, and the young—who might suffer as a result of arbitrary decision making.

Efforts to control the social costs of crime should have as a goal the just distribution of such costs. We recognize that crime policy is, as Inkeri Anttila notes, essentially political in nature. There is a complex set of factors working against the poor and powerless, ranging from the drafting of penal sanctions, selective surveillance, detection, and investigation practices, on through trial, execution of sentence, and control of ex-offenders.[40]

The effect of institutionalized racism is reflected in William Nagel's study, "On Behalf of a Moratorium on Prison Construction" (1977), which found that race strongly affects rates of imprisonment. For each 10 percent increment in black population, the states confine 37.6 more prisoners per 100,000 population, although this correlation is not reflected in crime rates. This statistic suggests that in a state with the racial composition of Georgia, for example, the existence of racist patterns in the various steps of the selective enforcement process might account for as many as 4,400 prisoners—or a number large enough to fill five prisons.[41]

3. *A law-abiding career must be seen as a viable alternative to a career in crime.* This obvious fact seems to have been ignored by social planners. Full employment, which many see as inflationary, might be less expensive to society than increasing crime and repressive crime policy. As Wilson suggests, to increase the cost (penalties) of crime without improving the benefits of work is to assume young people are irrational.[42]

However, jobs alone are not sufficient. We need to distinguish between jobs and careers. The failure to do so is a factor in both the ineffectiveness of most prisons and in the alternative to prison, vocational training. Even with our highly automated productive work force, there are still many menial jobs that might seem rewarding to outsiders but may be considered a drag to those locked into them. *Careers* involve choice, as well as rewards or gratifications such as meaning, competence, belonging, security, and future expectations. Jobs are more likely to be transitory and do not ordinarily inspire commitment.[43] Admittedly, it is utopian to talk about full employment in times of "stagflation" and recession. Yet to the extent that the ability to choose jobs and legitimate careers becomes a reality to more persons, including the young and the powerless, crime might be reduced. In times of excessive unemployment, differences between social strata are sharpened, and those on the bottom often take out their bitterness against one another as their aggression is turned inward. For instance, Marvin Ross found that unemployment was the

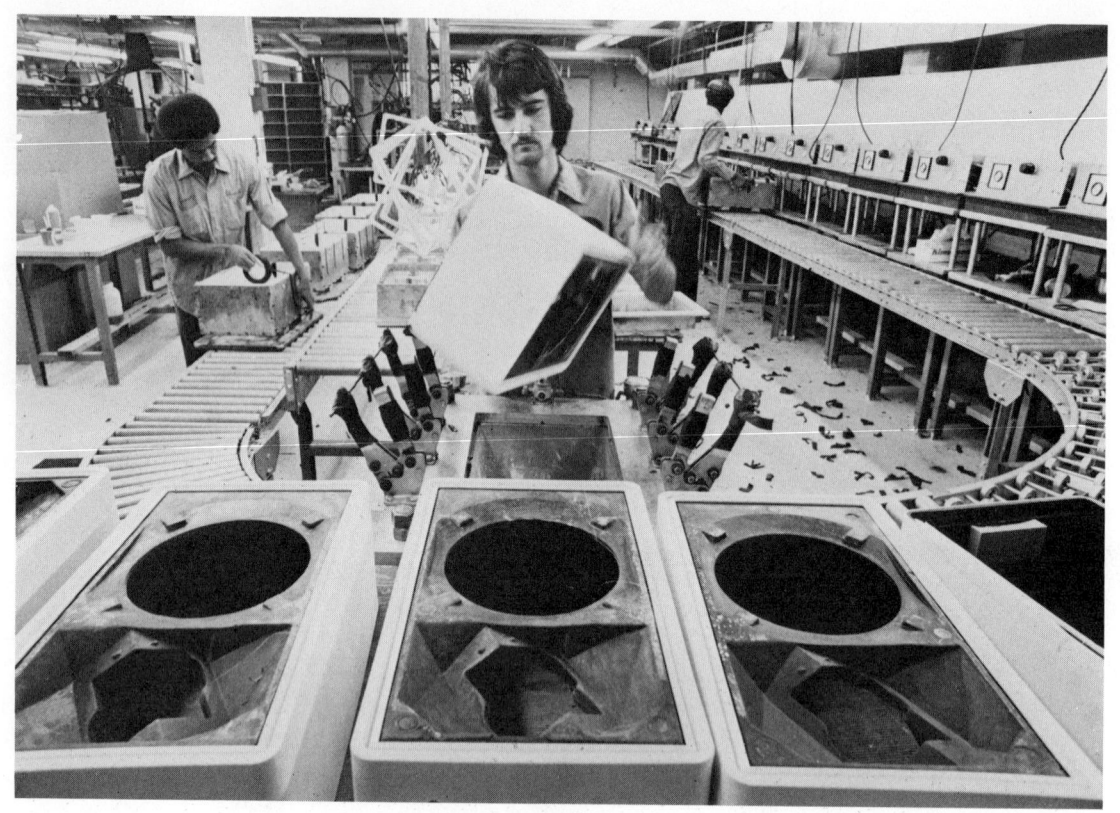

Is this a job or a meaningful career?

most important variable correlated with crimes of violence in Toronto. It accounted for 63 percent of the variance in violent crime rates between areas of the city.[44] Using statistical analysis, Nagel predicted that each 1 percent increase in unemployment would result in 266.4 more crimes per 100,000 population. In a state with a population of four million, he suggests that we might expect a 1 percent decline in unemployment to prevent over 10,000 index crimes a year.[45]

However, there is a growing body of literature suggesting that the guarantee of a job is hardly sufficient by itself to reduce crime very much. The nature of work must also change. As Arthur Pearl has suggested, work should not be defined by market factors, but in terms of what it contributes to the quality of life without placing an unnecessary drain on scarce resources.[46]

In sum, we feel that a just criminal justice apparatus in the larger society will not come into being as a result of an attitude of grim determination to hold the line, but by a social policy that assumes a potentiality for human freedom and participation. An emphasis on repression and law and order will do nothing to change the context in which the individual acquires a stake in the moral order of society.[47]

A JUST CRIMINAL JUSTICE SYSTEM AS A POLICY TO CONTROL CRIME

The consumer perspective cuts through the dilemma created by oversimplified conservative or liberal perspectives. Conservatives demand "certain and severe" punishments, while liberals call for treatment of the offender. Both focus on the offender rather than on the violation. Both assume that by doing something to the criminal they will be doing something about the crime problem. Yet criminologists have produced a great deal of evidence on the effects of different punishments. This evidence tends to support the generalization that it makes very little difference what we do with offenders. Their return, or nonreturn, to crime does not seem to be determined by treatment measures.

The consumer perspective focuses attention not only on the system of societal reaction, but also on those caught up in the various phases of the criminal justice apparatus: the offender, social control agents (police, prison guards, probation personnel), the victim, and not least, the taxpayer. With the conflicting outlooks, needs, and interests of these various individuals, there is little wonder that some criminologists and policymakers find that they are not as confident as they once were regarding what constitutes a just system.

How Might the Criminal Laws Be Made More Just?

Decriminalization. Would criminal law become more effective if laws regulating morality were to be repealed? It might, but who knows? Decriminalization would, in all probability, be more economic, decent, and fair and result in justice less biased by racism and sexism. Gilbert Geis has estimated the cost of enforcing laws regulating morality at about $3.4 billion per year. But he concludes, even if decriminalization were to create more problems than it solves, a more narrow definition of the law should be sought that does not deprive minorities of their liberty.[48]

It is our position that an *extensive* rewriting of the law should take place, encompassing more than the removal of victimless crimes from the statutes. *Crime, under a rewritten statute, should be defined as some actionable behavior that deprives a person of property, harms him or her physically, or damages the quality of his or her life.*[49] The recent attempt to recodify the federal criminal code, which passed the Senate in January 1978 as S1437 and was tied up in the House Judiciary Committee as HR6869, failed in this regard. Under this law, obscenity and prostitution would for the first time become federal crimes.

Decriminalization would lessen the overreach of the criminal law through the repeal of so-called victimless crimes. Among the laws that might be repealed are laws prohibiting gambling, consensual sexual relationships between adults, substance use including alcohol and narcotics (though sale other than by licensed pharmacists would be a criminal offense), disorderly conduct, vagrancy, and juvenile status offenses. The removal of the last category of juvenile offenses would, by itself, decrease the volume of the juvenile court by about 50 percent. The others would diminish arrests by about three million per year, or almost 40 percent. The law enforcement resources freed by such legal modifications might be used to devise ways of enforcing laws against professional and organized criminals.

Criminalization. Laws regulating professionals, business executives, and government officials would be included within the criminal code. Penalties would be as severe as they are for comparable crimes committed by offenders from the lower classes. They might, however, include restitution and fines.[50]

What Is the Role of the Police in the Community? To Whom Are They Accountable?

From the consumer perspective, the taxpayers in a community should be involved in evaluating police effectiveness and productivity. Police departments of large cities should be decentralized in those functions that relate to community service and maintenance of order. At the same time, the police must guard against being used by competing groups for intergroup vendettas. Unless police organizations can identify with the problems of minority and poorer communities, they will be perceived as alien control agents rather than legitimate representatives of the authority of the state. Perhaps the ultimate dilemma of law enforcement is to find a way to narrow police discretion and still maintain a police force responsive to the community. One way to avoid the horns of this dilemma might be to improve both the quality and quantity of police-citizen interaction.

Limiting Judicial Discretion and Promoting Justice as Fairness

Two contrasting models for the administration of justice were outlined by Herbert Packer. They are the "Crime Control Model" and the "Due Process Model," and they depict competing goals and means of administering justice. The first emphasizes efficiency, speed, and finality, or "assembly-line justice." The "Due Process Model" is more like an obstacle course, with challenges occurring at each stage. The accused is presumed innocent until proved guilty through an adversarial proceeding, and the model assumes an impartial judge and jury. The first describes the reality, although the system does not move all that swiftly, except perhaps in the misdemeanor and traffic courts. The second represents the ideal.[51]

If the judicial process is to approach the ideal, some of the following reforms should be sought:

1. The discriminatory, arbitrary nature of judicial decision making must be curbed. Thus, vague laws which contribute to the excessive use of discretion by sentencing judges should be eliminated.[52]
2. The volume of cases jamming the court dockets should be diminished by eliminating or decriminalizing vice crimes.

3. Excessive case bail should be abolished, and the activities of the nefarious bail bondsman should be restricted. Those awaiting trial, except those for whom there is a strong presumption that they might commit violent crime before trial, should be released on ROR.[53]
4. A swift trial should be made possible by adequate court staff. At the same time, "assembly-line" justice should be abolished, though not at the expense of fairness.[54]
5. Plea bargaining ultimately should be abolished. In the meantime, it should be carefully regulated, involving the judge, the accused, and possibly the victim in the process.[55]
6. The punishment (sentence) meted out must fit the crime and not be lengthened to fit the treatment needs of the individual. The indeterminate sentence should be replaced by short (five-year) "flat" sentences with length mitigated only by "good time credit." [56]
7. Sentencing alternatives such as probation, conditional discharge, restitution, and fines should be considered before incarceration, which should be the sanction of last resort.[57]
8. The sentence should represent a deprivation of liberty in which the offender loses only those freedoms or rights necessary to maintain restraint.[58]

Alternatives to Corrections

1. Prisoners should be treated in a lawful manner while incarcerated, both because it is their right and because it may well be one of the more productive ways of teaching law violators how to become law abiding.

2. The offender's rights include the right to be treated as a responsible person. These rights include opportunities for self-improvement, education, and counseling, which should be made available but not tied to release date or made a condition of being paroled.[59]

3. Meaningful work should be available and seen as one way to promote a measure of normality. However, prisoners should be paid at prevailing rates in the marketplace. Prisoners could be charged reasonable rates for meals and lodgings and have monies set aside for their release.[60]

4. The "monster," fortress-type prisons that now exist should be phased out as rapidly as possible. Newer, smaller institutions with a maximum capacity of about three hundred, divided into small living units, should be established. This could be accomplished by locking fewer people up for shorter periods of time. However, chronic violent offenders should be segregated in maximum security, humane prisons located in or near urban centers.[61]

5. Prisons, it has been noted, overprogram for custody. As a result the public tends to retain a dark stereotype of the "atrocious, dangerous convict." Consequently, if we deal humanely, safely, and sensibly with the "irreducible minimum" of residual, career, dangerous offenders (estimates vary between 10

Criminals: Doing Good Instead of Time

BOX 1

More and more judges are looking with favor at restitution programs, which allow criminal offenders to work their way back while compensating the victims of their crimes.

By NINA MCCAIN

Mrs. Hanah Moore and her sister were only away from the house in Billerica about a half hour that January night, just long enough to pick up a loaf of bread, milk and cigarettes. But Jim, who lived down the street, saw them drive off and knew their house was empty.

Jim (not his real name) was 15. He already had begun to dabble in petty theft and he needed money. He hurried down the street in the early winter darkness, opened a back porch window and crawled in. The old house was chock full of knick-knacks and china figurines but nothing you could sell to a fence for $20.

Jim went upstairs and found a metal box on top of one of the bureaus. Inside was a brown envelope and inside that a thick sheaf of $10 and $20 bills. Jim didn't stop to count. He grabbed the envelope and scooted off into the night.

When Mrs. Moore (not her real name) and her sister got back, they spotted the break right away and started checking for missing items. The minute they saw the open box on the bedroom bureau, they knew: The $1200 they had taken out of the bank that morning to pay property taxes and insurance was gone.

"That money just happened to be here that night," Mrs. Moore said. "I was going to the town hall first thing in the morning . . . I never thought we'd see any of it again."

But Mrs. Moore and her sister did see their money again, at least $800 of it. And Jim, who had gotten on the legal elevator that goes past misdemeanors and felonies and stops at "five to ten" in Walpole, got a break.

Instead of getting a crash course in crime at the taxpayers' expense, Jim found his way into Earn-It, the kind of program that is beginning to change the way some offenders are handled in courts throughout the country.

Earn-It, which is sponsored by the Lowell Chamber of Commerce, is one of about a dozen restitution programs in the state that is giving young people like Jim a chance to stay out of jail and pay back what they have stolen or the damages they have caused.

Restitution is hardly a new idea, but it has had an upsurge in popularity recently as judges try to find alternatives to jail terms or the slap on the wrist of suspended sentences. Just last week, Massachusetts received a $3 million federal grant to put some 350 young offenders to work in community service jobs. They will be paid $3 an hour and one fourth of their wages will go to repay their victims.

Jim's employer, Richard Codling, is an enthusiastic supporter of the concept of restitution. Codling, the president of a small data processing firm called Envirodata, was one of the first businessmen to volunteer a job to the Earn-It program.

"To me it's the most beautiful way to help somebody who's screwed up without costing the state money," Codling said. "The businessman gets to try a new young person who needs help. . . . The victim gets some money back. It's so simple, so beautiful. Everybody's a winner."

Jim didn't have much time to enjoy Mrs. Moore's money. The same night he stole it, a friend found him counting the money and took $400 from him. Most of the rest he blew on a spree in New Hampshire. Then the police, who suspected Jim in the Moore robbery, caught him breaking into another house on a nearby street. He still had some of the stolen cash in his pocket.

Jim confessed and on May 18, 1977, in Lowell District Court Judge Arthur Williams gave him a one-year suspended sentence and ordered him to pay back $800.

"He more or less said if he saw us in there again, he'd send us away," Jim remembers.

Jim got a series of what he calls "weird" odd jobs but none of them paid enough to add up to $800 in a year. He was getting desperate when he saw a story in the Lowell Sun about Earn-It. He went to see Robert Houde, who runs the program, and Houde sent him to Codling. Codling hired him for $85 a week and Jim paid $50 to the court for Mrs. Moore.

"He had a debt and we made a deal," Codling says. "I told him, 'If we like you, you'll be assured of a good job. After you've paid off your debt, you'll get a raise and, in six months, you'll get another raise.' He kept his part of the deal and I kept mine."

It took Jim about four months to pay off his debt. When the payments were completed, he went to see Mrs. Moore to make sure she had received the money. He says he had to work up the courage to knock on the door.

"It wasn't a long conversation," Jim said. "I told her I was sorry and she said OK. I didn't expect her to be too polite, but she was."

Mrs. Moore says she doesn't bear any grudges against Jim.

"I never really hated him," she said. "It's just that I worked hard all my life, worked in the mills, for that money. It really gets you when somebody comes and takes it all.

"But, hey, live and let live. If he came by now, I'd say 'Hi.' I think he's going to make it. He just got in with a bad gang."

Jim, who is 17, figures that without Earn-It he would still be trying to pay back the $800. And, by now, he'd probably be in more trouble.

"The kids I hung around with, I know they kept on breaking into houses and stealing cars. But everything is different for me now. I've got my own car. I don't have to hang around."

Jim, an open-faced young man with sandy red hair, likes his job, which involves scanning miles of squiggly lines on graph paper and translating them into language the computer can understand.

"I never thought I'd be doing anything like this," Jim said. "I figured I'd be roofing or something. I didn't like school. I was good at it, but I didn't like it."

Jim says the idea of doing any more stealing is "the farthest thing from my mind. I'm doing all right for myself now. Plus I've got a lot of responsibilities here."

There was a bad moment a while ago when some money was stolen from the petty cash box.

"I thought if they accused me of it, I'd leave," Jim said. "But they didn't. Working here is so relaxed. Everybody trusts everybody."

Codling says he could tell after the first few weeks that Jim was going to make it.

"If you put extra effort into your work — and he did — you'd have to be pretty stupid to do anything that would jeopardize the job. I don't think Jim is going to be dishonest again."

Not all restitution cases turn out as happily as Jim's. Some of the young offenders can't find jobs and some don't show up once they are hired. Every once in awhile, to the great chagrin of program sponsors, one of the offenders stumbles again.

Houde, who steered Jim to his job, remembers another, less successful case. The young man got arrested the first night he was on his new job.

In spite of the problems and occasional failures, restitution programs are increasingly popular.

A recent study found 11 programs in Massachusetts and several more are planned. They range from those in which the judge simply orders the defendant to pay and leaves him on his own to find a job, to the more elaborate programs that provide jobs either in private industry or public service, counseling and other services. Some programs have panels in which the victims, or their representatives, meet the defendant and participate in setting the amount and the terms of payment.

One of the first restitution programs — and still the largest — is the Quincy District Court's Earn-It (Lowell adopted the name). Last year, 670 adults and 323 juveniles repaid a total of $81,713 to the victims of crimes they had committed. This year, the repayment will be more than $100,000.

Andrew Klein, who was the first director of Quincy Earn-It and is now chief of probation for the court, says that Judge Albert Kramer started the program three years ago when it became clear to him that some alternative to nothing or jail was needed.

The judge went to the South Shore Chamber of Commerce and asked each business to donate 100 hours of paid work. About 40 signed up. More than 75 participate now.

"In most cases, first and second offenders were not even tried," Klein said. "The case was continued without a finding. That encouraged the behavior. If you did get caught, nothing happened.

"Earn-It gives kids a chance to earn their way back. If they fail, that tells you something. One kid kept the money he made and spent 10 days in jail. He earned his way into jail."

Restitution seems to work best when the defendant is a young first offender, although older persons and repeat offenders are not ruled out. In Quincy, if the judge and the probation officer don't think the defendant is ready to be trusted in a private business, he is sent to work at the MDC's Peddocks Island.

Quincy also attempts to fit the job to the crime. One kid who set off a series of false alarms was sentenced to paint the fire station. Drunk drivers are assigned to four weekends at the alcohol detoxification center where they can see what alcoholism looks like at close range. There are no statewide figures on the number of persons involved in restitution programs and no follow-up studies have been done to see if they are effective in keeping the offenders from getting into trouble again.

Xandra Kayden, who did a study of alternative court programs for the Shaw Foundation of Sturbridge, says the nature of the district court system makes such information hard to obtain.

"A kid could get arrested one week in Dorchester and the next in Quincy and no one would ever know," she said in a phone interview.

Kayden also found that most offenders were assigned to menial jobs and that neither employers nor offenders seemed to worry about whether they showed up on time or at all.

"At best, it is transient employment and the employer does not expect more," she wrote.

But, in a survey of 50 employers participating in the Quincy Earn-It, Kayden found that some 70 percent gave the program a favorable rating. Most said they participated because they wanted to "help the kids."

In the Quincy program, the amount of money the offender has to pay is set by the Earn-It staff after consulting with the victim. The victim and offender do not have to meet, although they sometimes do.

In the Lowell Restitution program, which is separate from but cooperates with Lowell Earn-It, the amount is determined by a panel made up of the victim, the offender, staff members and probation officers. In the Dorchester Urban Court program, community representatives sit on the panel.

Supporters of the panel say it helps the offender realize what he has done. They admit that it is a time-consuming process and that some victims simply are not able to face those who harmed them.

"Defendants often commit crimes in a vacuum," Bryan Callery, director of the Urban Court program, says. "They don't understand the consequences of what they've done. This humanizes the event."

"I've seen some pretty dramatic cases," Callery continued. "We had one where a 15-year-old kid stole a car with lots of athletic equipment in the trunk. The owner was a guy involved in youth work in Fall River. He came up here before the panel and told the kid he had thought first of breaking both his legs. Then he told him how he had hurt the kids in Fall River who were in the sports program.

"The defendant at first couldn't look at the owner. After he heard the story, he offered to fix up a '53 Chevy he had and give it to the guy. That kid has never been arrested again."

Source: The *Boston Globe*, Oct. 22, 1978. Reprinted courtesy of the Boston Globe.

to 25 percent) as in paragraph 4, then we might be able to develop sufficient public confidence to support the greatest possible use of community corrections as the "least-restricted" punishment for the great numbers of avocational and conventional car thieves, drug users, and others classified as "nondangerous." Programs such as those specified in paragraphs 1 to 3 are more effective if based in the community. Yet if community-based alternatives and programs are increased without doing something radically different in the way we deal with those left in the fortress prisons, these prisons might become even more explosive. Thus, we must plan rational sentencing legislation and new environments for the less safe offenders, while we plan the maximum use of "least restricted" sentences and community-based programs for the "safer" offender.[62]

Parole and Reentry: Should Parole Be Abolished? Should Ex-offenders Receive Amnesty?

Parole boards tend to base their decision on when to release on the idea that behavior in a controlled prison environment is related to readiness to function in a free society. Their decisions are based on the specious belief that they can predict whether or not the individual will behave in a law-abiding manner. This approach should be abandoned if a more just and effective alternative is to be developed.

The imposition of definite sentences combined with the abolition of parole is favored by the Committee for the Study of Incarceration. Standard sentences close to the median term now served could be set, with procedural restrictions placed upon the sentencing judge to narrow the degree of discretion in sentencing. Parole boards could be abolished, since the offender would serve his or her sentence less good credit time. For instance, one day of good time could result in one day being subtracted from the sentence.[63]

Reentry facilities, or half-way houses, should be made available on a voluntary basis for those offenders who feel they are needed. During the transitional period, parole staff could be used to provide employment counseling and other assistance for the ex-offender. Funds now being expended on parole might be used to strengthen social services in communities with large numbers of returning ex-offenders. The reentry facility might serve as a referral service on a drop-in basis for ex-offenders in such communities.[64]

Amnesty for Offenders. It is well known that arrest records and prison records serve as serious handicaps to those who desire to "straighten up their hand" when they return to the street and seek legitimate employment. We have "status degradation ceremonies," such as public trials, in which the individual is publicly stigmatized. But we have no comparable process in which the offender is cleared and fully reintegrated into society. "Once a thief, always a thief" or "once a con, always a con" are phrases with which we are familiar. To ex-offenders, this stereotyping of them as "evil" follows them in their postprison careers and provides a cruel hurdle to their becoming conventional members of the community.

Why is he unlikely to be an ex-offender?

As one study by the American Bar Association disclosed, there are 1,948 separate statutory provisions under which persons with an arrest or conviction record may be denied a license to practice a given occupation or profession. The average number of restrictions for each state is thirty-nine. Connecticut leads the nation with eighty such restrictions, while New Hampshire has the fewest, twenty-two. Barbering, for instance, is one of the occupations most restricted to former offenders. Forty-six states and the District of Columbia have laws restricting the licensing of former offenders as barbers.[65]

Two things can be done to remedy these liabilities faced by the former offender. *First,* legislation can be enacted by the various states that will remove or modify these arbitrary restrictions on the licensing of persons with a record of arrest or conviction. Illinois adopted such a law in 1971, and recent legislation in Florida and California has specified that a criminal conviction shall not be a barrier to such a license unless it directly relates to the occupation. Hawaii recently passed a law forbidding discrimination in employment against former offenders.[66] *Second,* laws can be passed that make it possible to clear an offender's record once he has satisfactorily served his sentence. Even if the police continue to argue that the ex-offender's record is needed to maintain a list of suspects, this need could be satisfied by allowing such records to be available only for use by law enforcement agencies. However, these agencies should not be allowed to make such records available to nonlaw enforcement persons or agencies. And a person who has repaid society for his or her crime should not be required to make it known when applying for a job.

BY WAY OF CONCLUSION

Social policy that will deal effectively with the crime problem must recognize that the problem is far wider in scope than the issue of dealing with apprehended criminals. Policymakers must deal with more than symptoms, for crime and the criminal often are indicators of problems created by our social structure. Choices for action-policy must relate to the general social organization of society.

The plain truth is that there is no easy way to control crime. We, as a society, face the problems of larger and ever more impersonal political and economic organizations. We need to find some way to control and make manageable these large social units, to make work and jobs not only available but more meaningful. Not only must many jobs be created, but work must be revitalized so that it is a real alternative to a career of crime. Opportunity, training, and credentials for satisfying career work must be made widely available so that minority groups, the poor, and the young will develop feelings of competence, usefulness, and belonging. Participation works better than prevention. We might seek to eliminate the status of powerlessness, although this would be to the disadvantage of powerful and privileged groups. Only as we promote participation and justice will we have the stability that will decrease lawlessness.

Until we move toward a "just" society, a social policy that makes law-abiding behavior both possible and gratifying to virtually all members of society will be impossible. Yet we can move toward a more positive criminal justice system by abolishing unnecessary laws, building justice and equity into our criminal laws and trial procedures, and establishing a correctional system that improves justice by consistent adherence to lawful means. By encouraging a bigger criminal justice system and promoting a greater reliance on formal means of social control, we might further reduce more effective means of informal or primary control.

The ultimate crime control policy might lie not in new, bigger, and more powerful control organizations, but rather in scaling down those that already exist. In the end, such organizations must be made visible and responsive to the needs of ordinary citizens. A social policy that encourages participation by all those concerned with the crime problem can point the way toward a criminal justice system that will reflect a more just and free society rather than a repressive, controlled one. As Norman Cousins so eloquently wrote: "Nothing about human life is more precious than that we can define our own purpose and shape our own destiny."

ADDITIONAL READINGS

Gardiner, John A., and Michael A. Mulkey, eds. *Crime and Criminal Justice.* Lexington, Mass.: D. C. Heath, 1976.

This collection of essays focuses on the definition of policy analysis and goals of crime policy as well as on the participants in crime policymaking. Common themes are the need to recognize conflicting social goals, the development of indicators to measure the impact of programs, and the implications of various policy alternatives.

Hood, Roger, ed. *Crime, Criminology and Public Policy.* New York: Free Press, 1974.

This collection of twenty-nine essays conveys some of the diversity of scholarship on crime and public policy over the past several decades. Aside from the usual topics, the book illustrates the interplay between crime, punishment, and official policy in different cultural and political contexts, including the USSR, South Africa, Sicily, and East and West Germany.

Krisberg, Barry. *Crime and Privilege: Toward a New Criminology.* Englewood Cliffs, N.J.: Prentice-Hall, 1975.

The author argues that our present justice system punishes only some of the people some of the time. He maintains that the system has created an uneven, unhealthy social climate that is weighted on the side of the privileged and thus serves to suppress entire groups of individuals, mostly minorities, who threaten the status quo.

Radzinowicz, Leon, and Joan King. *The Growth of Crime.* New York: Basic Books, 1977.

This comparative, international analysis of all aspects of the crime problem sums up what has been tried, what works, and what does not. The authors conclude that the system functions poorly in most places; nowhere does it work well.

Reiman, Jeffrey H. *The Rich Get Richer and the Poor Get Prison: Ideology, Class, and Criminal Justice.* New York: Wiley & Sons, 1979.

This examination of the ideology and economic bias inherent in the criminal justice system provides a wide-ranging analysis of numerous important topics, among them, patterns of enforcement and imprisonment, the "noncriminal" but dangerous acts overlooked by the system. Reiman sets forth cogent reasons for the failure of the system and argues that it seems predesigned to fail.

Silberman, Charles E. *Criminal Violence; Criminal Justice.* New York: Random House, 1978.

The author of *Crisis in Black and White* provides a critical analysis of crime and punishment in America. His six-year study of the system leads to the conclusion that, in the long run, the eradication of poverty and discrimination will result in the decline of violent crime. In the meantime, Silberman puts forth some practical and provocative recommendations that he argues would improve the situation.

NOTES

Chapter 1

1. James A. Inciardi, *Reflections on Crime: An Introduction to Criminology and Criminal Justice* (New York: Holt, Rinehart and Winston, 1978), pp. 13–22; see also, Doris A. Graber, "Idiological Components in the Perception of Crime and Crime News," a paper presented at the annual meeting of the Society for the Study of Social Problems (September 1977); see also, M. E. Grenander, "The Heritage of Cain: Crime in American Fiction," *Annals of the American Academy of Political and Social Science* 423 (January 1976):47–66.
2. Ron Goulart, *Cheap Thrills: An Informal History of the Pulp Magazines* (New Rochelle, N.Y.: Arlington House, 1972), pp. 114–15; see also, Inciardi, *Reflections on Crime,* pp. 13–22.
3. A. A. Berger, *The Comic-Stripped American* (Baltimore: Penguin Books, 1974), pp. 112–33; see also, Inciardi, *Reflections on Crime,* pp. 13–22.
4. Horace Newcomb, *TV, The Most Popular Art* (Garden City, N.Y.: Doubleday, 1974); see also, Inciardi, *Reflections on Crime,* p. 22.
5. Inciardi, *Reflections on Crime,* pp. 24–25.
6. John E. Conklin, *The Impact of Crime* (New York: Macmillan Co., 1975), pp. 20–21.
7. A survey conducted by Yankelovich, Skelly, and White Inc., for the National Center for State Courts. Reported in the *Boston Globe,* March 19, 1978, p. 20. Actually, these figures are considerably higher than other polls in the 1970s; in 1975 the Associated Press found that 45 percent of those interviewed in cities over 200,000 population were fearful of walking alone at night on their streets, and in 1977 NBC found that 49 percent of those questioned expressed similar fears; see also, *New York Times,* June 1975 and September 1977.
8. President's Commission on Law Enforcement and Administration of Justice, *Task Force Report: Crime and Its Impact on Assessment* (Washington, D.C.: U.S. Government Printing Office, 1967), p. 19.
9. Daniel Bell, "Crime as an American Way of Life," in Bell, ed., *End of Ideology,* rev. ed. (New York: Free Press, 1962), pp. 128–29.
10. Conklin, *The Impact of Crime,* pp. 18–20.
11. Edwin M. Schur, *Law and Society* (New York: Random House, 1968), pp. 51–52.
12. Martin Luther King, Jr., *Why We Can't Wait* (New York: Harper & Row, 1963), pp. 84–85.
13. Schur, *Law and Society,* p. 51; see also, Inciardi, *Reflections on Crime,* p. 2.
14. Raffaele Garofalo, *Criminology* (Boston: Little, Brown & Co., 1914), p. 5.
15. Hermann Mannheim, *Comparative Criminology* (Boston: Houghton Mifflin, 1965), p. 47.
16. Jerome Michael and Mortimer Adler, *Crime, Law and Society* (New York: Harcourt Brace Jovanovich, 1933), p. 5.
17. Schur, *Law and Society,* pp. 43–44.
18. Wilfrid E. Rumble, Jr., "Legal Realism, Sociological Jurisprudence and Mr. Justice Holmes," *Journal of the History of Ideas* 26 (October–December 1965):458.
19. Paul W. Tappan, "Who Is the Criminal?" *American Sociological Review* 12 (February 1947):100.
20. Paul W. Tappan, *Crime, Justice, and Correction* (New York: McGraw-Hill, 1960), p. 10.
21. Schur, *Law and Society,* p. 50; see also, Roscoe Pound, *Interpretations of Legal History* (New York: Macmillan Co., 1923), especially chapter 3.
22. Thorsten Sellin, *Culture Conflict and Crime* (New York: Social Science Research Council, 1938), p. 32.
23. Howard S. Becker, *Outsiders: Studies in the Sociology of Deviance* (New York: Free Press, 1963), pp. 9–20.
24. Austin T. Turk, *Criminology and the Legal Order* (Chicago: Rand McNally, 1969), p. 25; see also, Austin T. Turk, "Prospects for Theories of Criminal Behavior," *Journal of Criminal Law, Criminology and Police Science* 55 (December 1964):454–61.
25. Richard Quinney, *The Social Reality of Crime* (Boston: Little, Brown & Co., 1970), pp. 4–10; see also, George Vold, *Theoretical Criminology* (New York: Oxford University Press, 1958).
26. Quinney, *The Social Reality of Crime,* p. 16; see also, Inciardi, *Reflections on Crime,* p. 8.
27. Herman and Julia Schwendinger, "Defenders of Order or Guardians of Human Rights?" *Issues in Criminology* 5 (Summer 1970):123–57.
28. Richard Quinney and John Wildeman, *The Problem of Crime: A Critical Introduction to Criminology,* 2nd ed. (New York: Harper & Row, 1977), pp. 6–9; see also, Richard Quinney, *Class, State and Crime* (New York: David McKay Co., 1977), pp. 30–33, 60–65.
29. Tappan, *Crime, Justice, and Correction,* pp. 20–22; see also, Robert G. Caldwell, *Criminology* (New York: Ronald Press, 1965), p. 97.
30. Edwin H. Sutherland, *White Collar Crime* (New York: Dryden Press, 1969), p. 11.
31. C. Ray Jeffery, "The Structure of American Criminological Thinking," *Journal of Criminal Law, Criminology and Police Science* 46 (1956):658; see also, C. Ray Jeffery, "The Historical Development of Criminology," in Hermann Mannheim, ed., *Pioneers in Criminology* (Montclair, N.J.: Patterson Smith, 1973), pp. 464–65; see also, Turk, "Prospects for Theories of Criminal Behavior," p. 459.
32. Justin Miller, *Handbook of Criminal Law* (St. Paul: West Pub. Co., 1934), p. 16; see also, Turk, "Prospects for Theories of Criminal Behavior," pp. 454–61.
33. Abraham S. Blumberg, "Crime and the Social Order," in Blumberg, ed., *Current Perspectives on Criminal Behavior* (New York: Knopf, 1974), p. 19; see also, Jerome Hall, *General Principles of Criminal Law,* 2nd ed. (Indianapolis: Bobbs-Merrill, 1960), especially pp. 14–26.
34. Edwin H. Sutherland and Donald R. Cressey, *Criminology,* 10th ed. (Philadelphia: J. B. Lippincott, 1978), pp. 5–9.
35. Barry Krisberg, *Crime and Privilege* (Englewood Cliffs, N.J.: Prentice-Hall, 1975), pp. 1–5.
36. Tappan, *Crime, Justice, and Correction,* p. 178.
37. Emile Durkheim, *The Rules of Sociological Method* (New York: Free Press, 1938), pp. 68–71; see also, David Matza, *Becoming Deviant* (Englewood Cliffs, N.J.: Prentice-Hall, 1969), pp. 13–14.
38. Richard Quinney, *Critique of the Legal Order* (Boston: Little, Brown & Co., 1974), pp. 6–7.
39. Quinney, *The Social Reality of Crime,* pp. 16–25.

40. Vold, *Theoretical Criminology,* p. vi.
41. Tappan, *Crime, Justice, and Correction,* pp. 20–22.
42. Walter C. Reckless, *The Crime Problem* (New York: Appleton-Century-Crofts, 1967), p. 10.
43. Inciardi, *Reflections on Crime,* pp. v–vi.
44. Turk, "Prospects for Theories of Criminal Behavior," p. 454.
45. Vold, *Theoretical Criminology,* pp. v–vi.
46. Leon Radzinowicz, *Ideology and Crime* (New York: Columbia University Press, 1966), pp. 1–4.
47. Ibid., pp. 4–7.
48. Ibid., pp. 8–13.
49. Ibid., pp. 19–20.
50. Ian Taylor, Paul Walton, and Jock Young, *The New Criminology: For a Social Theory of Deviance* (New York: Harper & Row, 1973), pp. 37–38.
51. Marvin Wolfgang, "Cesare Lombroso," in Mannheim, *Pioneers in Criminology,* pp. 232–35.
52. Ibid., pp. 244–46.
53. Gina Lombroso-Ferrero, *Criminal Man: According to the Classification* of Cesare Lombroso (with an introduction by Cesare Lombroso), reprint of 1911 ed. (Montclair, N.J.: Patterson Smith, 1972), pp. xxiv–xv.
54. Radzinowicz, *Ideology and Crime,* pp. 31–38.
55. Francis A. Allen, "Raffaele Garofalo," in Mannheim, *Pioneers in Criminology,* p. 321.
56. Vold, *Theoretical Criminology,* pp. 35–39.
57. Jeffery, "The Historical Development of Criminology," p. 488; see also, Radzinowicz, *Ideology and Crime,* pp. 56–59.
58. Radzinowicz, *Ideology and Crime,* pp. 31–38.
59. Taylor et al., *The New Criminology,* pp. 222–36.
60. Emile Durkheim, *The Division of Labor in Society,* trans. by George Simpson (New York: Free Press, 1933), pp. 102–04.
61. Radzinowicz, *Ideology and Crime,* pp. 72–74; see also, Durkheim, *Division of Labor in Society,* pp. 1–15, 64–68, 70; see also, Matza, *Becoming Deviant,* chapters 4 and 5.
62. Nicholas N. Kittrie, *The Right to Be Different: Deviance and Enforced Therapy* (Baltimore: Johns Hopkins Press, 1971), pp. 38, 355.
63. Peter K. Manning, "Foreword," in Peter Wickman and Phillip Whitten, eds., *Readings in Criminology* (Lexington, Mass.: D. C. Heath, 1978).
64. Jeffery, "The Historical Development of Criminology," p. 464.
65. We are indebted to Charles E. Reasons, "Social Thought and Social Structure: Competing Paradigms in Criminology," *Criminology* 13, no. 3 (November 1975):332–65, for this current rendering of "kinds-of-people" and "kinds-of-environment" paradigms. This approach was earlier developed by Albert K. Cohen, *Deviance and Control* (Englewood Cliffs, N.J.: Prentice-Hall, 1966), especially chapters 2 and 3. Reasons incorporates these into T. S. Kuhn's concept of paradigms as the dominant means for analyzing the major elements within a theory—a paradigm is more inclusive than a theoretical model and more specific than a perspective. See Thomas S. Kuhn, *The Structure of Scientific Revolutions,* 2nd ed. (Chicago: University of Chicago Press, 1962).
66. Matza, *Becoming Deviant,* pp. 114–15.
67. Cohen, *Deviance and Control,* pp. 52–53.
68. Matza, *Becoming Deviant,* p. 17.
69. Edwin H. Sutherland and Donald R. Cressey, *Criminology,* 9th ed. (Philadelphia: J. B. Lippincott, 1974), pp. 75–76.
70. Edwin H. Sutherland, "White Collar Criminality," in Gilbert Geis, ed., *White Collar Crime,* rev. ed. (New York: Free Press, 1977), pp. 38–39.
71. Becker, *Outsiders,* p. 9.
72. Quinney, *The Social Reality of Crime,* p. 207.
73. Taylor et al., *The New Criminology,* p. 267.
74. Turk, *Criminology and the Legal Order,* p. 35; see also, Turk, "Prospects for Theories of Criminal Behavior," pp. 454–61.
75. Ibid.
76. Gresham Sykes, "The Rise of Critical Criminology," *Journal of Criminal Law and Criminology* 65 (1974):209–11; see also, Taylor et al., *The New Criminology,* p. 267.
77. Stanton Wheeler, "Trends and Problems in the Sociological Study of Crime," *Social Problems* 73, no. 5 (June 1976):525–34.
78. Isidore Silver, "Crime and Conventional Wisdom," *Society* 13, no. 3 (March/April 1977).
79. Taylor et al., *The New Criminology,* chapter 9, passim.
80. Patrik Tornudd, "The Futility of Searching for Causes of Crime," in Nils Christie, ed., *Scandinavian Studies in Criminology,* vol. 3 (Oslo: Scandinavian University Books, 1971), pp. 21–32.
81. Roger B. Parks, "Sources and Limitations of Data in Criminal Justice Research," in John A. Gardiner and Michael A. Mulkey, eds., *Crime and Criminal Justice* (Lexington, Mass.: D. C. Heath, 1976).
82. Sue Titus Reid, *Crime and Criminology* (New York: Dryden Press, 1976), pp. 97–98; see also, Turk, "Prospects for Theories of Criminal Behavior"; see also, Matza, *Becoming Deviant,* pp. 67–69.
83. Blumberg, "Crime and the Social Order," p. 31. This theme is developed more fully in chapter 15.
84. Marvin E. Wolfgang, "Making the Criminal Justice System Accountable," *Crime and Delinquency* 18 (January 1972):15–22; see also, Reasons, "Social Thought and Social Structure."
85. Sutherland and Cressey, *Criminology,* 9th ed., pp. 61–70.
86. Reasons, "Social Thought and Social Structure," pp. 353–54.
87. Manning, "Foreword," in Wickman and Whitten, eds., *Readings in Criminology.*
88. Nils Christie, "Scandinavian Criminology Facing the 1970s," in Christie, *Scandinavian Studies in Criminology,* pp. 121–45.

Chapter 2

1. Edwin H. Sutherland, *Criminology* (Philadelphia: J. B. Lippincott, 1924), p. 11; see also, Gilbert Geis, "Editorial: Revisiting Sutherland's Criminology," *Criminology* 14, no. 3 (November 1976):303–06.
2. William J. Chambliss, "Introduction, the Creation of the Legal Norms," in Chambliss, ed., *Criminal Law in Action* (Santa Barbara, Calif.: Hamilton, 1975), pp. 2–3.
3. C. Ray Jeffery, "The Historical Development of Criminology," in Hermann Mannheim, ed., *Pioneers in Criminology* (Montclair, N.J.: Patterson Smith, 1973), pp. 489–91.
4. Edwin H. Sutherland and Donald R. Cressey, *Criminology,* 10th ed. (Philadelphia: J. B. Lippincott, 1978), p. 3.
5. Jerome Michael and Mortimer J. Adler, *Crime, Law and Social Science* (Montclair, N.J.: Patterson Smith, 1971), pp. 2–5; see also, Austin Turk, *Criminality and Legal*

Order (Chicago: Rand McNally, 1969), pp. 9–10.

6. Lawrence M. Friedman, *Law and Society: An Introduction* (Englewood Cliffs, N.J.: Prentice-Hall, 1977), pp. 2–11.

7. F. James Davis, "Law as a Type of Social Control," in Davis et al., eds., *Society and the Law* (New York: Free Press, 1962), p. 43.

8. Max Weber, *On Law in Economy and Society,* edited and trans. by Max Rheinstein (Cambridge, Mass.: Harvard University Press, 1954), pp. 5, 14, 16.

9. Phillip Selznick, "Legal Institutions and Social Controls," *Vanderbilt Law Review* 17 (December 1963):88; see also, Richard Quinney and John Wildeman, *The Problem of Crime: A Critical Introduction to Criminology,* 2nd ed. (New York: Harper & Row, 1977), p. 15.

10. Bronislav Malinowski, *Crime and Custom in Savage Society* (London: Routledge & Kegan Paul, 1926), p. 55; for a narrower anthropological view of the law, see E. Adam on Hoebel, *The Law of Primitive Man* (Cambridge, Mass.: Harvard University Press, 1954).

11. Harold J. Berman, *Justice in the U.S.S.R.,* rev. ed. (New York: Vintage Books, 1963), chapters 1 and 2; see also, Edwin M. Schur, *Law and Society* (New York: Random House, 1968), pp. 116–21.

12. Dennis Lloyd, *The Idea of Law* (Baltimore: Penguin Books, 1976), chapters 4 and 5; see also, Schur, *Law and Society,* pp. 27–28, 37–38.

13. Friedman, *Law and Society,* pp. 77–78.

14. William E. Nelson, "Emerging Nations of Modern Criminal Law in the Revolutionary Era," *New York University Law Review* 42 (May 1967):450–85.

15. Eric Goode, "Drugs and the Law," in Goode, ed., *Drugs in American Society* (New York: Knopf, 1972), pp. 181–210; see also, Howard S. Becker, *Outsiders: Studies in the Sociology of Deviance* (New York: Free Press, 1963), pp. 147–64.

16. Kurt Wolff, "Social Control," in Julius Gold and William L. Kolb, eds., *Dictionary of the Social Sciences* (New York: Free Press, 1964), pp. 650–52.

17. Georg Simmel, "Custom, Law Morality," in *The Sociology of Georg Simmel,* trans. by Kurt H. Wolff (New York: Free Press, 1950), pp. 99–104.

18. C. Ray Jeffery, "The Development of Crime in Early English Society," *Journal of Criminal Law, Criminology and Police Science* 47 (March/April 1957):66.

19. Jerome Hall, *Theft, Law and Society,* 2nd ed. (Indianapolis: Bobbs-Merrill, 1952), p. 33.

20. William J. Chambliss, "The Law of Vagrancy," in Chambliss, ed., *Criminal Law in Action,* pp. 9–25; see also, Francis Fox Piven and Richard A. Cloward, *Regulating the Poor* (New York: Vintage Books, 1970).

21. Becker, *Outsiders,* pp. 135–46; see also, Donald Dickson, "Bureaucracy and Morality: An Organizational Perspective on a Moral Crusade," *Social Problems* 16 (Fall 1968):143–56.

22. Joseph R. Gusfield, "Moral Passage: The Symbolic Process in the Public Resignation of Deviance," *Social Problems* 15 (Fall 1967):178.

23. Stuart L. Hills, *Crime, Power and Morality—The Criminal Law Process in the United States* (New York: Chandler, 1971), pp. 8–9; see also, Joseph R. Gusfield, *Symbolic Crusade* (Urbana: University of Illinois Press, 1903), p. 177.

24. R. Bryce Young, *Criminal Law: Codes and Cases* (New York: McGraw-Hill, 1972), pp. 22–23.

25. Quoted in Sutherland and Cressey, *Criminology,* 10th ed., pp. 10–11.

26. Edwin H. Sutherland, "The Sexual Psychopath Laws," *Journal of Criminal Law, Criminology and Police Science* 40 (January–February 1950):543–54; see also, Edwin H. Sutherland, "The Diffusion of Sexual Psychopath Laws," *American Journal of Sociology* 56 (September 1950):142–48.

27. Roscoe Pound, "A Survey of Social Interests," *Harvard Law Review* 57 (October 1943):39.

28. Becker, *Outsiders;* see also, Richard Quinney, *Critique of Legal Order* (Boston: Little, Brown & Co., 1974); see also, George Vold, *Theoretical Criminology* (New York: Oxford University Press, 1958); see also, Austin Turk, *Criminology and Legal Order;* see also, William J. Chambliss and Robert B. Seidman, *Law, Order and Power* (Reading, Mass.: Addison-Wesley, 1971).

29. Richard Quinney, *Crime and Justice in Society* (Boston: Little, Brown & Co., 1969), pp. 25–31; see also, Quinney, *Critique of Legal Order,* pp. 22–25.

30. Jerome Hall, *General Principles of Criminal Law* (Indianapolis: Bobbs-Merrill, 1947), p. 1.

31. Ian Taylor, Paul Walton, and Jack Young, *The New Criminology* (New York: Harper & Row, 1973), p. 237; see also, Gresham Sykes, "The Rise of Critical Criminology," in *The Aldine Crime and Justice Annual, 1974* (Chicago: Aldine, 1975), pp. 31–32.

32. Edwin H. Sutherland and Donald Cressey, *Principles of Criminology,* 7th ed. (Philadelphia: J. B. Lippincott, 1966), p. 11; see also, Schur, *Law and Society,* p. 131.

33. Robin Williams, *American Society: A Sociological Interpretation,* 2nd ed. (New York: Knopf, 1960), chapter 10.

34. Edwin M. Schur, *Crimes Without Victims* (Englewood Cliffs, N.J.: Prentice-Hall, 1965); see also, Edwin M. Schur, *Our Criminal Society* (Englewood Cliffs, N.J.: Prentice-Hall, 1969), pp. 191–228.

35. Schur, *Our Criminal Society,* pp. 139–40.

36. Quinney and Wildeman, *The Problem of Crime,* pp. 17–19.

37. Young, *Criminal Law: Codes and Cases,* pp. 22–23.

38. Austin Turk, "Prospects for Theories of Criminal Behavior," *Journal of Criminal Law, Criminology and Police Science* 55 (December 1964):454–61.

39. Alan A. Stone, *Mental Health and Law: A System in Transition* (Rockville, Md.: National Institute of Mental Health, Center for Studies of Crime and Delinquency, 1975), pp. 218–19.

40. Richard Maran, "Awaiting the Crown's Pleasure: The Case of Daniel M'Naghten," *Criminology* 15, no. 1 (May 1977):7–10.

41. N. Walker, *Crime and Insanity in England,* vol. 1 (Edinburgh: Edinburgh University Press, 1968), chapter 5.

42. Durham v. United States, 214 F.2d 862 (D.C.Cir. 1954); see also, Stone, *Mental Health and Law,* pp. 221–22.

43. Durham v. United States, 214 F.2d 862 (D.C.Cir. 1954); see also, Joseph Goldstein, "The Brawner Rule," *Washington University Law Quarterly* (1973):126.

44. Rita Simon, *The Jury and the Defense of Insanity* (Boston: Little, Brown & Co., 1967); see also, Stone, *Mental Health and Law,* p. 227; see also, American Law Institute, *Model Penal Code,* sec. 4.01.

45. Edwin H. Sutherland, *White Collar Crime* (New York: Dryden Press, 1969); see also, Stanton Wheeler, "Trends and Problems in the Sociological Study of Crime,"

Social Problems 25, no. 5 (June 1976):525–33.

Chapter 3

1. Peter K. Manning, "The Police: Mandate Strategies and Appearance," Jack D. Douglas, ed., *Crime and Justice in American Society* (Indianapolis: Bobbs-Merrill, 1971), p. 169; see also, John E. Conklin, *The Impact of Crime* (New York: Macmillan Co., 1975), pp. 15–19.
2. Roger Hood and Richard Sparks, *Key Issues in Criminology* (New York: McGraw-Hill, 1970), p. 45.
3. Richard Quinney and John Wildeman, *The Problem of Crime* (New York: Harper & Row, 1970), p. 122; see also, Gresham M. Sykes, "The Rise of Critical Criminology," *Journal of Criminal Law and Criminology* 65 (1974):210.
4. Conklin, *The Impact of Crime*, pp. 18–19; see also, Richard Quinney and John Wildeman, *The Problem of Crime*, 2nd ed. (New York: Harper & Row, 1977), p. 96.
5. Hood and Sparks, *Key Issues in Criminology*, p. 43.
6. Harry Best, *Crime and the Criminal Law in the United States* (New York: Macmillan Co., 1930), p. 134.
7. Don C. Gibbons, *Society, Crime and Criminal Careers*, 2nd ed. (Englewood Cliffs, N.J.: Prentice-Hall, 1973), p. 100.
8. Edwin H. Sutherland and Donald R. Cressey, *Criminology*, 10th ed. (Philadelphia: J. B. Lippincott, 1978), p. 29.
9. Hood and Sparks, *Key Issues in Criminology*, pp. 43–45; see also, Quinney and Wildeman, *The Problem of Crime*, pp. 107–09.
10. Manning, "The Police: Mandate Strategies and Appearance," p. 169.
11. James A. Inciardi, *Reflections on Crime: An Introduction to Criminology and Criminal Justice* (New York: Holt, Rinehart and Winston, 1978), pp. 54–55.
12. FBI, *Uniform Crime Reports, 1970 & 1975* (Washington, D.C.: U.S. Government Printing Office, 1971, 1976), p. 59 (1970), pp. 3–4 (1975). Unless otherwise noted crime data cited in this chapter will be drawn from the 1975 *Uniform Crime Reports*.
13. Conklin, *The Impact of Crime*, pp. 20–21; see also, Leslie T. Wilkins, *Social Deviance: Social Policy, Action and Research* (Englewood Cliffs, N.J.: Prentice-Hall, 1965), p. 142.
14. Jack D. Douglas, "Crime and Justice in American Society," in Douglas, *Crime and Justice in American Society*, p. 4.
15. Jessica Mitford, *Kind and Unusual Punishment* (New York: Knopf, 1973), pp. 64–68; see also, Hazel Erskine, "The Polls: Politics and Law and Order," *Public Opinion Quarterly* (Winter 1974–1975):23–39.
16. Inciardi, *Reflections on Crime*, pp. 78–79; see also, Manning, "The Police: Mandate Strategies and Appearance," p. 169.
17. President's Commission on Law Enforcement and Administration of Justice, *The Challenge of Crime in a Free Society* (Washington, D.C.: U.S. Government Printing Office, 1967), pp. 26–27. Hereafter referred to as Crime Commission.
18. Daniel Bell, "The Myth of the Crime Wave," in Bell, *The End of Ideology* (New York: Free Press, 1960), p. 38.
19. Manning, "The Police: Mandate Strategies and Appearance," pp. 168–75.
20. Eugene Doleschal, "Crime—Some Popular Beliefs," *Crime and Delinquency* 25, no. 1 (January 1979):7–8.
21. Manning, "The Police: Mandate Strategies and Appearance," pp. 168–75.
22. Thorsten Sellin, "The Significance of Records and Crime," *The Law Quarterly Review* 67 (October 1951):498.
23. Inciardi, *Reflections on Crime,* pp. 59–62.
24. Rita J. Simon, *The Contemporary Woman and Crime* (Rockville, Md.: National Institute of Mental Health, Center for the Studies of Crime and Delinquency, 1975), p. 3.
25. Ibid., pp. 40–42.
26. Crime Commission, p. 44.
27. Lynn A. Curtis, *Criminal Violence* (Lexington, Mass.: D. C. Heath, Lexington Books, 1974), pp. 82–92.
28. Lynn A. Curtis, *Violence, Race and Culture* (Lexington, Mass.: D. C. Heath, 1975), pp. 17–18; see also, Lee Rainwater, *Behind Ghetto Walls: Black Families in a Federal Slum* (Chicago: Aldine, 1970).
29. Crime Commission, p. 44.
30. Albert Biderman and Albert J. Reiss, Jr., "On Exploring the Dark Figure of Crime," *Annals of the American Academy of Political and Social Science* 374 (November 1967):12.
31. Crime Commission, p. 21.
32. Albert D. Biderman, "Surveys of Population Samples for Estimating Crime Incidence," *Annals of the American Academy of Political and Social Science* 374 (November 1967):17.
33. Ibid., pp. 25–26.
34. National Crime Panel Surveys of Chicago, Los Angeles, New York and Philadelphia, *Criminal Victimization Surveys in the Nation's Five Largest Cities* (Washington, D.C.: U.S. Department of Justice, National Criminal Justice Information and Statistics Service, 1975), pp. 63–67.
35. U.S. Department of Justice, National Criminal Justice Information and Statistics Service, *Criminal Victimization Surveys in Eight American Cities* (Washington, D.C.: U.S. Government Printing Office, 1976), pp. 1–131 passim.
36. Hood and Sparks, *Key Issues in Criminology*, pp. 20–21.
37. A. L. Porterfield, *Youth in Trouble* (Austin, Texas: Leo Polishman Foundation, 1946).
38. F. J. Murphy et al., "The Incidence of Hidden Delinquency," *American Journal of Orthopsychiatry* 16 (October 1946):686–95.
39. J. A. Wallerstein and C. J. Wyle, "Our Law-abiding Law Breakers," *Federal Probation* 25 (April 1947):107–12.
40. James F. Short, Jr. and F. I. Nye, "Scaling Delinquent Behavior," *American Sociological Review* 22 (June 1957):326–31.
41. Hood and Sparks, *Key Issues in Criminology*, pp. 20–21.
42. M. L. Erickson and L. T. Empey, "Court Records, Undetected Delinquency and Decision-Making," *Journal of Criminal Law, Criminology and Police Science* 54 (1963):456–69.
43. H. L. Voss, "Ethnic Differentials and Delinquency in Honolulu," *Journal of Criminal Law, Criminology and Police Science* 54 (1963):322–27.
44. D. P. Farrington, "Self-Reports of Deviant Behavior: Predictive and Stable," *Journal of Criminal Law, Criminology and Police Science* 64 (1973):99–110.
45. Travis Hirschi, *Causes of Delinquency* (Berkeley: University of California Press, 1969), pp. 57, 77.
46. B. R. McCandless et al., "Perceived Opportunity, Delinquency, Race and Body Build Among Delinquent

Youth," *Journal of Consulting and Clinical Psychology* 38 (1972):281–87.

47. Kristen Elmhorn, "Study in Self-Reported Delinquency Among School Children in Stockholm," in K. O. Christiansen, ed., *Scandinavian Studies in Criminology*, vol. 1 (London: Tavistock, 1965), pp. 117–46.

48. Nils Christie et al., "A Study of Self-Reported Crime," in Christiansen, *Scandinavian Studies in Criminology*, pp. 86–116.

49. Hood and Sparks, *Key Issues in Criminology*, p. 46.

50. Crime Commission, p. 32.

51. Ibid., pp. 32–35.

52. Norval Morris and Gordon Hawkins, *The Honest Politician's Guide to Crime Control* (Chicago: University of Chicago Press, 1970), p. 38.

53. Crime Commission, p. 32.

54. Edwin H. Sutherland, "White Collar Criminality," *American Sociological Review* 5 (February 1940):1–12.

55. Doleschal, "Crime—Some Popular Beliefs," p. 5.

56. Crime Commission, p. 33.

Chapter 4

1. David Matza, *Delinquency and Drift* (New York: John Wiley & Sons, 1964), pp. 1–5.

2. Ibid.; see also, Frank Tannenbaum, *Crime and the Community* (New York: Columbia University Press, 1938).

3. Edwin Schur, *Radical Non-Intervention: Rethinking the Delinquency Problem* (Englewood Cliffs, N.J.: Prentice-Hall, 1973).

4. Matza, *Delinquency and Drift,* p. 22; see also, Edwin Powers and Helen Witmer, *An Experiment in the Prevention of Delinquency: The Cambridge-Somerville Youth Study* (New York: Columbia University Press, 1951); see also, Joan McCord and William McCord, "A Follow-up Report on the Cambridge-Somerville Youth Study," *Annals of the American Academy of Political and Social Science* (March 1959):89–96.

5. David F. Greenberg, "Delinquency and the Age Structure of Society," in Peter Wickman and Phillip Whitten, eds., *Readings in Criminology* (Lexington, Mass.: D. C. Heath, 1978), pp. 66–81.

6. Howard Becker, *Outsiders: Studies in the Sociology of Deviance* (New York: Free Press, 1963), p. 176.

7. Thorsten Sellin and Marvin Wolfgang, *The Measurement of Delinquency* (New York: John Wiley & Sons, 1964), pp. 71–86.

8. Condensed and slightly rephrased from Frederick B. Sussman, *Law of Juvenile Delinquency* (Dobbs Ferry, N.Y.: Oceana, 1959), p. 21.

9. President's Commission on Law Enforcement and Administration of Justice, *Task Force Report: Juvenile Delinquency and Youth Crime* (Washington, D.C.: U.S. Government Printing Office, 1967), p. 4. Hereafter referred to as *Task Force Report: Juvenile Delinquency*.

10. FBI, *Uniform Crime Reports, 1975* (Washington, D.C.: U.S. Government Printing Office, 1976), pp. 188–89. Unless otherwise noted, offense data in this chapter is from the UCR.

11. A summary of such studies appears in Chapter 3. Especially see, Austin Porterfield, *Youth in Trouble* (Fort Worth, Texas: Leo Patisham Foundation, 1946); see also, inter alia F. J. Murphy, M. M. Shirley, and H. L. Witmer, "The Incidence of Hidden Delinquency," *American Journal of Orthopsychiatry* 16 (1946):686–96.

12. James F. Short and F. Ivan Nye, "Extent of Unrecorded Delinquency: Tentative Conclusions," *Journal of Criminal Law, Criminology and Police Science* 49 (November–December 1958):296–302.

13. Richard Quinney, *The Social Reality of Crime* (Boston: Little, Brown & Co., 1970), pp. 8–11.

14. Peter L. Berger and Thomas Luckmann, *The Social Construction of Reality* (Garden City, N.Y.: Anchor Books, Doubleday & Co., 1966), pp. 58–63.

15. Ibid., p. 61.

16. Peter S. Venezia, "Delinquency as a Function of Intrafamily Relationships," *Journal of Research in Crime and Delinquency* 5 (July 1968):148–73; see also, Joan McCord and William McCord, "The Effects of Parental Role Model on Criminality," *Journal of Social Issues* 14 (1958):66–75.

17. Karen Wilkinson, "The Broken Family and Juvenile Delinquency: Scientific Explanation or Idiology," *Social Problems* 21, no. 5 (June 1974):726–37.

18. Travis Hirschi, *Causes of Delinquency* (Berkeley: University of California Press, 1969), pp. 3–10.

19. D. H. Scott, "Family Situations Conducive to Behavior Disturbances in Delinquents," *Social Work* 10 (April 1965):14–17, in Elmer H. Johnson, *Crime, Correction and Society*, 3rd ed. (Homewood, Ill.: Dorsey Press, 1974), p. 108.

20. Walter E. Schafer and Kenneth Polk, "Delinquency and the Schools," in *Task Force Report: Juvenile Delinquency*, p. 222.

21. Ibid., pp. 258–60.

22. Bernard Rosenberg and Harvey Silverstein, *The Varieties of Delinquent Experience* (Waltham, Mass.: Blaisdell, 1969), pp. 135–37.

23. Martin Gold, *Delinquent Behavior in an American City* (Belmont, Calif.: Brooks/Cole, 1970), pp. 124–25.

24. Hirschi, *Causes of Delinquency,* pp. 120–32.

25. Schafer and Polk, "Delinquency and the Schools," pp. 259–60.

26. *New York Times,* June 23, 1977, p. 13.

27. Joseph P. Fitzpatrick, S.J., "The Role of Religion in the Prevention and Correction of Crime and Delinquency," in *Task Force Report: Juvenile Delinquency*, pp. 323–30.

28. Kahlil Gibran, *The Prophet* (New York: Knopf, 1961), p. 32.

29. Wilbur Schramm et al., *Television in the Lives of Our Children* (Stanford, Calif.: Stanford University Press, 1961).

30. "Five Acts of Violence Per Hour," *Saturday Review,* March 14, 1970, p. 104.

31. Surgeon General's Scientific Advisory Committee on TV and Social Behavior, *TV and Adolescent Aggressiveness,* vol. 3 (Washington, D.C.: U.S. Government Printing Office, 1972).

32. Seymour Feshback and Robert A. Singer, *Television and Aggression: An Experimental Field Study* (New York: Jossey Boss, 1971); see also, Robert B. Snow, "How Children Interpret TV Violence in Play Context," *Journalism Quarterly* 5 (Spring 1974):13–21.

33. David Matza, "Position and Behavior Patterns of Youth," in Robert L. L. Farris, *The Handbook of Sociology* (Chicago: Rand McNally, 1964), pp. 192–94; see also, David Matza, *Delinquency and Drift,* pp. 33–37, 56, 62.

34. Matza, *Delinquency and Drift,* chapter 2.

35. Anthony Platt, *The Child Savers: The Invention of Juvenile Delinquency* (Chicago: University of Chicago Press, 1969); see also, LaMar Empey, "The Social Construction of Childhood, Delinquency and Social Reform," in Malcolm Klein, ed., *The Juvenile Justice System* (Beverly

Hills: Sage Publications, 1976), pp. 27–54.

36. Nicholas N. Kittrie, *The Right To Be Different: Deviance and Enforced Therapy* (Baltimore: Penguin Books, 1971), pp. 104–06.

37. Platt, *The Child Savers*, p. 296; see also, Kittrie, *The Right To Be Different*, p. 110.

38. Kittrie, *The Right To Be Different*, pp. 110–11; see also, David Matza, *Becoming Deviant* (Englewood Cliffs, N.J.: Prentice-Hall, 1969), pp. 90–91.

39. Matza, *Becoming Deviant*, chapters 5–7; see also, Peter K. Manning, "On Deviance," *Contemporary Sociology* 2 (March 1973):124–25.

40. Sheldon and Eleanor Glueck, *Physique and Delinquency* (New York: Harper & Row, 1956); see also, E. A. Hooton, *Crime and the Man* (Cambridge, Mass.: Harvard University Press, 1939); see also, William Sheldon, *Varieties of Delinquent Youth* (New York: Harper & Row, 1949). For an analysis of such studies of delinquency see Travis Hirschi and Hanan C. Selvin, *Delinquency Research: An Appraisal of Analytic Methods* (New York: Free Press, 1967), pp. 96–97.

41. Karl Schuessler and Donald Cressey, "Personality Characteristics of Criminals," *American Journal of Sociology* (March 1950):476–89; see also, Gordon Waldo and Siven Dinitz, "Personality Attributes of the Criminal: An Analysis of Studies, 1950–1965," *Journal of Research in Crime and Delinquency* 2 (July 1967):185–202.

42. William and Joan McCord, *The Psychopath* (New York: D. Van Nostrand, 1964), pp. 3, 85; see also, Robert M. Lindner, *Rebel Without a Cause* (New York: Grune & Stratton, 1944).

43. Schur, *Radical Non-Intervention*, pp. 38–40.

44. Matza, *Becoming Deviant*, pp. 94–99.

45. Clifford Shaw, Henry McKay et al., *Delinquency Areas* (Chicago: University of Chicago Press, 1929); see also, Clifford Shaw and Henry McKay, *Jack Roller* (Chicago: University of Chicago Press, 1930); see also, Clifford Shaw and Henry McKay, *The Natural History of a Delinquent Career* (Chicago: University of Chicago Press, 1931).

46. Matza, *Becoming Deviant*, pp. 94–95; see also, Solomon Kobrin, "The Formal Logical Properties of the Shaw-McKay Delinquency Theory," in H. Voss and D. Peterson, eds., *Ecology, Crime and Delinquency* (New York: Appleton-Century-Crofts, 1971).

47. Robert Merton, "Social Structure and Anomie," in Merton, ed., *Social Theory and Social Structure* (New York: Free Press, 1957).

48. Ibid.; see also, Matza, *Becoming Deviant*, pp. 96–98; see also, David Matza, "Poverty and Disrepute," in Robert Merton and Robert Nisbet, eds., *Contemporary Social Problems* (New York: Harcourt Brace Jovanovich, 1966), chapter 12.

49. Robert W. Winslow, "Anomie and Its Alternatives: A Self-Report Study of Delinquents," *The Sociological Quarterly* 8 (1967):468–80; see also, Rosenberg and Silverstein, *The Varieties of Delinquent Experience*, pp. 135–37.

50. Matza, *Becoming Deviant*, pp. 101–02.

51. Ibid., pp. 104–07; see also, Ian Taylor, Paul Walton, and Jock Young, *The New Criminology* (New York: Harper & Row, 1973), pp. 126–32.

52. Edwin H. Sutherland and Donald R. Cressey, *Criminology*, 10th ed. (Philadelphia: J. B. Lippincott, 1974), pp. 80–82.

53. Albert K. Cohen, *Delinquent Boys* (New York: Free Press, 1955), passim.

54. Albert K. Cohen and James Short, "Crime and Juvenile Delinquency," in Merton and Nisbet, *Contemporary Social Problems*.

55. Walter B. Miller, "Lower Class Culture as a Generating Milieu of Gang Delinquency," *Journal of Social Issues* 14 (1958):5–19.

56. Richard A. Cloward and Lloyd Ohlin, *Delinquency and Opportunity* (New York: Free Press, 1960).

57. Hirschi, *Causes of Delinquency*, pp. 3–10.

58. Michael Hindelang, "Causes of Delinquency: A Partial Replication and Extension," *Social Problems* 20 (Spring 1973):471–87.

59. Kenneth Polk, "Schools and the Delinquency Experience," *Criminal Justice and Behavior* 2, no. 4 (December 1975):315–38.

60. Walter E. Schafer, Carol Olexa, and Kenneth Polk, "Programmed for Social Class: Tracking in High School," *Transaction* 7 (October 1970):39-46.

61. Short and Nye, "Extent of Unrecorded Delinquency: Tentative Conclusions"; see also, Martin Gold, "Undetected Delinquent Behavior," *Journal of Research in Crime and Delinquency* 3 (January 1966):27–46; see also, Gold, *Delinquent Behavior in an American City*.

62. LaMar T. Empey and Steven G. Lubeck, *Explaining Delinquency* (Lexington, Mass.: D. C. Heath, 1971), p. 48.

63. Greenberg, "Delinquency and the Age Structure of Society," p. 79.

64. Ibid.

65. Paul C. Friday and Jerold Hage, "Youth Crime in Postindustrial Societies: An Integrated Perspective," *Criminology* 14, no. 3 (November 1976):347–68, especially 366.

66. Matza, *Delinquency and Drift*, pp. 62–63; see also, Empey and Lubeck, *Explaining Delinquency*, p. 171.

67. Matza, *Becoming Delinquent*, pp. 143–56.

68. Ronald Christensen, "Projected Percentage of U.S. Population with Criminal Arrest and Conviction Records," in President's Commission on Law Enforcement and Administration of Justice, *Task Force Report: Science and Technology* (Washington, D.C.: U.S. Government Printing Office, 1967), pp. 216–28.

69. Richard Perlman, "Juvenile Court Statistics, 1964," in *Children's Bureau Statistical Series No. 83* (Washington, D.C.: U.S. Government Printing Office, 1965); see also, Edwin M. Lemert, *Instead of Court: Diversion in Juvenile Justice* (Rockville, Md.: National Institute of Mental Health, 1971), p. 1.

70. Empey and Lubeck, *Explaining Delinquency*, pp. 170–72.

71. Nathan Goldman, "The Differential Selection of Juvenile Offenders for Court Appearance," in William J. Chambliss, ed., *Crime and the Legal Process* (New York: McGraw-Hill, 1969), pp. 264–90; see also, Malcolm Klein, *Police Processing of Juvenile Offenders: Toward the Development of Juvenile System Rates* (Los Angeles: L.A. County Subregional Board, Criminal Justice Planning Projects, California Council on Criminal Justice, 1970), part III.

72. James Q. Wilson, "The Police and the Delinquent in Two Cities," in Peter G. Garabedian, ed., *Becoming Delinquent: Young Offenders and the Correctional System* (Chicago: Aldine, 1970), pp. 111–17.

73. Donald J. Black and Albert J. Reiss, "Police Control of Juveniles," *American Sociological Review* 35 (February 1970):63–77.

74. Robert M. Terry, "The Screening of Juvenile Of-

fenders," *Journal of Criminal Law, Criminology and Police Science* 58 (June 1967):173–81; see also, Goldman, "The Differential Selection of Juvenile Offenders for Court Appearance."

75. Irving Piliavin and Scott Briar, "Police Encounters with Juveniles," *American Journal of Sociology* (September 1964):206–14; see also, Goldman, "The Differential Selection of Juvenile Offenders for Court Appearance"; see also, Black and Reiss, "Police Control of Juveniles."

76. Malcolm W. Klein et al., "The Explosion in Police Diversion Programs: Evaluating the Structural Dimensions of a Social Fad," in Klein, ed., *The Juvenile Justice System* (Beverly Hills: Sage Publications, 1976), pp. 101–20.

77. Harold Garfinkle, "Conditions of Successful Degradation Ceremonies," *American Journal of Sociology* 61 (1956):420–24.

78. Kai T. Erickson, "Notes on the Sociology of Deviance," in Howard S. Becker, ed., *The Other Side* (New York: Free Press, 1964); see also, Greenburg, "Delinquency and the Age Structure of Society."

79. Edwin M. Lemert, "Juvenile Justice: Quest and Realities," in Abraham S. Blumberg, ed., *The Scales of Justice* (Chicago: Aldine, 1970), pp. 141–62.

80. U.S. Department of Health, Education and Welfare, *Juvenile Court Statistics* (Washington, D.C.: U.S. Government Printing Office, 1975), p. 1.

81. Jay R. Williams and Martin Gold, "From Delinquent Behavior to Official Delinquency," *Social Problems* 20 (1972):209–29; see also, Anthony Platt, "The Triumph of Benevolence: The Origins of the Juvenile Justice System in the United States," in Richard Quinney, ed., *Criminal Justice in America: A Critical Understanding* (Boston: Little, Brown & Co., 1964), pp. 356–89.

82. Gene Kassebaum, *Delinquency and Social Policy* (Englewood Cliffs, N.J.: Prentice-Hall, 1974), p. 85.

83. Kittrie, *The Right To Be Different,* p. 121.

84. *A Study of the Administration of Juvenile Justice in California* (Sacramento: Governor's Special Study Commission on Juvenile Justice in California, 1960), part I, p. 12.

85. Kent v. United States, 383 U.S. 541 (1966) in Re Gault, in *Task Force Report: Juvenile Justice;* see also, in Re Winship, 396 U.S. 85, 90 S Ct. 1068 (1970).

86. Charles Cayten, "Emerging Patterns in the Administration of Juvenile Justice," *Journal of Urban Law* 49 (1971):377–98; see also, W. V. Stapleton and L. E. Teitelbaum, *In Defense of Youth* (New York: Russell Sage Foundation, 1972).

87. Robert M. Emerson, *Judging Delinquents; Context and Process Juvenile Court* (Chicago: Aldine, 1969), pp. 83–91; see also, Aaron V. Cicourel and John I. Kitsuse, *The Educational Decision-Makers* (Indianapolis: Bobbs-Merrill, 1963), p. 74; see also, Aaron V. Cicourel, *The Social Organization of Juvenile Justice* (New York: John Wiley & Sons, 1968).

88. Terrence P. Thornberry, "Race, Socioeconomic Status and Sentencing in the Juvenile Justice System," *Journal of Criminal Law and Criminology* 64, no. 1 (1973).

89. Ibid.

90. LaMar T. Empey, "Juvenile Justice Reform: Diversion, Due Process and Deinstitutionalization," in Lloyd E. Ohlin, ed., *Prisoners in America* (Englewood Cliffs, N.J.: Prentice-Hall, 1973), pp. 13–14.

91. Edwin M. Lemert, "Juvenile Justice: Quest and Realities," pp. 27–48.

92. Empey, "Juvenile Justice Reform: Diversion, Due Process and Deinstitutionalization," pp. 27–48.

93. Schur, *Radical Non-Intervention,* pp. 166–71; see also, Matza, *Delinquency and Drift,* pp. 106–14.

Chapter 5

1. There are several reviews of the relatively limited literature on women and crime which we have relied on; these include Dorie Klein, "The Etiology of Female Crime: A Review of the Literature," *Issues in Criminology* 8 (Fall 1973):3–30; Stephen Norland and Neal Shover, "Gender Roles and Female Criminality: Some Critical Comments," *Criminology* 15, no. 1 (May 1977):87–104; Dorie Klein and June Kress, "Any Women's Blues: A Critical Overview of Women, Crime and the Criminal Justice System," *Crime and Social Justice* 5 (Spring/Summer 1976):34–49.

2. See Freda Adler, *Sisters in Crime: The Rise of the New Female Criminal* (New York: McGraw-Hill, 1975). For a critique of this position, see Norland and Shover, "Gender Roles and Female Criminality," pp. 98–101; see also, Klein and Kress, "Any Women's Views," pp. 34–36.

3. The first of these models will rely on Adler, *Sisters in Crime,* and earlier sources as well as current data from the popular press. The second model, as well as the criticisms of the emphasis on sex gender as an explanation, will rely upon analysis by Rita Simon, *Women and Crime* (Lexington, Mass.: D. C. Heath, 1975), as well as the critique by Joseph G. Weis, "Liberation and Crime: The Invention of the New Female Criminal," *Crime and Social Justice* 6 (Fall/Winter 1976):17–27. These sources, official data from the FBI's *Uniform Crime Reports,* and the literature reviews and critiques cited in note 1 also provide the basis for our analysis throughout this chapter.

4. Sigmund Freud, *Female Sexuality* (London: Hogarth, 1931). For a critique of Freud's sexism, see Kate Millett, *Sexual Politics* (New York: Doubleday, 1970); see also, Cesare Lombroso, *The Female Offender* (New York: Appleton-Century-Crofts, 1970), originally published in Italian in 1903.

5. Sheldon and Eleanor Glueck, *Five Hundred Delinquent Women* (New York: Knopf, 1934), p. 96.

6. Ibid., pp. 308–18.

7. Otto Pollak, *The Criminality of Women* (Philadelphia: University of Pennsylvania Press, 1950).

8. Weis, "Liberation and Crime," p. 18.

9. Klein and Kress, "Any Women's Views," p. 41; see also, Dale Hoffman-Bustamante, "The Nature of Female Criminality," *Issues in Criminology* 8, no. 2 (1973):117–36.

10. Lombroso, *The Female Offender;* see also, Weis, "Liberation and Crime," p. 18; see also, Simon, *Women and Crime,* p. 9.

11. Sigmund Freud, *New Introductory Lectures on Psychoanalysis* (New York: W. W. Norton, 1933); see also, Millet, *Sexual Politics,* pp. 180–201.

12. Adler, *Sisters in Crime,* p. 87.

13. Ibid., p. 251.

14. Ibid., pp. 85–110.

15. Nancy B. Wise, "Juvenile Delinquency Among Middle-Class Girls," in Edmund D. Vaz, ed., *Middle-Class Delinquency* (New York: Harper & Row, 1967), pp. 179–88.

16. Weis, "Liberation and Crime," pp. 19–23.

17. Ibid., pp. 23–24; see also, Joseph G. Weis, "Delinquency Among the Well-to-Do," unpublished Ph.D. dissertation, University of California, Berkeley, 1973; see also, David F. Greenberg, "Delinquency and the Age Structure

of Society," in Peter Wickman and Phillip Whitten, eds., *Readings in Criminology* (Lexington, Mass.: D. C. Heath, 1978), pp. 66–86.

18. Weis, "Liberation and Crime," pp. 19–25.

19. Adler, *Sisters in Crime*, p. 3.

20. Mary Owen Cameron, *The Booster and the Snitch* (New York: Free Press, 1964); see also, Darrell J. Steffensmeier and Robert M. Terry, "Deviance and Respectability: An Observational Study of Reactions to Shoplifting," *Social Forces* 51, no. 4 (June 1973):417–26. This study, which takes exception to Pollak's argument that women are less apt to be detected, found that neither the sex of the shoplifter nor of store customers had any effect on the extent of reporting shoplifting offenses.

21. Klein and Kress, "Any Women's Blues," pp. 39–42.

22. Pollak, *The Criminality of Women*.

23. I. W. Thomas, *The Unadjusted Girl* (New York: Free Press, 1923).

24. Pollak, *The Criminality of Women*.

25. Kingsley Davis, "The Sociology of Prostitution," in Robert K. Merton and Robert A. Nisbet, eds., *Contemporary Social Problems* (New York: Harcourt Brace Jovanovich, 1961).

26. Klein and Kress, "Any Women's Blues," p. 41.

27. Simon, *Women and Crime*, p. 2.

28. Adler, *Sisters in Crime*, p. 24.

29. Klein and Kress, "Any Women's Blues," pp. 36–37.

30. W. H. Chafe, *The American Woman* (New York: Oxford University Press, 1972), p. 115.

31. Simon, *Women and Crime*, p. 16.

32. Klein and Kress, "Any Women's Blues," p. 37.

33. Ibid., p. 38.

34. Simon, *Women and Crime*, p. 18.

35. "Women Talk About Being Ex-Cons," *The Fortune News*, February 1977, p. 4.

36. Klein and Kress, "Any Women's Blues," pp. 38–39.

37. Simon, *Women and Crime*, p. 18.

38. Weis, "Liberation and Crime," pp. 18–19; see also, Klein and Kress, "Any Women's Blues," p. 41.

39. W. C. Reckless and B. A. Kay, *The Female Offenders*, in the President's Commission on Law Enforcement and Administration of Justice, 1967, and David Ward and E. Ward, "Crime and Violence by Women," *Crimes of Violence* 13, Appendix 17, President's Commission on Law Enforcement and Administration of Justice, 1968.

40. Angus Campbell, "The American Way of Mating, Marriage: Children Only Maybe," in Peter Wickman, ed., *Readings in Social Problems: Contemporary Perspectives* (New York: Harper & Row, 1977), pp. 125–29.

41. Paddy Quick, "Women's Work," *Review of Radical Political Economies* 4, no. 3 (July 1972):13.

42. Simon, *Women and Crime*, pp. 19–32. We have relied on Simon's summary of the changing status of women, although there are many other good sources. See also, Chafe, *The American Woman*.

43. Norland and Shover, "Gender Roles and Female Criminality," p. 96.

44. Simon, *Women and Crime*, pp. 40–45.

45. Ibid., p. 46.

46. Norland and Shover, "Gender Roles and Female Criminality," p. 93.

47. Pollak, *The Criminality of Women*.

48. Simon, *Women and Crime*, p. 47.

49. Camille Le Grand, "Rape and Rape Laws: Sexism in Society and Law," *California Law Review* 61 (May 1973):919–41.

50. Simon, *Women and Crime*, p. 49.

51. S. S. Nagel and L. J. Weitzman, "Women and Litigants," *The Hastings Law Journal* 23 (November 1971): 171–98.

52. Meda Chesney-Lind, "Judicial Enforcement of the Female Sex Role: The Family Court and the Female Delinquent," *Issues in Criminology* 8, no. 2 (Fall 1973):51–69.

53. Ibid., p. 63.

54. Simon, *Women and Crime*, p. 54.

55. Ibid., pp. 55–59.

56. Ibid., pp. 75–76.

57. L. Temen, "Discriminatory Sentencing of Women Offenders," *American Criminal Law Review* 11 (Winter 1973):353.

58. Simon, *Women and Crime*, pp. 60–63.

59. Klein and Kress, "Any Women's Blues," p. 43.

60. Rose Giallombardo, *Society of Women: A Study of a Women's Prison* (New York: John Wiley & Sons, 1966).

61. Klein and Kress, "Any Women's Blues," p. 44.

62. Rob Wilson, "U.S. Prison Population Sets Another Record," *Corrections Magazine* 3, no. 1 (March 1977):3–22.

63. Simon, *Women and Crime*, pp. 74–100.

Chapter 6

1. Richard Quinney, *The Social Reality of Crime* (Boston: Little, Brown & Co., 1970), p. 103.

2. Austin Turk, "Prospects for Theories of Criminal Behavior," *Journal of Criminal Law, Criminology and Police Science* (December 1964):454–61.

3. John M. Gillith and James M. Reinhardt, *Current Social Problems* (New York: American Book Company, 1933), pp. 652–53; see also, Richard Moran, "The Future of Crime and Its Control," paper presented at the annual meeting of the American Society of Criminology, Toronto, 1975.

4. Leon Radzinowicz, *Ideology and Crime* (New York: Columbia University Press, 1966), pp. 29–30.

5. Ibid., pp. 30–59.

6. N. J. Davis, *Sociological Constructions of Deviance: Perspectives and Issues in the Field* (Dubuque, Iowa: Wm. C. Brown Co., 1975), pp. 15–73; see also, Don C. Gibbons and Peter Garabedian, "Conservative, Liberal and Radical Criminology: Some Trends and Observations," in Charles E. Reasons, ed., *Crime and the Criminal* (Pacific Palisades, Calif.: Goodyear, 1974), pp. 51–53; see also, Radzinowicz, *Ideology and Crime*, pp. 103–28.

7. Radzinowicz, *Ideology and Crime*, pp. 103–28; see also, Gibbons and Garabedian, "Conservative, Liberal and Radical Criminology," p. 55.

8. Gibbons and Garabedian, "Conservative, Liberal and Radical Criminology," p. 55.

9. Ibid.

10. Richard L. Henshel and Robert A. Silverman, *Perception in Criminology* (New York: University of Columbia Press, 1975), pp. 3–4.

11. Ian Taylor, Paul Walton, and Jock Young, *The New Criminology* (New York: Harper & Row, 1973), p. 26; see also, Alvin W. Gouldner, Foreword to *The New Criminology*, p. xiv.

12. Marvin E. Wolfgang, "Cesare Lombroso," in Hermann Mannheim, ed., *Pioneers in Criminology*, 2nd ed. (Montclair, N.J.: Patterson Smith, 1972), pp. 232–91; see also, Radzinowicz, *Ideology and Crime*, p. 46; see also,

Gina Lombroso-Ferrero, *Criminal Man, According to the Classification of Cesare Lombroso*, reprinted with a new Introduction (Montclair, N.J.: Patterson Smith, 1972), pp. 7–19.

13. David Matza, *Becoming Deviant* (Englewood Cliffs, N.J.: Prentice-Hall, 1969), pp. 90–93.

14. Richard Dugdale, *The Jukes* (New York: Putnam, 1910); see also, Henry Goddard, *The Kallikaks* (New York: Macmillan Co., 1912). For a criticism of such studies of heredity, see Ashley Montagu, *Human Heredity* (New York: World, 1959), p. 125.

15. Quoted in Simon Dinitz and John P. Conrad, "Thinking About Dangerous Offenders," *Criminal Justice Abstracts* (March 1978):111.

16. Ernest A. Hooton, *Crime and the Man* (Cambridge, Mass.: Harvard University Press, 1939), pp. 396–97.

17. William H. Sheldon, in collaboration with E. M. Hart and E. McDermott, *Varieties of Delinquent Youth* (New York: Harper & Row, 1949); see also, Edwin H. Sutherland, "Critique of Sheldon's Varieties of Delinquent Youth," *American Sociological Review* 316 (1951):10–14.

18. Sheldon Glueck and Eleanor Glueck, *Physique and Delinquency* (New York: Harper & Row, 1956); see also, Albert Cohen, *Deviance and Control* (Englewood Cliffs, N.J.: Prentice-Hall, 1966), pp. 52–53.

19. Johannes Lange, *Crime and Destiny* (New York: Charles Boni, 1930).

20. National Institute of Mental Health, Center for Studies of Crime and Delinquency, *Report on XYZ Chromosomal Abnormality* (Washington, D.C.: U.S. Government Printing Office, 1970).

21. Alfred Lindesmith and Yale Levin, "The Lombrosean Myth in Criminology," *American Journal of Sociology* 42 (1973):670.

22. Vernon H. Mark, M.D., and Frank Ervin, M.D., *Violence and the Brain* (New York: Harper & Row, 1970), pp. 65, 108.

23. Dinitz and Conrad, "Thinking About Dangerous Offenders," pp. 111–12.

24. Kate Friedlander, *The Psychoanalytic Approach to Juvenile Delinquency* (New York: International Universities Press, 1947).

25. Franz Alexander and Hugo Staub, *The Criminal, the Judge and the Public* (New York: Free Press, 1956), pp. 52–85.

26. George B. Vold, *Theoretical Criminology* (New York: Oxford University Press, 1958), pp. 117–25.

27. Karl Schuessler and Donald Cressey, "Personality Characteristics of Criminals," *American Journal of Sociology* (March 1950):476–88.

28. Gordon P. Waldo and Simon Dinitz, "Personality Attributes of the Criminal: An Analysis of Research Studies, 1950–1965," *Journal of Research in Crime and Delinquency* 4 (July 1967):185–201.

29. Ibid.; see also, Vold, *Theoretical Criminology*, pp. 137–38.

30. Alan H. Saranson, "Sexual Psychopath Statutes," *Journal of Criminal Law, Criminology and Police Science* 51 (July–August 1970):215–18.

31. Edwin H. Sutherland, "The Diffusion of Sexual Psychopath Laws," *American Journal of Sociology* 56 (September 1950):145.

32. Edwin M. Schur, *Labeling Deviant Behavior* (New York: Harper & Row, 1971).

33. Friedlander, *The Psychoanalytic Approach to Juvenile Delinquency;* see also, Alexander and Staub, *The Criminal, the Judge and the Public.*

34. Emile Durkheim, *The Rules of Sociological Method,* trans. by Sarah A. Solovay and John H. Mueller, edited by George E. G. Catlin (New York: Free Press, 1938), pp. 1–13, 65–68; see also, Radzinowicz, *Ideology and Crime,* pp. 71–72.

35. Durkheim, *The Rules of Sociological Method,* pp. 65–68, 70; see also, Radzinowicz, *Ideology and Crime,* pp. 73–74.

36. Davis, *Sociological Constructions of Deviance,* pp. 41, 92–93, 121; see also, Taylor et al., *The New Criminology,* pp. 67–79.

37. Clifford R. Shaw, *Delinquency Areas* (Chicago: University of Chicago Press, 1929); see also, Clifford R. Shaw and Henry D. McKay, *Juvenile Delinquency and Urban Areas* (Chicago: University of Chicago Press, 1942); see also, Frederic Thrasher, *The Gang* (Chicago: University of Chicago Press, 1927), especially pp. 381–82; see also, Taylor et al., *The New Criminology,* pp. 115–24.

38. Davis, *Sociological Constructions of Deviance,* pp. 54–61; see also, Taylor et al., *The New Criminology,* p. 125.

39. Robert K. Merton, "Social Structure and Anomie," in Merton, *Social Theory and Social Structure,* rev. ed. (New York: Free Press, 1957), p. 134; see also, Taylor et al., *The New Criminology,* pp. 92–93; see also, Davis, *Sociological Constructions of Deviance,* pp. 96–110.

40. Taylor et al., *The New Criminology,* pp. 94–96; see also, Merton, "Social Structure and Anomie," p. 157.

41. Bernard Rosenberg and Harry Silverstein, *The Varieties of Delinquent Experience* (Waltham, Mass.: Blaisdell, 1969), passim.

42. Albert K. Cohen, *Delinquent Boys: The Culture of the Gang* (New York: Free Press, 1955).

43. Richard A. Cloward and Lloyd E. Ohlin, *Delinquency and Opportunity: A Theory of Delinquent Gangs* (New York: Free Press, 1960).

44. Walter P. Miller, "Lower Class Culture as a Generating Milieu of Gang Delinquency," *Journal of Social Issues* 14 (Summer 1958):5–19.

45. Travis Hirschi, *Causes of Delinquency* (Berkeley: University of California Press, 1969), pp. 4–10; see also, David J. Bordua, "A Critique of Sociological Interpretations of Gang Delinquency," *Annals of the American Academy of Political and Social Science* 338 (November 1961):120.

46. Matza, *Becoming Deviant,* chapter 5.

47. Ibid., pp. 101–02.

48. Ibid., p. 116.

49. Ibid., pp. 116–42.

50. Edwin H. Sutherland and Donald R. Cressey, *Criminology,* 10th ed. (Philadelphia: J. B. Lippincott, 1978), pp. 80–85.

51. Davis, *Sociological Constructions of Deviance,* pp. 132–34; see also, Albert Cohen, Alfred Lindesmith, and Karl Schuessler, eds., *The Sutherland Papers* (Bloomington: Indiana University Press, 1956), pp. 16, 103–05, 117–18.

52. Sutherland and Cressey, *Criminology,* 10th ed., pp. 87–93; see also some of the critical evaluations found in Daniel Glaser, "The Differential Association Theory of Crime," in Arnold Rose, ed., *Human Behavior and Social Process* (Boston: Houghton Mifflin, 1962), pp. 425–42; see also, Reed Adams, "The Adequacy of Differential Association Theory," *Journal of Research in Crime and Delinquency* 11 (January 1974):1–8; see also, James F. Short, Jr.,

"Differential Association and Delinquency," *Social Problems* 4 (1957):233–39.

53. Daniel Glaser, "Criminality Theories and Behavioral Images," *American Journal of Sociology* 61 (March 1956):433–44; see also, J. R. Stratton, "Differential Identification and Attitudes Toward Law," *Social Forces* 46 (December 1967):256–62.

54. Daniel Glaser, *Crime in Our Changing Society* (New York: Holt, Rinehart and Winston, 1978), pp. 126–27.

55. Melvin DeFleur and Richard Quinney, "A Reformulation of Sutherland's Differential Association Theory and a Strategy for Empirical Verification," *Journal of Research in Crime and Delinquency* 3 (January 1968):1–22.

56. Robert Burgess and Ronald Akers, "A Differential Association Reinforcement Theory of Criminal Behavior," *Social Problems* 3 (Fall 1966):28–47.

57. Ibid.

58. Taylor et al., *The New Criminology*, pp. 130–32.

59. Ronald Akers, *Deviant Behavior; A Social Learning Approach*, 2nd ed. (Belmont, Calif.: Wadsworth, 1977), pp. 42–57; see also, Rand Conger, "Social Control and Social Learning Models of Delinquency: A Synthesis," *Criminology* 14 (May 1976):17–40.

60. Matza, *Becoming Deviant*, p. 107; see also, Davis, *Sociological Constructions of Deviance*, pp. 136–37.

61. Matza, *Becoming Deviant*, pp. 112–48; see also, Howard S. Becker, *Outsiders: Studies in the Sociology of Deviance* (New York: Free Press, 1963), pp. 41–58; see also, Taylor et al., *The New Criminology*, pp. 189–90.

62. Matza, *Becoming Deviant*, pp. 107–08; see also, Taylor et al., *The New Criminology*, pp. 128–29.

63. Matza, *Becoming Deviant*, chapter 7.

64. Turk, "Prospects for Theories of Criminal Behavior," p. 454; see also, Matza, *Becoming Deviant*, Part I, passim.

65. Frank Tannenbaum, *Crime and Community* (Lexington: Ginn & Co., 1938), pp. 19–21.

66. Becker, *Outsiders*, pp. 33–34.

67. Ibid.; see also, Kai T. Erickson, "Notes on the Sociology of Deviance," *Social Problems* 9 (Spring 1962):307–14; see also, John Kitsuse, "Societal Reaction to Deviant Behavior: Problems of Theory and Method," *Social Problems* 9 (Winter 1962):247–57.

68. Edwin Lemert, *Social Pathology* (New York: McGraw-Hill, 1951), pp. 75–76.

69. Ibid.

70. Ibid.; see also, Edwin Lemert, *Human Deviance, Social Problems and Social Control*, rev. ed. (Englewood Cliffs, N.J.: Prentice-Hall, 1972), pp. 62–79; see also, Matza, *Becoming Deviant*, chapter 7.

71. Becker, *Outsiders*, pp. 34–39.

72. Lemert, *Social Pathology*, p. 43.

73. Egon Bittner, "The Police on Skid Row: A Study of Peace Keeping," *American Sociological Review* 32 (October 1967):699–715.

74. Jerome Skolnick, *Justice Without Trial*, 2nd ed. (New York: John Wiley & Sons, 1975).

75. Marvin Wolfgang, *Crime and Race: Conceptions and Misconceptions* (New York: Institute of Human Relations Press, 1964); see also, Irving Piliavin and Scott Briar, "Police Encounters with Juveniles," *American Journal of Sociology* 69 (September 1964):204–14.

76. Robert A. Scott, *The Making of Blind Men* (New York: Russell Sage, 1969).

77. Tannenbaum, *Crime and Community*, p. 18.

78. Aaron Cicourel, *The Social Organization of Juvenile Justice* (New York: John Wiley & Sons, 1968), pp. 121–22. Also, for a description of assumptions employed in ethnomethodology, see Cicourel, "The Acquisition of Social Structure: Toward a Developmental Sociology of Language and Meaning," in Jack D. Douglas, ed., *Understanding in Everyday Life* (Chicago: Aldine, 1970).

79. Schur, *Labeling Deviant Behavior*, chapter 3.

80. Robert M. Emerson, *Judging Delinquents* (Chicago: Aldine, 1969), pp. vii–viii.

81. Ibid., pp. 89–100.

82. Howard Becker, ed., *The Other Side: Perspectives on Deviance* (New York: Free Press, 1964), Introduction.

83. Schur, *Labeling Deviant Behavior*, p. 21.

84. Davis, *Sociological Constructions of Deviance*, p. 186; see also, Alfred Lindesmith, *Opiate Addiction* (Bloomington: Indiana University Press, 1965).

85. Davis, *Sociological Constructions of Deviance*; see also, Cicourel, *The Social Organization of Juvenile Justice*, pp. 335–36. Also, for a further critique regarding the imperative need for clear conceptual development and study by those using the labeling perspective, see Peter K. Manning, "Survey Essay on Deviance," *Contemporary Sociology* 2 (1973):123–28.

86. Ibid., pp. 171–72, 187–88.

87. Vold, *Theoretical Criminology*, pp. 203–08; see also, Taylor et al., *The New Criminology*, p. 238.

88. Thorsten Sellin, *Culture Conflict and Crime* (New York: Social Science Research Council, 1938).

89. Taylor et al., *The New Criminology*, p. 241.

90. Austin Turk, *Criminality and the Legal Order* (Chicago: Rand McNally, 1969), p. 53; see also, Turk, "Prospects for Theories of Criminal Behavior," pp. 454–61.

91. Turk, *Criminality and the Legal Order*, pp. 58–59; see also, Turk, "Conflict and Criminality," *American Sociological Review* 31 (June 1966):338–52.

92. John Lofland, *Deviance and Identity* (Englewood Cliffs, N.J.: Prentice-Hall, 1969), pp. 14–19.

93. Taylor et al., *The New Criminology*, pp. 253–55.

94. Richard Quinney, *The Social Reality of Crime*, pp. 14–15; see also, Peter L. Berger and Thomas Luckmann, *The Social Construction of Reality* (New York: Doubleday, 1966).

95. Quinney, *The Social Reality of Crime*, pp. 15–16.

96. Ibid., p. 23.

97. Ibid.; see also, Richard Quinney, *Criminology: Analysis and Critique of Crime in America* (Boston: Little, Brown & Co., 1975), p. 41.

98. See R. Serge, R. Denisoff, and Charles McCaghy, *Deviance, Conflict and Criminality* (Chicago: Rand McNally, 1973); William J. Chambliss and Robert B. Seidman, *Law, Order and Power* (Reading, Mass.: Addison-Wesley, 1971); Quinney, *The Social Reality of Crime*; Quinney, "Crime Control in Capitalist Society: A Critical Philosophy of Legal Order," *Issues in Criminology* 1 (Spring 1973):75–99; William Chambliss, ed., *Criminal Law in Action* (Santa Barbara, Calif.: Hamilton Pub. Co., 1975), pp. 5–6; and David Gordon, "Capitalism, Class and Crime in America," *Crime and Delinquency* 19 (April 1973):163–86.

99. Tom Wicker, "The Rich Get Richer," *New York Times*, June 29, 1972.

100. See Paul Hirst, "Marx and Engels on Law, Crime and Morality," *Economy and Society* 1 (February 1972):28–56; see also, Stephen Mugford, "Marxism and Criminality:

A Comment on the Symposium on the New Criminology," *Sociological Quarterly* 15 (Autumn 1974):591–96.

101. William J. Chambliss, *Functional and Conflict Theories of Crime* (New York: MSS Modular Publications, Module 17, 1974), pp. 1–23, especially p. 7.

102. Ibid., pp. 16–23.

103. Gordon, "Capitalism, Class and Crime in America," especially pp. 175–78.

104. Ibid., pp. 181–84.

105. Quinney, *Criminology: Analysis and Critique of Crime in America*, p. 41. Compare with his *Social Reality of Crime*, pp. 40–41.

106. Richard Quinney, *Critique of the Legal Order* (Boston: Little, Brown & Co., 1974), pp. 15–19.

107. Chambliss and Seidman, *Law, Order and Power*, pp. 54–74; see also, Quinney, *Critique of the Legal Order*, p. 16.

108. Peter K. Manning, "Deviance and Dogma," *British Journal of Criminology* 15 (January 1975):12–14, especially p. 14.

109. Gresham Sykes, "The Rise of Critical Criminology," *Journal of Criminal Law and Criminology* 65 (June 1974):206–13.

110. Stanton Wheeler, "Trends and Problems in the Sociological Study of Crime," *Social Problems* 23, no. 5 (June 1976):525–33; see also, Taylor et al., *The New Criminology*, pp. 170–71.

111. Don C. Gibbons, *Society, Crime and Criminal Careers*, 3rd ed. (Englewood Cliffs, N.J.: Prentice-Hall, 1977), p. 209.

112. Taylor et al., *The New Criminology*, p. 267.

113. See Turk, "Prospects for Theories of Criminal Behavior," p. 454.

114. See Matza, *Becoming Deviant*, Part II, passim; see also, Lemert, *Social Pathology*; see also, Becker, *Outsiders*.

115. See Quinney, *Critique of the Legal Order*; see also, Chambliss, *Functional and Conflict Theories of Crime*; see also, Gordon, "Capitalism, Class and Crime in America."

116. Marshall B. Clinard and Richard Quinney, *Criminal Behavior Systems: A Typology*, 2nd ed. (New York: Holt, Rinehart and Winston, 1973), p. 13.

117. See Herbert A. Bloch and Gilbert Geis, *Man, Crime and Society*, 2nd ed. (New York: Random House, 1970), pp. 167–379; see also, Sutherland and Cressey, *Criminology*, 10th ed., pp. 77–98; see also, Gibbons, *Society, Crime and Criminal Careers*, pp. 239–63.

118. See Clinard and Quinney, *Criminal Behavior Systems*, pp. 3–5. We rely on their rationale for the need for criminal typologies as a means for the organization of variations among offender types in this section.

119. Ibid., pp. 10–13.

120. Glaser, "Criminal Theories and Behavioral Images."

121. John Irwin, *The Felon* (Englewood Cliffs, N.J.: Prentice-Hall, 1970), p. 167.

122. Clinard and Quinney, *Criminal Behavior Systems*, p. 13; see also, Irwin, *The Felon*, pp. 3–4.

123. Clinard and Quinney, *Criminal Behavior Systems*; see also, Matza, *Becoming Deviant*, chapter 7.

124. Clinard and Quinney, *Criminal Behavior Systems*, pp. 14–21; see also, Matza, *Becoming Deviant*, chapters 5–7, passim.

Chapter 7

1. Edwin M. Lemert, *Human Deviance, Social Problems and Social Control*, 2nd ed. (Englewood Cliffs, N.J.: Prentice-Hall, 1972), pp. 62–94.

2. John Irwin, *The Felon* (Englewood Cliffs, N.J.: Prentice-Hall, 1970), pp. 3–4. Irwin suggests that the terms "action" or "behavior system" will be used interchangeably to refer to the social world of the actor. He or she may move in and out of membership in this action system, and thus act upon these and other beliefs and identities, criminal or noncriminal.

3. James A. Inciardi, *Careers in Crime* (Chicago: Rand McNally, 1975), p. 1.

4. Ibid., p. 2.

5. Frank Aydelotte, *Elizabethan Rogues and Vagabonds* (Oxford, England, 1913), p. 1; see also, Frank Gibney, *The Operators* (New York: Harper & Row, 1960), p. 111.

6. Inciardi, *Careers in Crime*, p. 9; see also, Arthur V. Judges, *The Elizabethan Underworld* (London: George Routledge, 1930), pp. 149–78.

7. Inciardi, *Careers in Crime*, pp. 9–11.

8. Edwin H. Sutherland, ed., *The Professional Thief* (Chicago: University of Chicago Press, 1937), pp. vii–viii.

9. Inciardi, *Careers in Crime*, pp. 12–13.

10. Neal Shover, "External Relations of Burglars," *Social Problems* 10 (1973):499–513.

11. Bruce Jackson, *A Thief's Primer* (New York: Macmillan Co., 1969), passim.

12. Harry King, *The Box Man: A Professional Thief's Journey*, as told to and edited by Bill Chambliss (New York: Harper & Row, 1972), p. 51.

13. Joint Economic Committee, U.S. Congress Press Release, Washington, D.C., December 20, 1976.

14. Jackson, *A Thief's Primer*, pp. 19–24; see also, King, *The Box Man*.

15. Sutherland, *The Professional Thief*.

16. Mary O. Cameron, *The Booster and the Switch: Department Store Shoplifting* (New York: Free Press, 1964).

17. Inciardi, *Careers in Crime*, pp. 18–19; see also, Cameron, *The Booster and the Switch*.

18. Cameron, *The Booster and the Switch*, p. 161.

19. Inciardi, *Careers in Crime*, p. 21.

20. Sutherland, *The Professional Thief*, p. 56.

21. David Maurer, *The American Confidence Man* (Springfield, Ill.: Charles C Thomas, 1974), p. 6; see also, Maurer, *Whiz Mob: A Correlation of the Technical Argot of Pickpockets with their Behavior Pattern* (Gainesville, Fla.: American Dialect Society, 1955); see also, Maurer, *The Big Con* (Indianapolis: Bobbs-Merrill, 1940); see also, Erving Goffman, "On Cooling the Mark Out: Some Aspects of Adaptation to Failure," *Psychiatry* 15 (November 1952):451–63.

22. Maurer, *The American Confidence Man*; see also, Sutherland, *The Professional Thief*, pp. 56–57.

23. FBI, *Uniform Crime Reports, 1975* (Washington, D.C.: U.S. Government Printing Office, 1975), p. 6. Unless otherwise noted, crime statistics are from this volume of the UCR.

24. Lemert, *Human Deviance, Social Problems and Social Control*, 2nd ed., pp. 150–61; see also, Sutherland, *The Professional Thief*; see also, Jackson, *A Thief's Primer*, especially note, p. 229.

25. Joint Economic Committee, press release, Dec. 20, 1976.

26. Irwin A. Berg, "A Comparative Study of Forgers," *Journal of Applied Psychology* 28 (June 1944):232–38.

27. James A. Inciardi, "Vocational Crime," in Daniel Glaser, ed., *Handbook of Criminology* (Chicago: Rand Mc-

Nally, 1974), p. 317.

28. Sutherland, *The Professional Thief*, pp. 79–80.
29. Jackson, *A Thief's Primer*, pp. 143–44.
30. Ibid., pp. 123–25.
31. John Irwin and Donald R. Cressey, "Thieves, Convicts and the Inmate Culture," in Irwin, *The Felon*, p. 71.
32. CBS, "Sixty Minutes," September 10, 1977; see also, Irwin, *The Felon*.
33. Inciardi, *Careers in Crime*, p. 74; see also, Sutherland, *The Professional Thief*.
34. Inciardi, *Careers in Crime*, p. 33.
35. King, *The Box Man*.
36. Jackson, *A Thief's Primer*, p. 130.
37. Duncan Chappell and Marilyn Walsh, "No Questions Asked: A Consideration of the Crime of Criminal Receiving," *Crime and Delinquency* 20, no. 3 (April 1974):157–68.
38. President's Commission on Law Enforcement and the Administration of Justice, *Task Force Report: Crime and Its Impact—An Assessment* (Washington, D.C.: U.S. Government Printing Office, 1967), p. 99.
39. Carl B. Klockars, *The Professional Fence* (New York: Free Press, 1974), p. 87; see also, Gerald Howson, *Thief-Taker General* (New York: St. Martins Press, 1971).
40. Inciardi, *Careers in Crime*, p. 69.
41. Ibid., p. 70; see also, Jackson, *A Thief's Primer*, pp. 67–122; see also, Maurer, *The Big Con*, pp. 150–53.
42. Peter Letkemann, *Crime as Work* (Englewood Cliffs, N.J.: Prentice-Hall, 1973), chapter 4.
43. Inciardi, *Careers in Crime*, p. 74; see also, Sutherland, *The Professional Thief*.
44. Inciardi, "Vocational Crime," pp. 345–56.
45. Ibid., pp. 356–59.
46. Ibid., pp. 357–59; see also, Werner J. Einstadter, "The Social Organization of Armed Robbery," *Social Problems* 17 (Summer 1969):64–83.
47. Klockars, *The Professional Fence*, pp. 28, 171–72.
48. Letkemann, *Crime as Work*, chapter 4; see also, Jackson, *A Thief's Primer*, pp. 67–120.
49. Inciardi, *Careers in Crime*, p. 105.
50. President's Commission on Law Enforcement and the Administration of Justice, *Task Force Report: Organized Crime* (Washington, D.C.: U.S. Government Printing Office, 1967), p. 5.
51. Frederick Sondern, Jr., *Brotherhood of Evil: The Mafia* (New York: Farrar, Straus & Giroux, 1959), p. 71.
52. George B. Vold, *Theoretical Criminology* (New York: Oxford University Press, 1958), pp. 279–80.
53. Ibid., p. 240; see also, Thomas C. Schelling, "Economic Analysis of Organized Crime," in President's Commission, *Task Force Report: Organized Crime*, pp. 114–15.
54. Thomas Plate, *Crime Pays* (New York: Ballantine Books, 1977), p. 162.
55. Donald R. Cressey, "Methodological Problems in the Study of Organized Crime as a Social Problem," *Annals of the American Academy of Political and Social Science* (November 1967):105.
56. President's Commission, *Task Force Report: Organized Crime*, pp. 7–10.
57. Ned Polsky, "Research Method, Morality and Criminology," in *Hustlers, Beats and Others* (Chicago: Aldine, 1967); see also, John Irwin, "Participant-Observation of Criminals," in Jack Douglas, ed., *Research on Deviance* (New York: Random House, 1972), pp. 117–39.
58. William J. Chambliss, "Vice, Corruption, Bureaucracy, and Power," *Wisconsin Law Review* (1971):1150–73.
59. Joseph L. Albini, *The American Mafia: Genesis of a Legend* (New York: Appleton-Century-Crofts, 1971).
60. Francis A. J. Ianni, *A Family Business: Kinship and Social Control in Organized Crime* (New York: Russell Sage Foundation, 1972).
61. Albini, *The American Mafia*, p. 8.
62. Inciardi, *Careers in Crime*, p. 105.
63. Sondern, *Brotherhood of Evil*, p. 69.
64. Ibid.
65. Schelling, "Economic Analysis of Organized Crime," pp. 114–15.
66. Inciardi, *Careers in Crime*, p. 107.
67. Ibid., pp. 120–21; see also, Cressey, "Methodological Problems in the Study of Organized Crime as a Social Problem."
68. Norval Morris and Gordon Hawkins, *The Honest Politician's Guide to Crime Control* (Chicago: The University of Chicago Press, 1970), pp. 231–33; see also, Cressey, "Methodological Problems in the Study of Organized Crime as a Social Problem"; see also, Schelling, "Economic Analysis of Organized Crime," pp. 114–15.
69. Inciardi, *Careers in Crime*, pp. 118–28.
70. Ibid.; see also, Daniel Bell, "Crime as an American Way of Life," in Bell, ed., *End of Ideology* (New York: Free Press, 1960), p. 20.
71. Ianni, *A Family Business*, p. 11; see also, Francis A. J. Ianni, "New Mafia: Black, Hispanic, and Italian Styles," *Society* 11 (March–April 1974):26.
72. Donald R. Cressey, *The Theft of a Nation* (New York: Harper & Row, 1969), p. x.
73. Ibid., pp. x–xi.
74. See Bell, *End of Ideology*; see also, Albini, *The American Mafia*; see also, Gordon Hawkins, "God and the Mafia," *Public Interest* 14 (Winter 1969):24–51; see also, Ianni, *A Family Business*.
75. Hawkins, "God and the Mafia," pp. 67–70.
76. John F. Galliher and James A. Cain, "Citations in Support for the Mafia Myth in Criminology Textbooks," *American Sociologist* (May 1974):68–74.
77. Ianni, "Black, Hispanic, and Italian Styles," pp. 26–28.
78. Edmund Bergler, *The Psychology of Gambling* (New York: Hill and Wang, 1957); see also, Herbert A. Block and Gilbert Geis, *Man, Crime and Society*, 2nd ed. (New York: Random House, 1970), pp. 199–201.
79. Francis A. J. Ianni, *Black Mafia: Ethnic Succession in Organized Crime* (New York: Simon & Schuster, 1974); see also, Ianni, "New Mafia: Black, Hispanic, and Italian Styles," pp. 34–50.
80. S. Drake and H. R. Cayton, *Black Metropolis* (New York: Harcourt Brace Jovanovich, 1945), chapter 17.
81. Ianni, "Black, Hispanic, and Italian Styles," pp. 30–35.
82. President's Commission on Law Enforcement and the Administration of Justice, *The Challenge of Crime in a Free Society* (Washington, D.C.: U.S. Government Printing Office, 1967), pp. 190–91; see also, Joint Economic Committee, press release, Dec. 20, 1976.
83. Gilbert Geis, *Not the Law's Business?* (Washington, D.C.: U.S. Government Printing Office, 1972), p. 245.
84. Plate, *Crime Pays*, pp. 130–35.
85. Ibid., pp. 136–39; see also, Ianni, "Black, Hispanic, and Italian Styles," pp. 29–30.
86. Mark H. Moore, *Buy or Bust?* (Lexington, Mass.:

D. C. Heath, 1977), pp. 51–54, 205.

87. Ibid.; see also, Plate, *Crime Pays,* pp. 140–41; see also, Schelling, "Economic Analysis of Organized Crime"; see also, Lawrence J. Redlinger, "Marketing and Distributing Heroin: Some Sociological Observations," in Peter Wickman and Phillip Whitten, eds., *Readings in Criminology* (Lexington, Mass.: D. C. Heath, 1978), pp. 277–79.

88. Moore, *Buy or Bust?* pp. 59–61.

89. Ianni, "Black, Hispanic, and Italian Styles," pp. 31–32.

90. *New York Times,* July 31, 1977, p. 31.

91. Ibid.

92. Bell, "Crime as an American Way of Life," chapter 3.

93. Ianni, "Black, Hispanic, and Italian Styles," pp. 34–35.

94. Bell, "Crime as an American Way of Life," pp. 131, 141.

95. Ibid., p. 131; see also, David Matza, "Latency and Irony," in Matza, *Becoming Deviant* (Englewood Cliffs, N.J.: Prentice-Hall, 1969), pp. 68–80.

96. President's Commission, *Task Force Report: Organized Crime,* p. 4.

97. Plate, *Crime Pays,* p. 138.

98. President's Commission, *Task Force Report: Organized Crime,* pp. 4–5.

99. *New York Times,* May 22, 1977, p. 1.

100. Plate, *Crime Pays,* p. 142.

101. *New York Times,* March 3, 1977, p. 1.

102. Cited in Plate, *Crime Pays,* pp. 143–44.

103. Plate, *Crime Pays,* pp. 142–43; see also, Stuart Hills, *Crime Power and Morality: The Criminal Law Process in the U.S.* (Scranton, Pa.: Chandler, 1971), p. 144.

104. Plate, *Crime Pays,* p. 144; see also, President's Commission, *Task Force Report: Organized Crime.*

105. Ianni, "Black, Hispanic, and Italian Styles."

106. President's Commission, *Task Force Report: Organized Crime,* pp. 61–79.

107. Chambliss, "Vice, Corruption, Bureaucracy, and Power," pp. 1172–73.

108. *New York Times,* August 26, 1977.

109. *New York Times,* March 17, 1977, p. 16.

110. Plate, *Crime Pays,* p. 144.

111. Robert K. Merton, *Social Theory and Social Structure* (New York: Free Press, 1957), pp. 71–72; see also, Matza, *Becoming Deviant,* pp. 53–61.

Chapter 8

1. Task Force Report on Violent Aspects of Protest and Confrontation of the National Commission on the Causes and Prevention of Violence, *The Politics of Protest* (New York: Simon & Schuster, 1969), pp. 8–21.

2. Quoted in Marvin Wolfgang, "Contemporary Perspectives on Violence," in Duncan Chappell and John Monahan, eds. *Violence and Criminal Justice* (Lexington, Mass.: D. C. Heath, 1975), pp. 1–2.

3. D. J. Mulvihill, M. M. Tumin, and L. A. Curtis, *Crimes of Violence,* vol. II, Staff Report to National Commission on the Causes and Prevention of Violence (Washington, D. C.: U.S. Government Printing Office, 1969), p. 4; see also, Chappell and Monahan, *Violence and Criminal Justice,* pp. xv–xvi.

4. FBI, *Uniform Crime Reports, 1975* (Washington, D.C.: U.S. Government Printing Office, 1975), pp. 12–20. Unless otherwise noted, FBI data are from this source throughout this chapter.

5. Roger Lane, "Criminal Violence in America: The First Hundred Years," *Annals of the American Academy of Political and Social Science* 423 (January 1976):1–13.

6. Hans Toch, *Violent Men* (Chicago: Aldine, 1969). This is a sophisticated approach that seeks to describe violent-prone individuals; see also, W. Lindsey Neustatter, *The Mind of the Murderer* (New York: Philosophical Library, 1957).

7. Toch, *Violent Men.*

8. Truman Capote, *In Cold Blood* (New York: Random House, 1966); see also, Irving Malin, *Truman Capote's In Cold Blood: A Critical Handbook* (Belmont, Calif.: Wadsworth, 1969).

9. Marvin E. Wolfgang, "A Sociological Analysis of Criminal Homicide," *Federal Probation* 25 (March 1961): 48–55; see also, M. E. Wolfgang, *Patterns of Criminal Homicide* (Philadelphia, University of Pennsylvania Press, 1958, for a more complete description.

10. See Clifford R. Shaw and Henry McKay, *Juvenile Delinquency in Urban Areas* (Chicago: University of Chicago Press, 1942); see also, Daniel Glaser, "Criminality Theories and Behavioral Images," *American Journal of Sociology* 61 (March 1956):433–44; see also, V. L. Swigert and R. G. Farrell, *Murder, Inequality and the Law* (Lexington, Mass.: D. C. Heath, 1976), pp. 39–58.

11. Marvin E. Wolfgang and Franco Ferracuti, *The Subculture of Violence* (New York: Barnes & Noble, 1967).

12. Ibid.

13. Marvin E. Wolfgang, Robert M. Figlio, and Thorsten Sellin, *Delinquency in a Birth Cohort* (Chicago: University of Chicago Press, 1972), pp. 221–42.

14. Harold Garfinkel, "Research Note on Inter- and Intra-Racial Homicides," *Social Forces* 27 (1949):369–81; see also, G. Myrdal, *An American Dilemma* (New York: Harper & Row, 1944).

15. President's Commission on Law Enforcement and the Administration of Justice, *The Challenge of Crime in a Free Society* (Washington, D.C.: U.S. Government Printing Office, 1967). Hereafter referred to as Crime Commission.

16. *Boston Globe,* September 9, 1977, p. 16.

17. Shaw and McKay, *Juvenile Delinquency and Urban Areas.*

18. Wolfgang, "Contemporary Perspectives on Violence," p. 3.

19. Mulvihill et al., *Crimes of Violence,* vol. II, p. 86.

20. Wolfgang, "Contemporary Perspectives on Violence," p. 4; see also, Wolfgang, *Patterns of Criminal Homicide,* for a discussion of subculture of violence. For a more specific revision of this concept, see Lynn A. Curtis, *Violence, Race and Culture* (Lexington, Mass.: D. C. Heath, 1975), chapters 3–5.

21. Curtis, *Violence, Race and Culture,* chapters 3–5; see also, Lynn A. Curtis, *Criminal Violence: Inquiries into National Patterns and Behavior,* Ph.D. dissertation, University of Pennsylvania, 1972. Cited in Curtis, above (published by D. C. Heath, Lexington Books, 1974).

22. David Matza, *Delinquency and Drift* (New York: John Wiley & Sons, 1964), pp. 62–63; see also, Curtis, *Violence, Race and Culture,* pp. 9–10.

23. Curtis, *Violence, Race and Culture,* pp. 49–53.

24. David F. Greenberg, "Delinquency and the Age Structure of Society," *Contemporary Crisis* 1, no. 2 (1977):206–07.

25. M. Amir, *Patterns of Forcible Rape,* Ph.D. dissertation, University of Pennsylvania, p. 70. Cited in Franco

Ferracuti and Graeme Newman, "Assaultive Offenses," in Daniel Glaser, ed., *Handbook of Criminology* (Chicago: Rand McNally, 1974), p. 182.

26. Greenberg, "Delinquency and the Age Structure of Society," p. 208.

27. Law Enforcement Assistance Administration, *Criminal Victimization in the U.S.: A Comparison of 1973 and 1974 Findings* (Washington, D.C.: U.S. Government Printing Office, 1976), No. SD-NCP-N3.

28. John E. Conklin, *Robbery and the Criminal Justice System* (Englewood Cliffs, N.J.: Prentice-Hall, 1972), chapter 5.

29. John E. Conklin, "Robbery, the Elderly and Fear: An Urban Problem in Search of a Solution," in Jack and Sharon Goldsmith, eds., *Crime and the Elderly* (Lexington, Mass.: Lexington Books, D. C. Heath, 1975), pp. 99–110.

30. Conklin, *Robbery and the Criminal Justice System*, chapter 5.

31. Wolfgang, *Patterns of Criminal Homicide*; see also, Wolfgang, "A Sociological Analysis of Criminal Homicide"; see also, Swigert and Farrell, *Murder, Inequality and the Law*.

32. Mulvihill et al., *Crimes of Violence*, vol. II, p. 1244.

33. Conklin, *Robbery and the Criminal Justice System*, pp. 79–100.

34. Amir, *Patterns of Forcible Rape*, p. 112.

35. Paul H. Gebhard, John H. Gagnon, Wardell Pomeroy, and Cornelia V. Christenson, *Sex Offenders: An Analysis of Types* (New York: Harper & Row, 1965), pp. 192–94.

36. Howard Erlanger, "The Empirical Status of the Subculture of Violence Thesis," *Social Problems* 22 (December 1974):280–92.

37. R. Bryce Young, *Criminal Law: Codes and Cases* (New York: McGraw-Hill, 1972), p. 153.

38. Ibid.
39. Ibid.
40. Ibid.
41. Ibid.

42. Herbert A. Bloch and Gilbert A. Geis, *Man, Crime and Society* (New York: Random House, 1970), p. 226.

43. Preben Wolf, "Crime and Development: An International Comparison of Crime Rates," in Nils Christie, ed., *Scandinavian Studies in Criminology*, vol. 3 (Oslo: Scandinavian University Books, 1971), p. 111.

44. Edwards Veleri and Graeme Newman, "International Crime Statistics: An Overview from a Comparative Perspective," *Abstracts on Crime and Penology* 1, 2, 3 (May–June, 1977):258–59.

45. Marvin E. Wolfgang, " 'Victim-Precipitated' Criminal Homicide," *Journal of Criminal Law, Criminology and Police Science* 4 (1957):1–11.

46. Swigert and Farrell, *Murder, Inequality and the Law*, pp. 39–46.

47. Ibid., pp. 46–47.
48. Ibid., pp. 50–51.
49. Ibid., pp. 47–48.
50. Ibid., pp. 45–56.
51. Ibid., pp. 54–58.

52. Suzanne K. Steinmetz and Murray Straus, "The Family as a Cradle of Violence," in Peter Wickman and Phillip Whitten, eds., *Readings in Criminology* (Lexington, Mass.: D. C. Heath, 1978), pp. 59–65.

53. Ibid., p. 60; see also, FBI, *Uniform Crime Reports, 1975*, pp. 225–27.

54. Steinmetz and Straus, "The Family as a Cradle of Violence," pp. 61–62.

55. *New York Times,* August 11, 1977.

56. Steinmetz and Straus, "The Family as a Cradle of Violence," pp. 61–62.

57. Maure Hurt, *Child Abuse and Neglect: A Report on the Status of Neglect*, U.S. Department of Health, Education and Welfare (Washington, D.C.: U.S. Government Printing Office, 1974), DHEW # COHD 74-20, p. 5.

58. Ibid., p. 7.
59. Ibid., p. 8.
60. Ibid., p. 5.

61. C. Henry Kempe et al., "The Battered Child Syndrome," *Journal of the American Medical Association* 181 (July 1962):17–24; see also, C. Henry Kempe, "The Battered Child and the Hospital," *Hospital Practice* 4 (October 1969):44–57.

62. David Gil, *Violence Against Children* (Cambridge, Mass.: Harvard University Press, 1970), pp. 60–67, 141.

63. Hurt, *Child Abuse and Neglect*, pp. 6–7.

64. Richard J. Light, "Abused and Neglected Children in America," *Harvard Educational Review* 43 (November 1973):566–98.

65. Conrad G. Paulson, "The Law and Abused Children," in Ray E. Helfer and C. Henry Kempe, eds., *The Battered Child* (Chicago: University of Chicago Press, 1968), p. 176.

66. Hurt, *Child Abuse and Neglect*, p. 8.

67. William J. Goode, "Force and Violence in the Family," *Journal of Marriage and the Family* 33 (November 1971):624–36.

68. Suzanne K. Steinmetz, "Occupational Environment in Relation to Physical Punishment and Dogmatism," in Suzanne Steinmetz and Murray K. Straus, eds., *Violence in the Family* (New York: Dodd, Mead & Co., 1974).

69. Brian Lauer et al., "Battered Child Syndrome," *Pediatrics* 54 (July 1974):67–70; see also, Serapio R. Zalba, "Battered Children," *Transaction* 8 (July–August 1971):58–61.

70. Hurt, *Child Abuse and Neglect*, p. 12.

71. Stephen J. Pfohl, "The Discovery of Child Abuse," in Wickman and Whitten, *Readings in Criminology*, pp. 214–25.

72. Ibid., pp. 216–18; see also, Anthony M. Platt, *The Child Savers: The Invention of Juvenile Delinquency* (Chicago: University of Chicago Press, 1969); see also, S. J. Fox, "Juvenile Justice Reform: An Historical Perspective," *Stanford Law Review* 22 (June 1970):1187–1239.

73. Gil, *Violence Against Children.*

74. Pfohl, "The Discovery of Child Abuse," pp. 219–23.

75. Toch, *Violent Men.*

76. Ibid.

77. James Fitzjames Stephen, *History of the Criminal Law in England*, vol. I (London: Butterworths, 1886), pp. 117–18, quoted in Duncan Chappell, "Forcible Rape and the Criminal Justice System," *Crime and Delinquency* (April 1976):126.

78. Kate Millet, *Sexual Politics* (New York: Avon Books, Equinox Edition, 1971), p. 44.

79. Eldridge Cleaver, *Soul on Ice* (New York: McGraw-Hill, 1968), p. 14.

80. Susan Brownmiller, *Against Our Will: Men, Women and Rape* (New York: Simon & Schuster, 1975), pp. 423–24.

81. U.S. Department of Justice, Criminal Victimization Surveys in Eight American Cities: A Comparison of 1971/

72 and 1974/75 Findings (Washington, D.C.: U.S. Government Printing Office, 1976), pp. 15–131, passim. The earlier studies by the National Victimization Study, conducted for the Crime Commission in 1967 showed a ratio of between 3 and 4 as contrasted with UCR data, except for homicide and motor vehicle theft.

82. Chappell, "Forcible Rape and the Criminal Justice System," p. 131.

83. FBI, *Uniform Crime Reports, 1975,* p. 23; see also, Young, *Criminal Law: Codes and Cases,* pp. 224–25.

84. Chappell, "Forcible Rape and the Criminal Justice System," pp. 131–33.

85. J. Betrus, "Rape: An Act of Possession," *Battle Acts* (April–May 1972):93.

86. Gebbard et al., *Sex Offenders: An Analysis of Types,* cited in J. Gagnon, "Sexual Conduct and Crime," in Glaser, *Handbook of Criminology,* p. 264.

87. Richard L. Jenkins, "The Making of the Sex Offender," in Clyde B. Vedder et al., eds., *Criminology: A Book of Readings* (New York: Dryden Press, 1953), pp. 293–300.

88. These items were abstracted from accounts in newspapers and news magazines, e.g., *Detroit Daily News, New York Times, Newsweek,* and *Time* for dates cited.

89. Colin Sheppard, "The Violent Offender: Let's Examine the Taboo," *Federal Probation* 35 (December 1971):12–22.

90. E. Wenk, J. Robinson, and G. Smith, "Can Violence Be Predicted?" *Crime and Delinquency* 18 (1972):393–402.

91. Norval Morris, *The Future of Imprisonment* (Chicago: University of Chicago Press, 1974), pp. 67–71.

92. Henry Steadman and Joseph Cocozza, *Careers of the Criminally Insane* (Lexington, Mass.: D. C. Heath, 1974).

93. John Monahan, "The Prediction of Violence," in Chappell and Monahan, *Violence and Criminal Justice,* p. 20.

94. Morris, *The Future of Imprisonment,* pp. 80–84.

95. Swigert and Farrell, *Murder, Inequality and the Law,* p. 58.

Chapter 9

1. Nanette J. Davis, *Sociological Constructions of Deviance* (Dubuque, Iowa: Wm. C. Brown, 1975), p. 150.

2. Bruce Jackson, *A Thief's Primer* (New York: Macmillan Co., 1969), pp. 19–44.

3. Davis, *Sociological Constructions of Deviance,* pp. 140–41.

4. Marshall B. Clinard and Richard Quinney, *Criminal Behavior Systems: A Typology,* 2nd ed. (New York: Holt, Rinehart & Winston, 1973), pp. 18–19, 57–131.

5. Peter Letkemann, *Crime as Work* (Englewood Cliffs, N.J.: Prentice-Hall, 1973), p. 36.

6. David Matza, *Delinquency and Drift* (New York: John Wiley & Sons, 1964), p. 60; see also, Gresham Sykes and David Matza, "Techniques of Neutralization: A Theory of Delinquency," *American Sociological Review* 22 (December 1957):664–70.

7. Data on the incidence of crime in this chapter, unless otherwise noted, are from FBI, *Uniform Crime Reports, 1975* (Washington, D.C.: U.S. Government Printing Office, 1976); see also, William E. Cobb, "Shoplifting," in L. D. Savitz and N. Johnston, eds., *Crime in Society* (New York: John Wiley & Sons, 1978), pp. 923–24.

8. President's Commission on Law Enforcement and Administration of Justice, *The Challenge of Crime in a Free Society* (Washington, D.C.: U.S. Government Printing Office, 1967), p. 30.

9. Mary Owen Cameron, *The Booster and the Snitch: Department Store Shoplifting* (New York: Free Press, 1969), passim and p. 110.

10. Erhard Blankenburg, "The Selectivity of Legal Sanctions: An Empirical Investigation of Shoplifting," *Law and Society* 11 (Fall 1976):109–30; see also, Robert E. Kraut, "Deterrent and Definitional Influences on Shoplifting," *Social Problems* 23 (February 1976):358–68.

11. Special Report, "Ripoffs: New American Way of Life," *U.S. News & World Report,* May 31, 1976, pp. 29–31.

12. FBI, *Uniform Crime Reports, 1975,* pp. 6, 43.

13. Harrison Salisbury, *The Shook-Up Generation* (New York: Harper & Row, 1958); see also, President's Commission, *The Challenge of Crime in a Free Society,* p. 43.

14. President's Commission, *The Challenge of Crime in a Free Society,* p. 43.

15. Carl Werthman, "The Function of Social Definitions in the Development of Delinquent Careers," in President's Commission on Law Enforcement and Administration of Justice, *Task Force Report: Juvenile Delinquency and Youth Crime* (Washington, D.C.: U.S. Government Printing Office, 1967), p. 156.

16. *U.S. News & World Report,* May 31, 1976, p. 30.

17. Edwin Lemert, "An Isolation of Closure Theory of Naive Check Forgery," *Journal of Criminal Law, Criminology and Police Science* 44 (October 1953):296–307.

18. Walter B. Miller, "Violent Crime in City Gangs," *Annals of the American Academy of Political and Social Sciences* 364 (1966):96–112.

19. Lemert, "An Isolation of Closure Theory of Naive Check Forgery," p. 305.

20. Albert Cohen, *Delinquent Boys: The Culture of the Gang* (New York: Free Press, 1955).

21. Gilbert Geis, "Avocational Crime," in Daniel Glaser, ed., *Handbook of Criminology* (Chicago: Rand McNally, 1974), p. 291.

22. Cameron, *The Booster and the Snitch,* pp. 147–48.

23. Andrew L. Wade, "Social Processes in the Act of Juvenile Vandalism," in Clinard and Quinney, *Criminal Behavior Systems,* pp. 98–108.

24. Lemert, "An Isolation of Closure Theory of Naive Check Forgery."

25. Cameron, *The Booster and the Snitch.*

26. William Wattenberg and James Balistrieri, "Automobile Theft: A Favored Group Delinquency," *American Journal of Sociology* 57 (May 1952):575–79.

27. Sykes and Matza, "Techniques of Neutralization," pp. 664–70.

28. Bertram Spiller, "Delinquency and Middle Class Goals," *Journal of Criminal Law, Criminology and Police Science* 56 (December 1965):463–78.

29. Sykes and Matza, "Techniques of Neutralization," pp. 667–68; see also, Lemert, "An Isolation of Closure Theory of Naive Check Forgery," pp. 304–06.

30. Sykes and Matza, "Techniques of Neutralization," p. 669.

31. Ibid., pp. 669–70.

32. Ibid., p. 676; see also, Kraut, "Deterrent and Definitional Influences on Shoplifting," pp. 358–68.

33. Sykes and Matza, "Techniques of Neutralization," pp. 670–71; see also, Lemert, "An Isolation of Closure Theory of Naive Check Forgery."

34. Blankenburg, "The Selectivity of Legal Sanctions"; see also, Kraut, "Deterrent and Definitional Influences on Shoplifting."

35. David Matza, *Becoming Deviant* (Englewood Cliffs, N.J.: Prentice-Hall, 1969), pp. 155–58.

36. Letkemann, *Crime as Work*, p. 29.

37. FBI, *Uniform Crime Reports, 1975*, p. 6.

38. Ibid.

39. David F. Greenberg, "Delinquency and the Age Structure of Society," *Contemporary Crises*, 1, no. 2 (1977):189–91.

40. Marvin Wolfgang, Robert Figlio, and Thorsten Sellin, *Delinquency in a Birth Cohort* (Chicago: University of Chicago Press, 1972), pp. 163–64.

41. Gerald D. Robin, "Gang Delinquency in Philadelphia," in Malcolm Klein, ed., *Juvenile Gangs in Context: Theory, Research and Action* (Englewood Cliffs, N.J.: Prentice-Hall, 1967).

42. John Allen, "The Education of John Allen," excerpted from a forthcoming book, *Assault with a Deadly Weapon*, in *Psychology Today* 2, no. 5 (October 1977): 98–103.

43. Ibid.

44. Letkemann, *Crime as Work*, p. 22.

45. Robert E. Clark, *Reference Group Theory and Delinquency* (New York: Behavioral Publications, 1972), pp. 19–22.

46. Letkemann, *Crime as Work*, p. 29.

47. John E. Conklin, *Robbery and the Criminal System* (Philadelphia: J. B. Lippincott, 1972), p. 104.

48. Andre Normandeau, "Violence and Robbery: A Case Study," *Acta Criminologica* 5 (1972):83; see also, Robert Lejeune, "Management of a Mugging," *Urban Life* 6, no. 2 (July 1977):123–48.

49. Letkemann, *Crime as Work*, p. 23.

50. Roger Feldman and Glenn Weisfeld, "An Interdisciplinary Study of Crime," *Crime and Delinquency* 19, no. 2 (April 1973):159–60.

51. Letkemann, *Crime as Work*, p. 29.

52. Greenberg, "Delinquency and the Age Structure of Society," pp. 201–11; see also, the autobiography of a thief, Jack Black, *You Cannot Win* (New York: Macmillan Co., 1927), pp. 112–13.

53. Walter C. Reckless, *The Crime Problem*, 4th ed. (New York: Appleton-Century-Crofts, 1961), p. 286; see also, Richard A. Cloward and Lloyd E. Ohlin, *Delinquency and Opportunity* (New York: Free Press, 1960), p. 23.

54. Feldman and Weisfeld, "An Interdisciplinary Study of Crime," p. 158; see also, Werthman, "The Function of Social Definitions in the Development of Delinquent Careers," p. 111.

55. Cloward and Ohlin, *Delinquency and Opportunity*.

56. President's Commission, *The Challenge of Crime in a Free Society*, p. 38.

57. Bernard Rosenberg and Harry Silverstein, *The Varieties of Delinquent Experience* (Waltham, Mass.: Blaisdell, 1969), p. 97.

58. Allen, "The Education of John Allen," p. 98; see also, Gerald Suttles, *The Social Order of the Slum: Ethnicity and Territory in the Inner City* (Chicago: University of Chicago Press, 1968). Although slum life is often associated with blacks, there are white southerners from Appalachia in such circumstances as Rosenberg and Silverstein noted. See also, Todd Gitlin and Nanci Hollander, *Uptown: Poor Whites in Chicago* (New York: Harper & Row, 1970).

59. Clifford R. Shaw, *The Natural History of a Delinquent Career* (Chicago: University of Chicago Press, 1931), pp. 230–31; see also, James F. Short, Jr. and Fred L. Strodtbeck, *Group Processes and Gang Delinquency* (Chicago: University of Chicago Press, 1965), p. 283.

60. Shaw, *The Natural History of a Delinquent Career*; see also, James F. Short, "Gang Delinquency and Anomie," in Marshall B. Clinard, ed., *Anomie and Delinquent Behavior* (New York: Free Press, 1964), pp. 98–127.

61. Letkemann, *Crime as Work*, p. 29.

62. Conklin, Robbery and the Criminal System, pp. 58–79.

63. Clarence Schrag, "Some Foundations for a Theory of Corrections," in Donald R. Cressey, ed., *The Prison* (New York: Holt, Rinehart & Winston, 1961), pp. 34–56.

64. Greenberg, "Delinquency and the Age Structure of Society," pp. 191–92.

65. Matza, *Delinquency and Drift*, pp. 195–99; see also, Cohen, *Delinquent Boys*. This theory has been roundly criticized, and Cohen himself has revised it as noted in Chapter 6. For criticism, see David Bordua, "Delinquent Subcultures: Sociological Interpretations of Gang Delinquency," in William H. Rushing, ed., *Deviant Behavior and Social Process* (Chicago: Rand McNally, 1975), pp. 45–57.

66. Greenberg, "Delinquency and the Age Structure of Society, pp. 196–97.

67. Ibid., pp. 197–99; see also, T. R. Fyvel, *Troublemakers: Rebellious Youth in an Affluent Society* (New York: Schocken Books, 1961), for a description of youth in Great Britain and other affluent societies.

68. Greenberg, "Delinquency and the Age Structure of Society," pp. 198–99; see also, Joseph Weis, "Liberation and Crime: The Invention of the New Female Criminal," in Peter Wickman and Phillip Whitten, eds., *Readings in Criminology* (Lexington, Mass.: D. C. Heath, 1978).

69. Richard Quinney and John Wildeman, *The Problem of Crime*, 2nd ed. (New York: Harper & Row, 1977), pp. 135–45.

70. Feldman and Weisfeld, "An Interdisciplinary Study of Crime"; see also, Reckless, *The Crime Problem*, pp. 284–85.

71. FBI, *Uniform Crime Reports, 1975*, pp. 41–42.

72. Conklin, *Robbery and the Criminal System*, pp. 182–84.

73. John Irwin, *The Felon* (Englewood Cliffs, N.J.: Prentice-Hall, 1970), pp. 23–24; see also, Reckless, *The Crime Problem*, pp. 284–86.

Chapter 10

1. Edwin H. Sutherland, *White Collar Crime* (New York: Holt, Rinehart & Winston, 1949), pp. 9–10.

2. Vilhelm Aubert, "White-Collar Crime and Social Structure," in Gilbert Geis and Robert F. Meier, eds., *White-Collar Crime: Offenses in Business, Politics and the Professions*, rev. ed. (New York: Free Press, 1977), pp. 168–79.

3. Gilbert Geis, "Avocational Crime," in Daniel Glaser, ed., *Handbook of Criminology* (Chicago: Rand McNally, 1974), p. 282.

4. Edwin H. Sutherland, "Crime of Corporations," in Geis and Meier, *White-Collar Crime*, p. 84.

5. Sutherland, *White Collar Crime*, p. 9.

6. Ibid., pp. 236–38.

7. Geis and Meier, *White-Collar Crime*, pp. 12–13.

8. James A. Inciardi, *Reflections on Crime: An Introduc-*

tion to *Criminology and Criminal Justice* (New York: Holt, Rinehart & Winston, 1978), p. 146; see also, Donald J. Newman, "White-Collar Crime: An Overview and Analysis," in Geis and Meier, *White-Collar Crime,* pp. 52–54.

9. Newman, "White-Collar Crime: An Overview and Analysis," p. 52.

10. Marshall B. Clinard, *The Black Market: A Study of White-Collar Crime* (New York: Holt, Rinehart & Winston, 1952).

11. Richard Quinney, "The Study of White-Collar Crime: Toward a Reorientation in Theory and Research," *Journal of Criminal Law, Criminology and Police Science* 55 (June 1964):208–14.

12. Marshall B. Clinard and Richard Quinney, *Criminal Behavior Systems: A Typology* (New York: Holt, Rinehart & Winston, 1973), pp. 154–84; see also, Inciardi, *Reflections on Crime,* p. 147.

13. Sutherland, *White Collar Crime,* pp. 23–24.

14. Geis, "Avocational Crime," p. 273; see also, Geis and Meier, *White-Collar Crime,* pp. 23–26.

15. These typologies have been adapted from the three types of criminal behaviors delineated by Clinard and Quinney, *Criminal Behavior Systems,* pp. 19–20; see also, John E. Conklin, *Illegal But Not Criminal: Business Crime in America* (Englewood Cliffs, N.J.: Prentice-Hall, 1977), p. 10.

16. Clinard and Quinney, *Criminal Behavior Systems,* pp. 154–59, 187–91, 206–10; see also, Nanette J. Davis, *Sociological Constructions of Deviance* (Dubuque, Iowa: Wm. C. Brown, 1975), pp. 143, 147–48.

17. "A $40 Billion Crime Wave Swamps American Business," *U.S. News & World Report,* February 21, 1977, pp. 47–48.

18. *New York Times,* October 10, 1977, sect. 4, pp. 1–3.

19. *New York Times,* February 20, 1977, p. 36; September 29, 1977, p. 1; March 5, 1978, p. 1.

20. Samuel E. Morison and Henry S. Commager, *The Growth of the American Republic,* quoted in Clinard and Quinney, *Criminal Behavior Systems,* p. 208.

21. Sutherland, *White Collar Crime,* pp. 17–28.

22. Morton Mintz, *The Therapeutic Nightmare: A Report on Prescription Drugs, the Men Who Take Them, and the Agency that Controls Them* (Boston: Houghton Mifflin, 1965), p. 41.

23. Ibid., pp. 45–46; see also, Richard Quinney, *The Social Reality of Crime* (Boston: Little, Brown and Co., 1970), pp. 79–81.

24. Stuart H. Hills, *Crime, Power and Morality* (New York: Chandler, 1971), pp. 150–51; see also, Quinney, *The Social Reality of Crime,* p. 81.

25. Ralph Nader, "Foreword," in John Esposito, *Vanishing Air* (Washington, D.C.: The Center for Study of Responsive Law, 1970).

26. *New York Times,* September 15, 1977, pp. 1, 20.

27. Charles H. McCaghy, *Deviant Behavior, Crime Conflict and Interest Groups* (New York: Macmillan Co., 1976), p. 195.

28. *Newsweek,* June 14, 1976, p. 22. (Obviously this covers only up to the above date.)

29. John A. Gardiner, "Wincanton: The Politics of Corruption," in President's Commission on Law Enforcement and Administration of Justice, *Task Force Report: Organized Crime* (Washington, D.C.: U.S. Government Printing Office, 1967), pp. 61–79; see also, Lincoln Steffens, *The Shame of the Cities* (1904).

30. Knapp Commission Report, "Police Corruption in New York City," in Jack D. Douglas and John M. Johnson, eds., *Official Deviance Readings in Malfeasance, Misfeasance, and Other Forms of Corruption* (Philadelphia: J. B. Lippincott, 1977), pp. 270–83.

31. Bryce Nelson, "24 Indicted as Chicago Police Scandal Grows," *Los Angeles Times,* December 26, 1972; see also, Robert Davis, "Braasch, 18 Others Found Guilty in Police Shakedown Trial," *Chicago Tribune,* October 6, 1973, cited in Martin R. Haskell and Lewis Yablonsky, *Criminology: Crime and Criminality* (Chicago: Rand McNally, 1978), p. 187.

32. *Newsweek,* June 14, 1976, p. 21.

33. Anthony Lewis, "I am the Law," *New York Times,* May 30, 1977, p. 41. © 1977 by The New York Times Company. Reprinted by permission.

34. Rockefeller Commission, Special Operations Group, "Operation CHAOS," in Douglas and Johnson, *Official Deviance Readings in Malfeasance, Misfeasance, and Other Forms of Corruption.*

35. Sutherland, *White Collar Crime,* pp. 218–20.

36. Geis and Meier, *White-Collar Crime,* p. 67.

37. Sutherland, *White Collar Crime,* p. 221.

38. Geis, *Handbook of Criminology,* p. 273.

39. Geis and Meier, *White-Collar Crime,* pp. 117–23.

40. Donald R. Cressey, *Other Peoples' Money: A Study in the Social Psychology of Embezzlement* (New York: Free Press, 1953).

41. Harry V. Ball, "Social Structure and Rent Control Violations," *American Journal of Sociology* 65 (May 1960):603.

42. James McNaughton et al., "Agnew and Nixon: Three Views," in Geis and Meier, *White-Collar Crime,* pp. 222–39.

43. *New York Times,* May 29, 1977, p. 1.

44. *New York Times,* November 1, 1977, pp. 1, 20.

45. *New York Times,* November 10, 1977, p. 10.

46. David Matza, *Becoming Deviant* (Englewood Cliffs, N.J.: Prentice-Hall, 1969), pp. 101–08.

47. Edwin H. Sutherland, "White-Collar Criminality," in Geis and Meier, *White-Collar Crime,* pp. 47–48.

48. Daniel Bell, "Crime as an American Way of Life," chapter 3 in *End of Ideology* (New York: Free Press, 1962).

49. Clinard, *The Black Market.*

50. Frank E. Hartung, "White Collar Offenses in the Wholesale Meat Industry in Detroit," *American Journal of Sociology* 56 (July 1950):25–32.

51. Sutherland, "White-Collar Criminality," p. 40.

52. Richard Quinney, "Occupational Structure and Criminal Behavior: Prescription Violations by Retail Pharmacists," in Geis and Meier, *White-Collar Crime,* pp. 189–96.

53. Gilbert Geis, "The Heavy Electrical Equipment Antitrust Case of 1961," in Geis and Meier, *White-Collar Crime,* pp. 120–21.

54. Ibid., p. 125.

55. Douglas and Johnson, *Official Deviance Readings in Malfeasance, Misfeasance, and Other Forms of Corruption,* pp. 1–12.

56. James M. McNaughton et al., "How Agnew Bartered His Office To Keep from Going to Prison," in Geis and Meier, *White-Collar Crime,* pp. 222–23.

57. John R. Silber, "The Thicket of Law and the Marsh of Conscience," in Geis and Meier, *White-Collar Crime,* pp. 235–39.

58. Renata Adler, "Searching for the Real Nixon Scandal," *The Atlantic Monthly,* December 1977, pp. 76–95.

59. Kirkpatrick Sale, "The World Behind Watergate," in Geis and Meier, *White-Collar Crime,* p. 248; see also, Jack D. Douglas, "Watergate: Harbinger of the American Prince," in Douglas and Johnson, *Official Deviance Readings in Malfeasance, Misfeasance, and Other Forms of Corruption,* pp. 109–11.

60. Sutherland, "White-Collar Criminality," p. 40.

61. Robert Claiborne, "The Great Health Care Rip-Off," *Saturday Review,* January 7, 1978, pp. 10–16; see also, Peter Bonventre et al., "Rx for Med. Fraud," *Newsweek,* November 10, 1977, p. 11.

62. Claiborne, "The Great Health Care Rip-Off."

63. *New York Times,* November 17, 1977, pp. 1, 2.

64. William N. Leonard and Marvin Glenn Weber, "Automakers and Dealers: A Study of Criminogenic Market Forces," in Geis and Meier, *White-Collar Crime,* pp. 138–42.

65. Special Report; "Ripoffs: New American Way of Life," *U.S. News & World Report,* May 31, 1976, p. 32.

66. Leonard and Weber, "Automakers and Dealers: A Study of Criminogenic Market Forces," p. 147.

67. Donn B. Parker, *Crime by Computer* (New York: Charles Scribner's Sons, 1976), pp. 45, 295–96; see also, Conklin, *Illegal But Not Criminal,* pp. 62–64.

68. Edwin Schur, *Our Criminal Society* (Englewood Cliffs, N.J.: Prentice-Hall, 1969), p. 185.

69. Gilbert Geis and Robert F. Meier, "Corporate and Business White-Collar Crime," in Geis and Meier, *White-Collar Crime,* p. 69.

70. Sutherland, "White-Collar Criminality," pp. 29–32.

71. "Taking Care of Business," *New York Times,* June 24, 1977, p. 21.

72. Geis, "The Heavy Electrical Equipment Antitrust Case of 1961," pp. 130–31.

73. *Mother Jones,* July 1977, p. 42; see also, Garney Breckenfeld, "Multinationals at Bay: Coping with the Nation-State," in Peter Wickman, ed., *Readings in Contemporary Social Problems* (New York: Harper & Row, 1977), pp. 170–76; see also, Conklin, *Illegal But Not Criminal,* pp. 55–56.

74. Sutherland, *White Collar Crime,* pp. 29–32.

75. Edward Cowan, "The Case Against the Big 4 Cereal Makers," *New York Times,* January 1, 1978, pp. 2–3.

76. Sutherland, *White Collar Crime,* p. 116.

77. John P. Cohane, "The American Predicament: Truth No Longer Counts," *Los Angeles Times,* October 1, 1972, quoted in Haskell and Yablonsky, *Criminology: Crime and Criminality,* p. 172.

78. Gilbert Geis and Robert F. Meier, "Political White-Collar Crime," in Geis and Meier, *White-Collar Crime,* p. 211.

79. See Albert K. Cohen, Alfred Lindesmith, and Karl Schuessler, eds., *The Sutherland Papers* (Bloomington: Indiana University Press, 1956), p. 102.

80. Aubert, "White-Collar Crime and Social Structure," pp. 178–79.

81. Edwin H. Sutherland, "Is 'White-Collar Crime' Crime?" in Geis and Meier, *White-Collar Crime,* p. 267.

82. Donald R. Taft and Ralph W. England, *Criminology,* 4th ed. (New York: Macmillan Co., 1964), pp. 205–06.

83. Stanton Wheeler, "Trends and Problems in the Sociological Study of Crime," *Social Problems* 23, no. 5 (June 1976):531–32; see also, Gilbert Geis and Robert F. Meier, "What Is White-Collar Crime?" in Geis and Meier, *White-Collar Crime,* pp. 23–26.

84. Ibid.

85. Sutherland, "Is 'White-Collar Crime' Crime?" p. 269.

86. Ibid., p. 261.

87. Marshall B. Clinard, "The Black Market," in Geis and Meier, *White-Collar Crime,* pp. 85–101.

88. Geis, "The Heavy Electrical Equipment Antitrust Case of 1961," pp. 122–26.

89. President's Commission on Law Enforcement and Administration of Justice, *The Challenge of Crime in a Free Society* (Washington, D.C.: U.S. Government Printing Office, 1967), p. 104.

90. Blake Fleetwood and Arthur Lubow, "America's Most Coddled Criminals," in Wickman, *Readings in Contemporary Social Problems,* p. 190.

91. Ibid., pp. 184–85.

92. Howard R. and Martha E. Lewis, *The Medical Offenders* (New York: Simon & Schuster, 1970), pp. 21–22.

93. Ibid., pp. 312–20; see also, Richard D. Schwartz and Jerome H. Skolnick, "Two Studies of Legal Stigma," *Social Problems* 10 (Fall 1962):133–42.

94. "Ripoffs: New American Way of Life," *U.S. News & World Report,* May 31, 1976, p. 32; see also, Gerald D. Robin, "The Corporate and Judicial Disposition of Employee Thieves," *Wisconsin Law Review* (Summer 1967):685–702.

95. Albert E. McCormick, "Rule Enforcement and Moral Indignation: Some Observations on the Effects of Criminal Antitrust Convictions upon Societal Reaction Processes," *Social Problems* 25, no. 1 (October 1977):30–39.

96. "The Embattled Businessman," *Newsweek,* February 16, 1976, pp. 58–59; see also, Geis and Meier, *White-Collar Crime,* pp. 2–3.

97. McCormick, "Rule Enforcement and Moral Indignation," p. 36.

98. *New York Times,* September 15, 1977, pp. 1, 20.

99. Sale, "The World Behind Watergate," pp. 240–52; see also, Douglas, "Watergate: Harbinger of the American Prince"; see also, Arthur J. Vidich, "Political Legitimacy in Bureaucratic Society: An Analysis of Watergate," in Douglas and Johnson, *Official Deviance Readings in Malfeasance, Misfeasance, and Other Forms of Corruption,* pp. 112–20, 145–70.

100. Adler, "Searching for the Real Nixon Scandal," p. 94.

101. *New York Times,* January 1, 1978.

102. Vidich, "Political Legitimacy in Bureaucratic Society," pp. 148–67.

103. Geis and Meier, *White-Collar Crime,* pp. 5–8.

Chapter 11

1. Norval Morris and Gordon Hawkins, *Letter to the President on Crime Control* (Chicago: University of Chicago Press, 1977).

2. President's Commission on Law Enforcement and Administration of Justice, *The Challenge of Crime in a Free Society* (Washington, D.C.: U.S. Government Printing Office, 1967), pp. 233–34.

3. Richard Quinney, "Who Is the Victim?" *Criminology* 10 (November 1972):315.

4. Edwin M. Schur and Hugo A. Bedau, *Victimless Crimes: Two Sides of a Controversy* (Englewood Cliffs, N.J.: Prentice-Hall, 1974), pp. 6–7.

5. Edwin H. Sutherland and Donald R. Cressey, *Principles of Criminology,* 6th ed. (Philadelphia: J. B. Lippincott, 1960), p. 11.

6. Schur and Bedau, *Victimless Crimes,* pp. 7–8; see also, Edwin M. Schur, *Crimes Without Victims: Deviant Behavior and Public Policy* (Englewood Cliffs, N.J.: Prentice-Hall, 1965), pp. 169–70.

7. Troy Duster, *The Legislation of Morality* (New York: Free Press, 1970), pp. 23–28; see also, Schur and Bedau, *Victimless Crimes,* p. 8.

8. Schur and Bedau, *Victimless Crimes,* p. 9.

9. Laud Humphreys, *Tearoom Trade,* enlarged ed. (Chicago: Aldine, 1975), pp. 84–88; see also, Schur, *Crimes Without Victims;* see also, Schur and Bedau, *Victimless Crimes.*

10. See Schur, *Crimes Without Victims,* pp. 171–72; see also, Schur and Bedau, *Victimless Crimes,* p. 31; see also, Howard S. Becker, *Outsiders: Studies in the Sociology of Deviance* (New York: Free Press, 1963); see also, Harold Garfinkel, "Conditions of Successful Degradation Ceremonies," *American Journal of Sociology* 61 (March 1956):420–24; see also, Erving Goffman, "The Moral Career of the Mental Patient," in Erving Goffman, *Asylums* (New York: Doubleday/Anchor Books, 1961).

11. See Howard S. Becker, "Moral Entrepreneurs," chapter 8 in Becker, *Outsiders.*

12. Lord Devlin, *The Enforcement of Morals* (1959), cited in Sanford H. Kadish, "The Crisis of Overcriminalization," *Annals of the American Academy of Political and Social Science* 374 (November 1967):159.

13. Ibid.

14. Norval Morris and Gordon Hawkins, *The Honest Politician's Guide to Crime Control* (Chicago: University of Chicago Press, 1970), p. 15.

15. Stanton Wheeler, "Sex Offenses: A Sociological Critique," in John H. Gagnon and William Simon, eds., *Sexual Deviance* (New York: Harper & Row, 1967), pp. 78–80.

16. Cited in Kadish, "The Crisis of Overcriminalization," p. 160.

17. Kingsley Davis, "The Sociology of Prostitution," *American Sociological Review* (October 1937):746–55.

18. Fernando Henriques, *Prostitution and Society* (New York: Grove Press, 1963), p. 21; see also, Charles Winick and Paul Kinsie, *The Lively Commerce: Prostitution in the United States* (New York: Signet Books, 1971), chapter 1.

19. Winick and Kinsie, *The Lively Commerce,* p. 13.

20. Henriques, *Prostitution and Society;* see also, Humphreys, *Tearoom Trade,* pp. 25, 47.

21. Harry Benjamin and R. E. L. Masters, *Prostitution and Morality* (New York: Julian Press, 1964), pp. 21–22, 76; see also, Winick and Kinsie, *The Lively Commerce,* pp. 29, 89–90.

22. F. C. Esselstyn, "Prostitution in the United States," *Annals of the American Academy of Political and Social Science* 376 (March 1968):127.

23. Mary McIntosh, "Societal Context and the Homosexual Role," in William Rushing, ed., *Deviant Behavior and the Social Process* (Chicago: Rand McNally, 1975), p. 237.

24. John Gagnon, ed., *Human Sexuality: An Age of Ambiguity* (Boston: Little, Brown & Co., 1975), p. 52; see also, Humphreys, *Tearoom Trade,* p. 84.

25. Schur, *Crimes Without Victims,* pp. 78–79; see also, J. H. Gallo et al., "The Consenting Adult Homosexual and the Law: An Empirical Study of Enforcement and Administration in Los Angeles County," *UCLA Law Review* 13 (March 1966):831–32.

26. Joseph Gusfield, *Symbolic Crusade* (Urbana: University of Illinois Press, 1963).

27. Salme Ahlstrom-Laakso, "Arrests for Drunkenness: Two Capital Cities Compared," in Nils Christie, ed., *Scandinavian Studies in Criminology,* vol. 3 (Oslo: Universitetsforloget, 1971), pp. 89–106.

28. Gerald Stern, "Public Drunkenness: Crime or Health Problem?" *Annals of the American Academy of Political and Social Science* 374 (November 1967):148–49.

29. David F. Musto, *The American Disease* (New Haven: Yale University Press, 1973), p. ix.

30. Carl Chambers, "Some Epidemiological Considerations of Opiate Usage in the United States," in Eric Josephson and Eleanor Carrol, eds., *Drug Use: Epidemiological and Sociological Approaches* (New York: Holsted Press, 1974), pp. 65–82; see also, Ronald Akers, *Deviant Behavior: A Social Learning Approach,* 2nd ed. (Belmont, Calif.: Wadsworth, 1977). This taxonomy has been adapted from Akers, pp. 75–83, and also from Erich Goode, *Drugs in American Society* (New York: Knopf, 1972), chapters 2 and 4.

31. Akers, *Deviant Behavior,* pp. 77–78.

32. Ibid., pp. 78–80; see also, Alfred R. Lindesmith, *The Addict and the Law* (Bloomington: Indiana University Press, 1967), pp. 129–30.

33. Goode, *Drugs in American Society,* chapter 2; see also, Akers, *Deviant Behavior,* pp. 81–84.

34. Akers, *Deviant Behavior,* pp. 81–84.

35. Goode, *Drugs in American Society,* pp. 181–82.

36. Ibid., pp. 182–83; see also, Joel Fort, *The Pleasure Seekers* (Indianapolis: Bobbs-Merrill, 1969).

37. Goode, *Drugs in American Society,* pp. 183–86.

38. See Becker, *Outsiders,* pp. 135–46; see also, Donald Dickson, "Bureaucracy and Morality," *Social Problems* 16 (Fall 1968):143–56.

39. Marshall B. Clinard and Richard Quinney, *Criminal Behavior Systems,* 2nd ed. (New York: Holt, Rinehart & Winston, 1973), pp. 83–84; see also, Goode, *Drugs in American Society,* p. 184.

40. Lindesmith, *The Addict and the Law,* pp. 3–4.

41. Ibid., pp. 5–11.

42. Schur, *Crimes Without Victims,* pp. 130–44.

43. Ibid., pp. 133–35.

44. Ibid., pp. 152–55.

45. Andrew Scull, "Social Control and the Amplification of Deviance," in Robert A. Scott and Jack D. Douglas, eds., *Theoretical Perspectives on Deviance* (New York: Basic Books, 1972), pp. 282–314.

46. Schur, *Crimes Without Victims,* pp. 169–71.

47. Winick and Kinsie, *The Lively Commerce,* p. 29; see also, Diana Gray, "Turning Out: A Study of Teenage Prostitution," *Urban Life and Culture* 4 (January 1973):401–24.

48. Edwin M. Lemert, "Prostitution," in Edward Sagarin and Donald E. MacNamara, eds., *Problems of Sex Behaviors* (New York: Thomas Y. Crowell, 1968), p. 405; see also, James H. Bryan, "Occupational Ideologies and Individual Attitudes of Call Girls," *Social Problems* 13 (Spring 1966):441–50.

49. Norman R. Jackman, Richard O'Toole, and Gilbert Geis, "The Self-Image of the Prostitute," in Gagnon and Simon, *Sexual Deviance,* pp. 133–46.

50. Wayland Young, "Prostitution," in Gagnon and Simon, *Sexual Deviance,* p. 132.

51. Bryan, "Occupational Ideologies and Individual Attitudes of Call Girls," pp. 447–48.

52. Paul H. Gebhard, "Misconceptions About Female Prostitution," *Medical Aspects of Human Sexuality* (March 1968):28–29.

53. *New York Times,* November 9, 1978, and November 11, 1977.

54. James H. Bryan, "Apprenticeships in Prostitution," in Gagnon and Simon, *Sexual Deviance,* pp. 146–64.

55. Ibid.; see also, John H. Gagnon, "Sexual Conduct and Crime," in Daniel Glaser, ed., *Handbook of Criminology* (Chicago: Rand McNally, 1974), p. 260.

56. Gagnon, "Sexual Conduct and Crime," pp. 254–58.

57. Alfred C. Kinsey, Wardell B. Pomeroy, and Clyde E. Martin, *Sexual Behavior in the Human Male* (Philadelphia: W. B. Saunders, 1949), p. 640.

58. Gagnon, *Human Sexuality,* pp. 48–55.

59. Excerpt from *20 Questions About Homosexuality,* quoted in Gagnon, *Human Sexuality,* p. 48.

60. Grace Lichtenstein, "Teachers on Coast and in Jersey Lose Disputes over Homosexuality," *New York Times,* October 4, 1977, p. 41.

61. Richard H. Blum, *Society and Drugs* (San Francisco: Jossey-Bass, 1969), pp. 36–37; see also, Gusfield, *Symbolic Crusade,* pp. 175–77.

62. Harold Mulford and Donald E. Miller, "Drinking in Iowa, Preoccupations with Alcohol, and Definitions of Heavy Drinking and Trouble Due to Drinking," *Quarterly Journal of Studies on Alcohol* 21 (1960):81; see also, Marshall B. Clinard, *Sociology of Deviant Behavior,* 3rd ed. (New York: Holt, Rinehart & Winston, 1968), pp. 412–14.

63. Clinard, *Sociology of Deviant Behavior,* pp. 414–15.

64. President's Commission, *The Challenge of Crime in a Free Society,* p. 234.

65. David J. Pittman, "Drugs, Addiction and Crime," in Daniel Glaser, ed., *Handbook of Criminology* (Chicago: Rand McNally, 1974), pp. 218–19.

66. President's Commission on Law Enforcement and Administration of Justice, *Task Force Report: Drunkenness* (Washington, D.C.: U.S. Government Printing Office, 1967), appendix G, p. 90; see also, Earl Rubington, "Variations in Bottle Gang Controls," and Samuel Wallace, "The Skid Row Subculture and Routes to Skid Row," in Earl Rubington and Martin S. Weinberg, eds., *Deviance: The Interactionist Perspective* (New York: Macmillan Co., 1968).

67. M. M. Miller, "Arrests for Intoxication in Cleveland, Ohio," *Quarterly Journal of Studies on Alcohol* 3 (1942):38; see also, Stern, "Public Drunkenness: Crime or Health Problem?"

68. Division of Alcoholic Rehabilitation, *Criminal Offenders and Drinking Involvement* (Sacramento: California State Department of Public Health, 1964), cited in Martin R. Haskell and Lewis Yablonsky, *Criminology: Crime and Criminality,* 2nd ed. (Chicago: Rand McNally, 1978), p. 334.

69. Goode, *Drugs in American Society,* p. 164.

70. Harold Finestone, "Cats, Kicks and Color," in Howard S. Becker, ed., *The Other Side* (New York: Free Press, 1964), pp. 281–97; see also, Isodore Chein et al., *The Road to H* (New York: Basic Books, 1964), pp. 78–108.

71. Goode, *Drugs in American Society,* p. 167; see also, Chein, *The Road to H.*

72. Goode, *Drugs in American Society,* pp. 169–71; see also, David Matza, *Becoming Deviant* (Englewood Cliffs, N.J.: Prentice-Hall, 1969), chapter 6.

73. Seymour Fiddle, *Portraits from a Shooting Gallery* (New York: Harper & Row, 1967), p. 82; see also, Edward Preble and John J. Casey, Jr., "Taking Care of Business: The Heroin User's Life on the Street," *International Journal of Addiction* 4 (1969):1–24.

74. Charles Winick, "Physician Narcotic Addicts," *Social Problems* 9 (1961):174–86.

75. *New York Times,* May 23, 1977, pp. 29, 46.

76. Goode, *Drugs in American Society,* pp. 237–49.

77. Alfred Lindesmith, *The Addict and the Law* (Bloomington: Indiana University Press, 1967).

78. Norval Morris, "Crime Without Victims: The Law is a Busybody," *New York Times Magazine,* April 1, 1973; see also, Schur and Bedau, *Victimless Crimes,* pp. 32–38.

79. Jerome H. Skolnick, *Justice Without Trial,* 2nd ed. (New York: John Wiley & Sons, 1975), pp. 100–04; see also, Paul Chevigny, *Police Power: Police Abuses in New York City* (New York: Vintage Books, 1969).

80. Skolnick, *Justice Without Trial;* see also, Gagnon, "Sexual Conduct and Crime," pp. 259–60.

81. Gagnon, "Sexual Conduct and Crime," p. 260.

82. Ibid.

83. Ibid., p. 250.

84. Gagnon, *Human Sexuality,* pp. 51–52.

85. Ibid., p. 51.

86. J. H. Gallo, "The Consenting Adult Homosexual and the Law," pp. 657–85; see also, Chevigny, *Police Power,* pp. 121–28.

87. Humphreys, *Tearoom Trade,* pp. 87–90; see also, Schur, *Crimes Without Victims,* p. 83.

88. Gagnon, *Human Sexuality,* p. 52; see also, Schur and Bedau, *Victimless Crimes,* pp. 4–5.

89. President's Commission, *The Challenge to Crime in a Free Society,* pp. 256–57.

90. Pittman, "Drugs, Addiction and Crime," pp. 225–26.

91. Stern, "Public Drunkenness: Crime or Health Problem?" pp. 154–56.

92. Pittman, "Drugs, Addiction and Crime," pp. 221–22.

93. Ibid., p. 224; see also, Eckart Kuhlhorn, *Effekter Av Behandling* (Vanersborg, Sweden: Sober Forlogs AB, 1974), English summary pp. 218–35 and interview with Eckart Kuhlhorn by one of the authors.

94. Pittman, "Drugs, Addiction and Crime," pp. 225–26.

95. Ibid., p. 226; see also, Schur, *Crimes Without Victims,* pp. 138–45. For some empirical data which raise some questions about this theory, see William E. McAuliffe and Robert Gordon, "A Test of Lindesmith's Theory of Addiction," *American Journal of Sociology* 79 (January 1974):795–840.

96. Schur, *Crimes Without Victims,* pp. 120–22, 136–37.

97. Pittman, "Drugs, Addiction and Crime," p. 228; see also, Schur, *Crimes Without Victims,* pp. 150–51.

98. *New York Times,* May 23, 1977, pp. 29, 46.

99. Robert E. Carr, "The Potvote," in Peter Wickman, ed., *Readings in Social Problems* (New York: Harper & Row, 1977), pp. 223–27.

100. *New York Times,* May 23, 1977, pp. 29, 46.

101. Morris and Hawkins, *The Honest Politician's Guide to Crime Control,* p. 56; see also, Schur and Bedau, *Victimless Crimes,* pp. 3–54.

102. Gilbert Geis, "The Criminal Justice System Without Victimless Crimes," in Wickman, *Readings in Social Problems,* pp. 215–16.

103. Ibid., pp. 215–16.

104. Ibid., p. 213.
105. Quoted in ibid., p. 213.

Chapter 12

1. George L. Kelling, "Police Field Services and Crime: The Presumed Effects of a Capacity," *Crime and Delinquency* 24, no. 2 (April 1978):173–84, especially p. 174; see also, footnotes 4 and 6 below.
2. U.S. Department of Justice, *Trends in Expenditure and Employment Data for the Criminal Justice System, 1971–1975* (Washington, D.C.: U.S. Government Printing Office, 1977); see also, FBI, *Uniform Crime Reports, 1975* (Washington, D.C.: U.S. Government Printing Office, 1976). Unless otherwise noted, crime data in this chapter are from the UCR.
3. Robert P. Rhodes, *The Insoluble Problems of Crime* (New York: John Wiley & Sons, 1977), p. 76.
4. Nicholas Alex, *Black in Blue: A Study of the Negro Policeman* (New York: Appleton-Century-Crofts, 1969), pp. 5–8; see also, Charles Reith, *The Police Idea: Its History and Evolution in England in the Eighteenth Century and After* (London: Oxford University Press, 1938), p. 188. Note: although women comprised less than 3 percent of the total sworn officer personnel in 1974, we use the term "police officer" rather than "policeman" throughout this chapter. Since there are no conclusive studies indicating that the "style of policing" of women police is distinguishable from that of men, we do not treat female police as a separate entity.
5. Michael Banton, *The Policeman in the Community* (New York: Basic Books, 1964), pp. 1–2.
6. Jerome H. Skolnick, *Justice Without Trial* (New York: John Wiley & Sons, 1975), pp. 6–10; see also, Alex, *Black in Blue*, pp. 3–5; see also, President's Commission on Law Enforcement and Administration of Justice, *Task Force Report: The Police* (Washington, D.C.: U.S. Government Printing Office, 1967), pp. 3–12; see also, Wilbur R. Miller, *Cops and Robbers: Police Authority in New York and London* (Chicago: University of Chicago Press, 1977), pp. 1–8.
7. Skolnick, *Justice Without Trial*, pp. 1–4; see also, Reith, *The Police Idea*; see also, Miller, *Cops and Robbers*, chapter 1; see also, Peter K. Manning, *The Social Organization of Policing* (Boston: MIT Press, 1977), pp. 39–81.
8. Banton, *The Policeman in the Community*; see also, Miller, *Cops and Robbers*, pp. 12–16; see also, Manning, *The Social Organization of Policing*, pp. 74–81.
9. Jerome Skolnick, "Professional Police in a Free Society," in Jerome Skolnick and Thomas Gray, eds., *Police in America* (Boston: Little, Brown & Co., 1975), pp. x–xvi; see also, Banton, *The Policeman in the Community*, chapter 1; see also, Miller, *Cops and Robbers*, chapter 1.
10. Skolnick, "Professional Police in a Free Society."
11. Cyril D. Robinson, "The Deradicalization of the Policeman: A Historical Analysis," *Crime and Delinquency* 24, no. 2 (April 1978):135–42; see also, C. Hackey Barton, "The United States Army as a National Police Force: The Federal Policing of Labor Disputes, 1877–1898," *Military Affairs* (April 1969):260.
12. Peter K. Manning, "The Police: Mandate, Strategies and Appearance," in Jack D. Douglas, ed., *Crime and Justice in American Society* (Indianapolis: Bobbs-Merrill, 1971), p. 151.
13. Richard Quinney, *Criminology: Analysis and Critique of Crime in America* (Boston: Little, Brown & Co., 1975), pp. 166–68; see also, Rhodes, *The Insoluble Problems of Crime*, pp. 58–71.
14. James A. Kaklik and Sorrel Wildhorn, *Private Police in the United States: Findings and Recommendations*, vol. 1 of the Rand Study; see also, Center for Research on Criminal Justice, *The Iron Fist and the Velvet Glove* (Berkeley, Calif.: Center for Research on Criminal Justice, 1975), p. 104.
15. Banton, *The Policeman in the Community*, p. 89.
16. Morris Cobern, "Some Manpower Aspects of the Criminal Justice System," *Crime and Delinquency* 19 (April 1973):198–99.
17. Ibid.; see also, National Institute of Law Enforcement and Criminal Justice, *The National Manpower Survey of the Criminal Justice System, Law Enforcement* (Washington, D.C.: U.S. Government Printing Office, 1978), p. 1.
18. Cobern, "Some Manpower Aspects of the Criminal Justice System"; see also, Tony Platt and Paul Takagi, "Intellectuals for Law and Order: A Critique of the Law Realists," *Crime and Social Justice Issues in Criminology* 8 (Fall/Winter 1977):1–16.
19. Cobern, "Some Manpower Aspects of the Criminal Justice System," p. 198.
20. Quoted in Arthur Niederhoffer, *Behind the Shield* (New York: Doubleday, 1967), pp. 12–13.
21. Cited in Alex, *Black in Blue*, p. 4.
22. John P. Clark and Richard E. Sykes, "Some Determinants of Police Organization and Practice in a Modern Industrial Democracy," in Daniel Glaser, ed,, *Handbook of Criminology* (Chicago: Rand McNally, 1974), pp. 455–94.
23. William K. Muir, Jr., *Police: Street Corner Politicians* (Chicago: University of Chicago Press, 1977), pp. 3–4.
24. Manning, *The Social Organization of Policing*, pp. 311–12; see also, Albert J. Reiss, Jr., *The Police and the Public* (New Haven: Yale University Press, 1971); see also, Paul G. Chevigny, *Police Power* (New York: Pantheon Books, 1969).
25. Reiss, *The Police and the Public*, pp. 100–04.
26. Clark and Sykes, "Some Determinants of Police Organization and Practice in a Modern Industrial Democracy," pp. 456–60.
27. Reiss, *The Police and the Public*, pp. 64, 88–89; see also, Donald J. Black and Albert J. Reiss, "Police Control of Juveniles," in Robert A. Scott and Jack D. Douglas, eds., *Theoretical Perspectives on Deviance* (New York: Basic Books, 1972), pp. 119–41.
28. Kelling, "Police Field Services and Crime," pp. 174–78.
29. Clark and Sykes, "Some Determinants of Police Organization and Practice in a Modern Industrial Democracy," pp. 460–61.
30. James Q. Wilson, *Varieties of Police Behavior* (Cambridge, Mass.: Harvard University Press, 1968); see also, Kelling, "Police Field Services and Crime," p. 174.
31. Reiss, *The Police and the Public*, pp. 63, 64, 71.
32. Manning, *The Social Organization of Policing*, pp. 313–14; see also, Clark and Sykes, "Some Determinants of Police Organization and Practice in a Modern Industrial Democracy," pp. 462–64.
33. Manning, *The Social Organization of Policing*, pp. 111–13.
34. Ibid., pp. 31–35, 314–15.
35. Ibid., pp. 316–17; see also, Clark and Sykes, "Some Determinants of Police Organization and Practice in a Modern Industrial Democracy," pp. 364–65.
36. Manning, "The Police: Mandate, Strategies and Ap-

pearance," pp. 155–56.

37. Ibid., p. 156. The ten assumptions he notes have been drawn from the following works: Banton, *The Policeman in the Community*; Albert J. Reiss, David Bordua, and John H. McNamara in David Bordua, ed., *The Police: Six Sociological Essays* (New York: John Wiley & Sons, 1967); Niederhoffer, *Behind the Shield*; Skolnick, *Justice Without Trial*; William A. Westley, "Violence and the Police," *American Journal of Sociology* 59 (July 1953):34–41; William A. Westley, "Secrecy and the Police," *Social Forces* 34 (March 1956); and Wilson, *Varieties of Police Behavior*.

38. Manning, "The Police: Mandate, Strategies and Appearance," pp. 156–57; see also, Manning, *The Social Organization of Policing*, chapter 4, pp. 111–22, for a discussion of institutional contradictions and sentiments associated with the role of policing.

39. Banton, *The Policeman in the Community*, pp. 105–09.

40. Niederhoffer, *Behind the Shield*, pp. 18–19.

41. Ibid., p. 17.

42. James Q. Wilson, "The Police and Their Problems: A Theory," *Public Policy* 12 (1963):189–216.

43. *Municipal Police Administration Handbook, Institute for Training in Municipal Administration*, 5th ed. (Chicago: National City Managers Association, 1961), p. 61; cited in Banton, *The Policeman in the Community*, pp. 92–93.

44. President's Commission on Law Enforcement and Administration of Justice, *The Challenge of Crime in a Free Society* (Washington, D.C.: U.S. Government Printing Office, 1967), pp. 107–10.

45. Niederhoffer, *Behind the Shield*, pp. 21–23.

46. Kelling, "Police Field Services and Crime," pp. 181–83.

47. Skolnick, "Professional Police in a Free Society," pp. xi–xviii.

48. David J. Bordua and Albert J. Reiss, Jr., "A Command Control and Charisma: Reflections on Police Bureaucracy," *American Journal of Sociology* 72 (July 1966):68–76.

49. Peter K. Manning, "Foreword," in Peter Wickman and Phillip Whitten, eds., *Readings in Criminology* (Lexington, Mass.: D. C. Heath, 1978). This provides a concise review of some of the literature on studies of the police. See also: Banton, *The Policeman and the Community*; Skolnick, *Justice Without Trial*; Peter Greenwood, J. Chaiken, and J. Petersilia, *The Criminal Investigation Process* (Lexington, Mass.: D. C. Heath, 1977); George Kelling et al., *The Kansas City Preventive Patrol Report* (Washington, D.C.: Police Foundation, 1974); Wilson, *Varieties of Police Behavior*; and James Q. Wilson, *Thinking About Crime* (New York: Basic Books, 1975).

50. O. W. Wilson, *Police Administration* (1950), p. 59; cited in Bordua and Reiss, "A Command Control and Charisma," p. 69.

51. Daniel Walker, *Rights in Conflict* (New York: E. P. Dutton, 1968).

52. President's Commission, *Task Force Report: The Police*, p. 44.

53. National Institute for Law Enforcement and Criminal Justice, *The National Manpower Survey of the Criminal Justice System, Law Enforcement*, pp. 81–82.

54. U.S. Department of Justice, Law Enforcement Assistance Administration, *Higher Education Programs in Law Enforcement and Criminal Justice, PR 71-2* (Washington, D.C.: U.S. Government Printing Office, 1972), p. 57; see also, Peter M. Wickman and Joseph D. Yenerall, *Final Report: Regional Jail Study*, vol. 2, Grant Award C57591 (New York: State Office of Criminal Justice Planning, 1972), p. 7.

55. President's Commission, *Task Force Report: The Police*, pp. 44–46.

56. Center for Research on Criminal Justice, *The Iron Fist and the Velvet Glove*, pp. 85–86.

57. Reiss, *The Police and the Public*, pp. 3–11.

58. Ibid., p. 104.

59. Albert Reiss challenged the idea of preventive patrol in the 1960s in *The Police and the Public*. See also: James Press, *Some Effects of an Increase in Police Manpower in the 20th Precinct of New York City* (New York: Rand Institute, 1971); Donald Fisk, *The Indianapolis Police Fleet Plan* (Washington, D.C.: Urban Institute, 1970); Kelling et al., *The Kansas City Preventive Patrol Report*. Irving Piliavin reported on *Police-Community Alienation: Its Structural Roots and a Proposed Remedy* (Andover, Mass.: Warner Modular Publications, Module 14, 1973), pp. 1–25.

60. Herman Goldstein, *Policing in a Free Society* (Cambridge, Mass.: Ballinger, 1977).

61. Reiss, *The Police and the Public*, p. 104.

62. Ibid., p. 113.

63. Skolnick, *Justice Without Trial*, pp. 120–38.

64. Ibid., pp. 127–28.

65. Hugh D. Graham and Ted Gurr, eds., *The History of Violence in America* (New York: Bantam Books, 1969), p. xiv; see also, Frank R. Prassel, *Introduction to American Criminal Justice* (New York: Harper & Row, 1975), pp. 80–81.

66. Prassel, *Introduction to American Criminal Justice*, p. 81; see also, Greenwood et al., *The Criminal Investigation Process*, pp. 58–59, 210–11.

67. Banton, *The Policeman in the Community*, pp. 45–47; see also, Arthur Niederhoffer and Alexander B. Smith, *New Directions in Police Community Relations* (Hinsdale, Ill.: Dryden Press, 1974), pp. 1–7; see also, Muir, *Police: Street Corner Politicians*, pp. 48–49.

68. W. F. Whyte, Street Corner Society (Chicago: University of Chicago Press, 1943), p. 139.

69. O. W. Wilson, *Police Administration*, 2nd ed. (New York: McGraw-Hill, 1963), p. 182; see also, Niederhoffer and Smith, *New Directions in Police Community Relations*, p. 9.

70. Skolnick, "Professional Police in a Free Society," pp. xvii–xxi.

71. Niederhoffer and Smith, *New Directions in Police Community Relations*, pp. 35–72.

72. President's Commission, *The Challenge of Crime in a Free Society*, p. 99.

73. Ibid., p. 100.

74. James F. Ahern, *Police in Trouble* (New York: Hawthorne Books, 1972), p. 221; see also, Niederhoffer and Smith, *New Directions in Police Community Relations*, pp. 52–65.

75. Leonard Ruchelman, "Police Policy," in John A. Gardiner and Michael A. Mulkey, eds., *Crime and Criminal Justice* (Lexington, Mass.: D. C. Heath, 1976), pp. 117–18.

76. Niederhoffer and Smith, *New Directions in Police Community Relations*, pp. 60–62.

77. Ahern, *Police in Trouble*, pp. 222–24.

78. James R. Hudson, "Organizational Aspects of Internal and External Review of the Police," in Skolnick and Gray, *Police in America*, pp. 279–87.

79. "ABA Standards for Criminal Justice Relating to the Urban Police Function," in Skolnick and Gray, *Police in America*, pp. 291–300.
80. Herbert L. Packer, "The Courts, the Police and the Rest of Us," *Journal of Criminal Law, Criminology and Police Science* 57 (1966):238–43.
81. Ibid.; see also, Manning, *The Social Organization of Policing*, pp. 229–31.
82. Prassel, *Introduction to American Criminal Justice*, pp. 88–89.
83. Herman Goldstein, "Police Discretion: The Ideal versus the Real," in Skolnick and Gray, *Police in America*, pp. 96–106; see also, Manning, *The Social Organization of Policing*, p. 251.
84. Kenneth C. Davis, *Discretionary Justice: A Preliminary Inquiry* (Baton Rouge: Louisiana State University Press, 1969), pp. 52–96.
85. Arnold S. Trebach, *The Rationing of Justice: Constitutional Rights and the Criminal Justice Process* (New Brunswick, N.J.: Rutgers University Press, 1964).
86. FBI, *Uniform Crime Reports, 1970 and 1975* (Washington, D.C.: U.S. Government Printing Office, 1971 and 1976), p. 119 (1971) and p. 176 (1976); see also, Trebach, *The Rationing of Justice*, p. 5.
87. Trebach, *The Rationing of Justice*, pp. 4–7.
88. Ibid., pp. 6–7.
89. Ibid., p. 7; see also, *Report and Recommendations of the Commissioner's Committee on Police Arrests for Investigation* (District of Columbia, 1962), pp. 34, 69.
90. Davis, *Discretionary Justice*, pp. 84–86.
91. Ibid., pp. 90–91; see also, Greenwood et al., *The Criminal Investigation Process*, p. 10.
92. Reiss, *The Police and the Public*, pp. 93–94.
93. Mapp v. Ohio 367 U.S. 643 (1961); see also, Trebach, *The Rationing of Justice*, pp. 12–18.
94. Niederhoffer, *Behind the Shield*, pp. 161–63.
95. Ibid.; see also, Greenwood et al., *The Criminal Investigation Process*, pp. 10–11; see also, Leon Radzinowicz and Joan King, *The Growth of Crime: An International Experience* (New York: Basic Books, 1978), p. 175.
96. Trebach, *The Rationing of Justice*.
97. Westley, "Violence and the Police."
98. Walker, *Rights in Conflict*, especially pp. 215–82.
99. President's Commission, *The Challenge of Crime in a Free Society*.
100. Albert J. Reiss, Jr., "Police Brutality: Answers to Key Questions," in Michael Lyssky, ed., *Police Encounters* (Chicago: Aldine, 1970), pp. 57–84.
101. Chevigny, *Police Power*, pp. 137–43, 280.
102. W. Knapp, *The Knapp Report on Police Corruption* [in New York City] (New York: Braziller, 1972), p. 3.
103. F. R. Stoddard, "The Informal Code of Police Deviance: A Group Approach to Blue Coat Crime," *Journal of Criminal Law, Criminology and Police Science* 59 (June 1968):201–05.
104. Manning, *The Social Organization of Policing*, pp. 355–56.
105. Skolnick, *Justice Without Trial*, pp. 246–51; see also, Goldstein, "Police Discretion: The Ideal versus the Real"; see also, Robert M. Fogelson, *Big-City Police* (Cambridge, Mass.: Harvard University Press, 1977), pp. 284–88.
106. Arthur Niederhoffer, "Criminal Justice by Dossiers' Law, Enforcement Labeling and Liberty," in Abraham S. Blumberg, ed., *Current Perspectives on Criminal Behavior* (New York: Knopf, 1974), pp. 47–67; see also, Kelling et al., *The Kansas City Preventive Patrol Report*, pp. 181–82; see also, Kelling, "Police Field Services and Crime," 173–84.
107. Bernard L. Garmire, "The Police Role in an Urban Society," in Robert F. Steadman, ed., *The Police and the Community* (Baltimore: Johns Hopkins University Press, 1972), p. 3.
108. See citations, footnote 49.
109. Manning, "The Police: Mandate, Strategies and Appearance," p. 191.
110. Kelling, "Police Field Services and Crime," pp. 173–87. In the pages that follow, we will adapt Kelling's analysis to prompt us to view more cogently the need to reformulate a more effective police mandate.
111. Ibid., pp. 173–75; see also, Manning, "The Police: Mandate, Strategies and Appearance," p. 191.
112. Kelling, "Police Field Services and Crime," pp. 174–75; see also, Reiss, *The Police and the Public*; see also, Richard C. Larson, *Urban Police Patrol Analysis* (Cambridge, Mass.: MIT Press, 1972).
113. Kelling, "Police Field Services and Crime"; see also, Kelling et al., *The Kansas City Preventive Patrol Report*; see also, President's Commission, *Task Force Report: The Police*; see also, Piliavin, "Police-Community Alienation," pp. 1–25.
114. Kelling, "Police Field Services and Crime," pp. 177–78; see also, D. K. Betram and A. Vargo, "Response Time Analysis Study: Preliminary Findings on Robbery in Kansas City," *The Police Chief* (May 1976):74–77; see also, Pate et al., *Police Response Time: Its Determinants and Effects* (Washington, D.C.: Police Foundation, 1976).
115. Kelling, "Police Field Services and Crime," p. 178.
116. Ibid., pp. 178–80.
117. Ibid., pp. 179–80; see also, Alfred I. Schwartz and Summer N. Clarren, *Evaluation of Team Policing in Cincinnati* [after 30 months experimentation] (Washington, D.C.: Police Foundation, in press).
118. Kelling, "Police Field Services and Crime," p. 181; see also, Goldstein, "Police Discretion: The Ideal versus the Real"; see also, Peter B. Bloch and James Bell, *Managing Investigation: The Rochester System* (Washington, D.C.: Police Foundation, 1976); see also, Greenwood et al., *The Criminal Investigation Process*.
119. Kelling, "Police Field Services and Crime," pp. 181–82.
120. Ibid., p. 182; see also, Joseph H. Lewis, *Evaluation of Systems Effectiveness* (Washington, D.C.: Police Foundation, 1964).
121. Kelling, "Police Field Services and Crime," p. 180; see also, Bloch and Bell, *Managing Investigation: The Rochester System*; see also, Greenwood et al., *The Criminal Investigation Process*; see also, Tony Pate et al., *Three Approaches to Criminal Apprehension in Kansas City: An Evaluation Report* (Washington, D.C.: Police Foundation, 1976).
122. Kelling, "Police Field Services and Crime."
123. Ibid., pp. 174–75, 183; see also, Manning, *The Social Organization of Policing*, pp. 108–09; see also, Manning, "The Police: Mandate, Strategies and Appearance," pp. 190–93.
124. Kelling, "Police Field Services and Crime," p. 184.
125. Ibid.; see also, Joseph H. Lewis, "Evaluations of Systems Effectiveness," shortened version, in J. K. Lawrence, ed., *Operation Research and the Social Sciences* (London: Tavistock, 1966), p. 46.

Chapter 13

1. Richard Quinney, *The Social Reality of Crime* (Boston: Little, Brown & Co., 1970), pp. 15–25.
2. President's Commission on Law Enforcement and Administration of Justice, *The Challenge of Crime in a Free Society* (Washington, D.C.: U.S. Government Printing Office, 1967), p. 125.
3. The following eight stages are adapted from James H. Inciardi, *Reflections on Crime: An Introduction to Criminology and Criminal Justice* (New York: Holt, Rinehart & Winston, 1978), pp. 161–71; see also, Livingston Hall, Yale Kamisar, Wayne R. LaFave, and Jerald Israel, *Modern Criminal Procedure*, 3rd ed. (St. Paul, Minn.: West Pub. Co., 1969), Supplement (1973), chapter 13.
4. See also, Donald J. Newman, *Conviction: The Determination of Guilt or Innocence Without Trial* (Boston: Little, Brown & Co., 1966).
5. President's Commission, *The Challenge of Crime in a Free Society*, p. 7.
6. American Bar Association, *New Perspectives on Urban Crime* (Washington, D.C.: ABA Special Committee on Crime Prevention and Control, 1972), p. 1.
7. William L. Hickey, "Depopulating the Jails," *Crime and Delinquency Literature* (June 1975):234–55.
8. Harry E. Allen and Clifford E. Simonsen, *Corrections in America* (Beverly Hills, Calif.: Glencoe Press, 1975), p. 93.
9. President's Commission, *The Challenge of Crime in a Free Society*, p. 262.
10. National Advisory Commission on Criminal Justice Standards and Goals, *Courts* (Washington, D.C.: U.S. Government Printing Office, 1973), pp. 3–16.
11. FBI, *Uniform Crime Reports, 1975* (Washington, D.C.: U.S. Government Printing Office, 1976), pp. 37–41, 49. Unless otherwise noted, data on offenses reported to the police and arrests are from the UCR. See also, Stephen Gettinger, "U.S. Prison Population Hits All-Time High," *Corrections Magazine* (March 1976):9–20.
12. John F. Klein, "Inducements to Plead Guilty: Frontier Justice Revisited," in John F. Klein, *Let's Make a Deal* (Lexington, Mass.: D. C. Heath, 1976); see also, Donald J. Newman, "Plea Bargaining," *Trial* (March/April 1973): 11–15.
13. Commission on Standards and Goals, *Courts*, p. 42.
14. Project STAR, Survey of Role Perceptions for Operational Criminal Justice Personnel: Data Summary, 238, 243 (1972), in Commission on Standards and Goals, *Courts*, p. 43.
15. Ibid., pp. 43, 44.
16. Norval Morris, *The Future of Imprisonment* (Chicago: University of Chicago Press, 1974), p. 52.
17. Commission on Standards and Goals, *Courts*, pp. 27–28. The statement made by Arnold Hopkins was at a conference on Criminal Law and Pretrial Programs, State University of New York, Potsdam, New York, April 1973.
18. Alexander B. Smith and Arthur Niederhoffer, "The Psychology of Power," *Crime and Delinquency* 19, no. 3 (July 1973):406–13; see also, J. Skelly Wright, "Law for the Poor," *New York Times Magazine*, March 9, 1967, pp. 26–27.
19. Commission on Standards and Goals, *Courts*, pp. 110–11.
20. Harry Kalven, Jr. and Hans Zeisel, "The American Jury Study," in Harry Kalven, Jr. and Hans Zeisel, eds., *The American Jury* (Boston: Little, Brown & Co., 1966), pp. 35–52; see also, Fred L. Strodtbeck et al., "Social Status in Jury Deliberations," in Richard D. Schwartz and Jerome H. Skolnick, eds., *Society and the Legal Order* (New York: Basic Books, 1970), pp. 353–60.
21. Smith and Niederhoffer, "The Psychology of Power," pp. 408–09.
22. Commission on Standards and Goals, *Courts*, pp. 110–11.
23. Inciardi, *Reflections on Crime,* pp. 174–76; see also, Robert O. Dawson, *Sentencing: The Decision as to Type, Length, and Conditions of Sentence* (Boston: Little, Brown & Co., 1969).
24. Smith and Niederhoffer, "The Psychology of Power," pp. 409–11.
25. Ibid.
26. Commission on Standards and Goals, *Courts*, pp. 145–51.
27. Smith and Niederhoffer, "The Psychology of Power," pp. 406–07.
28. Ibid.
29. David Sudnow, "The Public Defender," in Schwartz and Skolnick, *Society and the Legal Order*, pp. 389–402.
30. Smith and Niederhoffer, "The Psychology of Power," p. 412; see also, Abraham Blumberg, "Criminal Justice in America," in Jack D. Douglas, ed., *Crime and Justice in American Society* (Indianapolis: Bobbs-Merrill, 1971), pp. 66–67.
31. Kalven and Zeisel, *The American Jury*, pp. 55–59.
32. Ibid., pp. 59–62.
33. Ibid., pp. 375–94; see also, Fred L. Strodtbeck, Rita M. James, and Charles Hawkins, "Social Status in Jury Deliberation," *American Sociological Review* 22 (December 1957):713–19.
34. Strodtbeck et al., "Social Status in Jury Deliberation."
35. Commission on Standards and Goals, *Courts*, pp. 99–102.
36. Ibid., p. 160.
37. Ibid., pp. 112–15.
38. R. Bryce Young, *Criminal Law: Codes and Cases* (New York: McGraw-Hill, 1972), pp. 7–8.
39. Ibid., pp. 10–13; see also, Commission on Standards and Goals, *Courts*, pp. 160–63.
40. Commission on Standards and Goals, *Courts*, pp. 160–61; see also, President's Commission, *The Challenge of Crime in a Free Society*, pp. 128–29.
41. President's Commission, *The Challenge of Crime in a Free Society*, pp. 129–30.
42. Ibid., pp. 128–29.
43. Commission on Standards and Goals, *Courts*, pp. 162–63.
44. Kent v. United States, 383 U.S. 556 (1966).
45. Anthony M. Platt, *The Child Savers: The Invention of Delinquency* (Chicago: University of Chicago Press, 1966), p. 169; see also, Nicholas N. Kittrie, *The Right To Be Different: Deviance and Enforced Therapy* (New York: Penguin Books, 1971), pp. 3–11.
46. Harold K. Becker and Elnor O. Hjellemo, *Justice in Modern Sweden* (Springfield, Ill.: Charles C Thomas, 1976), pp. 107–09.
47. Kittrie, *The Right To Be Different,* chapter 3; see also, William Hickey, "Status Offenses and the Juvenile Court," *Criminal Justice Abstracts* (March 1977):91–122.
48. President's Commission, *The Challenge of Crime in a Free Society*, pp. 85–86; see also, Aaron V. Cicourel, *The*

Social Organization of Justice (New York: John Wiley & Sons, 1968).

49. Fred D. Fant, "Impact of the Gault Decision on Probation Practice in Juvenile Courts," *Federal Probation* 33 (September 1966):14–17; see also, *In re Gault,* 387 U.S. 1 (1967).

50. Edwin M. Lemert, "Legislating Change in the Juvenile Court," *Wisconsin Law Review* 2 (1967):421–49.

51. Jessica Mitford, *Kind and Usual Punishment* (New York: Random House, 1971), pp. 81–83.

52. David Fogel, *We Are the Living Proof: The Justice Model for Corrections* (Cincinnati: W. H. Anderson, 1975), pp. 193–94.

53. Marvin E. Frankel, *Criminal Sentences* (New York: Hill & Wang, 1973), p. 112.

54. Michael S. Serrill, "Determinate Sentencing: History, Theory, Debate," *Corrections Magazine* 3, no. 3 (September 1977):8; see also, President's Commission, *The Challenge of Crime in a Free Society,* pp. 25–26.

55. President's Commission, *The Challenge of Crime in a Free Society,* pp. 25–26.

56. Serrill, "Determinate Sentencing," p. 8.

57. Pierce O'Donnell et al., *Toward a Just and Effective Sentencing System* (New York: Praeger, 1974); see also, Serrill, "Determinate Sentencing."

58. John Hagen, "Extra-Legal Attributes and Criminal Sentencing: An Assessment of a Sociological Viewpoint," *Law and Society Review* 8 (Spring 1974):379. For recent empirical data challenging this study, see A. L. Lizotte, "Extra-Legal Factors in Chicago's Criminal Courts Testing the Conflict Model of Criminal Justice," *Social Problems* 25, no. 5 (June 1978):564–80.

59. Sol Rubin, *The Law of Criminal Correction* (St. Paul, Minn.: West Pub. Co., 1973), pp. 162–64.

60. Richard A. McGee, "A New Look at Sentencing: Part II," *Federal Probation* (September 1974):7–8.

61. Quoted in Serrill, "Determinate Sentencing," pp. 9, 13.

62. Fogel, *We Are the Living Proof,* pp. 242–45.

63. McGee, "A New Look at Sentencing: Part II," pp. 7–8.

64. The American Law Institute's *Model Penal Code* (1963); see also: President's Commission, *The Challenge of Crime in a Free Society,* p. 142; the National Council on Crime and Delinquency's *Model Sentencing Act* (1972); and the Board of Directors, NCCD, "The Nondangerous Offender Should Not Be Imprisoned; A Policy Statement," *Crime and Delinquency* 21, no. 4 (October 1975):315–22.

65. President's Commission, *The Challenge of Crime in a Free Society*; see also, Fogel, *We Are the Living Proof,* pp. 244, 247.

66. The American Law Institute's *Model Penal Code,* 8 section 7.01 (1963); see also, Andrew von Hirsch, *Doing Justice: The Choice of Punishments* (New York: Hill & Wang, 1976).

67. Fogel, *We Are the Living Proof,* p. 245; see also, von Hirsch, *Doing Justice.*

68. Stephen Gettinger, "Three States Adopt Flat Sentences; Others Wary," *Corrections Magazine* 3, no. 3 (September 1977):16–33, 36.

69. Charles L. Black, Jr., *Capital Punishment: The Inevitability of Caprice and Mistake* (New York: W. W. Norton, 1974), pp. 10–11.

70. Ibid., p. 12.

71. Furman v. Georgia, 408 U.S. 238 (1972), section 253.

72. Black, *Capital Punishment,* pp. 11–13.

73. Hugo A. Bedau, *The Case Against the Death Penalty* (New York: American Civil Liberties Union, 1977), p. 3.

74. Black, *Capital Punishment,* p. 24.

75. Bedau, *The Case Against the Death Penalty,* pp. 1–3; see also, William Bowers, *Executions in America* (Lexington, Mass.: D. C. Heath, 1974).

76. Daniel Glaser and Max S. Zeigler, "Use of the Death Penalty v. Outrage at Murder," *Crime and Delinquency* 20, no. 4 (October 1974):333–38.

77. Abe Fortas, "The Case Against Capital Punishment," *The New York Times Briefing Papers for Public Affairs* 2 (May 1978):12.

78. Thorsten Sellin, *The Death Penalty* (Philadelphia: The American Law Institute, 1959); see also, Frank Zimring and Gordon Hawkins, *Deterrence* (Chicago: University of Chicago Press, 1973).

79. Glaser and Zeigler, "Use of the Death Penalty v. Outrage at Murder," pp. 336–37.

80. Isaac Ehrlich, "The Deterrent Effect of Capital Punishment: A Question of Life and Death," *American Economic Review* 65 (June 1975):397–417; see also, Gary Kleck, "Capital Punishment, Gun Ownership, and Homicide," *American Journal of Sociology* 84, no. 4 (January 1979):882–910; see also, William F. Graves, "The Deterrent Effect of Capital Punishment (A Doctor Looks at Capital Punishment)," in Hugo A. Bedau, ed., *The Death Penalty in America* (New York: Doubleday/Anchor Books, 1964), pp. 322–32.

81. Bedau, *The Case Against the Death Penalty,* p. 23; see also, Fortas, "The Case Against Capital Punishment"; see also, Marc Riedel, "Discrimination in the Imposition of the Death Penalty," *Temple Law Quarterly* 49 (1976):261–87.

82. Bedau, *The Case Against the Death Penalty,* p. 24.

83. Ibid.

84. *New York Times,* January 15, 1978.

85. Bedau, *The Case Against the Death Penalty,* p. 5.

86. Charles W. Thomas and Robert G. Howard, "Public Attitudes Toward Capital Punishment," in Norman Johnston and Leonard Savitz, eds., *Justice and Corrections* (New York: John Wiley & Sons, 1978), pp. 407–20; see also, Gregg v. Georgia (1976).

87. *New York Times,* July 4, 1978, p. 8.

88. Thomas and Howard, "Public Attitudes Toward Capital Punishment," p. 410; see also, Furman v. Georgia (1972), Gregg v. Georgia (1976), and Lockett v. Ohio (1978).

Chapter 14

1. William G. Nagel, *The New Red Barn: A Critical Look at the Modern American Prison* (New York: Walker & Co., 1973), p. 17. (Published for the American Foundation, Inc., Institute of Corrections, Philadelphia.)

2. Ibid.

3. Ibid., p. 159.

4. Ibid., pp. 17–18, 159–60.

5. Joseph Fishman, *Crucibles of Crime* (New York: Cosmopolis Press, 1973); see also, National Commission on Law Observance and Enforcement, *Report on Penal Institutions, Probation and Parole,* Report of the Advisory Committee on Penal Institutions, Probation and Parole (Washington, D.C.: U.S. Government Printing Office, 1931). (Report to the Wickersham Commission of Law Observance and Enforcement hereafter called Wickersham Com-

mission.) See also, Richard A. McGee, "Our Sick Jails," *Federal Probation* 35, no. 1 (March 1971):3–8.

6. Law Enforcement Assistance Administration (LEAA), *The Nation's Jails, 1970* (Washington, D.C.: U.S. Government Printing Office, 1970), pp. 6–7.

7. Law Enforcement Assistance Administration (LEAA), *The Nation's Jails, 1975* (Washington, D.C.: U.S. Government Printing Office, 1975), pp. 22–24.

8. Robert M. Carter, Richard McGee, and E. Kim Nelson, *Corrections in America* (Philadelphia: J. B. Lippincott, 1975), pp. 73–74.

9. Hans W. Mattick and Alexander B. Aikman, "The Cloacal Region of American Corrections," *Annals of the American Academy of Political and Social Science* 381 (January 1969):109–18.

10. Billy Wayson, Gail S. Funke, Sally F. Familton, and Peter B. Meyer, *Local Jails* (Lexington, Mass.: D. C. Heath, 1977), pp. 3–4.

11. Ibid., p. 4.

12. Ibid.; see also, P. D. Jordan, "The Close and Stinking Jail," in *Frontier Law and Order: Ten Essays* (Lincoln: University of Nebraska Press, 1970), pp. 140–41.

13. Wayson et al., *Local Jails*, p. 4; see also, Orlando F. Lewis, *The Development of American Prisons and Prison Customs, 1776–1845* (Montclair, N.J.: Patterson Smith, 1967), p. 278.

14. Wayson et al., *Local Jails*, pp. 6–7; see also, Nicholas N. Kittrie, *The Right To Be Different* (New York: Penguin Books, 1971), pp. 50–113.

15. Wayson et al., *Local Jails*, pp. 4–5; see also, Lewis, *The Development of American Prisons and Prison Customs*, p. 269.

16. Louis Robinson, *Penology in the United States* (Philadelphia: J. C. Winston, 1923), pp. 29–44, cited in Wayson et al., *Local Jails*, p. 4.

17. Fishman, *Crucibles of Crime*, pp. 82, 14.

18. Wayson et al., *Local Jails*, p. 5.

19. Wickersham Commission; see also, Joseph C. Hutcheson, "The Local Jails," in *Proceedings of the Attorney General's Conference on Crime, December 10–13, 1934* (Washington, D.C.: U.S. Government Printing Office, n.d.), p. 233; see also, President's Commission on Law Enforcement and the Administration of Justice, *Task Force Report: Corrections* (Washington, D.C.: U.S. Government Printing Office, 1967), p. 75; see also, National Advisory Commission on Criminal Justice Standards and Goals, *Corrections* (Washington, D.C.: U.S. Government Printing Office, 1973), p. 309.

20. LEAA, *The Nation's Jails, 1970*, and *1975*.

21. LEAA, *The Nation's Jails, 1975*.

22. Hans W. Mattick, "The Contemporary Jails of the United States: An Unknown and Neglected Area of Justice," in Daniel Glaser, ed., *Handbook of Criminology* (Chicago: Rand McNally, 1974), pp. 777–79.

23. Ibid., pp. 785–89.

24. McGee, "Our Sick Jails," pp. 3–8.

25. LEAA, *The Nation's Jails, 1975*.

26. American Civil Liberties Union, *The Seeds of Anguish: An ACLU Study of the D.C. Jail* (Washington, D.C.: ACLU, 1972), p. 1, cited in Commission on Standards and Goals, *Corrections*, p. 275.

27. Nagel, *The New Red Barn*, pp. 20–21.

28. Mattick, "The Contemporary Jails of the United States," p. 802.

29. Ibid., p. 803.

30. LEAA, *The Nation's Jails, 1975*, pp. 23–24.

31. Mattick, "The Contemporary Jails of the United States," pp. 804–07.

32. Ibid., pp. 810–13; see also, LEAA, *The Nation's Jails*, p. 28.

33. LEAA, *The Nation's Jails, 1975*, p. 15.

34. Allen J. Davis, "Sexual Assaults in the Philadelphia Prison Systems and Sheriffs Vans," *Transaction* 6 (1968):9.

35. Commission on Standards and Goals, *Corrections*, p. 98; see also, President's Commission, *Task Force Report: Corrections*, pp. 79–80.

36. Commission on Standards and Goals, *Corrections*, pp. 103, 296–97.

37. William L. Hickey, "Depopulating the Jails," *Crime and Delinquency Literature* (June 1975):237–39.

38. Nagel, *The New Red Barn*, pp. 160–61.

39. Ibid., pp. 103–04.

40. Jerome Skolnick, "Judicial Response to Crisis," in Jerome Skolnick, ed., *The Politics of Protest* (New York: Simon & Schuster, 1969).

41. Commission on Standards and Goals, *Corrections*, pp. 274–76.

42. Manhattan Bail Project, cited in Commission on Standards and Goals, *Corrections*, p. 100; see also, Charles Ares, Anne Rankin, and Herbert Sturz, "The Manhatten Bail Project: Interim Report on the Use of Pretrial Parole," *New York University Law Review* 38 (1968):67, 85.

43. Anne Rankin, "The Effect of Pretrial Detention," *New York University Law Review* 39 (1964):654; see also, Commission on Standards and Goals, *Corrections*, p. 100.

44. Commission on Standards and Goals, *Corrections*, p. 109.

45. Paul B. Wice, *Freedom for Sale: A National Study of Pretrial Release* (Lexington, Mass.: D. C. Heath, 1974), cited in Commission on Standards and Goals, *Corrections*, pp. 244–45.

46. American Friends Service Committee, *Struggle for Justice* (New York: Hill & Wang, 1971), p. 2.

47. Hickey, "Depopulating the Jails," pp. 248–51.

48. U.S. National Law Enforcement and Criminal Justice Research Operations Division, *Case Screening and Selected Case Processing in Prosecutors Offices* (Washington, D.C.: U.S. Government Printing Office, 1973).

49. National Center for Prosecution Management, *The Prosecutor's Screening Function: Case Evaluation and Control* (Chicago: National District Attorney's Association, 1973).

50. Elizabeth W. Vorenburg and James Vorenburg, "Early Diversion from the Criminal Justice System," in Lloyd E. Ohlin, ed., *Prisoners in America* (Englewood Cliffs, N.J.: Prentice-Hall, 1973), pp. 151–83.

51. Ibid., pp. 153–54.

52. Ibid., pp. 154–66, 172.

53. Rosemary C. Sarri, National Assessment of Juvenile Corrections, *Under Lock and Key: Juveniles in Jails and Detention* (Ann Arbor: University of Michigan, 1974), p. 5.

54. *Juvenile Detention in Wisconsin, 1976, Final Report* (Madison: Wisconsin Health and Social Service Department, 1976), pp. 5, 70–71.

55. Andrew Rutherford, "The Dissolution of the Training Schools in Massachusetts," in Calvert R. Dodge, ed., *A Nation Without Prisons* (Lexington, Mass.: D. C. Heath/Lexington Books, 1975), pp. 57–75, especially pp. 67–74; see also, Lloyd E. Ohlin, Robert B. Coates, and Allen D. Miller, "Radical Correctional Reform: A Case Study of the

Massachusetts Youth Correctional System," *Harvard Educational Review* 44 (1974).

56. Vorenburg and Vorenburg, "Early Diversion from the Criminal Justice System," pp. 160–61.

57. Franklin Zimring, "Measuring the Impact of Pretrial Diversion from the Criminal Justice System," *University of Chicago Law Review* 41 no. 2 (1974):224–41, cited in Hickey, "Depopulating the Jails," p. 243.

58. Commission on Standards and Goals, *Corrections*, pp. 95–96.

59. *Source Book on Pretrial Criminal Justice Intervention Techniques and Action Programs* (Washington, D.C.: American Bar Association, National Pretrial Intervention Service Center, 1974). Also see their *Summary Report, Pretrial Intervention Strategies: An Evaluation of Policy-Related Research and Policy-Maker Perceptions* (Washington, D.C.: 1974).

60. Hickey, "Depopulating the Jails," p. 244.

61. Vorenburg and Vorenburg, "Early Diversion from the Criminal Justice System," p. 183; see also, Commission on Standards and Goals, *Corrections*, pp. 73–97.

62. LEAA, *The Nation's Jails*.

63. Board of Directors, NCCD, "The Nondangerous Offender Should Not Be Imprisoned," *Crime and Delinquency* 21, no. 4 (October 1975):313–22.

64. Ibid.

65. Sol Rubin, *The Law of Criminal Corrections* (St. Paul, Minn.: West Pub. Co., 1973), pp. 195–96.

66. Mattick, "The Contemporary Jails of the United States, p. 827; see also, Harold K. Becker and E. O. Hjellemo, *Justice in Modern Sweden* (Springfield, Ill.: Charles C Thomas, 1976), p. 12.

67. President's Commission, *Task Force Report: Corrections*, p. 1; see also, Hickey, "Depopulating the Jails," pp. 254–58. For a summary of studies regarding the effectiveness of probation compared with other sentencing alternatives, see Roger Hood and Richard Sparks, *Key Issues in Criminology* (New York: McGraw-Hill, 1970), pp. 178–92.

68. Mattick, "The Contemporary Jails of the United States," p. 826.

69. Carter et al., *Corrections in America*, pp. 79–80.

70. David F. Greenberg, "The Correctional Effects of Corrections," in David F. Greenberg, ed., *Corrections and Punishment* (Beverly Hills, Calif.: Sage Publications, 1977), p. 123; see also, A. Rudoff and T. C. Esselstyn, "Evaluating Work Furlough: A Follow-Up," *Federal Probation* 27 (June 1973):48–53.

71. Greenberg, "The Correctional Effects of Corrections"; see also, A. D. Witte, *Work-Release in North Carolina: An Evaluation of Its Post Release Effects* (Chapel Hill, N.C.: Institute for Research in Social Science, 1975).

72. Greenberg, "The Correctional Effects of Corrections," pp. 123–24; see also, R. Jeffrey and S. Woolpert, "Work Furlough as an Alternative to Incarceration: An Assessment of its Effect on Recidivism and Social Cost," *Journal of Criminal Law and Criminology* 65 (1974):405–15.

73. Commission on Standards and Goals, *Corrections*, p. 235.

74. Ibid., chapter 7; see also, Hickey, "Depopulating the Jails," pp. 202–53.

75. Commission on Standards and Goals, *Corrections*.

76. LEAA, *The Nation's Jails, 1975;* see also, Wayson et al., *Local Jails*, pp. 13–15, 37.

77. Commission on Standards and Goals, *Corrections*, pp. 389–90; see also, Wayson et al., *Local Jails*, pp. 14–17.

78. Nagel, *The New Red Barn*, p. 168; see also, Andrew Scull, *Decarceration: Community Treatment and the Deviant; A Radical View* (Englewood Cliffs, N.J.: Prentice-Hall, 1977).

79. Commission on Standards and Goals, *Corrections;* see also, Wayson et al., *Local Jails*.

80. Mattick, "The Contemporary Jails of the United States," pp. 842–43; see also, Hickey, "Depopulating the Jails," pp. 254–55; see also, Edith E. Flynn, "Jails and Criminal Justice," in Lloyd E. Ohlin, ed., *Prisoners in America* (Englewood Cliffs, N.J.: Prentice-Hall, 1973), pp. 49–88.

81. Mattick and Aikman, "The Cloacal Region of American Corrections."

Chapter 15

1. Austin Turk, *Criminology in the Legal Order* (Chicago: Rand McNally, 1969), p. 18.

2. For recent studies of corrections and the female offender see: Freda Adler, *Sisters in Crime: The Rise of the New Female Criminal* (New York: McGraw-Hill, 1975); Rose Giallombardo, *Society of Women: A Study of Women's Prisons* (New York: John Wiley & Sons, 1966); Rose Giallombardo, *The Social World of Imprisoned Girls* (New York: John Wiley & Sons, 1974); Walter Reckless and Barbara Kay, Report to the President's Commission on Law Enforcement and Administration of Justice, *The Female Offender* (Washington, D.C.: U.S. Government Printing Office, 1967); Rita Simon, *Women and Crime* (Lexington, Mass.: D. C. Heath, 1975).

3. Rob Wilson, "U.S. Prison Population Again Hits New High," in Peter Wickman and Phillip Whitten, eds., *Readings in Criminology* (Lexington, Mass.: D. C. Heath, 1978), pp. 352–61.

4. Law Enforcement Assistance Administration (LEAA), *Expenditures and Employment Data for the Criminal Justice System: 1975* (Washington, D.C.: U.S. Government Printing Office, 1977), cited in *Newsletter of the National Moratorium on Prison Construction* 1, no. 11 (September/October 1977):10.

5. President's Commission on Law Enforcement and Administration of Justice, *Task Force Report: Corrections* (Washington, D.C.: U.S. Government Printing Office, 1967), p. 1.

6. Leslie T. Wilkins, *Evaluation of Penal Measures* (New York: Random House, 1969), chapter 1; see also, National Advisory Commission on Criminal Justice Standards and Goals, *Corrections* (Washington, D.C.: U.S. Government Printing Office, 1973), p. 535.

7. David J. Rothman, "Decarcerating Prisoners and Patients," *Civil Liberties Review* (1973):22.

8. Norval Morris, *The Future of Imprisonment* (Chicago: University of Chicago Press, 1974), pp. 21–22.

9. Robert Martinson, "What Works? Questions and Answers About Prison Reform," *The Public Interest* 22 (Spring 1974):35; see also, D. Lipton, R. Martinson, and J. Wilkes, *The Effectiveness of Correctional Treatment: A Survey of Treatment Evaluation Studies* (New York: Praeger, 1975); see also, American Friends Service Committee, *Struggle for Justice; A Report on Crime and Punishment in America* (New York: Hill & Wang, 1971), pp. 46–47.

10. Commission on Standards and Goals, *Corrections*, p. 224.

11. American Friends Service Committee, *Struggle for Justice*, pp. 22–23, 48–49.

12. Nils Christie, "Changes in Penal Values," in Nils Christie, ed., *Aspects of Social Control in the Welfare State: Scandinavian Studies in Criminology,* vol. 2 (London: Tavistock Publications, 1968).

13. David Fogel, *We Are the Living Proof: The Justice Model for Corrections* (Cincinnati: W. H. Anderson Co., 1975), pp. 6–13.

14. Ibid., pp. 18–21.

15. David Rothman, "The Invention of the Penitentiary," *Criminal Law Bulletin* 8 (September 1972), cited in Fogel, *We Are the Living Proof,* p. 22.

16. Fogel, *We Are the Living Proof,* p. 27.

17. The Official Report of the New York State Special Commission on Attica, *Attica* (New York: Bantam Books, 1972), pp. 92–96. (Hereafter referred to as the Report on Attica.)

18. Fogel, *We Are the Living Proof,* pp. 34–35.

19. Commission on Standards and Goals, *Corrections,* pp. 343–44.

20. Donald R. Cressey, "Adult Felons in Prison," in Lloyd E. Ohlin, ed., *Prisoners in America* (Englewood Cliffs, N.J.: Prentice-Hall, 1973), pp. 117–23.

21. American Friends Service Committee, *Struggle for Justice,* pp. 20–21.

22. Cressey, "Adult Felons in Prison."

23. Fogel, *We Are the Living Proof,* pp. 57–58.

24. Jessica Mitford, *Kind and Usual Punishment* (New York: Random House, 1971), p. 6.

25. Cressey, "Adult Felons in Prison," p. 131.

26. Charles McKendrick, "Custody and Discipline," in Paul W. Tappan, ed., *Contemporary Corrections* (New York: McGraw-Hill, 1951), pp. 159–60; see also, Fogel, *We Are the Living Proof,* p. 55.

27. Report on Attica, pp. 488–89; see also, Fogel, *We Are the Living Proof,* p. 57; see also, Cressey, "Adult Felons in Prison," pp. 131–32.

28. James B. Jacobs and Harold G. Retsky, "Prison Guard," in Robert G. Leger and John R. Stratton, eds., *The Sociology of Corrections* (New York: John Wiley & Sons, 1977), pp. 49–65.

29. George Jackson, *The Village Voice,* September 10, 1970, as cited in Fogel, *We Are the Living Proof,* p. 105.

30. Fogel, *We Are the Living Proof,* pp. 88–89, 92.

31. "The Cantos of Mutability Revisited—Opportunities for the new C.O.," *Corrections, Compendium* 2, no. 7 (January 1978):1–3. This survey is lacking in accuracy, since it reports both California and New York state prison systems as having no union for custodial staff. California has an effective local union, and New York State prison guards are affiliated with a Teamsters Union. See also, Fogel, *We Are the Living Proof,* p. 92.

32. John Irwin, "The Changing Social Structure of the Men's Prisons," in David F. Greenberg, ed., *Corrections and Punishment* (Beverly Hills, Calif.: Sage Publications, 1977), pp. 36–37.

33. Ibid., pp. 25, 35–37.

34. Donald Clemmer, *The Prison Community* (New York: Holt, Rinehart & Winston, 1940), pp. 98–118.

35. See, for instance, Hans Reimer, "Socialization in Prison," in *Proceedings of the Sixty-Seventh Annual Congress of the American Prison System,* 1937, and Clarence Schrag, "Social Types in a Prison Community," unpublished Master's thesis, University of Washington, 1944, cited in John Irwin, *The Felon* (Englewood Cliffs, N.J.: Prentice-Hall, 1970), p. 61.

36. Irwin, "The Changing Social Structure of the Men's Prisons," pp. 22–23.

37. Cressey, "Adult Felons in Prison," pp. 133–34.

38. Ibid., p. 134; see also, Irwin, "The Changing Social Structure of the Men's Prisons"; see also, Peter Garabedian, "Social Rules and Processes of Socialization in the Prison Community," in R. G. Leger and J. R. Stratton, eds., *The Sociology of Correction; A Book of Readings* (New York: John Wiley & Sons, 1977), pp. 201–16.

39. Irwin, *The Felon,* pp. 61–85; see also, John Irwin and Donald Cressey, "Thieves, Convicts, and the Inmate Culture," *Social Problems* 10, no. 3 (1963), pp. 142–55; see also, Irwin, "The Changing Social Structure of the Men's Prisons," p. 24.

40. Irwin, "The Changing Social Structure of the Men's Prisons," p. 25; see also, Stanton Wheeler, "The Determinants of Normative Patterns in Correctional Institutions," in Christie, *Aspects of Social Control in the Welfare State,* pp. 173–83.

41. John Irwin and A. Holder, "History of the Prisoner's Union," *The Outlaw: Journal of Prisoners Union* 2 (January/February 1973):2.

42. Ibid.

43. C. Ronald Huff, "Unionization Behind the Walls," *Criminology* 12, no. 2 (August 1974):184–85.

44. Ibid., p. 185; see also, Thomas Mathiesen, *The Politics of Abolition: Scandinavian Studies in Criminology,* vol. 4 (Oslo: Scandinavian University Books, 1974), pp. 39–43.

45. Information gathered by one of the authors while on study tour of Scandinavian prisons in 1974.

46. Goodwin v. Oswald, 46 2F 2nd 1937 (1972); see also, Huff, "Unionization Behind the Walls," p. 186.

47. Jones v. North Carolina Prisoner's Labor Union, Inc., Supreme Court, 1977, 433 U.S. 97S Ct. 2532, 53 L.Ed. 2d 629.

48. Ibid., pp. 25–36; see also, Gerald Suttles, *The Social Order of the Slum* (Chicago: University of Chicago Press, 1968).

49. Rothman, "Decarcerating Prisoners and Patients," pp. 22–24; see also, Morris, *The Future of Imprisonment,* pp. 21–22, 57.

50. ABA and Council of State Governments, *Compendium of Model Correctional Legislation and Standards* (July 1972), Part V, pp. 1–11; see also, Council of Judges, NCCD, *Model Sentencing Act,* 2nd ed., *Crime and Delinquency* 18 (1972):335; see also, Commission on Standards and Goals, *Corrections,* Standard 5.2.

51. Council of Judges, NCCD, *Model Sentencing Act.*

52. Report of the Committee for the Study of Incarceration, Andrew Von Hirsch, ed., *Doing Justice: The Choice of Punishments* (New York: Hill & Wang, 1976), pp. 10–12.

53. American Friends Service Committee, *Struggle for Justice,* pp. 44–45.

54. New York State Division of Parole, Department of Corrections, "Parole Adjustment and Prior Educational Achievement of Male Adolescent Offenders, June 1957–January 1961" (September 1964), cited in Martinson, "What Works? Questions and Answers About Prison Reform," p. 28.

55. Cited in David F. Greenberg, "The Correctional Effects of Corrections," in Greenberg, *Corrections and Punishment,* p. 121.

56. Ibid.

57. Ibid., p. 122.

58. Lipton et al., *The Effectiveness of Correctional Treat-*

ment, p. 206.

59. Martinson, "What Works? Questions and Answers About Prison Reform," p. 28.

60. E. S. Guttman, "Effects of Short-Term Psychiatric Treatment on Boys in Two California Youth Authority Institutions," Research Report #36, California Youth Authority, also cited in Greenberg, *Corrections and Punishment,* p. 125.

61. Lipton et al., *The Effectiveness of Correctional Treatment,* pp. 214–15.

62. Cited in Martinson, "What Works? Questions and Answers About Prison Reform," p. 30.

63. Greenberg, *Corrections and Punishment,* pp. 125–26; see also, Jew et al., "Effectiveness of Group Psychotherapy with Character Disordered Prisoners," Research Report #56, California Department of Corrections, also cited in Greenberg, *Corrections and Punishment,* pp. 126–27.

64. Gene Kassebaum, David Ward, and Daniel Wilner, *Prison Treatment and Parole Survival* (New York: John Wiley & Sons, 1971).

65. Mitford, *Kind and Usual Punishment,* p. 131.

66. Ibid.

67. Wayne Sage, "Crime and Clockwork Orange," *Human Behavior* (September 1974):16–25.

68. "Identification and Treatment of Incarcerated Dangerous Offenders and the Politization of Inmate Populations: Rehabilitation or Repression?" in Peter W. Lewis and Kenneth D. Peoples, eds., *The Supreme Court and the Criminal Process: Cases and Comments* (Philadelphia: W. B. Saunders, 1978), pp. 749–98.

69. Ibid.

70. Greenberg, *Corrections and Punishment,* p. 130.

71. Morris, *The Future of Imprisonment,* pp. 23–24.

72. Greenberg, *Corrections and Punishment,* pp. 122–23.

73. Ibid., pp. 118–20.

74. Martinson, "What Works? Questions and Answers About Prison Reform," p. 40.

75. Ibid., p. 41.

76. Attorneys General's Survey of Release Procedures 11 (1939), quoted in Sol Rubin, *Law of Criminal Corrections* (St. Paul, Minn.: West Pub. Co., 1973), p. 620.

77. Lipton et al., *The Effectiveness of Correctional Treatment,* pp. 116–36.

78. Greenberg, *Corrections and Punishment,* pp. 137, 139–40.

79. Roger Hood and Richard Sparks, *Key Issues in Criminology* (New York: McGraw-Hill, 1970), pp. 188–90; see also, Martinson, "What Works? Questions and Answers About Prison Reform," p. 36.

80. Martinson, "What Works? Questions and Answers About Prison Reform," p. 37.

81. Ibid.

82. Nigel Walker, *Crimes, Courts and Figures* (New York: Penguin Books, 1971), pp. 120–22.

83. Nigel Walker, "The Interchangeability of Criminal Sanctions," as cited in Leonard Orland, *Justice, Punishment and Treatment: The Correctional Process* (New York: Free Press, 1973), pp. 5–6.

84. Eugene Doleschal, "Sentencing Practices of the U.S. Compared with Three Northern European Countries," *Crime and Delinquency* 23, no. 1 (January 1977):51–56.

85. Norman Bishop, "Aspects of European Penal System," in Louis Blom-Cooper, ed., *Progress in Penal Reform* (Oxford: Clarendon Press, 1974), pp. 84–88.

86. Bengt Borjeson, "Om pafoljders verkningar," with English summary (Stockholm: Almquist and Wiksell, 1966).

87. Bishop, "Aspects of European Penal System," pp. 84, 88–90.

88. *Sveriges Officiella Statestik, Kriminalvarden, 1974* (Stockholm: Kriminalvardsverket, 1975), pp. 20–21.

89. Inkeri Anttila, "Conservative and Radical Policy in the Nordic Countries," in *Scandinavian Studies in Criminology,* vol. 2, pp. 9–22.

90. Ibid.; see also, Bishop, "Aspects of European Penal System," pp. 97–98.

91. From field notes of a conversation between Norman Bishop and one of the authors, Stockholm, Sweden (November 1974).

92. Michael S. Servill, "Profile Sweden," *Corrections Magazine* 3, no. 2 (June 1977):26.

93. Bishop, "Aspects of European Penal System," p. 98.

94. Martinson, "What Works? Questions and Answers About Prison Reform," p. 34.

95. Conversation with Danish forensic psychiatrists, field notes (December 1974).

96. Bishop, "Aspects of European Penal System," pp. 98–99.

97. Correspondence with Finnish prison official, July 1976.

98. Svante Mycander, in *The Swedish Dialogue: Criminal Welfare—Voices from Newspapers, Magazines and Books* (Stockholm: The Swedish Institute, 1973).

99. Cited in William Nagel, *The New Red Barn: A Critical Look at the Modern American Prison* (Philadelphia: The American Foundation, Institute of Corrections, 1973), p. 148.

100. Morris, *The Future of Imprisonment,* pp. ix, 17–22.

101. See Ted Palmer, "Martinson Revisited," *Journal of Research in Crime and Delinquency* (July 1975):133–52; see also, Robert Martinson, "California Research at the Crossroads," *Crime and Delinquency* (April 1976):178–91; see also, Donald E. J. MacNamara, "The Medical Model in Corrections: *Requiescat in Pace,*" *Criminology* 14 (February 1977):439–48; see also, *Criminology* (May 1978), for a response to this article.

102. American Friends Service Committee, *Struggle for Justice,* p. 23.

103. David Rothman, "Society and Its Prisons," a review of *Discipline and Punish: The Birth of the Prisons* by Michel Foucault in the *New York Times Book Review,* February 19, 1978, pp. 1, 2, 6, 7.

104. Nagel, *The New Red Barn,* pp. 148–49.

105. Quoted in *Jericho, Newsletter of the National Moratorium on Prison Construction* 1, no. 12 (November 1977–January 1978):2.

106. Ernst von den Haag, *Punishing Criminals: Concerning a Very Old and Painful Question* (New York: Basic Books, 1975); for the reaction to this book, see Clarence Schrag's review of *Punishing Criminals,* in *Criminology* 14 (February 1977):569–73.

107. James Q. Wilson, *Thinking About Crime* (New York: Vintage, 1977), p. xix.

108. Ibid., pp. 169–70.

109 Martinson, "What Works? Questions and Answers About Prison Reform"; see also, Judith Wilkes and Robert Martinson, "Is the Treatment of Criminal Offenders Really Necessary?" *Federal Probation* 40 (March 1976):7–9.

110. William Nagel, "On Behalf of a Moratorium on Prison Construction," *Crime and Delinquency* 23, no. 2

(April 1977):154–72.

111. Irwin, "The Changing Social Structure of the Men's Prisons," pp. 38–39.

112. Morris, *The Future of Imprisonment*.

113. von Hirsch, *Doing Justice*, pp. 107–09.

114. Fogel, *We Are the Living Proof*, pp. 180–202.

115. Ibid., pp. 203–04.

116. Ibid., pp. 188–89.

117. *Prisons: The Price We Pay* (Hackensack, N.J.: National Council on Crime and Delinquency, 1978), pp. 1–4. 7–8.

118. Ibid., pp. 13–16.

119. Ibid., p. 17

120. Joan Petersilia and Peter W. Greenwood, "Mandatory Prison Sentences: Their Projected Effects on Crime and Prison Populations," *Journal of Criminal Law and Criminology* 69, no. 4 (Winter 1978):604–15.

121. von Hirsch, *Doing Justice*, p. 149.

Chapter 16

1. Samuel Walker, "Reexamining the President's Crime Commission's, *The Challenge of Crime in a Free Society*, After Ten Years," *Crime and Delinquency* 24, no. 1 (January 1978):11.

2. Center for Research on Criminal Justice, *The Iron Fist and the Velvet Glove* (Berkeley, Calif.: Center for Research on Criminal Justice, 1977), pp. 7–9; see also, Tony Platt and Paul Takagi, "Intellectuals for Law and Order: A Critique of the New 'Realists,' " *Crime and Social Justice* 8 (Fall/Winter 1977):2.

3. U.S. Department of Justice, *Trends in Expenditure and Employment Data for the Criminal Justice System, 1971–1975* (Washington, D.C.: U.S. Government Printing Office, 1977); see also, Platt and Takagi, "Intellectuals for Law and Order," p. 2.

4. David L. Bazelon, "A Federal Judge on Political Integrity," paper delivered before the annual meeting of the American Society on Criminology, Atlanta, Georgia, November 1977, by Judge Bazelon, Chief Judge of the U.S. Court of Appeals for the District of Columbia, printed in *Fortune News*, September 1977, p. 6.

5. Walker, "Reexamining the President's Crime Commission's, *The Challenge of Crime in a Free Society*, After Ten Years," pp. 7–8.

6. Ibid., p. 12.

7. Edwin H. Sutherland and Donald R. Cressey, *Criminology*, 10th ed. (Philadelphia: J. B. Lippincott, 1978), p. 3.

8. Emile Durkheim, *The Rules of Sociological Method*, 8th ed., translated by Sarah A. Solovay and John Mueller, and edited by George E. G. Catlin (New York: Free Press, 1938), pp. 69–73.

9. Karl Marx, *Selected Writings in Sociology and Social Philosophy*, translated by T. B. Bottomore (New York: McGraw-Hill, 1956), pp. 158–59.

10. Richard Quinney, *Criminology: Analysis and Critique of Crime in America* (Boston: Little, Brown & Co., 1977), pp. 283–84.

11. Daniel Glaser, *Strategic Criminal Justice Planning* (Rockville, Md.: National Institute of Mental Health, Center for Studies of Crime and Delinquency, 1975), p. 3.

12. Charles Reasons and Russell L. Kaplan, "Tear Down the Walls? Some Functions of Prisons," *Crime and Delinquency* 21, no. 4 (October 1975):366–72.

13. Quinney, *Criminology*.

14. Don C. Gibbons and Peter Garabedian, "Conservative, Liberal and Radical Criminology: Some Trends and Observations," in Charles E. Reasons, ed., *The Criminologists: Crime and the Criminal* (Pacific Palisades, Calif.: Goodyear Pub. Co., 1974), pp. 51–65; see also, Quinney, *Criminology*, chapter 5.

15. Patrick Törnudd, "The Futility of Searching for the Causes of Crime," in *Scandinavian Studies in Criminology*, vol. 3 (Oslo: Universitetsforlaget, 1971), pp. 23–24; see also, Bazelon, "A Federal Judge on Political Integrity."

16. Barry Krisberg and James Austin, *The Children of Ishmael: Critical Perspectives on Juvenile Justice* (Palo Alto, Calif.: Mayfield Pub. Co., 1978), pp. 576–77.

17. Thomas Mathiesen, "The Politics of Abolition: Essays in Political Action Theory," in *Scandinavian Studies in Criminology*, vol. 4 (Oslo: Universitetsforlaget, 1974), pp. 3–31.

18. A. C. Germann, "Criminal Justice Leadership: Bankrupt Forever?" *Criminology* 15, no. 1 (May 1977):3–6.

19. Richard Harris, *The Fear of Crime* (New York: Praeger, 1968), pp. 15–17.

20. Michael S. Serrill, "LEAA Part II," *Corrections Magazine* 2, no. 5 (September 1976):3–12, 25–26, 34.

21. Ibid.

22. Center for National Security Studies, *Law and Disorder*, IV (Washington, D.C.: Center for National Security Studies, 1976), pp. 4–30.

23. Richard Quinney, *Critique of the Legal Order* (Boston: Little, Brown & Co., 1974), pp. 105–09.

24. Richard Quinney, "The Ideology of Law: Notes for a Radical Alternative to Repression," *Issues in Criminology* 7 (Winter 1972):1–35; see also, Quinney, *Critique of the Legal Order*, pp. 109–32.

25. Gibbons and Garabedian, "Conservative, Liberal and Radical Criminology," pp. 63–65; see also, J. H. Reiman, *The Rich Get Richer and the Poor Get Prison; Ideology, Class and Criminal Justice* (New York: John Wiley & Sons, 1979).

26. Michael S. Serrill, "LEAA: A Question of Impact," *Corrections Magazine* 2, no. 4 (June 1976):3–12, 17–29.

27. Ibid., p. 3.

28. Ibid., pp. 4–5.

29. Cited in Platt and Takagi, "Intellectuals for Law and Order," pp. 2–3.

30. Serrill, "LEAA Part II," pp. 4, 34–36.

31. Ibid.

32. Nils Christie, "Main Trends in Criminology," paper presented to the 7th International Congress on Criminology, Belgrade, Yugoslavia, September 17–22, 1973, p. 20; see also, Krisberg and Austin, *The Children of Ishmael*, pp. 576–77.

33. James Q. Wilson, *Thinking About Crime* (New York: Basic Books, 1975), p. 59.

34. Ibid., pp. xiii, 202.

35. Andrew von Hirsch, *Doing Justice: The Choice of Punishment* (New York: Hill & Wang, 1976), p. 144.

36. Richard Quinney and John Wildeman, *The Problem of Crime: A Critical Introduction to Criminology*, 2nd ed. (New York: Harper & Row, 1977), pp. 166–72.

37. C. Ronald Chester, "Relative Deprivation as a Cause of Property Crime," *Crime and Delinquency* 22 (January 1976):17–30.

38. Paul W. Tappan, "Objectives and Methods in Corrections," in Paul W. Tappan, ed., *Contemporary Correction* (New York: McGraw-Hill, 1951), pp. 5–6. Also, for the "consumer perspective," see Edmond Cohn, *Confronting*

Injustice (Boston: Little, Brown & Co., 1966), p. 15.

39. Wilson, *Thinking About Crime*, pp. 62–63; see also, Törnudd, "The Futility of Searching for the Causes of Crime," pp. 31–33.

40. Inkeri Anttila, "Punishment versus Treatment—Is There a Third Alternative?" *Abstracts in Criminology and Penology* 13, no. 3 (May/June 1973):287–90.

41. "Nagel's Study Re-analyzed," *Jericho: Newsletter of the National Moratorium on Prison Construction* 1, no. 12 (November 1977–January 1978):6–7.

42. Wilson, *Thinking About Crime*, p. 202.

43. Arthur Pearl, "Public Policy or Crime: Which Is Worse?" in Peter Wickman and Phillip Whitten, eds., *Readings in Criminology* (Lexington, Mass.: D. C. Heath, 1978), pp. 373–79, especially p. 376.

44. Marvin Ross, *Economics, Opportunity and Crime* (Toronto: Renouf Pub. Co., 1977).

45. Cited in *Jericho: Newsletter of the National Moratorium on Prison Construction*, p. 6.

46. Pearl, "Public Policy or Crime: Which Is Worse?" pp. 376–77.

47. Lamar T. Empey, "Crime Prevention: The Fugitive Utopia," in James A. Inciardi, *Crime: Emerging Issues* (New York: Praeger, 1977). pp. 92–116.

48. Gilbert Geis, "The Criminal Justice System Without Victimless Crimes," in Peter Wickman, ed., *Readings in Social Problems* (New York: Harper & Row, 1977), pp. 212–17.

49. "Ex-Con Coalition Offers Blueprint," *Fortune News*, June 1974, p. 2.

50. Norval Morris and Gordon Hawkins, *The Honest Politician's Guide to Crime Control* (Chicago: University of Chicago Press, 1970), pp. 3–4.

51. Herbert L. Packer, *The Limits of the Criminal Sanction* (Stanford, Calif.: Stanford University Press, 1968), pp. 149–239.

52. Norval Morris, *The Future of Imprisonment* (Chicago: University of Chicago Press, 1974), pp. xi, 50–57.

53. American Friends Service Committee, *Struggle for Justice: A Report on Crime and Punishment in America* (New York: Hill & Wang, 1971), pp. 143–44.

54. Ibid., pp. 138–44.

55. Ibid.; see also, Morris, *The Future of Imprisonment*, pp. 50–57.

56. David Fogel, *We Are the Living Proof,* (Cincinnati: W. H. Anderson Co., 1975), pp. 246–48.

57. Ibid., pp. 250–60.

58. Ibid., pp. 202–03.

59. Ibid., pp. 204–05.

60. Ibid., p. 261; see also, Reiman, *The Rich Get Richer and the Poor Get Prison*, pp. 193–97.

61. von Hirsch, *Doing Justice*, pp. 98–106, 124–31; see also, Fogel, *We Are the Living Proof*, pp. 274–87.

62. Fogel, *We Are the Living Proof,* pp. 275–76.

63. David T. Stanley, *Prisoners Among Us: The Problem of Parole* (Washington, D.C.: The Brookings Institute, 1976), pp. 184–91.

64. James Hunt, James Bowers, and Neal Miller, *Laws, Licenses, and the Offender's Right To Work* (Washington, D.C.: ABA National Clearinghouse on Offender Employment Restrictions, 1973), pp. 5–13.

65. Ibid., p. 13.

66. Ibid.

INDEX

Adler, Freda, 137, 138
Adler, Mortimer, 7, 36
Adler, Renata, 352
Advertising fraud, 359–361
Affiliation theory: of avocational crime, 311–312; of criminal behavior, 184–189; of juvenile delinquency, 116–117; of white-collar crime, 349–352
Affinity: and anomie theory, 179–182; biological, 114, 167–171; defined, 114, 167; psychological, 114–115, 171–178; sociological, 115; subcultural, 182–184
Agnew, Spiro T., 263, 264, 343, 348, 357
Akers, Ronald, 187, 188
Albini, Joseph, 240
Alcohol use, 379–380, 389–391, 398–399; and violent crime, 278
Alexander, Franz, 172
Allen, John, 317, 318
American Corrections Association, 533
Amnesty for offenders, 589–590
Anomie: and affinity, 179–182; and crime rate, 24; and juvenile delinquency, 115, 116
Arson, 257, 337–338
Atavism, 18
Aubert, Vilhelm, 362
Automobile fraud, 356–357
Automobile theft, 310, 321–322
Avocational crime, 307–315, 330; affiliational aspects of, 311–312; characteristics of, 307; check forgery, 309, 311; and conventional behavior patterns, 313–314; criminal self-concept, 310–311; shoplifting, 217–218, 220, 308–309, 312; societal reaction to, 314–315; vandalism, 309, 311, 312. *See also* White-collar crime
Aydelotte, Frank, 214, 215

Bail, 457, 507–508
Ball, Harry, 348
Banton, Michael, 408, 423
Baxstrom v. *Herold*, 301, 304
Beccaria, Cesare, 15, 16, 17
Becker, Howard S., 25, 42, 97, 190, 191, 384
Behavior modification, 549
Bell, Daniel, 6, 66, 250, 254, 256
Bentham, Jeremy, 17
Berger, Peter, 103
Berkowitz, David, 175–178
Biderman, Albert, 82
Bio-psychological determinism, 19
Bishop, Norman, 555
Blackmail. *See* Extortion

Black market activities, 350
Blacks: arrest rates for, 80; in organized crime, 254; and sentencing patterns, 477; and violent crime, 274, 275, 276, 277
Blackstone, William, 17
Blankenburg, Erhard, 309
"Blue laws," 53
Bonger, William, 21
Booth, Charles, 21
Bribery, 360
Brockway, Z. B., 21
Brownmiller, Susan, 295
Burgess, Robert, 187
Burglary, 215–216, 229, 316

Cain, James, 250
Cameron, Mary, 138, 217, 220, 308
Capital punishment, 478–490
Career crime. *See* Professional crime
Carrier Case (1473), 41–42
Case screening, 458, 510
Central Intelligence Agency (CIA), 264, 344, 345–346, 348, 369
Chambliss, William, 42, 199, 240, 263
Chappell, Duncan, 227
Check forgery, 309, 311
Chesney-Lind, Meda, 155
Chevigny, Paul, 442
Child abuse, 279, 291–294
Christie, Nils, 31, 527, 578
Cicourel, Aaron, 192
Civil law, 47–48
Clark, John, 416
Classical school of criminology, 15–17
Cleaver, Eldridge, 295
Clemmer, Donald, 540
Clinard, Marshall B., 336, 363
Cloward, Richard, 24, 120, 183
Cocozza, Joseph, 301, 302
Cohen, Albert, 117, 182
Commonplace crime, 315–330, 331; affiliational aspects of, 323–325; and conventional behavior patterns, 325–326; criminal self-concept, 316–323; and juvenile delinquency, 316–318, 320, 324; societal reaction to, 326, 329–330; types of, 315–316
Computer crime, 357
Comte, Auguste, 18, 178
Confidence swindling, 222–223
Conflict theory: of crime, 26–27, 195–202; of criminal law, 43–46; of juvenile delinquency, 102
Conklin, John, 5, 278
Corporal punishment in schools, 287
Corporate crime. *See* White-collar crime
Corrections system, 521–566; European perspectives on, 553–559; goals of, 525–527, 532–533; guards, 535–539; history of, 527–532; inmate culture in, 540–545; organizational structure of, 532–535; reformatories in, 530; reform movements for, 560–566, 585–589; rehabilitation programs, 516–518, 545–551; scope of, 522–525; women and, 158
Cosa Nostra, La, 243, 245, 247–249
Counterfeiting, 223–224
Court system: discretionary aspects of, 457–461; major roles in, 465–470; pretrial procedures, 454–461; structure of, 470–474; trial procedures, 461–465
Cressey, Donald, 114, 185, 225, 243, 245, 348, 532, 542
Crime and criminality: in American history and folklore, 4; competing perspectives of, 6–9, 11, 25–27; conflict perspective of, 26–27, 195–202, 210; cost estimates of, 87–91, 92; early theories of, 13–15; economic impact of, 571; factors affecting rate of, 75–76; index, 64, 68, 70, 91; labeling perspective of, 26, 189–195, 209; legal definition of, 10–12; of public order, *see* Victimless crime; public perception of, 5–6; relativity of, 10–11; unemployment and, 581–582; unofficial estimates of, 82–89. *See also* Avocational crime; Commonplace crime; Female crime; Organized crime; Professional crime; Victimless crime; Violent crime; White-collar crime
Crime control policy, 569–591; alternatives to corrections, 585–591; "consumer-oriented," 579–582; decriminalization, 583–584; efforts of LEAA, 574–577; limiting judicial discretion, 584–585; police role in, 584; and social policy, 591
Crime data, 62–63; on female criminality, 144–153; homicide, 281–282, 282–285; *Uniform Crime Reports*, 64, 67–79; use and misuse of, 63–67; variations in sex, age, and race, 79–82, 274, 275
Criminal behavior: affiliation theories, 116–120, 184–189; and alcohol use, 393; bio-psychological theories of, 18–19, 23–24, 114, 167–178; defined, 9; personality tests and, 173–175; prescientific theories of, 164; sociological theories of, 115, 178–179; subcultural affinity, 182–184; typological approach to, 204–208, 210

625

Criminal justice system: corruption of, 259–265; court procedures in, 454–465; discretionary aspects of, 457–461, 477–478; police as extension of, 417–419; and sexist patterns, 153–158. *See also* Corrections system; Jails

Criminal law: classifications of, 52; consensus and conflict theories of, 43–46; decriminalization, 583–584; and definition of crime, 7, 8, 10–12; as form of social control, 36–43; "liberal doctrine" of, 15; limits of individual responsibility, 52–56; over- and underreach of, 56–57; procedural, 48, 49, 52; sources of, 48–49; substantive, 48, 49, 52; versus civil law, 47–48

Criminology: classical school of, 15–17; contemporary theories in, 25–27; development of, in America, 22–25; dimensions of, 12–13; positive school of, 17–22, 165, 167; radical-critical perspectives, 166, 199–202; research in, 28–31

Curtis, Lynn, 80, 276

Dahrendorf, Rolf, 195, 196
Davis, Allen, 504
Davis, Edward, 574
Davis, Kenneth, 437
Davis, Kingsley, 139
Defense lawyers, 467–468
De Fleur, Melvin, 187
Delinquency. *See* Juvenile delinquency
Dershowitz, Allen, 364
Determinism: biological, 23–24; cultural, 8; legalistic, 7; social, 24–25
Dickson, Donald, 42
Differential association, 116–117, 184–186, 335, 350
Dinitz, Siven, 114
Discretionary powers: of judges, 475–477; of police, 437–438; of prosecutors, 458
Diversion programs, 460–461, 511–513
Doleschal, Eugene, 553
Drugs and drug use: in behavior modification, 549; and crime rate, 394; and organized crime, 252–253; regulation of, 341; societal reaction to, 395, 399–401; subculture of, 393–394; types of, 380–383
Drunkenness. *See* Alcohol use
Dugdale, Richard, 23, 168
Durham rule on insanity, 55
Durkheim, Emile, 11, 21, 178, 179
Duster, Troy, 375

Education, relationship to juvenile delinquency, 106–108
Ehrlich, Isaac, 485
Elmhorn, Kerstin, 87

Emerson, Robert, 126, 193
Empey, L. T., 86, 121
Employee theft, 365
English common law, 40–41
Environmental protection laws, 341, 342
Erickson, Kai, 124
Erikson, M. L., 86
Ervin, Frank, 171
Ethnomethodology, 192
Extortion, 224

Family: interpersonal violence in, 286–294; and relationship to juvenile delinquency, 104–106
Farrington, D. P., 86
Federal Bureau of Investigation (FBI), 67, 68, 73, 344
Felicity calculus, principle of, 17
Female crime: arrest rates for, 78, 144–153; contemporary theories of, 135–144; early theories of, 134–135; economic status of women, 143–144; and sexist patterns in criminal justice system, 153–158; and women's movement, 135, 137, 140–141
Ferri, Enrico, 18, 19, 21
Fishman, Joseph, 497
Fogel, David, 478, 563
Forgery, 223–224; of checks, 309, 311
Frankel, Marvin, 475
Fraud, as occupational crime, 339, 340
Freud, Sigmund, 137, 172
Friday, Paul, 121
Furman v. *Georgia,* 479

Galliher, John, 250
Gambling, 250–251
Garabedian, Peter, 165
Gardiner, John, 263, 342
Garfinkle, Harold, 124
Garofalo, Raffaele, 7, 18, 19
Gault decision, 474
Geis, Gilbert, 335, 344, 347, 351, 358, 363, 402, 583
Giallombardo, Rose, 157
Gibbons, Don, 165
Glaser, Daniel, 187, 205, 485, 551
Glueck, Eleanor T. and Sheldon, 24, 114, 134, 135, 168
Goddard, Harry H., 23
Goddard, Henry, 168
Gold, Martin, 107, 108
Goldfarb, Ronald, 511
Goldman, Nathan, 123
Goode, Erich, 383
Gordon, David, 199, 200
Goring, Charles, 23
Greenberg, David, 96, 121, 277, 326, 515, 549
Greenwood, Peter, 565
Gregg v. *Georgia,* 479, 486, 488
Guerry, A. M., 17, 19
Guilty pleas, 457, 459–460. *See also*

Plea bargaining
Gusfield, Joseph, 42, 379

Hage, Jerold, 121
Hagen, John, 477
Half-way houses, 551
Hall, G. Stanley, 112
Hall, Jerome, 41, 42, 44
Harrison Act (1914), 381, 386, 399
Hartung, Frank, 350
Hawkins, Gordon, 89, 243, 246, 376, 526, 552
Heavy Electrical Equipment Case, 347, 351
Helms, Richard, 348, 349
Hijacking, 230–231, 233–235
Hindelang, Michael, 120
Hirschi, Travis, 86, 106, 107, 108, 120
Hoffman, Julius, 466
Homicide: rates of, 281–282; types of, 279–281; victims of, 282–285
Homosexual behavior, 376, 378–379, 389–391, 397–398
Hood, Roger, 86, 551
Hooten, E. A., 168
Hoover, J. Edgar, 416
Howard, John, 497
Howson, Gerald, 227

Ianni, Francis, 240, 245, 250
Inciardi, James, 214, 244
Insanity defense, 54–56
Irwin, John, 225, 542

Jackson, George, 536
Jacobs, James B., 536, 537
Jails, 493–519; alternatives to, 513–515; conditions in, 499–504; depopulation of, 505–513; functions of, 493–495; historical perspective on, 495–498; organization and administration of, 498–499; reform programs, 516–518; sentence options, 515–516
Jeffrey, C. Ray, 9, 23, 40
Jenkins, Richard, 299
Judge, Arthur, 215
Judges, 465–466
Juries, 463, 468–470; grand, 456
Juvenile correctional system, 127–128; reforms, 128–130
Juvenile court. *See* Juvenile justice system
Juvenile delinquency: affiliation theory of, 116–117; consensus and conflict theories of, 102; legal definitions of, 54, 97–99; psychological and sociological theories of, 114–116; and signifying agents, 122–124; social correlates of, 102–112; statistics on, 100–102; subculture theory of, 117, 120; and vandalism, 309; and youth gangs, 118–119
Juvenile justice system, 99, 113, 472–

626

474; diversion programs in, 511–512; processing of delinquents, 124–127, 155

Kempe, Henry C., 291
Kennedy, Edward M., 478
Kerner, Otto, 343
King, Harry, 216, 226
King, Martin Luther, 7
Kleck, Gary, 485
Klein, Dorie, 138, 140, 157
Klein, Malcolm, 124
Klockars, Carl, 227
Knapp Commission, 442, 443
Kress, June, 138, 140, 157

Lange, Johannes, 23
Law Enforcement Assistance Administration (LEAA), 83, 413, 426, 427, 569, 574–577
Le Grand, Camille, 153
Lemert, Edwin, 191, 213
Loansharking, 251–252
Lofland, John, 196, 197
Lombroso, Cesare, 18, 19, 20, 136, 167, 214
Lotteries. *See* Gambling
Lubeck, Steven, 121
Luckman, Thomas, 103

McCormick, Albert, 365
McGee, Richard, 477, 487, 499
McKay, Henry, 105, 115
McKendrick, Charles, 535
Mafia, 243–244, 246
Mala en se, principle of, 43
Mala prohibita, principle of, 43
Mallory v. *Hogan*, 574
Malpractice suits, 365
Mandel, Marvin, 264
Manhattan Employment Project, 512
Manilowski, Bronislaw, 38
Mannheim, Herman, 7
Manning, Peter, 63, 201
Mapp decision, 439
Marijuana, 42, 381, 383, 384, 385, 394, 395
Mark, Vernon, 171
Marshall, Thurgood, 490
Martinson, Robert, 562
Marx, Karl, 21, 195, 571
Mathiesen, Thomas, 573
Mattick, Hans, 499, 501, 517
Matza, David, 24, 112, 114, 115, 167, 188, 189, 276, 308, 313, 314
Maurer, David, 222, 228
Medical fraud, 339–340, 353–356
Merton, Robert K., 21, 24, 115, 179, 180, 181, 182, 256
Michael, Jerome, 7, 36
Miller, Walter, 120, 183, 184, 311
Millet, Kate, 295
Mills, C. Wright, 23
Minnesota Multiphasic Personality Inventory (MMPI), 174

Miranda v. *Arizona*, 49, 50–51, 439, 440, 574
Mitchell, John, 64
Mitford, Jessica, 548
M'Naghten rule on insanity, 17, 54–55
Monroe, Eric, 326, 327–328
Moore, Mark, 252
Morality legislation, 42–43, 374, 376–377
Morris, Norval, 89, 243, 376, 396, 460, 477, 552, 563
Murphy, F. J., 85

Nader, Ralph, 335, 341
Nagel, S. S., 154
Nagel, William, 531, 560, 581
Narcotics. *See* Drugs and drug use
National Opinion Research Center (NORC), 83
Natural law, concept of, 6–7
Newman, Donald J., 336
New York State Identification and Intelligence System (NYSIIS), 445
Niederhoffer, Arthur, 424, 461
Nixon, Richard M., 343, 348, 352, 367
Norland, Stephen, 144
Nullen poena sine lege, principle of, 17
Nullum crimen sine lege, principle of, 17, 97
Nye, F. Ivan, 102

Occupational crime. *See* White-collar crime
Ohlin, Lloyd E., 24, 120, 183, 512
Operation CHAOS, 345–346
Organized crime, 213, 235–240; activities of, 250–254; code of silence, 240; and corruption of criminal justice system, 259–265; history of, 241–243; infiltration of legitimate businesses, 254–259; Mafia and La Cosa Nostra, 240, 243–250; structure of, 243–245

Packer, Herbert, 526, 584
Parens patriae, doctrine of, 22, 54, 113, 294, 473
Parker, Donn B., 357
Parole, 530, 550–551, 589
Perlman, Richard, 122
Personality tests, and criminal behavior, 173–175
Petersilia, Joan, 565
Pickpocketing, 215, 220–222
Platt, Anthony, 113
Plea bargaining, 457, 460
Police, 407–450; abuse of power, 416–417, 441–442; arrest powers of, 436–438; code of ethics, 418; and community relations, 431–435; corruption, 259–262, 343, 442–443; early history of, 409–411; and juvenile delinquents, 122–124; legal restrictions on, 438–441; levels of agencies, 411–414; new technologies of, 444–445, 448; occupational culture of, 422; operational patterns, 428–435; organizational structure, 423–427; politicization of, 443–444; primary functions of, 414–422; review of present strategies, 446–448
Political corruption, 263–264
Polk, Kenneth, 108, 121
Pollack, Otto, 135
Polsky, Ned, 240
Pornography, 257
Porterfield, A. L., 85
Positive school of criminology, 17–22
Pound, Roscoe, 44
President's Crime Commission, 83, 87, 89, 99, 227, 237, 308, 323, 364, 398, 432, 433, 458, 525
Prisons. *See* Correctional system
Probation, 514–515, 550
Procedural laws, 48, 49
Prohibition era, and development of organized crime, 241–243
Professional crime, 213–235, 307; affiliation systems of, 226–227; behavior systems of, 215–224; "heavy," 229–235; history of, 214–215; self-concept, 224–225; societal reaction to, 229; status system of, 228
Prosecutors, 462, 463, 466–467; discretionary powers of, 458
Prostitution, 158, 254, 377–378; behavior system of, 388, 399; recruitment for, 388–389; self-concept of prostitute, 387; societal reaction to, 396–397
Punishment, deterrent effect of, 363–364, 551–552. *See also* Capital punishment

Quetelet, Adolphe, 17, 19, 75
Quinney, Richard, 9, 11, 26, 44, 62, 187, 197, 198, 200, 208, 336, 350, 374

Radzinowicz, Leon, 15, 22, 165
Rape, 153, 278, 295–299
Recidivism rates, 545, 546, 549, 550, 552, 556
Reckless, Walter, 12, 325
Reformatories. *See* Correctional system
Regulatory agencies, 362–363
Rehabilitation, 526, 545–551
Reidel, Marc, 486
Reiss, Albert, 82
Release on recognizance (ROR), 457, 509
Religion, and relationship to juvenile delinquency, 109–110
Retsky, Harold, 536, 537
Rizzo, Frank, 434
Robbery: in professional heavy crime, 229, 230, 235; as traditional crime, 316, 329

627

Robinson, Louis, 497
Romilly, Samuel, 17
Rosenberg, Bernard, 107, 115, 182, 323
Ross, Marvin, 581
Rothman, David, 526, 544
Rubin, Sol, 514

Salisbury, Harrison, 309
Schafer, Walter, 108
Schelling, Thomas, 243
Schuessler, Karl, 114
Schur, Edwin, 45, 129, 175, 357, 374
Scoll, Andrew, 517
Securities and Exchange Commission (SEC), 359, 367
Self-reports, as estimate of crime rate, 85–89
Sellin, Thorsten, 8, 70
Sentencing, 464–465; alternative, 513–516; discretion in, 477–478; disparities in, 474–477; effectiveness of, 551–552
Sexual psychopathy laws, 43
Shaw, Clifford, 105, 115
Sheldon, William, 168
Sherman Anti-Trust Act (1890), 340, 365
Shoplifting, 217–218, 220, 308–309, 312
Short, James, 102
Shover, Neal, 216
Signification, 122, 189–190; and labeling perspective of crime, 190–195; and victimless crime, 395–401
Silver, Isidore, 27
Silverstein, Harry, 182, 323
Silverstein, Harvey, 107, 115
Simmel, Georg, 40, 195
Simon, Rita, 77, 78, 139, 140, 143, 155, 156
Skolnick, Jerome, 430, 443
Slums, and crime patterns, 323–324
Smith, Alexander, 461
Snow, Robert, 112
Socialization process, and relation to juvenile delinquency, 103–107
Social reform movements, 21–22
Somatotypes, 168
Sparks, Richard, 86, 551
Spenkelink, John A., 489
Spouse battering, 286, 287, 288–290
Stare decisis, principle of, 48
Status offenses, 97–99
Staub, Hugo, 172
Steadman, Henry, 301, 302
Street gangs. *See* Youth gangs
Steffens, Lincoln, 342, 442
Stephen, James F., 295
Substantive laws, 48, 49
Sudnow, David, 468
Sumner, William Graham, 8
Sutherland, Edwin H., 9, 10, 25, 35, 45, 89, 116, 117, 184, 185, 186, 215, 217, 223, 333, 334, 335, 344, 358, 361, 362, 363
Sykes, Gresham, 201, 313, 314, 541
Sykes, Richard, 416
Syndicated crime. *See* Organized crime

Taft, Donald R., 362
Tannenbaum, Frank, 190, 192
Tappan, Paul, 7, 8, 11, 579
Tarde, Gabriel, 21
Television, impact of, on juvenile delinquency, 110–112
Terry, Robert, 123
Thomas, I. W., 139
Trebach, Arnold, 437
Trial procedures, 461–463; speedy, 509–510
Turk, Austin, 26, 196

Unemployment, and crime rate, 581–582
Unions, prisoner, 543–544
Uniform Crime Reports (UCR), 64, 67–79, 91; index crimes, 64, 68, 70, 91; juvenile delinquency, 100; and police data, 414, 438

Vagrancy laws, 42
Valachi, Joseph, 247–249
Vandalism, 309, 311, 312
Van den Haag, Ernst, 27, 561
Vesco, Robert, 359
Victimless crime, 56, 373–404; alcohol use, 379–380, 391–393, 398–399; decriminalization of, 403–404; drug use, 380–386, 393–395, 399–401; homosexual behavior, 378–379, 389–391, 397–398; police investigation of, 430; problems in regulating, 402; prostitution, 158, 254, 377–378, 387–389, 396–397
Victim surveys, 83–85
Violent crime, 269–304; child abuse, 279, 291–294; forcible rape, 278, 295–299, 304; identification, control, and prediction of, 299–302; interpersonal, 271–273; public concern over, 271, 272; and race, sex, and age, 274–275; and socioeconomic status, 274; spouse battering, 286, 287, 288–290; subculture of, 273–274, 275–278, 303
Vold, George B., 13, 26, 195, 238
Von Hirsch, Andrew, 563, 565
Voss, H. L., 86

Wade, Andrew, 312
Waldo, Gordon, 114
Walker, Nigel, 552
Walsh, Marilyn, 227
Watergate, 343, 344, 352, 367
Weber, Max, 38
Weis, Joseph G., 137
Weitzman, L. J., 154

Wheeler, Stanton, 201
White-collar crime, 9, 89, 333–370; affiliational aspects of, 349–352; corporate, 340–342, 357–359, 365–367; and conventional behavior patterns, 352–361; defined, 334–335, 339; occupational, 339–340, 353–357, 364–365; official, 342–344, 367–369; Operation CHAOS, 345–346; self-concept of white-collar criminal, 344–349; social control of, 362–369; societal reaction to, 361–362
Whyte, William, 432
Wice, Paul B., 509
Wife beating. *See* Spouse battering
Wild, Jonathan, 227
Wilkenson, Karen, 106
Williams v. *Florida,* 470
Wilson, James Q., 27, 123, 420, 423, 561, 578, 579, 580, 581
Wilson, O. W., 425
Wolfenden Report, 376
Wolfgang, Marvin E., 30, 278, 283
Women's movement, and female criminality, 135, 137, 140–141
Woodson v. *North Carolina,* 479
Work release programs, 515–516, 549–550

XYY chromosomal abnormality, 24, 169–171

Youth, social position of, 111
Youth gangs, 118–119, 120, 324

Zeigler, Max, 485
Zimring, Franklin. 526